The Papacy and Political Ideas
in the Middle Ages

Professor Walter Ullmann

Walter Ullmann

The Papacy and Political Ideas in the Middle Ages

VARIORUM REPRINTS
London 1976

ISBN 0 902089 87 0

Published in Great Britain by *Variorum Reprints*
21a Pembridge Mews London W11 3EQ

Printed in Great Britain by   *Kingprint Ltd*
Richmond Surrey TW9 4PD

VARIORUM REPRINT CS44

TABLE OF CONTENTS

This volume contains a total of 408 pages

PREFACE

The central issues of this volume – closely linked as it is with its predecessor *The Church and The Law in The Earlier Middle Ages* (Variorum Reprints 1975) – are focused on the chief ideas which propelled the medieval papacy, on the influence they exercised and the reaction they evoked. What sustained the institution was the conception that Christ had founded *uno ictu* a new society (the Church) as well as its government (Matt.XVI.18f.). Throughout the medieval period the papacy made this the pivot of all its numerous governmental, jurisdictional and religious pronouncements. Entrance into this papally governed society was obtained through the legally crucial act of baptism. It replaced the natural-carnal *generatio* of man by his *regeneratio* effected through divine grace. Through this rebirth or renaissance man became a new creature, a *homo novus* or *renatus* and received new norms of living. He became incorporated into the Church.

From this fundamental *point d'appui* the three main papal themes emerged: that of unipolarity – the Christian as a member of the Church had one aim and end only, that of transcendental salvation and eternal life to which all other ends and measures and actions were subordinated; that of totality – Christianity of which the Church was the corporate and public manifestation, claimed the whole of man, and the distinction between religious, moral, political, social, and other sets of norms was not merely irrelevant, but also beyond the contemporary papal purview; that of universality of papal jurisdiction and law – the disregard of linguistic, ethnic, biological, geographical, in short of all physical features, the immediate effect of the conquest of nature by grace in baptismal rebirth. In applying these basic themes the papacy elaborated the principle of division of labour – the Pauline groundwork served as a basis for the formulation by Gelasius I in the late fifth century – according to which each member of society had definite functions allocated, so that the whole was integrated and all members worked towards the same end directed by the papal *auctoritas* and by means of the law. Hence the preponderance of the descending theme of government and of the view that faith constituted the material ingredient of the law.

The introduction of secularist modes of thought in the twelfth century, mainly on the basis of the Roman law, facilitated the

Aristotelian absorption in the thirteenth, when the naturalist standpoint regained its position, a new category of 'Politics' came into being and with it a new science, the *scientia politica*. Thereby the individual as a subject — in theory at least — changed into an autonomous citizen who created law himself by exercising his own consent. Unipolarity gave way to bipolarity (and later multipolarity); totality was replaced by atomism and the consequential autonomy of the religious, moral, political and other sets of norms; universality yielded to national sovereignty with the consequence that what on an ecclesiological foundation was once one undivided whole, now become fragmented and disintegrated into its component autonomous parts. As the natural took its place next to the supranatural, so did the ascending theme of government take its place next to its descending counterpart.

The essays in this volume depict the theoretical and intellectual background of these topics. They should be seen as preparatory examinations on which my relevant books rested, and they also reflect the stages of my own penetration into the matrix of papal thought and the structure of papal mechanics. Many years of intensive research and analysis of a vast source material have gradually made me realize and eventually convinced me that the papacy as an institution operated with a comprehensively conceived programme which mirrored the comprehensiveness of the Christian theme itself. And this programme of the medieval papacy was claimed to be the divine scheme of things merely translated into terms of human government. The medieval papacy was an institution *sui generis.* Its history is a classic instance of the interplay of cosmology, abstract ideas and concrete facts. An adequate understanding of the working of the papacy postulates a firm grasp of the very criteria fixed and formulated and applied as they were by the papacy itself in the thousands of its decretals and pronouncements. In a word, the papacy must be seen from within itself, if its operation on the plane of reality is to be understood. May these essays stimulate further research into fields which have far too long suffered from insufficient, because antiquated forms of approach and hence an inevitable staleness of results. What is needed is both integrative analysis and synthesis. And a by-product of this will be the furtherance of the never ending historical quest to discover what we were before we have become what we are today.

Once more I would like to express my sincere thanks to the Editors and Publishers for their permission — readily and generously given — to reproduce the essays.

WALTER ULLMANN

Cambridge
Autumn 1975

I

CARDINAL HUMBERT AND THE ECCLESIA ROMANA

The dynamic and creative forcefulness, the characteristically individualistic style and expression, the profound argumentation in his literary products, the conciseness of legal work — all these features have rightly secured Cardinal Humbert a permanent place in the history of the medieval papacy. The illuminating researches of Professor Anton Michel have indeed thrown into clear relief the prominent part that the learned Cardinal has played in shaping precisely those foundations upon which the future medieval papacy was to rest securely. A perusal of the various works of the Cardinal cannot but create the impression that the fifth century is re-enacted dramatically in the eleventh century with the ideological armoury and resources of the ninth century. In more than just one respect Humbert resembles Anastasius, the great and influential savant of the mid-ninth century.

The pivotal point in the programme of Humbert is the closely reasoned, sharp hitting and high-spirited attack against the prevailing *Rex-Sacerdos* ideas and practices. In launching his frontal assault the learned and enthusiastic Cardinal draws skilfully on ancient material and equally skilfully blends this with the reality of the mid-eleventh century. The avenue chosen by him to show how the *ordo rationis* or the prevention of *confusio*[1] should be realized was that of a recourse to the ancient Roman tradition.[2] That, incidentally, is the reason why the Cardinal relied so heavily

---

[1] See *Adv. Simoniacos*, in MGH., *Libelli de lite*, I, 205: *Ad totius ... religionis conculcationem praepostero ordine omnia fiunt*; see also HUMBERT's *Sententiae* (the former *Diversorum patrum sententiae*, or *collectio minor* have now been identified, thanks to the most minute investigation of A. Michel, as Humbert's work, see A. MICHEL, *Die Sentenzen des Kardinals Humbert, das erste Rechtsbuch der päpstlichen Reform*, in *Schriften des Reichsinstituts f. ältere deutsche Geschichtskunde (MGH.)*; idem, *Pseudo-Isidor* etc., in *Studi Gregoriani*, III (1948), 149 ff; against Michel there is the lonely voice of Father F. PELSTER S. J., in *Studi Gregoriani*, I (1947), 347 ff), in THANER, *Anselmi ... Collectio Canonum* (c. 31), at Anselm's IV, 8, p. 195.

[2] Cf. MICHEL, op. cit., p. 64; *Die Restauration altkirchlicher Verhältnisse*.

on Pseudo-Isidore, the pantheon of papal prerogatives, in a way the influential pathmaker of hierocratism.[3] And just like the great popes of the fifth century, so also with Humbert — either as a literary author, or as a draughtsman of official papal communications[4] — we witness that the lever with which the right order could most effectively be implemented was the primacy of the Church of Rome. This indeed was the strongest tool in the hands of all those who attempted to implement the effective government of the Christian world through the *ecclesia Romana*. Humbert invokes the time-honoured commission « Thou art Peter... » and basing himself on the equally time-honoured doctrines comes to the conclusion that the Roman Church is the hinge and head — *cardo et caput* — of all other churches.[5] The Roman Church is the mother of all churches, and hence like a mother cares for the oppressed children, in the same way all oppressed Christians have the right to appeal to their spiritual and ideological mother.[6] In a word, the Roman Church is the *e x o r d i u m* of Christianity: it is the *principium* and the *fons* of all ecclesiastical life, embracing as it does *universam terram*.[7] The *ecclesia Romana* is the epitome of all Christianity: *Romana ecclesia... afficit totius Christianitatis membra*.[8]

To Cardinal Humbert, then, the world, as far as it was Christian, was synonymous with Christendom: standing as he does on the ancient roads, to Humbert this Christian world was nothing but an *ecclesia*, the *congregatio fidelium* which is epitomised in the Roman Church. It is therefore perfectly in keeping with this axiomatic view that not only the Gelasian *mundus*[9] is here exchanged for *ecclesia*, but also that the secular power becomes, ideologically, part and parcel of this *ecclesia*. The Cardinal's distinctive terminology, *ecclesia* on the one hand, and *sacerdotium* on the other hand, enables him to lay down a neat and tidy delineation within the larger framework of Christendom: for this, according to him, consists of

[3] MICHEL, op. cit., p. 97: *Die unerschöpfliche Fundgrube, der eigentliche Steinbruch*; see also MICHEL, in *Studi Greg.*, I, 72.

[4] On this see MICHEL, *Humbert und Kerullarios*, Paderborn 1925.

[5] *Sententiae*, cc. 2, 12 (THANER's *Anselm*, I, 20, p. 7; I, 9, p. 10); cf. also LEO IX's letter in Corn. WILL, *Acta et Scripta* etc., c. xxxii, pp. 81-2; furthermore, MICHEL, *Sentenzen*, p. 18.

[6] *Sententiae*, c. 3 (THANER, II, 6, p. 77).

[7] *Fragmentum B*, printed by Percy SCHRAMM, *Kaiser, Rom und Renovatio*, II (Leipzig 1929), 133.

[8] ibid., p. 131.

[9] In the famous *Duo quippe* letter, see A. THIEL, *Epistolae Romanorum Pontificum*, ep. 12, pp. 350 ff.

two agencies. If we wish to compare, he says, the sacerdotal and royal dignity, one should say

sacerdotium in praesenti ecclesia assimilari animae, regnum autem (*scil.* in praesenti ecclesia) corpori, quia invicem se diligunt et vicissim sese indigent... ex quibus sicut praeeminet anima et praecipit, sic sacerdotalis dignitas regali, utputa coelestis terrestri.[10]

The Christian world, in a word, was a Church.[11] Under this presupposition that the world is an *ecclesia*, the *sacerdotium* quite logically and naturally assumes the leadership of the whole *ecclesia*.

It is natural and logical, furthermore, that the *clericalis ordo* within the Church has to fulfil functions which its laical counterpart is incapable of fulfilling: as an eighth-century pope had said, and as Humbert no doubt would have endorsed, the former alone have the *sensus Christi* [12] and consequently the guidance of the Christian body is a matter for the clerics, and not for the laical component parts. The inevitable consequence was, on the one hand, the fiery attack on lay investiture which as plainly as possible was the concrete manifestation of the *Rex-Sacerdos* idea in practice, and, on the other hand, the concentration of the powers and rights, diffused as they were throughout the churches, in the Roman Church. The *ecclesia Romana* was, as we termed it, the epitome of all Christianity. Or differently expressed, the primacy of the Church of Rome was an indispensable requisite for the proper functioning and working of the Christian body, called a Church. Every other arrangement was bound to lead to a perversion of the right order.

For our present purpose we may leave aside the magisterial primacy of the Roman Church and concentrate our attention on the jurisdictional primacy. It will be recalled that the principle of jurisdictional primacy had been theoretically and ideologically hammered out by the time of Gelasius I, and it is needless to point out that this principle played a most conspicuous rôle in the thought of Cardinal Humbert. But in order to set the original contribution of the Cardinal into a proper perspective, that is, in order to show what, according to him, was the *ecclesia Romana*, it will be profit-

---

[10] *Adv. Sim.*, loc. cit., p. 225.

[11] See especially the stimulating study of J. Rupp, *L'idée de Chrétienté*, pp. 53-71.

[12] See Gregory II's letter in Mansi, XII, 977: *quoniam Christi sensum nos habemus.* On this see also E. Caspar, in *Zeitschrift f. Kirchengeschichte*, 1933, p. 86, and P. Schramm, *Sacerdotium und Imperium* etc., in *Studi Gregoriani*, II (1947), 415.

able to review briefly the fate of the principle of the jurisdictional primacy since its formulation by Gelasius I. This will be all the more advisable since the principle of the pope's immunity, to whose modification Humbert contributed so much, stands in closest proximity to the jurisdictional primacy of the Roman Church.

Despite the inimitable conciseness of Gelasius's language, the forger working a few years after this pope's death (circa 501) considered it necessary to give the Gelasian statements a more popular and more easily appealing form. The forger invented a synod held under Silvester in 324, and this synod passed the socalled *Constitutum Silvestri* decreeing in canon XX this:[13]

Nemo judicabit primam sedem justitiam temperare desiderantem. Neque enim ab Augusto, neque ab omni clero neque a regibus neque a populo, judex judicabitur.

The forger thus gave the jurisdictional primacy of the Roman Church his own peculiar flavour, without receding too much from his papal source.[14] Being the juristic expression of an important principle, it became a traditional axiom that weathered many a storm.[15] Its inclusion in Pseudo-Isidore[16] ensured its longevity and its canonical authority. A pope of Nicholas I's calibre obviously saw its great ecclesiastico-political value when he rendered the principle in this way:[17]

Cum enim Christi munere propter primatum ecclesiae Romanae in beato Petro concessum nemini sit de sedis apostolicae judicio judicare aut illius sententiam retractare permissum.

It is clear that this principle rendered in a typical Nicholean language

---

13 MANSI, II, 632; MIGNE, *PL.*, VIII, 839. On the series of Symachan forgeries, see P. COUSTANT, *Epp. Rom. Pontificum,* = *PL.*, VIII, 841-45; DUCHÈSNE, *Liber Pontificalis,* I, pp. cxxxii ff.; MAASSEN, *Geschichte der Quellen und Literatur des canonischen Rechts im Abendland,* pp. 411 ff.; E. CASPAR, *Geschichte des Papsttums,* II, 107 ff.; A. KÖNIGER, *Prima sedes a nemine judicatur,* in *Festschrift f. Ehrhard,* pp. 273 ff., at pp. 298 ff.

14 About the barbarous Latinity of the fake, its notorious ignorance in matters canonical, see the brilliant study by St. KUTTNER, *Cardinalis. The history of a canonical concept,* in *Traditio,* III, 191.

15 The *Constitutum Silvestri* was incorporated in at least three canonical collections of the sixth century, the *Coll. San Blasiana, Coll. Theatina,* and the collection in MS. Vat. Lat. 1342; on this see MAASSEN, op. cit., pp. 411 ff., 506 ff., 515, 526 ff.; C. H. TURNER, *Chapters* etc., in *Journal of Theological Studies,* XXXI (1931), 9-20; E. LOWE, *Cod. Lat. Antiquiores,* I, 34, 44, and especially KUTTNER, art. cit., p. 190.

16 P. HINSCHIUS, *Decretales Pseudo-Isidorianae,* pp. 449-50, 463. On the pre-Pseudo-Isidorian transmission, see preceding note and KUTTNER, p. 203.

17 *MGH., Epistolae,* VI, 606.

had become a fundamental axiom whenever the primacy of the Roman Church was defended. We find this principle, naturally, also in Humbert's *Sententiae,* apparently modelled on Nicholas I, but slightly re-arranged in its formulation, re-arranged, that is to say, to make it suitable for juristic consumption.[18]

Nemini *est* de sedis apostolicae judicio judicare, aut illius sententiam retractare permissum: *videlicet* propter Romanae ecclesiae primatum, Christi munere in beato Petro *apostolo divinitus collocatum.*

The Humbertine juristic formulation of the jurisdictional primacy of the Roman Church went into Anselm's collection,[19] into Ivo's collection,[20] and finally into Gratian.[21] At the same time the Cardinal was also a mere transmitter of the formula employed by the Symmachan forger in the 20th canon of the *Constitutum Silvestri.* Humbert incorporated this canon in his *Sententiae* without any change [22] and from here the formula went into Anselm's collection,[23] into Ivo's [24] and into Gratian [25] to mention only the main stages of post-Humbertine transmission.

The principle of the jurisdictional primacy of the Roman Church must not be confused with the pope's personal immunity from any sort of accusation. The two principles must strictly be separated, as in fact Humbert did, a feature that is usually overlooked. It is true that papal immunity stands in close proximity to the jurisdictional primacy of the Roman Church, but each concerns different aspects. The one is concerned with the Roman Church as exercising supreme jurisdiction, from which there lies no appeal to any other authority — *Roma locuta, causa finita est* — and the other concerns the pope personally as the object of a judicial trial and examination. As regards the latter principle, Humbert's contribution was fundamental and as far-reaching as Gelasian dicta had become in the political field. Far-reaching, that is to say, within the internal constitu-

---

[18] *Sententiae,* c. 17 (THANER's *Anselm,* I, 21, p. 16). The words italicized indicate Humbert's change in wording. On this moulding process cf. E. PERELS, in *Neues Archiv der Gesellschaft f. ältere deutsche Geschichtkunde,* XXXIX (1914), 72, 111, 119, and MICHEL, *Sentenzen,* p. 13, note 2.

[19] I, 21, except that *enim* is inserted between *nemini* and *est.*

[20] *Panormia,* IV, 10.

[21] *Decretum,* XVII. IV, 30, attributing it to Nicholas I.

[22] c. 8, THANER, p. 15, ad c. 19, note 1.

[23] I, 19.

[24] *Panormia,* IV, 5.

[25] IX, III, 13.

tion of the Church, and hence perhaps not so noticeable to medieval contemporaries and still less noticeable to the modern historian. But in order to bring Humbert's contribution into clear relief, we must examine the historical background. Humbert sets forth his views on the personal immunity of the pope not in the *Sententiae,* but in the fragment *De sancta Romana ecclesia.*[26] In it the Cardinal employs his own language. With every justification this fragment has been called a « hymne »,[27] the « höchste Leistung » in the defence of the Roman primacy,[28] written « in leuchtender Sprache ».[29] But this literary product of Humbert is, as we hope to show, even more. It not only programmatically and concisely sums up in little more than a printed page the ideological development of previous centuries, but it also opens up the future constitutional development within the Roman curia. All this is achieved with an economy of words and an incisiveness of expression which cannot find a parallel. In a way it may be what Schramm has called the « Posaunenstoss, der die Katastrophe von Canossa einleitet ».[30] But this literary piece of Humbert assumes a special significance because of the modification of the principle of the pope's personal immunity. When we attempt to trace the genesis of this principle of papal immunity, the same forger who has just attracted our attention, will once again have to serve as the « point d'appui ». In the same *Constitutum Silvestri* purporting to be the record of the synod held under Silvester, we find the following stipulation in canon III:

Neque praesul summus judicabitur a quoquam, quoniam scriptum est: Non est discipulus super magistrum.[31]

Just like the complementary principle of the jurisdictional primacy of the Roman Church, so also was this principle of the pope's per-

---

[26] See SCHRAMM, op. cit., I, 238 ff.; II, 126 ff.; and identified by MICHEL, ibid., II, 134 ff.

[27] H. X. ARQUILLIÈRE, *Grégoire VII, essai sur la conception du pouvoir pontifical,* p. 314.

[28] SCHRAMM, op. cit., II, 125

[29] MICHEL, in *Studi Gregoriani,* I, 67.

[30] vol. I, p. 241.

[31] Text in MANSI, II, 623, also in COUSTANT, op. cit., app. 44; the biblical reference is to Matth., X, 24. The text is also printed by KUTTNER, art. cit., p. 190, with critical notes, note 57.

It should be borne in mind that whilst canon XX of the *Constitutum* deals with the jurisdictional primacy of the Roman Church, canon III is concerned with the personal immunity of the pope from any sort of accusation. This distinction is not always clearly made resulting in considerable confusion.

sonal immunity nurtured by collectors.[32] We have in fact the testimony of Alcuin how the lapse of 300 years — or from Alcuin's point of view, the lapse of nearly 500 years — had increased the authority of canon III of the *Constitutum*. Before Charlemagne sat in judgment over Leo III in December 800, Alcuin had written to his friend Arn of Salzburg pointing out the inadmissibility of trying a pope; he protests against the pending trial and says:[33]

If I remember rightly I had read in the canons of St. Silvester that a Bishop can be accused only on the testimony of 72 witnesses... and I also read in other canons that the apostolic see must not be judged, but that it judges everyone.

When then in actual fact Charlemagne did sit in judgment over Leo III at Christmastide 800, the episcopal participants of the synod — the trial was conducted in the manner of a synod [34] — declared:[35]

Nos sedem apostolicam, quae est caput omnium ecclesiarum, judicare non audemus. Nam ab ipsa nos omnes et vicario suo judicamur, ipsa autem a nemine judicatur quemadmodum et antiquitus mos fuit.

The Fathers of that synod reiterated the idea of the Symmachan forger and changed his wording only insignificantly. They and the forger therefore maintained that the pope's personal immunity was u n c o n d i t i o n a l : under no circumstances whatsoever was a pope to be tried for any crime and for any reason. The papal pronouncement of Nicholas I which is in fact a literal copying of the third canon of the *Constitutum*, endorses the unconditional papal inviolability.[36] That Pseudo-Isidore also reported this important principle, needs no explanation.[37]

And yet, despite his thorough familiarity with Nicholas I, with the Symmachan forger and the Frankish forger, Cardinal Humbert in the *De sancta Romana ecclesia* makes a statement that although purporting to fix the pope's personal immunity, has a very significant addition.

[32] On the transmission see supra note 15.
[33] *MGH., Epistolae*, IV, 296. See also E. CASPAR, *Das Papsttum unter fränkischer Herrschaft*, in *Zeitschrift f. Kirchengeschichte*, 1935, pp. 223-4.
[34] CASPAR, art. cit., p. 226.
[35] *Liber Pontificalis*, II, 7: Vita Leonis III.
[36] *MGH., Epistolae*, VI, 466.
[37] Headed: *Excerpta quaedam ex synodalibus gestis s. Silvestri papae*, c. 2, at HINSCHIUS, *Decr. Ps. Isid.*, p. 449. The forged decree was also incorporated in the *Capitula Angilramni*, c. 51 (2), HINSCHIUS, p. 766.

Cuius (*scil.* papae) culpas redarguere praesumit mortalium nullus, quia cunctos ipse judicaturus a nemine est judicandus, n i s i f o r t e d e p r e h e n d a t u r a f i d e d e v i u s .

In this form the statement went into the collection of Cardinal Deusdedit,[38] into that of Ivo,[39] and finally into Gratian.[40] Since Anselm so largely relied on Humbert's *Sententiae*, he did not incorporate this statement: Humbert did not have it in his *Sententiae*. Nor, significantly enough, did he have the *Neque praesul summus* (can. III of the *Constitutum Silvestri*) which, incidentally, may be further proof for the identity of the author of the *Sententiae* and of the *De sancta Romana ecclesia*.[41]

When one realizes what great importance this statement had to play in later canonistics and particularly in the interminable constitutional quarrels concerning the Church government, we can perhaps then measure the contribution and the influence of Cardinal Humbert. Nevertheless, the Humbertine fixation of papal immunity is an astonishing piece: does it not throw out of gear the whole papalist-hierocratic machinery? Can this still be reconciled with the basic thought of Humbert? Or is it nothing but a colossal blunder the implications of which its author had not seen? The whole tenor, diction and composition of this document militates against even considering this last-mentioned possibility. But then, how is one to explain a statement like this coming from a convinced hierocrat and curialist such as Humbert was? Perhaps his position as a curialist will give us the clue, but first we must again enquire into the genesis of the so-called heresy clause: *nisi forte deprehendatur a fide devius.*

Whether or not inspired by the forged Symmachan decrees, Isidore of Seville in his *Sententiae* laid down that a superior should not be judged by his ecclesiastical inferior; that only if the superior fails in his faith he should be reproved (« corrected ») by his inferiors; any moral failings should be tolerated.[42] Stern as Pseudo-Isidore's views were on the hierarchical ordering, he deals in several places with the problem of accusation by ecclesiastical inferiors of their

---

[38] I, 231, see Wolf von GLANVELL, *Die Kanonessammlung des Cardinals Deusdedit*, p. 177, although strangely enough he also had the *Neque praesul summus*, I, 89, p. 74.

[39] *Decretum*, V, 23, and *Coll. Tripart.*, III. 9 (3).

[40] Dist. 40, c. 6.

[41] If any further proof were needed after Michel's conclusive evidence.

[42] *Liber Sententiarum*, III, xxxix, 5, MIGNE, *PL.*, LXXXIII, 710: *Rectores ergo a Deo judicandi sunt, a suis subditis nequaquam judicandi sunt*; no. 6: *Quod si a fide exorbitaverit rector, tunc erit arguendus a subditis: pro moribus vero reprobis tolerandus magis distringendus a plebe est.*

superiors, and he makes a number of popes say that if a Bishop should deviate from the faith he should be corrected secretly by his inferiors, and only if he is incorrigible, h e s h o u l d b e r e p o r t - e d t o t h e a p o s t o l i c s e e.[43] In substance Isidore and Pseudo-Isidore are identical: both are insistent that moral defects of the superior should be suffered by the inferiors; both agree that deviations from the faith should be put right. Pseudo-Isidore adds, however, that in the case of an incorrigible adherence to unorthodoxy report should be made to the apostolic see.[44] About the pope himself both were silent. And it is with respect to the pope that Humbert's innovation emerges so fully, an innovation, however, that was reserved for the *De sancta Romana ecclesia* and which we will not find in his *Sententiae* where he closely follows the old models.[45]

What Humbert did in *De s. Romana ecclesia* was to combine canon III of the *Constitutum Silvestri* with the Isidorian and Pseudo-Isidorian provisions of the superior's heresy, and in this way he arrives at a true immunity of the pope from accusations of a moral nature. Humbert excluded from the immunity the pope's deviation from the faith. Purely moral failings on the part of the pope are the object of papal immunity. The novelty was that Humbert infused into the (hitherto unconditional) immunity of the pope (can. III of the *Const. Silv.*) the Pseudo-Isidorian provision of a Bishop's accusation before the apostolic see. The immunity of the pope, according to Humbert, was conditional in that he was not accused of heresy: in this case all immunity vanishes and the pope is answerable. For moral defects — simony, adultery and the like — papal immunity remains, and nobody can judge him.

---

[43] *Si incorrigibilis, quod absit, apparuerit, tunc erit a c c u s a n d u s ad primates suos aut a d a p o s t o l i c a m s e d e m ,* Fabian, ep. II, c. 23 (Hinschius, p. 166), see also Clement I, ep. I, c. 42 (Hinschius, p. 45), Anacletus, ep. III, c. 39 (p. 85). See also Fabian, c. 22 (p. 165): *Apostolica auctoritate iubemus ne pastorem suum oves, quae ei commissae fuerant, nisi a fide erraverit, reprehendere audeant ... neque potest esse discipulus super magistrum.* Cf., furthermore, Eusebius, c. 11 (p. 237), Johannes, ep. I (p. 694), and Symachus synod (p. 676).

[44] See preceding note. Burchard does not open the way to the apostolic see, cf., e. g., I, 136; *Doctor autem vel pastor ecclesiae, si a fidelibus exorbitaverit, erit a fidelibus corrigendus. Sed pro reprobis moribus magis est tolerandus quam distringendus;* and c. 139: *Oves, quae pastori suo commissae fuerint, eum nec reprehendere, nisi a recta fide exorbitaverit, debent nec ullatenus accusare possunt,* PL., CXL, 589, 590. See furthermore Gratian, *Decretum,* II. vii. 13 (= Anselm: III, 44, Thaner, p. 136; Ivo, *Panormia,* IV, 39).

[45] c. 74, at Anselm, III, 37, Thaner, p 134, where we find the agreement with Isidore, Anacletus in Pseudo-Isidore, c. 38, p. 85 (and Burchard); see also c. 78, at Michel, *Sentenzen,* p. 35, no. 12.

Every difficulty of interpreting this statement would disappear if, as has once been suggested, the *nisi* clause could be made to refer to *mortalium nullus,* and not to *judicandus.*[46] Freely rendered the Humbertine statement might then read: « only he who is devoid of faith can have the temerity of judging the pope for his faults, for he judges all and is not judged by anyone ». This interpretation, however ingenious, not only does violence to Humbert's diction, for nothing justifies us to juggle about with the construction of an undoubtedly carefully built up sentence, but also contradicts the very tenor of the immediately preceding sentences. In the preceding sentence Humbert says that it depends on the pope whether he will make the whole world run after God in ecstacy and enthusiasm, or whether, when useless, unmindful of his duties and negligent of his and his brethren's spiritual well-being, he will drag innumerable nations down to hell: and then follows the enigmatic sentence that, namely, « whose (scil. the pope's) defects in these affairs no mortal presumes to judge, because he will judge... » It is clear, then, that Cardinal Humbert considers the pope's negligence of his duties and so forth as these defects (the *culpae*) which no mortal can judge. In so far he moves entirely within Isidore's, Pseudo-Isidore's (and also Burchard's) *reprobi mores.* But it is not a mere *culpa,* our Cardinal thinks, if the pope should deviate from the faith — that is something entirely different from a personal defect, such as the commission of a crime and the like. And for this he may be judged. That this is the meaning follows also from the immediately succeeding sentence. Here the possibility that the pope can fall into heresy is openly admitted when he says that the *universitas fidelium* prays all the more ardently for the pope's ever-lasting government, because they — the faithful — consider that, after God, their salvation depends on the pope's safety (scil. in matters of faith). There can be no guarantee for the pope's orthodoxy, and therefore the prayers of the faithful are necessary. There is, then, nothing to justify the interpretation that the heresy clause does not refer to the pope.[47]

Another interpretation has been attempted. It is suggested that the Cardinal's meaning will become clear if a distinction is made between his official and his private capacity.[48] This argumentation

---

[46] So MICHEL, in SCHRAMM, op. cit., II, 136. But see the cautious approach of SCHRAMM, ibid., p. 126, and also K. HOFMANN, *Der Dictatus Papae Gregors VII.,* p. 125.

[47] MICHEL himself (*Sentenzen,* p. 32, note 1) has since withdrawn this interpretation.

[48] Idem, ibid., and in *Studi Gregoriani,* I, 68.

is based on the interpretation of letters of Leo IX which, in fact, were drafted by Humbert. The Humbertine passage, in other words, is to be explained by a recourse to official papal communications. Surely, this kind of interpretation violates the canons of historical analysis. Nothing entitles us to set this literary product of Humbert lightly aside, for it is — as Professor Michel is only too ready to admit — a programmatic declaration, and not the result of some pious, momentary inspiration: its diction, its conciseness, its extremely well chosen biblical allusions and borrowings — all these compel us to consider the fragment on its own merits. We are not forced to go outside it and to make a loan in official papal documents, if we wish to interpret Humbert himself. Apart from this, it m a y be that the distinction between the private and official capacity of the pope was implied in the letters adduced by Michel, but these letters had not gone into the canon law.[49] What has gone into it is the passage from the fragment, and that is what matters. If the distinction had been operative in Humbert's mind, then there is every reason to assume that he had expressed it in the fragment. Humbert was not at a loss for the right word in the right place. The attempt to interpret Humbert's product by a recourse to extraneous matter is at the same time a degradation of the very man to whom his modern rescuer had devoted years of his life.[50]

Having rejected the two interpretations of the important passage, what can we offer in their place? Is there a t e r t i u m ? We think there is. This literary product of Humbert is all of a piece. After stating the function and the basis of the Roman Church Humbert continues: « As a matter of fact » — *revera* — all Christians look with such awe and reverence to the apex of this Church that they prefer to accept the interpretation of doctrine from his own mouth to the sacred writings themselves. Here the Cardinal does not say that all Christians s h o u l d look at the pope in this way, but he merely states a fact, of which he no doubt approves. And the opening of the immediately following sentence gives us the opinion of the Cardinal himself: the operative words are *quod si*. Freely rendered our author says: « That is true, if the pope strives to be irreproachable to God and man, in his works and speech, for then he will indeed

---

[49] Except the one in Ivo's *Decretum*, V, 44.
[50] See MICHEL himself in *Studi Gregoriani*, III, 161, and *Savigny Zeitschrift*, Kanonist. Abtlg, XXXV, 339.

make the world run after God ecstatically, but if he should be forgetful of his position he will drag innumerable people to hell ».[51] Humbert then leaves this part dealing with the pope and reverts to the Roman Church,[52] to which — and not to the pope — may be attributed the words of Job: « He breaketh down and it cannot be built again; he shutteth up a man, and there can be no opening; he withholdeth the waters, and they dry up; also he sendeth them out, and they overturn the earth ». For the Roman Church is the mother of all the faithful in Christ. What matters is t h e s e e of him to whom Christ had spoken the words « Thou art Peter... » — *sedes illius, cui dictum est: Tu es Petrus...* The Roman Church in a special sense, not the pope, fulfills the Petrine commission: *ipsa specialius in Petro coeli terraeque retentet habenas.* Through the medium of St. Peter the Roman Church was divinely endowed with the functions attributed to it. It is the see of Rome that matters: the emphasis is on the Church of St. Peter, on his see, at the expense of the pope who, by virtue of being Bishop of this apostolic Church, is its apex.

Humbert speaks as a curialist in the most literal meaning of the term. The Roman Church is to him the curia in whose birth he himself had such a large share.[53] Our passage is not only the programmatic declaration of a hierocrat concerning the Roman Church, but also the programmatic vindication of the rights of the Roman curia. As far as the Cardinals were concerned, Roman Church and Roman curia were identical terms. For from the time of Leo IX onwards the Cardinals assume that function that has since been the one attributed to them, namely, they participate in the primacy of the Roman Church.[54] And when we look at Leo's letters — for corroborating evidence only — we shall see that the cardinal-curialist

---

[51] *Quod si, ut summopere sibi et omnibus expedit, zelo domus Dei sine intermissione tabescens, fidelis dispensator et prudens existens, Deo et hominibus opere et sermone irreprehensibilem sese conservare studuerit, ut vere fatear, universum pene mundum secum attonitum et sollicitum post Deum currere facit, ex utroque sexu populos diverse professionis, condicionis et etatis catervatim domino suo super omnia bona ipsius constituendus ducit. Si vero sue et fraterne salutis...*

[52] *Salvo enim divine omnipotentie misterio....*

[53] See MICHEL, *Papstwahl und Königsrecht*, pp. 13 ff.; idem, in *Studi Gregoriani*, I, 86; see, furthermore, J. B. SÄGMÜLLER, *Die Tätigkeit und Stellung der Cardinäle bis auf Bonifaz VIII.*, pp. 128 ff., idem, *Lehrbuch des katholischen Kirchenrechts*, (4th ed.), I, 4, p. 517; cf. C. JORDAN, *Le sacré Collège au m. a*, in *Revue des cours et des conferences*, XXIII, 128 ff.; H. W. KLEWITZ, *Die Entstehung* etc., in *Savigny Zeitschrift*, Kanonist. Abt., XXV, 115 ff., and KUTTNER, in *Traditio*, III, 172 ff.

[54] See especially, KUTTNER, art. cit., p. 176.

pattern emerges here too. To take only one example of Leo's letters: to the patriarch in Constantinople he writes in a language that shows the modification of the term Roman Church, or rather the clarification of this institution when he says: « Like the immovable hinge that sends the door forth and back, thus Peter and his successors have the free judgment over the entire Church... Therefore his clerics are named cardinals, f o r t h e y b e l o n g m o r e c l o s e l y t o t h e h i n g e b y w h i c h e v e r y t h i n g e l s e i s m o v e d ».[55] Humbert as the draughtsman of this letter expresses exactly the same idea which he had conveyed in De s. R. ecclesia. The Roman Church consists of the cardinals and the pope. It is the Church of the apostle to which Christ's words were directed.

Humbert is as convinced of the primacy of the Roman Church as he is of the rights of the Cardinals. The De s. Romana ecclesia contains the germ of all the later constitutional quarrels between the pope on the one hand and the College of Cardinals on the other hand; but it also contains the germ of the later canonistic theory that the Roman Church was a corporation to which all the consequences of a properly developed corporation theory could be applied.[56] In a word, the Roman Church had become the corporate epitome of universal Christendom. The pope is merely the head of this corporate epitome, and it is in this function, as the apex of the apostolic see, that he addresses the faithful. They have every reason to see in him the actual Ruler — revera, says the Cardinal, « they look at him with reverence and prefer his interpretation to the sacred writings themselves »; but although this is a matter of fact, the point in theory is that the pope as an individual may fall into error. When therefore Gregory VII in Dictatus Papae 22 lays axiomatically down that « the Roman Church has never erred », he expresses exactly the same idea as Humbert: Gregory does not evade the question at all.[57] According to Humbert, the pope virtually appears to the universal Church as the true Ruler, but there is, theoretically, just the chance — forte — that he deviates from the faith, in which case, theoretically, he is subject to judgment. The pope partakes in the

---

[55] LEO IX's letter in C. WILL, Acta et Scripta etc., cap XXXII, pp. 81-2.

[56] O. GIERKE, Deutsches Genossenschaftsrecht, III, 251 ff.; SÄGMÜLLER, Cardinäle, pp. 225 ff.; B. TIERNEY, A Thirteenth-Century Conciliarist, in Catholic Historical Review, XXXVI (1951), 426 ff.

[57] As MICHEL (op. cit., p. 32, note 1) would have it: « Der DP 22 u m g e h t die Frage, insofern er die Unfehlbarkeit der 'römischen Kirche' zuschreibt ».

function of the Roman Church, but only in so far as he is a member of this corporation.[58]

What reasons might the Cardinal have had to dwell at such inordinate length on the possible moral defects of the pope, whilst the — dogmatically at least — much more important issue of the pope's orthodoxy is given so little prominence? The latter is subordinated to a mere *nisi* clause, whilst the pope's moral deviations are painted in rhetorically bleak terms. The reason for this stands in closest proximity to the fundamental opposition of Humbert to the *Rex-Sacerdos* idea. The dealings of Henry III were still fresh in the memory of the curia, and Henry's removal of the two popes for what Cardinal Humbert indubitably would have called a *culpa* was unjustifiable by reason of the relevant canons purporting to safeguard the immunity of the pope. There was *mortalium nullus* who had the right to sit in judgment over the pope's moral failings. The accountability of the pope for heresy is almost tucked away — surely a far more important aspect than a simoniacal or otherwise immoral pope. The importance of this pronouncement would have warranted a statement which would not have been so disproportionate in comparison with the preceding lengthy exposition of his moral deviations. Admitting the legal possibility of subjecting the pope to a judgment for his aberration from the faith — the question at once arises: who is to judge him? And, who is to watch the pope's orthodoxy? It is certainly strange that Humbert deals with a negative point at such great length, whilst the positive point is, so to speak, only half-made.

We may perhaps find the answer in the source from which he derived the *nisi* clause. As we pointed out before, this heresy clause was the exception which permitted inferiors to charge their ecclesiastical superior and to notify their heresy to the apostolic see. The step which Humbert took in applying the heresy clause — which, we should bear in mind, had never been used in connexion with the *Prima sedes a nemine judicatur* — to the pope would indicate that he also accepted the apostolic see as the last resort. The tenor and the fundamental ideas of the *De s. Romana ecclesia* leave little room for doubt as to who was to sit in judgment over the pope,

---

[58] This, indeed, may later lead, in a rather tortuous and circuitous route to the distinction between private and official capacity, but in the *De s. Romana ecclesia* there is absolutely no support for this distinction.

who was to control his orthodoxy, and who in fact was to deal with him if he deviated from the faith: the Roman Church. As the corporate epitome of the universal Church the Roman Church, that is, the curia as constituted by the Cardinals, has the right to judge the pope's heresy. Moreover, if there is *mortalium nullus* who should sit in judgment over the pope's moral deviations, there must be some mortals who can do so in the case of his heresy. It would have been most imprudent on the part of the learned Cardinal to say all this explicitly, but how else is one to justify, firstly, the peculiar construction of this literary product, beginning with the Roman Church, then going over to the pope, and reverting again to the Roman Church; and, secondly, the novel combination of the immunity of the pope (hitherto unconditional) with the heresy clause (hitherto applicable only to non-papal ecclesiastics)? To the initiated it must have been clear enough what the author of the *De s. Romana ecclesia* wished to say — and none understood the Cardinal better, that is, Dist. 40, c. 6 of the *Decretum,* than the leading canonist of the following century, Huguccio, who had no qualms in saying: *Cardinales possunt deponere papam propter haeresim.*[59]

We suggest, therefore, that *De s. Romana ecclesia* constitutes an entirely new departure, in so far as the internal constitutional government of the Church is concerned. It created what might be called the problem of the cardinalate, that is, the function and position of the Cardinals within the Roman Church. The canonical status of the Cardinals was a problem that was to emerge as soon as the College of Cardinals came into being, and this problem was inconspicuously tucked away in *De s. Romana ecclesia.* To anyone acquainted with the endless disputes within the curia as to the standing of the Cardinals, it must be plain that the seeds of this controversy were contained in this literary product. Sometimes this problem smouldered under the surface, sometimes it broke out with elemental force and with a fury which characterizes a repressed tension, as it was the case in the eventful year 1378. It was a problem that was to engage the attention of the leading canonists in the centuries following Humbert's own.[60]

---

[59] Huguccio's *Summa* ad Dist. 63, c. 23. For further details see the present writer's *Origins of the Great Schism,* Appendix: *Cardinal Zabarella and his position in the Conciliar Movement.*

[60] See esp. Tierney, art. cit., pp. 429 ff., and Sägmüller's articles in *Theologische*

To say, however, that Humbert's piece began to exercise influence in the canonistic sphere only by virtue of its inclusion in Gratian's *Decretum* would be accurate in one sense only, namely, in so far as the theory of corporation was to evolve the corporate nature of the Roman Church with the pope as a mere head of this corporate body. The echo of Humbert's piece can be felt, however, almost immediately. We have in fact two witnesses, each obviously focussing their attention on this weighty document. The one is the author of the *Dictatus* of Avranches, who in cap. 2 gives a direct reply to Humbert and flatly contradicts the Cardinal's statement: *A nemine papa judicari potest, etiamsi fidem negaverit.*[61] And it may well be that DA. should be dated earlier than has hitherto been assumed, namely, to the very beginning of Gregory VII's pontificate.[62] The other witness as strongly endorses the view of the *De s. R. ecclesia* as the DA. denies it. Cardinal Hugh asserts, like his greater colleague, that what matters is the see of Rome, not the pope.[63] The pope, according to Hugh, is merely the mouthpiece of the Holy See.[64] Lastly, the Roman Church being the Cardinals together with the Pope, the former have the right to depose the latter, as, according to Hugh's reading of history, they had done so in the cases of Anastasius and Liberius: *Liberius et Anastasius... a cardinalibus sanctae sedis ut profani dampnati sunt.*[65]

The controversy regarding as to who constitutes the Roman Church naturally came only to the fore, when circumstances favoured the open eruption of the problem. As the machinery of Church government grew more complicated as time went on, so also increased the opportunities for friction between pope and cardinals: the succeeding centuries show this all too clearly, especially when such land marks are given their proper historical evaluation as Frederick

---

Quartalschrift, LXXX, 6.18; LXXXIII, 45 ff.; LXXXVIII, 595. See also V. MARTIN, *Comment s'est formée la doctrine de la superiorité du concile*, in *Revue des sciences religieuses*, XVII, 121 ff.

[61] S. LÖWENFELD, *Der Dictatus Papae* etc., in *Neues Archiv* etc., XVI, 198.

[62] So SACKUR, in *Neues Archiv*, XVIII, 150; see also HOFMANN, op. cit., p. 21.

[63] *MGH., Libelli de lite*, II, 404 (Ep. Ugonis, no. IV), and p. 419 (Ad Mathildam). ... *verbum Domini dicentis Petro et per Petrum Romanae sedi 'Quodcumque ligaveris super terram ...' est autem privilegium Romanae sedis semper assistere per cardinales ... ipsi pontifici vel vicario ipsius sedis, id est, q u e m i p s a s e d e s s a c r o s a n c t a o s s u u m facit, per quem et cum quo praedicat, per quem sacramenta administrat..*

[64] See the preceding note.

[65] ibid., p. 418.

II's appeal to the cardinals,[66] the Colonna troubles during Boniface VIII's time,[67] the Avignonese re-organisation of curial business culminating in the disaster of 1378 which was primarily concerned with this particular constitutional issue.[68]

We cannot omit to mention that amongst the most extreme papalists of later days we also find at the same time the staunchest attackers of papal absolutism within the curia: whether or not it is a coincidence, it is a fact nevertheless that this dichotomy — an extreme papalism directed outwards vis-à-vis the universal Church, and a rigid constitutionalism directed inwards, that is, within the curia — can usually be observed with canonists who were cardinals. It is the beginning of this very same dichotomy which we find with Cardinal Humbert — an enthusiastic defender of papalism as well as of the constitutional restriction of the pope's function at least as far as his orthodoxy was concerned. Once this breach was admitted it was only a matter of resolving a theory, particularly the one based on the concept of corporations, that other constitutional restrictions of the pope within the curia followed as a matter of course. The stimulus given to these later developments by Cardinal Humbert in particular and by the Gregorian era in general is an aspect that would merit closer attention than it has hitherto received.

Cambridge (Engl.), Trinity College

---

[66] See B. SÜTTERLIN, *Die Politik K. Friedrichs II. und die Kardinäle;* and H. WEIRUSCOWSKI, *Vom Imperium zum nationalen Königtum,* pp. 179, 189, 191.

[67] It is not without significance that Boniface VIII in his *Unam Sanctam* said this: *Si deviat spiritualis minor, a suo superiori (judicabitur). Si vero suprema, a solo Deo, non ab homine, poterit judicari,* in *Extravag. Comm.,* I, viii, 1.

[68] See *Origins of the Great Schism,* pp. 170 ff. Cf. also Professor R. P. E. de Moreau S. J., *Une nouvelle théorie sur les origines du grand schisme d'Occident,* in *Bulletin de l'Académie royale de Belgique,* Classe des Lettres, XXXV (1949), 182 ff.

II

Von Canossa nach Pavia

Zum Strukturwandel der Herrschaftsgrundlagen
*im salischen und staufischen Zeitalter**

Die Erschütterungen, die der Investiturstreit auslöste, hatten bekanntlich tiefe Spuren nicht nur in der Papstgeschichte hinterlassen, sondern auch in der deutschen und gesamteuropäischen Geschichte, weil die aufgeworfenen Probleme an den Grundfesten der bestehenden Ordnung rüttelten. Das im Titel kurzschriftlich durch die Ortsnamen angedeutete Thema soll zum Ausdruck bringen, daß sich eine klare staatsrechtliche Verbindung herstellen läßt zwischen dem Geschehen in Canossa 1077 und dem Konzil in Pavia 1160, das nach etwas mehr als 80 Jahren dort abgehalten wurde. Trotz der schier unübersehbaren Sekundärliteratur möchte es scheinen, daß die Bedeutung, die diese beiden Ortsnamen hinsichtlich der herrscherlichen Stellung einnehmen, noch nicht voll erkannt ist. Canossa und Pavia können als die symbolischen Eckpfeiler von zwei Herrschaftssystemen angesehen werden, die sich in ihren Voraussetzungen und Zielrichtungen grundsätzlich unterschieden.

Diese Feststellung zwingt allerdings, in gedrängtester Kürze die königliche und die päpstliche Stellung im Investiturstreit zusammenzufassen. Das Papsttum war im Anschluß an die Maßnahmen des jüngst verstorbenen dritten Heinrich mit einer nahezu beispiellosen Dynamik und einer Wucht emporgewachsen, die die im Schoß der römischen Kirche aufgestauten Energien bald zum Durchbruch bringen sollten. Das Papsttum hatte ein Programm und hatte auch die Männer, die keinen Zweifel aufkommen ließen an ihrem Eifer, ihrer Fähigkeit und Entschlossenheit, ihr Programm in die Tat umzusetzen. Das Papstwahldekret von 1059 war eine unmißverständliche Maßnahme, die dem bisherigen Zustand ein Ende bereiten sollte[1]. Dazu kommt die Verbindung, die das Papsttum mit der Mailänder Pataria angeknüpft

---

* Leicht erweiterte Fassung eines Vortrages, den der Verfasser an der Philosophischen Fakultät I der Universität München am 4. Juni 1973 hielt. Für die ehrende Einladung, den Vortrag dem Historischen Jahrbuch zur Verfügung zu stellen, sei dem hochverdienten Herausgeber wärmstens gedankt.

[1] Darüber vgl. zuletzt H. G. K r a u s e , Das Papstwahldekret von 1059 und seine Rolle im Investiturstreit (1960); W. S t ü r n e r , Salvo debito honore et reve-

hatte[2]. Diese Verbindung verrät einen tiefen ideologischen Hintergrund: sie zeigt, daß das Papsttum keineswegs abgeneigt war, sich einer Gruppe oder einer Partei anzuschließen, die sich nicht in das bisherige soziale Gefüge einordnen ließ. Die Patarini waren weit davon entfernt, die gesellschaftlichen und herrscherlichen Grundlagen der überkommenen Ordnung anzunehmen. Im Gegenteil, sie wandten sich ab von den konservativen, traditionsgebundenen Schichten und setzten ein radikalisierendes, wenn nicht sogar ein teilweises revolutionäres Programm dem Establishment entgegen. Die enge Interessengemeinschaft zwischen Kurie und Pataria läßt sich unschwer erklären: beide beabsichtigten, die bisher geltenden gesellschaftlichen und herrscherlichen Grundlagen zum Teil zu beseitigen, und zum Teil zu modifizieren. Dazu kommt noch ein anderer erheblicher Umstand. Die Patarini rekrutierten sich überwiegend, wenn nicht ausschließlich, aus der städtischen Bevölkerung, und in dieser Zusammensetzung liegt ein Schlüssel zum Verständnis: die Spitze richtete sich gegen die konservativen Kreise, die im Landadel ihre mächtigste Stütze hatten[3].

Der Landadel hatte aber einen starken Rückhalt im deutschen König und ganz besonders in Oberitalien. Wenn daher die Kurie gegen Simonie, gegen die von Königtum und Hochadel entscheidend beeinflußten bischöflichen und erzbischöflichen Ernennungen Stellung nahm[4], und den Konkubinat und die vielen anderen Mißstände verurteilte, so fand sie bei den Patarini ein williges Ohr und kräftige Unterstützung[5]. Der Zusammenschluß von Kurie und Pataria schuf eine völlig neue gesellschaftliche Konstellation. Dadurch kamen die bisher vernachlässigten

---

rentia: ZRG Kan. Abt. 54 (1968), dazu H. G r u n d m a n n, Eine neue Interpretation des Papstwahldekrets von 1059: DA 25 (1969) 234—6. Ferner W. U l l m a n n, A short history of the papacy in the Middle Ages (1972) 135 f.

[2] Darüber G. M i c c o l i, Per la storia della Pataria milanese, in dessen Chiesa Gregoriana (1967) 101—60; H. E. J. C o w d r e y, The papacy, the Patarenes and the Church of Milan: Transactions of the Royal Historical Society, 5. Serie, 18 (1968) 25—48.

[3] Obgleich von ganz anderen Voraussetzungen ausgehend, deutet K. B o s l, Mensch und Gesellschaft in der Geschichte Europas (1972) aus gesellschaftlich-anthropologischer Sicht diese Situation in ähnlichem Sinne (hier 131–2).

[4] Über deren tatsächlichen Umfang unterrichtet grundlegend L. S a n t i f a l l e r, Zur Geschichte des ottonisch-salischen Reichskirchensystems: SB. Wien, Phil. Hist. Kl., Bd. 229, 1. Abh. (1954); 2. Aufl. (Wien 1964). Erst nach Fertigstellung des Textes erhielt ich Kenntnis von der jüngst erschienenen und sehr bedeutsamen Studie von G. K o c h, Auf dem Weg zum Sacrum Imperium (1972) (freundlicher Hinweis von Herrn Professor G. Baaken [Tübingen]). Zum Reichskirchensystem vgl. nunmehr zusätzlich G. K o c h, 30 ff., bes. 41 ff.

[5] Über das Programm der Patarini vgl. C. V i o l a n t e, La Pataria milanese e la riforma ecclesiastica, I: le premesse 1045–1057 (1955); vgl. dazu F. J. S c h m a l e in seiner Rezension in HZ 187 (1959) 376 ff., der das religiöse Element der Pataria stark in den Vordergrund rückt (besonders 379 f.).

städtischen Massen – die sog. silent majority – ins kuriale Blickfeld. Die Zielsetzung der Kurie war sicherlich reformatorisch, trug aber gewiß auch revolutionäre Merkmale an sich, und zwar nicht im Hinblick auf das Programm, das doch schon Jahrhunderte alt war, sondern im Hinblick auf die Mittel, deren sie sich bediente, um das Ziel zu erreichen[6]. Man denke hier bloß an die Proklamation eines Laienstreiks, der vom Papsttum gegen die simonistischen und beweibten Kleriker postuliert und zum Teil auch in Szene gesetzt worden war[7]. Wenn daher die gewählten Mittel vielleicht nicht der Tradition entsprachen, so versprachen sie dennoch eine erfolgreiche Ausführung des Gesamtplanes. Von entscheidender Bedeutung war, daß das Papsttum die Beseitigung der traditionellen Herrschaftsstruktur als eine wesentliche Voraussetzung für die erfolgreiche Durchführung seines Planes betrachtete.

Diese Herrschaftsstruktur hatte die durch das Eigenkirchenwesen geförderten, wenn nicht verursachten, Übelstände gezeigt, wie etwa Simonie usw., die eine fruchtbare Entfaltung der in der Christenheit schlummernden Potentialitäten nach päpstlicher Auffassung nicht zuließen. Dem Papsttum erschien die Christenheit in einem Zustand der Unfreiheit zu leben, der durch das geltende Herrschaftssystem bedingt war. Die Überwindung dieser Unfreiheit und die Herstellung der Freiheit sei aber nur möglich, wenn an die Stelle der Grundlagen, auf denen das herrschende System aufgebaut war, andere und zwar mit dem Wesen des Christentums und der Kirche verträglichere träten[8]. Der Stein des Anstoßes war das traditionell praktizierte monarchische Herrschaftsprinzip auf Seiten der zeitgenössischen Könige, das aber vor allem beim deutschen König in besonders akzentuierter Weise in Erscheinung trat. Das Papsttum verfocht die Ansicht, die Monarchie und die daraus fließende Souveränität der Könige in ihrem Königreich seien mit der kirchlicherseits vertretenen Auffassung vom Christentum nicht nur nicht vereinbar, sondern dem innersten Wesen einer christlichen Gemeinschaft zuwider.

Diesen monarchischen Herrschaftsgedanken innerhalb der christlich orientierten Gemeinschaft zu bewältigen war daher das Ziel der päpst-

---

[6] Einzelheiten bei W. U l l m a n n , The Growth of papal government in the Middle Ages (4. Aufl. 1970) Kap. 8 passim.

[7] Vgl. etwa Gregors Register IV. 2 und 10, usw. Die Zustände werden lebhaft geschildert von Sigbert von Gembloux in seiner Apologia: MGH. Libelli de Lite II. 438–9; siehe auch seine Chronica, in MGH. VI. 362–3: »Gregorius papa celebrata synodo symoniacos anathematizavit et uxoratos sacerdotes a divino officio removit et laicis missam eorum audire interdixit novo exemplo . . .«

[8] Dies scheint mir der wesentliche Inhalt der Kampflosung zu sein, die im Schlachtruf der *libertas ecclesiae* gipfelt. Darüber vgl. W. U l l m a n n , Growth of papal government, bes. 297 Anm. 2 mit weiterer Literatur.

lichen Politik. Das Papsttum hatte auch das Mittel parat, nämlich den päpstlichen Primat, der sich seiner Struktur nach als monarchisches Herrschaftsprinzip verstand. Seit frühester Zeit war die primatiale Rolle des Papsttums der Angelpunkt der von ihm betonten Herrschaftslehre in einem christlichen Gemeinwesen[9]. Der päpstliche Primat war der Urgrund und Mittelpunkt der christlichen Gesellschaftsauffassung, wie sie vom Papsttum in tausenden von Quellen seit dem 4. Jahrhundert proklamiert worden war. Und um diese vortrefflich verbürgte Funktion des Papstes zu verwirklichen, bedurfte es nicht nur gewisser Berichtigungen und Begradigungen im Funktionsbereich der weltlichen Herrscher, sondern einer radikalen Strukturveränderung des von den weltlichen Herrschern geübten Herrschaftssystems. Im Rahmen der gegebenen Wirklichkeit bedeutete dieser Plan einen Frontalangriff auf den mächtigsten der zeitgenössischen Herrscher, den deutschen, nicht weil er deutsch war[10], nicht weil er möglicherweise römischer Kaiser werden konnte, nicht weil er in irgendeiner Weise Glaubenssätze verletzt hätte, sondern weil er geradezu unverfälscht eine Tradition verkörperte und darstellte, die der vom Papsttum geplanten Herrschaft in einem christlichen Gemeinwesen diametral entgegengesetzt war und der Anwendung päpstlicher Grundsätze im öffentlichen Bereich sehr wirksam im Wege stand. Auf den deutschen König Heinrich IV. konzentrierte sich der Frontalangriff, weil er dem Papsttum als das Sinnbild einer *damnosa haereditas* galt, die sich zusätzlich im italischen Herrschaftsbereich eindrucksvoll bemerkbar machte. In Heinrich IV. waren in der Tat alte deutschrechtliche Herrschaftsgrundsätze und theokratische Gedanken zu einer glänzenden, wenn nicht vorbildlichen Symbiose und Einheit verschmolzen. Nach päpstlicher Ansicht waren allerdings die gegeißelten Mißstände das Produkt dieser innigen Verschmelzung gewesen.

Dieser nahezu nahtlosen Verklammerung verdankte aber das theokratisierte Herrscheramt seine Stärke, die freilich auch zur Schwäche werden konnte. Die Stärke lag darin, daß es den König vermöge der Salbung weit über alle seine Untertanen emporhob, und die Schwäche zeigte sich darin, daß der Herrscher seine gehobene Stellung und Funk-

---

[9] Darüber vgl. W. U l l m a n n , Leo I and the theme of papal primacy: Journ. of theological studies, new series, 11 (1960) 25 ff., und über den Hintergrund vgl. W. U l l m a n n , The cosmic theme of the Prima Clementis and its significance for the concept of Roman rulership, in: Texte und Untersuchungen zur Geschichte der altchristlichen Literatur, 108 (1972) (= Studia Patristica XI) 84 ff.; W. U l l - m a n n , Papst und König (1966) 13–19.

[10] Diese These wurde in überspitzter, möglicherweise zeitbedingter Art vorgetragen von G. K a l l e n , Der Investiturstreit als Kampf zwischen germanischem und romanischem Denken: Jahrb. des Kölnischen Geschichtsvereins 19 (1937) 89–110.

tion den Mittlern dieses Sakramentes verdankte[11], denen er, wenn sie einmal kräftig zupackten, unbarmherzig ausgeliefert war. Diese theokratisierte Herrschaft war zur Tradition geworden. Und hier ist es wie bei jeder traditionsgebundenen Einrichtung – sie besteht und gedeiht so lange nicht an ihren Grundfesten gerührt und sie nicht einer erbarmungslosen kalten rationellen Kritik ausgesetzt wird. Wenn das geschieht, dann zerbröckelt und zerfällt die Tradition und mit ihr auch die von ihr getragene Institution. Das aber war gerade der Fall im Investiturstreit. Die Argumentation, es sei doch schon immer so gewesen, konnte nicht verfangen, weil sie vor der Kritik, die sich auf rationelle Überlegungen stützte, in ein Nichts zerfloß. Dazu kommt noch, um das Bild zu vervollständigen, die eingangs berührte Machtkonstellation in Oberitalien, wo die Verbindung zwischen Kurie und Pataria ihre besondere Note und ihren historischen Sinn erhält.

Gewiß hatte der deutsche Herrscher, wie jeder andere zeitgenössische, ein Programm, das sich in der Erhaltung des bestehenden Rechtszustandes und der überkommenen Herrschaftsmaxime, in der Festigung der sozialen Schichtungen erschöpfte. Die Aufgabe des Königs war, die natürlich entwickelte und gewordene Ordnung zu verfestigen und vor Schaden zu bewahren. In jeder Hinsicht war dieses Programm konservativ und traditionsgebunden. Es verpflichtete den Herrscher, weil die Vorfahren den Weg vorgezeichnet und beschritten hatten. Gewohnheit, Tradition, Herkommen, waren die Quadern des königlicherseits vertretenen Programms. Mir ist keine Schrift bekannt, die in konstruktiver Art einen gedanklichen Unterbau dieses Programms geliefert oder ein positives Herrschaftsprogramm entworfen hätte.

Worin bestand nun dieses traditionsgebundene Herrschaftssystem? Es war vor allem ein gewordenes, nicht erdachtes, sondern eines, das

---

[11] Die Königssalbung galt bis ins 13. Jahrhundert hinein als echtes Sakrament, und Sakramente konnten verständlicherweise nur von den hierzu befugten kirchlichen Amtsträgern vermittelt werden. Über den Sakramentscharakter der Königsweihe im 12. Jahrhundert vgl. etwa Otto von Freising, Gesta Friderici: MGH, SS. Rer. Germ. II. 3, S. 104, Z. 28 (anläßlich der Königsweihe Barbarossas); Petrus Blesensis Ep. 10: Migne PL 207. 28 B und 29; im 13. Jahrhundert vgl. etwa den Lincolner Bischof Robert Grosseteste in seinem Brief an König Heinrich III., hrsg. von L. Wickham L e g g , English Coronation Records (1901) 67, sowie auch Papst Alexander IV, siehe die Stelle bei P. E. S c h r a m m , Der König von Navarre: ZRG, Germ. Abt. 68 (1951) 110 ff., hier S. 147. Zur Salbung siehe insbes. E. M ü l l e r , Die Anfänge der Königssalbung im Mittelalter: Hist. Jahrb. 58 (1938) und C. A. B o u m a n , Sacring and Crowning: the development of the Latin ritual for the anointing of kings and the coronation of an emperor before the 11th century (1957). Über die Bedeutung der Königssalbung im Rahmen der karolingischen Erneuerung vgl. W. U l l m a n n , The Carolingian Renaissance and the idea of kingship (1969) 71 ff., sowie die bisher noch unveröffentlichte Cambridger Dissertation meiner Schülerin J. N e l s o n , »Early medieval royal inauguration rites«.

immerhin in seiner damaligen Gestaltung auf eine mehrhundertjährige Entwicklung und Übung zurückblicken konnte und das seine konkrete strukturelle Substanz im fränkischen Zeitalter erhalten hatte. Dieser Herrscher, der sich, was häufig nicht erkannt wird, während des 9. Jahrhunderts im Zuge der karolingischen Erneuerung oder Renaissance entwickelt hatte, war eine Gestalt, die der Taufe nachgebildet worden war. Das heißt, wie der Christ durch die Taufe zu einer *nova creatura* wurde, wie die Taufe den *homo naturalis,* den Naturmenschen, in ein anderes Wesen verwandelte (ich gebrauche hier paulinische Ausdrücke) und zu einer Wiedergeburt auf höherer als der natürlichen Ebene führte[12], ebenso erlebte der König vom 9. Jahrhundert an eine Wiedergeburt als Ergebnis der Salbung, die, wie bekannt, gewisse Taufelemente einer früheren Zeit in sich aufgenommen hatte[13]. Diese Wiedergeburt des Königs war eine ideologisch wie auch religiös notwendige Folge des sozialen Erneuerungsgedankens, der, wie erinnerlich, die fränkische Gesellschaft von Grund aus erneuern, neu gestalten, und zu einer wahren christlichen Gesellschaft machen sollte: das Ziel war die Wiedergeburt der Gesellschaft als des *populus Dei*[14]. Die Salbung erreichte im Rahmen der Königssphäre genau dasselbe, was die Taufe beim Einzelnen bewirkte, d. h. eine Wiedergeburt, und zwar war die Wiedergeburt des Königs zwingend und engst mit der Wiedergeburt der Gesellschaft selbst verknüpft.

Die Wirkung dieser königlichen Wiedergeburt bestand nicht bloß in einem Verblassen der bisherigen grundsätzlichen Herrschaftsvoraussetzungen, sondern war eine wahrhaftige Transformation des hiermit wiedergeborenen Königs. Genau wie der Täufling wurde auch der König zu einer *nova creatura.* Diese *Wesens*veränderung stellte sich im Alten Testament unzweideutig dar. Wie das Taufwasser das natürliche Wesen im Menschen wegspülte, und ihn an den göttlichen Gnaden teilnehmen ließ[15], in eben demselben Maße erwirkte die Salbung (die Chrismatio) die Ersetzung des »natürlichen« Herrschers durch einen, der an der göttlichen Herrschaft der Menschheit besonderen Anteil haben sollte. Das machen die Krönungsordines, insbesondere die Ge-

---

[12] Vgl. etwa Paulus in I Kor. 2. 14; II Kor. 5. 17; Gal. 5. 24; 6. 15; Kol. 2. 12; Tit. 3. 5.

[13] Darüber vgl. W. U l l m a n n , Carolingian Renaissance, Kap. 4.

[14] Ebda, Kap. 1 und 2. Ferner G. L a d n e r , Erneuerung: Realencyklopädie f. Antike und Christentum 6 (1966) 262 ff.

[15] Über die Taufe vgl. vor allem O. H e g g e l b a c h e r , Die christliche Taufe als Rechtsakt nach dem Zeugnis der frühen Christenheit (1953). Vgl. noch P. E. S c h r a m m in ZRG , Kan. Abt. 68 (1951) 395: »Die Taufsalbung ist also eine spirituelle Königssalbung.« S. auch L. M i t c h e l l , Baptismal Anointing (1966), 121, 129 f.

betstexte, unmißverständlich klar[16]. Die Hauptwirkung war jedoch diese: das bisher durch Geblüt vermittelte Recht zur Herrschaft wurde ersetzt durch das durch Gnade vermittelte Recht zur Herrschaft. An die Stelle des Charismas des Blutes trat das Charisma der göttlichen Gnade. Der Herrscher ist zum *Rex Dei gratia* geworden, wobei der Akzent auf der *gratia Dei* liegt. Es ist überflüssig zu betonen. daß dieses wiedergeborene Herrschertum nur gegen den religiösen Hintergrund voll erfaßt werden kann. Das paulinische *Dei gratia sum id quod sum* erhielt im König von Gottes Gnaden seine konkrete Verwirklichung. Es war diese stärkstens ausgeprägte religiöse Komponente, die die besondere ekklesiologische Wirkung im Herrschaftsbereich erzeugte[16a].

Das bedeutet jedoch, daß das Herrscherantlitz ekklesiologisch bestimmt wurde und der Herrscher in stetig steigendem Maße an den ekklesiologischen Attributen teilzunehmen begann. Anders ausgedrückt: der Herrscher, der seine Stellung der von der Hierarchie vermittelten Gnade verdankte, wurde nunmehr in den kirchlichen Organismus inkorporiert[17]. Damit setzte er sich von den Laiengewalten sichtlich ab. Auch hier finden wir eine klare Parallele zur Taufe, die die Eingliederung des Täuflings in die Kirche als Heilsanstalt bewirkte, genau wie hier beim König, der zur *persona ecclesiastica* wurde oder zum *rex canonicus*[18], was seine enge Verknüpfung mit dem geistlichen

---

[16] Deshalb auch die Bezeichnung des Königs als eines *Athleta Christi* oder vielleicht noch einprägsamer die Kennzeichnung als *Typus Christi*, was schon in dem Sieben Formeln Ordo des späten 9. Jahrhunderts vorkommt: C. E r d m a n n , Forschungen zur politischen Ideenwelt des Frühmittelalters, (hrsg. F. Baethgen) (1951) 89; genau dasselbe im Mainzer Ordo I und in allen englischen Ordines. Vgl. noch W. U l l m a n n , Der Souveränitätsgedanke in den Krönungsordines: Festschrift f. P. E. Schramm I (1964) 72–90, bes. 82. Die Bedeutung des gesalbten Königs als eines Mitstreiters Christi kommt überzeugend in dem teleologisch gefaßten Text der Schwertformel zum Ausdruck: »... quatinus cum mundi salvatore, cuius tipum geris, sine fine merearis regnare«, aber ebenso in dem unmittelbar nach der Salbung gesprochenen Gebet *Deus, Dei filius* und in der Thronsetzungsformel *Sta et retine.* Besonders lehrreich ist das Gebet *Prospice,* das auf geniale Weise Teleologie mit christlicher Herrscherideologie verknüpfte.

[16a] Vgl. etwa Heinrich V. (anno 1099–1100): »Heinricus Dei gratia id quod sum« (Cod. Udalrici, nr. 94, S. 182).

[17] Verwiesen sei auf das Weihegebet *Omnipotens aeterne (sempiterne) Deus, creator omnium,* das u. a. die Übernahme des Königs in den Rahmen des Klerus zum Ausdruck bringt.

[18] Darüber insbes. A. S c h u l t e , Deutsche Könige, Kaiser und Päpste als Kanoniker an deutschen und römischen Kirchen: Hist. Jahrb. 54 (1934) 137 ff. (auch separat Darmstadt 1960); auch J. F l e c k e n s t e i n , Rex canonicus: Festschrift f. P. E. Schramm (wie oben Anm. 16) 57–72. Nicht weniger als 11 deutsche Könige wurden formell Kanoniker an deutschen Domkapiteln, zwei Männerstiften und am Lateran und in St. Peter zu Rom. Der König hatte Sitz und Stimme. Ähnliches trifft auch für die englischen Könige zu.

Stand ausdrücken sollte. Das wurde er, weil er das Herrscheramt von der Hierarchie förmlich übertragen erhielt durch die von derselben Hierarchie vermittelte göttlichen Gnade[19]. Es ist nunmehr verständlich, warum das Herrscheramt den König zum kirchlichen Amtsträger machte – es versteht sich, daß ich auf die Synode von Hohenaltheim (916) anspiele[20] – weil das Amt sich auf die Leitung einer ekklesiologisch verstandenen Gesellschaft – der *Christianitas* oder der *societas christiana*, usw. – bezog. Der König wurde damit zum Treuhänder eines ihm von Gott anvertrauten Gutes: das ist der Sinn des ständig wiederkehrenden *regnum nobis commissum*. Dieses Gut wurde ihm anläßlich der Salbung zur Leitung ausgehändigt. Ganz gewiß zeigt eine Tiefenanalyse dieses christlichen Königs vom 9. bis zum 11. Jahrhundert eine große Zahl von entscheidenden und unzweifelhaft wirksamen deutschrechtlichen Elementen in der Herrschaftsstruktur, aber diese wurden überlagert von dem theokratischen Herrschaftsgedanken, so daß man von einem theokratisierten Herrscher zu sprechen befugt ist.

Nun, dieser Herrscher hatte wenig Profil, noch weniger Konturen, und fast keine scharf ausgeprägten Merkmale. Ich möchte nicht, wie man das zuweilen liest, von einem sakralen Königtum sprechen, weil der Begriff zu schillernd ist und dabei Ober- und Untertöne mitschwingen, die das Bild zu verzerren geeignet sind. Der theokratisierte Herrscher hatte aber trotz der erwähnten Nachteile einen sehr großen Vorteil. Er war der *Christus Domini*[21], der Gesalbte des Herrn, der seinen eigenen Stand innehatte; denn er stand über dem ihm anvertrauten Volk[22] und der gerade dadurch einen uns heute im 20. Jahrhundert nahezu unvorstellbaren öffentlichen Schutz genoß. *Noli tangere christos meos*[23] war kein bloßes biblisches Schlagwort, sondern war ein im öffentlichen Recht anerkannter Grundsatz, mit einer gewichtigen Einschränkung, auf die ich sogleich zurückkommen werde. Diese theokratisierte Stellung des Herrschers war eine der Voraussetzungen für

---

[19] Auch hier sprechen die Gebetstexte bei der Krönung eine deutliche Sprache, vgl. etwa das Gebet bei der Schwertübergabe oder die Krönungsformel »per officium nostrae benedictionis«.

[20] Einzelheiten W. U l l m a n n , Carolingian Renaissance 128 ff. M. H e l l - m a n n , Die Synode von Hohenaltheim. In: Die Entstehung des deutschen Reiches (1956), 289 ff., hat zum ersten Male auf diese Entwicklung aufmerksam gemacht.

[21] I Kge 26. 9.

[22] Deshalb kommt dem Thron und der Thronsetzung in den Ordines besondere Bedeutung zu: der Thron symbolisiert die Höherstellung, die *superioritas*, des Herrschers, der von dieser hohen Warte das ihm anvertraute Königreich überblicken konnte. Warum es bei der mittelalterlichen Kaiserkrönung keinen Thron gab vgl. W. U l l m a n n , Carolingian Renaissance, 173 ff. und W. U l l m a n n , Short History of the Papacy in the Middle Ages (1972) 187 f., 211.

[23] Ps. 105. 15.

die Ausdehnung seiner Herrschaft auf den kirchlichen Organismus, was sich praktisch im Eigenkirchenwesen und -recht manifestierte. So sah der König aus, der dem Papsttum in den 70er Jahren des 11. Jahrhunderts gegenüberstand. Was stand ihm zur Verfügung, um die päpstlichen Ansprüche abzuwehren? Ich fürchte, im Grunde genommen nicht mehr als die Tradition und das Herkommen, die seine theokratisierte Herrscherstellung zwar geschichtlich verankerten[24], aber noch nichts über die Richtigkeit dieses Systems im Rahmen einer reflektierenden christlichen Herrschaftsstruktur aussagten. Vermag Tradition, Gewohnheit, Alter Unrecht in Recht zu verwandeln? Das war die entscheidende Frage, auf die die Antwort lautete: trotz und nicht wegen der auf religiöser Grundlage aufgebauten Herrschaft war dieses System einer christlichen Gemeinschaft nicht angemessen und widersprach ihr in grundsätzlichen Belangen. Es ist bekannt, wie sehr Heinrich IV. auf seine Stellung als *Christus Domini* gepocht hatte[25], womit er Gregor VII. des Sakrilegs zeihen wollte, aber es war ein Schlag ins Wasser, weil der Königssalbung niemals ein *character indelebilis* zuerkannt wurde[26] und im Gegensatz zur Bischofssalbung keinen sakrosankten Charakter verliehen hatte. Und über diese dem König verliehene Gnade hatten deren Spender zu befinden, was symbolisch in den zwei Gebeten Gregors VII. an die beiden Apostelfürsten in 1076 und 1080 bei der Bannung und Absetzung des Königs zum Ausdruck kam[27]. Ferner berief sich Heinrich IV. ebenso richtig wie wirkungslos auf die Gewohnheit und die Tradition, worauf ihm Gregor eine klassische Antwort erteilte: *Dominus non dixit Ego sum consuetudo, sed dixit Ego sum veritas*[28].

---

[24] Hier sei bemerkt, daß die Krönungsliturgie selbst stark den auf väterlicher Sitte beruhenden Herrschaftsgedanken zum Ausdruck brachte. Vgl. etwa den früh-deutschen Ordo, hrsg. von C. E r d m a n n , Forschungen 84 nr. 7: »... princeps interrogatur ab episcopis ... si ... cunctum populum sibi subiectum iuste et religiose regali providentia *iuxta morem patrum suorum* defendere ac regere velit.«

[25] »Me quoque, qui licet indignus inter christos ad regnum sum unctus, tetigisti, quem sanctorum patrum traditio soli Deo iudicandum docuit nec pro aliquo crimine, nisi a fide quod absit exorbitaverim, depondendum asseruit« (MGH. Const. I. nr. 62, S. 111 = C. Erdmann, Die Briefe Heinrichs IV.: Deutsches Mittelalter, Kritische Studientexte des Reichsinstituts für ältere deutsche Geschichtskunde 1 (1937) nr. 12; übersetzt von K. Langosch, in: Die Briefe Kaiser Heinrichs IV. (1954) 49). Zur Stelle selbst sei bemerkt, daß der zweite Teil (»nec pro aliquo crimine«) wahrscheinlich z. T. wenigstens aus Isidors Sententiae stammt (Migne PL 83. 710). Die Möglichkeit einer Benutzung des Humbertinischen Fragments in Rücksicht auf »nisi a fide ...« ist durchaus nicht ausgeschlossen. Zu dieser Terminologie und deren Ableitung vgl. W. U l l m a n n , Cardinal Humbert and the Romana Ecclesia: Studi Gregoriani, IV (1952) 109 ff., bes. 118 ff. [26] Vgl. die Literatur oben Anm. 11; ferner J. L. N e l s o n in: Studies in Church History VII (1970) 209 ff.

[27] Reg. III 10a (hrsg. E. Caspar, 270 f.); VII. 14a, S. 483 ff.

274

Wenn also Heinrich IV. – wie jeder andere zeitgenössische König – nichts anderes dem Papsttum entgegenzusetzen hatte als Thesen, die im Grunde seine Stellung nur verschlechterten, so kommt noch ein weiterer Umstand hinzu, der innig mit der theokratisierten Herrschaftsidee zusammenhängt, und das ist die einsame, auf dem Königsthron sitzende isolierte Figur des Herrschers, der sich eben vermöge seiner allen anderen unerreichbaren hohen Stellung (seiner *Majestas)* den Laienfürsten entfremdet hatte[28a]. Der König war doch in den kirchlichen Organismus eingebaut und hatte damit, jedenfalls ideologisch, eine Trennungslinie zwischen sich und den Laiengewalten gezogen. Keines der ihm zustehenden ekklesiologischen Attribute kam einem Laienfürsten zu.

Auf der anderen Seite stand dem Papsttum ein fest gefügtes und geschlossenes Programm zur Verfügung. Es war ein Programm, das sich auf grundsätzliche Erwägungen stützte, sich aus der Bibel ableitete oder jedenfalls die Bibel in seinem Sinne auslegte, sich auf Dekrete, Statuten, Synodalschlüsse usw. berufen konnte, und auf unzähligen Väteraussagen aufgebaut worden war – kurz, es war ein gedankliches, abgerundetes und fest umrahmtes System, das stets die Bibel als letzten Zeugen anzurufen bereit war. Man könnte wohl mit Recht hier sagen: im Anfang war das Wort, und nicht die Tat.

Hier ist besonders zu beobachten, daß das Papstprogramm auf den Begriff der Ordnung, des *ordo,* großes Gewicht legte. Das Papsttum behauptete, weil der in der christlichen Lehre fundierte *ordo* gestört sei, herrschte Unfreiheit[29]. Ordnung in diesem Sinne hieß aber Gliederung der Gesellschaft nach dem Grundsatz der Über- und Unterordnung, der *superioritas* und *inferioritas,* und damit stand im Zusammenhang die Idee des Rechts, das diese Ordnung erzeugt, erzwingt und erhält. Da es aber hier um die Ordnung einer rein christlichen Gemeinschaft ginge, könne das Recht setzende Organ nur ein solches sein, das über die nötige Qualifikation, das nötige Rüstzeug und Wissen um christliche Dinge verfüge. Die verbindlichen Leitsätze in der Form des Rechts konnten und sollten nach der Papstauffassung nur von den hierzu qualifizierten Amtsträgern fixiert werden. Dem Laien, auch wenn er ein gesalbter König war, wurde diese Qualifikation abgesprochen, was auch immer Gewohnheit, Herkommen und Tradition überliefert hätten. Und unter den befugten Amtsträgern ragte in ganz besonderer

---

[28] Dazu vgl. G. L a d n e r , Two Gregorian Letters: Studi Gregoriani V (1958) 225–42. G. K o c h 79 ff., 94, schien die Antwort Gregors entgangen zu sein.
[28a] Richtig hervorgehoben von G. K o c h 130.
[29] Darüber vgl. W. U l l m a n n , Growth of papal government 297 ff.

Weise der Papst selbst heraus. Das ist der Sinn des von Gregor vertretenen Anspruchs auf das *universale regimen*[30], ein Begriff, der den
primatialen Gedanken und damit die monarchische Papstidee unmißverständlich in den Vordergrund stellte und in einen sachlichen Zusammenhang mit der zeitgenössischen Gesellschaft brachte, auf die diese
Herrschaftsidee Anwendung finden sollte. Die Oberaufsicht über die
christliche Gemeinschaft, die Fixierung und Wahrung der ihre wesentliche Substanz betreffenden Grundlagen, zu denen verständlicherweise
die Besetzung der Kirchenämter gehörte, sollte den dafür Berufenen ob-
liegen. Zu diesen gehörte aber nicht der König. Dieses Papstprogramm
gipfelte in der Idee des Rechts, das die richtige Ordnung in der christlichen Gesellschaft erzwingen sollte. Erst diese Erkenntnis klärt die
volle Bedeutung des Investiturstreits; denn hier wurde die Idee des
Rechts in unzertrennliche Verbindung mit der Gemeinschaft gebracht,
auf die das Recht anzuwenden sei. In dieser Betonung der gesell-
schaftsbezogenen Rechtsidee[31] liegt vielleicht die wichtigste und
tiefste Bedeutung des Investiturstreits, in dem das königlich gesetzte
Recht sowie die Rechtsübung nicht als richtiges Recht anerkannt wurden. Kurz, die Lehre vom richtigen Recht ist nicht eine Erfindung des
19. oder 20. Jahrhunderts, sondern wurde schon im 11. Jahrhundert
auf die Probe gestellt.

Ein solches Recht setzt aber spezifische Kenntnis der die Gesellschaft
tragenden Grundsätze voraus, und das heißt hier der christlichen Maxime. Die christliche Gesellschaftsordnung entsprang nicht einer natür-

---

[30] Vgl. etwa Gregors Reg. II. 51, S. 193: »... ex universali regimine quod nobis
commissum est«; oder ebda II. 44, S. 280: »ex universalitate suscepti regiminis, omnibus qui in Christo sunt.« Auch in sog. Dictatus von Avranches scheint derselbe
Gedanke auf, diesmal mit Recht aus Gelasius I. abgeleitet, siehe cap. 10: »Papae omnis potestas mundi subdi debet Clemente Gelasio teste. Regna mutare potest ut Gregorius Stephanus Adrianus fecerunt.« Der hier genannte Klemens ist offenbar iden-
tisch mit dem Träger des Namens, der in der sog. Epistola Clementis als Bericht-
erstatter im Vordergrund stand; darüber vgl. W. Ullmann, The significance
of the Epistola Clementis in the Pseudo-Clementines: Journ. theol. studies, n. s. 11
(1960) 295 ff.
[31] Das hatte schon Kardinal Humbert von Silva Candida in seinen wuchtigen
und scharf formulierten Sätzen zum Ausdruck gemacht, als er von der *confusio* in der
christlichen Gemeinschaft sprach, die die Verwirklichung des *ordo rationis* verhin-
dere: Adversus simoniacos: MGH. Lib. de Lite, I. 205. Daher steht von jetzt ab auch
die Gleichsetzung der *anima* mit dem Recht und der Rechtsidee hoch im Kurs, während dem Begriff des *corpus* in dieser Gegenüberstellung die christliche Gesellschaft
entspricht; daher auch der funktionelle Vorrang der Geistlichkeit. Über den tiefen
rechtsideologischen Sinn der *anima-corpus* Allegorie vgl. W. Ullmann, Papst
und König (1966), 37 ff. mit Belegstellen. Und die Sempiternität der Kirche stützte
sich in diesem Gedankenschema auf die Verheißung in Matt. 16. 18 f., weil darin
die Uridee von der Wirkkraft des von Christus selbst gesetzten Rechts ausgedrückt
wurde (das »Bauen« der Kirche wurde im nomologischen Sinn verstanden).

lichen, intuitiven Einsicht, sondern war ein gedanklich aufgebautes System, das seinem Wesen nach all-umfassend kosmologisch war und sich auf aus der Bibel ableitbare Grundthesen berufen konnte. Mit anderen Worten, Tradition und Herkommen spielen in diesem Rahmen eine sehr untergeordnete Rolle. Darin erscheint mir der tiefere Sinn des päpstlichen Programms im 11. Jahrhundert (wie auch in früheren und späteren Zeiten) zu liegen. Und auf den Streit mit dem deutschen König angewandt, heißt dies auf andere Ebene transponiert eine Auseinandersetzung zwischen Natur und Gnade, die Natur symbolisiert in dem gewordenen, sich natürlich entwickelten Königtum, die Gnade dargestellt in der gedanklichen, systematisierten, organisierten kirchlichen Struktur, die im Papst ihre oberste Spitze hat. Dieser vom Papsttum nachhaltig vertretenen und kristallklaren Rechtsidee hatte das zeitgenössische Königtum nichts Gleichwertiges entgegenzusetzen. Denn das überlieferte Recht wurde zum Un/Recht deklariert, weil es auf un/rechten Voraussetzungen ruhte. Einen aussichtsreichen Kampf konnte auf so ungleicher Ebene ein theokratischer König nicht führen. Und darin liegt die ungeheure historische Bedeutung von Canossa[32]. Es rückte das äußerlich imposante, in seiner inneren Struktur aber brüchige theokratische Herrschertum ins grelle Lampenlicht. Der Schein konnte nicht mehr über die Wirklichkeit hinwegtäuschen.

Der Eintritt des römischen Rechts in die Arena dieses bitteren Kampfes gehört zu den epochalen Ereignissen des europäischen Mittelalters. Das römische Recht begann nunmehr als geistige Waffe für das deutsche Königtum herangezogen zu werden. Den Anfang machte der Ravennater Jurist Petrus Crassus in den frühen 80er Jahren des 11. Jahrhunderts[33]. Die Bedeutung liegt darin, daß ein als unübertroffen geltendes Rechtssystem in den Dienst des Königtums gestellt wurde, und hiermit wurde dieses römische Recht ein Kampfmittel in einer Auseinandersetzung, die die grundsätzliche Funktion eines Königs und des Papsttums betraf. Gleichzeitig verlagerte sich die Auseinandersetzung auf die Ebene gleichwertiger Rechtsordnungen. Diese Bedeutung wird noch dadurch erhöht, daß das benutzte römische Recht das Rechtsbuch eines Laien war, von dem man sagte, er hätte alle superlativen Eigenschaften wahren Römertums in sich vereinigt. Petrus Crassus wußte vortrefflich mit dem römischen Recht umzugehen und versuchte mit

---

[32] Zur Auslegung vgl. noch W. U l l m a n n , A short history of the papacy 157 ff.

[33] Über Ravenna vgl. F. C a l a s s o , Medio evo del diritto (1954) 281 ff. Der Traktat ist ediert in MGH. Lib. de Lite, I. 434 ff. Einzelheiten bei K. J o r d a n , Der Kaisergedanke in Ravenna zur Zeit Heinrichs IV.: DA 2 (1938) 315 ff., Papal government, 382 ff., sowie W. U l l m a n n , History of political ideas in the Middle Ages, 2. Aufl. (1970), 117 ff.

dessen Hilfe zu beweisen, daß die vom Papsttum vertretene Herrschaftsidee keineswegs mit dem Recht in Einklang zu bringen wäre. Im
Gegenteil, das päpstliche Programm sei dem Recht zuwider und die
vom Papst getroffenen oder angedrohten Maßnahmen seien rechtlich
durchaus zu verurteilen. Er schlug vor, daß sich Gregor wegen seines
verbrecherischen Verhaltens zu verantworten habe: Hildebrand sei der
hostis legum, der *hostis pacis* und *totius christianitatis*.
    Dieser Traktat ist lebhaft geschrieben. Der Verfasser zitiert recht
geschickt, und seine Argumentation verrät einen klaren Kopf und einen
scharfen Denker, der dem Gegner die Waffen zu entwinden sucht, und
zwar mit den Mitteln des Rechts, das das Papsttum als oberste Richtschnur auf öffentlich-rechtlichem Gebiet postuliert hatte. Nun ist dieser
Appell vom Recht aufs Recht gewiß sehr bedeutsam, doch erheben sich
bei näherer Analyse nicht zu unterdrückende Bedenken. Vor allem, war
das römische Recht wirklich ein geeignetes Mittel, um die päpstlichen
Ansprüche abzuwehren? Der Titel des Traktats – »Zur Verteidigung
König Heinrichs« – verrät unzweideutig den Defensivcharakter: gewiß
wollte er mit Hilfe des römischen Rechts Gregor der Rechtsverletzung
zeihen und das Gregorianische Herrschaftsprogramm in ein Vernichtungsprogramm der bestehenden öffentlichen Ordnung umwandeln,
nicht weil es der Tradition widersprach, sondern weil es Unrecht war,
wie eben durch das römische Recht bewiesen werden sollte. Aber war
das römische Recht das richtige Recht? Nirgends im römischen Recht
gab es einen König, nirgends las man etwas von jenen tiefgreifenden
und weitreichenden Problemen, die die Christenheit gerade in den letzten Jahrzehnten des 11. Jahrhunderts so tief erschüttert und ergriffen
hatten[34]. Es ist kaum möglich, ein Paradox von größerem Ausmaß sich
zu denken als den deutschen König mit Hilfe des Codex und der Novellen Justinians verteidigen zu wollen. Wohlgemerkt, der Streit ging
doch nicht um die Funktion eines römischen Kaisers in einer christlichen Gesellschaft, sondern betraf ausschließlich königliche Rechte[35].
Die Investiturfrage und die vielen anderen Probleme und Mißstände
hatten gar nichts mit einem römischen Kaiser zu tun, sondern betrafen
königliche Rechte, die im letzten Urgrund auf deutschrechtliche Vorstellungen zurückgingen, welch letztere durch die theokratisierte Verbrämung verdeckt waren.

----

[34] In der höchst verdienstvollen Arbeit von K. J o r d a n vermißt man eine Erwähnung dieser Bedenken, die mir auch nicht aufstiegen, vgl. W. U l l m a n n ,
Growth of papal government, doch vgl. jetzt W. U l l m a n n , A short history
of the papacy 183.

[35] Das hat mit Recht H. G r u n d m a n n in einem anderen Zusammenhang besonders hervorgehoben (oben Anm. 1); vgl. auch W. U l l m a n n , A short history
of the papacy 161.

Diese Einsicht soll aber keineswegs die weitergehende Bedeutung des wohl gezielten Wurfes des Ravennater Juristen schmälern. Er zeigte, daß Zeitgenossen gar wohl die Schwäche des herkömmlichen Königtums erkannt hatten. Dazu kommt noch eine weitere Überlegung. Die päpstliche Herrschaftsidee ging von der Voraussetzung aus, daß Herrschaft im christlichen Gemeinwesen und damit Rechtssetzung und Rechtsgestaltung ausschließlich Sache der hierzu qualifizierten Organe sei, jedenfalls so weit grundlegende das Wesen der christlichen Gemeinschaft betreffende Verhältnisse in Frage standen. Das aber involvierte nicht bloß die Geltung und Wirksamkeit des päpstlichen Primats, sondern vor allem die grundsätzliche, verfassungsmäßige und rechtliche Scheidung der Laien von den Klerikern. Und hier hatte das Papsttum eine mächtige Stütze in dem seit Jahrhunderten sich angesammelten Material, das sich als imposantes Lehrgebäude darstellte[36]. Es ist überflüssig, Einzelbelege anzuführen: es genügt, auf die scharf geschliffenen Sätze Gregors VII. in seinen beiden Rechtfertigungsschreiben an Hermann von Metz zu verweisen, die doch in der Tat nichts an Deutlichkeit und Bestimmtheit zu wünschen ließen[37]. Das bisher bloß schwelende Problem manchmal kurz an der Oberfläche erscheinend, aber gewöhnlich unterschwellig, war durch den Investiturstreit zu einem zentralen und offenen Problem geworden: es betraf die Stellung der Laien innerhalb der christlichen Gemeinschaft[38]. Und gerade in diesem Punkte war das Papsttum mit festem und lehrmäßig unterbautem Rüstzeug in den Kampf eingetreten – das königliche Lager hatte dem allen wenig entgegenzuhalten. Auch hier gilt, daß das eine System auf natürlicher, gewordener Entwicklung ohne viel gedankliche Arbeit und begriffliche Untermauerung ruhte, während das andere auf grundsätzlichen Überlegungen und der Interpretation des in der Bibel enthaltenen göttlichen Wortes fußte. Zwei Welten standen sich in der Tat auch in diesem Rahmen gegenüber, die kurzschriftlich und summarisch mit den Begriffen des Laien und Klerikers, des ordinierten und nichtordinierten Mitglieds der Kirche sich ausdrücken ließen, was selbstverständlich nicht bedeutet, daß auf der einen Seite ausschließlich Laien und auf der anderen ausschließlich Kleriker

---

[36] Darüber W. U l l m a n n , Growth of papal government 272–343, 360.

[37] Reg. IV. 2, S. 293–97; VIII. 21, S. 546–62.

[38] Es sei daran erinnert, daß dieses Problem als solches richtig erkannt wurde in dem Augenblick, in dem die karolingische Wiedergeburtsidee sich in die Tat umzusetzen begann. So weit mir bekannt, war Jonas von Orléans der erste, der einen Traktat unter dem Titel *De institutione laicali* verfaßte (Migne PL 106. 121 ff.). Es war derselbe Jonas, der den ersten Traktat über die Stellung eines Königs in einem christlichen Gemeinwesen schrieb. Über ihn vgl. W. U l l m a n n , Carolingian Renaissance 59 ff. mit weiterer Literatur.

gewesen wären. Aber hier handelt es sich um grundsätzliche Ordnungs-
fragen.

Die Berufung des Petrus Crassus auf das römische Recht verfolgte
neben der Abwehr des päpstlichen Anspruchs den Zweck, der von den
Klerikern formulierten Rechtsidee ein von Laien nicht bloß formulier-
tes, sondern auch in geschliffener und reifer Sprache gesetztes Recht
gegenüberzustellen, das auf eine jahrhundertlange ehrenvolle Geschichte und ein noch höheres Alter zurückblicken konnte. Das römische Recht war ein System, das von Laien stammte, deren tief religiöses
und christliches Wesen nicht in Frage zu stellen war. Das trifft selbstverständlich auf den Codex und die Novellen Justinians zu. Im Codex
vor allem waren die christlichen Vertreter echten Römertums reprä-
sentiert – von Konstantin dem Großen ganz zu schweigen waren sie
alle da, die Theodosii, die Valentiniani und so weiter. Dem Traktat
des Crassus kommt nach allen diesen Überlegungen eine Bedeutung zu,
die mir noch nicht entsprechend gewürdigt zu sein scheint. Er erkannte
das Potential des römischen Rechts im Rahmen der Rechtswirklichkeit
und der Anwendbarkeit auf zeitgenössische Herrschaftsverhältnisse.

Geistesgeschichtlich macht sich in den Anfangsjahren des 12. Jahrhunderts eine kräftig einsetzende Wendung bemerkbar. Hier kann ich
auf Einzelheiten nicht eingehen, möchte bloß unterstreichen, daß die
wissenschaftliche Erfassung des römischen Rechts durch die zeitgenössischen Wirren einen sehr mächtigen Impuls empfangen hatte. Wir wissen heute, daß es in Ravenna eine Anzahl von *legis doctores* gegeben
hatte, die dem Laienstande angehörten, was bei dem allseits zu beobach-
tenden hohen Bildungsstand in Oberitalien nicht überrascht[39]. Wir wissen auch, daß kurz nach der Jahrhundertwende in Bologna eine Rechtsschule sich entwickelte, von der wir gesicherte und feste Nachrichten
haben. Zwei Umstände sollen besonders in diesem Rahmen unter-
strichen werden. Erstens, daß das römische Recht von jetzt ab mit einer
Intensität studiert wurde und zwar auf einer wissenschaftlichen Höhe,
wofür es kein voraufgehendes Beispiel oder Muster gibt[40]; und zweitens, daß diese gewordene (nicht gestiftete oder gegründete) Akademie
– vielleicht sollte man den Begriff der Universität noch nicht auf Bo-

---

[39] C. G. M o r , Legis Doctor, In: Atti del convegno internazionale di studi
Accursiani, hrsg. G. Rossi, I (1968) 193 ff.

[40] Noch immer grundlegend E. G e n z m e r , Die justinianische Kodifikation und
die Glossatoren. In: Atti del congresso internazionale di diritto romano, I (1933)
347 ff. Ferner F. C a l a s s o 530 ff., und B. P a r a d i s i , Storia del diritto italiano (2. Aufl. 1967), II. 84 ff.; A. S o r b e l l i , Storia dell università di Bologna, I
(1944) bes. 35 ff.; W. T r u s e n , Die Anfänge des gelehrten Rechts in Deutschland:
ein Beitrag zur Geschichte der Frührezeption (1962), 102 ff., bes. 107 f.; F. W i e -
a c k e r , Privatrechtsgeschichte der Neuzeit (2. Aufl. 1967), 45 ff. (leider mit vielen

logna in seinen Anfangsstadien anwenden – ausschließlich von Laien unterhalten, von Laien organisiert, von Laien besetzt worden war. Schüler und Lehrer waren Laien. Die Erklärung für diese einmalige Erscheinung dürfte in denselben Gründen liegen, die Crassus einige Jahre vorher bewegten, seinen Traktat zu schreiben.

Bologna, seine Entwicklung und seine ungeheure ideengeschichtliche Bedeutung können nur gegen den Hintergrund der damaligen bewegten Zeit verstanden werden. Wie sollte man sonst den raschen Aufstieg und die Zugkraft des neuen wissenschaftlichen Fachs, des Rechtsstudiums, erklären? Weder entstehen Ideen im luftleeren Raum, noch können Studien, Lehranstalten, Bildungszwecke ohne Rücksicht auf zeitgenössische Probleme von Herrschaft und Gesellschaft verstanden werden. Das ist ein Gebot historischer Erkenntnis. Das römische Recht wurde gerade damals vorzüglich als eine schicksalhafte Vereinigung von christlichem und römischem Gedankengut mit besonderer Anwendbarkeit auf die zeitgenössische herrschaftliche Problematik angesehen. Diese reichhaltige Symbiose von Christentum und Römertum erklärt wenigstens zum Teil den gewaltigen vorwärtsdrängenden Einfluß des römischen Rechts und die Überflutung aller geistigen Bereiche mit römisch-rechtlichen Ideen. Die Durchdringung dieses Rechts wurde zum Erfordernis der Stunde; denn hier hatte man vor sich das Recht der römisch-christlichen Kaiser, die damals, wie schon vorher und auch nachher, als die Apotheose reinsten und unverfälschten Römertums galten. Und ebenso erblickte man in ihrem Recht das reifste und auf höchster Stufe stehende, das zwar nachahmungswürdig war, doch nie nachgeahmt werden konnte.

Aber auch die Wirkung des Rechtsstudiums eröffnete bisher unbekannte Perspektiven. Man wurde vertraut mit einer eleganten Jurisprudenz, einer ausgereiften Terminologie, dem Problem des Anwendungs- und Geltungsbereichs des Rechts und vor allem mit dem Problemkreis der Rechtserzeugung. Man begann hier, und wiederum ist in erster Linie an den Codex zu denken, eine Welt des Begrifflichen zu erkennen, die vieles klärte und die die Struktur der Herrschergrundlagen in einer bisher ungeahnten Schärfe erfassen ließ. Der gedankliche Reichtum, der im römischen Recht verborgen lag, wurde nunmehr den Studierenden zugänglich und hiermit stellte sich die Notwendigkeit der wissenschaftlich fundierten Anpassung dieses Rechts auf zeitgenössische Verhältnisse von selbst.

---

ungenauen Angaben behaftet). Siehe noch P. C l a s s e n , Die hohen Schulen und die Gesellschaft: A. f. Kulturgeschichte 48 (1966), 155 ff., 169 ff. P. K o s c h a k e r , Europa und das römische Recht (2. Aufl. 1954) 69 ff., obgleich vielleicht ein wenig pointiert, bringt das hohe Ethos der Bologneser Schule magistral zur Darstellung.

Nun ist allerdings zu beobachten, daß eine Anzahl von Umständen
das Studium des römischen Rechts begünstigt hat, ganz abgesehen von
dem als auslösendes Moment wirkenden Investiturstreit. Zum ersten
war die privatrechtliche Anwendung des römischen Rechts in Italien
nie ausgestorben. Dazu kommt, daß gewisse römisch-rechtliche Begriffe,
wie etwa *tuitio* und dergl. sich unschwer mit deutschrechtlichen Begriffen wie etwa der *munt* verbinden ließen und aufs öffentliche Recht
übertragen wurden, was wieder die Aufnahmebereitschaft wesentlich
förderte[41]. Zweitens war, wie kürzlich gezeigt wurde, die Vulgata mit
römisch-rechtlichen Begriffen durchtränkt, die die Rezeptionsfähigkeit
des Bodens im ausgehenden 11. und anhebenden 12. Jahrhundert in
sehr erheblichem Maße erhöhte. Viele Begriffe waren dem Vulgatatext
und dem römischen Recht, wenigstens terminologisch, wenn auch nicht
immer bedeutungsmäßig, gemeinsam, was zur Folge hatte, daß viele
römisch-rechtliche Begriffe gar nicht als Neuigkeit erschienen, weil man
mit ihnen eben schon durch die Bibel vertraut war[42]. Den Anteil, den
das Papsttum selbst hatte an der Förderung des römischen Rechts, soll
man auch hier in Anschlag bringen[43]. Als weitere Voraussetzung
kommt insbesondere in Betracht die Idee eines römischen Kaisertums.
Gewiß, das römische Kaisertum, wie es im Westen seit dem 9. Jahrhundert in Erscheinung trat, war gedacht als ein päpstliches Macht-
instrument vornehmlich im Rahmen der gegen Konstantinopel gerichteten Papstpolitik. Dieses Kaisertum war, wie Hampe es einmal pla-
stisch ausgedrückt hatte, dem deutschen Königtum aufgepfropft. Aber
die deutschen Herrscher blieben trotz des römischen Kaisertitels ihrem
Wesen nach deutsche Herrscher, ganz unleugbar im Heimatboden ver-
wurzelt. Das dem Kaisertum zeitlich vorgelagerte Königtum war, wie
angedeutet, vorwiegend theokratisiertes Herrschertum. Es verdient
vielleicht betont zu werden, daß Heinrich III. hin und wieder in seinen
Urkunden gewiße Bruchstücke oder Teile von Rechtssätzen dem römischen Recht entnahm, aber sie nehmen sich aus wie Fremdkörper oder
Verzierungen, die wenig innere Beziehung zur Sache hatten. Ferner
hatte Otto III. zum Beispiel das Majestätsverbrechen als Sonderver-
brechen nach römischem Muster unter Strafe gestellt, desgleichen Heinrich III. Aber all das ist noch weit entfernt von einer konkreten und
konsequenten Nutzanwendung des römischen Rechts.

Von entscheidender Bedeutung scheint zu sein, daß mit Heinrich III.

---

[41] Darüber vgl. W. U l l m a n n , Carolingian Renaissance 175 ff.

[42] Über diese viel zu wenig beachtete Erscheinung siehe W. U l l m a n n , The
Bible and Principles of Government in the Middle Ages. In: Settimana Spoleto, X
(1962) 185–229)

[43] Ausgezeichnete Übersicht bei A. van H o v e , Prolegomena ad Codicem Iuris
Canonici (2. Aufl. 1945) 225 ff.

282

eine Entwicklung einsetzt, die gerade für die uns interessierende Frage
wesentlich ist, aber bisher ungenügend beachtet wurde. Wie bekannt,
war er nachweislich der erste deutsche Herrscher, der sich *Rex Romanorum* nannte[44]. Die Bezeichnung geht ursprünglich auf ein Mißverständ-
nis in der Kanzlei zurück[45]. Der Titel selbst aber war gewiß ein sonder-
bares Irrlicht; denn einen römischen König hat es doch seit der mehr
oder weniger sagenhaften vor-republikanischen Zeit nicht gegeben[46],
und auch das *Corpus iuris civilis* wußte vom römischen König herzlich
wenig. Kein Zweifel dürfte bestehen, daß der mittelalterliche König
der Römer mit dem mystischen und geschichtlich zwielichtigen römischen König schon gar nichts gemein haben konnte. Ob man sich zu
Heinrichs III. Zeiten bestimmte Vorstellungen über diesen schwange-
ren Titel machte, wird wohl kaum mit Sicherheit festzustellen sein.
Jedenfalls hat weder er noch sein Sohn diesen Titel konsequent geführt.
So weit ich sehen kann, gebrauchte ihn Heinrich IV. nur ein einziges
Mal[47]. Es ist aber höchst interessant zu sehen, daß dieser Titel mit
Heinrich V. immer mehr in Gebrauch kommt[48] und bei Lothar, Kon-
rad III. und Friedrich Barbarossa finden wir ihn ständig in Gebrauch[49].

---

[44] Vgl. darüber W. U l l m a n n , Dies ortus imperii, in: Atti Accursiani 661 ff.,
bes. 685 ff.
[45] J. F i c k e r in MIÖG. 6 (1885) 225 ff., auf 244 f., und H. B r e s s l a u ad
DH. II. 170 (MGH. Diplomata III. 201). Siehe jetzt auch O. E n g e l s , Beiträge
zur Geschichte der Staufer: DA. 27 (1971), 373 ff., bei 385 f.
[46] Vgl. A. H e u s s , Römische Geschichte (2. Aufl. 1964) 9: »Von ihrer Königszeit
haben die späteren Römer so gut wie nichts gewußt.« Das meiste war »ungeschicht-
liches Fabulieren«; ferner Cambridge Ancient History, VII (1928) 407 (eine »Fik-
tion«); P a u l y - W i s s o w a , RE., 2. Reihe, s. v. Rex, S. 714, (»traditionelle
Legende von den sieben Königen«).
[47] Siehe C. E r d m a n n , Die Briefe, nr. 5, S. 8 (= Gregors Reg. I. 29a). Möglicherweise käme noch in Betracht DH. IV. 262 (undatiert) wo er sich nach des
Vaters Muster »Tertius Heinricus divina favente clementia Romanorum rex«
nannte. Das Diplom bedarf aber noch genauerer Untersuchung. Nach seiner Kaiserkrönung in 1084 nannte er sich »Heinricus tertius Romanorum imperator«. Gregor
selbst nannte ihn nie *Rex Romanorum*, sondern stets *Rex Teutonicorum* (oder *Teutonicus*), vgl. etwa Reg. II. 52a, S. 196; II. 63, S. 218, Z. 29, und an vielen anderen
Stellen. Während in Reg. VII. 14a, S. 486 Heinrich das *regnum Teutonicum et Italiae*
entzogen wurde, schrieb Gregor dem Gegenkönig Rudolf bloß die Herrschaft über
das *regnum Teutonicum* zu (ebda, Z. 23–4); vgl. schon E. C a s p a r , Anm. 3. Dazu
jetzt auch G. K o c h 111–3, mit weiterer Literatur. Die tiefere Bedeutung scheint
ihm entgangen zu sein, vgl. S. 185, 217, und unten bei Anm. 66.
[48] Siehe Codex Udalrici (hrsg. Ph. J a f f é , Bibliotheca Rerum Germanicarum
(Neudruck 1964) V. nr. 140, S. 257 (anno 1107); nr. 142, S. 259; nr. 148 (anno
1110).
[49] Es soll besonders hervorgehoben werden, daß der sog. Staufische Kaiserordo
aus dem Ende des 12. Jahrhunderts zum ersten Male im Krönungseid den Titel *Rex
Romanorum* verwendet: »Ego enim rex Romanorum futurus annuente Domino imperator promitto...« in R. E l z e (ed.), Ordines coronationis imperialis: MGH.

Das sind Tatsachen, an denen man nicht vorbeikommt. Sie bedürfen
einer Erklärung. Mir will scheinen, daß zwischen dem Gebrauch des
Titels, dem rasch anschwellenden Studium des römischen Rechts in Bologna und der dadurch geförderten Strukturveränderung des deutschen
Herrschers ein enges Verhältnis besteht. Der Titel war ein zeitweiliger,
d. h. der erwählte und geweihte deutsche König war nicht wie ehedem
ein schlichter *Rex* oder *Rex Francorum* oder *Langobardorum* oder *Italicorum* oder *Rex Teutonicorum*, sondern wurde vermöge der Wahl sozusagen kurzschlüssig König der Römer. An sich genommen deutete
der Titel in gar keiner Weise darauf hin, daß der ihn tragende Herrscher ein deutscher König war. In der konsequenten Benutzung des
Titels sehe ich einen sehr gewichtigen Fingerzeig für die sich voll-
ziehende Strukturveränderung der Herrschaftsgrundlagen.

Wie bekannt, wurde auf die Formulierung des Titels stets harte Ge-
dankenarbeit verwendet, weil sich das Wesen und die innerste Substanz, der Inbegriff der Funktionen des Titelträgers darin äußern
sollte. Schließlich ist es doch keine geringfügige Maßnahme, den un-
bestrittenermaßen deutschen einfach in einen römischen König zu verwandeln. Zu einem solchen gewichtigen Schritt mußte ein zwingender
Grund Veranlassung gegeben haben. Einen Teil der Erklärung glaube
ich schon angedeutet zu haben, als ich auf die Ungleichheit der päpstlichen und königlichen Grundlagen verwies. Einen erfolgversprechen-
den Weg zeigte Crassus, aber von entscheidender Bedeutung war die
durch das Studium des römischen Rechts eröffnete und geradezu er-
drückende Wucht der darin verankerten Herrschaftsgrundsätze. Vor
allem der einzigartig entwickelte monarchische Gedanke; die sog. ab-
steigende (deszendente) These von Herrschaft und Recht[50]; die im
römischen Kaiser vertretene Machtfülle, seine Sakralität und die sich
daraus ergebende Unverletzbarkeit sowie der Charakter seiner Gesetze als *leges sacratissimae* usw., und schließlich seine Autonomie.
Weder das Papsttum noch das Christentum noch göttliche Gnade hatten etwas mit dem Werden des römischen Kaisers zu tun gehabt. Er
war autonomer Herrscher in seiner Funktion als *dominus mundi*[51] und
Autokrator und daher auf dem Weg einer gedanklichen Konstruktion

---

Fontes iuris germanici antiqui IX (1960), nr. XVII, 6, S. 63. Bis dahin hieß er bloß
Rex. Vgl. den voraufgehenden Ordo XIV, 4, S. 37. Wie auch in anderen Fragen
spiegeln die Krönungsordines die ideologische Entwicklung getreulich wieder. Ob
nicht diese bislang unbeachtete Tatsache zu einer Klärung der Datierungsfrage von
Ordo XIV beitragen könnte?

[50] Über diese These vgl. W. U l l m a n n in Revue d'histoire du droit, 26 (1958)
360 ff. (Buchrezension) und W. U l l m a n n , Principles of Government and Politics in the Middle Ages (2. Aufl. 1966) 20 ff.

[51] Siehe insbes. die *Lex Rhodia* in Dig. 14. 2, bes. lex 9.

284

Vertreter des Pantokrator auf Erden. Das war nun einmal eine wahre Staatslehre, die ebenso verfeinert wie erprobt war. Und das alles, wie ich betonen möchte, im Rahmen des gesetzten positiven Rechts. Man kann nicht umhin in der ersten Hälfte des 12. Jahrhunderts eine beträchtliche Verschiebung der Herrschergrundlagen wahrzunehmen. Sie zeichnet sich deutlich ab gegen den Hintergrund der wissenschaftlichen Durchdringung des römischen Rechts, die sie begleitete und beschleunigte. Sollte es denn wirklich bloßer Zufall gewesen sein, daß der große und einflußreiche Irnerius ein *amicus curiae* Heinrichs V. war, der schon urkundlich 1112 zum ersten Mal greifbar wurde? Sollte es blindes Walten gewesen sein, daß er zusammen mit Heinrich V. gebannt wurde vom Papst, und zwar als *fautor* der dem Kaiser angelasteten Vergehen[52]? Die Möglichkeit, daß Irnerius, der übrigens in der Bannsentenz Gwarnerius genannt wurde, ein Deutscher war, ist keineswegs von der Hand zu weisen. Burchard von Ursperg nannte ihn schlechthin Werner[53]. Irnerius war eine der Leuchten am juristischen Himmel Bolognas in den ersten Dezennien des Jahrhunderts[54].

Die Erkenntnis des ideologisch gesättigten römischen Rechts trug begreiflicherweise viel zum raschen Aufstieg und zur Blüte der Bologneser Rechtsschule bei. Eine bisher unbekannte Welt tat sich hier auf und neue gedankliche Dimensionen und Perspektiven fügten sich in den wissenschaftlichen Rahmen ein. Von unmittelbarem Interesse ist der Niederschlag dieser römischen Jurisprudenz in den amtlichen Kundgebungen der deutschen Herrscher, doch gibt es hier noch viel Forschungsarbeit zu tun. Der stetig steigende Einfluß der römischen Rechtssprache, römischer Sprachbilder, römischer Grundsätze und Topoi lassen sich in den Urkunden und Briefen Lothars, Konrads und Friedrichs erkennen. Hier sind insbesondere die Arengen noch einmal auf ihren Aussagewert hinsichtlich der Herrschergrundsätze zu untersuchen[55]. Ich glaube kaum, daß es genügt, wie das hin und wieder geschieht, dieses hier aufgegriffene römische Gedankengut als Schlag-

---

[52] W. Holtzmann in NA 50 (1934) 301 ff., bes. 317 und 319, wo er in der Liste der Gebannten »Gwarnerius Bononiensis legis peritus« geheissen wurde. Ferner G. Cencetti, Bononiae fuit studium. In: Studi Medievali, 3. Serie, 7 (1966) 781 ff., bes. 795 ff. P. Weimar in H. Kantorowicz – W. W. Buckland, Studies in the Glossators of the Roman Law (Neudruck 1969) 333 Anm. 97.

[53] Burchard von Ursperg, Chronicon, hrsg. O. Holder-Egger – B. v. Simson: MGH. SS. Rer. Germ. (2. Aufl. 1916) 15, Z. 38: »Dominus Wernerius libros legum ... ad petitionem Mathilde comitisse renovavit.«

[54] G. Pescatore, Die Glossen des Irnerius (1888); E. Besta, L'opere d' Irnerio (1896); A. Rota, Lo stato e il diritto nella concezione d'Irnerio (1954). E. Genzmer 367 f.: »Mit Irnerius beginnt etwas Neues«.

[55] Tüchtige Vorarbeit leistete H. Fichtenau in seiner Studie Arenga (Erg. Bd. 18 der MÖIG 1957).

worte der Propaganda abzutun oder es als bloßes Vocabularium zu
kennzeichnen. Als ob nicht alle Sprache und daher Gedanken aus einem
Vocabularium bestünden. Mit solchen Erklärungen erklärt man eben
nichts[56]. Es handelt sich nicht um ein Gekräusel an des Wassers Oberfläche, das keinen Aufschluß auf Denkprozesse zu geben imstande
wäre. Wie dem auch sei, ein Vergleich der amtlichen Schriftstücke Konrads oder Friedrichs mit jenen der Herrscher des 11. Jahrhunderts zeigt
den Unterschied in Fassung, Ausblick, Präzision des Ausdrucks und
Glätte der Formulierung. Damit trifft sich gut eine verstärkt einsetzende und mit Nachdruck verfolgte Italienpolitik, und vor allem die
gerade in diesem Zusammenhang wesentliche Bevorzugung der Laienfürsten und -gewalten.

Hier stellt sich zwingend die Frage nach dem Sinngehalt des amtlichen Titels der deutschen Könige. Was sollte der *Rex Romanorum*
zum Ausdruck bringen? Während der deutsche König einen mehr oder
weniger fest umrissenen Machtbereich hatte, möchte es scheinen, daß
der römische König nur schwer in seiner begrifflichen Gestalt zu fassen
ist. Wenn nicht alles täuscht, dürfte es sich hier um eine Verdichtung
früherer königlicher Funktionen handeln. Der *Rex Romanorum* dürfte
sich aus dem *Rex Langobardorum* und dem *Rex Italicorum* heraus-
geschält haben. Weil aber diese Herrschaftsfunktion eine tatsächliche
Herrschaftsgewalt auf italischem Boden konkretisierte, schwangen
beim König der Römer hochbedeutsame Ober- und Untertöne ideolo-
gischer Art mit, die des geschichtlichen Zusammenhangs nicht entbeh-
ren, denn jedenfalls seit dem 9. Jahrhundert war der Kaiser der Römer
stets vor seiner Kaiserkreierung im Besitz italischen Bodens und be-
herrschte ihn als König. Das konnte unschwer zu einer gedanklichen
Rückprojektion führen, und zwar so, daß der Kaiser der Römer den
König der Römer aufsog. Mit anderen Worten, man stellte sich den
Kaiser der Römer gedanklich als König der Römer vor der Kaiserkrönung vor, obwohl er faktisch ein Langobardenkönig oder König
der Franken usw. gewesen war. Und diese königliche Herrschaft in
Oberitalien wurde als italisches Königreich verstanden, wie es in den
Urkunden vom 9. bis zum 12. Jahrhundert geheißen hatte und wie
sich leicht aus Konrads III. Bezugnahme auf *nostrum regnum itali-*
cum[57] in unserer Zeitspanne nachweisen läßt[58].

---

[56] Dazu H. K r a u s e , Kaiserrecht und Rezeption (1952) 33.
[57] DK. III. 255, S. 443, Z. 2.
[58] Eine Generation später wird der erwählte deutsche König zum Herrscher über
das *regnum Romanum*, wie die Wahlanzeige der deutschen Fürsten die Wahl Ottos
IV. kundtat: Reg. de neg. Romani imperii (ed. F. Kempf) nr. 10: »ad *Romani regni*
fastigium iuste et rationabiliter elegimus.« In ebendemselben Sinne sprachen Philipps Anhänger, indem sie sich auf seine Wahl *in imperaturam Romani solii* bezogen

Hiermit trat die Funktion des italischen Herrschers ins Blickfeld, die genau bis ins 9. Jahrhundert zurückreicht. Es war die Funktion des Königs als Schutzherrn der römischen Kirche als deren *patronus et defensor,* die, wie erinnerlich, Heinrich III. besonders stark in seiner Stellung als *patricius Romanorum* hervorkehrte[59]. Und vom *patricius Romanorum* ließ sich leicht eine Brücke zum *Rex Romanorum* schlagen. Das dürfte auch die Erklärung dafür sein, daß das Papsttum selbst den Begriff des *Rex Romanorum* in unserem Zeitabschnitt verwendete, vornehmlich Innozenz II. im Jahr 1130, als er sein Schreiben an Lothar richtete, um in nichts hinter seinem Gegenpapst Anaklet II. zurückzustehen[60]. Damit dürfte auch die Rolle der Stadtrömer sich erklären, die neuerdings auf ihre Macht zu pochen begannen, indem sie sich anboten, ihren König – den *Rex Romanorum* – durch ihre Wahl zum *Imperator Romanorum* zu erheben. Hier reiht sich Arnold von Brescia unschwer in den Zusammenhang ein[61]. Um das Bild abzurunden, soll Konrads III. herrscherlicher Verfügungen als *Rex Romanorum* in Deutschland gedacht werden. Aus eigener Machtvollkommenheit hob er das Interdikt über ein Kloster auf (Quedlinburg)[62]; auf derselben königlichen Grundlage entschied er die bischöfliche Doppelwahl in Eichstätt[63] und setzte auf den Würzburger Stuhl den als Anti-Gregorianer bekannten Gebhard als Bischof[64]; darüber hinaus bezog

---

(ebda nr. 14). Auch hier soll angemerkt werden, daß der Terminus regnum Romanum schon früher gebraucht wurde (vgl. etwa DH. III. 80 vom 3. Juni 1041 in MGH. Diplomata V. 105, Z. 7), aber erst im Zusammenhang mit dem *Rex Romanorum* seine volle Bedeutung erhielt.

[59] Einzelheiten s. W. U l l m a n n , Growth of papal government, 250 ff. und W. U l l m a n n , Short History of the Papacy 127 ff.

[60] Codex Udalrici nr. 247 und 244. Siehe aber auch Eugenius III. an Konrad III. vom 6. Oktober 1149, ebda nr. 197, S. 315, wo Konrad als *patronus b. Petri* bezeichnet wurde, *weil er Rex Romanorum* wäre. Ebenso derselbe Papst an Friedrich I. in seinem Antwortschreiben an dessen Wahlanzeige in MGH. Const. I. nr. 139, S. 194 und in den folgenden Jahren vor der Kaiserkrönung.

[61] Schon 1128 wandten sich die Römer an Lothar: Cod. Udalrici, nr. 237.

[62] Ph. Jaffé (ed.) I: Wibald, Ep. 196, S. 314–5 (anno 1149).

[63] J. G r e t s e r , Opera omnia (1734), X. 812 E (Adelbert Heiderheims Relatio): »Quod scisma diu duravit, sed rege Cunrado, obsequio Gerhardi comitis, in partem Burchardi episcopi inclinato, nulla synodali discussione habita, sed *regia potentia* adhibita praedictus Burchardus . . . permansit.«

[64] H. K r a b b o , Der Reinhardsbrunner Briefsteller aus dem 12. Jahrhundert: NA 32 (1907) 53 ff., bes. 62 ff. über die selbständige königliche Ernennung Gebhards zum Bischof, der schon viele Jahre vorher angesichts der kraftvollen gregorianischen Opposition den Stuhl nicht länger halten konnte (S. 65): »Hier (findet) die Ansicht der deutschen Laienkreise, wie sie um die Mitte des Jahrhunderts bestand, ihren Ausdruck. Von irgendwelcher Bezugnahme auf die Bestimmungen des Konkordates von 1122 findet sich auch nicht die geringste Spur.« Friedrich befand sich unter den einflußreichen Ratgebern Konrads und »war schon damals (d. h. 1150) der Führer der antiklerikalen Partei.«

er sich auf die *sacra imperialia scripta* – für einen *Rex Romanorum* eine sehr beachtenswerte Formulierung[65]. Das alles waren Maßnahmen und Äußerungen, die den Kompetenzbereich, der einem König im 12. Jahrhundert zustand, in sehr beträchtlichem Maße überschritten und an die Herrschergewalt eines oströmischen Kaisers erinnerten.

In schärfstens profilierter Art kommt die Verwandlung des deutschen in einen römischen König bei Barbarossa zum Ausdruck. Auch er wurde durch die Königswahl und -weihe funktionell *Rex Romanorum*. Wie sein unmittelbarer Vorgänger Konrad, so machte auch er sich sogleich in dieser Funktion aller Welt kund[66]. Und auf diese Funktion gründete er nicht nur den Rechtsanspruch auf Ausübung königlicher Rechte in Italien, sondern auch auf die Kaiserkrone selbst. Obwohl grundsätzlich auch bei ihm der *Rex Romanorum* eine zeitweilige Funktion hatte, war er dennoch kühn genug, diesen Titel nicht weniger als zweieinviertel Jahre vor der Kaiserkrönung durch den Kaisertitel zu ersetzen. Ich beziehe mich auf seine Bestätigungsurkunde des Konstanzer Vertrags[67]. Doch bestand noch eine gewisse herrscherliche Unsicherheit, denn von einem konsequenten Gebrauch des *Imperator Romanorum* an Stelle des zuständigen *Rex Romanorum* kann nicht die Rede sein. Die Möglichkeit, daß der *Rex Romanorum* eine Rückübersetzung des Byzantinischen *Basileus ton Romaion* war, soll wenigstens angedeutet werden[67a]. Der nachmalige Westkaiser hätte damit seinen Rivalen überspielen und seine eigene Vorrangstellung sichern können. Angesichts der Restorationspolitik des Manuel Komnenos in diesen Jahren könnte diese Möglichkeit an Bedeutung gewinnen.

Nun ist es gerade hier zum Verständnis wesentlich, sich die besonders starke Betonung des aus dem römischen Recht gewonnenen Gedankengutes zu vergegenwärtigen, das bei Friedrich so auffallend im

---

[65] E. Lindenbrog, Scriptores Rerum Germanicarum Septentrionalium (1706): Privilegia, nr. XLV, S. 155: Konrad III. in einem Diplom an Bischof Hartwig 1145 unter Berufung auf die *sacra imperialia scripta testantur*.

[66] In seinem grundlegenden Werk Papato e impero: dalla elezione di Federico I alla morte di Adriano IV (1152–59) (1959) 13 ff. entging M. Maccarrone die Bedeutung des Titels Friedrichs offenbar vollends. Nirgends findet sich ein Hinweis darauf. Für Einzelheiten der Wahl vgl. O. Engels 399 ff.

[67] In der Bestätigungsurkunde des Konstanzer Vertrags und zwar in Abweichung von dem zwischen seinen und den päpstlichen Bevollmächtigten vereinbarten Entwurf: MGH. Const. I. nr. 145, S. 202, vom 23. März 1153. Auch das Eschatokoll hat das *Signum domini Romanorum imperatoris invictissimi*. Der Entwurf ebda nr. 144, S. 201 (vgl. auch Wibalds Eintrag nr. 407 in Jaffé (wie oben Anm. 48) S. 208. Wibald hatte schon lange vorher beim Papst Klage geführt über die Schwierigkeiten der Zusammenarbeit mit dem jungen Staufer, vgl. etwa ebda nr. 396, S. 529.

[67a] Diese Möglichkeit wurde von G. Koch nicht gewürdigt, doch sind seine Ausführungen hinsichtlich des Zusatzes *semper augustus* höchst bedeutsam (S. 219 ff.).

288

Vordergrund stand. Es ist der sonore Reichtum der spätrömischen Reichs- und Rechtssprache und die in die Arengen eingewobenen grundsätzlichen Ideen über die Herrschaftsgrundsätze Friedrichs, die seinen amtlichen Äußerungen ihr spezifisches Gepräge geben. Die Sättigung mit römisch-rechtlichen Maximen bei einem Herrscher, der in seiner Substanz deutscher, in seiner Funktion aber römischer König war, ist durchaus verständlich. Ebenso verständlich ist es, wenn der König der Römer beim römischen Recht, seinem eigenen Recht, Anleihen machte und sich darauf berief. Nur historischer Unverstand kann darin etwas Ungewöhnliches erblicken.

Die zeitweilige Phase oder das Übergangsstadium endete mit der Kaiserkrönung, die den *Rex* zum vollen *Imperator Romanorum* machte. Trotz der Anbiederung seitens der Stadtrömer, zog Friedrich es vor, die Kaiserkrone aus der Hand des Papstes entgegenzunehmen[68], was jedenfalls mit der Geschichte seit fränkischer Zeit in Einklang stand. Auf die vielen delikaten Reibungen nach der Kaiserkrönung kann ich in diesem Zusammenhang nicht eingehen, bloß bemerken, daß die allmählich sich anbahnende Entfremdung der kaiserlichen und päpstlichen Kurie[69] zu dem bekannten Zusammenstoß in Besançon führte. Dort kam mit voller Wucht und Deutlichkeit der Mittelpunkt allen Staatsrechts zum Vorschein – die Autonomie, die Eigen- und Selbständigkeit jedes Herrschertums[70]. Begreiflicherweise klafften kaiserliche und päpstliche Auffassungen in dieser fundamentalen das innerste Wesen des römischen Kaisertums betreffenden Frage weit auseinander.

---

[68] Zur Kaiserkrönung Friedrichs vgl. Liber Pontificalis, hrsg. L. Duchesne (Neudruck 1955) II. 392, Z. 6 ff.; E. E i c h m a n n , Die Kaiserkrönung im Abendland (1943) I. 255 f. sowie meine Rezension von E. E. Stengel, Abhandlungen und Untersuchungen zur Geschichte des Kaisergedankens im Mittelalter (1965) in Revue Belge de Philologie et d'Histoire, 45 (1967) 531 ff., wo ich mich auch (533 ff.) mit der These Stengels auseinandersetzte, »die Waffen der Deutschen sind der Besitztitel ihres Rechts auf das Kaisertum; mit ihnen haben sie sich es erworben, mit ihnen wissen sie es zu behaupten« (Stengel 93). Er stützt sich dabei auf Bezold: »Das Recht des Stärkeren ist kaum jemals mit so schneidender Energie vorgetragen worden« wie bei der Kaiserkrönung. Dabei wird vergessen, wie dies auch bei anderen geschieht, auf den *favor apostolicus* Bezug zu nehmen, der zum Zuge kommen mußte, bevor Friedrich Kaiser werden konnte. Darüber F. K e m p f , Favor apostolicus. In: Speculum Historiale (Festschrift J. S p ö r l) (1965) 469 ff.

[69] Insbesondere der Streit mit Hadrian IV. um die Auslegung des Konstanzer Vertrags (1156). Darüber am besten M. M a c c a r r o n e 105 ff.

[70] Darüber vgl. W. U l l m a n n , Cardinal Roland in Besançon. In: Misc. Historiae Pontificiae 18 (1954) 107 ff.; M. M a c c a r r o n e 173 ff. Über die innige Verknüpfung von *beneficium* und *favor apostolicus* hat nur unklare Vorstellungen W. H e i n e m e y e r , Beneficium – non feudum, sed bonum factum: A. f. Diplomatik 15 (1969) 155 ff.

Es war aber auch zur selben Zeit, daß man sich im staufischen Lager anschickte, die Transformation der Herrschergrundlagen unmißverständlich zu formulieren und zu deklarieren. Die Bezeichnung des Reiches als *sacrum imperium*[71] bezeugt das sachliche Verständnis der staufischen Ratgeber für die Anwendung römisch-rechtlicher Grundsätze auf die Herrschaftsstruktur. Diese Bezeichnung ist wohl bekannt, die zwar in allen Lehrbüchern steht, über deren Aussagewert aber man recht wenig findet. Dem Umstand, daß das Adjektiv *sacrum* irgendwie die Unterschiedlichkeit zu einem *sanctum imperium* kennzeichnen sollte, wird, so viel ich sehe, keine Beachtung geschenkt. An eine Gegensätzlichkeit des *sacrum imperium* zur *sancta ecclesia* hatten gewiß weder Eberhard noch Rainald noch Friedrich gedacht. Ihnen ging es um viel weiter gesteckte Ziele als einer alten Sache einen neuen Namen zu verleihen. Es ging ums Ganze. Der Begriff des *sacrum imperium* diente als Ausdrucksmittel der Rechtsnachfolge des alten römischen Reiches. Ein Blick auf das römische Recht genügt, um eine viel zu wenig, wenn überhaupt beachtete Rechtstatsache gehörig zu würdigen[72]. Nach dem unverfälschten römischen Recht war der Kaiser der Urgrund, die Quelle allen öffentlichen Rechts. Nun dieses römische öffentliche Recht, das vom Kaiser stammt, erstreckt sich auf alle jene öffentlichen Angelegenheiten, die dem Wohl des *imperium* oder der *res publica* dienen. Ulpian gibt die klassische Definition des öffentlichen Rechts, als dessen wesentlichen Bestandteil er das *ius in sacris* ansieht, was die Stellung des alten römischen Kaisers als *Pontifex maximus* genügend erklärt. Aber hören wir einmal, was Ulpian wörtlich sagt:

Publicum ius est, quod ad statum rei Romanae spectat.

Publicum ius in sacris, in sacerdotibus, in magistratibus consistit[73].

---

[71] Erscheint zuerst in dem Schreiben Friedrichs an die Fürsten, worin sie zum Feldzug gegen Mailand aufgerufen wurden: Otto von Freising, Gesta, II. 50, S. 158. Man sollte nicht darauf vergessen, daß alles, was mit dem altrömischen Kaiser in Verbindung stand, Sakralität besaß.

[72] Auch M. M a c c a r r o n e in seinem höchst verdienstlichen Werk läßt sich darüber nicht aus. Vgl. etwa Th. M a y e r , Papsttum und Kaisertum im hohen Mittelalter: HZ. 187 (1959), 1 ff., auf S. 28: die Bezeichnung »stellt ein politisches Programm, den Anspruch des Kaisertums unmittelbar von Gott herzustammen, auf.« Da kommt doch K. J o r d a n der Sache näher, wenn er sagt, Investiturstreit und frühe Stauferzeit, in: Gebhardts Handbuch der deutschen Geschichte (9. Aufl., hrsg. H. Grundmann 1970), I. 391: »Seit 1157 kommt in der Sprache der Reichskanzlei der Begriff des sacrum imperium auf. Die Heiligkeit des Reiches ist darin begründet, daß Friedrich nicht nur die Tradition Karls d. Gr. und seiner Nachfolger, sondern auch die der ersten christlichen Kaiser weiterführt. Die deutschen Herrscher sind die rechtmäßigen Erben der römischen Imperatores und dürfen deshalb auch die alten imperialen Rechte in Italien wahrnehmen.« Die These G. K o c h s , der Begriff des *sacrum imperium* hätte sich gegen »den Hintergrund des Feudalstaates« vollzogen, scheint mir nicht überzeugend (vgl. S. 271 ff.).

[73] Dig. 1. 1. 1 § 2. Vgl. auch Institutionen I. 1 § 4. Zum spätrömischen *imperium*

Justiz, Religionswesen und Kirchenangelegenheiten waren in moderner Terminologie die von Ulpian besonders herausgegriffenen Grundpfeiler des öffentlichen Rechts. Mit der kurzen Bezeichnung *sacrum imperium* wollte Friedrich die Übertragung der unverfälschten öffentlichen Grundsätze auf seine Herrschaft anzeigen und sich damit auf römisch-rechtlicher Grundlage zum Nachfolger der römischen Kaiser ausweisen. Das hat primär durchaus nichts mit einer Gegensätzlichkeit zum Papsttum zu tun, sondern der Begriff verkündete die Absicht, mit der Idee des römischen Reiches und seiner Verfassung Ernst zu machen. Das aber bedeutete die Absage an den ekklesiologisch orientierten, theokratisierten Herrscher und die An- und Übernahme eines Herrschaftssystems, das von Laien erdacht und in die Praxis auch erfolgreich umgesetzt worden war. Und diese Laien – die römischen Kaiser – wurden so im Rechtssinne zu den glänzendsten deutschen Vorfahren, die das vorbildliche römische Recht geschaffen hatten.

In der Tat zeichnete sich dieses staufische System scharf von dem früheren theokratisierten ab. Es hatte gerade jene Konturen, jenes profilierte Wesen und jene gedankliche Schärfe, die den theokratisierten Herrschern fehlten. Zweitens bot dieses System unvergleichlich weniger Angriffsflächen dem Papsttum als das theokratisierte, weil es eben auf Grundlagen aufgebaut war, die mit dem päpstlicherseits vertretenen nichts gemein hatten. Verglichen mit dem theokratisierten war dieses Herrschaftssystem ein begriffliches *aliud*.

Die Bedeutung dieses staufischen Schrittes war groß. Man kann die Probe aufs Exempel machen. Einer der wesentlichen Beschlüsse auf dem roncalischen Reichstag von 1158 – die *Habita*, die die kaiserliche Schutzfunktion gegenüber der Rechtsschule in Bologna zum Gegenstand hatte[74] – wurde auf Geheiß des Kaisers dem Codex einverleibt[75].

---

sacrum, das die gottgewollte Ordnung garantierte und das sich in der amtlichen und poetischen Sprache findet, vgl. F. C h r i s t , Die römische Weltherrschaft in der antiken Dichtung (1938) S. 166–7.

[74] Über die *Habita* vgl. W. U l l m a n n , The medieval interpretation of Frederick I's Authentic »Habita«. In: Europa e il diritto Romano, hrsg. A. B. Schwarz (1952) I, 101 ff. Vgl. ferner G. C e n c e t t i 819 ff. mit weiterer Literatur. Zur Vorgeschichte noch immer am besten H. S i m o n s f e l d , Jahrbücher des deutschen Reichs unter Friedrich I. (1908) 313 ff. Die epische Einkleidung des anonym überlieferten Berichtes im Gedicht *Gesta de Federico I in Italia*, entdeckt und hrsg. von E. Monaci in: Fonti per la storia d'Italia: scrittori secolo XII (1887) 21, Z. 495 ff. Dieser Bericht hat freilich bloß die Repressalien zum Gegenstand, nicht aber die legislatorischen Maßnahmen der *Habita*, insbesondere nicht den Gerichtsstand der Scholaren. Über das Verhältnis von Rahewin zu dem Gedicht siehe R. H o l t z - m a n n in NA 44 (1922) 253 ff. (hier auch über die Rolle, die Rainald bei einer amtlich inspirierten Geschichtsschreibung spielte).

[75] Cod. IV. 13 am Ende. Neuausgabe von H. Koeppler in English Historical Review 54 (1939) 607. Die Ausgabe in MGH Const. I. nr. 178, 249 ist ungenau.

Das war ein überzeugender Beweis der nunmehrigen These, daß der mittelalterliche Kaiser der Erbe und Rechtsnachfolger der antiken Kaiser war. Diese Einfügung gewisser mittelalterlicher Gesetze und Verordnungen in den justinianischen Codex – es handelt sich immerhin um ein gutes Dutzend – über Auftrag des Kaisers ist nicht bloß unwiderlegbarer Beweis für die Behauptung der Nachfolge, sondern auch, und vor allem, dafür, daß von nun ab das römische Recht zum ureigenen Recht der mittelalterlichen Kaiser geworden war. Wie könnte man sonst diese Einfügung kaiserlicher Gesetze ins römische Rechtsbuch erklären? Dieser Tatsache mißt die moderne Mediävistik viel zu wenig Bedeutung zu. Von den Satzungen der fränkischen, sächsischen und salischen Herrscher wurde keine einzige dem römischen Rechtsbuch einverleibt. Mit der Übernahme der römischen öffentlich-rechtlichen Grundsätze wurde auch das Rechtssystem als solches übernommen und es als das dem *imperium* entsprechende und angemessene aufgenommen.

Gerade in diesem Zusammenhang verdienen die roncalischen Beschlüsse weitere Beachtung, weil sie sich mühelos in das Schema des römischen öffentlichen Rechts einfügen lassen. Da Gerichtsbarkeit ein wesentlicher Bestandteil des öffentlichen Rechts war, beabsichtigte Friedrich eine Festlegung der Regalien, eben der öffentlichen Reichsrechte, deren Inhalt dann von der berühmten Kommission bestehend aus den führenden Köpfen der Universität von Bologna und den Kommunen fixiert worden ist[76]. Ihre neulich dafür verwendete Bezeichnung als »Mischrecht« geht am Kern der Sache vorbei[77], denn genau so gut könnte man die in Bologna und späteren Universitäten gepflegte Jurisprudenz als Mischjurisprudenz bezeichnen, was wenig zur Sachkenntnis beiträgt. Worauf es ankam, war die Fixierung der herrscherlichen Hoheitsrechte, wie Ernennungsrecht der Beamten, hohe Gerichtsbarkeit, Straßen-, Markt-, Münz-, Steuerhoheit usw.[78].

Die Angleichung der kaiserlichen Rechtssprache an das römische Vorbild scheint mir das hervorragendste Merkmal der staufischen Satzungen zu sein. Auf Einzelheiten kann ich hier nicht eingehen, möchte bloß auf ein paar markante Dinge verweisen, wie etwa die Benennung der Bologneser Lehrer als »divinarum et *sacrarum legum* professores« in der eben erwähnten *Habita*, die sich selbst, wohlgemerkt, als *sacra lex* bezeichnete. Ein Jahr vorher, als das *imperium* zum *sacrum* erklärt

---

Einige Beobachtungen auch in P. C l a s s e n (oben A. 40), 173 f.

[76] Einzelheiten bei M. M a c c a r r o n e 271 ff.

[77] H. A p p e l t , Die Kaiseridee Friedrich Barbarossas: SB Wien, Phil. Hist. Kl. 252 (1967), Heft 4.

[78] Aufgezählt in MGH. Const. I. nr. 175, S. 244–5.

wurde, hält im selben Atemzug die *diva res publica* ihren Einzug, die man zwar richtig als synonym mit dem *sacrum imperium* neuerdings ansieht, sie aber in etwas naiver Art als christliches Reich verstanden wissen will, um dann das Maß voll zu machen und sogleich darin den Ausdruck einer nicht weniger naiv verstandenen Zweigewaltenlehre zu erblicken[79]. Da ist die sehr bemerkenswerte häufige Angleichung der mittelalterlichen Kaiser an die *divi reges et imperatores* und deren Charakterisierung als *nostri predecessores*. Da sind die voll ausgereiften römisch-rechtlichen Sprachgebilde, etwa die *edictalis lex*[80] und die zahlreichen anderen Wendungen und Entlehnungen, wie etwa die Anleihe beim theodosianischen Edikt *Cunctos populos,* dessen Wortlaut Friedrich übernahm[81]. Wenn es einmal drüben in Byzanz geheissen hatte, »Ein Staat, ein Gesetz, ein Kaiser«, dann hieß es jetzt unter Friedrich *Unus Deus, unus papa, unus imperator, una ecclesia*[82].

Man könnte wohl einwenden, daß schon früher ähnliche sprachliche Wendungen gebraucht wurden, wie etwa unter Otto III. die *sacra lex*[83], desgleichen unter Heinrich II.[84] und III. Aber dieser Einwand zieht nicht, weil es sich hier um isolierte Fälle handelt, während es bei den Staufern um ein System, um eine grundsätzliche Anschauung ging, die ihr Substrat aus dem römischen Recht empfing. Was früher einmal Floskel oder Verzierung war, wurde nunmehr wesentlicher Bestandteil. Identität der Sprache beweist noch nicht Identität der sprachlichen Bedeutung.

---

[79] H. A p p e l t , Friedrich Barbarossa und das römische Recht: Römische Hist. Mitteilungen 5 (1962) 18 ff. Mit Recht nimmt K. J o r d a n (oben Anm. 72) Stellung gegen die ungerechtfertigte Abwertung des römischen Rechts durch H. Appelt (siehe J o r d a n 393 Anm. 4).

[80] Z. B. MGH. Const. I. nr. 176, S. 245. Die Auslegung von W. O h n s o r g e , Das Zweikaiserproblem im frühen Mittelalter (1947) 102 ist unverständlich: Friedrich hätte eindeutig die germanische Herrscherauffassung gezeigt, die eine »romfreie« Interpretation des römischen Kaisertums gewesen sei, »und diese Auffassung war nicht gewonnen aus der neuen Belebung des römischen Rechts, sondern einzig und allein aus dem Beispiel Byzanz.« Wie reimt sich germanische Herrscherauffassung mit Byzanz?

[81] MGH. Const. I. nr. 223, S. 315. Im Edikt des Theodosius, das die christliche Religion als Staatsreligion einführte, hieß es: »Cunctos populos, quos clementiae nostrae regit imperium« (Cod. I. 1. 1), und bei Friedrich hieß es in dem Rundschreiben betreffend die ausschließliche Anerkennung des Gegenpapstes ebenso (ebda nr. 223, S. 315 und nr. 224, S. 317): »cunctis populis quos clementiae nostrae regit imperium.«

[82] MGH. Const. I. nr. 182, S. 253. Hier sei zusätzlich an den Begriff des *honor imperii (regni)* erinnert, den P. R a s s o w »Honor Imperii« (Neuausgabe 1960) herausgearbeitet hat, der aber auch in anderen Reichen modisch geworden war. Dazu jetzt auch G. K o c h 141 ff.

[83] Er nannte Justinian seinen *sanctissimus antecessor:* MGH. Leges, IV. 662.

[84] Vgl. auch seine Benennung Justinians als *divus Iustinianus,* ebda, IV. 584.

Aber neben diesen urkundlichen leicht vermehrbaren Zeugnissen für die staufische Aneignung römischrechtlicher Grundsätze gibt es auch herrscherliche Maßnahmen Friedrichs, die im faktischen Rahmen die Anwendung derselben Grundsätze erweisen. Wie bekannt, brach ohne Zutun des Kaisers im September 1159 das Schisma aus zwischen Alexander III. und Viktor IV.[85]. Diese Doppelwahl stellte den Kaiser vor eine von ihm nicht vorausgesehene Situation. Der Schismen hat es viele vorher gegeben; sie waren auch von nicht geringem Interesse für den deutschen Herrscher, insbesondere wenn er schon oder fast Kaiser war. Aber was in diesem Zusammenhang interessiert, ist die herrscherliche Reaktion darauf. Als Kaiser der Römer war er in ganz besonderem Maße Schutzherr der römischen Kirche. Aber diese hatte jetzt nicht ein Haupt, sondern zwei. Das war ein untragbarer Zustand. Die Einheit der Christenheit war dadurch gefährdet und vielleicht in höherem Grade und auf unmittelbarere Weise als dies früher einmal im spätrömischen Reich bei reinen Glaubensstreitigkeiten der Fall war. Welche Maßnahmen ergriff nun der Kaiser, um die Situation zu meistern? Nicht Gewalt, sondern Recht wollte er walten lassen, wie es sich einem Nachfolger der römischen Kaiser geziemte. Das hieß aber, den Rechtsweg beschreiten und das Schisma als reine Rechtsfrage behandeln. Damit wahrte er auch den Grundsatz, daß *papa a nemine iudicatur*[86]. Das Mittel lag zur Hand: das römische Recht, das nunmehr des Kaisers eigenes Recht war, und hier insbesondere das öffentliche Recht, aus welchem die spätrömischen Kaiser die Befugnis ableiteten, Konzilien einzuberufen. Und diese kraft alten römischen Verfassungsrechts einberufenen Konzilien gingen als allgemeine Konzilien in die Geschichte ein[87]. Der kaiserlich verfolgte Zweck war, die für das römische Reich notwendige Glaubenseinheit herzustellen.

Nun die Reaktion Friedrichs glich der altrömischen aufs Haar. Nur handelte es sich diesmal nicht um Glaubenseinheit, sondern um die Entwirrung eines undurchsichtigen Rechtszustandes[88]. Die Frage lautete: Wer war rechtmäßiger Papst, und nicht, was war rechtmäßige Lehre? Dem Vorbild der spätrömischen Zeit getreu, in der die Kaiser

---

[85] Liber Pontificalis, ed. L. Duchesne II. 397 ff.; Bericht bei Migne PL 200. 70 f.; Rahewin, Gesta Friderici, ed. Waitz-Simson (1912) IV. 52, 59 ff.; S. 291, 296 ff.

[86] Das betont im besonderen Rahewin, IV. 64, S. 309. Auch die spätere Geschichtsschreibung hob diesen Punkt hervor, vgl. etwa Burchard von Ursperg, S. 40–1: Friedrich bestellte beide nach Pavia, »non ut eos iudicaret aut causam sedis apostolicae sed ut a prudentibus viris addisceret, cui electo potius obedire deberet ... die iure quoque satis adiectum est, ut reprobata electione Rolandi Octavianus verus presul Romanae ecclesiae iudicaretur.«

[87] Darüber W. U l l m a n n , A short History of the Papacy 7 f., 11, 23.

[88] Die Sachlage wird verkannt von P. R a s s o w 87 f., der die Einberufung der Synode mit dem *honor imperii* in Zusammenhang bringt: »Oktavian als Papst durch-

die wichtigsten Konzilien versammelten, berief nun auch Kaiser Friedrich I. ein Konzil[89]. Diese Situation ermöglichte es ihm, seine römisch-kaiserliche Funktion vollends zur Geltung zu bringen. Er hielt sich für berechtigt 1.) einen Generalkonvent, d. h. ein Konzil, einzuberufen, und 2.) die diesbezüglichen Maßnahmen und Vorgänge, wie sie die spätrömischen Kaiser beginnend mit Konstantin dem Großen beobachteten, zum Muster zu nehmen. Das Wesentliche an der Einberufung des Konzils von Pavia, das dann auch im Februar 1160 tagte, war die kraft des alten römischen Verfassungsrechts ihm zustehende Befugnis, aus der im großen und ganzen klaren Sachlage einen Rechtsentscheid zu erwirken. Über diese im römischen Recht gegründete Befugnis Kaiser Friedrichs kann es keinen Zweifel geben. Darüber hinaus wurde Friedrich auch insoferne seiner kaiserlichen Stellung gerecht, als er in seiner universalen Funktion nicht nur die deutschen, italischen und burgundischen Bischöfe vorlud, sondern auch eine Anzahl von Königen[90] einlud, Vertreter zum Konzil zu entsenden. Und wie es das Recht verlangte, wurde auch Alexander III. geladen, doch gleicht die Sprache der kaiserlichen Einladung eher einer gerichtlichen Vorladung: der Kaiser befiehlt und ordnet das Erscheinen Alexanders an; da der legitime Papst formell noch unbekannt ist, wird Alexander in seiner bisherigen Funktion als Kanzler der römischen Kirche apostrophiert und ihm befohlen, das Urteil in Pavia zu vernehmen[91]. An Deutlichkeit läßt der Wortlaut nichts zu wünschen übrig, was vielleicht dadurch bedingt war, daß der Kaiser peinlich bedacht war, den oben erwähnten Grundsatz nicht zu verletzen.

War die Einberufung des Konzils dem spätrömischen Vorbild nachgeformt, so diente insbesondere das erste allgemeine Konzil, jenes von Nicäa, als unmittelbares Muster. Hier wie dort eröffnete der Kaiser die Versammlung; hier wie dort überließ der Kaiser die Entscheidung

---

setzen war gleichbedeutend mit Durchsetzung der kaiserlichen Ansicht vom *honor imperii*. Dem diente die Synode von Pavia.« Den *honor imperii* kannten weder das römische Recht noch die Verfassung.

[89] MGH. Const. I. nr. 181, 182, S. 252, 253 f. Rahewin und Gerhoch von Reichersberg, De investigatione antichristi, I. 55: MGH Lib. de Lite, III. 365.

[90] MGH. Const. I. nr. 183, S. 254. Die anderen sind erwähnt in den Schreiben nr. 181, 182, 184.

[91] Ibid., nr. 184, S. 256 (= Rahewin, IV. 65, S. 309). Der Eingang ist sehr interessant: »Quoniam divina preordinante clementia Romani imperii gubernacula suscepimus, oportet ut in omnibus viis nostris ipsius legem custodiamus, cuius munere, cuius voluntate dignitatis nostrae apicem adepti sumus. In hoc itaque sacratissimo proposito constituti ... ad quam (scil. generalem curiam et conventum) evocavimus totius imperii nostri et aliorum regnorum ... Proinde eruditioni vestrae mandamus et *ex parte Dei omnipotentis et totius ecclesiae catholicae* praecipimus, ut ad eandem curiam sive conventum veniatis, ecclesiarum sententiam personarum audituri et recepturi.«

den versammelten Bischöfen; hier wie dort griff an entscheidénden Stellen der Kaiser selbst ein und steuerte die Versammlung, mit dem Ergebnis, daß die Entscheidung (die kaum unerwartet kommen konnte) zugunsten Viktors ausfiel. Ich betone, daß die Sachlage wenig Schwierigkeiten machte; was schwierig war, war die Rechtsfrage, die Friedrich den kirchlichen Vertretern überlassen zu wollen erklärte, die aber angesichts der klaren Sachlage gewiß nicht leicht zu entscheiden war, und um die er dann auch von den Bischöfen um Rat gefragt wurde[92].

Von ganz außerordentlichem Interesse ist die Eröffnungsansprache des Kaisers, auf die zwar auch wieder alle modernen Darstellungen verweisen, sie resümieren und sogar deren staatsmännischen Weitblick hervorheben, ohne aber die tiefere Bedeutung dieser Rede zu erkennen. Die Bedeutung der Ansprache liegt darin, daß sie in unmißverständlicher Weise zeigt, wie Friedrich nunmehr die Funktion eines spätrömischen Kaisers auszuüben gedachte. Die Ansprache ist, was bisher völlig unbeachtet geblieben ist, eine zum Teil wörtliche Wiedergabe der Eröffnungsrede Konstantins d. Gr. beim Konzil von Nicäa im Jahre 325 und zum Teil eine Angleichung des konstantinischen Textes an die Situation im Jahre 1160[93]. Darüber hinaus erklärte der Kaiser, daß ihm vermöge des kaiserlichen Amtes und der damit verbundenen Funktion das Recht zustehe, Konzilien zu berufen, wie es eben Konstantin, Theodosius, Justinian sowie Karl und Otto getan hätten. Über die urkundliche Vorlage seiner Rede bei der Konzilseröffnung kann kein Zweifel bestehen. Das Gerüst der Rede stammt entweder unmittelbar aus Rufinus von Aquileja oder mittelbar aus Pseudo-Isidor[94]. Auch die Berichterstattung selbst (durch Rahewin) folgte getreu und genau der Vorlage[95]. Das Wesentliche ist, daß Friedrich hier die ver-

---

[92] Siehe A. H a u c k , Kirchengeschichte Deutschlands (4. Aufl. Neudruck 1956) IV. 252 Anm. 6.

[93] Rahewin IV. 74, S. 319. »Quamvis noverim officio ac dignitate imperii penes nos esse potestatem congregandorum conciliorum, presertim in tantis aecclesiae periculis ... *auctoritatem* tamen diffiniendi huius maximi et summi negotii vestrae prudentiae *vestraeque potestati committo*.« Wie in so vieler anderer Hinsicht, sind auch hier die neuesten Arbeiten über Friedrich I. arg enttäuschend. Weder P. M u n z, Frederick Barbarossa: a study in politics (1969) 214 ff. noch M. P a c a u t , Frédéric Barbarousse (1970) erkannten den Bericht in seiner Bedeutung.

[94] Rufinus, Historia ecclesiastica, X. 2, hg. Th. Mommsen in Ed. Schwartz, Eusebius Werke: Kirchengeschichte, in: Die griechischen christlichen Schriftsteller IX. 2 (1903) 961 (auch in Migne PL 21. 468–9). Pseudo-Isidor, hg. P. Hinschius, Decretales Pseudo-Isidorianae (Neudruck 1956): Epistola vel praefatio Niceni concilii, S. 256. Vgl. über diese pseudo-isidorische Stelle jetzt auch H. F u h r m a n n , Einfluß und Verbreitung der pseudo-isidorischen Fälschungen: von ihrem Auftauchen bis in die neuere Zeit (1972) 184.

[95] Rahewin, IV. 74, S. 319 (die kursiv gedruckten Worte wörtlich mit Rufinus

sammelten Bischöfe mit seiner eigenen *auctoritas* ausstattete. Der Schluß ist zwingend, daß sie sonst nicht ermächtigt gewesen wären, die ihnen vorgelegte Rechtsfrage gültig zu entscheiden. Es handelt sich hier um eine stillschweigende Übernahme und entsprechende Korrektur gelasianischer Gedanken, die gar wohl der Justinianischen in der 6. Novelle nachgebildet sein konnte[96]. Pavia bildet sozusagen den Abschluß einer Phase in der Transformation der Herrschergrundlagen. Aus dem theokratisierten, wiedergeborenen oder neugeborenen König ist ein antikisierender, romanisierender Kaiser geworden. Was sich geändert hatte, war der gedankliche Aufbau, die ideelle Struktur der Herrschaftsgrundlagen.

Welches vorläufige Fazit können wir aus diesen Überlegungen ziehen? Die m. E. unbestreitbare Tatsache, daß Friedrich seine Herrschaft auf römisch-rechtlichem Boden aufbauen wollte, findet ihre Erklärung darin, daß er nur auf dieser Grundlage die volle ungehinderte Entfaltung der monarchischen Regierungsgewalt als möglich und gesichert betrachtete. Dadurch fand die Herrscherstellung einen Schutzwall, einen Panzer, einen Schirm gegen päpstliche Interventionen, weil diese Grundlage gar nichts mit der überlieferten Ekklesiologie, mit der aus der geistlichen Rüstkammer stammenden Theokratie, mit mittelalterlichen kirchlichen Anschauungen oder dem Kirchenrecht zu tun hatte, sondern der unverfälschte Ausdruck christlicher Laienherrscher war. Der Akzent liegt auf dem Laienherrscher. Mit dem alten römischen Recht hatte das Papsttum nichts zu tun gehabt. Im Gegenteil, das Papsttum wuchs ins römische Reich und Recht hinein. Das römische Recht sollte für den Staufer Garantie sein, daß die Herrschermacht dem Zugriff des Papstes entzogen war. Mit dieser Grundauffassung

---

übereinstimmend): »Deinde convocato in unum concilio, *cum resedisset, ait ad episcopos ... Deus* enim *vos constituit sacerdotes et potestatem vobis dedit de nobis quoque iudicandi.* Et quia in his quae ad Deum sunt non est nostrum de vobis iudicare ... *cum haec dixisset,* ipse se concilio subtraxit.«

[96] Über diese »stillschweigende Korrektur« durch Justinian in seiner Novelle VI, vgl. H. R a h n e r , Kirche und Staat im frühen Mittelalter (1964) 286. Friedrich machte eine ähnliche Korrektur eines anderen gelasianischen Grundsatzes zwei Jahre vorher in dem Schreiben, das er an die deutschen Bischöfe absandte: MGH. Const. I nr. 167, S. 233 = Rahewin III. 17 S. 187 ff. Darüber vgl. W. U l l m a n n , Über eine kanonistische Vorlage Friedrichs I.: ZRG Kan. Abt. 46 (1960) 430 ff. Bemerkt sei hier, daß die besonders beeindruckende Terminologie des Kaisers – er wolle sich über das überkommene Recht nicht hinwegsetzen – schon in einem Brief Eugenius III. an Konrad III. (6. Okt. 1149) anklingt. Eugenius sagte hier u. a.: »Quoniam sacrorum canonum et sanctae Romanae ecclesiae sanctionibus contraire non possumus nec debemus« (Ph. Jaffé, wie oben Anm. 48) I. 315, nr. 197. Es ist möglich, wenn nicht sogar wahrscheinlich, daß Eugenius' Brief eine gewisse Verwandtschaft mit Gratian (XXV. 1. 16) verrät. Sollte dies zutreffen, dann wäre dies ein Beweis für die frühe Benutzung von Gratians Dekret in der päpstlichen Kanzlei.

hängt auch zusammen, daß die *lex regia* des römischen Rechts in der Rechtstheorie sehr hoch im Kurs zu steigen begann[97]. Damit aber sollte die Autonomie, die Eigenständigkeit der kaiserlichen Herrschaft und des Reiches erwiesen werden. Die folgenden Jahre sollten zeigen, wie Friedrich trotz des Pavia-Fehlschlages seine Grundsätze in die Tat umzusetzen versuchte – es genügt auf Würzburg und die darauf beruhende Entwicklung zu verweisen[97a], sowie sich seine anmaßende Stellung gegenüber dem Ostkaisertum zu vergegenwärtigen. Von jetzt ab wurde, was betont werden soll, der Streit zwischen Papsttum und Kaisertum auf einer völlig anderen Ebene und auf anderen Voraussetzungen ausgetragen als dies im Investiturkampf der Fall war.

Die tiefe historische Bedeutung dieser Transformation liegt darin, daß das Herrschertum aus der theokratischen Umklammerung und Verflechtung befreit und sie auf säkulärer Grundlage aufgebaut werden sollte. Der nunmehr kräftig einsetzende Säkularisierungsprozeß der Herrschergewalt, der öffentlichen Funktionen, der herrscherlichen Rechte, geht Hand in Hand mit dem auch auf rein geistigem Gebiet ebenso kräftig einsetzenden Säkularisierungsgedanken, der dann während des 13. Jahrhunderts im wiedererstandenen aristotelischen System und im mächtig nach vorwärts drängenden Naturalismus auf allen Gebieten seinen triumphalen Siegeszug hielt[98]. Darin scheint mir die tiefere Bedeutung des staufischen Herrschaftsgedankens zu liegen, weil er die säkuläre Komponente der Herrschermacht als die allein maßgebliche erklärte, und damit die auch anderweits im 12. Jahrhundert zu beobachtende Säkularisierungstendenz kraftvoll vorwärts trieb[99]. Die Folge war, daß die religiösen, theokratischen Attribute des Herrschertums immer mehr an Bedeutung einbüßten und nur mehr im Hintergrund wahrnehmbar waren[100]. Höchst bezeichnend und nur in diesem Zusammenhang erklärbar ist die bisher ebenso ungebührlich ver-

[97] Darüber vgl. W. U l l m a n n , Principles of Government and Politics in the Middle Ages 223 f. und 296 f. Die bevorzugte Behandlung der *lex regia* war offenbar vereinbar mit einer theokratischen Einstellung, wie sich doch auch Justinian auf sie berief in seinem Edikt *Deo auctore*, das die Kodifikationskommission einsetzte (§ 7). Diese Auffassung erreichte in der Lehre des Cynus de Pistoja ihre prägnante Formulierung in dem Satz *Imperium a Deo, imperator a populo* (darüber 297 f.).
[97a] Ob nicht doch Verbindungslinien aus dieser Zeit zum englischen Heinrich II. führten, die dann 1169 in den jüngst edierten scharfen Dekreten Gestalt annahmen? Vgl. D. K n o w l e s et al. in: Engl. Hist. Rev. 87 (1972) 757 ff., bes. 764 ff.
[98] Darüber vgl. W. U l l m a n n , Individual and Society in the Middle Ages (1967) Kap. 3.
[99] Siehe vor allem T. G r e g o r y , Platonismo medievale (1958) 135 ff.; T. G r e g o r y , L'idea di natura nella filosofia medievale (1965) 17, 26.
[100] Das trifft auch für das englische und französische Königtum zu im 13. Jahrhundert. Diese regionalen Probleme bedürfen noch der genaueren Untersuchung. Daß

nachlässigte Bedeutung der Änderung in der Zählung der Regierungsjahre des Herrschers. Während bisher – ganz in Übereinstimmung mit
dem theokratischen Herrschaftsgedanken – die Regierungsjahre vom
Tag der Salbung (Krönung) gerechnet wurden, wurden sie jedenfalls
seit Philipp von Schwaben (der übrigens einer der ersten mittelalterlichen Herrscher gewesen zu sein scheint, dessen Kanzlei die Änderung vornahm) vom Tag der Wahl an gerechnet[101]. Diese Änderung
in der Berechnung der Regierungsjahre ergab sich zwingend aus der
Bestimmung des römischen Rechts, dergemäß der sog. *dies ortus imperii*
der Tag des tatsächlichen Regierungsantritts war[102].

Die Wiedererstehung des Bürgers, des *civis,* und die dadurch be-
dingte Ablösung des Unter/tanen, des *sub/ditus,* durch den Bürger im
13. Jahrhundert wurde durch diese im herrscherlichen Bereich sich voll-
ziehende Entwicklung sehr erheblich gefördert. Man könnte in der Tat
versucht sein, eine Parallele zwischen herrscherlichem und individuel-
lem Bereich zu sehen. Denn genau so wie sich der staufische Herrschafts-
gedanke aus der Betonung des Laientums und der damit verbundenen
Berufung auf das römische Recht erklären läßt, in ebendemselben
Maße läßt sich die Umwandlung des Individuums als eines Unter/tanen
in einen Bürger, der begrifflich nichts mit dem Christentum zu tun
hatte, erklären. In beiden Bereichen handelt es sich um eine Rückkehr
zum vor-christlichen, vor-kirchlichen, zum rein natürlichen *humani-*
stischen Zeitalter (worin der Akzent auf dem *homo* → *humanitas*
liegt), was so viel heißt, daß das humanistische Denken und der humanistische Wiedergeburtsgedanke die mittelalterliche Kosmologie zu un-
terwandern und auszuhöhlen begannen. Es war der Beginn der Renaissance, die wie ihre Vorgängerin im fränkischen Zeitalter, ebenso zuerst

auch hier das römische Recht eine große Bedeutung spielte, dürfte wohl keinem
Zweifel unterliegen. Die Entwicklung in England wurde durch das sog. common
law gefördert, das gleich dem römischen Recht reines Laienrecht war.

[101] Siehe MGH. Const. II. nr. 1, S. 2, datiert 29. Juni 1198 (»anno primo«), also
weit über zwei Monate vor der Krönung am 8. Sept. 1198; er war am 8. März ge-
wählt worden. Vgl. ferner nr. 15, S. 18, ebenso konsequent. Die englischen und fran-
zösischen Könige folgten 70 Jahre später. Der englische König Eduard I. trat die
Regierung mit dem Tag des Begräbnisses seines Vaters Heinrichs III. an (20. Nov.
1272), wurde aber erst am 19. August 1274 gesalbt und gekrönt. Ähnliches gilt für
Philipp III. von Frankreich.

[102] Siehe Cod. III. 12. 7 (5) und meinen Beitrag zu den Atti Accursiani (wie oben
Anm. 39), 662 ff. Als dieses Gesetz erlassen wurde (3. August 389), gab es selbstverständlich keine Salbung oder Krönung. Daß sich in der juristischen Literatur des
13. und 14. Jahrhunderts eine große Diskussion über die Rechte des Herrschers *vor*
der Krönung entspann, ist bekannt, aber noch ganz ungenügend untersucht (vgl. W.
U l l m a n n , Medieval Idea of Law [Neudruck 1968] 176 f. [Cynus, Jacobus de
Arena, Bartolus, Lucas de Penna]).

auf herrscherlichem, öffentlichem und gesellschaftlichem Gebiet sich zu Wort meldete.

Aber man kann füglich fragen, wie stand es denn mit dem staufischen Herrschaftsgedanken selbst? War das Ziel, die päpstliche Umklammerung abzuschütteln, erreicht? War die Berufung auf das Laienrecht, auch wenn es das römische Recht war, genügend abgestützt und auch ein tragfähiges Fundament? Im gegenwärtigen Rahmen kann ich nicht auf diese vielen Fragen eingehen. Bloß einige flüchtige Bemerkungen seien vielleicht am Platze. Das päpstliche Pochen auf das Recht im Investiturstreit erwies sich als zweischneidig. Man könnte der Versuchung unterliegen und sagen, die Geister, die es rief, die ward das Papsttum nimmer los, denn der ungleiche Rechtszustand im Zeitalter Gregors VII. führte zur Wiederbelebung des römischen Rechts und zu dessen Studium. Damit erwuchs aber dem Papsttum ein sehr eindrucksvoller und auf dieser rechtlichen Ebene auch gleichwertiger Gegner. Doch für diesen Gegenspieler des Papsttums ergaben sich dabei andererseits mancherlei Fragen. Wie sehr man auch die römischen Kaiser als Vorgänger der mittelalterlichen Kaiser vor- und darstellte (ich erinnere etwa an den Archipoeta oder an Gottfried von Viterbo) und wie sehr man die Rechtsnachfolge der mittelalterlichen Kaiser zu erweisen sich bemühte – hinter diesen Behauptungen stand freilich eine Frage, die Verlegenheit bereiten konnte: wie wurde denn der deutsche König Kaiser der Römer? Es hat sowohl vor wie nach Friedrich I. keinen mittelalterlichen Herrscher gegeben, der ohne aktive Mitwirkung des Papsttums legitimer Kaiser der Römer geworden wäre[103]. Die Rolle, die das Papsttum dabei spielte, war konstitutiv. Daß man diese Rolle im Staufenlager leugnete, ist sattsam bekannt, aber damit war die Rolle des Papsttums doch noch nicht aus der Welt geschafft. Konnten die vielen staufischen und ghibellinischen Erklärungen, Manifeste usw. die konstitutive Rolle in eine deklaratorische umwandeln? Das sind Fragen, an denen man nicht vorbeikommt. Vor allem, konnte die Figur des *Rex Romanorum* den Anspruch auf das Kaisertum *rechtlich* begründen?[104] Da sich diese Figur auf eine rein gedankliche Rückprojektion stützte, lag da nicht in der Figur eines römischen Königs und

---

[103] Mit der möglichen Ausnahme von Ludwig IV. in 1328, der, zuerst von Sciarra Colonna im Namen des römischen Volkes gekrönt, aber doch eine Krönung durch den Gegenpapst nachholte.

[104] Im 14. Jahrhundert zur Zeit Ludwigs IV. Wahl (1314) wurde das *regnum Romanum* (= *Romanorum*) mit dem *imperium Romanum* gleichgesetzt: vgl. MGH. Const. V. nr. 102, S. 98 f. Daher auch die Identität von *rex Romanorum* und *imperator Romanorum* gemäß *Licet iuris* vom 6. August 1338, hrsg. K. Zeumer, Geschichte der deutschen Reichsverfassung im Mittelalter und Neuzeit (2. Aufl. 1913), I. nr. 142, S. 184.

des daraus fließenden *regnum Romanum* die Gefahr eines Trug-
schlusses? Daß man den Begriff ernst nahm und daß er ernst genommen zu werden verdient, darüber sollte es keinen Zweifel geben[105].
Aber alle diese Fragen zeigen, wie vielschichtig der Komplex ist. Eine
von mir unerwähnt gebliebene Schicht betrifft die Rolle, die das Ostkaisertum bei dieser Entwicklung spielte. Und bei der Analyse dieser
Schicht und ihrem Verhältnis zum westlichen Kaisertum tut sich eine
gewisse historische Tragik auf, die fürwahr auf geschichtlicher Ebene
starke Ähnlichkeiten mit einer griechischen Tragödie hat. War das
westliche Herrschertum nach staufischer Auffassung nicht dem östlichen
Kaisertum wesensgleich? Hier wie dort wurde die Kaiserkrönung als
deklaratorisch angesprochen. Hier wie dort war die Rolle der Hierarchie eine dienende und der Laiengewalt ein viel größerer Spielraum
eingeräumt als dies bisher im Westen der Fall war. Hier wie dort
gehörte das römische Recht zum Fundament der öffentlichen Gewalt.
Hier wie dort gab es einen Kaiser der Römer – aber gerade darin zeigt
sich, welch tiefe Kluft Ost und West trennte! Die Kaisermacht spitzte
sich auf den Begriff des wenn auch nur ideell verstandenen universalen
Jurisdiktionsanspruchs zu, aber hierin liegt der historisch faßbare Kern
der Tragödie, die im 5. Jahrhundert anhebt und die in dem Dreigestirn
Ostkaisertum, Papsttum, Westkaisertum ihren sichtbaren, konkreti-
sierten, historischen Ausdruck finden sollte.

---

[105] Das hatte Innozenz III. klar erkannt, indem er den Titel in dem langen
deutschen Thronstreit geflissentlich vermied, denn schon in der Benutzung eines Titels
liegt eine stillschweigende Anerkennung der darin ausgedrückten Funktionen. Darüber vgl. Studi Accursiani (wie oben Anm. 102), 661 ff. Daß sich die Verhandlungen Heinrichs VI. mit Coelestin III. über die Königssalbung des jungen Friedrich II. im Jahr 1196 gerade an diesem Punkt zerschlugen, dürfte wohl kaum zu
bestreiten sein, vgl. art. cit., 680 ff. mit Belegstellen und Literatur. In seiner Studie
steht H. S t e h k ä m p f e r , Der Kölner Erzbischof Adolf und die deutsche Königswahl (1195–1205): HZ. Beiheft 2 (1973) 1–83, der Tragweite dieses Begriffs sowie
den eben erwähnten Verhandlungen ganz verständnislos gegenüber. Auch G. B a a -
k e n , Die Verhandlungen zwischen Heinrich VI. und Coelestin III. in 1195–1197:
DA. 27 (1972) 457 ff., bes. 502 f. berührt die zur Erklärung des Scheiterns der Verhandlungen wesentliche Frage nicht.

III

THE PONTIFICATE OF ADRIAN IV[1]

O N Saturday, 4 December 1154, eight hundred years ago, Nicholas
Breakspear was elected pope. On the following day he was enthroned
and crowned at St Peter's, Rome. Adrian IV was the only 'pontifex
natione Anglicus' who has assumed the tiara.

I do not propose to give an account of Nicholas Breakspear's early life, to
speak of his abbatial career, to deal with his mission as a cardinal, or to go
into the details of his pontificate; there is no scarcity of books and essays
adequately treating of these matters. What I propose to do is to attempt to
show the historic importance of this pontificate in the wider setting of medieval
Europe, to portray it within the framework of the forces at work in the mid-
twelfth century, to delineate the reign of Adrian against a larger background
and to re-create some of the basic contemporary issues, believing that hereby
a better perspective and a better appreciation of this pontificate can be
obtained. Since his pontifical career left an imprint upon contemporary
Europe which is not yet fully recognized, it will be my task to draw attention
to the unpretentious and unostentatious manner in which Adrian acted. By
concrete implementation of the abstract papal theory the Englishman initiated
the age of the great medieval popes. Adrian, the pope of action, ranks in
importance in no wise below the popes of theory. He is, as it were, theory made
eminently practical. His pontificate begins the steep ascent of the papacy to
the dizzy heights of the Innocentian era.

The age in which Adrian took office was one that witnessed profound
changes in all spheres of life, and change always brings in its train restlessness,
crises, stress and tension, caused by the attempted displacement of the old by
the new. New forces were released which had hitherto had no opportunity of
asserting themselves and which challenged the traditional scheme of things
vigorously. The new forces—the educated lay element—made their impact
upon the age; multifarious and divergent in their character, they were at
once fresh, exuberant, youthful and progressive, and yet at the same time
immature, naïve and retrogressive.

It is the lay spirit, so powerfully engendered by the crusade, which begins
to assert itself most forcefully in the fifties. The century between the 1150's
and 1250's is characterized by the conflict of the lay element with its older
antagonist, and it is this background which makes accessible to understanding

[1] A lecture delivered before the University of Cambridge on 1 December 1954.

the conflicts of the Staufens and Plantagenets with the papacy. And in this conflict the figure of Adrian IV assumes its historic significance. He was the first pope against whom the newly released forces unleashed their attack; he was the pope who was faced with a serious challenge to the conception of the papal office by adversaries better equipped and better advised than papal opponents had so far been. By meeting the attack effectively in its initial stages, Adrian earned the gratitude of later popes—and none was more generous in recognizing the debt of the later papacy to Adrian than Innocent III.

The brief span of his bare five years' rule is somewhat disproportionate to its historic significance. It is a well-known fact that much depends on the handling of the opening phases of a conflict. Had Adrian IV not acted in the resolute and energetic manner in which he did, the physiognomy of the century that followed his pontificate would assuredly have been different. Having no inclination towards lengthy theoretical discussions, Adrian acted, and he acted on the firm basis of the papal-hierocratic ideology, which had by now reached its fully matured stage. Adrian is therefore not only the man of action; he is also the man of tradition, and by acting in conformity with tradition, he preserved tradition in an age of restless transition.

Indeed, the year 1154 might well seem symptomatic in several respects. On the one hand there was Adrian the pope, a traditionalist to the core. On the other hand, there were Henry II of England and Frederick I Barbarossa, classic examples of the reinvigorated royalist-lay ideology. Less than a fortnight after Adrian's assuming the office of tradition, Henry II became king of England. In the very week in which Adrian was elected and crowned, the mighty Staufen, Frederick I, on his way to Rome for the imperial crown, released the Furor Teutonicus on north Italian cities. It may well seem symptomatic that these three men should herald their entry onto the historic stage at the very same time. To the extent to which Adrian was the representative of the traditional hierocratic standpoint, epitomized in the monarchic function of the pope, to the same extent Frederick and Henry were representatives of the fundamentally opposed royalist-lay standpoint, epitomized in the monarchic function of the emperor or king.

In the same year 1154 there died Gilbert de la Porrée, whose great antagonist, the abbot of Clairvaux and uncrowned emperor of Europe, had preceded him into the grave a few months earlier. It is assuredly a symptom of the time that in the very same year 1154 Rome itself witnessed a renewed outburst of demagogic activity by Arnold of Brescia, an activity which, whilst largely negative and destructive, nevertheless manifested the signs characteristic of the temper of the time; his bombastic appeals to ancient Roman institutions kindled the imagination of the ever-receptive and emotional, if not entirely practical, Roman populace, and these appeals show how barely awakened forces can degenerate quickly and in a ludicrous manner. However, Arnold's fiery call for a return to apostolic poverty was a portent.

Again, not only England witnessed a change of government in this year 1154. The southern Norman kingdom of Sicily, in this same year 1154, also underwent a change, which likewise was to leave permanent traces. Upon the death of the great Roger II, William I succeeded, who himself was to play a major role in the curial policy of Adrian and thereby of the later papacy. Hardly less significant is it that in this year 1154 the troops of the eastern emperor Manuel had begun their operations, troops who in 1155 were to occupy the whole district from Ancona down south to Tarento: troops of the man who personified almost as long a tradition as Adrian; troops of the man whose avowed aim was the revival of the true Roman empire in its Constantinean and Justinianean shape, to whom the western emperor was a mere usurper and illiterate upstart.

Very little historical imagination is needed to appreciate the character of these events and the gravity of the situation at the accession of Adrian: the city of Rome in the throes of Arnold's régime; clear signs of restlessness in the patrimony of St Peter; the future west-Roman emperor, the *unicus filius Romanae ecclesiae*, somewhat menacingly working his way to Rome; the east-Roman emperor despatching his forces towards the same target—that emperor who, though he never dreamed of becoming the *unicus filius Romanae ecclesiae*, nevertheless held out the hope of a union between eastern and western churches.

It is tempting to draw parallels between the papacy in the fifties of the eleventh century and the papacy in the fifties of the twelfth century. In the former Hildebrand was the papal mentor who succeeded as Pope Gregory VII; in the latter it was Chancellor Roland who fulfilled the role of a mentor and also succeeded as pope. In each period the Normans of Sicily assume a major role; in each the Lombard cities in the north play a vital part; in each the orientation of western-imperial tradition is of decisive moment; in each there is the wider background of the eastern schism. However, there is this difference: Hildebrand was a self-made man, endowed with unique qualifications which enabled him almost instinctively to say the right word at the right time. Chancellor Roland, on the other hand, had no such natural gifts. Adrian's confidential adviser personifies a new class of officials in the papal curia, the class of the specialized and trained scholar. With Roland the close link between curia and Bologna is established, a link whose importance for the working of the papacy cannot be exaggerated. Roland was the first product of the canonistic school of Bologna to enter the service of the curia. Inevitably one is reminded of the pairs Felix–Gelasius, Nicholas–Anastasius, Leo–Humbert, Alexander–Hildebrand, when one considers the pair Adrian–Roland. But whilst earlier mentors were men of natural abilities, who created or materially contributed to the making of the papal programme, Roland's part consisted in giving practical advice based on the concrete application of the doctrines created by these earlier mentors. Adrian–Roland presented a perfect team, in which the one complemented the other: Adrian the man of tough energy, iron will, clear sightedness, in so many ways reminiscent of Nicholas I—Roland supplying the intellectual equipment drawn from the large armoury of juristic theology. The practical experience which Roland gained in the school of Adrian proved invaluable to Roland's own pontificate.

To the traditional programme of the medieval papacy Adrian did not make any substantial additions. This was a programme which had been tried, modified and hammered out in numerous situations and conflicts and to which very little could be added by Adrian's time. What he did was to apply this traditional programme to situations for which it appeared to have been prepared. In appraising the historic significance of Adrian's pontificate one must beware of overrating the role of the man himself; there is, in the medieval period, no other institution in which not so much the man and his character count as the office and the function which the man assumes. The medieval papacy was an office the bearer of which was instituted to govern, to lead, to direct. The authority and power of this office were conceptually independent of the man; the substance of the office was prescribed by an idea and circumscribed by tradition. It is of some historic interest that at this crucial time an Englishman should be the bearer of this office.

What Adrian as pope inherited was the papal theory of government in relation to the *societas christiana*. To use the technical term, it was the *gubernatio*, government, of this body politic that was the prime function of the pope. This direction, guidance, orientation, in short government, in order to be effective, could be undertaken only within the terms of an enforceable rule, in terms of the law. Hence the importance of law for the curia. The form of this government was monarchic. The papal monarchy was the translation of the Petrine commission into terms of government which was expressed by the names *principatus*, *primatus* or *monarchatus*. The contemporary allegorical designation of the Roman Church as the *caput et mater* of Christendom denoted its leadership in terms of government as well as its function as the foundation of Christendom.

In one of his earliest letters Adrian IV makes these points crystal clear.[2] Here he compares the body of Christians, the *Corpus Christi*, with the human body which, too, can function well only if all its parts dovetail and are directed to the same end, purpose, *finis* and *telos*. The *caput* of the human body is its directing organ, and so is the *caput* of the collective body of Christians, in other words the *monarchatus* of the pope. He considers himself alone entitled and bound to direct and govern the whole body of Christians in consonance with its underlying purpose or *telos*. In order to execute his *monarchatus* effectively, the pope appoints an auxiliary organ in the person of the emperor of the Romans, technically called the *brachium Romanae ecclesiae*, who has consequently no autonomous status. All this is nothing else but the

[2] *Ep[istola]* 9, of 3 January 1155.

doctrine of Hugh of St Victor, of Bernard of Clairvaux and of Adrian's own compatriot, Honorius of Canterbury.

It was in accordance with this papal-hierocratic conception that Adrian proceeded. One can appreciate the state of ideological preparedness and the measure of apprehension in the curia during this week eight hundred years ago when one recalls the rapid succession of events: on Friday Anastasius IV died; on Saturday Nicholas Breakspear was elected; on Sunday Adrian was enthroned. No doubt, the efficient handling of the difficult northern problems by Breakspear recommended him to the other sixteen cardinals who elected him unanimously. The election took place, not in the usual place, in the Lateran, presumably because the exequies for Anastasius were prepared there, but at St Peter's. A consecration of the newly elected pope was not necessary, for he had already been a bishop for six years, a somewhat unusual feature at the time, as many popes were not in orders at the time of their election.

The coronation of Adrian IV brings out the ideological content of the papal programme in an exquisite manner. His coronation followed the ceremonial of which we read in the immediately preceding as well as in the succeeding pontificates. Far too little stress is laid in our usual histories upon the profound symbolism to be witnessed in both papal and imperial coronation ceremonies. That symbolism revealed to contemporaries in a visible and hence easily comprehensible way the essential points of a programme much better than long tracts could have done. Symbolism was the means to express abstract theory by concrete actions which could not be misconstrued. If we do not take account of medieval symbolism, a good deal of medieval history eludes our understanding.

In the case of Adrian's coronation due emphasis is laid on the monarchic function of the pope which is shown by appropriately chosen actions and gestures. Moreover, his coronation brings into clearest possible relief the real difference between him as pope and monarch, and the emperor as his *filius* and *adjutor* who would be crowned six months later. Only a few of these symbolic actions can here be mentioned in passing. There is the clothing of the elected pope with the imperial scarlet mantle; there is the solemn elevation and enthronement of the pope upon the *cathedra beati Petri*—enthronement symbolizing taking physical possession of a dominion, a feature which we shall presently see, was conspicuously absent in the case of Frederick's coronation; there is the accompanying prayer at the enthronement that Christ may give the pope powers 'ad regendam ecclesiam et universam plebem'—assuredly a suitable frame for Hildebrand's formula of the *universale regimen* of the pope; there is the placing on Adrian's head of the papal crown, which by his time was already known as the tiara, but which had previously been designated as the *regnum* or the *corona*. This papal crown was a mitre modified by two rings, two *circuli*, which symbolized sacerdotal and regal powers, the very attributes of a medieval monarch. There is the solemn handing over of the straight staff,

III

238

the *pedum rectum*, the symbol of jurisdictional powers. There is the western transformation of the eastern proskynesis (the actual prostration before the *divina majestas* of the emperor) into the kissing of the pope's feet by the cardinals. Again, we note the symbolic incarnation of another Hildebrandine demand. The pope, seated so as to bring out his position of authority, receives the cardinals individually for the kiss of peace, one of the most distinctive papal prerogatives. In consonance with contemporary practice Adrian was given the twelve seals symbolizing the concentration of the power of all the twelve apostles in his own hands. I cannot strongly enough emphasize the pregnant nature of this symbolic act and of the number twelve, particularly when it is brought into relation with the Last Supper re-enacted at Easter, to which I will turn in a moment. There is also, to mention just one more symbolic feature, the handing over of the two keys and of the pallium—taken from St Peter's altar by the prior of the deacons, not by an ordained bishop or cardinal, but by a deacon, so as to avoid the suspicion that episcopal power had anything to do with the pope's receiving the pallium.

Because of the insecure situation in Rome created by Arnold's activity, Adrian stayed at St Peter's until Maundy Thursday, and therefore the perhaps even more significant acts at the Lateran were not carried out in his case, such as the pope's sitting in the *sedes stercoraria* (a symbolism which is so difficult for us moderns to grasp; it is the visible transformation of Ps. cxiii, 7–8, and Matt. xxiii. 12), his taking physical possession of the two curule chairs, the one signifying St Peter's, the other St Paul's chair, and so forth.

Whilst all this public symbolism, certainly that at his coronation, was to exhibit the true monarchic function of Pope Adrian, at his first Easter we find him, again following the practice of the last ten years, performing in the Lateran a ceremony that is important enough to be mentioned briefly. This ceremony at Easter demonstrated the pope as the vicar of Christ. Adrian IV is one of the first popes who, in an official communication[3], styles himself Vicar of Christ with the words 'We, however unworthy, are the vicegerents of Christ on earth' ('Nos, qui licet indigni, Christi vices in terris agimus').[4] This will become the standing phrase in Innocent III's as in all later papal correspondence. Adrian's thesis is important and needs emphasizing, because otherwise some of his actions cannot be properly understood. The concept of a papal vicariate of Christ—the title vicar of Christ was used by kings and emperors previously—brings to a close the long development towards the so-called mediatory role of the pope who, by becoming vicar of Christ, became thereby the vicar of Him Who was the one mediator between God and man.[5] Since, according to the accepted doctrine, Christ was *Rex* and

[3] *Ep.* 15, of 20 January 1155.
[4] Eugenius III designated himself 'domestically' as the 'vicarius Christi', cf. the curial officer's report in M[onumenta] G[ermaniae] H[istorica]: *Scriptores*, xx, 543. Cf. also his *Epistula* 575, of 10 April 1153, and M. Maccarrone, 'Vicarius Christi' (*Lateranum*, n.s. xviii, 1953) pp. 94 f.   [5] I *Tim.* ii. 5.

Sacerdos—the classic formulation of this theory is that of Gelasius I—and since furthermore 'nulla potestas nisi a Deo', the vicariate of Christ in the pope was a potent argument to assert the derivation of all power and, above all, of secular-imperial power, from the pope as the vicar of the true monarch, the *verus imperator*, Christ. From the point of view of government the concept of a visible vicar of Christ in the pope was a logical necessity. The concept was also equally important as an argument against the ever-threatening episcopalism—as vicar of St Peter the pope was still a mere vicar of an apostle, albeit the prince of the apostles, but when the Petrine commission could be considered to constitute a vicariate of Christ, the pope's position *vis-à-vis* the episcopacy was immeasurably strengthened; hence also from this time onwards the increasing exercise of papal confirmation of episcopal elections, so that shortly afterwards the theory could be developed that the bishops received their *potestas regendi* from the pope, whilst their *potestas ordinis* was derived from the apostles.

This is the meaning of the Easter ceremony, which symbolically re-enacted, in realist medieval fashion, the Last Supper. Here Pope Adrian plays the role of Christ, whilst eleven cardinals assume the function of the apostles. Judas is played by a Lateran official, the *basilicarius*. The lamb is brought in and blessed by the pope who breaks off small pieces from the lamb, handing the first to the Lateran official with the words of St John: 'That thou doest, do quickly.' Then the eleven cardinals are each handed a piece from the lamb: 'Et sic omnes comedunt.'[6] This is the meaning of the dry words in Adrian's biography: 'Pascha cum discipulis suis festive comedit.'[7]

These are a few revealing symbolic facets concretely manifesting the thesis of the pope's monarchic power. If we look at Adrian IV in this way, his relations with Frederick as well as with the East become in large measure understandable. There is a perfect concordance between Adrian's symbolic actions and his acts of government.

The passing of the first Eastertide in Adrian's pontificate heralded the approach of the proud Staufen who had undertaken his Italian campaign with a view to obtaining the imperial crown. It was certain that no man could call himself a Roman emperor unless the pope had personally placed upon his head the crown, which symbolized a conceptual universality of dominion. Nothing could change this, not even Frederick's assumption of the imperial title before the coronation.[8] Hence the pope, as the actual dispenser of Roman imperial dignity—before the crown was on Frederick's head he was constitutionally a mere *Rex Romanorum*—could not logically be denied the right to approve formally the candidate whom he was to crown; why Frederick should have been so annoyed at this what he called unwarranted approbation, is diffi-

---

[6] *Ordo Romanus* XI, cap. 48; repeated in *Ordo Romanus* XII, cap. 35.
[7] *Liber Pontificalis*, ed. L. Duchesne (Paris, 1892), II, 389, lines 27 f.
[8] See *MGH. Const.* I, no. 145, p. 202, and editorial note ibid.

cult to understand. But this was merely a minor inconsistency on Frederick's part, larger and more fundamental ones were soon to follow.

At Sutri, on 8 June 1155, there occurred the famous incident of Frederick's refusal to perform the service of a *strator*, i.e. of holding the reins of the pope's horse (there is no evidence for saying that the service of a stirrup holder was demanded). He pretended that this might be interpreted in the sense of a feudal dependence; it is very debatable indeed whether his refusal had any basis in feudal practice or theory. But Adrian insisted that this token of respect should be paid by the man who expressed the desire of being a Roman emperor, that is, a successor of Constantine.[9] And it was Constantine who in his Donation had laid down the service of a *strator*. No doubt sensing the role allocated to him, namely, the role of an *adjutor*, of an auxiliary organ, Frederick considered that service incompatible with the role he claimed for himself, not the role of an *adjutor*, but that of an autonomous Caesar, of a true monarch; and that service was not acknowledged by the Eastern emperors either. Yet Frederick was dependent on the pope, because there was no other way of obtaining the crown. It was Frederick's *desiderium*, to use his own words, to be crowned Roman emperor by Pope Adrian, a desire the fulfilment of which seemed jeopardized at Sutri by the firm stand of Adrian, until the seemingly self-willed German changed his mind and performed the service required.

Ten days after this episode the imperial coronation took place, a coronation whose fascinating symbolism revealed an inconsistency on Frederick's part which is quite remarkable. Every one of the symbolic actions showed that Frederick was not an autonomous Caesar but a mere auxiliary organ, whose imperial position was derivative. Moreover, the coronation of Frederick incorporated some very significant modifications introduced by Adrian IV.

For reasons which are irrelevant here, Frederick had to keep his coronation secret from the Roman population—it is a little ironical perhaps that the proud aspirant to universal dominion had to fear the Romans; it was for this reason that he entered the Leonine city with his German entourage from his camping place outside Rome not through the Porta Collina near the Castle of St Angelo, but through the Porta Viridaria which was, so to speak, the back entrance to St Peter's. Further, a Saturday was chosen in order to deceive the Romans, because the usual day for a coronation was a Sunday. For fear of the Romans the symbolic coronation acts outside St Peter's had to be omitted. But what took place inside St Peter's showed a number of alterations, all pointing to a diminution of the emperor's position.

The coronation ceremony that had hitherto been followed consisted of two distinctive parts, First came the consecration of the future emperor by the

---

[9] Cf. Frederick calling Constantine the Great one 'predecessorum nostrorum divorum imperatorum, magni Constantini videlicet et Justiniani et Valentiniani...' in *Const.* no. 227, p. 322, sub (3). For the designation of the ancient Roman emperors as *divi imperatores* see W. Ensslin, 'Gottkaiser und Kaiser von Gottes Gnaden' in *Sitzungsberichte der bayrischen Akademie der Wissenschaften* (1943), fasc. 6.

senior cardinals on the main altar of St Peter; in this anointing ceremony the pope was inactive. The second part was characterized by the sole activity of the pope and the inactivity of the cardinals. The second part was performed at a side altar, at that of St Maurice. In this second part the pope alone conferred the imperial insignia. But both parts took place within the coronation mass, between Introitus and Gloria.

Adrian IV changed this arrangement that had been in force since 1014. In order to show by manifest means that the unction did not constitute any ecclesiastical *ordo* whatsoever, Adrian arranged that Frederick's unction was to precede the coronation mass. I need not point out what a major change this was. The already considerably devalued imperial unction—devalued because the emperor was not anointed on the head with chrism, but between the shoulders and on the right arm, the seat of physical strength, with a lower grade oil—Adrian devalued still more by prescribing that it was to be administered before coronation mass began, the underlying reason being that only an ecclesiastical *ordo* was conferred during mass, but since the future emperor did not receive an *ordo*, the unction had to be performed before the mass. This change introduced by Adrian was incorporated by Innocent III in the last form of ceremonial for an imperial coronation to be devised in medieval times.

The second change introduced at Frederick's coronation concerned the altar at which he was anointed. It will be recalled that previously the future emperor was anointed at the main altar by the cardinals. According to the chief authority, Canon Mallius of St Peter, the decree of Gregory I (which is spurious) stipulated that nobody else but the pope was allowed to function at the main altar. But since it was not the pope but the cardinals who anointed the emperor, the unction had to be transferred from the main altar to a side altar. Boso's statement is therefore contradicted by Mallius's explicit declaration that at the side altar of St Maurice '*de antiqua consuetudine* Romanorum imperator a dominis episcopis cardinalibus benedicitur et ungitur'.[10]

The third change introduced by Adrian concerned the altar at which the imperial insignia were conferred. Since the unction was transferred to a side altar, the insignia were now conferred at the main altar by the pope; this arrangement brought the pope's position into the clearest possible relief. As far as the liturgical symbolism went, the conferment of the imperial insignia now became the main item of the whole coronation ceremony, because it was carried out during the mass, at the main altar, by the pope alone.

Frederick's coronation is also the first coronation at which the ring is omitted as an imperial emblem. Adrian introduced this further change, because the ring was the hallmark of episcopal functions, signifying the bishop's marriage with his diocese. But since Frederick could not claim this

---

[10] See Petrus Mallius, *Historia Basilicae Antiquae s. Petri*, II, 16 (in *Acta Sanctorum*, June VII–2, p. 39).

distinction, Adrian logically enough excised the ring, and never again did the ring appear as an imperial emblem.

There is no need to comment upon the deep symbolism which Adrian followed when fulfilling the *desiderium* of the Staufen. In an unspectacular manner the diminution of the emperor's position was carried several stages further. But Frederick, the proud Staufen, trembling in fear of the Romans, desirous of the crown, meekly went through the whole coronation ceremony, not seeing or perhaps not wanting to see the real meaning of the various acts which, to anyone endowed with a normal critical sense, would have shown that what aspirations he harboured could by no means be harmonized with the role he himself played on that 18 June 1155 in submissively following the coronation ceremony laid down by Adrian.

In order to receive the coveted crown, the Staufen raised no objection to submitting himself to the *scrutinium*, the formal examination by the pope (in parenthesis we may note that the Roman emperor did not know any Latin and that his prompters at the examination were two Lateran ecclesiastics who told him how to answer in Latin the pope's Latin questions). Nor did Frederick find it humiliating to perform the Western counterpart of the Eastern proskynesis. Nor, above all, did he notice that there was no provision for his enthronement—after all, what reason was there to enthrone an officer, an auxiliary organ, an *advocatus?*—nor did he show any misgivings that it was the pope personally who girded the sword on him, the sword which like the pallium, was taken from the altar of St Peter. Was not this an unmistakable way of showing how and where and from whom the self-styled *dominus mundi* received the sword? The sword is the sign of physical power and he was given the sword personally by the pope. When one brings the manner of conferring the sword into connexion with the unction and the places of the body that were actually anointed, one will have no difficulty in appreciating the exquisite way in which an ideology was symbolically enacted. The sceptre also, the sign of imperial jurisdiction, Frederick received from the hands of Adrian, who thereby gave his *filius* power in the bloodless sphere, in that of jurisdiction. That the Germans present at the ceremony shouted, as Cardinal Boso says, as if a thunderbolt had struck St Peter's, when Adrian placed the crown on Frederick's head thus fulfilling his *desiderium*, we can well believe. How and from whom, if not from the pope, did he receive the crown? What is in the pope's power to give is also in the pope's power to take away, as Frederick's grandson was to discover. This was the setting in which Frederick was made an emperor; an emperor whose imperial position was derivative, being derived from Pope Adrian. The imperial coronation was constitutive,[11] and

---

[11] The constitutive character of the imperial coronation was clearly established in the ninth century (cf. John VIII writing to Louis the Stammerer: *MGH. Epistolae*, VI, no. 87, p. 82, lines 27 ff.) and the coronation *Ordo C* which was applied since Henry II's coronation in 1014, makes it abundantly clear that not until the *Rex* has received the last imperial emblem, is he an *imperator*; he takes the coronation oath as 'rex et futurus imperator'. It was ob-

no arguing on the imperial side could change the constitutive meaning of the coronation and turn it into a merely declaratory ceremony.[12]

No doubt it was incongruous for a ruler to boast of his autonomous status, to emphasize the *Dei gratia* character of his emperorship, to declare himself the *christus Domini*, to act and speak as the true successor of the Roman Caesars,[13] to aim at the *reformatio totius orbis*,[14] and yet to be shown in such a palpable manner as that of the coronation that, after all, it was the pope alone who made him, created him, an emperor. From the human point of view the reaction to such an incongruous situation is understandable. It rankles in one's mind when one faces reality ruthlessly and sees that dreams do not accord with facts. It is this rankling in Frederick's mind which explains the otherwise inexplicable outburst at Besançon (Oct. 1157) with its famous *beneficium* episode, the episode which forms such a welcome relief for those who delight in sensational headlines. It will be recalled that Adrian IV used the term *beneficium* in his letter to Frederick; and that Rainald of Dassel, reading out the letter to the assembly, translated the term with 'fief', thereby making the pope say that the empire was a 'fief' of the papacy.

viously with these words of *Ordo C* in mind that Gregory VII wrote of Henry IV as '*Rex et Romae Deo annuente futurus imperator*' (*Reg[ister]*, ed. E. Caspar, I, 20). Hence in the fateful autumn days of 1076 he demanded prior notification of the elected candidate (*Reg.* IV, 3, p. 299: '*Negotium, personam et mores eius quamtotius potestis nobis indicare*'), so as to be in a position to approve the candidate for coronation; this confirmation of the election is based on the principle of suitability which was then classically expressed by Innocent III during the imperial dispute, see *Regestum super negotio Romani imperii*, no. 62 (ed. F. Kempf in *Miscellanea Historiae Pontificiae*, XII (1947), p. 169); cf. also nos. 21, 29, 48, 98 (*persona idonea*). For a literary source stating the constitutive character of the imperial coronation see, for instance, Ralph Glaber in *MGH. Scriptores*, VII, 59, lines 9 ff.: '...ne quisquam audacter Romani imperii sceptrum praeporerus gestare princeps appetat, seu imperator dici aut esse valeat, nisi quem papa sedis Romanea morum probitate aptum delegerit reipublicae eique commiserit insigne imperiale.' On the other hand, the papal coronation was declaratory; the constitutive act was that of the election itself. The placing of the tiara (*corona, regnum*) on the pope's head added nothing as regards his authority which he had not already possessed by virtue of being elected, cf. the election decree of 1059 in *MGH. Const.* I, 538, cap. 8, and the works of Eichmann and Wasner, cited in the bibliography below.

[12] For some imperial arguments of this sort cf., for example, Frederick's declaration in *MGH. Const.* I, no. 167, p. 233; the Speier manifesto of the Staufen princes incorporated by Innocent III in his *Regestum*, ed. cit., no. 14 with its significant term of *imperatura* (ed. cit. p. 35); the Staufen statement, ibid. no. 61 (ed. cit. p. 164: '*cum ad Romani imperii simus ascripti titulum*'); and the Staufen protest cited in the *Annales Stadenses* in *MGH. Scriptores*, XVI, 367, lines 12 ff.

[13] It is usually overlooked that in his first letter to the pope (*MGH. Const.* I, no. 137, p. 191) Frederick begins the arenga with these words: '*Patrem patriae decet veneranda priscorum instituta regum....*' The term *pater patriae* is culled from Roman law (Callistratus: *Dig.* 48, 22, 19) and was in fact used by the ancient Roman emperors. No earlier medieval evidence of the adoption of this phrase could be found. For another characteristic borrowing see Frederick's encyclical of 23 May 1165 (*MGH. Const.* I, no. 223, p. 315): '*Cunctis populis, quos clementiae nostrae regit imperium....*' This is borrowed from the famous imperial decree in Justinian's *Codex* I, i, 1: '*Cunctos populos, quos clementiae nostrae regit imperium....*' By this decree the Christian religion was enforced throughout the Roman empire in the year 380. Cf. also the arenga of *Const.* I, no. 228, p. 323 and its typical Justinianean phraseology.

[14] For these details and others relating to the text following, cf. my contribution to the *Misc[ellanea Historiae Pontificiae]*, XVIII (1954), pp. 107 ff.

244

There is no need to dub Adrian dishonest, because he is said to have withdrawn the feudal meaning of *beneficium*. He never employed the term in a feudal sense, but in that of a good deed, a *bonum factum*, a favour, since in this very same sentence he refers to the coronation of Frederick. What Adrian wished to express by this harmless enough term—taken in fact from Gelasius I, whose knowledge of feudal matters was certainly not profound— was that he conferred the imperial crown on Frederick as a favour; nobody has a *right* to demand or expect a good deed, a favour, and this is the whole meaning of Adrian's usage of the term *beneficium*. The imperial crown is not something Frederick has a right to expect. It was in fact the Latin word *favor* which the pope had used when approving Frederick as an imperial candidate: 'Benigno *favore* approbamus.'[15] Although the Germans at Besançon pretended to be so furious at the employment of the allegedly feudal term, strangely enough in subsequent statements and letters they never returned to this feudal interpretation. What they said afterwards was that the imperial crown was a divine benefice, a *divinum beneficium*, thereby making it only worse, as this assertion exposed them to the awkward question—from whom can a divine benefice be obtained, if not from the pope? It is at this point that the mediatory role of the pope, the concept of a papal vicariate of Christ, comes into full play.[16]

Sutri and Besançon reveal, like a flashlight, the medieval dilemma of the emperors. Frederick and Rainald of Dassel, despite all their vociferous protestations, were shown by Adrian the true meaning of Roman emperorship in cool and measured terms to which there was no answer. No wonder that Innocent III acknowledged so freely the historic significance of Adrian, who by his dignified stand against Staufen attacks appears like a rock in comparison with the clamorous Germans, ever ready, as Chancellor Roland had learnt at Besançon,[17] to threaten with the sword an opponent who has the better argument.

Force has to step in when arguments are not available. Humiliating the opponent by physical means is an alternative device. The confiscation of the personal property of Adrian's legates immediately after this incident, the minute search and inspection of their personal baggage, the humiliating despatch of the legates under imperial escort to the imperial frontier on the next day, the prohibition of appeals and visits to Rome and the consequential increase of frontier guards[18]—these are a few of the measures adopted by the

[15] See *Ep.* 504 of Eugenius III (*Patrologia Latina*, CLXXX, 1523).
[16] This was clearly understood in the protest sent to the pope: *MGH. Const.* I, no. 167, p. 234 [=Rahewin, *Gesta Friderici imperatoris*, ed. G. Waitz (in *Scriptores Rerum Germanicarum*), p. 189]. See also the passage of Gervase of Tilbury quoted in *Misc.* cit. p. 118; cf. also ibid. p. 120, n. 43.
[17] See the description of the incident by Rahewin, ed. cit. p. 177: 'Ob hoc dictum eo processit iracundia, ut unus eorum, videlicet Otto palatinus comes de Baioaria, ut dicebatur, exerto gladio cervici illius mortem intentaret.'
[18] Rahewin, ed. cit. p. 186.

pope's *filius* who, inflated by his dreams, could not bear the puncturing reminder that, after all, it was by a mere favour of Adrian that he became an emperor. Frederick's declaration that Adrian should be deposed because he was an uncanonical pope, being the son of a priest,[19] was indubitably a double-edged weapon; if Adrian was an uncanonical pope, then Frederick was an uncanonical emperor, and that seems the only reason why this point was not pressed further. The first hints of the coming schism are clearly discernible. But more important than all this, and more significant as a test for the strength of Adrian's pontificate, was the fabrication of a correspondence in the months following Besançon, according to which for the first time the plan was broadcast of a church in the empire separated from Rome.[20] This was a most significant development. The archbishop of Trier was to become the *Primas* on this side of the Alps, ruling 'vice Petri', the head of a church independent of the pope. Rome, in this correspondence, was a place where money ruled and not St Peter, a 'spelunca latronum et habitatio demonum', where there sits in the person of Adrian not only the mammon of iniquity, but also a Simon, who does not seek what is Christ's, but what is his—'Cuncta spiritualia habet venalia,'—calling us Germans stupid: 'vocantes nos stultos Alamannos.' Hence Trier was to be made a *secunda Roma*. All this seems very familiar to those who know of an earlier abortive attempt to create a *secunda Roma* on Germanic soil,[21] and yet it is somewhat fantastic in the mid-twelfth century to hear of a plan for an imperial church no longer in communion with Rome. That Rainald of Dassel stood behind this correspondence is not difficult to prove, as whole lines are identical with the official imperial correspondence, whose draftsman was Rainald.

Is not therefore the new designation of the Roman empire as *sacrum Romanum imperium*, the new name invented in these same months of 1157, a rather feeble compensation? The name was to bring out the monarchic function of Frederick, holy and imperial, by which terms the truly monarchic function of a medieval ruler could suitably be expressed. No contemporary had any doubt what the new name meant, least of all Adrian, as we know from John of Salisbury. It remained for modern historians, blinded as they are by the glitter of appearances, not to see in this new name the expression of the royal-lay ideology, according to which the *sacerdotium* was a mere branch of the imperial civil service. Can one be surprised at the effective help which on

---

[19] See Innocent III's statement in *Regestum*, cit. no. 29 (ed. cit. p. 85).

[20] See the three letters ed. by W. Wattenbach, 'Iter Austriacum' in *Archiv f. Kunde oesterreichischer Geschichts-Quellen*, XIV (1855), especially pp. 87–8.

[21] The reference is to Charlemagne's attempt to make Aix-la-Chapelle a *secunda Roma*. The canonization of Charlemagne in December 1165 was not therefore an act of sudden inspiration. The decree of canonization says that it was 'at the suggestion of the King of the English' (Henry II) that Charlemagne was canonized. Henry II and Rainald of Dassel had in fact met at Rouen in April 1165. For these details cf. R. Folz, *Le souvenir et la légende de Charlemagne* (Paris, 1950), pp. 204, 207. A MS. of the copy of the canonization decree is in the University Library of Bonn (S. 1559).

his very next visit to Italy, in September 1158, Frederick gave to Roman law studies at Bologna, to the codification of the model of all medieval monarchs, Justinian's collection of laws and decrees, to the *sacrae leges*? The decree *Habita* was a distinctly political document directed against the hierocratic exponents at Bologna.[22] All these are measures prompted by the virile and consistent stand of Adrian IV, measures which in their historic significance have not yet been fully evaluated. Nor has it been appreciated that as a direct result of Besançon and as a further challenge to the papal standpoint, Frederick's chancery tried to work out doctrinally the dualist theory of government characterized by a double vicariate of Christ, one in the pope, and one in the emperor.[23] This hybrid theory of dualism was the official Staufen programme, although, in disregard of the historical and doctrinal truth, a group of modern historians now attempts to persuade us that this dualism was the papal point of view.

Can one blame Adrian for thoroughly distrusting the intentions of the German Roman Caesar? Is it really a wonder that only the worst vituperative epithets were showered on Rainald? Is it really so very remarkable that Adrian, seeing what an obstreperous *filius* Frederick was proving himself, sought a reinsurance with the Sicilian king William I? Bent on executing the traditional papal programme Adrian was prompted to look for a more efficient protector than the emperor. The similarity of the configuration of circumstances in the fifties of the eleventh century and the fifties of the twelfth century is indeed striking. The reenfeoffment of the Sicilian king by Adrian was to be of decisive moment in the century that followed. Adrian's attitude towards Sicily is ideologically explicable: the view held by the curia was that which had been held exactly a hundred years earlier, the view, derived from the Donation, that all islands were given to the pope 'in jus et proprietatem'—in fact, the view which justified Adrian's letter to Henry II concerning Ireland. That letter contains the papal 'omni-insular' doctrine in classic terms, according to which 'omnes insulas ad jus b. Petri et s. Romanae ecclesiae pertinere.'

On account both of its immediate significance and of its influence, Adrian's ranks as one of the great medieval pontificates. Its importance, however, is by no means fully portrayed, if one looks only at the West. For the East demanded his attention to a degree that is too often overlooked; in fact he was concerned with its affairs no less than with those of the West. Here too Adrian is the man of tradition, if anything more so than in his dealings with the West.

For anyone who tries to pierce the entangled network of the vexatious

---

[22] For details cf. my contribution to the *Studi in memoria di Paolo Koschaker* (Milan, 1951), I, 101 ff.; also G. de Vergottini, 'Lo studio di Bologna, l'impero, il papato' in *Studi e memorie per la storia dell' Università di Bologna*, I (1954), pp. 27–42.

[23] For this cf. Frederick's communications in *Const.* I, no. 183, p. 254 and no. 240, p. 335.

relations between East and West and go beyond the tortuous and seemingly futile negotiations, campaigns, intrigues, charges, countercharges, which mark the long history of papacy and Eastern empire, the pontificate of Adrian IV witnesses a decisive development. The setting was familiar enough, the themes strike a very familiar chord, and yet there is a noticeable variation of the dominant theme; the bait offered by the Eastern emperor was more alluring and the actual military situation more serious than was the case earlier on. Adrian's denial of New Rome's aspirations vividly recalls the times when the problem of New Rome first emerged.

The full appreciation of Adrian's reaction presupposes a knowledge of the papal theme, a theme that had by his time hardened into tradition. According to it—and here we find the threads of Western and Eastern empires leading to Rome—the only true Roman emperor was one created as such by the pope. This curialist view therefore implied that the Eastern Emperor was a mere Greek king, and as such he was in fact designated in the pact of 1153,[24] the year before Adrian assumed the pontificate. This designation was not a play with words, but embodied a whole programme, because this very title denied the Greek king universality of rule which could be claimed only by a Roman emperor. And only he was a Roman emperor who was crowned by the pope, and therefore Adrian called the empire in the East not by the name it wished to be known by (Roman empire), but 'imperium Constantinopolitanum'.[25] This standpoint was fully adopted by the Western emperors who thereby unwittingly went along the papal-curialist road and consequently found themselves in their chronic dilemma. And by embracing the papal theme, Western emperors could raise the at times menacing claims that all other kings were mere *reguli* or *regulelli* (kinglings).

But Manuel, the Eastern ruler, in no way differing from the long line of his predecessors, would not recognize what, as his own historian, Cinnamus, untiringly tells us, he regarded as nothing more than the arrogant claims of a

---

[24] *MGH. Const.* I, no. 144, p. 201, sub (3) and (6) (papal copy), and no. 145, p. 203, sub (3) and (6) (royal confirmation). It is certainly worthy of notice that it was in this document (no. 145), in which the Eastern ruler was styled 'Rex Graecorum', that Frederick called himself 'Fridericus Dei gratia Romanorum imperator augustus' before he was actually crowned. Whilst this throws a highly significant light on Frederick's views as regards the position of the Greek king, it is no doubt somewhat incongruous that the royal confirmation reiterates the papal promise to crown him: 'Dominus papa...promisit et observabit quod eum sicut carissimum beati Petri filium honorabit et venientem pro coronae suae plenitudine sine difficultate et contradictione, quantum in ipso est, *imperatorem coronabit*.' And yet, in the intitulation Frederick styles himself Roman emperor and appends the 'signum domni Friderici Romanorum imperatoris invictissimi', but at the same time the dating line states: 'Datum...anno dominicae incarnationis MCLII, regnante domino Friderico *Romanorum rege* glorioso, anno vero *regni* eius primo.' The convention itself (no. 144) states quite correctly: 'Haec est forma concordiae et conventionis inter domnum papam Eugenium et domnum regem Romanorum Fridericum constituta....' In the royal document (no. 145) the term 'regem' was changed into 'imperatorem', although one cannot say that the chancery of Frederick was consistent: in the preamble and in point (1) the royal designations were not changed.

[25] *Ep.* 138.

would-be usurper. They, the Eastern rulers, were the true heirs of the first Christian emperor Constantine who in uninterrupted sequence had occupied the throne that Constantine had transferred from Rome to Constantinople. Hence, the determined attempt on the part of the Eastern rulers to re-create that empire that had been Constantine's, and it was Manuel who enacted the last attempt to translate these aims into reality. Manuel's plan to lead his troops personally in Italy must not be seen as an empty, vainglorious ambition. He was in deadly earnest about it. Again, to him as the man who considered himself to be the only true Roman emperor, it was vital that Old Rome should return to its legitimate place within the Roman empire, whose capital happened to be in New Rome. Indeed, in the first year of Adrian's pontificate not only had Byzantine troops occupied considerable portions of Italy, but the Balkans had been subjected and Hungary pacified, and at Kiew Manuel's own man was sitting on the throne. A little later we find Manuel entering into lively diplomatic and personal relations with Henry II of England.

The bait which Manuel offered was ecclesiastical union between East and West. I would not like to label the curial reaction to this bait political or religious, because it is so misleading to import our modern departmentalized categories of thinking into the mid-twelfth century. No doubt, Adrian's curia remembered the offer made shortly before by Manuel's predecessor to Pope Honorius II. This offer was made in the allegorical language to which the Easterners thought they could treat the crude and illiterate Western minds; this offer showed a profound misconception on the part of the Eastern Autokrator when he wrote that there were two swords, of which the one, the secular, was to be his, whilst the other, the spiritual, the pope was to wield over all Christians in the East and West.[26] It gives food for thought that the Eastern ruler adopted the very argument which several decades before had been invoked for the first time by the German Henry IV, who thus inauspiciously opened the Investiture Contest. That argument had been decisively rejected by Gregory VII, and it fared no better in the twelfth century. What is important, however, is that by borrowing this Western argument the Eastern ruler divested himself, so to speak, voluntarily of his true monarchic function, the very hallmark of the Eastern *Basileus ton Romaion, Autokrator kai Monokrator.* That the curia received Manuel's overtures with that scepticism which they deserved from the curial standpoint, is understandable.

For not only would the acceptance of the bait have entailed a complete overthrow of the traditional curial theme—pursued for exactly four hundred years, since the memorable visit of Stephen II to the Frankish kingdom in 754 —but it would also have presupposed an astonishing lack of memory on the part of the curia; the mere possibility of the Byzantine as (sole) Roman

---

[26] Cf. A. Theiner-Miklosich, *Monumenta spectantia ad unionem ecclesiarum graecae et romanae* (Rome, 1873), pp. 4 f.; G. Ostrogorsky, *Geschichte des byzantinischen Staates* (Munich, 1940), p. 273.

emperor recalled shuddering memories in the curia. Measured by the objective yardstick of the past, Manuel's offer of an ecclesiastical union and thus a healing of the schism, had a hollow ring. Were not the figures of a Vigilius and a Martin I sufficient warning to a clear-sighted man of Adrian's calibre, and a learned man, learned in history, like Roland? The contemporary history by Cinnamus shows how justified the curial scepticism was; here the thoughts of the Basileus stand nakedly revealed.

What guarantee was there that the schism was to be healed, except on the terms of the Autokrator who, so his secretary Cinnamus informs us, was the proper authority for appointing the pope of Rome?[27] Could the primatial authority of the pope be exercised even within the terms of Manuel's offer? That was the crucial point. Let us not forget the overriding consideration of the medieval papacy that Christianity concerned the whole of man, that man was an indivisible and integrated whole, that there could be no splitting up of human actions into certain departments. The papacy, rightly or wrongly, insisted that it alone had a right to lay down the rules of human conduct within Christendom. It was the totality of man and therefore of Christian society. and not certain items only, which was the object of papal primatial authority. On the other hand, the conception of the Eastern Autokrator, historically and ideologically conditioned, militated against this fundamental axiom of the papacy. This primatial authority, or in more familiar language, the monarchic idea of the pope, demanded unquestioned obedience to his mandates and decrees by all who did not wish to be labelled schismatics. This is the tenor of Adrian's letter to the archbishop of Salonika on this very point of the Eastern schism.[28] With a characteristic sureness of touch Adrian begins his letter with these words:

> From the time when the see of Constantinople separated itself from the holy Roman and apostolic church and from the time when the poisonous malice of man's enemy made the children of Rome secede from *obedience due to a mother* and substituted a double control for unity, the successors of Peter before me have striven hard to remove the schism (*ut schisma tolleretur*) and to restore to the unity of the Church those who have been separated from it.

He then goes on to say that union is essential and that all Christians must return 'ad b. Petrum *gubernatorem omnium fidelium*', to St Peter who 'jussu Domini' has been given the task of governing *all* Christians. The same emphatic insistence on Peter as *gubernator* who will not suffer 'scissuras et sectiones' occurs in Adrian's letter to the Patriarch of Grado with specific reference to the Church of Constantinople.[29]

The accent lies on obedience and the governance of all Christians by St Peter, the *gubernator*. Anyone who knows the earlier correspondence on

---

[27] John Cinnamus, *Historiarum libri septem*, ed. A. Meineke (Bonn, 1836), p. 229; cf. also ibid. pp. 171, 219.

[28] *Ep.* 198.   [29] *Ep.* 138.

this crucial point, hears the dominant theme reverberating anew in Adrian's letters. Inevitably one's mind turns back to the numerous earlier conflicts, caused (to use Adrian's term) by Byzantine disobedience to the Roman Church, appearing, it is true, under different names, but centring in the same fundamental issue. The road from Chalcedon ch. 28 and from the *Henoticon* of the Emperor Zeno winds its meandering path through the centuries to Adrian's vantage point, but never loses sight of its goal, that is, the exercise of monarchic functions in a Christian body politic by the Eastern Autokrator, an exercise in which as a matter of necessity lay disobedience to the Roman Church. That is the tenor of Adrian's letters with their emphasis on obedience and Eastern disobedience. They indeed recall Gregory VII's appeal for a crusade when he wrote: 'We are especially (*praemaxime*) moved to the undertaking of the crusade because the Church of Constantinople is separated from us.'[30] And, fifty years after Adrian, Innocent III writes with reference to the capture of Constantinople by the crusaders: 'The Church of Constantinople is now brought back to obedience to its mother, the Roman Church.'[31] The least one perceives in Innocent's letter is the unmistakable echo of Adrian's own words.

I am approaching the end of my discourse. I have tried, within the limited time at my disposal and with the limited resources available to a mere historian, to present the essential features of the pontificate of the English pope. I have tried to look at this pontificate from the point of view of a contemporary of Adrian. We may or may not approve of the premisses of his government. Approval or disapproval of the premisses of a historic institution, such as the medieval papacy, is wholly irrelevant. What is relevant is that a historic evaluation of a pontificate can be undertaken only within historic terms. That is why I have concentrated on topics and issues which to a contemporary of Adrian appeared essential: there was no need to say anything on what might be called the routine business of any medieval pope: enforcement of hierarchical discipline, insistence on freedom of elections, care for the regular clergy, confirmation of privileges and possessions, taking persons and places into St Peter's protection, maintenance of revenues, organizational measures within the Patrimony of St Peter, advice to kings about impending campaigns, judicial and binding decisions in matters of dispute, and so forth. Unlike any other governmental institution in the Middle Ages, the papacy had and pursued a definite programme based on Scripture and tradition which explains its enduring strength in the medieval period. The execution of this programme lay in the hands of Romans, Syrians, Greeks, Sicilians, Italians, Germans, Frenchmen and Spaniards. In this distinguished and cosmopolitan sequence of popes—merely reflecting the medieval universality of the institution itself—

---

[30] See Gregory VII's *Register*, II, 31 (ed. E. Caspar, pp. 166–7).

[31] Innocent III in *Register*, VIII, 153 (*Patrologia Latina*, CCXV, 728) and *Reg. super negotio Romani imperii*, no. 113 (ed. cit. p. 280).

THE PONTIFICATE OF ADRIAN IV

the only English occupant of the *cathedra beati Petri* takes his historic place. The pontificate of Adrian IV is the pontificate of an illustrious Englishman in a century which brought forth so many Englishmen of European renown.

SELECT BIBLIOGRAPHY

I. *Sources*

Ph. Jaffé. *Regesta Pontificum Romanorum*, 2nd ed. (Leipzig, 1888), nos. 9943 ff.

Vita Adriani IV (by Cardinal Boso) in *Liber Pontificalis* (ed. L. Duchesne, Paris, 1892), II, 388 ff.

Epistolae of Adrian IV in *Patr[ologia] Lat[ina]*, CLXXXVIII, cols. 1361 ff.

Otto of Freising and Rahewin, *Gesta Friderici Imperatoris*, 3rd ed. by G. Waitz in *M[onumenta] G[ermania] H[istorica]*: *Scriptores [Rerum Germanicarum]* (Hanover and Leipzig, 1912).

Romuald of Salerno, *Annales*, in *MGH. Scriptores*, XIX, 424 ff.

MGH., Constitutiones et Acta, I, nos. 137 ff.

W. Wattenbach (ed.), 'Iter Austriacum' in *Archiv f. Kunde oesterreichischer Geschichts-Quellen*, XIV (1855), pp. 86 ff.

Ordo Romanus XI and *XII*, in Mabillon, *Museum Italicum* (Paris, 1689), pp. 158 ff. (=*Patr. Lat.* LXXVIII, cols. 1025 ff.)

Petrus Mallius, *Historia Basilicae Antiquae s. Petri in Vaticano* (in *Acta Sanctorum*, June VII–2, pp. 37 ff.).

F. Dölger, *Regesten der Kaiserurkunden: Corpus der griechischen Urkunden des Mittelalters und der neueren Zeit* (Munich, 1925), nos. 1386 ff.

Johannes Cinnamus, *Historiarum libri septem* (in *Corpus Scriptorum Historiae Byzantinae*), ed. A. Meineke (Bonn, 1836).

II. *Secondary authorities*

R. Raby, *Pope Adrian IV* (London, 1849).

A. H. Tarleton, *Nicholas Breakspear, Englishman and Pope* (London, 1896).

J. D. Mackie, *Pope Adrian IV* (Oxford, 1907).

H. K. Mann. *Nicholas Breakspear* (London, 1914).

E. M. Almedingen, *The English Pope* (London, 1925).

R. Foreville, *Du premier Concile du Lateran à l'avènement d'Innocent III* (in Fliche-Martin, *Histoire de l'église*, IX–2, Paris, 1953).

H. Simonsfeld, *Jahrbücher des deutschen Reiches unter Friedrich I*, vol. I (Leipzig, 1908).

A. Werminghoff, *Nationalkirchliche Bestrebungen im deutschen Mittelalter* (vol. LXI of *Kirchenrechtliche Abhandlungen*, ed. by U. Stutz, Stuttgart, 1910).

P. Fedele, *Fonti per la storia di Arnaldo di Brescia* (Rome, 1938).

E. Eichmann, *Die Kaiserkrönung im Abendlande*, 2 vols. (Wurzbürg, 1943).

E. Eichmann, *Krönung und Weihe des Papstes im Mittelalter*, in *Münchener Theologische Studien: kanonistische Abteilung*, I, ed. by Kl. Mörsdorf, 1951.

G. Ostrogorsky, *Geschichte des byzantinischen Staates* (Munich, 1940).

H. W. Klewitz, 'Die Krönung des Papstes', in *Savigny Zeitschrift: kanonistische Abteilung*, XXX (1941), pp. 96 ff.

A. Marongiu, 'Un momento tipico de la monarquia medieval: el rey juez' in *Anuario de historia del derecho español*, XXIII (1953), pp. 677 ff.

W. Ohnsorge, 'Die Byzanzpolitik Friedrich Barbarossas', in *Deutsches Archiv*, VI (1943), pp. 122 ff.

J. Spörl, 'Rainald von Dassel und sein Verhältnis zu Johann von Salisbury', in *Festschrift f. Eduard Eichmann* (Munich, 1940), pp. 249 ff.

252

W. Ullmann, 'The medieval interpretation of Frederick I's Habita', in *Studi in memoria di Paolo Koschaker* (Milan, 1951), I, pp. 101 ff.

W. Ullmann, 'Cardinal Roland and the incident at Besançon', in *Miscellanea Historiae Pontificiae*, XVIII (1954), pp. 107 ff.

A. Vasiliev, 'Manuel Comnenus and Henry Plantagenet', in *Byzantinische Zeitschrift*, XXIX (1930), pp. 233 ff.

F. Wasner, 'De consecratione, inthronizatione, coronatione pontificis', in *Apollinaris*, VIII (1935), pp. 86 ff., 249 ff., 428 ff.

IV

CARDINAL ROLAND AND BESANÇON

Imperfection of language has at all times been a trouble-some source of misunderstanding, consequential ill-feeling and, in the larger political sphere, of serious repercussions. In the medieval period the student of history is only too familiar with such iridescent terms as *ecclesia, fidelitas, Romani, defensio, protectio, miles, militia, patronus, libertas, beneficium,* and so forth. This exasperating duplicity of meaning of such vital terms has caused a good deal of friction in the medieval period and a subsequent blurring of interpretation by modern historians. What the one party meant by using, for instance, the term *fidelitas,* did not always exactly correspond to what the other party ascribed to it : *fidelitas* may mean no more than faithfulness to one's promise given on oath — in which sense, for instance, the episcopal and imperial oaths must be taken [1] — or may mean fealty, the fully fledged feudal oath taken by a vassal (*juramentum fidelitatis*).

The assumption is not unjustified that a number of Latin terms were employed to express ideas which did not exist in ancient Rome, but were of fundamental importance in the medieval period. The original Latin term became, so to speak, assimilated and adjusted to a medieval idea, institution or fact, for which assimiliation and adjustment the original term gave no warrant. Nevertheless, this same term was still used to express the meaning originally denoted by it. The point which we wish to make is that since Latin was the universal diplomatic language in the medieval period, its expressions were used to denote medieval things and medieval ideas which were quite alien to the original Roman meaning. And since so many institutions in medieval times were Teutonic or had at least Teutonic roots

---

[1] And in which sense the modern canon law speaks of the *jusjurandum fidelitatis* of the bishop, cf. can. 332 (2).

and, since, on the other hand, there was only one « international » language, Latin was used to designate something Teutonic which by no stretch of imagination the original Latin word could be said to cover adequately. Some indication as to what a particular term was supposed to convey, can be obtained from the quarter which employed it : *prima facie* the assumption is justified that when the papal chancery used a term, it used it in the original (Latin) meaning; conversely, when the imperial (German) chancery used a term, the assumption in which sense it was used, cannot so easily be made.

The incident at Besançon in October 1157 [2] appears to us as a good example by which to demonstrate the duplicity of the term *beneficium*. *Beneficium* had a thoroughly plain meaning in its original sense — a good deed, a benefit, a favour. But by the twelfth century it also had acquired a technical feudal meaning, namely, that of a fief, or a benefice, a territory held in fief. It is our contention that in his first communication to Frederick I Pope Adrian IV had used the term *beneficium* — to which the Germans had taken such strong objection — in its original Latin meaning; that Adrian did not withdraw one jot or tittle in his second letter to Frederick; and that Adrian's usage of the term was historically and ideologically justified.

According to Rahewin [3] two points in particular aroused the wrath of the assembly at Besançon. Firstly, the pope's reference to his having conferred two years earlier the plenitude of dignity and honour on Frederick by way of placing the imperial crown on Frederick's head; and secondly, the pope's statement that he would have been happy if he could have conferred still greater *beneficia* on the Staufen [4]. Particularly the second point en-

---

[2] As this incident is so well known, we abstain from detailed references to modern literature.

[3] Rahewin's *Gesta Friderici Imperatoris*, ed. G. WAITZ, in MGH SS rer. germ. 1912[3].

[4] Rahewin, *op. cit.* (ed. cit. p. 176): « Praecipue tamen universos accenderat, quod in premissis litteris inter caetera dictum fuisse acceperant dignitatis et honoris plenitudinem sibi a Romano pontifice collatam et insigne imperialis coronae de manu eius imperatorem suscepisse, nec ipsum penitere, si majora beneficia de manu eius suscepisset ... » In his letter Adrian said this (we quote from Rahewin which seems to be the better edition; the letter is also in MGH Const. I no. 164, p. 229): « Debes enim, gloriosissime fili, ante oculos mentis reducere, quam gratanter et quam jocunde alio anno mater tua sacrosancta Romana ecclesia te susceperit, quanta cordis affectione tractaverit, quantam tibi dignitatis plenitudinem contulerit et honoris,

raged the Germans and the question which one of the legates, probably Roland himself, put to them, no doubt reveals a certain naive astonishment: « A quo ergo habet, si a domno papa non habet imperium? » [5].

Did Adrian's letter give any cause for the subsequent commotion? Did it, in any conceivable way, suggest that Adrian (and Roland) had spoken of the empire as a papal fief? No doubt, the situation was aggravated by the (all-too-sudden) recollection of the Lateran picture, according to which Lothar had done homage to the pope (Innocent II) — but there is no evidence that Lothar did homage to the pope in his capacity as an emperor: he became a vassal of the pope in respect of the Mathildine lands only, and not in respect of the empire [6]. No doubt also that the commission with which the two legates were charged, namely the visitation of the churches in Germany, was a measure that could not be viewed with equanimity by those in control of imperial policy, to wit by Frederick and Rainald of Dassel. This was a measure which blatantly violated the principles of the « reformatio totius orbis » so loudly and insistently proclaimed by the Staufen emperor [7], for the imperial church (the *Reichskirche*)

---

et qualiter imperialis insigne coronae libentissime conferens, benignissimo gremio suo tuae sublimitatis apicem studuerit confovere, nichil prorsus efficiens, quod regiae voluntati vel in minimo cognosceret obviare. Neque tamen penitet nos tuae desideria voluntatis in omnibus implevisse, sed, si majora beneficia excellentia tua de manu nostra suscepisset, si fieri posset, considerantes, quanta ecclesiae Dei et nobis per te incrementa possint et commoda provenire, non immerito gauderemus ».

[5] Rahewin, *op. cit.* (ed. cit. p. 177). There is absolutely no warrant for saying that Roland, at Besançon, suggested « that in all probability 'fief' was the meaning intended by the pope in using the term beneficium » as G. R. HICKS maintains, *Adrian IV*, Downside Review 64 (1946) 149 (here also some other questionable statements). But HICKS is not alone in maintaining this.

[6] Cf. MGH Const. I no. 117, pp. 169-70. See, furthermore, Rahewin, p. 177 and Gerhoh of Reichersberg, *De quarta vigilia noctis*, MGH Libelli de lite III 512. The picture was destroyed some time in the fourteenth century, cf. the reconstituted engraving (sixteenth century) in P. E. SCHRAMM, *Die deutschen Könige und Kaiser in Bildnissen*, Leipzig 1928 Table 129, and text pp. 148-9, 219-220, and G. LADNER, *Mosaici e affreschi nell'antico palazzo Lateranense*, Rivista di archeologia cristiana, 12 (1935) fig. 11 at p. 280, and text pp. 281-90.

[7] About Frederick's negotiations with Bishop Eberhard II of Bamberg « de *reformando* et componendo regni statu » and John of Salisbury's report that the young Staufen emperor intended « se totius orbis reformaturum imperium et urbi subjiciendum orbem » cf. our observations *Studi in memoria di Paolo Koschaker*, Milan 1953 I 110 note 1 with further literature.

was not to be controlled by the pope in Rome and his legates, but by the imperial government. In consonance with all medieval monarchic conceptions, Frederick's aim at the *reformatio* included of course a considerable tightening up of the imperial control over the (imperial) *sacerdotium*. Every medieval monarch intended to exercise this control and the envisaged visitation by the papal legates of the *Reichskirche* was a measure that could not but strike at the very roots of Frederick's monarchic conceptions [8]. And the employment of the term *beneficia* in the papal letter lent itself so easily to an interpretation with which the Germans were all too familiar, but which, we hold, was not intended by Adrian or Roland.

In fairness to Frederick and his able chancellor, it should be pointed out that in subsequent statements they did not stress the feudal meaning of the term. « Whoever says that we have received the imperial crown from the lord pope as a *beneficium*, contradicts the divine ordering of things and Petrine teachings » [9]. And in the letter which the German bishops sent to the pope and in which Frederick's reasoned reply was enclosed, there was no emphasis on the feudal meaning of the term: « Liberam imperii nostri coronam divino tantum *beneficio* ascribimus » [10]. This latter statement would in fact exclude the ascription of a feudal meaning to the term — but we will return to the point. In parenthesis it may be noted, however, that there is some ideological, if not verbal, similarity between these statements and the tract *De unitate ecclesiae conservanda,* written at the end of the preceding century [11]; the place taken by Gottschalk, the mentor of Henry IV and later provost of Achen [12], was now taken by Rainald of Dassel, the later archbischop of Cologne [13].

---

[8] The fusion of Justinianean (Roman) and Teutonic monarchic conceptions in Frederick's governmental system and ideology are still to be worked out. We take the term monarch in its literal sense.

[9] Rahewin, *op. cit.* p. 179, lines 11-14: « Quicumque nos imperialem coronam pro beneficio a domno papa suscepisse dixerit, divinae institutioni et doctrinae Petri contrarius est et mendacii reus erit ».

[10] Rahewin, *op. cit.* p. 188.

[11] MGH Libelli de lite II 173 ff.

[12] For this see C. ERDMANN and D. v. GLADISS, *Gottschalk von Aachen im Dienst Heinrichs IV,* Deutsches Archiv 3 (1939) 135 ff.

[13] The dichotomy between *ecclesia* and the *respublica imperii*; the *unitas* to be sought between *ecclesia* and the *imperium*; the use of the Two-Swords allegory, are reminiscent of Henry IV's letters, especially no. 13 in C. ERDMANN, *Die Briefe Heinrichs IV,* Berlin 1939 19 = *MGH Const.* I no. 63 (pp. 112-3), as well as of the tract itself, especially II, 3 (p. 214);

What Adrian IV wished to say in his letter was that the distinction of imperial dignity and honour was a *beneficium* in so far namely as the pope has no duty to confer this distinction, and the emperor no right to expect this « good deed » from the pope. It was Frederick's wish to be crowned and the pope fulfilled this wish, that is, the « desideria tuae voluntatis ». The pope in choosing the « specialis » or « unicus filius Romanae ecclesiae » — to use the appropriate terminology for the emperor — is free : he is not to be forced; he is not to be compelled to confer the plenitude of imperial dignity and honour upon any particular individual king. For the emperor, thus distinguished by the pope, is the special protector and defender of the Roman Church and herewith of the whole of Christendom; and it is for this reason and this reason alone, that the pope crowns him. This function of a protector and defender is the emperor's *raison d'être* : his dignity ascends to the then highest available dignity, that of the « imperator Romanorum ». By virtue of the Roman Church being the epitome of the whole of Christendom, itself a universal entity, the pope cannot confer any other dignity but a universal one. According to the papal theory of the empire, emperorship is not original; is not autonomous. It is derivative; it is derived from the act of the pope who, for understandable reasons, must in theory be free to confer this dignity and to select a suitable protector. The making of the suitable king an emperor of the Romans is expressed symbolically in the coronation *Ordo* with its *scrutinium,* in the approbation and confirmation of the elected candidate. And it is this which Adrian IV wished to say with the harmless enough term *beneficium*. It is a favour which the emperor receives when the pope places the crown on his head, but there is no right on the latter's part to demand the imperial crown —he can only express a *desiderium* — and there is no duty on the former's part to confer the crown. This is exactly the meaning which Adrian wished to convey in

---

this tract shows an extraordinary affinity with Henry IV's letters and the possibility that Gottschalk was its author, cannot be excluded; cf. also ERDMANN himself, *art. cit.* 172 sub no. 17. Should it be mere coincidence that Benzo of Alba's expression for Nicholas II as « ydolus » (of Hildebrand) should occur in Frederick's letter to the archbishop of Salzburg, cf. Rahewin, p. 329: « se contulerunt et *ydolum* sibi Rolandum cancellarium erexerunt ». See Benzo in MGH SS XI 672: « Corrumpens igitur Prandellus Romanos multisque perjuriis induxit synodum, ubi regali corona suum coronavit *hydolum* ».

the so-called *littera excusatoria* [14]. And this is exactly the same idea which was already expressed by Innocent II:

> Nos igitur imperatoriae dignitatis plenitudinem tibi concedimus [15].

As so much in medieval ecclesiastical-political thought, this idea of the empire being a *beneficium* was of Gelasian provenance. In Gelasius's letters we find the term and the corresponding idea of the *beneficium*. He had said that the emperor had the *privilegia potestatis suae* as a *beneficium* divinely conferred [16]. Of course, in a Christocentric world all rulership must be conceived to originate in Christ; equally, all rulership is a privilege. Imperial Christian power, according to Gelasius I, was indeed a *beneficium* conferred by Christ, and for this *beneficium* the emperor should not show himself ungrateful. The emperor surely recognizes « imperium tibi superna dispositione collatum » [17]. For in Gelasius's conceptual framework God is « summus et verus imperator » [18]. Already as draftsman of Felix III, Gelasius in a letter to the Emperor Zeno had expressed the idea that the emperor « temporalis culminis potestatem et aeternae vitae commercia de superna propitiatione pendere » [19]. Rulership, including emperorship, is a divine privilege, is, in other words, a divine favour, a *beneficium*, as Gelasius as pope declared.

---

[14] Rahewin, p. 196, lines 10 ff.: « Licet enim hoc nomen, quod est ' beneficium' apud quosdam in alia significatione quam ex impositione habeat, assumatur, tunc tamen in ea significatione accipiendum fuerat quam nos ipsi posuimus, et quam ex institutione sua noscitur retinere. Hoc enim nomen ex bono et facto est editum, et dicitur beneficium aput nos non feudum, sed bonum factum; in qua significatione in universo sacrae scripturae corpore invenitur, ubi ex beneficio Dei, non tamquam ex feudo, sed velut ex benedictione et bono facto ipsius gubernari dicimur et nutriri. Et tua magnificentia liquido recognoscit, quod nos ita bene et honorifice imperialis dignitatis insigne tuo capiti imposuimus; ut bonum factum valeat ab omnibus judicari. Unde quod quidam verbum hoc et illud, scilicet ' contulimus tibi insigne imperialis coronae' a sensu suo nisi sunt ad alium retorquere, non ex merito causae, sed de voluntate propria ... hoc egerunt ».

[15] Innocent II to Lothar, MGH Const. I no. 116 (p. 168).

[16] Ep. 1, cap. 10, in A. THIEL, *Epistolae genuinae pontificum Romanorum*, Braunsberg 1868 293: « Habet *privilegia* potestatis suae quae administrandis publicis rebus *divinitus* consecutus est et eius *beneficiis* non ingratus ... nil usurpet ... ne contra illius *beneficia* pugnare videatur, *a quo* propriam consecutus est potestatem ».

[17] Ep. 12, cap. 2 (p. 351); cf. also ibid, cap. 4 (p. 353).

[18] Ep. 10, cap. 6 (p. 345); the same terminology in Ep. 26, cap. 12 (p. 410). Cf. also Jud. 25: « Soli Deo salvatori nostro, per Jesum Christum, Dominum nostrum, gloria et magnificentia, imperium et potestas ... ».

[19] Ep. 1, cap. 1 (p. 223 in THIEL).

In that century, in which the papal theory of the (Western) empire was to be given its permanent foundations, that is, in the ninth century, the Gelasian statements were carefully heeded. According to Leo IV, God Himself had « elected » Lothar who was thus anointed by the pope : the great Hincmar was severely taken to task for having excommunicated the emperor, for the emperor is directly responsible to the pope and to nobody else [20]. In the ceremony of the unction the pope is a mere instrument of God's will, as John VIII declared in 877, referring to Charles the Bald : Christ through the pope's instrumentality had made Charles an emperor and constituted him a prince of the people [21]. Charles was anointed emperor « ad imitationem scilicet veri regis Christi filii sui, Domini nostri » [22]. What Christ possessed by nature, the emperor now possesses by grace, John VIII maintained : « Quod ipse possidet per naturam, iste consequeretur per gratiam ». The important point to bear in mind is the function of the pope as the instrument which confers this grace. For, according to John, he had elected and approved Charles; the emperor is « desideratus, optatus, postulatus a nobis et a Deo vocatus et honorificatus » [23]. Consequently, Charles should not think that he had received the empire as a mere human benefi- cium, but rather a divinum beneficium, which, however, is con- ferred through the instrumentality of the pope :

[20] Cf. Leo IV in 852, MGH Epp. V 605 to Lothar himself : « In unctum Domini, quem sedes apostolica benedictionis oleo publice consecravit, sibique proprium heredem fecit anathematis jaculum contra omnem, non solum di- vinam, immo humanam institutionem inferre praesumpsit ... mandamus, ut ... neque contra vos, quem Deus sibi principem et imperatorem elegit et per manus summi et apostolici pontificis sanctificatum benedictionis oleum super vestrum caput effudit ... ».

[21] MANSI, Conc. coll., XVII, appendix p. 172.

[22] MANSI, ibid.

[23] MANSI, ibid. : « Et quia pridem apostolicae memoriae decessori nostro papae Nicholao idipsum (Carolum) jam inspiratione coelesti revelatum fuisse comperimus, elegimus hunc merito et approbavimus una cum annisu et voto omnium fratrum et coepiscoporum nostrorum ... secundum priscam consue- tudinem ... proveximus et augustali nomine decoravimus ». Charles did not ask for the imperial crown, « sed tamquam desideratus, optatus, postulatus a nobis et a Deo vocatus et honorificatus, ad defendendam religionem et Christi utique servos tuendos humiliter et obedientia accessit ... promptus ad ipsius promotionem et hoc per sacerdotum Domini manus ministrorum eius officium, sicut David et Salomon ... ».

Quando ad *imperium* quod ei constat *non humano* collatum *beneficio*, licet *per* nostrae mediocritatis *ministerium,* sed *divino* pertingere potuisset [24].

The empire is a divine institution or, in the words of John VIII, it is « Dei omnipotentis ordinatio » [25], but conferred by the pope. « Vos auctore Deo, in imperium coronaverimus » [26]. The emperor is divinely preselected, and this divine preselection was revealed through John's predecessor, Adrian II :

> Divina majestas excellentiam vestram prae ceteris elegit Romani imperii altitudine sublimare augustalique voluit diademate coronare [27].

From these few examples it becomes clear that (Roman) imperial power could be had only from the pope [28], because the empire was a divine benefice, favour or good deed. Implicitly and in fact this point of view was confirmed by the Ottonians : the dignity of universal Roman emperorship can only be had from the hands of the pope. Roman emperorship can be held only by « Romans », not by Greeks; in this Roman-Christian world the special protector and defender of the (Roman) Church must be a Roman, not a Greek; the seat of the one universal empire must be Rome, not Constantinople. Writing at the middle

---

[24] MGH Epp. VI, Ep. 78 (p. 321, lines 20 ff); Ep. 8 (p. 324, lines 44 ff). Cf. Gelasius, Ep. 12, c. 2 (p. 351): « Imperium tibi superna dispositione collatum ».

[25] Ep. cit. (p. 325, line 23).

[26] Ep. 32 (p. 31, line 27).

[27] Ep. 56 (p. 51, lines 8-9).

[28] Cf. also John to Louis the Stammerer, Ep. 87 (p. 82, lines 27 ff): « ... matri vestrae, *a qua* et potum predilectionis in proavis et infulam imperii accepistis ». To Charles the Bald he had written, Ep. 22 (p. 20, lines 32-3): « *A qua* (scil. Romana ecclesia) non solum regnandi, sed et in unum Deum et verum credendi exordium percepistis ». ꟾefore him Louis II (and Anastasius) had confirmed the papal point of view in the famous letter to the Eastern basileus, MGH. Epp. VII 387: « *A qua* (scil. Romana ecclesia) et regnante prius et postmodum imperandi auctoritatem prosapiae nostrae seminarium sumpsit. Nam Francorum principes primo reges, deinde vero imperatores dicti sunt, hii dumtaxat, qui a Romano pontifice ad hoc oleo sancto perfusi sunt ». All these statements are of course Gelasian inspired, cf. his Ep. 1, cap. 10 (THIEL, p. 293; quoted supra n. 16): « ... ne contra illius beneficia pugnare videatur, *a quo* propriam consecutus est potestatem ». It was also this same Gelasian passage which served as the model for Nicholas I's letter to the Eastern emperor, MGH. Epp. VI Ep. 90 (p. 508, lines 30-2), and Ep. 91 (p. 530, lines 10-12): « Ingrati filii circa matrem vestram, *ex qua* imperandi fastigium vos et patres vestri ordine coelitus disposito percepistis, nullatenus appareatis ». Gelasius had said, Ep. cit. (p. 293): « Et eius beneficiis non ingratus contra dispositionem coelestis ordinis nil usurpet ».

of the eleventh century, Raoul Glaber states this which by now had become a truism, as clearly as one could possibly wish [29]. Whilst shortly afterwards the fiery enthusiast of the emperor's cause, Benzo of Alba, equally clearly senses the crucial rôle which the pope plays in the conferment of imperial dignity when he writes:

> Dixerat enim ille Sarabaita (Gregory VII) quod in sua potestate esset *quem vellet* ad imperium promovere et *quem nollet* removere [30].

Indeed, Benzo of Alba is a competent witness of the historic dilemma in which imperial ideology found itself placed [31].

---

[29] Raoul Glaber, *Historia*, MGH SS VII 59, lines 10 ff.: « Illud nihilominus nimium concedens ac perhonestum videtur atque ad pacis tutelam optimum decretum, scilicet ut ne quisquam audacter Romani imperii sceptrum praeporerus gestare princeps appetat, seu imperator dici aut esse valeat, nisi quem papa sedis Romanae *morum probitate aptum delegerit* reipublicae eique *commiserit* insigne imperiale ».

[30] MGH SS XI 670. We should note that the Henrician forgery of the eighties of the eleventh century, the *Privilegium Majus (MGH Const.* I 667 ff) avoids a discussion on the imperial coronation and we do not think that this was a mere omission on the author's part.

[31] Gregory VII had clearly laid down the constitutive part of the pope in the making of the emperor. In the fateful autumn days of 1076 he writes to all the faithful in Germany that if Henry should not repent, a new king should be elected who « shall bind himself unquestionably to carry out the measures » which the pope decrees, and at the same time Gregory demands, so as to be in a position to confirm the election, prior notification of the elected candidate: « Inform us at the earliest possible moment of the matter itself, the person and the character of the candidate » (Reg. IV 3 ed. E. CASPAR p. 299: « negotium, personam et mores eius quamtotius potestis nobis indicare »). The principle upon which this demand is based, is that of suitability: the pope alone is in a position to judge whether the elected candidate is suitable. And behind this there stands as a logical corollary the papal right of examining the election itself. The passage in Reg. cit. — « ut ... *novam ordinationem* nostris temporibus corroboremus, sicut a nostris patribus factum esse cognoscimus » — might possibly refer to the *scrutinium* of the coronation procedure. Cf. also Reg. I. 20 — « Rex et Romae Deo annuente *futurus imperator* » — which seems to point to the connexion between suitability and the making of the emperor. In this case, there would be additional support for the late EICHMANN's dating of *Ordo C* (formerly *Cencius II*) and its application in the eleventh century. The words « Rex et futurus imperator » are actually in the coronation oath of *Ordo C*. This *Ordo C* is printed in *Liber Censuum*, ed. P. FABRE & L. DUCHESNE Paris 1901 I pp. 1*-6*; by P. E. SCHRAMM, *Die Ordines der mittelalterlichen Kaiserkrönung*, Archiv f. Urkundenforschung 11 (1930) 375 ff; and by E. EICHMANN, *Die Kaiserkrönung im Abendlande*, Würzburg 1942 I 169 ff. As is well known, this *Ordo C*, its date and actual application formed the subject of a heated controversy. EICHMANN held that it was composed in the early eleventh century and was

The pope as the transmitter of divine benefices must needs play a crucial rôle in conferring the dignity of emperorship; and consequently he must be free in the selection of the emperor. We recall John VIII's emperor was « *postulatus* a nobis » and not so long before Adrian IV's pontificate it was said of Emperor Henry V that he « a pontifice imperator *designatus* est » [32]. Moreover, the biography of Pope Paschal II by Cardinal Peter of Pisa relates the old theme of the election by St Peter of the emperor (Henry V); with reference to the abortive coronation on 12 February 1111, the biographer says:

> Proceres, judices, advocati ... venerunt ... dicentes Henricum regem sanctus Petrus elegit [33].

In short, then, emperorship is a divine favour — indeed a commonplace enough axiom from which Staufen ideology could not and would not withdraw — but since the emperor is divinely pre-selected, the pope's rôle as the actual instrument cannot, by twelfth-century standards, be reasonably disputed. This empire is conferred — « contulimus » Adrian-Roland say in both letters — through the instrumentality of the pope. What the papal theory of the empire, certainly since the ninth century, wished to express was the mediatory rôle of the pope in conferring this *beneficium*. We recall John VIII's « *per* nostrae mediocritatis ministerium » when he spoke of the character of the empire as

---

first applied at the imperial coronation of Henry II, see EICHMANN, *Der Krönungsordo Cencius II*, in Miscellanea Francesco Ehrle II 322 ff; *Zur Datierung des sog. Cencius II*, Historisches Jahrbuch 52 (1932) 265-312; *Das Verhältnis von Cencius I und II*, in Festschrift f. Martin Grabmann, Paderborn 1935 I 204 ff. at 238-45; *Kaiserkrönung*, I 151 ff, 234 ff, II. 303; and in Historisches Jahrbuch 69 (1949) 613-15 (a reply to his critics). Against EICHMANN's point of view and for a later date (end of the twelfth century) and for the view that *Ordo C* was a mere programme that was not put into practice, see P. E. SCHRAMM, *art. cit.* 285 ff; idem, *Der Salische Kaiserordo*, Deutsches Archiv 1 (1937) 390 ff; M. ANDRIEU, *Le Pontifical Romain au Moyen Age*, (Studi e Testi 78) 1940 II 292 note 1 (« nature theorétique »); M. DAVID, *Le Serment du Sacre* (offprint from Revue du moyen âge latin 6 [1950]) 229 note 24; H. W. KLEWITZ, *Das Papsttum & Kaiserkrönung*, Deutsches Archiv 4 (1941) 421 (for second half of the eleventh century); idem, *Die Krönung des Papstes*, Savigny Zeitschrift, Kanon. Abt. 31 (1941) 96 ff. Cf. now also the attractive view of MA-THILDE UHLIRZ, *Die Quellen der Kaiserkrönung Otto III*, in Festschrift f. E. E. Stengel, Münster 1952 270, tentatively suggesting that *Ordo C* (or an early redaction) was used for Otto III's imperial coronation.

[32] *Relatio Registri Paschalis II*, MGH Const. I no. 99 (p. 147, line 40).
[33] I. M. WATTERICH, *Vitae Pontificum Romanorum*, II 8.

a divine favour; and for this there were the powerful precedents in Stephen II's numerous statements that St Peter through
the pope's instrumentality « unxit eum (scil. Pippinum) in
regem »[34]. Adrian IV's predecessor and pupil of St Bernard,
Pope Eugenius III had designated himself as « vicarius Christi »[35].
Since, as Gelasius I had said, imperial Christian power originates
in Christ, it is Christ's vicar who confers this *beneficium*. Differently expressed : Christ through the pope conferred on Frederick the plenitude of imperial dignity as a favour, as a *beneficium*. As we have said, from this Adrian does not and
can not detract one syllabe in the alleged *littera excusatoria*[36].

---

[34] Cf. *Codex Carolinus* (MGH Epp. III), no. 7 (p. 493, line 10):
« Ideo vos Dominus *per humilitatem meam mediante Petro* unxit in reges,
ut ... » Also no. 8 (p. 496, lines 15-6): « Sic adjutorium sumas a Deo omni-
potente, qui te unxit ... in regem ». Cf. also Paul I, ibid., no. 13 (p. 510,
lines 15-16): « Coram Deo vivo, qui vos in regem per suum apostolum
beatum Petrum ungui praecepit ».

[35] See the curial officer's report in MGH SS XX 543, referred to by
J. Rivière, *Le problème de l'église et de l'état au temps de Philippe le
Bel*, Louvain 1926 440 appendix VI. Moreover, already during the pontificate of Innocent II the Last Supper was symbolically and realistically
re-enacted at Easter when the pope in the company of 5 cardinals, 5 deacons, the « primicerius » and the « prior basilicarius » re-lived Our Lord's
last gathering with His 12 apostles; the « Prior basilicarius » played the
rôle of Judas. See *Ordo Romanus* XI, cap. 48 (PL 78 1044-5): « Judices
autem ducunt eum (*scil.* papam) illo die in basilicam magnam Leoninanam
in cameram, ubi sunt praeparata undecim scamna et unum subsellium circa
mensam domini pontificis, et lectus eius bene praeparatus in figura duodecim
apostolorum circa mensam Christi, quando comederunt pascha. Ibi jacent
in cubitis quinque cardinales, et quinque diaconi, et primicerius ad prandium,
dato prius presbyterio in camera cum manibus, sicut in die Natalis Domini.
Surgit inde, et venit ad locum qui dicitur Cubitorum, ubi agnus assus benedicitur, quem benedicit, et redit ad praeparatum lectum mensae. Prior
basilicarius sedet in subsellio ante lectum. Tunc dominus pontifex tollit
parum de agno, et prius porrigit priori basilicario dicens Quod facis, fac
citius (St John, XIII. 27), sicut ille accepit ad damnationem, tu accipe ad
remissionem; et mittit in os eius, accipit et comedit. Reliquum agni dat
undecim discumbentibus, et aliis quibus placet, et sic omnes comedunt ».
We should also bear in mind that Boso, who wrote his biography of Gregory VII during the pontificate of Adrian IV, called Gregory VII « ipsum
Christi vicarium dominum Gregorium papam » (*Liber Pontificalis*, ed. L.
Duchesne, II 362, lines 26-27), although Boso's model, Bonizo of Sutri, in
the relevant passage speaks only of « papa », see Libelli de Lite I 606. It
seems that Bazianus was one of the early canonists who designated the
pope as « vicarius Christi in terris », see the passage transcribed by A. M.
Stickler, Salesianum 15 (1953) 608.

[36] Nor Alexander III himself after he had become pope und often
enough in his subsequent letters referred to the episode at Besançon.

If anything, Adrian IV makes it worse for Frederick by rubbing in the nature of the papal conferment of the imperial crown, namely a *beneficium*: «Nos ita bene et honorifice imperialis dignitatis insigne tuo capiti imposuimus, ut *bonum factum* valeat ab omnibus judicari». A favour — a *bonum factum* — is not something one has a *right* to expect. And a favour can be withdrawn, as Frederick's grandson was to experience.

The confirmation of all this we find not only in the previously expressed papal thought, but also in the statement of Gervase of Tilbury who, writing to Innocent III's protegé, Otto IV, tells the newly crowned emperor that it was by the «gratia» of Innocent that he obtained his imperial dignity [37], and Gervase goes on to say [38]:

> Imperium tuum non est, sed Christi, non tuum, sed Petri. Non a te tibi obvenit, sed a vicario Christi et successore Petri ... Petro Constantinus imperium occidentis dedit, cui servierat regnum Francorum, regnum Teutonum, regnum Brittonum quin imo totus occidens et totus circumfusus orbis. Hic Petro voluit sub Christo totum servire occidentem. *Beneficio* papae, non suo, Roma tempore Karoli nomen recepit imperii; *beneficio* papae Francorum regi confertur imperium; *beneficio* papae regi nunc Teutonum et non Francorum debetur imperium. *Nec dedit imperium cui vult Teutonia, sed cui cedendum decrevit papa.*

Our interpretation, however, is also generously confirmed by the Staufen emperor himself. In the reply which the bishops forwarded to the pope [39], Frederick makes two important pronouncements. Firstly, in obvious allusion to Gelasius he holds that

> Duo sunt, quibus nostrum regi oportet imperium, leges sanctae imperatorum et usus bonus predecessorum et patrum nostrorum. Istos limites excedere nec volumus nec possumus; quicquid ab his discordat non recipimus.

What this passage makes clear is that pontifical authority as a means of government is excised, and its place is taken by the sacred laws of the emperor. In technical terms, the force of canon law is denied — there is, according to Frederick-Rainald,

---

[37] Gervase of Tilbury, *Otia imperialia*, MGH SS XXVII 379. On Gervase see W. HUNT in *Dictionary of National Biography*, s. v., and W. STUBBS in his introduction to Gervase of Canterbury's *Opera*, Rolls Series, I pp. XLI ff.

[38] Ibid. 382.

[39] MGH Const. I no. 167 (p. 233, lines 29 ff). We follow the reading of WEILAND which seems to us the better reading than that of WAITZ, cf. the latter's note (c) in Rahewin, p. 188.

no such a thing as a jurisdictional or legislative primacy of the Roman Church: the pope *qua* pope cannot issue binding instructions or decrees [40]. The empire is governed solely by the sacred civil laws [41] and by the ancient customs. As far as the *government* of the empire is concerned, the pope's laws display no validity. This brings Frederick and Rainald to the second and perhaps more important point, namely, the denial of the mediatory rôle of the pope in conferring the empire as a benefice:

> *Liberam* imperii nostri coronam divino TANTUM beneficio ascribimus.

Just as the pope as law-giver is excised, in the same way the pope's function as the instrument which confers the divine benefice is cut out [41a]. These are statements which blatantly disregard the genesis, history and ideology of Roman emperorship. And the immediately following statement of the election of the king-emperor together with the unction to be performed by the pope leaves no room for doubt that the papal action at the coronation was considered a mere formality, to which the elected candidate had a right: and consequently the pope a duty to perform. Indeed, from this point of view there is only a very short step to the *imperatura* at the end of this same twelfth century [42].

---

[40] Here again there is a striking resemblance with the tract *De unitate ecclesiae conservanda*, whose author reveals himself as an early antagonist of the binding character of canon law. There is also some resemblance with Peter Crassus and with Gerhoh of Reichersberg, cf. the latter's *De investigatione antichristi*, MGH Libelli de lite III 372: if the Gregorians had their way, all old law would vanish and they would make a new society, wiping out all distinctions, so that there would be « solum unum ovile, et unus pastor, solus Romanus pontifex », lines 25 ff.

[41] Hence Fredericks attempt at promoting the study of Roman law at Bologna, cf. our observations in *Studi in memoria di Paolo Koschaker*, I 102 ff.

[41a] The Staufen standpoint never changed. When in 1239 Gregory IX ordered the election of a new king in the place of Frederick II « quidam principum ei (Gregorio) rescripserunt: Non esse sui juris imperatorem substituere, sed tantum electum a principibus coronare » (*Ann. Stadenses*, MGH SS XVI 367, lines 12 ff).

[42] Announcing their election of Philip of Swabia, the German princes write to Innocent III and use this characteristic term, RNI 14 (ed. F. KEMPF, p. 35, line 15). For the meaning of *imperatura* see the late H. MITTEIS, *Die deutsche Königswahl*, 1943² 120, who was the first to draw attention to the correct reading. Attention should be drawn in this context to the significant terminology which Philip of Swabia, as a mere « Rex Romanorum », employed on 29 June 1198 in the treaty with Philip Augus-

In a round-about way the bishops themselves give a rather strong hint in the very last sentence of their letter at the real grievance, namely, the implied mediatory rôle of the pope. They implore the pope to calm the enraged emperor down so that « the empire may be raised still higher in its lofty position, *He Himself mediating and helping,* Who is made the mediator between God and men, the man Christ Jesus » [43].

tus of France, by designating his kingdom as « *imperium nostrum* », see MGH Const. II no. 1 (p. 1) § 2 (« Si aliquis de imperio nostro faceret eidem Philippo regi Francorum malum ... ») and § 3 (« Nos non retinebimus in imperio nostro aliquem hominem ... »). Philip of Swabia was not crowned king until 8 September 1198, hence more than 2 months after this treaty was made.

[43] « De caetero ... rogamus et obsecramus, ut ... imperium in suae sublimitatis statu glorietur, *ipso mediante* et adjuvante, qui mediator Dei et hominum factus est homo Christus Iesus ». We should note that the bishops not inadvertently and in obvious deference to the pope omit « unus ». Cf. 1 Tim. II. 5: « Unus enim Deus, unus et mediator Dei et hominum, homo Christus Iesus ». It is no doubt also interesting to note that Nicholas I in his Ep. 88 (MGH Epp. VI 486, lines 6 ff) very slightly modifies the famous Gelasian passage in *Tractatus IV,* cap. 11 (THIEL p. 568): whilst Gelasius had written « Quoniam Christus ... discrevit », Nicholas writes: « Quoniam idem mediator Dei et hominum homo Christus Iesus ... discrevit ». As a consequence of the clarification of the pope's vicariate of Christ Innocent III writes: « Nos, qui summi *mediatoris,* licet indigni, locum optinemus in terris » (RNI 185; *ed. cit.* p. 394, lines 29-30); cf. also Reg. I 335 and in many other places; also in his *Sermo II in consecratione pontificis* (PL 217 658 A) « inter Deum et hominem *medius* constitutus ». Cf. also Peter of Blois writing on behalf of Queen Eleanor to Celestine III and imploring the pope's help for the release of Richard I from captivity: St Peter « regnat et imperat et *in medio* constitutus est » (PL 206 1270). Gerhoh of Reichersberg designated Gregory VII (despite all his opposition) as vicar of Christ: « Christus per suum vicarium Petri successorem, Gregorium » (*loc. cit.* p. 325, cap. 19). However, we should bear in mind that the old conception of the vicariate of Christ was not yet dead in the late twelfth century; cf. the author of the *Summa Reginensis*: « Presbiter ... personam Christi habet, argumentum contra illos qui dicunt solum papam esse vicarium Christi. Nam quilibet sacerdos est vicarius Christi et Petri ... Dicebat cardinalis ss. Johannis et Pauli quod inde dominus papa dicitur Christi vicarius, quia Iesus Christus toto orbi preest ita et papa », ed. by A. M. STICKLER, *Vergessene Bologneser Dekretisten,* Salesianum 14 (1952) 489; about the Cardinal mentioned here, cf. *ibid.* note 68. In the middle of the thirteenth century a litigant who appeared personally before the pope, was advised to address him thus: « Mediator Dei et hominum, coram quo loqui praesumo, non considerabit meae scientiae parvitatem » (Aegidius Fuscararius, *Ordo judiciarius,* ed. L. WAHRMUND, Innsbruck 1916 III 259, under the heading: « Exordium coram domino papa »). From the point of view that all Christians form the Church, form, in other words, *unum corpus* (Rom. XII 4, 5, etc.) and that this unum corpus which is the Church, must

The episode at Besançon, therefore, has more significance than it is commonly credited with. In a nutshell, so to speak, it presents to us the papal theory of the genesis and function of the emperor; and on the imperial side it presents to us the hapless situation in which the proud Staufen found himself when reminded by Roland of the origin of the empire: to Roland's question there was no answer. How else but through the agency of the pope could Roman emperorship, which on Frederick's own admission was a *divinum beneficium,* be obtained?

Consequently, in using the term *beneficium,* Adrian IV moved entirely within the framework and thought pattern of the previous ideological development: there was no duplicity attached to it; the term was used in its original Latin sense; Adrian retracted not one syllable from his first letter. There is no need to dub Adrian IV dishonest or to sneer at him for withdrawing something which he had never said nor intended to say. If ever a papal statement was unambigious and harmlessly outspoken, it was Adrian's. For a Staufen emperor this was a humiliating reminder. The imperial reaction to Adrian's letter was, from the purely human point of view, understandable: the anger and rage revealed all too clearly the weakness of the imperial theme. It left out of account the genesis of the empire as well as the function of the emperor as the specially designated and selected protector and defender of the Roman Church. The incident at Besançon revealed the historic dilemma in which the medieval Roman emperors had placed themselves. Nevertheless, the visitation of the *Reichskirche* by the two papal legates was prevented.

Seen from a wider viewpoint, however, the divergencies between the papal and the imperial themes lie in that the former considered the emperor on the *functional* level: the emperor's *raison d'être* was the protection and defence of the Roman Church and therefore of the whole of Christendom. It was for this

---

be governed, the visible vicar of Christ was a logical necessity, hence: « Si quis autem dicat, quod unum caput et unus pastor est Christus, qui est unus unius ecclesiae sponsus, non sufficienter respondet » (St Thomas Aquinas, *Contra gentiles* IV, 76, nos. 3-4). Thomas's confrater, the Cambridge Doctor of theology and later English provincial, Simon of Boraston (*fl.* 1335) in his tract *De unitate ecclesiae* expresses the same thought: « Ipso corporaliter absente (*scil.* Christo) Petrum et in Petro omnes successores eius instituit capud ecclesiae et summum pontificem cum plenitudine potestatis » (MS. Trinity College, Cambridge, B. 15. 11, fol. 50va). On Simon cf. S. L. FORTE in Archivum Fratrum Praedicatorum, 22 (1952) 321-45.

reason that he was made. As the epitome of a universal entity, the Roman Church creates through the pope this universal defender, as witness the oaths of the emperors in the coronation *Ordines C* and *D*. Only a « Roman », that is one who acknowledges the primacy of the Roman Church, can fulfil this role, not a Greek. The emperor, thus made, is raised to the highest available dignity and enjoys certain privileges. As Roman emperor his dignity is universal. The universality of the (Roman) Church is reflected in the ideational universality of (Roman) emperorship. The emperor's universality is a reflection, not indeed in degree, but in kind, of that universality which is epitomized in the Roman Church [44]. The protector and defender of the Roman Church must needs be conceived on the plane of an ideational universality [45].

On the other hand, the imperial theory did not view the substance of Roman emperorship from this functional angle [46].

---

[44] It is from here, we think, that the later sun-moon allegory developed.

[45] As is well known, Innocent III shortly afterwards expressed in unsurpassable conciseness the genesis and function (purpose, finis, telos) of the emperor by the two terms *principaliter* and *finaliter* (cf. RNI 18, 29, 31, 33, 47 etc.). Therefrom arose his right to nominate the imperial candidate (RNI 62: « Ottonem reputamus et *nominamus* regem justitia exigente » and ibid: « (Ottonem) nos ad coronam imperii disponimus *evocare* »; also RNI 65 and 32: « Regiam magnificentiam ad suscipiendam imperii Romani coronam *vocabimus* ». This standpoint of Innocent III is based upon the principle of suitability (« persona idonea »), cf. RNI 29 p. t. and RNI 21: the princes should consider him who « ad regendum imperium est *idoneus* » since the (Roman) Church « nec debet *idoneo defensore* carere » (RNI 48, also RNI 62, 98). From this functionalist point of view the repeated complaints of Innocent (cf. e. g. RNI 15, 33, 85, 92) that malicious people impute to him the desire to destroy the empire, are of course perfectly justified. The imperial coronation at the hands of the pope is therefore constitutive, according to the papal theory, cf. Innocent II supra p. 110 and Innocent III in RNI 33: « *A nobis* imperator imperii recipit diadema in plenitudinem potestatis ». It should be noted that quite in consonance with the underlying papal theme, the designation of the emperor is « Electus » in *Ordo C* and in Innocent's *Ordo D* « Rex », until he has received the last imperial sign from the hands of the pope, when the *Ordines* designate him « imperator ». On the other hand, the coronation of the pope himself was merely declaratory, and not constitutive. The constitutive act was that of the election itself. The imposition of the *corona* on the pope's head added nothing as regards authority which he had not already possessed by virtue of being elected, cf. the election decree of 1059 (MGH Const. I 538, cap. 8); F. WASNER, *De consecratione etc.* in Apollinaris 8 (1935) 118-21; E. EICHMANN, *Weihe & Krönung des Papstes im Mittelalter* ed. by Kl. MÖRSDORF, (Münchener Theolog. Studien, kanonist. Abt. 1) 1951 36 ff.

[46] That the kind of oil and the place of its administration had already

To the Staufens, emperorship was universal, because it was Roman emperorship. They viewed the emperor from the monarchic level: the conception of the ancient Roman emperorship — particularly since the accelerated Roman law studies — engendered the view that emperorship was autonomous and monarchic. In fact, the Teutonic conception of kingship greatly facilitated the emergence of this imperial ideology. The glorification of Charlemagne precisely by the Staufens, above all by Frederick himself, reveals the metamorphosis which the conception of Charlemagne's emperorship had undergone: to the later medieval imperial generations Charlemagne was the idol [47], because they held that he had been a fully fledged and technical Roman emperor. That this was a tragic mistake [48] is less im-

been changed from *Ordo B* onwards, so as to indicate the « demotion » of the emperor, is too well known to need any comment. But the lack of a formal inthronization of the emperor on the occasion of his coronation is certainly noteworthy, especially as the *Ordines Romani* (XII-XIV) lay great stress on the pope's enthronement and elevation. Enthronement symbolizes the taking of physical possession of a dominion. This omission indicates the essential function which the emperor, according to the established papal doctrine, was to perform: he was created an *ad-vocatus*, a *defensor*, a *patronus*, and for this there was no need for an enthronement. As far as it is known, no emperor was ever enthroned in his capacity as an emperor. The much lamented EICHMANN, *Kaiserkrönung*, I 103, thought that the absence of an enthronement could be explained by a recourse to the Donation of Constantine (cap. 18), but it may be suggested that the papal view on the emperor's function affords an equally plausible explanation.

[47] For this see especially R. FOLZ, *Le souvenir et la légende de Charlemagne dans l'empire germanique médieval*, Paris 1950.

[48] The full understanding of the imperial conception of Charlemagne must be set against the Eastern background. This explains the *Renovatio* idea and the peculiar title he had chosen. « Roman empire » in both instances has no political significance. Charles's Roman empire was a *religious* conception: it was that entity which was held together by the spiritual element of the Christian faith as expounded by the Church of Rome. According to Charles, the political Roman empire was situated in the East, and he himself had spoken of an « imperium occidentale » and « orientale ». Roman empire for Charles was, roughly speaking, Latin Christendom, but, and this is the important point, it was governed (*gubernans*) by him as the supreme monarch. The Christmas coronation was a *fait accompli*, hence the long delay (5 months) before the appropriate title had been found and the acceptance of the previously used title after his visit to Ravenna in May 801 (see especially in P. CLASSEN, Deutsches Archiv 9 (1952) 105-112), because it came nearest to Charles's own conceptions, did not offend the pope and was to assuage the East. The Roman empire governed by him was *Europa*, was, in other words, Latin Christendom. And just as this Roman empire was a purely religious concept, so was the *Renovatio*. The idea was of biblical

portant than the fact that functionally, genetically and ideologically the emperor of the Romans was the defender and protector of the Roman Church; that he had grown out of the pat-
rician of the Romans; and that he was no more nor less than
the concrete realization of the profound abstract Pauline-Gelasian-
Isidorian ideas. The Staufen remonstration against the papal
theory of emperorship was undertaken with totally inadequate
weapons [49]. The papal view expressed in Adrian IV's letter to
Frederick was by no means, as Frederick-Rainald would have it,
an « inaudita novitas » [50] : on the contrary, it was old papal doctrine. The emperor was, as Alexander III in his first papal communication to Frederick I correctly expressed it, the advocate
and special defender of the Roman Church :

> Nos recognoscimus domnum *imperatorem* ex collato sibi debito
> dignitatis *advocatum* ac specialem sacrosanctae Romanae ecclesiae *de-*
> *fensorem* [51].

The virile and consistent stand which the papal curia, first
under Chancellor Roland and then under Pope Alexander III,

---

origin, Eccl. us XLVI. 16: « Samuel renovavit imperium et unxit principes
in gente sua ». The late EICHMANN was the first to draw attention to this, see
his *Kaiserkrönung*, I 113 note 15; cf. also H. FICHTENAU, *Das karolingische
Imperium*, 308 note 88. The coronation could not be undone and had to be
given a meaning which corresponded to Charles's conceptions and was no
offence to the pope. Through the coronation the Roman empire (in the
religious sense) was re-born. And the inner part of the seal with its
city gate overshadowed by a cross and the inscription *Roma* makes the
religious import sufficiently clear. But Charlemagne never was and never
styled himself « Imperator Romanorum »; he was an « imperator ». His
(religious) *imperium Romanum* was later taken in a political sense which
largely, though by no means exclusively, accounts for the metamorphosis
of his imperial conceptions. (We hope to deal with these aspects more
fully in a different context).

[49] One of the means of combatting the papal doctrine was that of
« dividing », so to speak, the vicariate of Christ. In his letter to King
Henry II of England, immediately after the outbreak of the schism (October 1159) Frederick conceded that the pope was « unius Dei et Petri vicarius » (Const. I no. 183; p. 254, line 20), whilst on the other hand he
claimed that « imperatoria majestas, quae regis regum et domini dominantium
vicem gerit in terris » (*ibid.*, no. 240; p. 335, lines 26-8). The background
of this was the old conception of Christ being « Rex regum et sacerdos
secundum ordinem Melchisedech ».

[50] In the manifesto issued immediately after the incident, Rahewin,.
op. cit, p. 179, line 22 = Const. I no. 165 (p. 231, line 39).

[51] *MGH Const.* I no. 185 (p. 256, line 24). About the two conceptions
of protection and defence cf. our paper « *The Origin of the Ottonianum* »,
Cambridge Historical Journal 11 (1953).

IV

took against the lay-monarchic tendencies of the time [52] was the first practical result of the new branch of learning, of canonistics, that science which propounded the *canon*, the *norma recte vivendi*, applicable within the *societas christiana*. The opposition against the curia was largely directed against the character of canon law as a norm binding all Christians, whether lay or clerical. To have weathered that storm and to have withstood the powerful combination of forces crystallized in Frederick and Rainald of Dassel, was, from the papal point of view, the great merit of the first canonist-pope.

---

[52] The aims of Frederick and Henry II of England were very much alike, namely the exercise of true monarchic rule. About Henry II John of Salisbury tells us (Ep. 201; PL 199 223) that in a kingdom one only can rule, and if it is the king alone, then the *sacerdotium* must obey him which means its end in a short time: « Si pastorale officium non nisi ad nutum principis liceat exercere, et procul dubio nec crimina punientur, nec tyrannorum arguetur immanitas, nec reipsa diu stabit ecclesia ». Cf. also his Ep. 239 (PL 199 271): Henry thinks that he has the pope and the cardinals « in his pocket » — « in bursa sua » — and glories in obtaining the position of his grandfather, « qui in terra sua erat rex, legatus apostolicus, patriarcha, imperator et omnia quae volebat ». For an attractive combination of John's and St Bernard's views by Robert Grosseteste cf. the latter's Ep. 23 and Ep. 72 * (Rolls Series, pp. 90-1 and pp. 217 ff.).

V

The significance of Innocent III's decretal «Vergentis»

Of all the brilliant expositions and analyses with which Gabriel Le Bras has enriched not only our knowledge, but also — and perhaps more so — our understanding of the intricate mechanisms and interdependent relations obtaining in the field of law, politics and social history, his examinations of the influence of Roman law and of the Roman empire ideology upon the papacy has always been credited with quite a special mark of distinction. With a superb skill of presentation, with a width of perception and a profundity of insight he has with an economy of strokes portrayed a picture which readily allows the spectator to appreciate the complex and involved nature of the papal government and its Roman roots, Roman in both the ecclesiastical and the pagan meanings of the term. Scores of researchers are indebted to him for the vistas which he has opened up -- may he accept this minute footnote as a token of a scholar's profound respect and gratitude for the stimulus and enlightenment he has received from the Master.

In the literature of medieval canon law the decretal of Innocent III issued in the first place to the people and clergy of Viterbo (1) does not seem to have attracted the attention which is its due. For its significance lies partly in the fixation of penalties laid down for heretics, and partly in the argument which Innocent III here adopts in order to bring the crime of heresy into the Roman law category of the *crimen laesae majestatis*. Let us quote the relevant passage from the decretal :

> *Cum enim secundum legitimas sanctiones reis laesae majestatis punitis capite, bona confiscentur eorum, filiis suis vita solummodo ex misericordia conservata, quanto magis, qui aberrantes in fide, domini Dei filium Jesum offendunt, a capite nostro, quod est Christus, ecclesiastica debent districtione praecidi, et bonis temporalibus spoliari, cum longe sit gravius aeternam quam temporalem laedere majestatem.*

(1) Potthast, 643 ; *Reg.* II.1 ; *Extra* : V.7.10.

The essential point which Innocent wishes to make is to put heresy, that is, the *aberratio in fide*, on the same footing as the *crimen laesae majestatis*, and the handle which enables him to effect this *aequiparatio*, is provided in the *legitimae sanctiones*. It is generally agreed that the latter refer to the chapter *Quisquis* in Gratian (2) which is in actual fact the law of the Emperors Arcadius and Honorius contained in *Cod. Just.* IX.8.5. (3) Everyone who has dealt with medieval heresy and its canonistic treatment knows what importance the complexion of heresy as a *crimen publicum* was to assume and what effects the construction of heresy as the crime of *lèse majesté* produced. However severe the sanctions were which heresy had hitherto attracted, the precise juristic construction of the crime itself as a public crime and one that bore all the features of the most serious of all crimes, that is, of the *crimen majestatis*, had not before Innocent's decretal been made. The juristic step which he took by using the categorisation of Roman law for treason, was both constitutionally and doctrinally of far-reaching importance. In fact, it was precisely this juristic categorisation which initiated the medieval treatment of heresy with all its known consequences.

Now the juristic advance made by Innocent III can perhaps best be appreciated, if due consideration is given to the incontrovertible legal fact that Roman law (in its Justinianean codification) had not in the strict juristic sense stigmatized heresy as a *crimen laesae majestatis*, though the sanctions threatened were severe enough, and secondly, that the imperial law on which Innocent based himself, dealt with the genuine *crimen laesae majestatis*, committed in the manner laid down. There is in this law nowhere any hint at any heretical ingredients as constitutive elements of the crime itself. Moreover, however widely-drawn the imperial law was, it presupposed some external manifestation of the intention to commit any of the acts mentioned in it (4), but Innocent's decretal does not at first sight seem to make this presupposition for heresy, because this was a crime that, in essence, was an *aberratio in fide* and therefore concerned exclusively internal, mental factors.

The question which engages the historian of medieval jurisprudence is how one can explain the stigmatisation of heresy as a *crimen laesae majestatis*, although the basic Roman law had fixed as the substance of the crime death or corporeal injury of the emporor or of any of the persons mentioned. *Prima facie* it would seem that juristically the substantive and constitutive elements of the two crimes were different : for the one it was the intended death or injury of the emperor and the other persons, for the other deviation from the established faith. Indeed, there are difficulties in justifying this adaptation of Roman law to the exigencies of medieval papal policy, since the presuppositions appear to belong to quite different

(2) Gratian, C.VI, qu.I, c.22.
(3) *Cf.* glosses on *Extra* cit.
(4) This seems also to have been at the root of Gratian's dictum ante c.22.

orders. And yet, as it is so often the case with medieval papal pronouncements, they are frequently misleading by virtue of their
conciseness and economy of words. What we are made to see in an
individual papal pronouncement is the result of an intensive, sustained and lengthy thought process, and the result is a brief formula
or a succinct statement, which in itself gives no indication how much
intellectual labour went into its making. It is this kind of what is in
reality a mere short-hand device which causes the interpreter difficulties and which is also responsible for a great many facile misinter-
pretations of papal views and ideas. The present problem is in fact
quite a good illustration of the difficulty facing the historian who
wishes to reconstruct and therefore to explain papal principles of
government. At the same time it is perhaps also symptomatic of the
present state of papal historiography that a problem of this magni-
tude has not even been recognized.

The solution of this problem has to set out from two principles
which nevertheless stand in closest relation to each other. The first
is the concept of the Church as the body of all the faithful, the
congregatio fidelium, the *corpus Christi quod est ecclesia catholica* (5),
and the second concerns the government of this body. Papal exegesis
of the Matthean passage (XVI. 18 f.) had always held that both the
body and its government were established by one and the same act
of Christ (6). In fact, the papal thesis of the pope as successor of
St Peter was, by means of a superb mastery of the Roman law, constructed by Leo I in the mid-fifth century when he made in an exclusively Roman-juristic sense the pope the *haeres beati Petri* (7). Now
this *corpus Christi* was formed and held together entirely by the
cementing bond of the faith : faith was, so to speak, the *anima* which
made the body alive and infused into it the material, that is, living
force (8). Faith in Christ was the welding element — at once intan
gible and yet tangible and concrete enough, at least as far as social
reality was concerned. But at the same time it should be realized
that this faith itself consisted of many diverse strains : the contents
of the faith were not, as it were, self-evident, but had to be enunciated and fixed by an authority that was charged with this task.
This enunciation and fixation of the individual articles of the faith
was, for reasons irrelevant to this inquiry, the right and duty of the

---

(5) *Cf.*, e.g., Gregory VII in his *Reg.*II.73 ; IV.6 ; etc. ; Gratian C.XXIII,
qu.III,c.4. *Cf.* also M. ROBERTI, *Studi in onore di Enrico Besta* (Milan, 1939),
IV.37 ff. ; A. EHRHARDT, Savigny Zeitschrift Kan. Abt., LXX (1953) 299 ff.

(6) For this see W. ULLMANN, *Principles of Government and Politics in the
Middle Ages* (London, 1961), pp. 32 ff. (abbr. : P.G.P.).

(7) *Cf.* W. ULLMANN, Journal of Theological Studies, n.s., XI (1960), 25 ff
and 295 ff.

(8) *Cf.*, e.g., Hebr.XI.6 : *Sine fide impossibile est placere Deo* ; Rom. XIV.8 ;
etc. Innocent III himself in his fourth consecration sermon : Christ as *animae
sapor* (*P.L.*, 217.667). In the fourteenth century we find : *Super fidem huma-
nitatis fundata est ecclesia*, Alvarus Pelagius, *De planctu ecclesiae* (Venice, 1560),
I.64, fol.80va.

pope in his capacity as its sole and unique guardian. The « building of the Church » — to use Matthean language — could be effected only by the determination and precision of the faith given by the pope holding the *primatus magisterii*.

If we keep this axiomatic tenet in mind, it will be easier to understand the thought-process which prompted Innocent III to equate heresy with the Roman law crime of *lèse-majesté*. To begin with, the reason why he adduced Cod. IX.8.5, and no other Roman law passage, was that this Codex-statement was easily at hand in Gratian (9), and for this reason this Roman law was also called *canonizata* by contemporary canonists. Although this Codex-passage dealt with the protection of those imperial counsellors and ministers who stood in intimate contact with the emperor himself, its declaration that the perpetrator should be treated *ut reus majestatis* made the task for Innocent III considerably easier in so far as it gave him a perfect handle to employ the ever favoured *argumentum a minori ad maius*. If even the attack on the emperor's intimate collaborators constituted treason, all the more so, the pope argues, does an attack upon divinity itself. However, there is some discrepancy between the decretal and its Roman law parent. It may perhaps be understandable why Innocent abstained from defining what actually constituted an *aberratio in fide*, but it is on the other hand rather difficult to put a deviation from faith on the same level as the offence enacted in Roman law, for the latter dealt with the intended physical death of the persons named and, according to general principles obtaining in Roman law, even in this category of crimes, there must have been an external activity manifesting the intention (10). In other words, there must be some outward manifestation to effect the killing of the individuals mentioned in the law, however much removed this manifestation may have been from the actual activity inflicting the death. Nevertheless, the structure of the *crimen laesae majestatis* and its commission would appear to be somewhat different from that crime that consisted in the *laesio divinae majestatis*. Jurist as he was, no doubt Innocent also demanded some external manifestation of heterodox belief, for instance, a statement or gesture, if only for evidential purposes, but even so, there still remains the difficulty of equating heresy with the Roman law adduced by him.

The essential element of the Roman law was the attack on the emperor's *majestas*. Moreover, the intimate connexion of the imperial counsellor with the person of the emperor gave him the special protection : in other words, it was the *majestas* of the emperor which

(9) See above note 2.

(10) *Cf.* Th. MOMMSEN, *Römisches Strafrecht* (in Bindings Handbuch der deutschen Rechtswissenschaft) (Leipzig, 1899), p. 97 : the principle was « dass die delictische Absicht aus dem Bereich des blossen Entschlusses und der Erklärung desselben hinaustritt in den Bereich der Handlung... das Staatsverbrechen darf angesehen werden als rechtlich vollzogen durch jedwede Betätigung der staatsfeindlichen Gesinnung ».

had distinguished the counsellor by his trust and confidence in appointing him, and it was this *majestas* which constituted the object of the attack. But this consideration does not and cannot apply to heterodox or heretical views and statements : they can never be said to have aimed at the death or physical injury of a person : they attacked divinity, not by concrete, physical actions, but by deliberately setting aside what was an article of faith, what was divine truth. The intention of the traitor in Roman law was the *laesio majestatis* of the emperor ; the intention of the heretic was the *laesio majestatis* of divinity itself by impugning the one or the other acticle of faith.

But as the *corpus Christi quod est ecclesia catholica* was held together by faith alone — and not by force, and the like — which faith emanated from Christ Himself and had exclusive reference to Him, deviation or aberration from this faith could indeed be viewed much more seriously than an indirect attack on the person of the emperor. For thereby the whole basis, the whole foundation, of the *corpus*, was attacked. As a purely mental element faith would appear to be in need of greater protection than the concrete personality of the emperor or of his counsellors.

The Innocentian reasonings lead to the conclusion that his view of stigmatizing heresy as a graver and more serious offence than the (ordinary) high treason has very much in its favour. For the operative term and concept is that of *majestas* and its violation. The *ratio legis* of penalizing an attack on the emperor or his collaborators was that his *majestas* was violated : this *majestas* was nothing else but his *majoritas*, that is, the manifest expression of his being *major* than his subjects, because he had received his *gubernacula* not from them, but from divinity : it was this distinction which divinity had conferred on him that made him — and not divinity — the target of treasonable activity. Divinity itself was in no way affected by any act that aimed at a diminution or *laesio* of imperial authority. His own *majestas* (= *majoritas*) was impugned. But heresy on the other hand, aimed at divinity itself, at the faith in divinity, at impugning the revealed truth. Christ had *majoritas* (= *majestas*), because He it was who had instituted the *corpus quod est ecclesia*, and it was through this faith in Him that this body actually became alive and into existence. What animates the body, what breathes life into it, what the *anima* of this corpus was, was faith in Christ, and if this is attempted to be diminished or violated, then indeed the whole corpus is threatened with collapse. The point is that the *anima* in the imperial field was the emperor and his law, hence the emperor as the *lex animata*, whilst in the field of the Church the *anima* was the papally enunciated faith in Christ and the law based upon it (11). What in fact both offences make abundantly clear is that they protect the sovereign status, sovereignty itself, in the one case, to use Innocent's own terminology, the *temporalis*

(11) For the concatenation of faith and law see P.G.P., pp. 95 ff.

majestas, in the other the *aeterna majestas*. For the Roman and the medieval concept of *majestas* (= *majoritas*) expresses exactly the same idea as does *superioritas* (— soveranitas — souveraineté). There is no power above the *major* or *superior* (12). We shall perhaps now also understand the profound implications of such papal terms and concepts as the pope being the *speculator omnium*, residing *in eminenti specula*, his being set *over* the nations and kingdoms, his possessing *omnis potestas in coelo et in terra*, his plenitude of power; and so forth. They all express in contemporary medieval language the sovereignty of the pope : there is nobody who is *superior* or *major* than the pope (13), and therefore there is nobody who could sit in judgment over him. It is this wholly juristic concept of *majoritas* (= *majestas* = *superioritas*) which explains the frequently misunderstood thesis that there is no one who could say to the pope : « *Cur ita facis* ? » (14) because it is the *voluntas principis* which is the material ingredient of his sovereignty (15).

It is only from the point of view of *majestas* that the function of the pope within the framework of heresy can properly be understood. It is here that the double function of the pope in its magisterial and jurisdictional primacy demonstrates itself fully. Because the pope is, as it were, the mouthpiece of divinity and as such not only fixes doctrine and articles of faith, but also watches over its purity and prevents its contamination with alien elements, the denial of this or that article of faith or persistent aberration from faith constitutes an attack on divinity and thereby on the function of the pope as supreme *magister fidei* : faith as expounded by the pope was held to be the truest expression of what Christ Himself had laid down — it is the clarification of a point hitherto doubtful or controversial. After all, it was the popes who had the *sensum Christi* (16). It is the legal identity between Christ and Peter and the pope, the essence of the petrinological theme (17), which explains this standpoint. The pope *is* Peter, succeeds the latter directly and without intermediaries, and continues his functions. A denial or a deviation from papal teaching amounted to a denial of the magisterial function of the pope, a function with which divinity itself had charged him, and in so far that denial or aberration revealed not only arrogance (18), but also the denial of the superior know-

---

(12) For this concept see also Th. MOMMSEN, *Römisches Staatsrecht* (Leipzig 1877), III.664 and note 1 ; *Strafrecht*, p. 538.

(13) *Cf.* also below at note 24.

(14) For instance, Tancred, Innocent's great contemporary Bologna canonist, see W. ULLMANN, *Medieval Papalism* (London, 1949), p. 55.

(15) *Cf.*, for instance, the Speculator, *Speculum Juris* (ed. Basle, 1574), I. De Legato, Nunc autem, no.51, p. 52 : « Apud eum (scil. papam) est pro ratione voluntas ».

(16) See W. ULLMANN, *The Growth of Papal Government in the Middle Ages*, 2nd ed. (London, 1962), p. 46, n.6 (Gregory II).

(17) For this see W. ULLMANN, Studi Gregoriani, VI (1959), pp. 261 ff.

(18) See below note 32.

ledge of the pope, as well as of his divine charge (19). Christ speaking through the pope as successor of St Peter could not have erred, and the assertion of any doctrine other than that held by the papacy, was of necessity erroneous (20).

But these considerations explain only, so to speak, one half of the problems raised in this decretal of Innocent III. The other half of the problem can be explained by a recourse to the jurisdictional primacy of the pope. In other words, both aspects of the papal function must be taken into account. Moreover, it is here within the jurisdictional primatial function that the concept ot the papal *majoritas* receives its juristic precision. As we have said, in his function as pope it is his duty to watch over the purity of the faith, but that supervisory function of the pope can adequately be fulfilled (not by pious advice or counsel or admonition, but) by bringing the law into play (21). How else could the pope build the Church ? How else is he to make sure that the faith will be maintained in its purity ? It was precisely in the context of the jurisdictional primacy that the concept of the papal *majestas* was worked out, and by no one less elegantly than by Innocent himself. At all times of its reflective thinking was the papacy anxious to emphasize its jurisdictional position and its possession of the *gubernacula* — indeed in so doing the papacy owed a very great debt to Roman law. It was in the process of elucidating the jurisdictional function of the pope that such characteristic maxims as *papa a nemine judicatur* or the automatism of the Petrine binding and loosening powers or the all-comprehensiveness of these powers, and the like, found their manifest expression. Indeed, one might go as far as to say that to the Roman-imperial maxim of *Princeps legibus solutus* corresponded the Roman-papal unaccountability expressed in *Prima sedes a nemine judicatur*. The essential point here is that the pope was in every respect a *major* or *superior*.

That is not to say that Innocent III in any way was the originator of this theme, but what he must be credited with is the succinct and concise utilisation of the Roman law for the purpose of clarifying the relationship between heresy and the jurisdictional function of the pope : his contribution had all the juristic touch of a former pupil of Bologna. He moved entirely within the broad stream of the traditional papal doctrine, according to which the pope in his func-

---

(19) *Cf.*, e.g., Luke XXII.32 : *Ego rogavi pro te ut non deficiat fides tua ;* Matt. XXVIII.20 ; etc.

(20) *Cf. D.P.*22 and P.G.P., p. 80 f, esp. note 1.

(21) This is what Innocent III himself indicated in *Extra* : III.34.9, where he speaks of the *idiotae*, who *sunt juris ignari*, a passage which was always interpreted in the sense that theology, morals etc. are insufficient for purposes of government. For the fourteenth century *cf.* Alvarus PELAGIUS, *op. cit.*, II.20, fol.54ra : *Praesumptuosum est asserere quod absque canonibus sacris per solam bibliam vel theologicam theoricam regi posset ecclesia sancta Dei, sed hoc tantum consueverant asserere jus canonicum ignorantes, praesertim viri religiosi superbi, qui ab Innocentio tertio idiotae vocantur...*

736

tion as pope did not belong to the Church, but stood outside and above it (22). The pope was the *Schnittpunkt* between heaven and earth, standing with one leg in heaven and with the other on earth. When Innocent declared in one of his consecration sermons that he was (23) :

> *Medius constitutus inter hominem et Deum... minor Deo, major homine, qui de omnibus judicat et a nemine judicatur,*

he gave thereby the succinctest possible expression of the pope's true sovereignty. This unsurpassably concise statement shows not only the mediatory role of the pope — that is, mediating divine favours, graces and benefits to man — but also the theme that *qua* pope he does not belong to the Church — standing in the middle, so to speak, between God and man — and is higher than man, occupying, so to speak, an estate of his own. Two corollaries at once can be derived from this sovereign status of the pope. First, that because he is *major*, he cannot be made responsible for any of his actions by his subjects who in this context become his *subditi* : this is in other words a re-statement of the ancient thesis (24). Second, because he is sovereign, he has the right to demand obedience from any Christian. The close link between the holder of sovereignty and his demand for obedience is here demonstrated most eloquently. The title in the decretal collections *De majoritate et obedientia* incorporates the individual decretals in which the interdependent themes of sovereignty and obedience are the paramount features (25).

The means to give effect to the sovereign status of the pope were provided by the power handed to St Peter by Christ to which the pope succeeded in a juristic fashion. Innocent's well-known decretals manifest the automatic effects of the Petrine binding and losening powers, and at the same time also bring into clearest possible relief the ancient Leonine *consortium potentiae* between Christ and the pope (26) : it is not man, but God who issues a decision when

---

(22) For this see P.G.P., pp. 48 ff.

(23) *P.L.*, 217.658.

(24) For Zosimus in the fifth century *cf. P.L.*, 20.677. *Cf.* also Innocent himself in *Reg*.II.105 : because the Roman Church is the *sedes justitiae*, its decision *nec potest ab alio retractari, sic aliis formam tribuit judicandi. Cf.* also the application of I Cor.IV.4 by Innocent : « he that judges me is the Lord » (*Sermo III*, in *P.L.*, 217.658). The sovereignty of the pope is also expressed by him thus : the Roman pontiff *post deum alium superiorem non habet* (*ibid.*, col. 664), to which he adds on another occasion : *quantumlibet evanescat, quis potest eum foras mittere aut pedibus conculcare* » ? (col. 670).

(25) A very neat and practical application of this theme is in Hostiensis, *Lectura* (ed. Paris, 1512), ad X : I.34.6, fol.158 : *Potestas pontificalis consistit in jure quo debet esse imbuta, regalis vero in potentia facti, quo debet esse suffulta, et sic patet, quod una eget reliqua et utraque adinvicem concordante omnia recte in regimine ecclesiae Dei. Debet tamen pontificalis precedere tamquam major et dignior et illuminatrix ad modum lucernae illuminationis, et regalis sequi tamquam minor sive rudior ad modum clave indevotos et rebelles percutientis seu malleantis.*

(26) *Cf. Journ. Theol. St.*, cit., XI (1960), pp. 32 ff.

V

the pope acts on this basis (27) ; it is not human, but divine power which the pope thus wields (28). There was indeed every justification for Innocent III to exhibit the pope as a true *vicarius Christi*. For governmental purposes there was juristic identity between Christ and the pope (29).

What these considerations will have made clear is that they exclusively concern juristic elements : evidently, the *majoritas* of the pope, his *superior* status, his being *medius* between God and man, can have reference only to his juristic function which is, in concrete terms, the function of a judge. It is here that the clarification of heresy as a *crimen laesae majestatis* by Innocent III assumes its full significance. Accordingly, it was solely the pope who by virtue of the self-same *majoritas* is qualified to pronounce whether or no divinity had been offended. In other words, the essential point here is the judicial function of the pope which is not however exercised merely in regard to positive law, but also in regard to the faith. What we are confronted with is the extension of the concept of judge in the pope : in the exercise of this capacity he does not necessarily base his decision upon positive law, but upon his knowledge, peculiar to him alone, whether or not a doctrine concerning the faith, amounts to an offence of the divine majesty itself. The announcement concerning heresy or orthodoxy is declaratory : it does not create *ex nihilo* an offence, if conduct has been declared heretical, that is, an offence against the divine majesty of Christ.

The principle *nullum crimen sine lege* cannot therefore be applied within the precincts of the pope's function as vicar of Christ and successor of St Peter (30). By virtue of his sovereign status he can create new law and thus stigmatize conduct as criminal, the basis being his insight and knowledge. Hence judge and law-giver flow here into one function. If any proof were needed, Innocent III would have furnished it by the decretal *Vergentis* that the Romanist thesis of the prince as the *lex animata* was fully applicable to the pope. The *anima* that held the *corpus (Christi)* together was faith in Christ, and he alone was functionally qualified to pronounce whether or not a certain conduct, statement, expression, etc. was orthodox or heterodox, and consequently also heretical (31). As the

(27) For instance, *Extra* : I.7.3.
(28) *Ibid.*, cap. 2.
(29) About this *cf.* our arguments in *Studi Gregoriani*, cit., p. 229 ff. *Cf.*, further Innocent III in *Reg.*I.75 ; I.88 : *qui (Christus) sit Dominus omnium... in nobis honoratur, cum honoramur, et contemnitur, cum contemnimur* ; I.320 : the pope *ita suas aliis vices distribuit, ut, ceteris vocatis in partem sollicitudinis, solus retineat plenitudinem potestatis, ut de ipso post Deum alii dicere possint : Et nos de plenitudine ipsius accepimus* (Joh.I.16) ; I.326 and 335 (the pope *non humana, sed divina auctoritate dissolvit*) ; I.485 : *Dei locum tenemus in terris* ; and so on.
(30) The principle *nulla poena sine lege* was in fact denied by Alexander III in *Extra* : I.29.4 in his instructions to judges delegates.
(31) About the biblical passages see above n. 8 ; *cf.* further Gratian, Dist.19, c.4 and 22, c.1 ; C.XXIV, qu.I, c.12 and also ead., I, c.14 ; see Innocent himself in X : III.42.3, also his *Reg.* II.220.

corpus was built on faith in Christ, received its *animating* sustenance from this faith, any deviation from it amounted to an attack on Christ Himself. The characterisation of heresy as a *crimen publicum* is wholly understandable and so is its nature as a *laesio divinae majestatis* : the very foundations of society were held to have been attacked.

The Innocentian legislation is in fact a classic demonstration of the essential and vital connexion between theology and jurisprudence : juristic theology found in this decretal its most persuasive and convincing testimony. Heresy was an offence against divinity, but it was also an offence against the pope himself, primarily an attack on his magisterial function (32) and secondarily on his juristic function. With good reasons has medieval juristic doctrine held heresy to be a crime directed against the Roman Church itself, which was considered the repository of the true faith and the *sedes justitiae*. In both respects, in its magisterial as well as in its jurisdictional, the Roman Church was impugned by heresy. It was an offence against the sovereign, because in accordance with the ancient derivational principle, the Roman Church was constitutionally the foundation on which the whole edifice of the *corpus Christi* was erected. The heretic was a rebel against his sovereign, the pope. No other legal feature shows the true *majoritas* of the pope better than the crime of heresy. To view it as high treason in the literal meaning of the term, committed against the sovereign, corresponds to the underlying conceptions of the medieval papacy. For because Christ was the *caput* of the *corpus*, as we read in *Vergentis*, because Christ was the *fundamentum et fundator ecclesiae* (33), and because there was the juristic identity between Christ and the pope through the intermediary of Peter, Innocent could well say that the Roman Church or its pastor was the *fundamentum et caput* (34) or the *fundamentum totius christianitatis* (35) or also *fundamentum legis totius christianitatis* (36), and that therefore attacks on the faith amounted to a *laesio* of divinity as well as of the papacy. Heresy offended in the pope divinity — and the further consequential implication is the threat to the *corpus Christi* itself (37). In the equation of heresy with high treason we may well witness the culmination of the petrinological theme, itself the religious-theological-political expression of the sove-

---

(32) *Cf.* Gratian, C.XXIV, qu.III, c.30 (Leo I) : teachers of error are those *qui ad cognoscendam veritatem aliquo impediuntur obscuro, non ad propheticas voces, non ad apostolicas litteras, nec ad evangelicas auctoritates, sed ad semetipsos recurrunt.*

(33) *Reg.*X.137.

(34) *Reg.*II.82.

(35) *Reg.*II.218 ; *RNI.*44.

(36) *Reg.*II.217 (the Latin translation of the Catholikos of Armenia's statement); *cf.* also *Reg.*II.209 and XVI.104 : *Caput et magistra totius christianitatis.*

(37) *Cf.* Innocent's statement : « Si caput fuerit infirmum, totum corpus languidum erit » in *Sermo I, P.L.* 217.650.

reignty of the ruler. Roman law was, if not the begetter, at all events a powerful assistant in the birth of the original petrinological thesis (38), and Roman law was to be of no lesser value in bringing this thesis to its logical conclusion.

Whilst Innocent III operated with the Roman-imperial decree, in order to construct by means of an *argumentum a minori* the crime of heresy as a *crimen laesae majestatis*, his succesor Honorius III, in 1225, modelled himself on the same decree when he placed the cardinals under a special protection : any kind of attack upon a cardinal rendered the perpetrator liable to most severe penalty measures, because he was « sicut reus criminis laesae majestatis » (39). The interesting feature of this decree is that it now transferred to the pope's intimate counsellors the protection which the imperial decree had given to the emperor's counsellors : the *ratio legis*, here as there, was the special protection of those who were in intimate contact with the sovereign. As a matter of fact, it was in this imperial law that the imperial counsellors were called *pars corporis nostri* (scil. imperatoris) — and we can readily understand why we find exactly the same designation for the Roman cardinals (40). It was the juristic skill of Innocent III which firstly clarified, with the help of Roman law, the concept of heresy as a *crimen laesae majestatis*, and which secondly influenced his immediate successor to apply this same Roman law and adopt it to the cardinals who had for so long been considered the senators of the pope. What served Innocent as a basis for an argument, served Honorius as a direct model. What is common to both is the idea of sovereignty manifesting itself in the pope. From the point of view of medieval *Staatslehre* the legislation of Innocent in this respect cannot be exaggerated in importance : it secured the protection of the monarch's true function, his sovereignty, and in so far the decretal *Vergentis* supplied that element which any other governmental system already had — the protection of the sovereign without which no public entity could exist (41).

The sanctions for an offence against the *majestas* are correspondingly similar in Roman and in canon law. The former decreed the physical death of the *reus majestatis*, the latter his spiritual and consequently social death by cutting him off « a capite nostro, quod est Christus », as Innocent III had it. Because Roman law had not decreed the death penalty for the descendants of the culprit of high treason, Innocent too abstained from inflicting upon them

---

(38) See *J.T.S.*, cit., pp. 25 ff.

(39) *Cf. Bullarium Romanum* (ed. Turin, 1863), III.410 ff. ; Boniface VIII incorporated the decree in the *Sextus* : V.9.5. *Cf.* also W. ULLMANN in *Essays in medieval history presented to A. Gwynn* (Dublin, 1961), p. 376, note 62.

(40) On this see W. ULLMANN, Ephemerides Juris Canonici, XII (1956), pp. 265 ff. ; *cf.* also gl. ord. on X : I.30.9, s.v. *commissam*, with a reference to Gratian, VI.I.22 (= *Cod.Just.*IX.8.5).

(41) It is certainly strange that this development did not take place before Innocent III, especially when due regard is had to the elaboration of the monarchical status of the pope himself in the preceding period.

spiritual death. It is equally instructive to see that precisely because heresy was in Innocent's view high treason, whilst in Roman law this crime was not put into the same juristic category, the canon law adopted the punishment of the Roman law *crimen majestatis* (and not that of the Roman law heresy punishment), that is, the confiscation of all the property and all the goods of the accusend, with the consequence that his descendants were disinherited — the *exhaeredatio filiorum* — which Innocent conceived to be an adequate temporal penalty measure. In no wise different from the Roman law high treason, the question of guilt was here not an issue at all — although innocent and possibly even quite unaware of the father's *aberratio in fide*, the descendants had to suffer for the misdeed of their progenitor (42), the reason being, according to Innocent, « cum in multis casibus filii pro patribus temporaliter puniantur » (43) Clearly, in Roman and canon law, the *exhaeredatio filiorum* was considered an additional and most suitable deterrent factor, though how far this tallied with the requirement that for punishment *culpa* had to be established, is not easy to say. On the other hand, in the Roman law crime of heresy (44) the question of guilt of the descendants played, as one would have expected, a major role : if they disproved of their parents' heresy, they remained capable of inheriting (45). That indeed was the rule in Roman law (46), which was so strongly impregnated with the principle of *Schuldhaftung* : the sole exception was made very late, in the very decree of Arcadius against high treason which served Innocent as his model and which, not without reason, has been stigmatised as *berüchtigt* (47). It is regrettable that Gratian saw fit to incorporate this juristically (even if not morally) detestable decree of the emperor who indeed knew better himself when in another decree he stated with singular clarity (48) :

(42) For the classical Roman law where there was no confiscation of property if the culprit had children, see *Dig.*48.4.9 (Hermogenianus).

(43) He continued : *et juxta canonicas sanctiones quandoque feratur ultio non solum in auctores scelerum sed etiam in progeniem damnatorum.* It may be worth pointing out that even when in criminal Roman law confiscation of property was decreed, one half still had to go to the children (MOMMSEN, *Strafrecht*, p. 1006), and Justinian abolished total confiscation altogether, except in the case of C.IX.8.5, see his *Nov.*17, c.2 and *Nov.*134, c.13 (incorporated as an authentic in C.IX.49 post legem 11). The *divinum judicium* and canonical sanctions adduced by Innocent to justify the measure were probably those in Gratian, D.p.c.11, C.I, qu.IV and D.a.c.1, C.XXIV, qu.III (biblical instances of vicarious liability) and C.XVI, qu.VIII, c. 3 and C.XXV, qu.II,c.25 ; *cf.* also his *De consecrat.*, I.41 : *Perit justus saepissime pro impio* but this was pseudo-isidorian (P. HINSCHIUS, *Decr. Ps.-Isidorianae* (Leipzig, 1869), p. 108, c.4).

(44) *Cod. Just.*I.5.4 ; *Nov.*115, c.3, § 14.

(45) *Cod.* cit., lex 4 : *nisi (filii) a paterna pravitate discesscint.*

(46) *Cf.*, e.g., *Dig.*48.19.20 (Paulus) and 26 (Callistratus) : *Crimen vel poena paterna nullam maculam filio infligere potest.*

(47) MOMMSEN, *Strafrecht*, p. 594. About this law *cf.* also J.B. BURY, *History of the later Roman Empire* (London, 1923) I.118 and II.410 ; E. DEMOUGEOT, *De l'unité à la division de l'empire Romain* (Paris, 1951), pp. 172 f.

(48) *Cod.*IX.47.22.

Sancimus ibi esse poenam ubi et noxia est... peccata igitur suos teneant auctores.

But it was not this imperial decree, but that dealing with treason which Innocent found in Gratian. That this pope should feel constrained to justify the punishment of innocent individuals, might well be seen as an *aberratio in jure* (49), and this is all the more regrettable as his immediate predecessor, Celestine III, had quoted, though without acknowledgement, in a decretal the very statement of Roman law *cum peccata suos auctores tenere debeant* (50). However much Innocent himself may have stressed that the descendants were to suffer merely in a temporal manner, the fact remains that even only a temporal punishment was a severe enough penalty. This is a standpoint which strikes some very harsh and discordant notes in those who considered the Roman Church as the *sedes justitiae*. Whether one views the assistance which Roman law rendered to canon law and to the papacy favourably or unfavourably, the stark and incontrovertible fact remains that by using the juristic category of the Roman *crimen laesae majestatis* Innocent adopted — and from his own contemporary point of view he was indubitably correct in so doing — the inhuman and very late Roman law sanctions concerning the descendants and thereby began a development in criminal law in the 13th century which extended this deterrent of punishing descendants to a number of other offences (51). It is one of the great legal-historical paradoxes that the thirteenth century on the one hand witnessed the height of medieval jurisprudential thought, and yet on the other hand also witnessed the adoption of such deterrents which cannot be justified by any juristic principle. One cannot be surprised that both civilians and canonists had considerable qualms and juristic scruples in their efforts to explain these drastic measures, and we may well sympathise with the sentiment which in dealing with this matter made Jacobus de Ravanis invoke Christ's statement : *Durum est contra stimulum calcitrare* (52).

---

(49) His justificatory plea is all the more unconvincing as he himself in the same year issued a letter in which he said that the addressee *sollicite debet attendere ne vel damnet innoxios vel noxios absolvet... non est nostrae intentionis innoxios cum nocentibus condemnare (Reg.*II.229).

(50) *Extra* : III.11.2.

(51) *Cf. Extra* : V.37.10 and 12 ; Honorius III, decr. cit. ; and Boniface VIII in *Sextus* : V.9.5 and V.2.15 ; etc. But *cf. De reg. juris*, c.22 : *Non debet aliquis alterius odio praegravari.*

(52) Jacobus de Ravanis, cited by Cynus, *Comm.ad.Cod.* (ed.Frankfurt, 1578), I.13, ad auth.*Gazaros* ; Acts, 9.5.

VI

'DIES ORTUS IMPERII'.
A NOTE ON THE 'GLOSSA ORDINARIA' ON C.III.12.7(5)

I

It might well seem somewhat anomalous that the question of the exact moment at which the medieval Roman emperor began to govern in this capacity, was not, in civilian literature, greatly discussed. In fact, to judge by the relevant glosses of Accursius himself, one might well be justified in saying that the civilians saw no problem in this question. There is no hint or allusion in the *gl. ord.* that there was any divergence of opinion on this point. In two places Accursius comes to speak of the *dies ortus imperii* and the laconic nature of his gloss is indeed noteworthy, and this all the more so, because there were, as we shall presently see, weighty opinions to the contrary.

In his gloss on *Bene a Zenone* Accursius states that([1])

> Non valet privilegium principis ante coronationem; item nota eum coronandum,

and in another gloss he maintained substantially the same when he declared that the *dies ortus imperii* was that day on which the prince was crowned([2]). From these two statements of Accursius it becomes clear that the imperial coronation assumes a constitutive function: whatever the emperor might have been before the coronation, he could not, in the opinion of the civilian, perform any governmental

---

([1]) Gl. «*Infulas*» ad l. *Bene a Zenone* (C. 7.37.3).

([2]) Gl. «Ortus imperii» ad l. *Omnes dies* (C. 3.12.7). Some decretists of the late 12th and early 13th centuries devoted a good deal of space to the question of the *dies ortus imperii*, cf. A.M. Stickler, *Imperator* p. 165 ff. E.g., p. 203, *Summa Et est sciendum*: «Item ante hodie potest imperator uti gladio quam consecretur in imperatorem, populi electione, qui (another MS has: per papae electionem, quae), ei et in eum omne jus et omnem potestatem transfert». Huguccio's opinion was similar. For the reasons why these and similar expressions on related topics cannot command much respect, see Stickler's observations, ibid., pp. 208-9: lack of clarity of fundamental conceptions (rex, imperator, princeps, etc.); ambiguity of diction; canonistic confusion of thought; etc. To these reasons may be added that as jurists the decretists had necessarily to confine themselves to the text of the Decretum and here they found nothing on this question. Hence the impossibility of answering it on a strictly juristic basis.

act specifically belonging to the emperor alone before he was crowned by the pope. This point of view would indeed tally with the meaning and significance of the imperial coronation (3).

Nevertheless, there are two exactly contemporary statements which flatly contradict the thesis expressed by Accursius. The one is a German verdict — a *Weistum* — of 1252 in which we read:

> Rex autem Romanorum ex quo electus est in concordia eandem potestatem habet quam et imperator nec dat ei inunctio imperialis nisi nomen (4).

This view clearly stands in direct contrast to that expressed by the glossator. Here the imperial coronation is nothing but a formality which though still of some importance, provides nothing more than a mere name: only after the coronation the *Rex Romanorum* is entitled to call himself an emperor, but imperial powers he has by virtue of the election performed « in concordia » (5).

Essentially not different is the doctrine which Innocent IV set forth in his commentaries on the *Extra*. Here he says:

> Credimus tamen quod si imperator coronam in debito loco recipere non potest, nihilominus auctoritatem ministrandi ab archiepiscopo Coloniensi posset recipere vel suam auctoritatem habet ex electione (6).

If anything, this declaration of Innocent IV is still more concrete than the *Weistum*, for Innocent does not demand that the election was performed *in concordia* and he further maintains that the *auctoritas ministrandi* can be derived either from the coronator of the king or from the election.

We have here quite explicit statements which on the surface do not admit of any doubt about their meaning. But how can we reconcile them? Can they in fact be reconciled? Or are they irre-

---

(3) Cf. W. ULLMANN, *Papal Government*, pp. 134 ff., 235 f.

(4) Reported by Hostiensis, *Lectura* (ed. Paris, 1512), V. 40. 26, fol. 127 rb. First discovered by K. Zeumer in *Neues Archiv*, 30 (1904), pp. 405 f.; for a discussion cf. H. MITTEIS, *Königswahl*, pp. 187 ff.

(5) That this does not mean unanimous, is explained by MITTEIS, *Königswahl* pp. 187 ff.

(6) INNOCENT IV, *Comm. ad Lib. Extra* (ed. Frankfurt, 1586), I. 6.34. This entry is, so to speak, sandwiched between topics which prima facie would seem to have little to do with the statement in the text.

concilable? Is, for instance, the point of view of Accursius a thorough-
going hierocratic-papal one? The very question would inevitably
put the possibility out of court, knowing as we do that his sympathies
certainly did not lie in that direction. Contrariwise, are we to say
that Innocent IV spoke Staufen language? For his point of view is
the Staufen thesis — and this alone makes any assumption in this
direction just as much inconceivable as in the case of Accursius. Or
are we to say that the *Weistum* merely is an isolated German expression to which no importance should be attached? This indeed would
be a very easy way out of all difficulties, but can obviously not be
adopted. But how are we to deal with the problem? There was no
imperial coronation since November 1220 — and hence all three statements were beyond a shadow of doubt made after this event, even
if we had not perfectly clear dates for the *Weistum* and Innocent IV's
commentary, and Accursius too cannot possibly have written the
gloss before this event, and so neither of the three statements could
be referred to some innovation in the coronation ceremonies, quite
apart from the fact that no new coronation ordo was produced in
the meantime.

It can readily be appreciated that if any satisfactory answer to
these questions can be given, some attempt must be made to elucidate
the meaning of Roman emperorship, for, assuredly, the notion is crucial in this context: what it stood for, and above all, what the imperial coronation was said to express. In other words, the problems
posed by these three statements make it imperative that the thesis
of Roman emperorship be more closely studied. It is obvious that
— as so often it is the case with important medieval statements —
their authors looked at their own contemporary reality, knowledge
of which was taken for granted, but which we so many centuries afterwards lack. It is perhaps not without significance that Innocent IV
made his important statement in a commentary on *Venerabilem*. This
decretal of Innocent III was considered in the thirteenth century to
declare the thesis of Roman emperorship classically: herein was expressed this theme in its most mature form and quite particularly in the
relation of the kind of kingship which was absorbed by Roman
emperorship. It would therefore seem advisable to re-open a number
of those problems of Innocent III which are directly connected with
the present analysis.

Having decided for Otto of Brunswick Innocent III coined the
term which henceforth becomes with him the official title of the

imperial candidate: *Rex in imperatorem Romanorum electus* (7). Every title is to a certain extent a short-hand device for expressing an underlying process of thought and may indeed even be somewhat misleading. Innocent III himself expanded the title (8) when on the occasion of explaining the function of the princes he said that they have « jus et potestatem *eligendi regem in imperatorem postmodum promovendum* ». It seems clear enough from this expansion that the election refers exclusively to kingship and that the « promotion » to emperorship is an act separate from, and yet connected with, the election. This is, furthermore, borne out by his immediately following statement that

> jus et auctoritas examinandi personam *electam* in regem et *promovendam* ad imperium ad nos spectat.

We keep therefore in mind that royal election and imperial promotion are two separate and independent, though closely connected, acts. The principles and criteria referring to the royal election are different from those which apply to the making of an emperor. Each has its own juristic complexion. The princes elect a king who is later — *postmodum* — to be advanced (promovendus) to emperorship by the only organ that is authorized to do so, the pope, « ad quem *negotium imperii* non est dubium pertinere » (9). Further, the royal election gives no title-deed nor a *jus ad rem* to emperorship, as again the same Innocent III makes abundantly clear when he says that the right of examining the elected king as to his suitability — intellectual, religious, ecclesiastical, governmental — belongs to him alone and therefore also the right of rejecting the applicant to emperorship. All of this has, according to Innocent III, applicability to the king to be promoted to emperorship, and not to any other king. Indeed, as every possession of rulership was the effluence of the divine good will, was a divine good deed, a *beneficium divinum*, so was emperorship, only in a more concrete and accentuated form (10).

---

(7) From *RNI.* 32 onwards.

(8) *RNI.* 62 = X:I.6.34.

(9) *RNI.* 33. Though Innocent himself refers to an *electio imperatoris* (e. g., *RNI.* 29, 30, 55), this should be read in the light of the considerations infra at n. 27.

(10) Cf. Innocent's use of *beneficia Romanae ecclesiae* in regard to Otto's kingship, cf. *RNI.* 107 to Otto: « Serenitatem tuam in Domino commendamus, quod *ingratitudinis* vitium fugiens et ecclesiae Romanae *beneficia* recognoscens nobis post

Nowhere, however, did Innocent III say explicitly that he claimed the right to examine the royal election itself([11]), but only the person elected. And yet, the exercise of his examining rights necessarily reflected back to the royal election. For the « promoted » candidate remained king and the « promotion » therefore affected kingship as such. By declaring that the king was to be promoted, the pope necessarily gave his approval to the result of the election, and this is exactly what Innocent III said when he declared that([12])

> te (Ottonem) *in regem recipimus* et *regalem* tibi praecipimus de cetero *reverentiam*

Precisely because the king had to undergo the papal examination, the papal « promotion » amounted to a confirmation of the election itself, as indeed contemporary opinion viewed it([13]), and as the pope himself also made clear by telling the German princes that([14])

> *is* sit a vobis *assumendus in regem*, quem nos in imperatorem possumus et debeamus merito coronare.

The implication was clearly that if a candidate was reproved, he was not to be legitimate king, however valid the election itself may have been. The reverse is also true: the deposition of an emperor by the pope deprived him not only of his emperorship, but of his kingship as well.

Deum profectum *suae promotionis ascribit* ». The same line of gratitude for *beneficia* already in *RNI*. 32. The idea itself came from Gelasius I, cf. W. ULLMANN, *Papal Government*, p. 22 f.

([11]) Though his examination of the *studia eligentium* and their *zelus, dignitas et numerus*, might be said to contain an implicit claim to this, nevertheless it is the subsequent promotion by the pope which explains his regard for the *studia eligentium* etc.

([12]) *RNI*. 32; repeated in *RNI*. 33 ff.

([13]) Cf. *RNI*. 5 (John of England to the pope): « Favore velitis apostolico consentire et regnum sibi Alemanniae auctoritate vestrae munimine confirmare, electionem ipsius (Otto) et coronationem approbantes »; *RNI*. 6 (John Rusca of Milan to the pope): « Pro eiusdem (Otto) consecratione, coronatione ac electione confirmanda »; *RNI*. 8 (Count of Daxbourg): « Rogamus, ut ... electionem domni nostri regis Ottonis confirmare... dignemini ». Cf. also the pope himself, *RNI*. 11.

([14]) *RNI*. 21.

Il

Two questions present themselves. First, is the procedure envisaged by Innocent III modelled on other similar procedures? Second, and perhaps more important, over whom was the *Rex in imperatorem Romanorum electus* set up as a king? Is it not rather strange that Innocent III, with his inimitable command of language and mastery of technical detail, never once referred to the king as *Rex Romanorum*, the very appellation by which he was commonly known?

Let us first deal with the possible model which Innocent may have applied. I believe the royal election procedure and the making of a king might well have served him as a pattern for his creation of an emperor, that, in other words, Innocent III's procedure was a continuation of the royal election procedure, with suitable adjustments. It is now generally agreed that — at least in theory — no finality was attached to the election of a king: what the election signified was the designation of a person held suitable for the kingly office (15). We should keep in mind that the royal office itself was not in the gift of the electors; that they could not modify or enlarge or in any way touch the office itself; that the office of the king existed before the particular vacancy and was to exist after the elected candidate had once again vacated it: what the electors did was to name a — to them — suitable office holder. Moreover, the royal office was in the widest possible sense an ecclesiastical office and above all it was on office that was conceded (or given) by divinity to the king. The electors simply designated or named a particular person to fill the vacant office. The election itself did not confer powers and did not therefore make the elected a king. The election was a means to an end: it was the vehicle through which the candidate was brought to the point of receiving his office — at the royal coronation. The election was merely designatory and preparatory to the formal and final conferment of the office. The usual expression employed in the sources was, significantly enough, that a candidate was elected *into* kingship — « electus est *in regem* » — a linguistic usage which is an indication of the principles obtaining in royal elections.

---

(15) Cf. W. ULLMANN, *Principles of Government and Politics,* pp. 145 t., with further literature, especially H. Mitteis.

Clearly, the designation of a candidate for kingship was nothing but a nomination by the electing body. And here we have the explicit statement in the very source on which we have so far drawn. On the one hand, it was the pope, Innocent III, who reproached the Germans for having *nominated* two kings([16]); on the other hand, it was Otto who wrote to the pope that certain princes had the temerity to have *nominated* as a king the excommunicated Duke Philip([17]). The procedure commonly known as election was in reality a presentation or a nomination of a candidate held suitable by the electors for filling the vacant office.

When we now turn to the royal coronation itself we shall — perhaps to our surprise — find a statement in a prayer-text which entirely bears out the thesis here propounded. We will of course keep in mind that the royal coronation was, in its structure, as well as in its purpose, a purely ecclesiastical matter. In the consecratory prayer-text the metropolitan — or other coronator — says of the elected king: « quem in regem *eligimus* » ([18]). Now a spectator who was unfamiliar with the acts preceding the coronation itself might be forgiven for thinking that the real election was carried out by the officiating hierarchy, notably the episcopacy on whose behalf the metropolitan spoke the text. Nowhere do we read of any antecedent electing procedure, and yet that an « election » had in actual fact taken place, is too obvious to need any comment. The reason why this far too little observed text was used seems clear: the royal coronation had constitutive effects. The acts which validly and finally made the king, which gave him the office, were those carried out by the officiating hierarchy. The nomination or presentation or designation of the king was followed by the hierarchy now finally electing the king within the framework of the highly elaborate liturgical ceremonial; further, we should note, the metropolitan speaks

---

([16]) *RNI*. 2: ... *duos* vobis *in reges* praesumpseritis *nominare* »; cf. also *RNI*. 1: « Quidam ... Phillippum ... *nominarunt* in regem ... *nominatione* Octonis ».

([17]) *RNI*. 3: « ... qui iamdictum Philippum ducem Sueviae in excommunicatione vestra detentum *in regem nominare* ... presumpserunt.

([18]) For some observations on this point cf. W. Ullmann in his contribution to the forthcoming *Festschrift f.P.E. Schramm*: « Der Souveränitätsgedanke in den mittelalterlichen Krönungsordines ». The text referred to was used throughout the medieval period since the coronation of 877. Commenting on this text C. Erdmann, *Forschungen*, p. 61, said: « die etwa vorausgehende weltlichen Wahlakte haben nur den Wert einer Designation ».

in the present, and not in the past, tense. And it was the anointing episcopally conferred on the king which in visible form gave the (divine) office of kingship — he was now fully « Rex *Dei gratia* ». It is therefore not without reason that in some of the best accounts concerning a royal coronation, we find the elected king before the coronation, in fact before the unction, referred to as a mere *designatus dux* or *designatus princeps*, a nomenclature which is taken from the coronation ordines themselves (19). It is furthermore of note that some royal coronation ordines, in order to bring out as clearly as possibly the role played by the « election » preceding the coronation, contain in the *Recognitio* the statement: « Fiat, fiat et vivat rex, *nomen dicti regis gratissime nominantes* » (20).

The essential point therefore is that the creative acts are the election by the hierarchy, the unction and lastly the coronation itself. Before this moment the king is merely a candidate or an aspirant, someone who is presented or nominated or designated for the office; but what matters is the office, and this the king receives from the hands of the coronator speaking and acting on behalf of the ecclesiastical hierarchy. The incontrovertible proof for this is that the king did not count his regnal years before the coronation: it was this which made him king, and for this reason he could not very well date any official documents before the event. The reckoning of regnal years seems to be first-class evidence for the constitutive, creative, effect of the (ecclesiastical) coronation.

One more observation seems called for. The elevation of a prince or duke into kingship may well be called a promotion: after all, he advances to the highest possible point within a kingdom and is in receipt of a divinely created and conferred office. It is not usually

---

(19) Cf. the evidence cited in art. cit. (Note 18). Most tentatively it might possibly be suggested that he problems raised in *RNI.* 10 by the signatures and the appended « elegi et ss. » on the one hand, the « consensi et ss. » of the Count of Huik on the other hand, may conceivably reflect the part played by the ecclesiastical contingent during the coronation of Otto (« quem in regem eligimus ») and by the consent given at the coronation by the « plebs » (the so-called *Recognitio*) *represented* by the Count. It is no doubt interesting to see that the *Liber Regalis* in England had in the allocution of the coronator to the *plebs* this: « inquirens voluntatem et consensum de dicti principis consecratione », see *Liber regie capelle,* p. 80-81, in other words, the hierarchy has the right to elect, the laity merely to give its consent.

(20) Cf. *Lib. Reg.,* p. 81. Surely, the verb one would have expected, is: *vocantes,* and the employment of *nominantes* appears rather significant.

recognized that this advancement or promotion was in fact called a *promotio*. There is easily available evidence for this. Alexander III writing to the archbishop of York refers to the custom that the kings of England were anointed and crowned by the archbishop of Canterbury: the beginning of the reign is here called by the pope the « principium suae *promotionis* » ([21]). That the acquisition was in fact taken to mean a *promotio*, emerges, moreover, from a twelfth-century coronation ordo, the so-called Ordo of Apamea. Here we read that the German king — the *rex teutonicus* — after having received his royal unction (and coronation) sends legates and letters to the pope informing the latter of his promotion, that is, to kingship ([22]). There is no need to point out that the terms *promotio* or *promovere* had belonged to the ecclesiastical vocabulary for a long time ([23]).

If we take all these elements together it will not be too difficult to see that the procedure envisaged by Innocent III continues, suitably adjusted, the procedure and machinery observable in royal creations. In other words, the procedure of creating an emperor of the Romans is an extension and continuation of that machinery pertaining to royal matters. Naturally, the procedure is considerably adjusted, but in its essential structural elements it shows great kinship with a royal creation. That instead of a metropolitan speaking and acting on behalf the ecclesiastical hierarchy there is now only the pope, is understandable, if the presuppositions of the medieval-imperial idea and institution are fully taken into account. Further, although the pope does not touch the royal election as such, his examination of Otto IV and « reception » of him as king, reflected back to the election in so far as it is now the pope — and not the electors — who, by virtue of his rights to promotion, replaces the (former) electors' nomination by his own nomination of Otto as king ([24]):

> Nos utique non Philippum, sed Ottonem reputamus et *nominamus regem* justitia exigente.

([21]) See *Thomas Becket*, V. 323.

([22]) « ... debet mittere honoratos nuntios ... ad Romanum pontificem significans ei ... promotionem suam et quod velit sibi omnimodis obedire tamquam patri », Ordo XV.1,in R. Elze, *Die Ordines*, p. 48. On this Ordo see also E. Eichmann, *Die Kaiserkrönung*, I.231-3.

([23]) Cf., e.g., Gregory VII's *Reg.*, ed. E. Caspar, Index *s.v.*

([24]) *RNI.* 62 = X:I.6.34.

In ther words, the pope takes the place of the former electoral body that had nominated a candidate. By recognizing a king as suitable for emperorship, the pope's decision necessarily casts its shadow back to the royal creation: the future emperor is, after all, still king of Germany, and the pope cannot leave any doubt on the position of the « king » who is reproved (25). The pope's nomination of the king — always under the presupposition of promoting him to emperorship — makes illegal the position of the « king » who was not found suitable (26).

The peculiarity of this procedural phenomenon may be expressed thus. We recall that one of the creative acts in a royal creation was the election by the hierarchy within the coronation ritual; this element upon closer analysis presents itself as an approval given by the ecclesiastical contingent to the pre-coronation election of the prince. In the case of an imperial creation this element is replaced by the pope's examination of the king's suitability, and having passed this examination, the king is then nominated — with the important observation that there is no place for the pope's decision in the imperial coronation ritual. In other words, what formed an essential part in the royal coronation service — the hierarchical election of the king — has been omitted in the imperial coronation service and made part of the extra-liturgical, purely juristic pre-coronation procedure. The decision of the pope of accepting the imperial candidate, called *nominatio,* therefore combines in the imperial sphere two elements observable in the royal sphere: the pre-coronation election by the princes and the coronation election by the hierarchy (27). The *nominare* of the pope in reality replaces the efficacy of the royal election and coronation for the purpose of an imperial coronation (28). Otto's own intitulation (29) as « King by the grace of God and by that of the pope » would seem to reflect quite accurately what the pope himself considered correct;

---

(25) Ibid.: « in reprobatione prefati Philipi ».

(26) Cf. in this context *RNI.* 44: Philip « nondum legitime dignitatem regiam est adeptus ».

(27) It should be pointed out that the royal prayer text *Omnipotens, sempiternus Deus, creator omnium,* which contained the ecclesiastical « election » of the king, was in no imperial Ordo. Also, for obvious reasons no imperial coronation Ordo contained anything approaching a Recognition.

(28) « districte precipias, ut eum, cuius nominatio per sedem apostolicam fuerit approbata, in regem recipiant », *RNI.* 1. Cp. with. this *RNI.* 55.

(29) *RNI.* 81, 106, 160, 187.

the same observation applies to the theme expressed by both Innocent and Otto that the *promotio* concerned his kingship (30) all this long before the imperial coronation of Otto, that is, long before he was actually promoted to emperorship. Because the king approved by the pope was also a German king, the decision of his approval necessarily affected the legitimacy of the king as a German king. If there had been no emperorship beyond kingship, there would have been no possibility for Innocent III to intervene in purely German governmental matters.

There is a further parallelism between royal and imperial coronation procedures. We know that the act which makes the *designatus princeps* (31) a king was the unction. When we now look at the imperial coronation ordo which was made, if not by Innocent III, at all events in his pontificate, we shall find that a similar arrangement obtained here too, though with a highly significant modification (which, as so much else in these matters, has not yet been recognized). The *Rex in imperatorem Romanorum electus* is called throughout the coronation service the *rex* until (not, as in the royal coronation, the unction, but) the kiss of the pope. It is the *rex* who is anointed by the cardinalbishop of Ostia at the side-altar of St Maurice, and after this has been performed, the anointed *rex* ascends the high altar of St Peter's, where the pope has remained, waiting for him to give him the kiss. Only this action changes the *rex* into the *imperator* (32). The conspicuously emerging and essential point is that in this imperial coronation ordo it was not the sacramental act of unction, but the pope's kiss which effected the metamorphosis of the king into an emperor, the intention of the redactor clearly being that the constitutive part played by the pope be still more stressed (33). We should also

---

(30) *RNI.* 53, 98, 105, 107, 160, etc.

(31) Cf., e.g., Mainz I and II, in P.E. SCHAMM, *Die Krönung,* p. 311 no. 6 and p. 326 no. 6.

(32) See Ordo XVIII, 19-20 (formerly D) in R. Elze's edit., pp. 76-7. The same in Ordo XVII. 18 and 19, pp. 65-66. It is instructive to see that in Ordo XIV (formerly C) the *Electus* becomes emperor only after having received the crown and before the conferment of the sceptre, see Ordo XIV. 41, p. 44.

(33) It should be pointed out that the singular role allocated to the pope in the creation of the emperor was begun in Ordo XIV (formerly C) which separated the unction (performed by the Hostiensis) from the actual coronation (performed by the pope); cf. on this also W. ULLMANN, *Papal Government,* pp. 253 ff. This is now in Ordo XVIII taken another step forward.

bear in mind that the *osculum pontificis* had in no earlier imperial coronation ordo formed a place after the unction: this novelty only heightens the significance of the feature which will remain with all subsequent ordines. But what is more immediately important is the appellation of the imperial candidate. Can it be merely coincidence that whilst in the chronologically preceding Ordo XIV (formerly C) we have the significant *electus imperator* (who throughout the ordo is referred to as *Electus*) whilst in our Innocentian Ordo XVIII there is not only a conspicuous absence of any *Electus* — only in the very beginning of the Ordo the rubric has: « Cum rex im imperatorem Romanorum electus pervenerit ad portam Collinam » — but there is a studied reference to the *rex* throughout the Ordo's rubrics. To brush aside these differences by saying that they merely concern terminological nuances, would be an easy way out of facing the reality as it was obviously seen by the redactors of the ordines. The implication of these noted differences is that prior to the Innocentian period the royal election (taken in the widest sense) had indeed the significance of an imperial election — a recognition which, once and for all, should do away with a « Staufen Kaiserwahl » thesis — whilst according to Innocent's ordo the « election » was the pope's nomination of the imperial candidate who had thereby become the one legitimate king. The coronation ceremonial rather faithfully reflects the considerations which prompted Innocent's nomination of a king.

III

Let us now turn to the second question which we have asked. It is not usually recognized that Innocent III nowhere speaks of a *Rex Romanorum*: in fact, I have not seen in the vast literary output on Innocent III's imperial thesis any reference to this feature. The term *Rex Romanorum* does not exist in his vocabulary. That the concept was nevertheless familiar to him, cannot possibly be doubted, because both Philip and Otto styled themselves as such in their respective communications to the pope immediately after their coronations (34). In no document did Otto or Philip call themselves in any

---

(34) Cf. *RNI.* 3 to Innocent III, and also Otto whilst still at Aachen in July 1198, in other words, immediately after his coronation: E. WINKELMANN, *Philipp,* p. 545, no. II, also p. 549 no. VIII (Philip); further *RNI.* 12,17; the heading

other way but *Rex Romanorum*, and yet the pope himself used no other appellation than *Rex in imperatorem Romanorum electus*. If I am not mistaken, the *rex* (reproved or approved by Innocent) is not qualified at all in any of the pope's official communications. Whose *rex* was he? Over whom was regal power recognized (or rejected)? It is remarkable that in his first letter on the disputed election (*RNI.*1) there is no mention of the fact over whom Philip and Otto were « nominated » kings by their followers; and not even in the pope's account of Otto's Aachen coronation is there any hint what sort of *regnum* the king had received by the crown (35). Often enough did the pope write to the *principibus Alemanniae*; often enough did he refer to *Teutonia* (36) to the *regnum Teutonicum* (37), to the *partes Germaniarum* (38), he is careful enough to speak, as one might well expect, punctiliously of the *Rex Francorum*, the *Regnum Franciae*, the *Rex Angliae*, the *Rex Danorum*, etc., but in the case of Otto (or for that matter of Philipp) we are left in the dark. Whose king, then, was Otto? Surely, the necessity to say over whom a king is set, had been long enough recognized, including Innocent III himself (39), who, we may be quite certain, was perfectly aware of the need to express rulership in appropriate language. Should it be coincidence that whilst in his very first communication to the pope Otto calls himself *Rex Romanorum*, the heading of this letter in the *RNI.* is: « Litterae *Regis* Ottonis » (40), though Otto was as yet far from being approved; and Philip far from being reproved, whose first letter has the simple heading: « Litterae Philippi » (41)? On the other hand, there are, as far as I can see, some small indications of the way in which Innocent's mind might have been moving. In *RNI.* 2 he says

---

of *RNI.* 77 on the one hand and the intitulation of Otto's letter in this entry is also revealing.

(35) « regni coronam imposuit »; for Philip: « ... regalem imposuit eidem coronam ».

(36) *RNI.* 34, 36, etc.

(37) *RNI.* 113.

(38) *RNI.* 48, etc.

(39) Evidenced by Innocent himself, cf. *Reg.* VIII.1.

(40) *RNI.* 3, which is the same heading as in *RNI.* 53 of August 1201. As *RNI.* 3 was entered in this Register in August-September 1199, the identity of heading is revealing for Innocent's mind.

(41) *RNI,* 12, in which Philip used exactly the same designation as Otto did: *Rex Romanorum et semper augustus*.

to the princes of Germany « ut duos *vobis* in *reges* praesumpseritis nominare » which might indicate a kingship to be exercised over Germany only, whilst in *RNI*. 15 he summarizes the relevant point of the Speyer protest in a most significant way (which has again not yet been noticed). The protest had: « Illustrem dominum nostrum Philippum in *imperaturam Romani solii* rite et solempniter elegimus », whilst Innocent summarizes this telling point thus: « Multi *principes Alemanniae* nobilem virum Philippum, ducem Sueviae, *sibi prefecerant* per electionem *in regem*. « This summary is all the more significant as the other points of the Speyer declaration are rendered concisely and sometimes in the original words (42). What strikes the attentive readers is that Otto, despite all his ingratiating attempts, not once used the appellation with which the pope had distinguished him (43). He was as consistent with his *Rex Romanorum* as was the pope with his own formula. Although it would be too much to maintain that Otto's implicit rejection of the Innocentian title revealed his eventual intentions, the point is nevertheless worth some reflexion. We are left with the rather clear assumption that Innocent III wished to avoid any precise appellation of the approved king. But when we ask ourselves why he omitted this, we must rely on inferences.

It is maintained that Innocent's model for the title was a communication of Gregory VIII sent « Heinrico (VI) illustri regi, electo Romanorum imperatori » (44). But serious reservations militate against accepting this as a model for Innocent III. First, the title is not the same: the *electus imperator* is hardly identical with an *electus in imperatorem*. A possible model for the title might in actual fact have been its employment in the imperial coronation ordo, i.e. Ordo XIV (formerly C) (45). But apart from this, in the letter which Gregory VIII

---

(42) In *RNI*. 10, Otto's electors told the pope that « dictum dominum Ottonem... ad Romani regni fastigium juste et rationaliter elegimus ». Of some interest appears to be the contradistinction between the *regnum teutonicum* and the *imperium* in *RNI*. 29: clearly the *imperium* is the wider concept. The immediately preceding « quantum in eo est » must be referred to Philip.

(43) In actual fact, and as far as I am able to establish, it was Frederick II who for a short time accepted this designation, cf. *M.G.H. Const.*, II.545, no. 414; 546, no. 415.

(44) *M.G.H. Const.*, I.586, no. 411. First pointed out by H. Bloch, p. 18 n. 1.

(45) See Elze, *Die Ordines*, Ordo XIV.1-2, p. 36.

wrote to Henry's father, Frederick I, he used an address which was most unusual ([46]):

> Gregorius, servus servorum Dei ... Friderico illustri *regi, Romanorum imperatori.*

Diplomatically speaking the address was faulty, because no emperor was ever addressed by a pope as *illustris rex* in addition to his emperorship ([47]). The irregularities which attach themselves to these two letters of Gregory VIII, make it very difficult to accept them in their transmitted form, and until further diplomatic examination has been undertaken on these two pieces, judgment on their probative value must be suspended ([48]). To use a double title in an address to a secular ruler was in any case unusual, and to have done so in the case of *rex* and *imperator* appears to provoke some misgivings ([49]).

But whatever the model for Innocent may have been, the real crux of the problem is why he so ostentatiously avoided the title *Rex Romanorum*. It is this title which demands attentation rather than the title used by Innocent. Hitherto examination and research have been exclusively attracted by Innocent's title, whilst the really interesting and vital point is why he used the new title or, which is the same question, why he refrained from using the traditional appellation. The title *Rex Romanorum* was not a technical or juristic one. True, it had been used virtually uninterruptedly since the mid-eleventh century by the Germans ([50]) and certainly in the twelfth century also by the papacy. What the title appeared to express was the exercise (or

---

([46]) *M.G.H.*, cit., p. 585, no. 410. I do not know of a diplomatic discussion of these two letters.

([47]) J. HALLER, *Heinrich VI*, p. 449 accepted without any qualms this letter of Gregory VIII, whilst the letter to Henry VI, contained in, and edited from, the same codex, is dismissed by him, because — according to him — it is merely part of a formulary collection, p. 598 n. o at end: « Das Stück ist nur in einer Formelsammlung überliefert »; if this is so, I am unable to understand why the other letter is above all suspicion.

([48]) These irregularites are all the more noteworthy as Gregory VIII was for two decades chancellor of the Roman Church and himself an outstanding canonist; cf. also H. Bresslau, *Urkundenlehre*, pp. 365 ff.

([49]) It is just conceivable that Gregory VIII intended a parallelism between Frederick I as *rex, imperator*, and Henry VI as *rex, imperator electus*, but there still remains the difficulty of explaining the most unusual form of address to an emperor..

([50]) Cf. further *infra* at note 79.

the claim to an exercise) of royal control over the non-German regions, above all, « imperial Italy », that is, *Reichsitalien*, significantly
enough designated from the eleventh century onwards as *nostrum
Italicum regnum* [51]. The title was no doubt intended to present
the German king as possessing regal rights over « our Italian kingdom », and in so far was also intended as a step preliminary to the
full imperial position: it was to give some shadow of a title-deed
to the imperial crown and was apt to reduce the significance of the
imperial coronation by the pope. As regards Staufens and Welfs there
was no fundamental difference at all in this respect — any possible
difference concerned the geographical extent of *Reichsitalien*.

That the significance of the omission of any reference to a *Rex
Romanorum* before the approval of the pope was given — or for that
matter, after Otto's approval by the pope — escaped contemporaries,
may be understandable. It is, however, very interesting that one of
Innocent's own notaries and a counsellor of the legation to Germany
missed the point, as is evidenced in the report of Master Philip to the
pope which begins thus [52]:

> Post pronuntiationem excellentissimi domni Ottonis Dei
> et vestra gratia illustris *Romanorum regis* semper augusti
> Coloniae in multorum presentia sollempniter celebratam.

It is equally interesting that even later popes failed to realise the
conspicuous omission of any qualification of the king. Thus, on the
next occasion on which the « problem of the empire » arose, i.e. in
Innocent IV's pontificate, we find that this pope obviously wished to
follow the lead given by his namesake earlier [53], but clearly without
seeing the implications meant to employ the formula in the way in
which it may well have appeared to him sensible and natural, but
which nevertheless expanded the original Innocentian formula in

---

[51] See, e. g. Henry IV (anno 1094), *M.G.H. Const.* I. 72, p. 122; Henry V
(anno 1111), ibid., 102, p. 153. Lothar III (anno 1136), ibid., 119, p. 172; Frederick
I (anno 1154), ibid., 150, p. 220; id., (anno 1177), 274, p. 375; Henry VI (anno
1197), 378, p. 527; Otto himself, ibid., II. 32, p. 39. The extent of the *Italicum
regnum* in Otto's pact is identical with that in Henry VI's pact.

[52] *RNI.* 52. The event referred to is 3 July 1201.

[53] Upon inquiry concerning the possible election of Henry VII from Conrad
of Metz, Honorius III in 1220 replied: « Nihil ad nos de electione Romanorum
regis pertinet », *M.G.H. Epp. sel. s. XIII*, I.127.

precisely the way in which it was not intended to be expanded. In his instructions to the electors Innocent IV said:

> Universitatem vestram monemus ... mandantes ... quatenus de gratia spiritus sancti confisi eundem lantgravium in *Romanorum regem*, in imperatorem Romanorum postmodum promovendum, cum prefatum imperium ad praesens vacare noscatur, unanimiter absque dilationis dispendio *eligatis* (54).

Obviously also believing to copy the crucial words from *Venerabilem*, Clement IV in his protest against Conradin sets forth the theme of the electoral princes and says:

> Porro non sine magna cordis amaritudine nuper accepimus, quod nonnulli ex hiis principibus et prelatis, ad quos jus pertinet *eligendi Romanorum regem*, in imperatorem postmodum promovendum... (55).

These examples could of course be easily multiplied (56). The point to be made it that the careful diction of Innocent III — who studiously abstained from saying into what sort of king the German electors had elected — was not heeded by his successors who read into his formula what he did not wish to be read into it (57). That there

---

(54) *M.G.H. Const.*, II.454, no. 346; in no. 347, p. 455 the same formula. Henry Raspe always called by Innocent IV *Rex Romanorum*, cf. no. 352, etc. Gregory X writes to Rudolf of Habsburg in January 1274: « Radolpho *in regem Romanorum electo* (ibid., III, no. 15; no. 35, p. 33), whilst on 26 September 1274 he writes to Rudolf: « ... te *regem Romanorum* de ipsorum concilio *nominamus* (ibid., p. 56, no. 66), and hence from now on Rudolf is addressed: « Gregorius ... R. regi Romanorum illustri » (p. 64, no. 77). Boniface VIII, after setting forth the translation theory and the thesis of the 7 electoral princes, says: « ut possint eligere *regem Romanorum*, qui est promovendus in imperatorem et monarcham regum omnium et principum terrenorum », ibid., IV.139, no. 173.

(55) *M.G.H. Const.*, II. 533, no. 406.

(56) Although the *RNI*. was carefully studied and perused in the papal chancery throughout the 13th century, it is nevertheless interesting to see that those who used it, also overlooked the Innocentian omission. The marginal notes are witnesses: they often enough refer to the *Rex Romanorum* in places in which Innocent III had taken so much trouble to avoid it, cf. e.g., *RNI*. 51, 74,189. About *RNI*. 74 infra at note 86.

(57) How irritated in fact he was by the title *Rex Romanorum*, emerges from his reply to a letter of Philip II: the withering contempt strikes the reader: « Per tuas nobis litteras intimasti, quod de Philippo quondam duce Sueviae, quem tu *regem Romanorum appellas*, conqueri poteras » (*RNI*. 165).

is nowhere any explicit statement of Innocent III over whom Otto (or Philip) was set as a king, cannot be taken as a mere whim or simple finesse, if due consideration is given to the fact that from the moment Frederick II was crowned at Palermo king of Sicily on 17 May 1198, his mother omitted in her official documents the hitherto customary intitulation (to which she herself had adhered previously) of Frederick as *Rex Romanorum*: from now on he was merely the *Rex Siciliae* ([58]). All this should be nothing but coincidence, chance, a mere title question?

Should it be mere coincidence — considering the avoidance by Innocent III of the title *Rex Romanorum* — that Henry VI's plan of 1196 came to naught? There is no doubt about the veracity and familiarity of the author of the Marbach Annals: they report that after the Diet of Würzburg in June 1196, Henry VI sent legates to Celestine III:

> Interim missis legatis suis, imperator cepit cum apostol- ico de concordia agere volens quod filium suum (Frederick II) baptizaret — nondum enim baptizatus erat — et quod *in regem ungeret* ([59]).

What this report makes clear it that Henry VI asked Celestine III to crown his son Frederick *Rex Romanorum*. It is not plausible that Henry's opposition to Cologne should have been his sole driving motive ([60]) for his petition to the pope. Moreover, Henry was planning a crusade ([61]) and his intention of having crowned Frederick as *Rex*

([58]) E. Winkelmann has pointed this out, *Philipp*, p. 120 — cf. his Excursus III with the Regesta of Constance — but did not link this up with the imperial question. See further Huillard-Bréholles, *Hist. Dipl. Frederici Secundi* I.10 f., 12 ff., 30, etc.; cf. Constance's intitulation before his coronation, e.g., pp. 5-6, and esp. p. 8, ordering the archbishop of Messina to attend to the coronation of « Frederici illustris *Romanorum et Siciliae regis* » (30 April 1198). Innocent of course called him merely « Rex Siciliae », cf. *RNI.* 15, 33, etc. That Constance acted in agreement with Innocent and that she had little liking for the Germans — a not insignificant point in this context — is too well known to need any comment.

([59]) *Ann. Marbacenses*, p. 68. Further M. Krammer, *Reichsgedanke*, pp. 9 ff.; J. Haller, *Heinrich VI*, at pp. 598 ff.; E. Perels, *Der Erbreichsplan*, pp. 5 ff.; J. Haller, *Das Papsttum*, II-2, pp. 318 ff.; Hampe-Baethgen, *Kaisergeschichte*, p. 229 n. 1; P. Zerbi, *Papato*, pp. 121 ff. Quite unsatisfactory, and in fact revealing a quite remarkable degree of lack of historical perception, is D. Waley, *Papal State*, p. 27.

([60]) So Haller, *Heinrich VI.*, pp. 634 ff.

([61]) Cf. also *Ann. Marb.*, p. 68: « Quod si fecisset, crucem ab eo aperte, ut putabatur, accepisset ».

VI

Romanorum would seem to be connected with this crusading plan, even if only to secure what alone mattered to him as a true Staufen, the preservation of *royal* succession which meant the exercise of royal rights over Italian regions which were, to put it no higher, in dispute between papal and imperial (royal) governments. That the Sicilian question provided an additional complication, seems clear. But we believe that it was primarily the question of royal, that is, of actual physical control over territories in Italy which were to be firmly settled — and this could be achieved by no better means than (1) by having recognized the position of the *Rex Romanorum* and (2) by the one who was directly involved, the pope. When we now take into account that it was barely four years earlier that Cencius had in his *Liber Censuum* marshalled all the lands in Italy which were alleged to be under direct papal jurisdiction (62) and which included whole duchies and the marches that were, certainly in Henry VI's time, under German control and jurisdiction, we begin to come nearer the core of the matter. In actual fact, the German control reached right down to the gates of Rome (63), in other words, into regions which at all events were possessed by the Roman Church on the basis of genuine and less genuine documents embodying territorial donations. That the Donation of Constantine with its deliberately vague references to Italy was ever present in curial memory and documentation, can hardly be a matter of surprise. It is these regions which were to constitute the policy of recuperations by the papacy, and it was precisely in these regions that German control was *de facto* exercised (64), a control that was to be legalised and to be made one *de jure* by the papal approbation of Henry's plan: no doubt could then

---

(62) FABRE-DUCHESNE, *Liber Censuum*, I.363 ff.; also FICKER, *Forsch. Reichs-Rechtsgesch. Ital.*, II.331-2.

(63) Cf. Innocent III in *RNI.* 29, Philip as « persecutor of the Church », because « olim enim patrimonium ecclesiae *sibi usurpare* contendens ducem Tusciae et Campaniae se scribebat (for this inaccuracy see HALLER, *Heinrich VI.*, p. 615 n. 3), asserens quod *usque ad portas urbis* acceperat potestatem et etiam *illa pars Urbis*, quae *trans Tiberim* dicitur, *eius* erat *jurisdictioni* concessa ».

(64) Cf. also HAMPE-BAETHGEN, *Kaisergeschichte*, p. 229; for the constitutional function of the German plenipotentiaries in Italy (who had charge of *negotia totius regni Italici*) and the special legates in Italy see the still fundamental exposition in J. FICKER, *Forsch.*, II.170 ff. We should keep in mind that a proper constitutional position of these officers can hardly be discerned before Frederick I (*ibid.*, pp. 133-5), but with his reign the full implementation of royal exercise in Italy was set on foot.

exist that — at any rate in these territories administered in 1196 by German officers — the exercise of royal control was lawful and legitimate. If one compares the entry in the *Liber Censuum* — which must be classed as claims at the time — and the actuality of the situation when German control was exercised over large parts of precisely those territories claimed as belonging to the Roman Church, the question is indeed justified: could any pope have agreed to a perpetuation of this actual state of affairs? And he would have agreed to it, if he himself had made the young Frederick *Rex Romanorum*, because there could then not have been a more convincing acknowledgement of royal powers in Italy exercised by the *Rex Romanorum*.

Our explanation of why the steps taken by Henry VI to have his son crowned *Rex Romanorum* by the pope, proved abortive, receives further confirmation from the fact that it was the same pope Celestine III who had refused Henry's request, who initiated the policy of papal recuperations, precisely that policy which Innocent III so masterfully was to execute[65]. What we are here presented with is a long-term policy aiming at substituting papal officers, papal administration, papal sovereignty for the hitherto existing German officers, German administration and German sovereignty. The instruments by which the papacy hoped to dislodge German control — epitomized as this was in the function of the *Rex Romanorum* — in the territories to be recovered, were the donations. The opportunity was provided by the double election in Germany. And not without surprise we hear the old battle cry of the *libertas ecclesiae* raised in precisely the context of the recuperation[66]. Differently expressed: the donations and

---

[65] This was again first pointed out by FICKER, II. 370. Further lit. in HAMPE-BAETHGEN, p. 239 n. 1. See P. ZERBI, *Papato*, pp. 135 ff. on the possible moving spirit behind Celestine III's steps. Insufficiently equipped as he is, D. WALEY, *Papal State*, p. 31 n. 1, rejects any « long-formed plan ».

[66] Of all the territories claimed — the whole of Tuscany, the duchy of Spoleto, the march of Ancona, Romagna as far north as Bologna and Ravenna, even leaving aside Lombardy (WINKELMANN, *Philipp,* p. 341), all of which was administered by German officers — only a stretch of Tuscany and the Mathildine inheritance were based on genuine titles, FICKER, *Forsch.*, II.326-7, 330-69. Quite insufficient in regard to the legality of these claims is D. WALEY. About the new battle-cry cf. Innocent III in his *Reg.*, I.27 to the archbishop of Ravenna and his suffragans: « Nusquam melius *ecclesiasticae* consulitur *'ibertati* quam ubi ecclesia Romana tam in temporalibus quam in spiritualibus plenam obtinet potestatem ... quanto amplius in eius (scil. Romanae ecclesiae) injuriam et ecclesiarum omnium praejudicium redundaret, si ecclesias in *eius patrimonio* constitutas non servaret

diverse privileges of the Roman Church were to serve as title-deeds for the Roman Church and with their help the title-deed of the Germans (contained in the *Rex Romanorum*) was to be supplanted. For the popes the title-deed to rule in the territories to be recuperated was based upon documents — whether genuine or spurious makes no difference in this context — and for the Germans the title-deed to rule was based on their Roman kingship. The refusal on the part of Celestine III to accede to Henry's request for a coronation of the *Rex Romanorum* and the refusal on the part of Innocent III to use the title of *Rex Romanorum*, rest upon exactly the same premisses and aims: to deny the claim to the control of Italian territories, a claim inherent in the *Rex Romanorum* [67].

It was very likely in pursuit of reducing German power in Italy that Innocent III used language which has always struck attentive readers of his correspondence [68]. That he speaks rather pointedly of the *Rex Alemannorum* (RNI. 74), a terminology which, if nothing else, is rather unusual at the time, is of less significance than his attempts to extol Italy and her place in the providential plan. In regard to the imperial question itself, he writes, for instance, to the Lombards (RNI. 92) that only he could be accepted as suitable who was in the service of Lombardy and the whole of Italy [69]. Part of the patrimony of St. Peter was Tuscany, which therefore must be

---

in statu debitae libertatis. Cum inter caetera, quae nos et fratres nostros inducunt exarchatum Ravenae, Marchiam et Tusciam ad dominium nostrum, ad quod pertinent, revocemus ... ». The same underlying theme in his Sermo VII, in Migne, *Patr. Lat.*, CCXVII, col. 481-2. For the *naturale dominium* see infra note 75.

[67] Which territories they were, is of no concern in this context, as their extent was to depend on Innocent. If I am not mistaken, J. Ficker, *Forsch.,* II.239, had expressed a very similar thought when he said that one of the intentions of Innocent was « einen in Deutschland anerkannten König, der auf seine Forderungen (in respect of the recuperations) nicht einging, *wenigstens in Italien nicht zur Herrschaft gelangen zu lassen,* dieses unter seiner Leitung zu halten » (italics mine). Although propounding a thesis that is at variance with ours M. Krammer, *Reichsgedanke,* p. 33, expresses the essence of Roman *King*ship well, maintaining its « bodenständige, deutsche Charakter » — despite its name.

[68] Cf. Ficker, *Forsch.,* II. 378-9.

[69] « ... ut persona talis assumeretur ad illud, quae pacem ecclesiae ac imperii affectaret, ut Urbis honores diligeret et servaret *toti Italie et Lombardie* specialiter libertatem » followed by the charge that many emperors had gravely oppressed the Roman Church, « Lombardiam et *universam Italiam* ».

taken from those who had unlawfully occupied it: Tuscany must be restored for the good of Italy (⁷⁰). And again in another letter to the Duchy of Tuscany he extols Italy as the country chosen by divinity to be the seat of supreme royal and sacerdotal power: by divine disposition Italy had merited its supremacy over all provinces and Italy speciality demands his solicitude, Italy,

> in qua Christianae religionis fundamentum existit et per apo-
> stolicae sedis primatum sacerdotii simul et regni praeeminet
> principatu (⁷¹).

On the other hand, there are frequent hits at the Germans, because of their oppression in Italy, because of their defrauding the Italians, because of the intolerable German tyranny, and so forth (⁷²).

How far these adulations of Italy should be taken at their face value, is not for the moment to say. That they were to a considerable extent attuned to the already existing animosities of the Italian popu- lation against the German administrators, cannot be seriously doubt- ed (⁷³). What in brief Innocent III intended was to supplant in the territories claimed, the German duke or count, by a rector of the Church. The scope of the envisaged papal administration was in the essentials not different from that of the German administrators (⁷⁴). And yet, if one tries to probe deeper into the papal policy of recupe-

---

(⁷⁰) *Reg.*, I.88: after striking up in Innocentian conciseness the theme of the vicariate of Christ in the pope he tells the rectors of Tuscany that he intends « ad profectum Italiae perpetuo » to restore to papal dominion the duchy.

(⁷¹) *Reg.*, I.401. Preceding this passage is the exposition of the sun-moon allegory symbolized by the *auctoritas pontificalis* and the *regalis potestas*. He then continues: « Utraque vero potestas sive primatus sedem in *Italia* meruit obti- nere, quae dispositione divina *super universas provincias* obtinuit principatum ... specialiter tamen *Italiae* paterna nos convenit sollicitudine providere, in qua ... » as text. Further examples in FICKER, *Forsch.*, II.379.

(⁷²) FICKER, *Forsch.*, p. 379; cf. also *Reg.*, I.566.

(⁷³) The hatred of the Italians against the Germans was not really national in a modern sense, but can be explained because the latter were the « bosses ». Cf. WINKELMANN, *Philipp*, p. 101: « Dieser Hass wurde ihnen nicht so wohl deshalb zuteil, weil sie Deutsche waren, sondern vielmehr, weil sie die Herrscher waren und vornehmlich weil sie die Herrschaft oft in rücksichtsloser Weise übten ». Hatred against the Germans in the sources — *furor Teutonicus, servitus Teutoni- corum* etc. — see FICKER, *Forsch.*, II.267. Cf. also infra note 92.

(⁷⁴) Although as a governing institution the Roman Church could say of itself, as Innocent III avowed, that « jugum meum suave est et onus meum leve » (*Reg.*, VII.228).

rations, one cannot fail to see come differences between the basis of this policy and the basis of that government which the recuperation were to replace. What is of immediate concern is that the papal claim was based on papal rights which were alleged to be embodied in documents — whether genuine or not makes again no difference — and it was these rights which were to be enforced. In short, the papal policy of recuperations shows once again the true physiognomy of the Roman Church — to stand on the law and the right order, a stand taken on the basis of alleged *verbriefte Rechte* (75).

Whilst this seems certain enough — the enumeration of the donation documents in the *Liber Censuum* proves it — there is far less certainty of the legality of the claim to government that was embodied in the *Rex Romanorum*. The function contained in this title was the exercise of dominion, that is, government over Italy. In origin, title and function are intimately linked with the German policy of subduing Italy and of consequently exercising German governmental power in Italian lands. That genetically — and perhaps even paradoxically — this policy of conquest had its roots in papal aspirations, is evident and is one more proof that the «liberator» may in course of time become or be seen as an unwonted usurper, when once the immediate danger had passed.

In substance it would appear that the *Rex Romanorum* was an offshoot of the *Rex Langobardorum* who by the ninth century gave way to the *Rex Italicorum*: the *regnum Italicum* (76) was in the hands of the German kings, and Otto I, after the conquest of Italy in 951, called himself *Rex Francorum et Italicorum* (77), whilst after his imperial coronation in 962 he designated himself frequently as « *Imperator* augustus *Romanorum* et Francorum » (78). Although the coinage of the title *Rex Romanorum* was quite obviously a chancery mistake in Henry II's (imperial) time (79), it certainly became established as the official and correct title of the German king by 1045 (80), in a

---

(75) Nevertheless, apart from this basis, Innocent also claimed that territory to be recuperated belonged to the « naturale (!) dominium apostolicae sedis », e.g., Ancona (*Reg.*, VII.228).

(76) Cf. ULLMANN, *Papal Government*, p. 163.

(77) DO.I.139, 140; further, WAITZ, *Deutsche Verfassungsgeschichte*, VI.141.

(78) For instance, DO.I.318, 322, 324, 326, 329, etc.

(79) Cf. H. BRESSLAU ad DH.II.170 (M.G.H., *Diplom.*, III.201) and esp. J. FICKER in *Mitt. oest. Inst. Gesch.* VI (1885), 225 ff., at 244 ff.

(80) My statement (*Papal Government*, p. 250) that Conrad was the first to bear the title, is incorrect: I based myself on DK.II.53 (*Dipl.* IV.62).

diploma of Henry III, issued the year before his imperial coronation in 1046; here we find([81]):

> Signum invictissimi *regis* Henrici *tertii*, Burgundionum *primi, Romanorum secundi.*

From now on the title becomes the usual designation for the German kings, although they were no longer crowned as Lombard kings. It designated (1) the actual and effective exercise of German royal control over more or less defined Italian territories; (2) the inherent claim to Roman emperorship, because only he could understandably call himself Emperor of the Romans who had at least some sort of control over the Italians, although not necessarily over the Romans in Rome who belonged to the *patrimonium b. Petri.* Both these meanings became in course of time intrinsically linked up, particularly in the Staufen period: *because* the German king *qua* king had control over Italy (*nostrum Italicum regnum*) — *Reichsitalien* — and *because* this control was contained in the title *Rex Romanorum*, a title-deed and actual claim to Roman emperorship was asserted ([82]). The *Herrschaft im italischen Königreich* was a pre-condition for the acquisition of the imperial crown ([83]). But for our immediate purpose the vital and essential point is that the claim to Italian dominion by the German king — who was hitherto known as *Rex Teutonicorum* — was based upon the incontrovertible fact of conquest by military means.

It should be pointed out, however, that, as has long been shown, notably by Ficker, the papal claims rested upon very shaky foundations. On the other hand, German power had, literally speaking, for centuries been exercised in Italian lands, and for this reason alone the good faith of the German kings as kings of the Romans cannot be impugned. But what was firm convinction with the Germans, resulting from a centuries-old domination of Italy, appeared to the same extent as firm conviction of the popes, and especially of Innocent III who, too, had no doubt on the veracity and genuineness of their claims based on documentary evidence. Yet, from a wider point of view

---

([81]) DH.III.134. Henry II was counted as first king of the Romans. Cf. also *Decretum Grat., Dist.* 63, c. 32 and also *RNI.* 61.

([82]) Cf. *Papal Government,* p. 163: the king of the Romans as the preliminary to the fully-fledged emperor of the Romans, further, FICKER, *art. cit.,* p. 320: « Tatsächlich war die Eignung zum römischen Kaiser vor allem abhängig vom Besitz der Herrschaft in Oberitalien ».

([83]) FICKER, *Mitt. oest. Inst. Gesch.,* VI (1885), p. 249.

the recuperation policy was significant in so far as the papacy based itself on claims resulting from legal evidence and Germany on claims resulting from the mere fact of conquest and domination. Perhaps nothing illustrates the papal position better than the way in which Innocent III referred to the territories to be « recuperated » and belonging to the patrimony, as having for a long time been oppressed and forcefully occupied by the Germans. This assertion can clearly mean one thing only: unlawfulness of the domination by the German government exercised in the patrimony of St Peter — *portio nostra* — as he maintains in his address to the peoples of the Duchy of Spoleto, Rieti, Gubbio, Perugia, Assisi and so forth ([84]). The recuperated territories belonged to the *jus et proprietas* of the Roman Church ([85]), which is the same as saying that the German kings had no *jus et proprietas* in these provinces.

Because the title-deed of the Germans in Spoleto, Ancona, Romagna, Tuscany as well as in Lombardy lay in the *Rex Romanorum* — which after all was simply a short-hand device to express royal government in Italy — Innocent III could hardly be expected to use that very title: this would have meant an implicit acknowledgment of the claims inherent in the title. Seen thus, the appellation chosen by him would indeed correspond to his intentions: the man « elected into emperorship of the Romans » was the king approved by him, and that king, we now can confidently assert, was for him no more than a mere German king, a *Rex Alemannorum*, as indeed Innocent made clear in a passage which again has not been properly appreciated. Reproaching the archbishop of Tarentaise for having crowned Philip in 1198, the pope says (which may well appear to be a dogmatic declaration):

> Cum enim dubium non existat coronationem *regem Alemannorum* ad venerabilem fratrem nostrum ... Coloniensem archiepiscopum pertinere ([86]),

---

([84]) *Reg.* I. 356: « (Dominus) patrimonium b. Petri, portionem videlicet nostram, desiderabile et praeclarum *haereditatis nostrae funiculum,* quae in oppressione diu posita, fuerat per violentiam occupata, nobis sperantibus... ». The same theme in *Reg.* I. 369 (to the city of Castello): « Cum dudum fuerit per violentiam occupata et per occupationem vehementer oppressa ... ». See also *Reg.* II.4 with the expression of certainty that the Lord repels « violentiam ab ecclesia ».

([85]) Cf. *Reg.* I.375; 426; II.33, 78; etc.

([86]) Of considerable interest is the marginal note from the 13th century on this entry (*RNI.* 74): « nota de jure Coloniensisi archiepiscopi in coronatione *regis Romanorum* » — precisely what Innocent III obviously had not meant to say.

and the significance of this appellation chosen by the pope contrasts rather starkly with the message which Otto's coronator (and elector) himself, that is, Adolf, the archbishop of Cologne, had to say on this:

> Dominum Ottonem in *Regem Romanorum* rationabiliter elegimus ... consecravimus ac coronavimus ([87]),

and one may reasonably assume that the archbishop knew what was the right and proper appellation of the king whom he himself had elected and crowned. Indeed, as we have pointed out, nobody on the German side ever called Otto or Philip in any other way but *Rex Romanorum*, just as the two rivals themselves constantly used this designation ([88]). The conclusion which strikes the discerning reader is that Innocent III attempted, by withholding the very meaningful title of *Rex Romanorum*, to withdraw from German control the domination of those parts of Italy which he claimed to belong to the patrimony of St Peter. In other words, the future state of affairs in Italy as envisaged by Innocent, was an extension of that state of affairs which in any case obtained in the patrimony of St Peter ([89]). To put the same thought differently: regal rights (*regalia*) of the pope — the *regalia beati Petri* — were to take the place of the regal rights of the German kings ([90]). German kingship was to be de-italianized or which is the same thing, was to be confined to Germany proper: the German

---

([87]) *RNI.* 9.

([88]) See supra at note 34. It is interesting that Innocent (*RNI.* 11) in his reply to Adolf (*RNI.* 10) thanks him for the message in which he had announced « et electionis modum et coronationis processum karissimi ... Ottonis, quem elegistis in regem ». For a similar method employed Innocent see supra at n. 42, his reply to *RNI.* 14.

([89]) Cf. *Lib. Cens.* I.363 ff., and the two promises of Otto of 1201 and 1209, *M.G.H. Const.* II.20, no. 16 and p. 27, no. 23, p. 36, no. 31 = *RNI.* 77 and 189. The constitutional state of affairs in the papal State was that which was apparently envisaged in the Treaty of Venice, according to which the emperor had no sovereign rights in the patrimony, but only specifically conceded rights on the occasion of his coronation and when called upon to act as *advocatus ecclesiae Romanae*, see FICKER, *Forsch.*, II. 307, 468-9.

([90]) Alexander II seems to have been one of the first to speak of the *regalia sancti Petri*, cf. DEUSDEDIT (ed. W.v. Glanvell), *Die Kanonessammlungs des Kardinals Deusdedit* (Paderborn, 1905), III.288, p. 396: feudal oath of Richard of Capua, whence it went to Gregory VII's *Reg.* I.21a, ed. cit., p. 36; the connexion *Papatus Romanus et regalia b. Petri* in Gregory's *Reg.* VI.17a (4), ed. cit., p. 429, whence also Innocent III, *Reg.* I.578, who explicitly links the *regalia b. Petri* with the recuperations.

king was no more than a *Rex Alemannorum*, and no longer a *Rex Romanorum*. For Innocent III the concept of the *Regnum Romanum* (or *Romanorum*) just as the *Rex Romanorum* and the *Italicum regnum* did not exist. What did exist as an operational instrument was the *imperium Romanum*.

Innocent III, consequently, sharply distinguished between royal and imperial powers of the German king. Royal powers were to be reduced in Italy (91). Royal power in Germany was in no wise touched by Innocent III, and it was this — and not the exercise of royal power in Italy — which was for him a pre-condition for emperorship, because the Roman Church had translated the empire from the Greeks to the Germans (92). Roman emperorship in his view apparently was — actually in consonance with the idea underlying the notion — conceived on a universal level and to be the proper reflexion of that universality which the Roman Church itself represented (93), and was the latter's prolonged arm: no royal powers were to be contained in this emperorship as far as Italy or the papal State was concerned, because here the pope himself meant to exercise it (94). That this Roman emperorship was by Innocent primarily seen in its bearing upon the East, is not an unreasonable assumption (95). The concept of Roman

---

(91) To what precise geographical extent it is hard to say nor really relevant.

(92) *RNI.* 62: « a Graecis transtulit in *Germanos* ». Most interesting is the utilisation of the translation thesis by Cynus, in order to abolish German power in Italy. « Nam ipse (scil. papa) ex causa transtulit imperium a Graecis in Germanos et eodem modo nunc posset *a Germanis in alios transferre vel ad se reducere* — quod utinam fieret, ut dira Germanorum barbaritas dulcem Italiam non vexaret », Lecture in Dig. 1. 3. 9, ed. D. MAFFEI, *Cino,* p. 56. For different reasons Gregory X had toyed with the idea of utilising the translation thesis, threatening to transfer the empire from the Germans to France, hence the electoral ultimatum to the Germans resulting in the election of Rudolf of Habsburg, cf. W. GOEZ, *Translatio,* p. 179.

(93) Hence also the invocation of the sun-moon allegory in precisely this context by Innocent. Cf. supra, n. 71.

(94) Cf. supra to Ravenna and the pope's *Sermo VII,* in MIGNE, *Patr. Lat.,* CCXVII., 480 f. A similar line of reasoning in regard to France may perhaps be revealed in *Reg.* V.128 = X: IV.17.13.

(95) Is it again a coincidence that it was Innocent III who presented the translation theory in its classsic form — the « translation of the empire » from the Greeks to the Germans? (*RNI.* 18, 29, 62). Was not in fact Innocent's pre-occupation with Constantinople, with the *Greeks,* the very point which Philip quite clearly perceived and which made him propose to Innocent as he did in 1203 (*M.G.H. Const.* II.9, no. 8, sect. 7) — a bait, no doubt, which Innocent considered still too low, just as his predecessor considered Henry VI's promise of a crusade too low

emperorship in the West was a papal offspring and was originally the answer to Byzantium — this was its original feature of which the papacy never lost sight (96). And this concept of Roman emperorship entailed not only rivalry between East and West on precisely this point (97), but also duties on a universal scale: on the other hand, this emperor of the Romans received *plenitudinem potestatis* as a result of his being crowned by the pope (98). If our interpretation of Innocent III's thesis in the context of the double election detracts a good deal from its supposed fundamental character and reduces it to a question of Italian royal control, his imperial thesis would nevertheless show his attempt to bring to fruition the pristine notion of the *dominus mundi*, at least seen from the point of view of his creator, the pope. And this is also why Innocent denied the (real) Roman emperor, that is, the one in Byzantium, the very title which only he who was crowned by the pope could bear. The emperor in the East was a mere *imperator Constantinopolitanus* (99).

For the Germans, however, the concept of empire does not seem to have only one meaning. For the Germans the *Rex Romanorum* was to all intents and purposes an emperor — indeed, this was what the Staufens meant with their *imperatura Romani solii* and what Otto's party meant with their *fastigium Romani regni* (100). Considering this indubitably carefully chosen language it is really hard to see any difference between the Staufen and the Welf standpoints in this respect. I do not know why the suggestion made for the meaning of the *imperatura* (101) can not and should not be equally valid for the *fastigium Romani regni*. What this language wished to express — and we must of course keep in mind that this terminology was used

---

(see supra n. 61), because the — to Innocent — essential and vital territorial question in Italy had priority before any other consideration — and it was the answer to this question for which Innocent looked in vain in Philip's offer.

(96) This is one of the main themes of my paper « Reflexions on the Medieval Empire » in the forthcoming *Transactions of the Royal Hist. Society* (1964).

(97) Cf. the highly significant statement by Frederick I quoted in the paper cited (note 96). Cf. also Innocent in *RNI.* 1: « necessitates terrae orientalis ».

(98) *RNI.* 33: « a nobis imperator diadema in plenitudinem potestatis recipit ».

(99) Cf., e.g., *Reg.* I.353; II. 211; etc., and compare the title of the Byzantine emperor himself, *Reg.* II.210.

(100) *RNI.* 10: « (Ottonem) ad *Romani* regni fastigium juste et rationabiliter elegimus... »; here also the statement that Otto was suitable for the « regimen *Romani imperii* ».

(101) H. MITTEIS, *Königswahl*, pp. 120 ff.

long before the pope had made any declaration on the « imperial » question and when the terminology itself was as yet uncontaminated — was that there was an indestructible link between the German king and his government over the Italian domains, as is evidenced by the identical use of the *Rex Romanorum* by both contestants. Here within the German sphere a distinction will have to be made between the *regnum Romanum* which expressed the king's royal control over Germany, Burgundy and Italy, and this dominion was somewhat loosely equated with the *imperium Romanum* ([102]), and the universal *imperium Romanum*. The *regnum Romanum* was thought to give a title-deed to Roman emperorship in the universal sense, a function which included the duty of protection of churches also outside the (narrow) empire, the duty to undertake a crusade, the duty to exterminate heretics, also outside the confines the (narrow) empire, and so on; on the other hand, only the true universal emperor of the Romans enjoyed certain privileges which were not possessed by a mere *Rex Romanorum*. As far as this correctly understood Roman emperorship went, no essential differences can be seen between the papacy and the Germans: for that universal Roman emperor did not come into being until he had been crowned by the pope.

In sum, then, Innocent III's efforts aimed at withholding regal rights of the German king in Italy, primarily, though not exclusively, in Central Italy, by withholding that title which customarily expressed the king's regal rights. To the Germans the *Rex Romanorum* was, as far as royal power in practice went, not only king of Germany (and Burgundy), but also king of Italy. For Innocent however the *Rex Romanorum* had shrunk and changed into a *Rex Alemannorum*: he became a national king, and as such he had no right to rule over Italian lands. It may well be that the later concept of a « Holy Roman Empire of the German Nation » is rooted in this territorial empire, comprising Germany, Burgundy, and Italy. It would have been quite unstatesmanlike, it would have been dangerous imprudence, if not

---

([102]) This was the original idea of Mitteis, *Königswahl*, pp. 124 f. He also most felicitously equated this empire in the narrow sense — the *imperatura* — with *Verwaltungshoheit* over Germany, Burgundy and Italy, precisely the claim which Innocent denied. One of the reasons for this equation of *regnum* and *imperium* may well be the German term *Reich* (*rîche*) which can mean kingdom as well as empire. It is not to be supposed that the Germans *thought* in Latin, but in German, terms.

outright folly, had Innocent conveyed his thoughts openly: he would have trodden on the susceptibilities of both contestants — he would have touched *heisses Eisen*. The tragedy for the Germans lay in that by linking the government over Italian lands automatically with their kingship over Germany, they offered the papacy a golden opportunity for deploying its scheme of territorial expansion (under the cloak of recuperations) — at a time when two kings vied for this Italian dominion. Hardly ever had a pope been presented with such a gift. And because German kingship embodied Italian kingship, and because the pope made the acknowledgement of reduction of German royal power in Italy by one of the rival kings the price of his approbation, his decision necessarily and automatically affected Germany itself. It would be quite anachronistic to say that had the Germans understood the implications of the meaningful withholding of the title *Rex Romanorum* by Innocent III, and had they acted in correspondence with the pope's intentions, none of the disasters of the thirteenth century would have befallen Germany. The problem of Italian domination was not a Staufen or a Welf problem, but one that was the bequest of the Saxon kings and emperors.

IV.

After this somewhat lenghty argumentation we should now be in a position to answer the question which we have posed at the beginning of this paper: how can these three statements be explained? For Accursius assuredly there was only one Roman emperor, and that was the one depicted in the Roman law books: there was no such unhistorical or weird thing as a *Rex Romanorum* in the corpus of civil law. And commenting upon the term *infulas* he could indeed consider them as imperial insignia which were conferred — in his time by the pope. As far as pure theory was concerned, Accursius was nothing but a civilian who could not have advanced any other point of view.

The German verdict (*Weistum*) of 1252 is a combination of the thesis contained in the *lex regia* with that thesis which we consider to be expressed in the title *Rex Romanorum* ([103]). Two points should be made. First, one concerning the significance of the election as it

---

([103]) As Mitteis, *Königswahl*, pp. 187 f., has pointed out, great caution is required in explaining the *Weistum*, as we do not know the actual wording, but have it only at second hand.

emerges from this *Weistum*. That the election had down to the end
of the twelfth century no constitutive significance is common knowledge: the king was not « Rex *Dei gratia* » until the anointing; he
was not therefore king in any full sense and this tallies with the practice of dating royal documents from the day of his coronation. It is
usually maintained that the practice of this dating ceased with the
French and English kings, almost at the same time, to wit by Philip
III in 1270 and by Edward I in 1272 ([104]), who began to govern from
the moment of accession. But this practice can again be antedated, for
Philip of Swabia began to date his documents also from the day of
his election, and not from that of his coronation. In his treaty with
Philip II of France of 29 June 1198 the dating reads: « anno dominico
incarnationis MCXCVIII, regni nostri primo » ([105]), although he was
not crowned until 8 September 1198. In other words, the *Weistum*
appears to reflect what by its time had become practice. And the consequence was the devaluation of the ecclesiastical coronation which became more and more a formal solemnity ([106]).

This brings me to the second point. In the same treaty with Philip II, the Swabian, although not even crowned king, used the title
« *Rex Romanorum et semper augustus* ». The implication clearly is —
and this follows also from the dating — that the election itself made
him *Rex Romanorum*, made him, in other words, king of Germany,
Burgundy and Italy, although the latter two had no means of participating in the election. It was, consequently, the same line of thought
which prompted the employment of the very term *imperium nostrum*
in the same document ([107]). This harmonizes perfectly with the *imperatura* of the Speyer protest, that is, the acquisition of a *Verwaltungshoheit* (Mitteis) over Germany and Italy as a result of his being *Rex
Romanorum*. And indeed, within this meaning of the empire —
embracing these three territories — there was no fundamental difference between the *Rex* and the *Imperator Romanorum*. What the

---

([104]) Cf. KANTOROWICZ, *Two Bodies*, pp. 328-9.

([105]) *M.G.H. Const.*. II.2, no. 1.

([106]) The interval between Otto's election and coronation was too short and
his own position so insecure that apparently no documents were issued between
9 June and 12 July.

([107]) Ibid., sect. 2 and 3: « Si aliquis de *imperio nostro* faceret eidem Philippo
malum ... »; « Nos non retinebimus in *imperio nostro* aliquem hominem *de regno
Franciae* ... ». As far as I can see, these details have not yet been observed.

Weistum seemed to signify was simply to confirm in a declaratory manner what had in any case been the German point of view ([108]).

These considerations should facilitate our understanding of Innocent IV's statement. In fact, virtually all of them can be applied to it. The *Verwaltungshoheit* of the elected can have reference only to Germany, Burgundy and Italy — this is what Innocent IV meant which the *auctoritas ministrandi* which the king-emperor received from the archbishop of Cologne ([109]). Two points may seem apposite. First, the *equiparatio* of emperor and king, for the *auctoritas ministrandi* can reasonably refer only to the empire in the narrow sense. In so far there is no difference between him and the *Weistum*, though the reduction of the empire to a territorial concept by a pope of Innocent IV's calibre is a noteworthy feature: it is no more and no less than a deviation from the hitherto prevailing papal point of view. Second, and no less important, is this pope's endorsement of the at any rate by then common devaluation of the royal coronation. That it was a pope who was to make these quite serious inroads into ecclesiatical strongholds, is again a feature worth pondering: the paradox emerges that whilst the civilian, Accursius, upheld the traditional point of view, though his reasons were exclusively juristic, his contemporary, the pope, lent support to a theme that in the end was to redound to the undoing of both empire and papacy.

These considerations once more would seem to emphasize the need for the integration of historical jurisprudence with historical analysis: it would be a somewhat dangerous undertaking to try to reconstruct reality from the abstract thought of a juristic thesis, and the three statements would seem to illustrate the risk of assessing reality exclusively by the instrumentality of the law or of legal opinion. The gloss of Accursius reflects the difficulty which confronted the glossator in the mid-thirteenth century, that is, to express by means of the pure Roman law legal elements which had no ancient ancestry, but all the greater medieval significance. And it was precisely these legal elements which were absent from the Justinianean codification. The gloss of Accursius is *kat exochen* a mirror (if I may use a modern and current

---

([108]) This seems also the opinion of Mitteis, *Königswahl*, p. 190: *Feststellungsurteil*, though he arrived at it by quite a different avenue.

([109]) Whether there is any dependence on Rufinus (who, it will be recalled, distinguished between the pope's *jus auctoritatis* and the emperor's *jus administrandi*, cf. *Papal Government*, p. 446 n. 2) must await further examination.

term) of a *reine Rechtslehre*. However dominant a feature the concept of a Roman emperor was in the Code, there is no gainsaying that it had undergone radical changes in the meantime. But how was a glossator in the thirteenth century to deal with it? The question itself is a reminder of the very serious difficulties besetting historical jurisprudence: how can Roman law, even in its Justinianean shape, be applied to problems of medieval *Staatsrecht* and *Staatslehre*?

Whilst Accursius represented unadulterated Romanist doctrine, with little bearing upon contemporary reality, the strength of the other two statements lies in their focussing attention upon the actuality observable at the time. For Accursius the empire was still the ancient universal entity, and no glossator could have conceived otherwise, but for the *Weistum* and Innocent IV the empire had shrunk to a territorial conception. Accursius with his gloss is a classic example of juristic traditionalism culminating in the concept of universal empire and emperor; his gloss is retrospective — the other two sources are prospective: they look ahead to a time which is not so distant when the empire was also given its appropriate territorial designation, thus making appear the problem of the *dies ortus imperii* in an entirely different complexion. These three statements reflect therefore a juristc reality of quite disparate orders and they may indeed serve as paradigmatic signs of the need to integrate historical jurisprudence with historical analysis, because the historical process demands that equal attention is paid to law and actual reality: within the precincts of medieval *Staatsrecht* both are essential.

SPECIAL BIBLIOGRAPHY

Ann. Marbacenses = *Annales Marbacenses*, ed. Bloch H., in *Scriptores Rerum Germanicarum*, Hannover 1907.

Bloch, *Kaiserwahlen* = Bloch, H., *Die staufischen Keiserwahlen*, Leipzig 1911.

Eichmann, *Kaiserkrönung* = Eichmann, E., *Die Kaiserkrönung im Abendlande*, Würzburg 1942.

Elze, *Die Ordines* = Elze, R., *Die Ordines für die Weihe und Krönung des Kaiser und der Kaiserin*, in *Fontes Iuris Germanici Antiqui*, Hannover 1960.

Erdmann, *Forschungen* = Erdmann, C., *Forschungen zur politischen Ideenwelt des Mittelalters*, Berlin 1951.

Fabre-Duchesne, *Lib. Cens.* = Fabre, J. — Duchesne, L., *Le Liber Censuum*, Paris 1905.

GOEZ, *Translatio* = GOEZ, W., *Translatio Imperii*, Tübingen 1958.

HALLER, *Heinrich VI.* = HALLER, J., *Heinrich VI. und die römische Kirche*, in *Mitt. oest. Inst. Gesch.*, XXXV (1914), 436 ff.

HALLER, *Papsttum* = HALLER, J., *Das Papsttum: Idee und Wirklichkeit*, Stuttgart 1938.

HAMPE-BAETHGEN, *Kaisergeschichte* = HAMPE, K., *Deutsche Kaisergeschichte in der Zeit der Salier und Staufer*, ed. BAETHGEN, F., Heidelberg 1949.

KANTOROWICZ, *Two Bodies* = KANTOROWICZ, E., *The King's Two Bodies*, Princeton 1957.

KRAMMER, *Reichsgedanke* = KRAMMER, M., *Der Reichsgedanke des staufischen Kaiserhauses*, Breslau 1908.

Liber regie capelle = *Liber regie capelle*, ed. ULLMANN, W., in Henry Bradshaw Society, vol. XCII (1961).

MAFFEI, *Cino* = MAFFEI, D., *La Lectura super Digesto veteri di Cino*, in *Quaderni di Studi Senesi*, vol. X (1963).

MITTEIS, H., *Königswahl* = MITTEIS, H., *Die deutsche Königswahl²*, Brünn, 1944.

PERELS, *Erbreichsplan* = PERELS, E., *Der Erbreichsplan Heinrichs VI.*, Berlin 1927.

Reg. = *Regestum Innocentii Tertii*, in MIGNE, *Patr. Lat.*, CCXIV-CCVI.

RNI. = *Regestum Innocentii Tertii Papae super Negotio Romani Imperii*, ed. KEMPF, F., in *Miscellanea Historiae Pontificiae*, XII (1947).

SCHRAMM, *Die Krönung* — SCHRAMM, P.E., *Die Krönung in Deutschland*, in *Z.S S. Kan. Abt.*, XXIV (1935), 276 ff.

STICKLER, *Imperator* = STICKLER, A.M., *Imperator vicarius papae*, in *Mitt. oest. Inst. Gesch.*, LXVII (1954), 165 ff.

Thomas Becket = *Materials for the History of Thomas Becket*, ed. Robertson, J.C., in *Rerum brit. med. aevi scriptores*, tom. V, London 1881.

ULLMANN, *Papal Government* = ULLMANN, W., *The Growth of Papal Government in the Middle Ages²*, London 1962.

ULLMANN, *Principles of Government* = ULLMANN, W., *Principles of Government and Politics in the Middle Ages*, London, 1961.

WALEY, *Papal State* = WALEY, D., *The papal State in the Thirteenth Century*, London, 1961.

WINKELMANN, *Philipp* = WINKELMANN, E., *Philipp von Schwaben*, in *Jahrbücher der deutschen Geschichte*, Leipzig 1873.

ZERBI, *Papato* = ZERBI, P., *Papato, Impero e Respubblica Christiana dal 1187-1198*, Milano 1955.

VII

THE DECLINE OF THE CHANCELLOR'S AUTHORITY IN MEDIEVAL CAMBRIDGE: A REDISCOVERED STATUTE

In accounts of the medieval constitution of the University of Cambridge insufficient attention is paid to the gradual decrease of the Chancellor's authority and the concomitant increase of powers of the regent masters. This development very clearly reflects the growing awareness of the University of itself as an autonomous institution, that is, a body with its own inherent rights and within which the supreme jurisdictional power resided. Although the premises and presuppositions are different, this development might well show some kinship with contemporary developments elsewhere, namely in the institutional growth of Parliament and in the conciliarist form of church government. This rather important evolution of the University constitution has not yet been properly appreciated, mainly because the individual statutory enactments by which the gradual transfer of authority from the (ecclesiastical) Chancellor to the whole University took place had not been known. What was known was one Statute, through which alone the stages of the development could not, of course, be recognized. Moreover, when touching upon this point, G. Peacock and C. H. Cooper[1] relied on a Statute which substantially differs in its wording and in its subject-matter from that printed by the Commissioners in 1852, on which J. B. Mullinger, Sir Stanley Leathes and Dean Rashdall drew.[2] Fortunately, the Statute in its original form has been preserved as an original document in the Archives of the University of Cambridge, and it enables us to trace, at least in rough outline, this process of displacement of authority which ended in the control by the regent masters (through their proctors) over the chancellor and vice-chancellor. As far as can be established, there was no corresponding development at the University of Oxford.

Generally speaking, jurisdictional and disciplinary powers were vested in the Chancellor or his deputy, the Vice-Chancellor. In a Statute passed certainly a considerable time before 1275, well-defined duties were conferred on the proctors; in this same Statute the jurisdictional and disciplinary powers of the proctors were confined to infringements of only those regulations which they themselves had issued in pursuance of the duties incumbent upon them, that is, the fixing of the time and place of University lectures, or disputations, inceptions, exequies and festivals. Offences committed in respect of these specific proctorial orders came

---

[1] G. Peacock, *Observations on the Statutes of the University of Cambridge* (1841), 23; C. H. Cooper, *Annals of Cambridge* (Cambridge, 1842), I, 55.

[2] *Statuta Antiqua* in *Documents relating to the University and Colleges of Cambridge* (ed. by the Queen's Commissioners (1852), I, 305 ff., at p. 342: stat. 57; J. B. Mullinger, *The University of Cambridge* (Cambridge, 1873), I, 143; *Grace Book A* (ed. Sir S. Leathes, in Luard Memorial Series I, Cambridge, 1897), p. xxxiv; H. Rashdall, *The Universities of Europe in the Middle Ages* (ed. F. M. Powicke and A. B. Emden, Oxford, 1936), III, 286.

within the competence of the proctors themselves. The bedells, too, were subject to the proctors' rulings.[3]

Even a superficial acquaintance with medieval University life will make it clear that there were many offences which were, according to this Statute, outside proctorial jurisdiction, and competently dealt with only by the Chancellor, or his deputy. The fact that a subsequent Statute actually made the Chancellor's most cherished prerogative powers devolve upon the proctors, proves that the Chancellor in dealing with offenders against a regent master did not always act in the way which the interests of the University would have warranted.[4] This neglect on his part led to the passing of the Statute of 17 March 1275 which constituted the first substantial increase in the powers of the regents and of the proctors, in so far as the Chancellor's authority devolved upon the latter and jurisdictional power upon the former.

Hitherto, the houses of regents and non-regents could be convoked only by the Chancellor: this was solely his prerogative.[5] But the new Statute gave the proctors alone the right of convoking the regent house, and this on two conditions: first, that an offence—the term is taken in its widest sense: *iniuria vel contumelia*— was publicly or privately committed against a regent master or against a whole 'community'[6]; and secondly, that the Chancellor had, despite a specific request, failed to deal with the offender. The convocation of the regent house, by even one of the proctors (or, as they were styled, rectors)[7] entailed that jurisdictional authority was now vested in this assembly. Consequently, the regent house could exercise its powers also over offenders who were not members of the University. This, taken in conjunction with the motive of passing the Statute—*pro bono pacis et tranquillitate universitatis*— would indeed indicate that the Chancellor had not preserved order within the University and the town, and that therefore the regent house itself was going to act as the disciplinary organ of the University. That the Chancellors must have been remiss in the exercise of their jurisdictional powers for a considerable time is shown by the wording of the Statute: since only the Chancellor could summon the regent house, and since he was, at any rate by custom, the sole jurisdictional authority, he

---

[3] *Statuta antiqua*, stat. 54, p. 340: 'Tempora et modus legendi et disputandi, exequias celebrandi et incipiendi et feriarum observantiae ad ipsos procuratores pertineant; in transgressores contra praedicta et in bedellos si mandatis eorum non paruerint, coercione concessa eisdem animadversione gravissima per cancellarium et magistros, si opus fuerit, nihilominus irroganda.' It is clear from this enactment that the duties of the bedells as officers of the University were regulated before this Statute was passed. What is doubtful, however, is whether the whole stat. 54 was originally passed in the form in which it has come down to us: it, too, may have undergone an expansion similar to that of stat. 57 (see below p. 178). There does not seem to exist an Oxford enactment corresponding to the Cambridge one, according to which the bedells were under the authority of the proctors.

[4] That the discipline at Cambridge about the middle of the thirteenth century left much to be desired was pointed out by H. Denifle (*Die Universitäten des Mittelalters*, Berlin, 1885, I, 371), although the otherwise omniscient Dominican, in his attempt to denigrate Cambridge, paid no attention to the measures taken by the University itself to remedy this state of affairs.

[5] The same holds good for Oxford, see Strickland Gibson, *Statuta antiqua Universitatis Oxoniensis* (Oxford, 1931), p. lxxi.

[6] It is by no means certain what the masters meant by this expression; it may be either the whole University, in which case the term is singularly inadequate, because the usual designation was either *studium* or *universitas*, or the town, which would correspond to the contemporary appellation of the municipality itself as a *communitas*. J. Heywood, *Collection of documents for the University of Cambridge* (1840), 103, translates the term *communitas* by 'assembly of regents'; cf. also his *Early Cambridge [University and College] Statutes* (1855), 42, a translation which I hesitate to accept as correct. In both these instances Heywood relied on the Statute in its later, amended form.   [7] On this point see H. Rashdall, op. cit., edn. cit., III, 58–9.

178

could always shield himself behind his prerogatives and thus also shield offenders —to the detriment of the peace and tranquillity of the whole University. It is this state of affairs which the regents dub *corruptelae preteritae* and which they are determined to remedy.[8] But the further significance of the Statute lies also in that it was passed not only by the regent and non-regent houses, but also by the *maiores bachalaurii* who can be none other than the bachelors in the higher faculties;[9] this goes to prove the advanced state of University teaching and organization in the thirteenth century as well as the importance which the University attached to this Statute.

Since the original of this Statute, now rediscovered, is so clearly of prime importance for the University's constitutional development, I have thought it worth editing and printing below (Appendix, pp. 180–2). The document measures $8\frac{1}{2}$ in. by 4 in. and is written on thin parchment (mounted probably in the nineteenth century, on modern paper) by a very neat and well-developed thirteenth-century charter hand; there is no heading and in one or two places (on the crease) the writing has almost faded away.

The Statute as printed in the Commissioners' edition of the *Statuta Antiqua* (stat. 57) corresponds to a later stage. It is an amended Statute which in two further respects expands the power of the regent masters and of the proctors. It is not yet possible to say whether both amendments were passed at the same or different congregations. The first permitted the testimony of one of the proctors to be sufficient evidence for the regent house to proceed to disciplinary measures against the offender. The second, and more important perhaps, enabled the proctors to convoke the regent house whenever the public interest—*utilitas communis*—warranted a congregation, and the Chancellor or Vice-Chancellor had refused a request oconvoke the regents. Moreover, in any of the cases which gave the proctors this right, the regents could by a majority demand the summoning of the house of non-regents. A flexible formula, such as 'the public interest', together with the possibility of asking for a congregation of the non-regents, gave, for understandable reasons, plenty of scope for the free display of all currents and undercurrents of University politics. This amended Statute was therefore a vigorous assertion of the powers of the regent masters and constituted an effective check on the Chancellor's and Vice-Chancellor's powers which were obviously considered by the University as too arbitrary. The real guardian of peace and order within Cambridge as well as of the interests of the University as a whole was the regent house exercising authority through its own officers, the proctors.

This amended Statute makes its first appearance in the Old Proctor's Book, the *Liber Procuratoris Antiquus*, preserved in the Archives. This is usually ascribed to a date *c.* 1390 and the palaeographical evidence bears this out or suggests an even slightly earlier date. The writing is in a very characteristic fourteenth-century book hand, with regular features, liberal spacing, well laid-out entries, and the whole makes a pleasing impression. It was probably the book carried by one of the proctors until it was superseded by the Senior and Junior Proctors' Books at the end of the

---

[8] The right of the proctors to convoke the regents seems to have been conceded at Oxford much later, on 2 Dec. 1322 (see *Statt. Antt.* cit. pp. 123–4). But neither of the two cases corresponds to the Cambridge ones. One enactment (p. 123) concerns the case of the insufferable chancellor (*intollerabilis cancellarius*), when the regent house could take disciplinary measures against the Chancellor himself; and the other (p. 124) deals with dissensions amongst the regents through which *pax et tranquillitas* could be disturbed, when either the Chancellor or the proctors had the right to summon the regents.

[9] Rashdall's doubt (op. cit., edn. cit., III. 280) can now be resolved.

fifteenth century. The suggested date of the *Lib. Proc. Ant.*, namely the late fourteenth century, would also fit in with a further development towards the autonomy of the University. As has been seen, our Statute aimed at exercising control over the Chancellor by the regents: the grant by Pope Boniface IX in 1401—according to which the election of the Chancellor no longer needed confirmation by the bishop of Ely[10]—may well mark the next and last stage in the emancipation of the University from 'outside' influence.[11]

From now onwards the amended Statute will be found in every book recording the Statutes in force. Thus it appears next in the so-called Register of Thomas Markaunt, of Corpus Christi, who was proctor in 1417. This book, which certainly was only a private collection and not written by a professional scribe, contains amongst a rather confused mass of ordinances, statutes, royal and papal privileges, letters, and so forth, both the original Statute (fo. 10v) and the Statute in its amended form (fo. 46v), although the latter's wording does not entirely agree with the one in the *Lib. Proc. Ant.*[12] The Statute in its amended shape is also in both the Senior and Junior Proctors' Books which date from the late fifteenth century. Both were written by a professional scribe and still preserve their clasps and chains; they were carried by the proctors until 1785 when they were superseded by the printed books of the Senior and Junior Proctor now in use. These two 'modern' books, still carried by the Proctors in public, contain the same stat. 57 in the precise form in which it was amended in the fourteenth century.[13]

Considering the paucity of early University records in general and the apparently quite divergent constitutional development of Oxford and Cambridge,[14] our resur-

[10] *Calendar of Papal Letters*, ed. W. H. Bliss & J. A. Twemlow (1904), v, 370–1 (12 Jan. 1401).

[11] That Boniface IX had every reason to show himself accommodating to the wishes of the Cambridge Masters is not surprising in view of the firm line which they had taken barely two years earlier in the matter of his recognition as the lawful pope. Cf. my 'The University of Cambridge and the Great Schism' in *Journal of Theological Studies*, ix (1958), 53ff.

[12] For personal details of Markaunt see *Historical Register*, ed. J. R. Tanner (Cambridge, 1917), 35; J. and J. A. Venn, *Alumni Cantabrigienses* (Cambridge, 1922), i, 3, 140; he died on 19 Nov. 1439. By inference it is possible to fix his age when he was proctor in 1417: he was witness in the notorious Barnwell trial (12–20 Oct. 1430) when he was 'aged 48 and more' (see Heywood, *Early Cambridge Statutes*, 195, where the whole proceedings are translated into English). Hence he was no more than 33 when proctor and 55 when he died. The surmise of Leathes (op. cit. p. xxxv) that the proctors must have been rather young is at least partly borne out in this instance. But there is really no prima facie evidence of an internal or external character to justify the ascription of this book to Thomas Markaunt. It is a paper volume of 81 folios, compiled without regard to chronology or subject-matter; for instance, our Statute in its original form (fo. 10v) is preceded by the agreement between the University and the rector of St Benedict's of 22 March 1273, concerning the ringing of the bells for lectures; it is succeeded by a writ of Richard II of 30 Jan. 1392 relating to the freeing of offenders imprisoned by order of the Chancellor. What would in fact militate against ascribing the book to Markaunt is that material subsequent to his death was entered, e.g. the letter of Nicholas V (fo. 31) to the bishop of Norwich, in 1450. The indefatigable sixteenth-century antiquarian Robert Hare transcribed from Markaunt (see Cambridge University Archives, Hare MSS. I, 28v), and Cooper and Peacock took the Statute from Hare.

[13] The books carried are actually the 1785 edition of the *Statuta Academiae Cantabrigiensis*: stat. 57 is at p. 29.

[14] The usual opinion that Cambridge followed Oxford closely in constitutional matters, would seem to be in need of revision. Cf. e.g. Denifle, op. cit. i, 251: 'Man war bisher gewohnt, Oxford und Cambridge unter einem Gesichtspunkte zu betrachten. Es geht dies an, wenn man die Verfassung beider Schulen vergleicht'; cf. Rashdall's statement (op. cit. iii, 285): 'The organisation of the University of Cambridge is so completely framed on the Oxford model that it will be enough to specify a few points' in which the constitutions differ.

rected Statute would seem to assume major importance. On the one hand it materially contributes to our scanty knowledge of the history of the Chancellor's office;[15] on the other, it indicates one of the principal stages by which the University came to regard the Chancellor no longer as a separate and distinct estate,[16] but as an organ of the University itself: by virtue of the regents' control the powers of the Chancellor, originally derived from the bishop of Ely, came to be viewed as pertaining to the regents. This gradual development almost classically exemplifies the transference of authority from one source to another, from the bishop of Ely to the regent masters, who henceforward regard themselves as possessing the sum total of all power and authority within the University of Cambridge.

APPENDIX

NOTES

The document is listed by H. R. Luard, 'List of the Documents in the University of Cambridge from 1266 to 1544' in *Communications of the Cambridge Antiquarian Society*, III (1876), 387, under no. 4 and described as: Decretum regentium et non-regentium etc. Johanne Hooke cancellario presente, quod rectores etiam habebunt coercitionem transgressionum et potestatem congregandi in quibusdam casibus, si cancellarius noluerit.

The following abbreviations will be used (unless otherwise stated, all the materials are in the Archives of the University of Cambridge):

O: original document, cf. above p. 178.

LPA: *Liber Procuratoris Antiquus:* parchment volume of the late fourteenth century; 48 folios. The Statutes are preceded by a *Calendarium* for the University, in which the so-called non-le, non-dis, and the like days are meticulously noted (a non-le day is a day on which no lectures must take place, a non-dis day one on which no disputation must be held). Our Statute is on fo. 20v. For further details cf. above, p. 178.

M: Thomas Markaunt's Register: paper volume of the fifteenth century. The Statute is on fo. 10v in its original form. For further details cf. above, p. 179.

MX: as M, but denoting the entry of the Statute in its amended form on fo. 46v.

P: G. Peacock, op. cit. 23, n. 1.

D: *Documents relating to the University of Cambridge*, cit. I, 342, stat. 57.

It does not seem necessary to indicate the quite insignificant variants in the Proctors' Books of the late fifteenth century (fo. 15v) and the currently used Proctors' Books, because their texts agree with D.

[15] Long ago Denifle, op. cit. p. xxvi, pointed out that the history of the Chancellor's office in medieval universities needed to be written.

[16] Cf. G. Peacock, op. cit. 19: 'He constituted a distinct estate in the academical commonwealth.'

STATUTUM UNIVERSITATIS CANTABRIGIENSIS
DE POTESTATE PROCURATORUM

17 March 1275

Convenientibus omnibus magistris regentibus et non regentibus nec non maioribus[1] baccalauriis[2] universitatis[3] presentibus[4] magistro Johanne Hooke[5] tunc[6] cancellario presente et auctoritatem prestante[7] pro[8] bono pacis et tranquilitate universitatis unanimi consensu est statutum, quod[9] liceat[10–] rectoribus suspendere tantum[11] transgressores statuti ad eorum officium spectantia, quod est tale: 'Tempora et modus legendi et disputandi et exequias celebrandi et incipiendi et feriarum observantie ad ipsos[12] pertineant: in transgressores contra[13] predicta ad eorum officia specialiter spectantia[14] et in bedellos si mandatis eorum non paruerint, cohercione concessa eisdem animadversione gravissima per cancellarium et magistros, si opus fuerit, nihilominus irroganda.'[–10] Si autem[15] presente cancellario [16–]in villa[–16] et [17–]ipsis rectoribus[–17] presentibus[18] vel altero eorum,[19] a quoquam iniuria vel contumelia publice vel privatim irrogata fuerit alicui regenti vel communitati,[20] si cancellarius requisitus correccionem adhibere dissimulaverit, neglexerit vel minus iuste distulerit,[21] procuratores vel alter eorum,[22] qui presens fuerit, irrequisito cancellario, convocent[23] universitatem regentium, que ex tunc in illa causa cognoscat et sententiet.[24] Si vero in absentia cancellarii presentibus rectoribus[25] vel altero eorum

---

[1] M and P om. *maioribus.*
[2] O: *bachilariis.*
[3] P adds: *predicte.*
[4] P om. *presentibus.*
[5] John Hooke was Chancellor 1270–5 (Venn, *Alumni Cantabrigienses,* I, 2 (Cambridge, 1922), 402).
[6] P: *tum.*
[7] M: *prestantem.*
[8] MX begins here.
[9] LPA and D begin here.
[10–10] LPA and D: *procuratoribus transgressores contra articulos ad eorum officium pertinentes suspendere et non alios; articuli vero predicti sunt 'Tempora et modus legendi etc.' ut supra capitulo xvij* (D: *ut supra, ibi 'Tempora et modus'*). The reference is to stat. 54.
[11] M and P: *tum.*
[12] scil. *rectores.*
[13] M, MX and P: *circa.*
[14] O, M and MX om. *spectantia;* P om. *specialiter.* Stat. 54 had neither:...*contra predicta et in bedellos*... that is, if the transcript in *Statt. Antt.* 340, is accurate.
[15] LPA and D: *Item si.*
[16–16] D: om.
[17–17] LPA and D: *eisdem procuratoribus.*
[18] D adds: *in villa.*
[19] LPA and D: *eorum altero.*
[20] LPA, MX and D add: *in quibus casibus per universitatem regentium extitit declaratum procuratorum vel alterius eorundem* (LPA: *vel eorum alterius aut eorundem*) *assertionem seu pretensionem debere* (MX: *assertionem debere*) *sufficere in hac parte.*
[21] Faded out in O, supplied from LPA.
[22] LPA and D: *eorum alter.*
[23] LPA, MX and D add: *vel convocet.*
[24] LPA and D add: *Pro utilitate etiam communi universitatis predicte valent* (D: *valeant*) *et debent iidem procuratores convocare magistros regentes, si cancellarius vel eius locum tenens requisitus hoc facere dissimulaverit, neglexerit seu distulerit minus iuste. Et si maior pars eorundem regentium super premissis vel aliquo eorum non-regentes fore vocandos decreverit, iidem procuratores vel eorum alter non-regentes convocent vel convocet indilate.*
MX adds (after *sententiet*): *Ad hoc statuendo discernimus, quod iidem procuratores vel eorum alter ob utilitatem communem universitatis predicte regentes ipsius, si cancellarius requisitus vel eius locum tenens hoc facere dissimulaverit, neglexerit seu distulerit minus iuste, valeant seu valet convocare. Et si*...(as LPA)...*ipsos non-regentes convocent vel convocet, faciant seu faciat convocari.*
[25] LPA, M, MX and D: *procuratoribus.*

aliquod tale delictum commissum fuerit, rectores[26] nullam cohercionem faciant, sed si vicecancellarius ab eis requisitus correccionem adhibere dissimulaverit, neglexerit vel minus iuste distulerit,[27] rectores[26] vel alter eorum[28] universitatem convocet sicut prius, omnibus consuetudinibus immo potius corruptelis preteritis huic statuto contrariis, hinc et in perpetuum minime valituris. [29]-Datum in ecclesia beate Marie, die sancte Wydburge, anno Domini millesimo ducentesimo septuagesimo quinto, tempore dicti cancellarii.-[29]

[26] LPA, M, MX and D: *procuratores.*
[27] D: *distulerit minus iuste.*
[28] LPA, MX and D: *eorum alter.*
[29-29] LPA, MX and D om.

VIII

The Curial Exequies for Edward I and Edward III

It is not generally known that solemn exequies were performed for Edward I at Poitiers in the presence of the pope, Clement V; that these exequies were the first exequies held in the curia for a king; that they supplied the model for the corresponding ceremonial in the office for the dead laid down in *Ordo Romanus* XIV[1] which was composed by cardinal James Gaetano Stefaneschi; and that, furthermore, the liturgical details of a canonisation ceremony shown in the same *Ordo Romanus* (OR.)[2] were modelled on the ceremonial actually observed at the canonisation of St. Thomas Cantelupe of Hereford in 1320. Lastly, attention must be directed to the apparently also unknown exequies solemnly performed for Edward III at Anagni on 3 September 1377, again in the presence of the pope, Gregory XI.

Apart from the last-mentioned item to which we shall return, the other details are transmitted in a unique MS. which is in the possession of the Museum Calvet at Avignon.[3] The first to draw attention to this MS. was the late cardinal Ehrle. Preparing a modern edition of the ORi., Ehrle searched for MSS. so as to obtain a firmer basis for his edition than Mabillon had at his disposal. This search led Ehrle to the Avignon MS., the rubrics of which he made known.[4] He also transcribed in full from this MS. the notes which cardinal Stefaneschi made on the first three sessions of the Council of Vienne (1311).[5] As regards the liturgical entries in this MS. Ehrle confined himself to a transcription of the rubrics only. Thus for f. 10v. of the MS. he noted the 'forma procedendi' in the canonisation of St. Thomas of Hereford which is followed by a detailed description of Celestine V's canonisation (5 May 1313). From f. 20r. Ehrle made known this rubric: Quid fuit servatum in exequiis regis Anglie.[6]

[1] We cite according to Mabillon's numeration of the *Ordines Romani*. See Mabillon, *Museum Italicum*, Paris 1689, ii–1. 1 ff.; *Ordo Romanus* XIV is on 246 ff. The fifteen *Ordines* of Mabillon were reprinted in Migne, P.L., lxxviii. 851 ff. The reference in the text is to cap. 114, P.L., lxxviii. 1254.

[2] Cap. 111, P.L., lxxviii. 1249–50.

[3] Museum Calvet, Avignon, MS. 1706. I desire to express my thanks to the Librarian, M. Georges de Loyes, for a microfilm.

[4] F. Ehrle, 'Zur Geschichte des päpstlichen Hofzeremoniells im 14. Jahrhundert' in *Archiv f. Literatur und Kirchengeschichte* v (1889). 565 ff.

[5] Ehrle, art. cit., 574 ff.   [6] Ehrle, art. cit., 569.

EXEQUIES FOR EDWARD I AND EDWARD III

Although he would not make a definite pronouncement, cardinal Ehrle considered it highly probable that the entries in this MS. came from the pen of cardinal James Gaetano Stefaneschi. It is an established fact that Stefaneschi was the author of OR.XIV which incorporates many liturgical items that seem to have such close relationship with the entries in this MS. In 1893 L. H. Labande published a penetrating study on this MS.[1] He concluded with convincing reasons that cardinal Stefaneschi was the author of these entries in the MS. They all have a strong personal character: for instance, in the entry concerning the canonisation of Celestine V we read this: Ego Jacobus sancti Georgii ad Velum aureum diaconus cardinalis domino pape a dexteris in predicta canonizatione et missa ministravi.[2] To Labande we owe the full transcription concerning the actual liturgy carried out in the case of St. Thomas of Hereford[3] as well as in that of Celestine V.[4] As far as the present writer could establish, this eye-witness account of the liturgical ceremonies observed at St. Thomas's canonisation does not appear to have been noticed. This liturgical ceremonial took an inordinately lengthy time, from 19 March till 17 April 1320, explicable no doubt by the vast amount of evidence collected by the special commission.[5] On the other hand, the canonisation procedure for Celestine V took a mere three days, from 2 to 5 May 1313. There can be no doubt that the respective entries in OR.XIV with regard to canonisation liturgy were directly based upon the ceremonies observed in these two cases.[6]

But Labande made no reference to the entry concerning the exequies of the king of England. The indefatigable historian of medieval liturgies, Mgr. Andrieu, in his minute examination of all the MSS. which he used for his editions, naturally enumerated this rubric of the Avignon MS.—a

---

[1] L. H. Labande, 'Le cérémonial Romain de Jacques Cajétan: les données historiques qu'il renferme' in *Bibl. de l'école des chartes*, liv (1893). 45 ff.

[2] MS. cit., f. 15v.; Labande, art. cit., 48. For other examples see ibid., 47. The cardinal's narrative of the canonisation of Celestine V in his *Opus metricum* (a biography of the canonised saint) is understandable only when this eye-witness report is taken into account, cf. F. X. Seppelt, *Monumenta Coelestiana* (in 'Quellen und Forschungen aus dem Gebiete der Geschichte', ix, Paderborn 1921), 14, 125–34, and editorial notes ibid.

[3] Labande, art. cit., 55–9.   [4] Ibid., 61–7.

[5] For the decree concerning the canonisation see *Lettres communes de Jean XXII*, ed. G. Mollat, Paris 1906, ii. 86, no. 11249; *Charters and Records of Hereford Cathedral*, ed. W. W. Capes, Hereford 1908, 190–4; *Extracts from Hereford Cathedral Registers*, ed. and translated by E. N. Drew, Hereford 1932, 50–2. For modern literature on Thomas see T. F. Tout in *D.N.B.*, s.v. Cantelupe; D. Douie, *Archbishop Pecham*, Oxford 1952, 217; Sir Maurice Powicke, *The Thirteenth Century*, Oxford 1953, 488–90; and D. Usher, *Two studies of medieval life*, Cambridge 1953, 89 ff. (a more popular account). The 17 miracles worked by St. Thomas and closely gone into by the special commissioners at Hereford, are examined in the manner of the 'advocatus diaboli' by A. T. Bannister, *The Cathedral Church of Hereford*, London 1924, 169–75. Altogether 221 miracles were said to have been worked by him. The voluminous evidence is set forth in the *Acta Sanctorum*, October, i. 539–610.

[6] See OR.XIV, cap. 111; Labande, art. cit., 55 n. 2; Ehrle, art. cit., 568 n. 3; and H. Leclercq in *Dict. d'archéologie chrétienne et de liturgie*, xii-2 (1936), col. 2434: 'Le MS. d'Avignon représente une copie du premier état de la rédaction de Jean Cajétan, lequel écrivait au fur et à mesure l'ordre et le détail des cérémonies auxquelles il venait d'assister.'

transcription of the whole entry was not called for considering Andrieu's object; he merely noted the Incipit and Explicit of this entry confining himself to the statement: 'Aucune date ni aucun nom propre.'[1] The opinion which Mgr. Andrieu puts forward as regards the character of this MS. is wholly convincing: according to him, it is a copy of cardinal Stefaneschi's own notes, a copy made in the second half of the fourteenth century. Cardinal Stefaneschi, great liturgist and writer as he was,[2] closely observed personally some of the liturgical ceremonies in which he either himself took part in some active manner or was a mere spectator.

It is understandable that the cardinal was especially interested in those ceremonies for which the earlier ORi. gave either insufficient information or no information at all. Intending as he was to compose a new OR. he was naturally anxious to observe ceremonies which were no more than *ad hoc* arrangements, but which gave him adequate material upon which to base the new OR. envisaged by him. It is thus clear why ceremonies for which the earlier ORi. contained no material particularly attracted his keen interest. One of these obvious gaps, to mention a rather conspicuous example, concerned the liturgy to be followed in the case of a royal coronation. Of imperial coronation *ordines* there was indeed no scarcity.[3] But the papal curia had no royal coronation *ordo* ready made. Hence when Charles of Anjou was to be crowned king of Sicily in 1289 by the pope, a royal coronation *ordo* was hastily put together. But because of its *ad hoc* nature, this *ordo* could not very well serve as a model for later royal coronations. Consequently, when the need arose to crown Charles's son, Robert of Naples, king, Clement V in 1309 appointed a commission under the chairmanship of cardinal Stefaneschi to compose a royal coronation *ordo*. The result of this commission's deliberations was the *ordo* applied at Robert's coronation on 3 August 1309 and this *ordo* also finds its place in the Avignon

---

[1] M. Andrieu, *Le Pontifical Romain au Moyen Age* (*Studi e Testi*, lxxxviii, Città del Vaticano 1940), iii. 41.

[2] For this see Ig. Hösl, *Kardinal Jacobus Gaietani Stefaneschi*, Berlin 1908, 96–105; also Leclercq, loc. cit., col. 2433. For other writings of Stefaneschi see Hösl, 34 ff. One of his chaplains in 1320–1322 was the Englishman Thomas of Wilton, canon of Wells and London (*Calendar of Papal Registers: Papal Letters*, ed. W. H. Bliss, ii. 82, 153, 206, 225) and a lecturer in theology at Paris (cf. *Chartularium Universitatis Parisiensis*, ed. Denifle-Chatelain, Paris 1891, ii. 240, no. 791). Dante appears to have been a friend of the cardinal; see Hösl, 127 f. Like so many high clerics at that time, the cardinal was never in priest's orders and remained all his life a deacon. He was created a cardinal by Boniface VIII and died on 23 June 1343, 73 years old. He was a witness of the Anagni outrage and a life-long opponent of France: in December 1304 he collected a number of votes as papal candidate in the same conclave that eventually elected Clement V. In parenthesis it may be mentioned that the English cardinal Walter Winterbourne—created by Benedict XI—was at the same time a strong papal candidate having received half of the votes of the College. For these details see H. Finke, *Aus den Tagen Bonifaz VIII*, Munster 1902, 283–4 and the report in document no. 14, pp. lix ff. The entry in *D.N.B.* s.v. Winterbourne, needs some rectification. Considering the anti-French attitude and Bonifacian loyalty of Stefaneschi the history of the fourteenth-century papacy would have been a little different, had he actually been elected pope.

[3] Cf. *Growth of Papal Government in the Middle Ages*, London 1954, 225 ff., 253 ff.

MS. It eventually re-appeared with some slight modifications in OR.XIV.[1]

But there was not only no royal coronation *ordo* in the earlier ORi.; there was also no liturgical regulation to be followed in the case of a canonisation; nor any ceremonial to be adopted in the case of exequies performed for a king (or an emperor) in the presence of the pope. These were lacunae which cardinal Stefaneschi was anxious to see filled. As regards the exequies there was a short entry in the ancient OR.X (cap. 36) for a *missa pro defunctis*, but this applied merely to deceased clerics of the local Roman province: there is no mention of the pope either as a celebrant or as a participant. Like the royal coronation *ordo* for 1289, the ceremonial arranged for 'the king of England' bears all the stamp of an *ad hoc* affair. Himself being the foremost liturgist of the curia at the time, Stefaneschi closely observed the exequies, precisely because they were a novelty.

It is plain that over a number of years the cardinal collected material with a view to the new OR.[2] What he saw in certain liturgical ceremonies, he took down in the shape of personal observations, whilst the ceremonies were still fresh in his memory. These notes were an *aide-mémoire* and they have all the appearance of personal jottings.[3] That is why the description of this eye-witness of the canonisation procedures in the cases of Thomas Cantelupe and Celestine V no less than his description of the coronation ceremony and of the exequies evoke so great an interest.

Mgr. Andrieu's assumption that these memos of cardinal Stefaneschi were on separate sheets, has everything in its favour; so also is his further assumption justified that an unknown copyist of the second half of the fourteenth century gathered these memos—quite in disregard of chronology—into one volume, the surviving MS. at Avignon, which in itself is not complete.[4] This copyist was neither intelligent nor a good latinist nor at times familiar with the technical terms, defects which have sufficiently been commented upon by Ehrle, Labande and Andrieu. In mitigation it

---

[1] See OR.XIV, cap. 107, P.L., lxxviii. 1245. For further details see Andrieu, op. cit., ii. 288 and iii. 41. The entry in the MS. is from fol. 18r–20r. OR.XIV, cap. 107, contains this statement: Rubrica, quae inferius ponitur, fuit ordinata de mandato domini Clementis pape V per aliquos cardinales, quibus hoc in consistorio commissum fuit, cum Robertus, rex Siciliae, cum sua conjuge peteret unctionem et coronationem apud Avinionem, ubi tunc Romana curia residebat. Nam nihil inveniebatur in litteris traditum, qualiter reges et reginae debent inungi et coronari, eo quod in pontificali Romano non habetur nisi de unctione et coronatione imperatoris et imperatricis. The MS. itself has this statement appended to the *ordo* composed for the coronation of Charles of Anjou: Sciendum quod multa ex supradictis quae acta sunt in coronatione prefati regis, non tam approbata quam tolerata fuerunt per dominum papam et fratres ipsius, unde non oportet quod omnia in exemplum trahuntur; transcribed by Labande, art, cit., 73.

[2] Cf. also Leclercq, quoted supra, 28 n. 2. The report of the coronation of Charles of Anjou in this MS. seems to have been the first notice of Stefaneschi. He was then a young chaplain of Nicholas IV; see Hösl, op. cit., 13, 101.

[3] These shorthand memos may be regarded as the forerunners of the fully-fledged diaries kept by the curial Masters of Ceremonies at a later period. One of these diaries (for December 1515) is dealt with by E. Bishop, *Liturgica Historica*, Oxford 1918, 435 ff.

[4] It has only 50 folios. For a full description see Andrieu, op. cit., iii. 35 ff.

may be pleaded that these memos of cardinal Stefaneschi were probably not written calligraphically and therefore the copyist might have had some difficulty in deciphering the cardinal's handwriting. That is why in some places he omitted terms, whilst in others when his deciphering ability failed him, he left a blank. Considering his failings in the other entries, the item concerning the exequies is quite competent.

Although, as Mgr. Andrieu has already noted, no date or proper name is given in this entry, the exequies can only refer to Edward I: the entry explicitly mentions the cathedral church of Poitiers, and it was at Poitiers that the papal curia stayed during the spring and summer months of 1307.[1] The immediate task which the pope had set himself was the arrangement of peace between Edward I and Philip IV.[2] The pope was expecting the young Edward (II) as the king's envoy, but whilst in London and preparing for the crossing, he was recalled by his father in June 1307.[3] On 7 July 1307 Edward I died. When did the exequies take place?

The silence of contemporary chroniclers may be explained by the purely 'domestic' character of exequies which were probably never known to outsiders. The Registers of the papal chancery by their very nature can give us no indication. All we learn from them is that the chancery knew of Edward I's death on 3 August 1307, because in a document issued on this day Edward seems to be referred to as dead.[4] This in itself gives no clue as to when the exequies were performed.

There is, however, a very welcome means which helps us in fixing the week within which the exequies for Edward I were held. They took place in the cathedral of Poitiers during the week ending 28 July 1307. Luckily, the detailed expenses accounts of the papal *camera* for the period in question are preserved. For two consecutive weeks there are entries of payment directly occasioned by the exequies for Edward I. In the fourth week of July, ending 28 July, payment was authorised for the transportation of certain articles from the papal residence to the cathedral of Poitiers and back, whilst in the subsequent week there are two entries recording payment and both expressly mention the exequies for Edward.[5]

---

[1] At the time of Edward II's death the curia had settled in Avignon.

[2] G. Lizerand, *Clément V et Philippe le Bel*, Paris 1910, 65 ff.

[3] Lizerand, op. cit., 67.

[4] See *Regestum Clementis papae V*, ed. cura et studio monachorum ordinis s. Benedicti, Rome 1885, no. 1845 of 3 August 1307. There may, of course, have been other letters before 3 August which took cognisance of the king's death, but none could be found in the Registers. Not all the letters were enregistered. Clement V's Registers are in no way different from the thirteenth-century papal Registers; cf. F. Bock, 'Einführung in das Registerwesen des Avignonesischen Papsttums' in *Quellen und Forschungen aus italienischen Archiven und Bibliotheken*, xxxi (1941). 1. For some Clementine Register fragments in later Register volumes and unknown to the editors, see E. Göller, 'Mitteilungen und Untersuchungen über das päpstliche Register und Kanzleiwesen im 14. Jahrhundert', ibid., vii (1904). 81–2.

[5] See *Reg.* cit., Appendix vol. i, Rome 1892, 42, for the week ending 28 July 1307: Item Andreutio domini Gentilis pro rebus portatis ad ecclesiam sancti Petri, clavis et reportatura ipsarum rerum ad cameram domini VII solidos et III denarios Turonensium parvorum. For the week ending 4 August the following two items are of interest (ibid., 43): Item Nicolao et Stephano spetiariis pro XV quintallis cum dimidio cere et II libris

EXEQUIES FOR EDWARD I AND EDWARD III

The inference is, therefore, that the pope heard of Edward's death round about 20/21 July 1307 and that the exequies were performed a few days afterwards. For this inference a possible corroboration may be had from an entry in the cameral expenses account for the week ending 21 July. This entry relates to the authorisation of payment occasioned by the arrival of three clerics from England in that week. It is not beyond the bounds of possibility that these three clerics reported Edward's death. He died on the Scottish border and the time the news would take to reach the pope at Poitiers would be about a fortnight.[1]

In Appendix (A) a transcription of cardinal Stefaneschi's eye-witness account will be found. As can readily be seen, this memo is not written with any particular regard for style, grammar or latinity; nevertheless, this blemish does not diminish the value of the account, which, just as in the cases of Thomas and Celestine, reads like a slow-motion picture of the ceremonial witnessed. It is clear that the cardinal focused his attention almost exclusively on the activity of the pope during the exequies, precisely the item which constituted a novelty. On the whole, the framework of the exequies followed the usual pattern of the ordinary masses for the dead.[2] It is certainly interesting to note that the cardinal bishop of Ostia— the senior of all the cardinals—was the celebrant of the exequies. Just as Stefaneschi made some slight modifications in the coronation *ordo* and in the canonisation procedure of OR.XIV, so here too he modified some items and condensed the whole procedure.[3] Naturally, some of the details

et III unciis ad XVIII florenos cum dimidio pro quintallo expensis pro exequiis domini E. regis Anglie de mandato domini nostri CCLXXXI florenos auri et II Turonenses grossos. The other entry follows: Item Tadiolo servienti pro operibus factis in ecclesia sancti Petri Pictavensi, quando fuerunt dicte exequie facte ibi VII libras, XVIII solidos et IX denarios Turonensium parvorum. About the contemporary value of these units cf. M. Tangl, 'Das Taxwesen der päpstlichen Kanzlei vom 13. bis Mitte des 15. Jahrhunderts' in *Mitteilungen d. oesterr. Instituts f. Geschichtsforschung*, xiii (1892). 13–15 (with further literature). For the expenses incurred by the *camera* see L. König, *Die päpstliche Kammer unter Clemens V und Johann XXII*, Vienna 1894, 56–68.

[1] See ibid., 40: Item pro feno III clericorum qui venerunt de Anglia XXXIII solidos et VI denarios Turonensium parvorum. There may be a clue to the identity of these three clerics. In *Calendar Pat. Rolls, 1301–1307*, 533, bishop William Gainsborough of Worcester obtained for 6 men, three of whom were clerics, on 28 June 1307, royal protection as they were to proceed with him 'to the court of Rome on the king's affairs'. These three clerics were: Gilbert de Aketoft, William de Stoketh, Robert de Wychio. Two days before his death, on 5 July, Edward wrote from Carlisle to Clement about the mission of William Gainsborough (Rymer, *Foedera*, ed. London 1816, i-2. 1017) and it is likely that the bishop himself was the bearer of this letter. Also on the same day Edward addressed the cardinals. Whilst there is at least a theoretical possibility that the bishop's three clerics may be the arrivals to whom the entry refers, it is certain that the bishop himself never reached the pope at Poitiers: he fell ill and died at Beauvais on 16 September 1307. About the consequences of his death and the wrong entry in Rymer, see Appendix (C).

[2] Cf. Durantis, *Rationale divinorum officiorum*, Lyons 1612, lib. vii, cap. 35, 452 ff.

[3] See OR.XIV, cap. 114, P.L., lxxviii. 1254. There was no stipulation here that the cardinal bishop of Ostia should be the celebrant: Notandum quod papa non consuevit celebrare solemniter missam pro defuncto, quantumcumque rege magno, sed facere celebrari solemniter et praedicari coram eo per unum episcopum vel presbyterum cardinalem, vocatis omnibus cardinalibus. At the exequies for Edward III it was the cardinal bishop of Glandève who was the celebrant: he did not become 'Ostiensis' until April 1378.

witnessed by the cardinal were of no intrinsic value and could be disregarded in the new OR.: there was no need permanently to record the change in the papal head gear necessitated by the rain falling before and after the exequies, or the change in the processional arrangements also conditioned by the rain, or the number of torches and candles burning during the ceremony, and so forth. What is important is that these exequies for Edward I were the first exequies for a king in which a pope solemnly and officially took part and which formed the basis of the respective ceremonial in OR.XIV witnessed by the author himself.

The OR. succeeding that of cardinal Stefaneschi was made by Peter Amelii in the closing years of the fourteenth century.[1] Now this OR.XV also contains a description of the ceremonial adopted in exequies for a king, but one that shows several more details and a greater refinement than its immediate predecessor. There is a strong likelihood that it was the exequies performed for Edward III at Anagni on 3 September 1377 which were the model on which Peter Amelii drew. It is, indeed, an astonishing parallel. The eighteenth-century liturgist, Johannes Gatticus, transcribed from certain Vatican MSS. entries one of which also contains the description of the exequies for Edward III.[2] Since they are not apparently known, it was thought advisable to reprint them here (Appendix (B)).

That this description of Edward III's exequies is an eyewitness account seems pretty obvious. And, since Peter Amelii was the author of OR.XV and since, furthermore, he was the curial librarian at the time,[3] it is very probable that he was acquainted with cardinal Stefaneschi's method of making a personal *aide-mémoire* of the ceremonies for the new OR. envisaged by him.[4] A comparison of the entry in MS.Vat.Urb.469—from

[1] He mentions himself in OR.XV, cap. 80 (P.L., lxxviii. 1324): Ita vidi ego Frater Petrus Amelii, Senegaliensis episcopus, observari tempore domini Urbani V, Gregorii XI et Urbani VI Romanorum pontificum. In cap. 90, 1336: Fuerunt facti illo anno (1378) per Fratrem Petrum episcopum Senegaliensem sacristam XXIV agnus. Cf. also cap. 139, 1348; cap. 142, 1349; cap. 150, 1358. A number of additions were made to this OR. in the fifteenth century. A modern critical edition of these later ORi. is very much wanted.

[2] See J. B. Gatticus, *Acta Selecta Caeremonialia Sanctae Romanae Ecclesiae*, Rome 1753, 170.

[3] For this see F. Ehrle, *Historia Bibliothecae Romanorum Pontificum*, Rome 1890, 735–7. Peter Amelii composed a valuable descriptive catalogue of the Avignonese library shortly before the curia returned to Rome: it is edited by Ehrle, ibid., 454–560. He also wrote the *Itinerarium* from Avignon to Rome to which he refers in OR.XV, cap. 142; P.L., lxxviii. 1349. The entries in C. Eubel, *Hierarchia Catholica Medii Aevi*, Munster 1893, i. 266, 473, relating to Peter, need some rectification.

[4] Thus the lengthy description of the canonisation of St. Bridget of Sweden in this OR.XV, cap. 153 (7 October 1391), follows the model provided by Stefaneschi's description of St. Thomas's and Celestine's canonisation. E. W. Kemp, *Canonization and Authority in the Western Church*, Oxford 1948, 128 n. 2, has drawn attention to the description of St. Bridget's canonisation. In cap. 75 (P.L., loc. cit., 1315), Peter quotes Stefaneschi as his authority: secundum Jacobum Gaietani. Cf. also cap. 77, 1319 and cap. 85, 1331. This OR.XV has in fact many more concrete details of ceremonies which occurred under Gregory XI, Urban VI and Boniface IX than OR.XIV. The author must have kept a very close watch on the ceremonies and detailed records. An interesting case is that of cap. 143. It describes the ceremonial which takes place when a pope is on his death-bed. Now Stefaneschi had in his notes his eye-witness report on the dying

which Gatticus transcribed—with the respective ceremonial in OR.XV[1] indicates how closely the latter was modelled on the former.[2] In view of the intimate relationship between OR.XIV and cardinal Stefaneschi's memo and between OR.XV and the entry in Vat.Urb. 469, the conclusion is justified that the death of Edward I occasioned the shaping of the curial liturgy relating to royal exequies, and the death of Edward III provided another opportunity of developing this liturgical ceremoniál. No doubt the gap in the official Roman liturgy, thus filled, is somewhat extraordinary, especially when one considers what minute attention was bestowed on all sorts of liturgical ceremonies in the curia: but this gap is no more extraordinary than the absence of a royal coronation *ordo* in the Roman pontifical or, for that matter, the absence of a proper liturgical ceremonial relating to the canonisation of a saint. Fortunately, the unique MS. at Avignon containing so much useful information has been preserved.

APPENDIX

(A)

Curial Exequies for Edward I at Poitiers, July 1307

MS. Museum Calvet, Avignon, no. 1706, f. 20r–v.

Quid fuit servatum in exequiis regis Anglie.

Notandum quod in missa fuerant magna tortitia, videlicet L et facule ante chorum et super altare multe, et ducente facule pape et cardinalibus et prelatis et aliis de camera pape. In obitu regis Anglie ut fuerat Pictaviis observatum, nam singuli cardinales dixerunt in domibus suis vesperas et vigilias mortuorum cum nota.[3] In mane sequenti celebravit Hostiensis[4] missam in ecclesia cathedrali pro defunctis pro anima regis. Dominus papa ibidem fuit et cardinales. Papa ivit in capa de scarleto ad ecclesiam

Benedict XI (f. 8r., MS. cit.), but in his OR.XIV there is no corresponding entry about this death-bed ceremonial. There is no doubt that Stefaneschi's notes served Peter Amelii as a useful guide for the composition of cap. 143. Cf. also Ehrle, art. cit., 584, and the transcript from the Avignon MS. ibid., 585–6.

[1] See OR.XV, cap. 132–4, 138.

[2] For a description of MS. Vat.Urb.469 see H. Ehrensberger, *Libri Liturgici Bibl. Apostolicae Vaticanae*, Freiburg 1897, 559. More details will be found in C. Stornajolo, *Codices Urbinatis Latini*, Rome 1902, i. 474–5. The first 72 folios contain OR.XIV of Stefaneschi. The passage on fol. 78v, describing Edward III's exequies, is immediately followed by reports about exequies performed in the presence of anti-popes at Avignon, such as Clement VII and Benedict XIII. The last date mentioned is 23 January 1408. But there is no indication at all that Peter Amelii had left Rome and gone over to Avignon: moreover, he died in 1401 (see Ehrle, op. cit., 737). What seems a possible explanation, without autopsy, is that this entry in the Vat. MS. was made by some Avignonese liturgist of the early fifteenth century who had conscientiously copied Peter Amelii's report and appended his own accounts. The description of Edward III's exequies is continued thus: Ita quoque servatum fuit Avinione tempore domini Clementis VII quando decesserunt. . . . All these exequies reported seem to have been based on the Edwardian ones. The whole passage will be found in Gatticus, loc. cit.

[3] That is 'chanted'. The terms 'cantus' and 'nota' were interchangeable, cf. M. Andrieu, op. cit., ii. 469 no. 19, note 1.

[4] This was Nicholas Alberti de Prato, O.P. (bishop of Spoleto), created by Benedict XI on 13 December 1303: C. Eubel, *Hierarchia Catholica*, i. 13.

cum capello papali[1] et portavit capellum, nam pluebat; alias portasset mitram simpliciter albam[2] cum capa de scarleto. In missa fuit cum capa predicta et mitra simpliciter alba. Veniens ad ecclesiam non adoravit in medio ecclesie nec fecit nomen,[3] et coram altari adoravit et obtulit pannum seu pannos sericos.[4] Ad *Introitus* accessit ad altare ut moris est. Et postmodum ad sedem, que post altare erat. Erant circumcirca diaconi tamen a dexteris, et episcopi et presbyteri cardinales a sinistris.

Cardinales cum eo dixerunt requiem et hinc in oratione debuit poni faldistorium et genuflectere, sicut in quadragesima.[5] Alie solempnitates facte sunt de incensando papam[6] et benedictio diaconi et benedictio predicantis, ut alias. Verum solus papa incensatur post evangelium, librum osculatur, et in ingressu misse et in offertorio tam celebrans quam papa debuit incensari. Dicto *Sanctus* cum cardinali genuflexit in faldistorio cum mitra usquequo sacerdos incipit facere cruces super oblatas, et tunc deposuit mitram usque ad elevationem calicis, et tunc resumpta mitra genuflexus incumbit faldistorio usque ad *Agnus*. Et tunc mitra deposita surgit juxta faldistorium et dicit *Agnus* cum cardinali. Et post iterum genuflexit sine mitra tantum usque sacerdos vinum perfusionis incipit sumere. Et incipiente sumere vinum perfusionis, papa cum mitra sedem ascendit sessurus. In oratione vero finali papa genuflectit cum mitra et oratione expleta ascendit ad sedem nec sedit. Et missa completa non dixit *Sit nomen*,[7] sed sedit cum mitra. Hostiensis vero venit ad pedem, indulgentiam non petiit nec debuit, predicavit, nec dictum est *Confiteor* nec alia absolutio facta nec fieri debuit. Et tunc dominus papa mantum accepit cum mitra frigiata, et sic ivit per ecclesiam. Et sic debuisset ad domum redire. Sed quia pluit, recessit in equo cum capa de scarleto et capello papali. Et notandum quod nullus cardinalis vel prelatus fecit orationem seu absolutionem consuetam cum corpus est presens, nec etiam dominus noster fecit absolutionem (sed si corpus non[8] fuisset presens, ultimam absolutionem

---

[1] This does not seem to have been a recognised liturgical or extraliturgical head gear: it is not mentioned in any earlier OR.

[2] For the three kinds of papal mitres see Gregory X's OR.XIII, cap. 12, P.L., lxxviii. 1114. For details of this OR. see Andrieu, op. cit., ii. 277 ff., especially 286 ff. The passage runs: Notandum est quod dominus papa tres mitras diversas habet, quibus diversis temporibus utitur, scil. unam albam totam, unam cum aurifrisio in titulo sine circulo et mitram aurifrisiatam in circulo et in titulo. For the historical development of papal head gears cf. *Growth of Papal Government*, 311 ff. See now also P. E. Schramm, *Herrschaftszeichen und Staatssymbolik*, Weimar 1954, 54 ff.

[3] This is obviously a shorthand and somewhat inelegant abbreviation for: nec dixit: Sit nomen Domini benedictum (the usual prayer text, cf. OR.XIV, cap. 45, P.L., lxxviii. 1140).

[4] For this see OR.XIII, cap. 11, P.L. lxxviii. 1113 = ed. Andrieu, ii. 540 sub no. 91: Nota quod semper papa offert pannum sericum super altare cuiuscumque ecclesie, cum primo eius altare ascendit. Would the statement in the text therefore indicate that the exequies for Edward provided the first opportunity of the pope's visit to the altar in the cathedral?

[5] Cf. OR.XIII, cap. 20, and OR.XIV, cap. 80 f.

[6] Cf. OR.XIV, cap. 53.   [7] See supra note 3.

[8] This is obviously a scribal mistake of the copyist. He either inserted thoughtlessly the 'non' or misread a 'nunc' or something like it. If the 'non' is excised, the sentence makes perfect sense.

fecisset dominus cum manto rubeo, et sic postmodum equitasset). Cardinales diaconi a dexteris in missa et episcopi et presbyteri a sinistris, sicut est consuetum.

(B)

Curial Exequies for Edward III at Anagni, 3 September 1377

MS. Vat.Urb.469, f. 78v. Edition: J. B. Gatticus, *Acta Selecta Caeremonialia Sanctae Romanae Ecclesiae*, Rome 1753, 170.

Quando celebratur pro rege vel imperatore mortuo.

Anno 1377, Dominus noster papa Gregorius XI, pontificatus sui anno VII, Anagniae existens pro tunc, tertia die mensis Septembris fecit fieri exequias in capella sua pro anima Domini Edwardi Regis Angliae defuncti, et Dominus cardinalis Glandatensis[1] fecit officium et sermonem, qui non portavit chirothecas[2] in toto officio nec anulum pontificalem nec sandalia, nec fuit dicta in missa nisi unica oratio, et dum dicta oratio dicebatur, dictus Dominus noster descendit ante altare ad orandum et etiam quando dicebatur ultima oratio, idem Dominus noster descendit ad orandum ante altare, sicut in quadragesima.

Fuit autem factus sermo statim post missam per eundem Dominum cardinalem, qui solum deposita casula accepit pluviale nigrum et mitram planam, et solum accepta benedictione a papa, et sine pedis osculo[3] accessit ad medium altaris pro sermone faciendo.

Non fuit facta absolutio post missam nec data benedictio, sed finito sermone recesserunt omnes. Venit autem ad capellam idem Dominus noster indutus capa de scarleto aperta a parte anteriori, et cum mitra plana, nec assistunt sibi cardinales, quia non est indutus vestimentis pontificalibus. Item est sciendum quod quando celebrat pro defunctis seu praelatus coram eo non debet dici *Trium puerorum*,[4] sed loco ipsius dicitur *De profundis*.

Sciendum est autem moris fuisse et esse in curia Romana, quod quando papa habet nova certa de morte imperatoris vel alicuius regis catholici tamen in obedientia papae permanentis, ante eum per modum supra positum facit dicere in sua praesentia per unum de dominis cardinalibus missam de Requiem aeternam, nec in ipsa missa ponitur aliqua repraesentatio funeris neque luminare candelarum vel intortitiorum,[5] nisi dumtaxat in locis consuetis quatuor vel sex intortitia sicut fit in aliis missis papalibus.

[1] This was cardinal bishop Bertrand de Lagery, O.M., who became Hostiensis the following April.
[2] About them cf. Andrieu, op. cit., ii. 368 no. 41; 367 note 12; 456 note 5 ad no. 7. For a liturgical explanation of the gloves see Durantis, *Rationale*, ed. cit., lib. iii, cap. 12, 75–6.
[3] Kissing of the pope's feet is mentioned in the eighth-century OR.IX, cap. 4, P.L. lxxviii. 1006.
[4] About this antiphon cf. OR.XIII, cap. 5, P.L., lxxviii, 1108 = ed. Andrieu, op. cit., ii. 530 no. 18.
[5] With this should be compared Stefaneschi's account of the illuminations provided at Edward I's exequies. Is this perhaps a reflexion of the financial position of the *camera* in 1377 as compared with that 70 years earlier? Cf. the expenses incurred, supra p. 30 n.5.

(C)

(i) Rymer, *Foedera*, ed. cit., ii. 1, has two letters of Clement V under the heading: 'Quae sequuntur bullae scriptae (inscio papa) Edwardo primo demortuo.' The one letter is addressed to the king of France, Philip, and the other to the king's chancellor. In both Clement V asks for safe conduct of the English envoys. Both letters are dated: 'Apud Villam novam Avenionensi diocesi, vii id. Augusti, pontificatus nostri anno secundo.' The ascription by Rymer of these two letters to Clement V is a mistake. This is Clement VI who writes to Philip VI (not Clement V to Philip IV) about the envoys of Edward III (not Edward I). Clement V was nowhere near Villeneuve on 7 August 1307, for he dates from Poitiers on 7 August 1307 (see *Reg.* cit., nos. 1842, 1891, 2150, 2153, 2164-7). Clement VI in his second pontifical year (1343) dates from Villeneuve in the way in which these two documents are dated, cf. *Analecta Vaticano-Belgica*, ed. U. Berlière, Rome 1924, vi. 324 ff. (nos. 928 ff.). No doubt the identity of names—Clement, Philip, Edward—misled Rymer, as also the coincidence of the second pontifical year. In the letters of 7 August 1343 to Philip VI and his chancellor, Clement VI complied with the request of Edward III for safe conduct of his ambassadors; see Edward III's letter to Clement VI of 6 July in Rymer, iii. 1228. Cf. also ibid., 1224 for the earlier letters of Edward and Clement.

(ii) The vacancy in the see of Worcester caused by William Gainsborough's death, occasioned, it seems, a very early implementation of the papal right of reservation as regards English bishoprics. Three weeks after William's death, on 5 October 1307, Clement V in a bull (*Ad perpetuam rei memoriam*) reserved himself the right to 'provide' for the vacant see (*Reg.* cit., no. 2273), the reason obviously being that William died during a journey to the curia, although the canonical grounds for the exercise of the right of reservation, i.e. death at the curia or at a place of two days journey's distance from the curia, did not seem to exist. Beauvais is some 220 miles from Poitiers (360 km. as the crow flies). The reaction of Edward II to this bull of Clement V is a classic example of the royalist attitude (see *The Register of the Diocese of Worcester: sede vacante*, ed. J. W. Willis-Bund, Oxford 1897, 104–107) and with its emphasis on 'the right of the crown' is reminiscent of Henry III's answer to Grosseteste (cf. *Ep.* cvii, ed. H. R. Luard, Rolls Series, 338–9). The attitude of the chapter of Worcester emerges from the entries in the *Register*, 107 ff. When, on 13 November 1307, Walter Reynolds was eventually elected by the chapter, the king petitioned the pope for confirmation of this election: the pope (*Reg.* no. 2464 of 12 February 1308, with 6 *a-pari* copies) quashed the election of Walter Reynolds ('electione contra reservationem praesumpta irrita') and himself appointed Walter as bishop. See also *Register of Worcester*, 111. About his chancellorship see the entry in Harley MS. 293, set ii, f. 21 v.

IX

A DECISION OF THE ROTA ROMANA ON THE BENEFIT
OF CLERGY IN ENGLAND

SUMMARY: The *privilegium fori* embraces not only criminal, but also civil causes — The situation in England in the XIII and XIV ss. — Apparent abrogation of the *priv. fori* in civil causes — The *Rota Romana* and its *Decisiones*, especially *Decis.* 840 — The personnel of the *Rota* in XIV s. — Some notable English *auditores* — The background to the decision of the *Rota* — The writ of prohibition and its connexion with the *priv. fori* in civil matters — The substance of the decision — Analysis of its main points: (1) Were the English clerics legally entitled to divest themselves of the *priv. fori* in civil matters? — (2) What juristic value had the pope's knowledge of the practice in England? — Juristic assessment of the decision — Two further specific cases of conflict of customary with positive law — (1) Royal conferment of certain offices and (2) Unction with chrism on the head of the king — Comparison of the function of the *Rota* as a tribunal of law with the function of the pope as legislator, judge and governor — The need for, and the scope of, further research — The controversies relating to the *priv. fori* exemplify rival jurisdictions within the Church, but do not represent a conflict between Church and State — King and cleric as *personae mixtae* — The decision itself an illustration of concrete historical jurisprudence [*W. U.*].

SUMMARIUM: *Privilegium fori* non solum ad causas criminales sed etiam ad causas civiles sese extendit. — De statu rerum in Anglia saeculis XIIIº et XIVº vigenti. — *Privilegium fori* in causis civilibus videtur abrogatum esse. — De *Rota Romana* eiusque *Decisionibus* praesertim de *Decisione* 840. — De *Auditoribus S. R. Rotae* perdurante saec. XIVº et praesertim de *Auditoribus* nationis Anglicae melioris notae. — De circumstantiis decisionis *S. R. Rotae* de qua sermo est. — De *Brevi regis de prohibitione* deque eius nexu cum *privilegio fori* in rebus civilibus. — Quid decisio dicat. — Eius capita principaliora analysi subiiciuntur: (1) possuntne clerici Anglici legitime abrenuntiare *privilegio fori* in causis civilibus? — (2) quid iuridice valeat factum quod R. Pontifex praxim Anglicam cognoverit? — Quid sub aspectu iuridico dicendum sit de *Decisione*. — De duobus aliis casibus specialibus in quibus ius consuetudinarium et ius positivum sibi contradicunt — (1) de approbatione regia quorundam officiorum et (2) de inungendo capite regis chrismate. — Instituitur comparatio inter officium *Rotae* qua est tribunal legis et inter R. Pontificem qua est legislator, iudex, rector. — Dicitur quod ulterior inquisitio necessaria est et quid efficere debeat. — Controversiae quae spectant ad *privilegium fori* exempla praebent iurisdictionum concurrentium in Ecclesia sed non significant pugnam inter Ecclesiam et Statum. — De rege et de clericis quatenus *personae mixtae* habentur. — De ipsa Decisione prout propriam iurisprudentiam historicam illustrat.

Every contribution to a *Festschrift* harbours some dangerous pitfalls. Ideally speaking the essay should not only be closely linked with the work of the savant in whose honour the *Festschrift* appears, but should take its cue from the main line of his research:

if it does not, he may justifiably feel aggrieved. On the other hand, when as in the present instance, the savant himself commands the towering height of sovereign and unrivalled mastery in a subject which to a large extent is his own creation and for which he has, powerfully and influentially, mapped out its direction, any contributor to his *Festschrift* must quite obviously be seized with the uncomfortable feeling that the *Jubilar* could himself have written each contribution so much better, so much more elegantly, and with so much more insight and penetration than the most strenuous efforts of others could ever hope to achieve. In offering Stephan Kuttner this tiny contribution I know very well how sadly I go astray from the ideal norm: for such pedestrian problems as the *privilegium fori* have not — and probably never could have — evoked his interest. Apart from this: *Rem non novam aggredimur.* In extenuation my plea is on the one hand *ignorantia invincibilis* in those matters in which he has, and can have, no peer — the classical age of canonistics, — and on the other hand I plead *brevitas temporis et ingens pondus negotiorum* for offering him so small and insignificant a contribution. I can only ask him to accept it in the spirit in which it is submitted to him.

I

Of the three great *privilegia clericorum* — the *privilegium canonis, immunitatis* and *fori* — the latter has always received the greater attention, especially in England where this *privilegium* had so dramatically stood in the forefront of the quarrel between King Henry II and Archbishop Thomas Becket (1). What characterizes, however, the historical treatment of the *privilegium fori* during and after the Henry II - Becket conflict is its concentration upon the criminal aspects and the virtual exclusion of the civil side of the matter. This so-called benefit of clergy is seen almost wholly from the angle of criminal proceedings against criminous clerks. For instance, in one of the more recent and most competent monographs on the subject we find this definition of the benefit of clergy:

---

(1) For the most recent discussion see Ch. Duggan, *The Becket Dispute and the Criminous Clerks* in: *Bulletin of the Institute of Historical Research*, XXXV (1962), 1 ff.

It may be defined as the exemption of members of the clergy from the jurisdiction of the temporal courts *in certain criminal cases* which normally would not have come within the competence of the ecclesiastical courts. The clerk charged with *felony* could, by pleading his " clergy " in the lay court, procure the transference of his case to the court of the bishop... (2).

And yet, here we also find the somewhat curious statement that

civil actions were outside the sphere of special privilege altogether (3).

Indeed, as far as the criminal side of the matter is concerned, by ransacking all the available evidence recent studies have thrown as much light on the question as it will probably ever be possible to do with any degree of historical certainty (4). Nevertheless, the virtually total neglect of civil actions and civil proceedings is certainly noteworthy: Maitland was — which can cause no surprise — one of the few who fully realized that personal actions were as much embraced in the *privilegium fori* as purely criminal proceedings, although he does not seem to have sufficiently evaluated the concrete evidence in this context (5). Admittedly, criminal proceedings have always had a much greater publicity appeal; by the very fact of a crime having been committed, public attention is much more easily arrested than is and was the case with civil actions, and quite especially if the culprit was a cleric in holy orders who had committed murder, robbery, theft, rape, and the like. It need not be specially emphasized here that civil actions, although less noisy,

---

(2) L. C. GABEL, *Benefit of Clergy in England in the later Middle Ages* (*Smith College Studies in History*) (Northampton, Mass. 1929), p. 7 (italics are mine).

(3) *Ibid.*, p. 59.

(4) Cf., for example, R. GÉNESTAL, *Le privilegium fori en France du Décret de Gratien à la fin du XIVe siècle*, 2 vols. (Paris, 1921-24); G. LE BRAS, *Le privilège du clergie en France dans les derniers siècles du Moyen Age* in: *Journal des Savants*, XX (1922), pp. 163 ff., 253 ff. (review of GÉNESTAL); for England see L. C. GABEL, *op. cit.*; W. HOLDSWORTH, *History of English Law*, 3rd ed. (London, 1923), III, 293 ff.; C. R. CHENEY, *The punishment of felonous clerks* in: *Engl. Hist. Rev.*, LI (1936), pp. 215 ff.; T. F. T. PLUCKNETT, *A Concise History of the Common Law*, 4th ed. (London, 1948), pp. 414 ff. Further literature in DUGGAN, *art. cit.*, p. 2 notes 1 and 2.

(5) See F. POLLOCK and F. W. MAITLAND, *History of English Law*, 2nd ed. (Cambridge, 1924), I.440; see also I.130.

460

can have far more severe and lasting consequences than criminal proceedings. As far as the canon law itself went, there can be no doubt whatsoever that civil proceedings were as much included in the *privilegium fori* as criminal ones (6). Moreover, imperial legislation strictly followed canon law: in his coronation edicts of November 1220 Frederick II declared:

> *Statuimus autem, ut nullus ecclesiasticam personam in criminali questione vel civili trahere ad iudicium seculare presumat contra constitutiones imperiales et canonicas sanctiones* (7).

And this part of the imperial edict was, most significantly, incorporated as an *authenticum* in the *Codex* itself (8).

The overwhelming evidence presented in canon (and civil) law was that criminal and civil proceedings were treated *pari passu* under the heading of the *privilegium fori*. That was the law; it was also the theory amongst the canonists: one authority must suffice. According to the report of the Archdeacon (Guido de Baysio), Huguccio had in his commentary on C. XI, qu. 1, c. 1 (9) unequivocally expressed the view that the term " accusare " should be taken in a wide meaning and should include criminal as well as civil proceedings (10). But as far as practice was concerned, at least in England, were the law and its theory also implemented? Although there are good reasons for holding that in criminal matters the *privilegium*

---

(6) For an easy orientation of the respective entries in Gratian, see DUGGAN, *art. cit.*, pp. 6 ff. See especially *D. p. c.* 47, C. XI, qu. 1: " Ex his omnibus datur intelligi, quod clericus ad publica iudicia nec *in civili* nec in criminali causa est producendus, nisi forte *civilem causam* episcopus decidere noluerit vel in criminali sui honoris cingulo eum nudaverit ". See further *ibid.*, c. 8 (" neque *pro civili* neque pro criminali causa "); c. 43 (" ... hic in criminali actione; *in civili* vero pendat... "), etc.; for decretal legislation cf., e.g., *X:* II.2.12, reenacting Gratian, C. XI.1.42 and 43; *VI:* II.2.2 and III.2.1 (" trahi non posse criminaliter aut *civiliter* ad iudicem saecularem "); etc.

(7) *M. G. H., Const.* II.85, cap. 4, p. 108.

(8) *Cod.* I.3, post legem 31. Baldus, *Commentaria ad Codicem* (ed. Venice, 1610), *ad Authent. Statuimus*, fol. 49v, tells us: " Dicunt canonistae, quod hoc non est ius novum, sed est recedere ab errore veterum legum ".

(9) Which ran: " Nemo unquam episcopum apud iudicem saecularem aut alios clericos accusare praesumat ". The passage actually comes from Ps.-Isidore, i. e. Ps.-Gaius in P. HINSCHIUS, *Decretales Pseudo-Isidorianae* (repr. Berlin, 1963), p. 214, cap. 3.

(10) See Archidiaconus, *Apparatus ad Sextum* (ed. Venice, 1577), ad *VI:* III.2.1, s. v. *condemnari*, no. 3, fol. 81: " Ubi (i. e. XI.1.1) dicit Hug. quod ibi accusare large sumitur, id est impetere *civiliter* vel criminaliter ".

fori was on the whole respected by the royal courts (11), there is far less evidence to the same effect in regard to civil actions (12). What one can safely say is that on balance it was certainly less respected than its criminal counterpart. Although there were complaints by the clergy which would indicate the disregard of the *privilegium fori*, as far as its civil side mattered, it would nevertheless be safe to say that the disregard of the civil protection afforded to the clerics by the *privilegium fori*, was less often made the point of a grievance than the purely criminal side. It is also true that, at any rate in the thirteenth century, there was the petition of the clergy in 1237 (13); there was also the ecclesiastical grievance at the Council of London in 1257 (14); above all, there was the legislation of the Council of Lambeth under Archbishop Boniface in 1261 (15). The most persuasive proof of the practice in the mid-thirteenth century, however, comes from Bracton himself who says that for debts (except litigations arising out of last wills or matrimonial causes) the competent court was the *forum laicale* for clerics whether in the role of plaintiffs or of defendants (16). Moreover, the same Bracton informs us that " quod videri poterit tota die ", clerics' contractual obligations, property disputes as well as feudal matters, " dum tamen *civiliter* agatur ", are also treated before the royal courts (17). That for indisputably civil cases, such as debts or other purely contractual stipulations

---

(11) Cf. C. R. CHENEY, *art. cit.*, p. 215: down to the fourteenth century " the punishment of felonous clerks was left entirely to the courts Christian "; also *ibid.*, pp. 235-6.

(12) In view of the decision of the *Rota*, the statement by W. A. PANTIN, *The English Church in the fourteenth Century* (Cambridge, 1955), p. 86, may be a shade optimistic: reviewing the situation created by the statutes of Provisors and Praemunire, he says: " Some conflicts had already been settled, such as the benefit of clergy ".

(13) See the quotation from the *Annales Monastici*, below note 52.

(14) F. M. POWICKE and C. R. CHENEY, *Councils and Synods with other Documents relating to the English Church* (Oxford, 1964), II.542-3, cap. 21: " Per eandem districtionem attachiantur et coguntur clerici in *actionibus personalibus* et in hiis, que *ex contractibus* oriuntur in foro seculari et etiam delictis, respondere querelantibus "; cf. also p. 541, cap. 8.

(15) *Ibid.*, pp. 669 ff., which the pope would not confirm who instead requested the king to pay heed to the demands of this council: POTTHAST 18483 of 30 January 1263, ed. *Councils*, 686. Cf. also POLLOCK and MAITLAND, *History*, cit., I.447 note 1 and *Councils*, p. 662.

(16) Bracton, *De Legibus*, ed. G. E. WOODBINE (New Haven, 1942), IV.249.

(17) *Ibid.*, p. 250. The king's response to the episcopal grievances of 1261 confirms the practice: art. VII: " Sistere solent prelati clericos iudicio seculari in causis contractuum quorum cognitio pertinet ad regem; et hoc iure usi sunt omnes reges Anglie a prima fundatione ecclesie Anglicane " (*Councils, cit.*, p. 688); see also *ibid.*, art. V and the king's reply. For the nature of the king's reply see p. 666.

or trespass, the king's courts directly summoned clerics through their respective bishops, and that the latter without demurring executed the summons, the fourteenth-century episcopal Registers give ample proof (18). And this practice, for which no more witnesses need be called upon, does seem to have given rise to the view that the protection of the clerics in civil proceedings had been abrogated by desuetude, and consequently that royal jurisdiction when clerics were involved in civil causes, had become law through customary observance. There is a very real cleavage between criminal prosecutions of clerics and civil proceedings taken by or against them: leaving aside some specific cases, the *privilegium fori* in regard to the former was observed; in regard to the latter custom had practically abolished it (19).

II

The decisions of the papal tribunal, the *Rota Romana,* have attracted far less attention than they deserve. Since the *audientia* had become a firmly established organisation in the curia by the decree

---

(18) Cf., for example, *Register of Walter Reynolds, Bishop of Worcester,* ed. R. A. WILSON (London, 1928), pp. 149 ff.; or later in the fourteenth century *Register Simon Langham* (Canterbury & York Society, 1956), p. 397 (anno 1367); etc.

(19) Always with the exception noted: civil obligations touching matrimonial or testamentary issues. In parenthesis it should be mentioned, however, that on the question of royal jurisdiction in civil matters of clerics, there was also considerable trouble in Portugal. See Albericus de Rosciate, *Super Codice* (ed. Lyons, 1545), ad *Authent. Statuimus,* no. 4, fol. 30: " De hoc fuit magna quaestio inter regem Portugaliensem, rege asserente iurisdictionem suam esse in civitate et de hoc debere cognoscere quoad bona temporalia episcopo autem eius iurisdictionem declinante ". Although Albericus himself does say " ratione rerum temporalium clerici legibus subsunt, ut XI qu. 1 § fin. (*D. p.* c. 10), sicut et in causa feudi ", he notes numerous qualifications and exceptions to the former; his discussion sheds interesting light on the arguments advanced in this case, nos. 6-7, fol. 30-30v. However some noted civilians (e. g. Guil. de Cuneo) maintained that litigations concerning immobile goods were exempted from this authentica and therefore that these causes were to be tried by the secular courts. See Paulus Castrensis, *Commentaria in Codicem* (ed. Venice, 1594), ad *Auth. Statuimus,* no. 1, fol. 18v: " De civilibus causis dicunt quidam habere locum quando clericus conveniretur actione personali, quae afficit personam, secus si actione reali pro re immobili, quia illa est temporalis iurisdictionis et in realibus sortitur quis forum ratione rei in loco ubi est, secundum Guilelmum de Cuneo, qui dicit quod ratione possessionis est de foro saeculari ". He also refers to the Portuguese trouble.

of John XXII in 1331 (*Ratio iuris*) (20) the decisions of the *Rota Romana* now began to have the same authority and standing as individual papal decisions themselves (21). This fact would go far to explain the advisability of, if not the need for, collecting the decisions (or as they were also called: *conclusiones*) of the *Rota* by an individual auditor (22). The first such collection was made by Thomas Fastoli (or Fastolf) for the years 1336-37; Fastoli was one of the auditors in the papal curia under John XXII and became afterwards a canon

---

(20) Ed. by M. TANGL, *Die päpstlichen Kanzleiordnungen von 1200 bis 1500* (Innsbruck, 1894), pp. 83-91; and E. CERCHIARI, *Capellani papae et apostolicae sedis* (Rome, 1921), III. 69-78. In the papal palace at Avignon the court room, the *audientia sacri palatii*, was finished by 1352; it measured some 160 feet in length, 50 feet in width and 35 feet in height: " ein Saal von unvergleichlicher Pracht ", F. E. SCHNEIDER, *Ueber d. Ursprung u. die Bedeutung des Namens Rota* in: *Römische Quartalschrift*, XLI (1933), p. 36. The auditors' bench was round, hence *rota*, ID., *ibid.*, pp. 37 ff., but according to J. GEMMEL in: *Theolog. Quartalschrift*, CXVII (1947), pp. 418 ff., the name was derived from the *rota porphyretica* in (old) St. Peter's, where quasi-judicial proceedings, especially the scrutinium at an imperial coronation, had taken place. For a description of this *Rota*, see M. ANDRIEU, *La rota porphyretica de la Basilique Vaticane* in: *Mélanges d'archéologie et d'histoire*, LXVI (1954), pp. 189-218.

(21) The complaints of A. FLINIAUX, " *Les anciennes collections de Decisiones Rotae Romanae* in: *Rev. historique de droit français et étranger*, 4th ser., IV (1925), p. 61, n. 1: " La littérature est excessivement pauvre sur ce point spécial " (i. e. the decisions of the *Rota*); of CH. LEFEBVRE, *Dict. Droit Can.*, VII (1960), col. 762: " Les décisions de la Rota... constituent une littérature considerable et encore assez mal connue "; and of GABRIEL LE BRAS, *Histoire du droit et des institutions de l'église en Occident*, VII: *L'âge classique* (Paris, 1965), p. 561, n. 1: " jusqu'ici trop peu étudiée ", are thoroughly justified. For literature on the *Rota* itself, cf. G. PHILLIPS, *Kirchenrecht* (Regensburg, 1864), VI.449 ff., 472 ff.; J. B. SÄGMÜLLER, *Die Entwicklung der Rota bis zur Bulle Johanns XXII.* in: *Theologische Quartalschrift*, LXXVII (1895), pp. 97 ff.; and above all the excellent entry in *Dict. Droit Can.*, VII. 742 ff. by CH. LEFEBVRE. See further G. MOLLAT, *The Popes at Avignon*, Engl. translation (London, 1963), pp. 299 ff. For the *Rota* before *Ratio iuris* was issued, see G. MOLLAT in: *Rev. d'histoire ecclésiastique*, XXXII (1936), pp. 877-96. F. E. SCHNEIDER, *Die römische Rota* (1914) and E. GÖLLER's article in: *Archiv f. kathol. Kirchenrecht* (1911), were not accessible to me. For the character of the decisions of the *Rota* see CH. LEFEBVRE in: *Hist. du droit, cit.*, p. 246: " La jurisprudence de la Rote romaine prend naissance dans les années 70 (of the fourteenth century) et supplée ainsi dans une large mesure à la défaillance du pouvoir législatif. Au droit des décrétales se substitue progressivement le *ius commune pontificium*, qui est en grande partie le fruit de l'élaboration faite par les *auditores Rotae romanae* ".

(22) The so-called *Consuetudines curiae Romanae et Cancellariae* by Bonaguida Aretinus, made in the fifties of the thirteenth century, may have been conceived in a similar spirit; he himself was advocate in the curia. Cf. J. F. SCHULTE, *Geschichte der Quellen u. Literatur des canonischen Rechts* (Stuttgart, 1877), II.113; A. VAN HOVE, *Prolegomena ad Codicem Iuris Canonici*, 2nd ed. (Mechlin-Rome, 1945), p. 491; here also further literature and editions; see further E. CERCHIARI, *Capellani, cit.*, I.228 no. 21, and CH. LEFEBVRE in: *Hist. du droit, cit.*, pp. 213 f., 341-2.

of Dublin and eventually Bishop of St. David's in Wales (23). It is the collection called *Decisiones Antiquae* ostensibly covering the years 1372-75 which is of interest to us (24). Now this collection consists in actual fact of three parts of which the third and last part is immediately relevant. This part has as its author Bonaguida of Cremona, also an auditor of the *Rota* (25) at the time of Urban V from 1362 to 1370 (26). A number of the decisions collected by Bonaguida, however, had in fact formed part of another collection, that is, the *Decisiones Antiquiores*, the author of which was Bernardus de Bisgneto who was none other than the later Cardinal Bernardus de Bosqueto: he was auditor of the *Rota* from 1355 until 1365 when he was nominated bishop of Naples on 5 September 1365 and created a cardinal on 22 September 1368; he died in 1371 (27). And one of the decisions collected by Bernard and re-incorporated in the *Decisiones Antiquae* of Bonaguida is one that is subsumed under the title *De consuetudine* (28) and given the following heading:

> *Consuetudo Anglicana quod Rex habeat iurisdictionem in clericos solutos in actionibus civilibus et personalibus mere, vel criminalibus ubi agitur civiliter, non valet.*

This decision carries the consecutive number 840 in the *Decisiones Antiquae* and had formed originally in the *Decisiones Antiquiores* the second entry under the title *De consuetudine* (29).

---

(23) See F. M. POWICKE and E. B. FRYDE, *Handbook of British Chronology*, 2nd ed. (London, 1961); 22 October 1352; *ob*. June 1361; further, VAN HOVE, *op. cit.*, p. 403.

(24) For a useful conspectus of the fourteenth-century collections of the decisions, see VAN HOVE, *op. cit.*, pp. 402-3; A. M. STICKLER, *Historia Iuris Canonici Latini* (Turin, 1950), p. 342, and LEFEBVRE, *D. D. C.*, 748. For the *Antiquae* see especially A. FLINIAUX, *art. cit.*, pp. 395-7.

(25) Not to be confused with Bonaguida of Arezzo, above note 22.

(26) See A. FLINIAUX, *art. cit.*, p. 388.

(27) For these details see FLINIAUX, p. 389-90. It is strange that not a single MS has survived. For incunabula see CH. LEFEBVRE, *D.D.C.*, VII.762.

(28) The material of the decisions was subsequently divided according to the titles in the *Extra*. The decisions of the *Rota* (in the way in which they were collected) strongly resemble English Law Reports: this is particularly noticeable in the *Decisiones Novae* (covering the years 1376-81). The *Antique* and *Antiquiores* are partly of the same character, and partly merely summaries or succinct statements concerning a special point of law (leaving out all details, concerning names and places). The (original) consecutive numbering without regard to subject-matter — probably day-by-day entries of the collecting (and officiating) *auditor* — recalls on a small scale the process observable in the post-Gratian period in regard to collections of the new law.

(29) I have used the edition of the *Decisions Rotae Romanae*, Lyons, 1567 (where the

As far as I can ascertain, this decision of the *Rota* does not seem to have excited much interest (30). The decision itself gives no indication of a date or of the actual circumstances which provoked the issue at all: no names are mentioned nor any details of fact which would allow us to venture at least some conjectures. The end of the judgment contains, however, some indication that the matter itself was discussed in detail and tried before the tribunal; here the proctor of one party is obliquely referred to by: " dicebatur per allegantem pro parte ista " (31). Juristically the decision is a first-class piece of work, crisp in its diction, concise in its arguments, economical in its references to the law and the relevant literature and, in its tone of finality and conclusiveness, reminds one of decisions on some constitutional problem by a contemporary supreme court.

A detailed analysis of the personnel of the *Rota* (32) in the sixties and seventies of the fourteenth century would reveal that there were quite a number of English auditors functioning in the *Rota* (33). Although it would be rash to attribute to an *auditor* any particularly decisive role — the principle of collegiality was firmly adhered to in the *Rota* (34) — it would nevertheless seem right at least to draw

---

decision is fol. 8v-9); Turin, 1579 (pp. 364-5), and Cologne, 1581 (pp. 364-5). All these editions seem to belong to group 4 of FLINIAUX's classification, *art. cit.*, pp. 86-9. That our decision had already been in Bisgneto's collection is clear, as all the editions have in Bisgneto's collection as the second entry under the title *De consuetudine* a reference to the same title in the *Decisiones Antiquae* no. X. See further FLINIAUX, *art. cit.*, p. 396 n. 1, who on the basis of edition of Lyons 1519 (not available to me) gave a concordance of those decisions which Bonaguida took from Bernard's collection; there are 16 altogether.

(30) There is, however, a casual reference to the decision in F. W. MAITLAND, *Roman Canon Law in the Church of England* (London, 1898), p. 62 n. 1.

(31) See below at note 81. For the actual procedure the details laid down in the recently discovered tract (*ca.* 1350) may well be applicable, see CH. LEFEBVRE, *Un texte inédit sur la procédure rotale au XIVe siècle* in: *Rev. de Droit Canonique*, X-XI (1961), pp. 174 ff., text pp. 184 ff.; see also ID., *D.D.C.*, VII.756-7.

(32) In parenthesis it should perhaps be mentioned that the usual statement that Oldradus died in 1335 (see SCHULTE, *op. cit.*, II.233; VAN HOVE, *op. cit.*, p. 489; and R. NAZ, *D.D.C.*, VI.1111) cannot be correct: in causa 32 (which bears the date 25 March 1337) of Thomas Fastoli's collection Oldradus still appears functioning in his official capacity as *auditor*, see ed. Cologne, p. 652. This is also mentioned by A. FLINIAUX, *art. cit.*, p. 404.

(33) One of the two patrons of the *Rota* was St. Augustine of Canterbury, see F. E. SCHNEIDER, *art. cit.*, p. 33; the other was St. Catherine, probably because she was martyred by a wheel (*rota*), *ibid.*, note 38.

(34) On this see F. E. SCHNEIDER in: *Römische Quartalschrift*, suppl. vol. XX (1913), pp. 20 ff., esp. pp. 34 f. Cf. also *Ratio iuris*, cc. 6, 7, 10, *ed. cit.* (TANGL), pp. 85, 86.

attention to the one or the other *auditor*. It would appear that the later Archbishop of Canterbury, Simon Sudbury, was officiating as an *auditor* on 27 March 1360 when he was designated in addition to the auditorship also papal chaplain and chancellor of Salisbury diocese (35); his assistant was a certain Rogerius, a Canterbury cleric and notary public (36). At the same time there was William Lenne (Lynn) on the staff of the *Rota*, soon to be promoted to the bishopric of Chichester (37). From 1362 onwards there was Robert Stratton (or Stracton) who seems to have held the office of an *auditor* until his death on 20 October 1380 (38): a civilian lawyer, he was the first Master of Trinity Hall, Cambridge, in 1350, became papal notary in 1354, joined the staff of the Hall's founder (himself, in 1332, an *auditor*) and was at Avignon with him until his death in 1355 (39).

---

(35) See E. CERCHIARI, *op. cit.*, II.31, no. 170.

(36) See the transcription from MS. Paris, B. N. fonds Doat, vol. 110, fol. 122 ff. by A. FLINIAUX, *art. cit.*, p. 401 n. o: " ... Innocentius divina providentia papa sextus causam... nobis Symoni de Subderia (*sic*), legum doctori, cancellario ecclesiae Sarisburiensis, capellano suo eiusque sacri palatii causarum auditori... commisit audiendus ".

(37) CERCHIARI, II.30, no. 158. He was dean of Chichester in 1349 and had permission to go to Avignon (? Rome) with three men and four horses in 1353; see A. B. EMDEN, *A Biographical Register of the University of Oxford* (Oxford, 1957-59), p. 1195.

(38) See FLINIAUX, p. 408, and the preface to the *Decisiones Novae*, dated 30 January 1376.

(39) For all these details and the numerous benefices and functions he held, see A. B. EMDEN, *A Biographical Register of the University of Cambridge to 1500* (Cambridge, 1963), s. v. Stratton alias Sutton, Robert, p. 562; for William Bateman, *ibid.*, p. 44 and E. CERCHIARI, II.26, no. 124, still functioning as *auditor* in 1337: Guilelmus de Norvico, and in 1339, see L. BOYLE, *The Summa Summarum...* in: *Proceedings II International Congress of Medieval Canon Law*, ed. S. KUTTNER and J. J. RYAN (Rome, 1965), p. 416 n. 7. In May 1380 Stratton was commissioned by Pope Urban VI with the drafting of a detailed report concerning the circumstances immediately before, during and after the election of this pope, see Raynaldus, *Annales Ecclesiastici*, ed. Bar-le-Duc, 1872, VII.391, sub anno 1380, no. 19. How high his reputation amongst the *Rota* judges stood, can be seen from the frequent and respectful references to his opinions in the *Decisiones Novae* (by William Horboch). Cf., e. g., *De Appellationibus*, no. 32 (originally no. 204), p. 247a: " Dominus vero Robertus non declinavit nec ad unam nec ad aliam partem, sed dixit se velle deliberare... "; *ibid.*, no. 17 (originally no. 114), p. 239a: " Dominus Robertus et ego contra... maior pars dominorum tenuit de rigore iuris quod non, sed de equitate sic, et dominus Robertus mutavit opinionem suam antedictam "; *ibidem*, no. 36 (orig. no. 267), p. 350a: " Licet Dominus Robertus tenendo contrarium dixerit... et dixit quod ita tempore Domini Innocentii sexti et Urbani V semper fuit observatum... "; *De officio delegati*, no. 12 (orig. no. 349), p. 93a: " in qua opinione fuit Dominus cardinalis sancti Angeli quando erat auditor, prout Dominus Robertus retulit nobis "; *De officio legati*, no. 3 (orig. no. 119), p. 99a: " Dominus Robertus contra, propter verbum ge-

Apart from these, there were John Mowbray (or Mombray) (40), Nicholas Boclesham (or Hoclesham) (41) and Thomas Sudbury (42), the archbishop's brother: these latter three do not appear as auditors before 1376 (43), whilst under Urban VI there function as English auditors Andrew Barrett and Thomas Walkyngton (44) as well as the later bishop of Hereford, John Trefnant (45). Although, as mentioned, it would be somewhat precipitate to link a particular name with the decision under discussion, the possibility that Robert Stratton was in some way connected with it, cannot be entirely dismissed. He certainly was an *auditor* of the *Rota* in the sixties when the decision was given. The very fact that (Cardinal) Bernardus de Bosqueto who ceased to be an *auditor* upon his appointment as

---

nerale... "; *De conc. praebendae*, no. 2 (orig. no. 95), p. 293b: " Et finaliter declinaverunt (scil. domini de Rota) in opinionem Domini Roberti... "; etc. (All page references are to ed. Cologne, 1581). The same respect for Stratton can be witnessed in the decisions collected by the *auditor* (and later bishop of Avignon), Aegidius de Bellamera, for the years 1374 to 1377 (I have used the ed. Lyons, 1508). Cf., e. g., *Decis.* 671, fol. 82va: " ...et hoc placuit Domino Nicolao de Cremona et Domino Roberto de Stratone (*sic*) auditoribus... "; in the difficult procedural problem of *Decis.* 689, fol. 87va, Robert Stratton again figured amongst the 9 other auditors who gave their opinion; see further *Decis.* 753, fol. 132vb. etc.

(40) An Oxford graduate, see EMDEN, *Oxford*, p. 1326.

(41) Nicholas Botlesham (should it not be: Bottisham?), a Cambridge Bachelor of civil and canon law, see EMDEN, *Cambridge*, s. v. He was elected one of the two proctors of the University of Cambridge for 1363-4, see *The Historical Register of the University of Cambridge to the year 1910*, ed. J. R. TANNER (Cambridge, 1917), p. 35.

(42) Cf. EMDEN, *Cambridge*, p. 566.

(43) Though according to CERCHIARI, II.31, no. 171, Thomas Sudbury was *auditor* already under Innocent VI (1352-62), which seems contradicted by the explicit statement in *Decisio* 452 of the *Novae* (*De electione*, no. 5) (ed. Cologne, 1581, p. 61): " Hic supervenit qui dem novus auditor Anglicus nomine Thomas de Sabaudia (*sic*), legum Doctor, frater Domini Simonis, Domini archiepiscopi Cantuariensis, anno domini MCCCLXXX, de mense Septembris, tempore Urbani Papae VI, pontificatus sui anno III ".

(44) CERCHIARI, II.35, nos. 198 and 201. The latter was an Oxford Doctor of canon law in 1374 and lectured on the *Extra* and the Clementines, see A. B. EMDEN, *Oxford*, p. 1965. See, further, L. BOYLE, *Proceedings*, cit. p. 417 and notes 13-16.

(45) He was an Oxford Doctor of civil law in 1376, who had equipped himself with a very fine library, right up to date (66 volumes on civil and canon law, 10 on theology and 13 service books); his library also included a collection " de decisionibus rote et aliis dubiis decisionibus et allegacionibus eiusdem episcopi in publicis relacionibus ", see EMDEN, p. 1901. The title would indicate that he himself collected the decisions whilst he was an *auditor* of the *Rota*. To these may be added John Trevor, also on Oxford graduate in both laws, who was an *auditor* towards the end of the century and became eventually bishop of St. Asaph in Wales; about his varied career see EMDEN, *Oxford*, pp. 1898-9.

bishop of Naples, had incorporated our decision in his own collection, would lend some force to the suggested possibility: as already indicated, the collection of Bernard covered in fact the decisions between the years 1355 and 1365 (46). But the suggestion that Stratton may have been one of the auditors in some way responsible for this decision, needs to be tested further.

I have mentioned that the decision gives no clue what particular *causa*, if any, had provoked the judgment of the *Rota*. However, that there must have been a pressing problem for bringing the matter before the *Rota*, goes without saying. That the presence of an experienced English *auditor* in the *Rota* may have provided an added stimulus, is a possibility which I think should not be overlooked. And that there must have been some reason additional to the (customary) extension of royal jurisdiction in civil cases (47), seems obvious enough, otherwise the *Rota* would hardly have been involved. There is some justification for saying that, since the decision is concerned with civil (as opposed to criminal) actions, the royal legislative measures ending with Edward III's ordinance *Pro clero* (1352) (48) and dealing with the definition of " clergyable " offences, can be safely left aside as determinant factors. Similarly, I do not think one could say that pleas of the crown came to be changed into common pleas, because the latter were, on the whole, concerned with civil actions: the distinction between the two kinds of pleas in a somewhat rough manner corresponded to criminal and civil actions (49). Nor do I think that the statutes of Provisors and Praemunire had anything to do with our problem. Where I believe a solution may lie is in the use of the writ of prohibition *by clerics*. This is one more topic which has attracted far too little attention, but which may further explain the recourse to the *Rota* as the highest tribunal in Christen-

---

(46) See A. FLINIAUX, *art. cit.*, p. 394 and CH. LEFEBVRE, *D. D. C.*, VII.762. It would be a highly rewarding task to establish the permanent English proctors at the curia in Avignon; for Andreas Sapiti who was proctor for Edward II and Edward III from 1317 until 1338, see J. P. KIRSCH in: *Hist. Jahrbuch*, XIV (1893), pp. 582-603, who has edited a number of otherwise inaccessible documents.

(47) See above at notes 14 ff.

(48) *Statutes of the Realm* (London, 1810) I. 325, *stat.* 6, s. 4: also in S. B. CHRIMES and A. L. BROWN, *Select documents of English Constitutional History* (London, 1961), pp. 78-9.

(49) Cf. T. F. T. PLUCKNETT, *Common Law*, cit., p. 398: " If some things which we regard as criminal could be dealt with more effectively under the form of civil litigation, they became common pleas. If other things which now seem indisputably civil, could only be effectively dealt with under criminal forms, then they became pleas of the crown ".

dom: it was a step which, *inter alia,* was to condemn the practice (stigmatized in the decision as an *abusus*) prevailing in England.

The writ of prohibition was a royal device to stop proceedings in an ecclesiastical court, as this court was alleged not to be competent to deal with the matter in hand (50). Now, it has been established that not only laymen, but also clerics came to make increasing use of this writ from the thirties of the thirteenth century onwards (51). Clearly, the bishops tried to stop this as early as 1237 (52), and throughout the subsequent period there were repeated attempts " to check clerics who had recourse to prohibitions. The bishops certainly viewed the abuse as grave enough to draw from them repeated warnings and protests " (53). For obvious reasons it was the cleric who as a defendant impetrated the writ. It was a practice that steadily grew, and in view of this growing practice the English bishops came to acquiesce in it and their protests diminished (54). By the fourteenth century this writ of prohibition obtained by a cleric had become a writ of course (*breve de cursu*). We may cite as a characteristic example one addressed to the bishop of Rochester (1323) in a case in which, paradoxically enough, a cardinal had appeared as a plaintiff (55). The evidence would indeed strongly sug-

---

(50) The fundamental — and admirable — clarification of the writ of prohibition is by G. B. Flahiff, *The use of prohibitions by clerics against ecclesiastical courts in England* in: *Medieval Studies,* III (1941), pp. 101 ff.; Id., *The writ of prohibition to the courts christian in the 13th century, ibid.,* VI (1944), pp. 261 ff.; VII (1945), pp. 229 ff. What is very badly needed is something approaching Flahiff's studies for the 14th century.

(51) Flahiff, III.102: " There is evidence to show that laymen availed themselves of the ecclesiastical courts when it was to their advantage. And clerics made use of the secular courts, if they could help themselves thereby ".

(52) See *Annales de Burton* (Rolls Series, in *Annales Monastici,* ed. H. R. Luard, London, 1864), I.254: " Petunt quod clerici non conveniantur *in actione personali,* quae non sit super re immobili, coram iudice saeculari, sed coram iudice ecclesiastico, et quod *prohibitio regis* non currat quominus hoc fieri non possit. Item quod innovetur poena in canone statuta contra clericos, qui impetrant in hoc casu *prohibitionem* domini regis ad iudices ecclesiasticos et in omnibus aliis in iure prohibitis... "; p. 255: " Ne clerici citentur coram iudice saeculari, responsuri coram eis quare causas tractaverunt in foro ecclesiastico *contra prohibitionem* domini regis ".

(53) Flahiff, III.107.

(54) Id., *ibid.,* pp. 109 ff.

(55) *Registrum Hamonis Hethe,* ed. Ch. Johnson (Canterbury & York Society, 1948), p. 296 (anno 1323): " Cum placita de catallis et debitis in regno nostro que non sunt de testamento vel matrimonio ad coronam et dignitatem nostram specialiter pertinent, ac Bertrandus cardinalis Ruffus magistrum Johannem de Bruton, archidiaconum Cantuariensem

gest that by the fourteenth century royal jurisdiction over clerics had customarily been extended partly by direct summonings (56), and partly indirectly through the working of the writ of prohibition (57). In both cases one could, with a semblance of justification, assert that this royal jurisdiction was one based upon law derived from customary practice and observed by the clerics themselves.

Of the effects of this decision of the *Rota* upon the practice in England there is extremely little evidence: in all likelihood there was, considering the long-standing practice, no effect at all. The Register of the bishop of Exeter, Thomas Brantyngham, contains under the year 1391 a complaint that " sons of iniquity " had brought personal actions against clerics before a secular judge (58). If the commentaries of William Lyndwood are a reliable guide, there does seem to be justification for assuming that this decision was not known to him, for although he deals fully with the *privilegium fori*, I have not found any reference to the case at all (59). This lack of knowledge on the part of so eminent a canonist as Lyndwood is all the more noteworthy, as he was extremely well versed with the literature down to his time (late twenties of the fifteenth century) (60), and what is still more noteworthy is that in a number of places he does

---

super huiusmodi catallis et debitis trahat in placitum coram vobis in curiam christianitatis, sicut ex relatu plurium accepimus, vobis prohibemus ne placitum illud teneatis in curia christianitatis, maxime cum huiusmodi placita ad nos et non ad alium pertineant in eodem regno ". The wording of the writ is entirely identical with that contained in the Register of Writs dating from the beginning of Edward I's reign (1272-74) which is analysed by FLAHIFF, III.113 n. 59. The phrase *ex relatu plurium* was a fig-leaf to cover up the fact that the writ was procured by a cleric, see on this FLAHIFF who was the first to have clarified the meaning of this otherwise enigmatic terminology: *ibid.*, pp. 109-15; also VI.304 f.

(56) See above at note 18.

(57) For this cf. FLAHIFF, III.115: " Ecclesiastics as a class were not all opposed to the use of prohibition. From the beginning, the lower clergy and religious availed themselves of it, if it promised something to their advantage ". For some almost comic cases in which one cleric delivered a prohibition to the other, see ID., VII.235, note 32.

(58) See *Register Thomas Brantyngham*, ed. F. C. HINGSTON-RANDOLPH (London 1901-6), II.737; see also L. C. GABEL, *op. cit.*, p. 121.

(59) See his *Provinciale* (ed. Oxford, 1679), I.13.2, s. v. " clericali ", pp. 68b-69a, where he enumerates 14 specific instances of clerical privileges; nor does he mention it when treating of customary law: I.3, *ed. cit.*, pp. 19 ff., nor in his glosses on Boniface's *Contingit*, II.2.1, pp. 92-3, where one naturally would have expected a reference, but he deals here only with criminal proceedings and cases of arrest for criminal offences.

(60) On him cf., F. W. MAITLAND, *Roman Canon Law*, *cit.*, pp. 1 ff.; also C. R. CHENEY, *William Lyndwood's Provinciale* in: *The Jurist*, XXI (1961), pp. 405 ff., at 406-10.

quote from, and refer to, the decisions of the *Rota* (61). But that on the Continent the decision was known, there can be no doubt. For instance, Hieronymus Gigans in his tract *De crimine laesae maiestatis* is thoroughly familiar with the decision, as he quotes from it literally (62). Towards the end of the sixteenth century the advocate in the Parliament of Paris, Antoine Hotman, also referred to the decision to show that the popes had never had cause for complaint in regard to France, in contrast to the grievances they had about English conditions concerning the observance of the clerical privilege (63).

III

Let us now turn to the decision itself. Its tenor and its argumentation reveal juristic maturity and that kind of firm grasp in juristic matters which one could expect from this supreme tribunal. What strikes the reader is the clarity of its theme and an almost transparent lucidity of the jurisprudential axioms. Nor does the decision evade delicate, if not tricky, questions in so far as they relate to the argument, obviously employed by one of the proctors, concerning the part which the popes themselves had played in not only not opposing the growing custom of disregarding the civil side of the *privilegium fori*, but in actually acquiescing in it. Reading this part of the decision creates the impression that the *Rota*, at any rate in this instance, did not shirk from pronouncing upon the pope's power in relation to customary law.

The decision is rightly subsumed under the title *De consuetudine*.

---

(61) Cf., for example, I.18.1, s. v. *reputetur* (*ed. cit.*, p. 78): " Hoc modo procedit dictum dominorum de rota in conclusione 63 et 64, ubi dicunt... "; also III.1.1, s. v. *dignitatibus* (*ed. cit.*, p. 117): " Et haec est conclusio dominorum de rota, conclusione 562 ".

(62) *Tractatus Illustrium Iurisconsultorum* (Venice, 1584), XI-1, fol. 49, no. 19; he wrote in the second half of the 16th century.

(63) See HOTMAN's tract *Traité des droits ecclésiastiques* in: *Traitez des droits et libertez de l'église Gallicane* (ed. Paris, 1731), I.133 ff.: book I, chapter 11, p. 138: " Et quant aux causes civiles et criminelles de personne de l'église, les juges ecclésiastiques en cognoissant et que la France l'ait toujours ainsi observé, il ne faut que voir la pleinte qu'à Rome (*sic*) on faisait contre les Anglois: Quod rex... decisio 840 Rotae in antiquis. Car jamais on n'a fait pareille pleinte contre les rois de France ". See also MAITLAND, *Roman Canon Law, cit.*, p. 62 n. 1, who had first noted this statement of HOTMAN.

It focuses attention entirely upon the question whether the *privilegium fori* — in so far as it relates to civil proceedings — could in fact and in theory be modified or abolished by the growth of a custom. Consequently, the decision falls into two parts: the first dealing with the question whether the English clerics could, from a juristic point of view, divest themselves of the *privilegium fori* by consenting to their case being tried in the king's court; the second part deals with what legal effects the connivance of the pope in this customary practice could have had.

Beginning with the question:

> *Utrum valeat consuetudo Anglicana quod rex possit recognoscere et habere iurisdictionem in clericos solutos in actionibus civilibus etiam personalibus mere, vel criminalibus, ubi agitur civiliter?*

the decision plunges straight *in medias res* by denying the legal validity of this custom — termed an *abusus* — which consequently cannot be the basis of any customary law. This custom the *Rota* declares was prejudicial to ecclesiastical liberty, devoid of any legal sanction and opposed to the enacted law:

> *quia contra libertatem ecclesiasticam et sanctorum patrum instituta,*

and in support of this contention the auditors invoke the view expressed by the Archdeacon (64) as well as in canon law itself (65), which makes it clear to them that this custom is explicitly directed against what they call *praeceptum prohibitivum et negativum*, and thus incapable of being renounced by a cleric — " cui renuntiari

---

(64) Archidiaconus, *Apparatus ad Sextum, cit.*, ad *VI:* II.2.1, s. v. *clericorum, ed. cit.*, fol. 61: " Nec credo valere consuetudinem quod clericus in alium iudicem consentiat sine sui dyocesani assensu, nam si papa illud intellexisset, illud expressisset ".

(65) *Extra:* III.11.1 (which is III *Lat.*, cap. 16) according to which any custom prevailing in a particular church is null and void, if contrary to the expressed majority view of the chapter of this church: the point which the *Rota* wishes to stress is clearly this statement in the decree: " Nec nostram constitutionem impediat, si forte aliquis ad conservandam ecclesiae suae consuetudinem iuramento se dicat adstrictum, non enim dicenda sunt iuramenta, sed potius periuria, quae contra utilitatem ecclesiasticam et sanctorum patrum veniunt instituta ". This is joined in the decision with *X:* II.2.2 (actually from Council of Paris, anno 614: *M. G. H. Concilia,* I.187, cap. 6), according to which no lay judge may exercise jurisdiction over clerics: " distringere aut condemnare " seems to be understood here as both civil and criminal proceedings.

expresse non potest " — as is laid down in Innocent III's decretal
Si diligenti (66). Operating with an *a fortiori* argument they declare
that clerics cannot divest themselves of this privilege by a tacit agreement either, for " prohibitive precepts " are always binding:

> *Ergo multo fortius* (the decision continues) *nec tacite. Prae-
> cepta enim negativa obligant semper et ad semper, ut furtum
> non facies, et similia* (67).

But above all, this custom is not only contrary to the law of the
Church and ecclesiastical liberty, it is also contrary to the structure
and well-being of the Church: the prohibition contained in the *privilegium fori* was introduced for the sake af the clerical *ordo,* and not
for the sake of some individuals or of a regional church, but for the
good of the universal Church order:

> *Item quia talis consuetudo est contra generalem statum ec-
> clesiae praesertim introductum in honorem totius ordinis
> clericalis, nedum clerici Anglicani, imo et universalis, ergo
> clericus Anglicanus tacite consentiendo aut assentiendo tali
> abusui non poterit praetextu talis consuetudinis ei derogare.*

The essential and juristically as well as constitutionally important
point here clearly is that this prohibitive precept belonged to public
law, and no private agreements, deals or steps can affect the scope
and extent of public law (68) and order. So much had already been

---

(66) *X:* II.2.12.

(67) Apparently, the view had been entertained at one time that clerics could tacitly
renounce their right. Cf. Goffredus de Trano, *Summa in Titulos Decretalium* (ed. Venice, 1586),
De foro compet., fol 73v, no. 11: " Quidam tamen dicunt quod clericus, etsi foro clericali renuntiare non posset expresse, tacite tamen potest, ut ff. De procur., l. filiusfamilias, § Veterani
(*Dig.* 3.3.8.2) et C. De iure cal., l. 2 (*Cod.* II.59.2), quod non puto verum ". Furthermore,
Huguccio was of the opinion that in civil litigations the cleric could, with his bishop's permission, agree to his case being tried before the lay court; see the report by the Archdeacon, ad
VI: III.2.1, fol. 81: after saying that " etiam de licentia episcopi iudicium saeculare non possunt clerici eligere " he continues: " Hug. dicit quod potest clericus duci coram iudice saeculari permissu episcopi, si ipse clericus voluerit, alias non, arg. 3, qu. 6, Non liceat (c. 14),
hoc enim non in favorem solum episcoporum, sed potius clericorum introductum est... et hoc
dumtaxat in causa civili, nam in criminali, quamvis episcopus consentiat, clericus non debet
produci coram iudice saeculari ". The matter was later dealt with by Innocent III in *X:*
II.2.12.

(68) This view goes back to Papinian: *Dig.* 2.14.38: " Ius publicum privatorum pactis
mutari non potest ". There was, however, another side to the problem to which Baldus draws
our attention: *Commentaria ad Codicem,* cit., ad *Auth. Statuimus,* no. 3, fol. 49v: " pone, nos

said by Innocent III in *Si diligenti*, when he declared "pacto privatorum iuri publico minime derogari" with specific reference to the *privilegium fori* (69). Innocent IV, to whom the *Rota* here appeals, had indeed made the juristic point that lawful custom presupposes a *res praescriptibilis*, and hence custom could not grow up in opposition to natural law or "contra statum ecclesiae" (70).

Moreover, this kind of custom cannot be squared with either divine law or positive law. As regards the former the *Rota* is, perhaps understandably, brief:

> *Talis consuetudo est contra legem divinam, per quam exempti sunt clerici a jurisdictione principum saecularium,*

referring us once again to the point of view expressed by Innocent IV in his commentary on *X:* I.33.2 (71). That this custom was in ex-

---

habemus statutum, quod si clericus declinaverit forum saeculare, quod sit exemptus a protectione communis et possit impune offendi. Modo clericus conventus coram Potestate dicit, Domine, ego non declino, imo libenter subiicerem me, et litigarem coram vobis, si possem, sed ego non possum, si vellem, quia decretalis me prohibet, scilicet Si diligenti, quae confirmatur per Auth. Statuimus ". Jacobus Butrigarius solved the problem by distinguishing between the cleric's inability to change (in which case he continued to enjoy the protection by the civic authorities) and his unwillingness to do so. This was rejected by Baldus, for whom the fact that the litigant was a cleric, made it impossible at all times to change the court and he thus remained protected by the civic authorities: " Ego dico cum reverentia, semper, quod eo ipso quod allegat se clericum declinat... et tene menti, quia ita vidi practicari in palatiis ". I mention the opinion of Baldus because he was then at the zenith of his academic standing.

(69) We should remember that this decretal not only made no difference between civil and criminal proceedings, but seems to have had in mind only *causae temporales:* cf. further *ibid.:* " Manifeste patet, quod non solum (scil. clerici) inviti, sed etiam voluntarii pacisci non possunt, ut saecularia iudicia subeant, cum *non* sit *beneficium* hoc *personale*, cui renuntiari valeat, sed potius toti collegio ecclesiastico sit *publice* indultum, cui privatorum pacto derogari non potest ". The *Gl. Ord. ad loc.* makes the point of renunciation crystal clear: " Dicas quod illi iuri quod est tantum introductum in favorem aliquorum, bene potest quis renuntiare (as is the case with the *S. C. Velleianum*), sed si aliquid ius introductum in favorem quorundam *pro utilitate publica* ipsorum et odio aliorum, nullus potest tali iuri renuntiare (as is instanced in the *S. C. Macedonianum*): est hoc de quo hic agitur, quod introductum est non tam in favorem clericorum quam in odium laicorum, ipsi enim clericis oppido sunt infesti ".

(70) Innocent IV, *Commentaria in Quinque Libros Decretalium* (ed. Frankfurt, 1570) ad *X:* I.4, *Rubrica*, no. 4, fol. 31v. It will be noticed that the *Rota* frequently appeals to Innocent IV's commentaries: was the reason for invoking him that he himself was at one time an *auditor*? See P. M. BAUMGARTEN, *Römische Quartalschrift*, suppl. vol. XX (1913), at p. 55; further E. CERCHIARI, *Capellani, cit.*, II.9, and J. A. CANTINI in: *D.D.C.*, VII (1960), 1030.

(71) Who in support of the view that the *privilegium fori* was grounded in divine law, cites only the statement made by Gelasius I to the emperor in Constantinople: " Dicimus

press contradiction to positive law, was not difficult to prove, since canon law itself denied any validity to a custom in direct opposition to what it called an *institutio ecclesiastica* (72). And there was no doubt for the *Rota* that in addition to being derived from divine law, the *privilegium fori* was an *institutio ecclesiastica* laid down in positive law (73). To these considerations concerning positive law, they append one of a general jurisprudential character, that is, that a law can only be changed by statute or custom if the legislator is entitled to do so: these positive canonical enactments can only be modified by the ecclesiastical authority which had first issued them: contrariwise, they cannot be subjected to a change by some extraneous authority which has no right to intervene in, or rather to inferfere with, ecclesiastical legislation:

> *Item contra praecepta non potest induci consuetudo, praesertim per eum, qui non potest contrariam legem vel praeceptum statuere* (74).

Behind these views there assuredly lies the generally entertained juristic thesis that a universal law cannot be changed by some provincial or regional or diocesan legislator or, as in this case, by customs which prevailed only within a province or region. For according to the view of the *Rota* a change or abolition of a positive law by customary practices presupposes that these practices were not only legitimate, but also emanated from organs which could have changed or abolished the universal law itself by a positive enactment. But the English Church or the English clergy could by no manner of means be said to be entitled to alter the universal law by a positive enactment or by custom. This is, from a purely jurisprudential

---

quod exempti sunt a Deo, 96 dist., Si imperator (c. 11) " (*ed. cit.*, fol. 156v). For the historical background of this Gelasian letter and its claim to the *privilegium fori*, cf. W. ULLMANN, *Growth of Papal Government in the Middle Ages*, 2nd ed. (London, 1962), pp. 26 ff.

(72) See *X:* II.11.2, to which we are referred.

(73) *X:* I.4.3: " consuetudo quae canonicis institutis obviat, nullius debet esse momenti ". The *Rota* states: " Item quia est contra institutionem ecclesiae: ergo etc. argumentum, De temp. ord. cap. 2. (*X:* I.11.2). Item, haec consuetudo videtur expresse reprobata, extra, De cons., c. Ad nostram (*X:* I.4.3) ".

(74) Referring us again to Innocent IV, ad *X:* I.4, *Rubrica*, no. 10, *ed. cit.*, fol. 32: " Vel dicas et melius quod contra iura et contra praecepta venire licet his quibus licitum est novam legem et specialem introducere contra illud ius vel praeceptum, similiter et novam consuetudinem ".

angle, a subtle thesis of considerable importance which, as far as I can see, was indeed first propounded by Innocent IV. The thesis created in fact a rather strong barrier to the corroding and undermining influence of customary practices in relation to positive law (75) and provided also, quite apart from the present topic, a not ineffective, albeit theoretical shield for the autonomy of the ecclesiastical legislator against the law — written or unwritten — emanating from any non-ecclesiastical government or body.

It is against this purely legal and jurisprudential background that the *Rota* approaches the delicate problem of the role which the pope had played in the growth of this custom. The auditors do not dispute that the pope knew of, and tolerated, the practices, but in their view this papal knowledge and toleration cannot serve as a valid juristic argument (which no doubt was one that was advanced). The law concerning the *privilegium fori* constituted, as they had already said, a *ius prohibitivum* which, moreover, was based upon the divine law. Hence, they say, a transgression of this cannot be condoned, no matter for how long a time this law may in fact have been abused. In other words, the mere knowledge of the pope of this abuse gives no warrant to anybody for acting in an unlawful manner (76). Nor can the toleration of this abuse by the pope be employed as a juristic instrument with which to turn an illegitimate practice into a legitimate one. Innocent III had already given the answer to this argument when he said:

> Cum multa per patientiam tolerantur, quae si deducta fuerint in iudicium, exigente iustitia non debeant tolerari (77).

Even if one were to assume that the pope had tolerated this abuse merely in order to avoid scandal, one can hardly deduce from this any kind of lawful approval of a conduct which in itself was not only

---

(75) Correctly understood, this thesis makes understandable, and adduces the essential justification for, the ancient (Constantinean) prohibition that custom could not do away with the *leges;* see *Cod.* VIII.53.2 = Gratian, Dist. 11, c. 4. For some observations on this topic, cf. W. ULLMANN, *Principles of Government and Politics in the Middle Ages*, 2nd ed. (London, 1966), pp. 281 ff.

(76) " Item quia papa hoc scivit et semper toleravit, quia cum fuerit ius prohibitivum et ab exemptione divina procedens (ut notat Innocentius, De maj. et ob., c. Si quis (*X:* I.33.2)), et per consequens contrarium esset peccatum, non possent dici ex hoc excusati, quantocumque etiam tempore in contrarium sint abusi ".

(77) *X:* III.5.18 in fine, to which the *Rota* refers.

legally reprehensible but also opposed to divine law. The thesis underlying this juristic consideration was clearly the view that the reasons and motives for the pope's toleration were, from the strictly juristic point of view, quite irrelevant.

> *Dato quod propter scandalum, quia a l i a s prohibere p o - t e r a t, toleravit, non propter hoc approbasse censeretur nec consuetudinem voluisse introduci.*

For saying this the auditors have very good authority in an ancient statement of Gregory the Great: papal silence and toleration should not be considered prejudicial for the future (78).

The decision, furthermore, invokes the divine law in order to counteract the argument (obviously also advanced) that the pope could not very well have privileged the English clergy to the prejudice and detriment of the English king's jurisdictional functions; the English king had admittedly, until the advent of Christ, possessed all jurisdictional powers (79) but it was Christ who had conceded this *privilegium fori* and ecclesiastical liberty to the clerics, and thereby had restricted the king's powers: after all, Christ had possessed, they declare, all *imperium et in temporalibus et spiritualibus.*

> *Nec obstat etiam si dicatur quod papa non potuit clerum Anglicanum privilegiare in praeiudicium regis Angliae, cui omnis antequam Christus veniret, iurisdictio competebat: quia istud privilegium et haec libertas concessa est clericis a Christo, in quem omne imperium fuit transmissum et in temporalibus et spiritualibus* (80).

---

(78) *X:* II.26.2 (from his *Reg.* III.57, in *M.G.H., Epp.* I. 216-7): " Sed illud scire vos volumus taciturnitatem atque patientiam nostram futuris post pontificibus in rebus pauperum praeiudicium non facturum ". It might possibly have strengthened the case of the *Rota,* if the decision had referred to *D. a.* c. 10, C. III. qu. 6, and c. 10 itself which was sometimes interpreted as toleration " pro vitando regis (Angliae) scandalo ". See the Archdeacon, *Rosarium* (ed. Venice, 1577), Dist. 10, c. 5, fol. 12, who refers to " Ro " in his gloss on *Comp.* I, *De jure patr., Ex diligenti* (III.33.6).

(79) Is this possibly a rejoinder to the king's reply (above n. 17)? Or is it a paraphrase of c. *Cum ad verum ventum?*

(80) The decision here refers us once more to Innocent IV on *X:* III.34.8 (*ed. cit.,* fol. 430, nos. 3-4), where he had dealt with the papal vicariate of Christ: " Credimus, quod papa qui est vicarius Iesu Christi, potestatem habet non tantum super christianos, sed etiam super omnes infideles, cum enim Christus habuerit super omnes potestatem, unde in psalmo Deus iudicium regi da (*Ps.* 71.2), non videtur diligens paterfamilias nisi vicario suo, quem in terra dimittebat, plenam potestatem super omnes dimisisset ". Further reference is made to In-

The sonorous re-affirmation of papal power in a context which *prima facie* would not have seemed to have called for this full blast, must have been intended to drown the argument propounded " per allegantem pro parte ista ", that is, that the papal legislator had himself in a case in which ecclesiastical and royal jurisdiction appeared to be in conflict, explicitly declared: " Ne videamur iuri regis Anglorum detrahere " (81). Clearly, the silence of the pope in the matter of the *privilegium fori* was not only played up as a means with which to argue for the legitimacy of the prevailing custom, but was also put forward to show the motivation and the reasoning behind the papally tolerated practice. And with the latter argument the *Rota* had very little patience: although they avoided — no doubt advisedly — any reference to a plenitude of power, their own stand seems plain enough: the pope could, in an individual instance, for extralegal reasons give a particular ruling, because he had the power to do so, but this could neither set aside a law which, according to their conviction (82), divinity itself had given nor could it endorse or create any (unlawful) custom (83). The decision ends with the statement that jurisdiction over clerics is essentially spiritual jurisdiction — " quia clerici sunt spirituales " as the *Rota* has it — which belongs exclusively to the pope alone or to the appropriate ecclesiastical tribunals: the conclusion the decision reaches, is that the custom is unlawful,

> *Quia, ut in praemissis patet, in clericos nullam iurisdictionem habet (scil.* rex), *nec habere potest.*

---

nocent IV ad: *X:* II.2.10 (*ed. cit.*, fol. 198, no. 4), where after invoking the same Psalm Innocent also dealt with the jurisdictional powers of the pope.

(81) Alexander III in *X:* IV, 17.7. The case concerned jurisdiction in a question of legitimate birth with which however questions of property were tied up. Alexander declared that the former was the principal *causa* and said: " Nos attendentes quod ad regem pertinet, non ad ecclesiam, de talibus possessionibus iudicare, ne... as text... qui ipsarum iudicium ad se asserit pertinere ".

(82) " Privilegium generale fuit datum a Deo " referring to *X:* II.1.17 and to Innocent IV's commentary ad *X:* V.39.49 (*ed. cit.*, nos. 1-2, fol. 558v).

(83) A similar problem seems to have confronted the *Rota* in the *Decis.* 752 recorded by Aegidius de Bellamera where we read: " Licet papa utitur plenitudine potestatis in uno articulo, non sequitur, quod velit in alio... " (*ed. cit.*, fol. 130rb).

IV

The issues raised in this decision of the *Rota* concerned above all the relation between enactments in positive law and customs which had grown up in opposition to them. Some additional remarks would seem to be in place here, since by its very generality the decision may convey a not wholly accurate picture of the actual as well as legal situation. Moreover, separate from the *privilegium fori,* and yet closely related to the juristic ingredients of the decision itself, there were some other features which should at least be mentioned in the present context.

The focal point of the decision is the competency of the ecclesiastical court *ratione personae:* the decision does not mention with one syllable the competency of the ecclesiastical court *ratione materiae.* But throughout the period antecédent to our decision the royal government always punctiliously observed the competency of the ecclesiastical courts (as far as civil litigations were concerned) in regard to testamentary and matrimonial questions. Bracton in the mid-thirteenth century is a trustworty witness to the practice already prevailing at his time (84), and however many writs of prohibition were issued by the king, they always affected only litigations which were not connected with testamentary or matrimonial matters (85). In other words, the royal courts did not in the numerous cases which in one way or another sprang from the myriads of quarrels connected with last wills or with marriages, claim any jurisdiction. The generality of the decision's tenor may well mislead one into thinking that even these causes had been encroached upon by the royal courts. And that in numerous instances clerics, especially those in lower orders, had been involved in this kind of litigation, is too self-evident to be specially mentioned.

Moreover, from a strict interpretation of this decision the conclusion may be drawn that all feudal matters of clerics also fell within the competency of the ecclesiastical courts. Certainly already at the time of Glanvill, that is, in the seventies of the twelfth century,

---

(84) See above at note 16.

(85) The standing phrase was: " Placita de catallis et debitis in regno nostro que *non* sunt de testamento vel matrimonio ".

the practice had been that for feudal litigations of clerics the royal courts alone were competent (86). Now it is certainly also true that Huguccio had maintained, perhaps not inconsistently, that no clerics may be brought before a secular tribunal in feudal matters (87), but common opinion was against him: " Multi tamen in hoc articulo contradicunt " (88). Moreover, the more recent decretal legislation concerning this point was interpreted in a sense contrary to that of Huguccio, and canonistic doctrine, too, appeared to side against him and to hold that feudal matters of clerics were to be legitimately within the competency of the secular courts (89). One of the main reasons given was that

> Episcopi et alii clerici tenentur venire ad vocationem regis, cum tenent ab eo temporalia, 23 qu. 8 § Ecce, et c. seq., 18 dist., Si episcopus (D. a. c. 21, C. XXIII, qu. 8, and c. 21; Dist. 18, c. 13) (90).

In other words, when what was called in England lay fee was in dispute, the clerics enjoyed no privilegium fori and had to plead before the royal courts (91), a practice which to a large extent seems to have accorded with canonistic doctrine, if not also the law. One can hardly assume that the Rota wished to present a point of view directly opposed to accepted theory as well as to law.

Let us enumerate two specific instances outside the privilegium fori, but still within the same precincts of the problem of customary

---

(86) Cf. also G. B. FLAHIFF, Med. Studies, cit., VI (1945), pp. 272-3; VII (1946), pp. 259 ff.

(87) See the report by the Archdeacon, App. Sext., cit., VI: III.2.1, no. 3, fol. 81 (continuing the passage cited above n. 10): "...et notat (Hug.) quod dicit ille canon (i.e. C. XI, qu. 1, c. 1) ' umquam ' quod exponitur, id est, in aliqua causa, ergo nec in causa feudi, quod verum est secundum Hug. prout notat ead. quaestione in summa, ubi dicit, quod idem est in causa feudi quod in aliis, et quicquid observetur inter laicos de iure ipsorum consuetudinario, tamen ratione feudi clericus numquam mutat forum ". On the question of " mutare forum " Iacobus de Arena had some interesting things to say, see the report by Cynus, Commentaria ad Codicem (ed. Frankfurt, 1578), ad Authent. Causa, nos. 7-10, fol. 18-18va.

(88) Archdeacon, ibid., immediately after the report quoted.

(89) See the Archdeacon who, apart from referring us to X: II.2.6, 7, 11 and II.1.5, mentions as representatives of the opinio communis Goffredus de Trano, Summa, cit., loc. cit., no. 13, fol. 73v, and Innocent IV ad X: II.2.15, ed. cit., no. 3, fol. 199v. The Archdeacon himself adhered to the communis opinio.

(90) Ibid. See also above at notes 17, 19.

(91) For details about the actual practice in England in the thirteenth century, see G. B. FLAHIFF, locc. citt.

law as opposed to enacted positive law. We must be brief and can
do no more than merely mention them. The one instance concerns
the custom according to which the English kings conferred prebends
and ecclesiastical offices, such as deaneries, upon whomsoever they
wished. It is William Lyndwood, the English canonist of the early
fifteenth century, who specifically and in a very long discussion refers
to this:

> *Reges Angliae licet non de iure scripto, tamen de c o n s u e -*
> *t u d i n e   l e g i t i m e   p r a e s c r i p t a conferunt quosdam*
> *decanatus et praebendas, quae sunt sui patronatus i u r e*
> *s u i , absque consensu episcopi saltem expresso* (92).

Now, in order to support his statement he sends us to a decretal of
Innocent III — the details of which, referring to a church in Nor-
mandy, are of no interest to us — according to which

> *Rex Angliae Johannes ratione ducatus sui Normanniae con-*
> *tulit decanatum et praebendas dictae ecclesiae s. Petri, ut ple-*
> *nius legitur in c. Cum inter, De consuetudine, in parte de-*
> *cisa* (93).

In this decretal Innocent III had said that " decanatum et praebendas ipsius ecclesiae idem rex et progenitores sui conferebant ". To
the eminent Tancred, however, this appeared not to accord with
canon law (94), but he comments thus:

---

(92) *Provinciale*, III.2.1, s. v. *beneficiati, ed. cit.*, p. 126.

(93) LYNDWOOD continues by saying " quae decisio habetur in compilatione antiqua,
quam vidi et perlegi in tertia compilatione, et notatur per Joh(annem), 10 dist. c. imperium ".
In parenthesis it may be noted that MAITLAND had observed this passage (*Roman Canon Law*,
cit., p. 5, n. 3) and asked whether this was " not a trait of a somewhat unusual erudition that
for an historical purpose he (LYNDWOOD) has gone behind the Gregorian collection ".
With all proper diffidence I am bound to question the relevance of the question.
LYNDWOOD was quite correct in quoting the *Gl. Ord.* of Johannes Teutonicus in the
shape given to it by Bartholomaeus Brixiensis, and for LYNDWOOD's purpose this
was necessary, if he wished to argue the existence of a *consuetudo legitime praescripta:* the point was that the decretal of Innocent III (*Reg.* VIII.212, in *P.L.* 215.795-6)
was in its entirety in the *Comp. III* (I.3.4: FRIEDBERG's edition (p. 106) here is misleading),
but the *Extra* (I.4.5) excised the part to which Johannes Teutonicus (and Barth. Brixiensis)
make reference. I have used MS. Caius College, Cambridge, 17:28, fol. 141. It is interesting
to note here that instead of the original " j " (for Johannes, the English king) this MS has
" h ", obviously referring to Henry III, which would not only give a clue to the time of
writing but might also indicate English provenance of this MS.

(94) MS. *cit.*, s. v. " conferebant ": " Et videtur quod male, per illa iura XVI, qu. ult.,
per laicos, si quis deinceps, et nullus (XVI.7.20, 12, 11) ".

> *Respondeo, quod rex Angliae p a t r o n u s e t d o m i n u s*
> *est omnium ecclesiarum cathedralium et aliarum maiorum*
> *ecclesiarum Normanniae et Angliae, et habent magna feuda*
> *ab ipso rege,*

and therefore by reason of either his patronage or of his feudal rights
the English kings had conferred prebends in those churches which
were either vacant or in others irrespective of a vacancy (95). In
other words, here within so fundamental an issue as the royal conferment of ecclesiastical offices and prebends in England there had
clearly evolved a *consuetudo legitime praescripta* in apparent contradiction to positive law: the juristic ingredients in this case do not
seem to be fundamentally different from those with which the decision of the *Rota* dealt (96).

To this instance of a custom we may append another one which
despite its importance of the subject, had not, perhaps, the same
topicality as the one just touched upon. This custom concerned the
anointing of the king on the occasion of his coronation. Now it
will be recalled that Innocent III had sent to the Bulgars a decretal
(in 1203) explaining the essential points of, amongst others, episcopal
and princely anointings (97). This decretal was also incorporated
in the *Compilatio III* and eventually in the *Extra* (98). After having
said that the head received unction " propter auctoritatem et dignitatem ", whilst the hands were anointed " propter ministerium et
officium ", Innocent III goes on to illustrate this by the difference
" inter pontificis et principis unctionem " declaring that the bishop's

---

(95) Tancred continues after the statement quoted in the text, MS. *cit.:* " Et ideo vel
ratione iuris patronatus et ratione feudorum conferunt reges praebendas ipsarum in quibusdam, dum sedes vacat, ut supra De iure patro., Ex diligenti in Ia (*Comp. I:* III.33.6), in quibusdam semper ut hic, et faciunt tamquam patroni; sed si facerent tamquam habentes aliquod ius spirituale tunc obtineret, quod dicitur in primis capitulis. T. '. The Archdeacon
had virtually wholly incorporated this gloss (in his *Rosarium, ed. cit.*, Dist. 10.5, fol. 12), and
it was he who had directed LYNDWOOD (and me) to Tancred's statement. For both the Archdeacon and LYNDWOOD it was therefore necessary to go " behind the Gregorian collection "
and to cite material not contained in it.

(96) The very long discussion of LYNDWOOD on the nature of the ecclesiastical benefice
conferred by the king, would repay detailed study; he is quite clearly ill at ease. For the
generally accepted point of view cf., e. g. Hostiensis, *Summa aurea* (ed. Cologne. 1612), III.7,
col. 785.

(97) *Reg.* VII. 3, in *P.L.* 215.282-7.

(98) *X:* I.15, c. un.

head was anointed with chrism, whilst the arm of the secular prince was anointed with oil only " ut ostendatur quanta sit differentia inter auctoritatem pontificis et principis potestatem " (99). It may possibly have been that Innocent III had only the imperial coronation in mind, but the fact remains that at any rate the English (and French) kings were before and after Innocent anointed on the head and also with chrism (100). How was one to reconcile this quite blatant discrepancy? Clearly, the principle underlying Innocent's decretal was in both England and France, if not openly flouted, at any rate quietly set aside. That this principle basically reflected the relative position of bishop and king is plain and needs no comment. It assuredly was the juristic acumen and ingenuity of Hostiensis who — so far as I can see — was the first to note the vital difference between Innocent's decretal and English (and French) practices in the matter of anointing. He is, perhaps understandably, brief: the difficulties would vanish, he thinks, if ancient custom were to be given its proper place:

> *Qualiter autem rex inungatur per librum pontificalem seu ordinarium poteris edoceri. Sed et c o n s u e t u d o a n t i - q u a c i r c a h o c o b s e r v a t u r , nam et supradictorum regum Angliae et Franciae capita inunguntur* (101).

The juristically relevant point here is that in a matter which, though not of the same topical interest as the *privilegium fori,* custom was quite plainly accorded, by doctrine at least a force which regionally anyway played its role, next to, and apart from, positive law.

---

(99) For practical instances of the anointing of the emperor on the occasion of his imperial coronation, see the respective *ordines* in R. ELZE, *Ordines coronationis imperialis* (in: *Fontes iuris Germanici antiqui* IX (1960)), nos. I.6, p. 2; IV B. 5, p. 11; VII.6, p. 17; X.6, p. 24; XIV.25, p. 41 (formerly called *Ordo C*); and XVIII.16, p. 75 (formerly called *Ordo D*, the *ordo* of the Roman curia: on this cf. ELZE, pp. XXV f. and the heading of XVIII, and esp. E. EICHMANN, *Die Kaiserkrönung im Abendlande* (Würzburg, 1942), I.253 (probably made in 1209 for the coronation of Otto IV and therefore an official curial *ordo*)); its rubric was: " Ostiensis episcopus ungat ei de oleo exorcizato brachium dextrum et inter scapulas ".

(100) For the twelfth century cf. Thomas Becket in *Materials for the life of Thomas Becket* (Rolls Series, 1891), V. 280; in general W. ULLMANN (ed.), *Liber regie capelle* (Henry Bradshaw Society, XCI (1960), pp. 30 ff. For France the same holds true: P. E. SCHRAMM, *Der König von Frankreich,* 2nd ed. (Darmstadt, 1960), I.157 f.

(101) *Summa, cit.,* ad I.15, no. 8, col. 187. In his *Lectura* ad *loc.,* I could not find any reference to this topic.

V

In conclusion two observations should be made, one of a particular, the other of a more general nature.

In order to assess this decision of the *Rota* I think one should bear in mind that it represents no more and no less than the purely juristic pronouncement of the highest tribunal on an important contemporary problem. The contrast to some rulings given in papal rescripts and decretals is one that is bound to strike the attentive reader: they were issued by the pope in his combined function as supreme judge, legislator and governor. Consequently, in the exercise of these functions the pope was at full liberty — the very hallmark of any *gubernator* — to be guided in his decisions by considerations and reflexions which, on closer inspection, could be regarded as extra-legal. The obvious instance is the one here which caused the *Rota* considerable difficulties, that is, the assertion that the motive of the pope in this or that case was the avoidance of scandal, and like. This wholly unavoidable and inescapable mixture of juristic and metajuristic considerations in the law-giver who is at the same time also judge and governor, is a theme that has not yet been appreciated in all its jurisprudential profundity and significance. In the more customary language, law and politics are intertwined and interlaced when the governing capacity of the Ruler also comprises judicial and legislative functions.

In confronting papal decretals with the decisions of the *Rota* the one striking and quite apparent difference is clearly that they are purely and exclusively juristic pronouncements into which considerations of a non-legal, i.e. " political " character did not infiltrate. In other words, a decision of the *Rota* — and the present one is quite a good illustration — did not and could not take into account any possible " political " implications, ramifications or repercussions: in this lies the essential and vital difference to the function from a legislator who is, by the very nature of his office, also a governor as well as judge. For government presupposes, of necessity, the application of criteria which are basically a-legal or ante-legal, whilst the function of a tribunal is, again by virtue of its nature, confined to the application of the law as laid down by the legislator. Hence the questions, whether the judgment of the *Rota* was " politically wise ", was opportune, was expedient, was advisable when thrown against the actual background, was not one that came into the professional or vocational purview of the *Rota*. The problem that urgently demands some attention, even if a solution will not readily be at hand, is the jurisprudential and constitutional significance of the establishment and subsequent working of the *Rota* as a firmly fixed tribunal, in relation to the functions and powers of the pope himself. Seen from a wider viewpoint, would it not be possible to discern some at least of the elements, albeit merely embryonically, which in a later age and under admittedly different conditions will characterize a system in which the judicial capacity came to be separated from the political and legislative functions? I do not know, but in its wholly juristic focus this decision of the *Rota* is so much devoid of all extraneous, non-legal and "political" considerations that its comparison with the judgment of some modern supreme constitutional court is not as farfetched as it might perhaps seem: in each case, it is the law pure and simple which is the sole ingredient of the judgment — and if the law needs changing in order to accommodate changed circumstances, this is not the function of a tribunal — be it called the *Rota* in the fourteenth century or a *Verfassungsgerichtshof* or *Staatsgerichtshof* in the twentieth century — but the business of the legislator: a tribunal has but one function only, to pronounce what the law in a concrete case is.

A presupposition for tackling this problem, however, is the availability of the source material. So far it has been, literally speaking, a mere handful of scholars who have done the preliminary spade work. We are, here, within the precincts of the working of the *Rota*, groping very much in the dark. The research carried out so far has, necessarily, concentrated upon the externals of the decisions, but not even they have been treated in such a way which would allow a final verdict. No attempt — apart from Fliniaux's pioneering work — has been undertaken to classify the numerous MSS containing the decisions of the *Rota*, to study the tradition and filiation of the MSS, to bring order into what is still largely chaos. Moreover, that there are quite noticeable divergencies between the MSS and the printed editions on the one hand, and within the editions themselves on the other hand, becomes clear to anyone who has had opportunity to enter this thorny, but highly interesting field. Rich and unexplored material is locked up in the decisions; virtually the whole canon law and the most recent contemporary literature are here subjected to a most rigorous analysis, an analysis

486

which was prompted by actual and practical exigencies: one comes to realize what an untapped source the *Rota* decisions also constitute in a purely *historical* respect. They contain evidence in regard to personages and matters which are otherwise hidden from the historian's view. The *materia* itself must be classified in such a way that the substance of the hundreds of decisions can be dealt with, in a systematic manner, from the legal-historical point of view. Further, it is high time that the question as to whether the *Rota* had *iurisdictio ordinaria* or *delegata* was properly examined, as this seems to me a problem that has first to be solved before one can fruitfully approach the larger jurisprudential questions. The light which this envisaged study necessarily must throw upon the relations between this practical and concrete jurisprudence and its academic counterpart should be of very great value to the intellectual history of the fourteenth century: what doctrines, what views, what interpretations advanced in the Universities, by civilians and canonists alike, did pass the rigorous standards of the judicial examination and application by the *Rota*? Vice-versa, what influence did its decisions exercise upon the academic study of law? Was there an interrelationship, and if so, of what kind was it, between *Spruchpraxis* and *Gelehrtenrecht*? Of particular interest are the *obiter dicta* of individual auditors cited in the decisions. A whole cluster of related questions would suggest itself: it is a field that is worthy of fuller exploration than has hitherto been the case. I cannot do better than conclude these observations with the words of the savant whom we honour, words spoken in a different, and yet closely related context which have particular force here: the historian, he said,

> will want to test the vital force of doctrine against the realities of ecclesiastical life in all their colourful variety, as they may be gleaned from archival and narrative sources — which means to co-ordinate the history of canonical jurisprudence and the history of canonical institutions (102).

And in this context the decisions of the *Rota* would seem to call for the closest possible attention.

Of the numerous controversial topics in the Middle Ages, the *privilegium fori* has in a quite pronounced degree prompted so many historians to present it as an issue of a conflict between Church and

---

(102) *Speculum*, XXIV (1949), p. 500.

State. But if ever there was a topic that showed none of the features commonly associated with a conflict of Church and State, it was precisely this claim of a privilege for clerics. The decision of the *Rota* itself makes this abundantly clear: the conflict was not one between two independent societies, but between two differing claims of jurisdiction in regard to the competency of the ecclesiastical courts *ratione materiae* as well as *ratione personae*. It was with special reference to the *privilegium fori* that the *Altmeister* of medieval law and institutions, has magisterially pronounced. Gabriel Le Bras said:

> Opposer simplement l'église et l'état, dans la société du Moyen Age, c'est commettre un véritable abus de langage: c'est transporter au XIIIe siècle l'état centralisé et l'église fortement unifiée de l'époque contemporaine (103).

Indeed, this conflicting claim to jurisdiction could only arise in a society which knew of no distinction between a State and a Church, for the chimerical conflict presupposes the existence of the State as a self-sufficient, autonomous, juristic body of citizens, but « this concept was as far removed from the medieval mind as the steam-engine and electricity " (104). The accent lies on the concept of the citizen: admittedly, since the eleventh century kings and emperors were groping towards this concept which in its turn presupposed, however, the existence of a conceptual framework that was, literally speaking, built upon foundations which were basically and ideologically vastly different from those upon which all medieval governments, including papal, royal and imperial, rested (105). The idea underlying the claim of royal jurisdiction in regard to the trial of clerics was assuredly the dimly conceived view that they were, next to being subjects of the king, also citizens of the kingdom itself, but this amorphously conceived idea never found legal or constitutional expression. What did find expression was the power

---

(103) Le Bras, *Journal des Savants, cit.*, p. 259.

(104) W. Ullmann, *History of Political Thought in the Middle Ages* (London, 1965), p. 137. See further, Carl F. Friedrich, *The Philosophy of Law in Historical Perspective* (Chicago, 1958), p. 43: " I regret the long established habit of speaking of medieval government as a State when nothing justifies this sort of anachronism. For medieval thought there were princes, lords, rule and government ".

(105) I have tried to analyse the respective development in *The Individual and Society in the Middle Ages* (Baltimore, 1966).

of the king over his subjects — and it was at this point that the sluices were opened up for controversies, because just as the king himself was a *persona mixta* (106), in the same way the cleric, only seen from a different angle, was also a *persona mixta* (107): but this situation reduced the whole problem of the *privilegium fori* to a mere conflict of rival jurisdictions — *within* the all-embracing body of the Church itself as the *congregatio fidelium*. Both king and cleric equally were members of this self-same body, however much their functions and offices differed: but the fundamental point here is that functions and offices were related to the purpose or end of the whole which was the Church. Differently expressed: the ecclesiological substratum of society in the Middle Ages militated against the atomisation of society and its divisions into different autonomous and autogenous compartments. The purely regional or territorial point of view could, in this respect, have little bearing. The issues raised by the *privilegium fori* gave rise to family disputes which were frequently fratricidal enough, but which never approached a conflict between a State and a Church, where wholly different criteria and postulates applied.

---

(106) See, for instance, LYNDWOOD himself, *Provinciale, ed. cit., loc. cit.,* p. 126: the " Rex unctus " was not " mere persona laica, sed mixta secundum quosdam et est expressum... ". See further, J. FLECKENSTEIN, *Rex Canonicus* in: *Festschrift für P. E. Schramm* (Wiesbaden 1964), I.57 ff.; also *ibid.,* p. 81 n. 38. That the properly installed (i. e. anointed and crowned) Ruler was often enough designated as an " ecclesiastical person " is well known. For the emperor, for instance, as a *persona ecclesiastica* in the *Summa Reginensis,* see the quotation in A. M. STICKLER in: *Salesianum,* XIV (1952), p. 493, reflecting possibly (imperial) *Ordo* XIV.19 (*ed. cit.,* p. 40): " Ibique fatiat (dominus papa) eum (the king to be crowned emperor) clericum et concedit ei tunicam et dalmaticam et pluviale et mitram, caligas et sandalia... et sic indutus stat ante dominum papam ". For the ideological background cf. also, *Principles of Government, ed. cit.,* pp. 147 ff.

(107) Particularly was this double character pronounced in regard to the episcopal status. A perhaps unusual example, given by Orderic Vitalis, refers to a French bishop who *qua* bishop was celibate, but *qua* baron was married; under Richard I the bishop of Coventry was summoned before the king's council to be judged as bishop by the bishops of the council, and as sheriff by the lay members of the council; perhaps most expressive was the statement of the royal court in Edward I's reign that the bishop of Durham " habet duos status, videlicet statum episcopi quoad spiritualia, et statum comitis palacii quoad tenementa sua temporalia ". These examples are given by J. CONWAY DAVIES, *The baronial opposition to Edward II* (Cambridge, 1918), pp. 22-3; and FRITZ HARTUNG, *Die Krone als Symbol monarchischer Herrschaft* in: *Corona Regni,* ed. M. HELLMANN (Weimar, 1961), p. 66. Cf. also E. KANTOROWICZ, *The King's Two Bodies* (Princeton, 1957), pp. 43-4, who links this mixed status with the noted view of the York Anonymous on the king's *persona gemina*.

The decision of the *Rota* reflects this properly medieval standpoint exceedingly well. It operated exclusively on the ecclesiological
level and with the law stemming from this ecclesiological premiss.
And yet, the very same age which witnessed this decision was also
the age which heralded and experienced the emergence and growth
of governmental principles in opposition to these ecclesiological
premisses. For the *Rota* there was no problem: it was called upon
to pronounce upon an issue on the basis of the *lex lata;* but the decision would seem, perhaps, once more to raise, though from another
viewpoint, the problem of law and politics, which is in this context
political ideology. And in so far the decision of the *Rota* was necessarily a pronouncement reflecting, not the present, but the past.
It was the built-in conservatism of law which prevented the decision
from being more than a mirror of an ecclesiologically conditioned
jurisprudence: it was in fact and in theory an almost classic illustration of concrete historical jurisprudence.

X

DE BARTOLI SENTENTIA :

CONCILIUM REPRAESENTAT MENTEM POPULI

I

The problem of the seat of legislative power and legislative competency is the medieval problem of the seat of political authority. Where does the *potestas condendi leges* reside? Who has *merum imperium?* In the terminology of modern political science this question is identical with where political sovereignty resides. In late Roman times as well as throughout the medieval period the significant notion of *jurisdictio* demonstrates the character and the nature of this sovereignty which therefore was exclusively legal.

In general, and without going into unnecessary details, two conceptions of the legislative competency can be discerned. This power may be ascribed to the community: it is the people assembled in a special gathering that decrees certain rules of action or, which is the more common historical experience, the people themselves adhere to certain conduct observed for a long time and through a variety of circumstances, a conduct that is to say which they hold binding and obligatory upon themselves. The formation of valid customary law, therefore, is, historically seen, the best test of the law-creating capability of a community. At the same time the people assembled in the Ting, and the like, can issue decrees which, to all intents and purposes, have the force of laws and may properly be called laws. The formation of the *Volksrechte* — because only a specific aspect of customary law — again would support the contention of the popular legislative capacity. Allegorically speaking, the law which is derived from the people is ascending, because it grows — whether in the form of a customary law or of a *Volksrecht* — from below upwards.

The other conception of legislative competency is that according to which the law comes, so to speak, from above and descends downwards. This kind of law is not made by the people, but given by a single individual who by virtue of his own position and legislative competency bestows upon the people the law. Within this descending conception there is strictly speaking no room for a customary or popular law. In a correctly understood christocentric society it is this descending conception that prevails and leads logically to the concept of a theocratic form of government, in which the Ruler constitutes an estate of his own and stands outside and above the community which he rules. This community is entrusted to the Ruler by divinity — it is the *populus* which is committed to the Ruler's care and government. The reverse is the case when the *populus* itself commits the government to the Ruler.

Whilst originally law was made by the people, the influence of late Roman governmental conceptions together with the overpowering strength of Roman Christianity entailed the gradual elimination of the people as a law-creating agency. From their point of view, neither pope nor emperor could, once having become aware of their own status within their respective societies, approve of, or even in a friendly spirit look at, the people themselves as law-making organs. *Mut.mut.* the same observation can be applied to kings who becoming gradually aware of their own power, begin to relegate the popular assembly to an inferior role and to try to excise it altogether eventually, with the result that the king's law became the sole law. This process may suitably be called the process of the king's emancipation from the people. This assumption of legislative omnipotence by the king was accompanied by the assumption of suitable titles in the papal, imperial and royal camps. That is to say, the political role of the legislator as monarch expressed itself in his being *vicarius Christi*, be he emperor or pope (1), or in the king being « Rex Dei gratia » or *divina favente gratia* which latter formula contains the double negation of the king's holding his power either from the people or from the pope. It is clear that, since within the prevailing christocentric conceptions, law could only come

---

(1) About the development of the papal title see M. MACCARRONE, *Vicarius Christi: storia del titolo papale* (Lateranum, n. s. XVIII: Rome, 1952). About the development of the corresponding royal and imperial titles there is still an exhaustive investigation outstanding; for some observations cf. MACCARRONE, and A. HARNACK, « Christus praesens - Vicarius Christi » in *Sitzungsberichte d. Preuss. Akad. d. Wiss.*, XXXIV (1927). The influence of Byzantium is especially noticeable in the Western adoption of the titles.

from « above » and be transmitted downwards through the (equally from above appointed) officials, this descending conception of law and government very greatly contributed to the strengthening of papal and royal and imperial power on the one hand, and also virtually, at least on the surface, suppressed the people as a law-creating agency (2). In other words, in the high Middle Ages the picture as regards the legislative competency is precisely the opposite of the early Middle Ages: there it was the popular assembly that pronounced and propounded the law; here it was the Ruler alone who gave it: the law is a « *donum* Dei ».

This exclusion of the people from legislation could not, however, affect the growth of usages and customs observed by the *populus* and endowed by it with a certain binding force. That customs, if they display the force of law, present a very serious challenge to the legislative competency of the monarchic Ruler, goes without saying. For if certain customs obtain this binding character, it follows conclusively that next to the creator of the written law, there is also a creator of the unwritten law which latter being a law in every respect must, from the point of view of its obligatory character, stand on the same level as its written counterpart. It is at this juncture that the two great legal systems, the Roman law and the Canon law, part company.

Classical Roman law had freely recognized the force of customs as a basis of the law: that is to say, that customs, provided certain obvious requirements were fulfilled, such as length of time, continuity of action, etc., displayed all the legal effects which otherwise pertained to written and enacted law. The Ruler himself *qua* legislator never entered into the process at all that eventually brought forth customary law. The actions of the multitude became law automatically: hence the people themselves were the actual law-creating organs, not however in the sense that they enacted in writing the individual abstract decree, but in the sense that their actual conduct became in course of time an enforceable rule, i.e. an (unwritten) law. That Roman law ascribed to the *populus Romanus* the function of a law-creating organ, follows from the contents of the *Lex Regia*, according to which it was the Roman people which had transferred their (at one time exclu-

---

(2) It is certainly significant that Constantine did not allow customary law the power to derogate the leges: *Cod.* VIII.LII.2.

sive) power to the *princeps*. Although they had handed over their governmental and legislative power to the emperor, they still may be said to have retained a modicum of law-creating capability in so far as their customs displayed full legal effects. There is no enactment in classical Roman law by which this residual power had been taken away from the (Roman) people. It was the thin end of the wedge.

Although it is not necessary for the present purpose to go into any details concerning canon law, it may suffice to say that the very nature of the canon militated against ascribing to the people that function which classical Roman law had done. On the contrary, it is in general correct to say that for the automatic transition from usage or custom into law there was no room within the conceptual framework of the canon law. Since, constitutionally, the Church was ruled monarchically by the pope and since he obtains his monarchic status directly from Christ, and since, lastly, the Church itself was a divine institution, there is indeed no possibility of even conceding to the Christian people any function resembling that which they have in Roman law. Whatever customs may develop within certain communities, they display no legal effects unless and until not only recognized, but also (explicitly or implicitly) approved by the supreme monarchic legislator, the pope. Also from another point of view there is an effective bar to crediting merely popular practices with automatic legal force: according to the axiomatic theme of canon law every law must embody in one form or another the idea of (Christian) *justitia;* the knowledge as to what does and what does not constitute *justitia* in the particular field of action, cannot be justifiably be presumed with the multitude, hence the insistence on the approval of a custom by the legislator.

Let us return to Roman law. Its acknowledgement of customary law as an equal of the written law anabled the Glossators and Post-Glossators to construct a fully-fledged theory of customary law. The details of this theory are of no concern to us in this context. What is of concern is the dawning realization on the part of a number of jurists that the *lex imperatoris* and the customary law show that they stem from entirely different roots and origins. The one comes from above, from the emperor *divina favente gratia* and descends downwards; the other comes from below, from the *populus* itself and ascends upwards, to use metaphorical language. And yet both display the same effects; both are validly enforceable; both may concern public and private law; both may affect civil and criminal law; both may relate to substantive and adjectival law. The realization by some jurists of this apparent dichotomy, for instance by Cynus, led to the theory that *imperator est a populo, imperium a Deo* (3) — a theory that does credit to the sagacious juristic mind, but does little to resolve the antinomy. There are, consequently, two law-creating organs — emperor as well as people.

II

It was no mere accidence that of all the fourteenth-century Post-Glossators Bartolus not only gave the most coherent doctrine of customary law, but also constantly adduced customary law as an object of comparison with the written law and, on this basis, drew consequences which may well appear obvious, but which were nonetheless not drawn by anyone before him: it was his comparison of customary and written law which enabled Bartolus to construct his theme of the *civitas sibi princeps*.

What, according to Bartolus, is it that converts a custom into an enforceable rule of action? He distinguishes between the *causa remota* and the *causa proxima* and declares that whilst the former consists of the actually observed conduct of the people, the latter presents itself in the tacit consent of the people to the obligatory character of the actions thus observed.

Usus et mores sunt causa consuetudinis: dico causa remota, nam proxima causa est tacitus consensus populi qui colligitur ex usu et moribus (4).

The essential point for our discussion is the consent of the people: it is this consent which automatically transforms a mere

(3) See W. ULLMANN, *The Medieval Idea of Law* (London, 1946), p. 175 n. 1, and the passage of Andreas de Isernia in the same sense, cited by E. KANTOROWICZ, *The King's Two Bodies* (Princeton, 1957), p. 297 n. 54.

(4) *Comm. ad Dig.* 1.3.23, fol. 19vb, and in other places. I have used the edition August. Taur., 1577, for all the works of Bartolus. For some details concerning his customary law see S. BRIE, *Die Lehre vom Gewohnheitsrecht* (Breslau, 1899), pp. 128 ff., and W. ULLMANN, « Bartolus on Customary Law » in *Juridical Review*, LII (1940), pp. 265 ff.

action into an enforceable rule. In another place Bartolus speaks of a popular convention which gives custom the force of law:

> Consuetudo sumit vigorem ex tacita populi conventione ... tacita civium conventione (5).

It is the people alone — no emperor, no king, no pope, had any say in this matter — who confer legal and obligatory character upon these factually observed customs.

Once the element that infuses into customs their enforceability was so clearly realized (6), the next step in the argument suggested itself at once: if the citizens can by tacit consent or tacit convention create unwritten law in the shape of customary law, what obstacle is there for not ascribing to them the same law-creating capability in the shape of written law? Bartolus realized that to credit the people with the power to make customary law, involved implicitly the logical conclusion that they had also the power to make written laws, i.e. *statuta*.

The great advance made by Bartolus was that he perceived the parallelism between written and unwritten law to lie in the element of the consent. It is at this point of the argument that the Bartolist conception of the *civitas sibi princeps* assumes it full significance (7). The kernel of a *civitas sibi princeps* is its non-recognition of a superior. Non-recognition, however, by its very definition — and Bartolus is thoroughly consistent in the appellation of a *civitas sibi princeps* as one *quae non recognoscit superiorem* — necessarily involves the all-pervading element of the will on the part of those who refuse recognition, it being understood that they *ought* to recognize, but in actual fact do not. One might go even so far as to say that non-recognition implies

---

(5) *Comm.* ad *Dig.* 1.3.33, fol. 21ra.

(6) Cf. Bartolus summarizing Petrus de Bellapertica's theory in *Comm.* ad C. VIII.LII.2, no. 4, fol. 114rb: « (Petrus de Bellapertica) dicit quod scriptura non est de esse legis nec etiam non scriptum de esse consuetudinis. Dicit ergo, quod tanta est differentia inter ea, quantum inter expressum et tacitum ».

(7) Reference should be made, once and for all, to the fundamental works of O. GIERKE, *Das deutsche Genossenschaftsrecht* (Berlin, 1881), III. 381 ff.; C.N.S. WOOLF, *Bartolus de Sassoferrato* (Cambridge, 1913), pp. 159 ff.; F. ERCOLE, *Da Bartolo all'Althusio* (Florence, 1932), pp. 49 ff.; cf. also the literature cited by F. BATTAGLIA, *Lineamenti di storia delle dottrine politiche*, 2nd ed. (Milan, 1952), p. 99 note 91. See also G. DE VERGOTTINI, *Lezioni di storia del diritto italiano: Il diritto pubblico italiano nei secoli XII-XV*, 2nd ed. (Milan, 1954), I. 273 ff.

a kind of defiant and rebellious attitude, but in any case it is the volitional element that gives non-recognition its peculiar complexion.

At all medieval times customary law was of paramount importance. Now classical Roman law had given, as we have seen, full force to customary law, but the essential point is that customary law could only come from the people. The analysis of the substantive elements of customary law necessarily leads to the full realization of the popular will — the *diuturnitas temporis* and the longuevity of the custom actually observed are not in themselves constitutive elements, but only elements proving the *tacitus consensus populi* which is therefore the really essential item in the creation of customary law. That the exercise of this popular will was in accord with Roman law, is evident, for the *Lex Regia* at no time excludes the capability of the people to live according to their own customs and usages. Moreover, the *Lex Regia* was by the time of Bartolus applied to the Roman populace as such — the « territorial » Romans — and left out of account the cities and kingdoms (8). But once the fundamental importance of the popular will and consent was recognised it was only a relatively small step to extend this to the making of statutes, that is, of written laws. As Bartolus unceasingly insists, the difference between the two kinds of law lies merely in the way in which the popular will finds its expression — either tacit or explicit — but the essence is the manifestation of the popular will demonstrated in consent. That citizenhood which acts upon its own will through tacit or express consent, is a *populus liber,* and for this reason refuses to acknowledge a superior: what they can do by tacit consent, they can also do by express consent, that is, to make laws. Consequently, there is no need for a superior's authorization of their statutes, *because* their customary laws also do not need this approbation.

> Quando populus habet omnem jurisdictionem, potest facere statutum, non expectata superioris auctoritate ... et quod isto casu non expectatur superioris auctoritas patet exemplo consuetudinis, quae inducitur ex tacito consensu populi et aequiparatur statuto (9).

---

(8) See WOOLF, op. cit., p. 35.

(9) *Comm.* ad *Dig.* 1.1.9, no. 4, fol. 9va; also cited in ERCOLE, op. cit., p. 83 n. 2.

Although maintained before, it was Bartolus who on the basis of his statement that « tacitus et expressus consensus aequiparantur et sunt *paris potentiae* » (10) constructed a fully-fledged theory of legislative popular sovereignty (11).

The juristic skill of Bartolus lay in that he extended the principles of customary law to written law by focusing his attention upon the *consensus populi*. It is again certainly no coincidence that the parallelism between written and unwritten law pervades his whole long and fundamental discussion on the *lex* « *Omnes Populi* ». It is therefore worth while pointing out that the Roman law description of customary law as a *conventio civium* (12) is used by Bartolus to designate a statute: like customary law, statute law too is « quaedam conventio civium » (13). By choosing the avenue of the tacit popular consent Bartolus is enabled to demonstrate and justify the full legislative powers of the *civitas sibi princeps*: the fact is undeniable that kingdoms and cities exercised fullest jurisdiction aside from that of the emperor as *dominus mundi*. Bartolus justified this fact juristically by the operation of the popular consent to which, from the strictly legal point of view, at no time any objection could be raised. Once due recognition is given to this in itself quite simple juristic thought process, the way lay open for this *civitas* to be a proper State, endowed with all the appurtenances of legal (and political) sovereignty. That *civitas* which is governed by the popular will and consent is distinguished by a *regimen ad populum* (14). What Bartolus did was to present the fact of not recognizing a superior as an effluence of the legally valid *consensus populi*.

Thereby the people's will was made an integral part of both legal and political theory. By virtue of the operation of the po-

---

(10) *Comm.* ad *Dig.* 1.4.1 § De quibus, no. 4, fol. 17ra.

(11) That the importance of the *consensus* of the people was recognized even by theologians, can be gathered from Bartolus' contemporary, William Ockham, who, though dealing with an entirely different topic, said: « Romanum imperium non potest minui nec dividi, saltem absque consensu tacito vel expresso communitatis mortalium », *Dialogus*, pars III, Tr. II, lib. I, cap. 31.

(12) *Dig.* 1.3.35 (Hermogenianus).

(13) *Comm.* ad *Dig.* 28.1.3, no. 4.

(14) Tractatus *De Regimine Civitatis*, no. 7. On this cf. also Woolf, op. cit., p. 174.

pular consent the *civitas sibi princeps* can legislate *prout sibi placet,* and above all on any matter affecting the public weal.

Nota quod statutum vel constitutio facta ... non valet nisi approbetur per superiorem. Sed contra hoc oppono, quia quilibet populus potest facere statutum, ut ff. de just. et jure, l. Omnes populi. Solutio: dicit Guil. (de Cuneo) quod illud est verum in his, quae privatam utilitatem respiciunt. In his vero, quae respiciunt publicam utilitatem principaliter, non possunt, ut hic. Sed ego dico aliter, in l. Omnes populi, nam quidem est populus liber, qui habet omnem jurisdictionem, et *tunc potest facere legem et statutum prout sibi placet,* ut. d. l. Omnes (15).

The essential feature of the Bartolist doctrine relating to the *civitas sibi princeps* is the full legislative sovereignty of the people or better, the full popular sovereignty expressed in legal terminology. This sovereign independence of the *civitas sibi princeps* shows itself in its capability to wage aggressive and defensive wars (16), to entertain an army (17), to erect its own fortifications (18), to conclude treaties and enter into leagues with other cities, to levy its own taxes and public charges (19), to confiscate property (20), to restitute to full civic status (21), and so forth. We must now enquire into how Bartolus envisaged the actual application of this doctrine, that is, how is this popular sovereignty to be practically realized in the shape of government? In so doing it should be stated that Bartolus, not a political theorist, but pre-eminently a jurist, employs a terminology which is wholly

---

(15) *Comm.* ad C. X.LXIII.5 (*Si quod*), no. 4, fol. 26.

(16) *Comm.* ad C. X.XXXI.2, fol. 16ra.

(17) *Comm.* ad *Dig.* 48.4.3, no. 2, fol. 165vb; *Tractus de Repressaliis,* qu. 1, no. 6, fol. 122va.

(18) *Comm.* ad *Dig.* 50.10.3, no. 4, fol. 241va.

(19) *Comm.* ad *Dig.* 49.14.2, no. 2, fol. 221va: « Sed debetis scire, quod quaedam sunt civitates, quae non recognoscunt superiorem et sic populus liber est et sic *ipsemet fiscus* ». Cf. also *Comm.* ad *Dig.* 37.1.3, no. 2, and *Consilium* CLXXX, no. 1-2, fol. 44vb.

(20) *Comm.* ad C.X.X.1, no. 11. It is noteworthy that shortly afterwards this Bartolist doctrine was embedded in the theory of *publica utilitas,* because this constituted a *justa causa* of expropriation. Cf. LUDOVICUS ROMANUS PONTANUS, *Consilia* (Frankfurt, 1577), *cons.* CCCX, fol. 153v: « Civitas so locum principis obtinet, rem privati auferre potest. Est autem justa causa *favor publicae auctoritatis* ... vel si aliquem remunerare velit de re publica benemerentem ».

(21) *Comm.* ad *Dig.* 48.1.7, no. 14, fol. 253vb.

taken from Roman law. The nomenclatures, though perhaps a little clumsy and unusual, matter less than the thing itself. Nor again should we expect a cut and dried theory of government, such as is presented to us in the many works of his contemporaries dealing *ex professo* with the scheme of political government.

Bartolus considers that the people as a whole assemble in what he calls the *Concilium majus* or the *Adunantia* or the *Parliamentum*. This is a real popular assembly in which the popular will finds its effective expression and which, in the last resort, is the concrete embodiment of power within the *civitas*. The prime object of this *Parliamentum* is the election of the governing body or Council. This Council in its turn appoints the actual governmental officers, and it is no doubt interesting to see that Bartolus refers here to the *jus commune* which determines this function of the governing body.

> Nota quod de jure communi ad concilium civitatis spectat facere electiones officialium et syndicorum. Facit infra, l. Procuratores, et sic non erit opus arenga vel adunantia generali. Arenga tamen illud seu parliamentum, ubi non est aliquis superior habet ab initio concilium eligere, ut lex 2, circa principium, ff. de orig. juris. Istud concilium sic electum postea repraesentat totum populum (22).

The important point here is the application of the principle of representation: the governing Council represents the whole people, because it is elected by them and therefore carries out the government on their behalf. This statement on the representative character of the Council — one might see in it the forerunner of the *conseil d'état* or the *Staatsrat* — is not an isolated one: it occurs in several places which only slightly modify the terminology, such as

> Concilium quod totam civitatem repraesentat (23).

---

(22) *Comm.* ad C. X.XXXI.2, fol. 16ra.

(23) *Comm.* ad *Dig.* 12.1.27, no. 2, fol. 17vb. Cf. also *Comm.* ad C. IV.XXXII.5, no. 3, fol. 158va: « Totus populus, quia *eius vicem concilium repraesentat* ». It may be that these populist opinions of Bartolus earned him later the distinction of his having pleased the lay people; cf. the statement of Baldus, reported by JASON DE MAYNO, *Dig. nov.*, De verborum oblig., l. 123, no. 37: « Semper tenebat opiniones multum placentes laicis, et hoc facit opinionibus suis multum honorem » (cited from F. SAVIGNY, *Gesch, d. röm. Rechts im Mittelalter*, 2nd ed. (Heidelberg, 1850), VI.149 note (c).

The idea that the Council represents the will of the people is perhaps best brought out in the statement of Bartolus that

Concilium repraesentat *mentem populi* (24).

The members of the Council are the *consiliarii* who are called — on the model of the available officers in Roman law — the *decuriones*.

Advertatis, quod concilium civitatis aequiparatur ordini decurionum; consiliarii decurionibus (25).

In them lies the whole governing capacity of the people manifesting itself primarily in legislation. It is they « per quos civitas regitur » (26) having bee entrusted through popular election with governmental business. Their government refers exclusively to ordering all issues pertaining to the public weal: they can issue laws only « de his, quae pertinent ad publicam utilitatem principaliter (27), though, as we have seen, not exclusively. Since the members of the Council are the representatives of the people, have therefore legislative power in public matters, they are somewhat restricted in their own private life: because they are the representatives of the community, they are not allowed to function in their private capacity as advocates and the like, or, if this is their calling, they are ineligible as public councillors (28).

Now the Council acting in the name of the people appoints those officers through whom the *civitas* is in actual fact administered. According to Bartolus, these officers fall into three categories — the judicial, the administrative and the economic ones. The judiciary comprises not only the judges in the technical sense, but also the officials who exercise a supervisory function over the entire subordinate official service. To the administrative

---

(24) *Comm.* ad *Dig.* 1.4.1, De quibus, no. 10, fol. 17ra. Is there an echo of Marsilius or of Bartolus in the statement by a Justice in Edward III's reign (anno 1365) that « Parliament represents the body of the whole realm », see F.W. MAITLAND, *Selected Essays* (Cambridge, 1936), p. 107 (from *Year-Books*, 39 Edw. III, fol. 7a).

(25) *Comm.* ad C. IV.XXXII.5, no. 5, fol. 158ra.

(26) *Comm.* ad. C. XI.XXX. Rubrica, fol. 35va.

(27) *Comm.* ad *Dig.* 50.1.3, no. 8, fol. 231va.

(28) *Comm.* ad. C. X.XXXI.34, fol. 17va: « Consiliarius non debet constitui procurator ... et forte male faciunt Perusini, qui nolunt quod aliquis notarius vel advocatus habeat officium prioratus vel camerae ».

officers belongs the actual management of public effairs — their
names vary according to the locality: *Priores, Antiani,* or *Consules* — whilst the economic functionaries are the *calculatores* and
the *revisores* upon whom falls the control of financial, economic
and food supplies as well as of the agricultural interests (29).
Into the judicial class of officers belong also what might be termed in modern parlance the police officials, that is, the syndics:
they too are constitutionally appointed by the Council, and not by
individual officers.

> Syndicos (id est denuntiatores) ad denuntiandum maleficia, seu
> milites ad capiendum malefactores concilium civitatis debet propo-
> nere, non judex solus sive potestas civitatis sive alius rector (30).

Whatever these appointed officers do, they do on behalf of the
Council so that it can be said that « ipsum concilium majus (id
est, parliamentum) hoc videtur fecisse per ipsos (scil. officiales) » (31).

The senior of the councillors — the *prior decurionum* (32)
— has the right and duty of convoking the Council: the summoning is done by the usual medieval method, namely by blowing
the trumpet or the ringing of the bells (33) or by the common
town crier. Hence it is not necessary that each individual councillor is summoned by name (34). The deliberations of the Council
must be in public, and for ordinary purposes the proper place
is the town hall, that is the *palacium publicum* (35):

---

(29) *Comm.* ad. C. X.I.2, no. 8, fol. 3rb: « (Civitas) habet officiales triplicis
generis. Quidam enim sunt calculatores et revisores rationum tantum ... quidam
sunt judices seu syndicatores qui habent omnes officiales condemnare vel absolvere ...
quidam sunt administratores, ut priores et consules seu antiani, secundum diversi-
tamen locorum ». The financial officers are not empowered to legislate on any financial matters, however important the proposed legislation would be or however
insignificant the actual sums involved may be, see *Comm.* ad *Dig.* 50.9.4, no. 21,
fol. 240rb.

(30) *Comm.* ad C X.LXXV. Rubrica, fol. 28ra.

(31) *Comm.* ad Dig. 50.9.4, no. 34, fol. 240vb.

(32) *Comm.* ad C. X.XXXI.2, fol. 16ra.

(33) This, incidentally, is still the custom in modern Cambridge: the bells
of the University Church are rung when the Senate or the House of Regents are
about to meet.

(34) *Comm.* ad Dig. 50.9.2, no. 1, fol. 239ra: « Utrum debent isti nominatim
vocari? Respondeo, sufficit, quod vocentur sono tubae vel campanae ».

(35) *Comm.* ad loc. cit., no. 1.

Nota quod concilium debet vocari in loco publico ... ubi publici officiales habitant et curiam tenent (36).

According to Bartolus the Council is properly convened if all are summoned: it is only necessary that those councillors who are actually in residence, appear at the meeting; conversely, the Council is properly constituted even if infirm or unavoidably absent or otherwise prevented counsellors do not take part in the deliberations. But it is essential that two-thirds of the whole Council are present (37). The voting on a particular proposal is — a vital difference to the usual medieval practice — by a simple numerical majority (38):

> Non valent decreta decurionum, si ibi non sunt duae partes decurionum seu duae partes concilii, et intellige, quod istarum duarum partium major pars consentiat.

In the case of elections to be carried out by the Council, the elected candidate may not vote for himself (39). Even in the way in which the proposal for a law is made, the idea of representation breaks through. Bartolus says that the senior councillor may either put the general question « quid placet vobis super tali facto statuere? » or he may submit a definite legislative draft proposal for discussion and ask: « An placeat populo quod sit talis lex vel statutum ». But in all cases whether election by the Council or legislation « quod placuerit majori parti, illud erit firmum » (40).

---

(36) *Comm.* ad C. X.XXXI. 2, no. 5.

(37) *Comm.* ad Dig. 1.1.9, no. 16, fol. 10ra: « Nec sufficit vocatos esse, nisi duae partes sint praesentes ».

(38) *Comm.* ad Dig. 50.9.2, no. 2, fol. 239ra. Cf. also *Comm.* ad C. X.XXXI.45, no. 2, fol. 18ra: « Sufficit duas partes consiliariorum adesse ... requiritur tamen quod omnes vocentur sono tubae vel campanae ... nota, quod sufficit quod major pars praesentium consentiat ... et notatur per Dyn. in cap. Quod omnes tangit ». The principle of quantitative majority shows that all the members of the Council had equal standing, a conclusion that is at once based on the correct appreciation of the implications of popular-legislative sovereignty and on the equality of the members of the *populus* itself. This marks an important advance towards a properly conceived individualism. The usual medieval practice, it will be recalled, was — except in papal elections — voting by a qualitative majority (the *pars sanior*, and the like).

(39) Cf. ibid., no. 3.

(40) *Comm.* ad Dig. 1.1.9, no. 16, fol. 10ra.

The consent may be express, though not necessarily given in words: it is sufficient if explicit signs convey the consent, such as standing up or remaining seated or by black or white balls (41). What is essential is that all vote in one act and in the same place, that is, that the councillors vote *ut universi*. If therefore everyone were to vote in his own house (in modern times this would amount to a postal ballot) and even if a notarial document were to confirm this individual voting, it would be without validity: what is required is « simul omnium consensus » (42). On the other hand, it is permissible — again assuredly only on the presupposition that the councillors represent *mentem populi* — that they can appoint specific officers charged with the drafting of the decrees; the reason for this delegation is that the people and through them the Council possess ordinary jurisdiction, that is, full legislative sovereignty, and can therefore legally entrust the making of statutes to experts, the assumption being that residual control remains with the people (43).

> Quaero, numquid possit aliquibus committi, quod faciant statuta? Tu dic, aut judices seu domini, qui habent auctoritatem hoc faciendi, volunt delegare, et non possunt, quia hoc eis ut majoribus est concessum ... aut populus vult hoc committere et potest ... Vel dic, quod ratio est, quia ille cui committitur a populo, videtur ordinarius, et non delegatus, quia populus potest dare ordinariam jurisdictionem ... sed alii judices non dant ordinariam, istud autem non potest delegari.

The latter assumption is borne out by Bartolus' view on the interpretation of a statute that is or has become obscure in its

---

(41) Loc. cit., no. 19: « Quaero, qualiter explorabitur talis voluntas populi? Et videtur, quod requiratur expressus consensus verbis ... cum in hoc differant statuta a consuetudine, quia unum venit ex consensu expresso, aliud ex consensu tacito ... Non requiruntur verba sed sufficiunt signa consensus secundum quod propositum fuit in partito sive de levando vel de sedendo, sive de fabis albis vel nigris ».

(42) Ibid., no. 18: « Quaero, quod si omnes de populo consentiunt separatim in domo sua, et hoc constat per publicum instrumentum, an valeat »? The answer is in the negative « primo in his, quae pertinent ad plures ut universos, requiritur simul omnium consensus ... secunda regula est in his, quibus consensus majoris partis praejudicat minori etiam si pertineat ad plures ut singulos, requiritur ut fiat simul ... ergo hic cum praedicta concurrant, requiritur, quod fiat simul. Nec obstat quod dicitur de consuedine, quia pluralitas actuum et cursus temporis succedit loco talis consuetudinis ».

(43) Ibid., no. 20.

meaning. Who is to interpret the meaning of such a statute? Is it those who actually drafted the statute or those whose will the statute in question is said to embody? Bartolus puts the problem very succinctly:

> Ubi vero statutum est adeo obscurum, quod non potest haberi congrua expositio, tunc fateor, quod recurritur ad statuentes.

Perhaps nowhere emerges the pervading view of Bartolus on the popular will as the bearer of legislative sovereignty with greater clarity than in his answer to this question: Who are the *Statuentes?* The draftsmen or the people through the Council? « Sed an recurratur ad ipsum populum, an recurratur ad illos homines, quibus commissum fuit a populo, ut conderent statuta?» The answer can surely only be the people or the Council whose will was to be found out, and not the *statutarii* who have inadequately drafted the statute (44):

> Populus seu concilium interpretatur, cum illi sapientes statutarii sint functi officio suo, nec habent amplius imperium et sic non habent jus interpretandi.

Imperium, in other words belongs to the people, and not to the draftsmen (45).

Bartolus' discussion on the legislative powers of the Council drives home the idea of popular sovereignty in a practical manner. What, in other words, is the legislative competency of the Council? In general, Bartolus' answer is, they have as much or as little power as the electing *populus* has given them, for the councillors exist solely by the will of the people: it is they who confer upon the councillors the *arbitrium* (scil. regendi). The general principle is that the extent of this *arbitrium* is determined by the original warrant given to the Council by the people (46).

> Quod habentes arbitrium super aliquo, possunt omnia facere, quae principaliter spectant ad id, super quo habent arbitrium.

---

(44) Ibid., no. 56. There is no need to recall that this is exactly the procedure followed in modern times.

(45) *Comm.* ad Dig. 50.9.4, no. 8, fol. 239va: « Ipsae (civitates) in se habent imperium ». *Comm.* ad Dig. 3.1.1 § De quare, no. 3, fol. 98va: « Apud eosmet dicitur esse imperium sui ipsius ».

(46) *Comm.* ad Dig. 50.9.4, no. 18, fol. 240ra.

From this fundamental principle follow four subsidiary principles (47). Bartolus specifies a number of governmental actions to which the councillors are not constitutionally entitled on the basis of the *arbitrium*, unless these actions are specifically made a charge upon them by the people. Thus, release from outlawry and re-instatement into full civic status; stay of execution beyond three months and general pardons; constitutional changes — « non possunt ex virtute dicti arbitrii vel alicuius eorum mutare ordines et regimina civitatum ... nam arbitrium quod habent super bono et pacifico statu civitatis, intelligitur de praesenti » ; changes of statutes made by the whole people (48); alienation of immobile public property (49); denial of a legitimately acquired private right « licet enim totus populus hoc posset » ; levying of new taxes, etc., in ordinary times (50); waging wars of aggression, but defensive wars are legitimately authorized by the Council (51); other issues which Bartolus enumerates, but which do not directly bear upon our topic, cannot be legitimately decreed, unless the Council had been given a specific warrant from the people or at least from the *concilium majus*, that is, from the popular assembly. What it therefore amounts to is that the *populus* may give full powers to the *concilium*, but the people nevertheless retain control at all times.

(47) Ibid., no. 18: « Quod possunt statuere et facere omnia antecedentia propter quae ad illud (scil. arbitrium) perveniri potest ... quod possunt statuere et facere omnia consequentia sine quibus illud commode explicari non potest ... quod non possunt aliquid facere vel statuere super eo, quod non spectat ad id super quo eis concessum est arbitrium ... quod non possunt facere aliquid vel statuere super eo quod est accessorium alterius, quod non spectat ad id, super quo eis concessum est arbitrium ».

(48) Ibid., no. 11: « Ex vigore dicti arbitrii non possunt statuere aliquid, quod sit contra statuta et ordinem factum *a toto populo a quo ipsi auctoritatem habent* ».

(49) Ibid., no. 10: « Item immobilia civitatis non possunt alienare, nisi specialiter hoc eis permittatur ».

(50) Ibid., no. 15: « Si quidem in illa civitate vectigalia et gabellae non sunt solitae imponi, ordo (scil. decurionum) eas imponere non poterit, nisi specialiter sit eis permissum, hic enim est casus, qui reservatus est *populo*, qui *in sua civitate imperium* habet seu *obtinet vicem principis*, sicut reservatur principi universali ... Si vero civitas consuevit tempore necessitatis imponere gabellas, tunc imponere poterunt (scil. decuriones) ».

(51) Ibid., no. 16: « An possit ex virtute alicuius arbitrii de praedictis institui nova guerra? Respondeo, potest pro defensione civitatis et suorum jurium. Alias autem pro recuperatione rerum perditarum ex intervallo ut pro invadendo res alterius, non posset sine auctoritate populi ».

From this it becomes quite clear that the scope and extent of the councillors' jurisdiction depends entirely on the will of the people, *a quo ipsi auctoritatem habent*. Hence also the responsibility of the councillors for their actions to the people and also the latter's constitutional right to rescind decrees of councillors which are *ultra vires* (52). For the government was entrusted by the people « secundum vices et secundum circulum aliquibus per tempus » (53). Differently expressed, the councillors representing the *mens populi*, are within their constitutional rights and their decrees are binding as long as they fulfil their functions as representatives of the people — the extent and the limits of these representative functions depend upon the *arbitrium* which in its turn stems from the people.

There is no gainsaying the practicability, fruitfulness and flexibility of this Bartolist idea: and it is precisely these features which ensured that the idea succeeded in practice and that its theoretical appeal never lost its force. But above all, by demonstrating the *populus liber* as the ultimate bearer of legislative competency and, rightly, equating it with the *princeps*, Bartolus at the same time established the people as the sovereign: for the absence of a *superior* has a deeper meaning than merely non-recognition of some overlord. This *superior* who is not recognized is, as it were, an outsider, constituting a separate and distinct estate which imposes its legislative will upon the people, entrusted to him. The *superioritas* of this *superior* is not derived from the people, and therefore he stands apart from it. But the *civitas sibi princeps*, by not recognizing a *superior*, has made itself its own *superior*. Positively expressed, the non-recognition of a *superior* is the people's assertion of its being its own *superior* — and etymologically too the (Latin) *superior* is nothing else but the (Italian) *sov(e)rano* and the (French) *souvrain* (54). What must be emphasized is that Bartolus operated entirely

---

(52) Ibid., no. 6.

(53) *De regimine civitatis*, no. 18, fol. 156vb: « Istud itaque regimen appellamus regimen ad populum seu regimen multitudinis, ut dictum est. Istud autem regimen dictum est, quando jurisdictio est apud populum seu multitudinem, non autem quod tota multitudo simul aucta regat, sed regimen aliquibus per tempus committit secundum vices et secundum circulum ».

(54) Cf. H. REHM, *Gesch. d. Staatsrechtswissenschaft* (Leipzig, 1896), p. 193 n. 2; also M. DAVID, *La souveraineté et les limites juridiques du pouvoir monarchique du ix au xv siècle* (Paris, 1954), pp. 16-7, also pp. 279-81.

with legal and juristic means: it was through the combination of his interpretation of Roman law with his taking account of the actual conditions in the Italian city-states that he came to envisage the *civitas sibi princeps* as a fully-fledged State (55), based upon the popular will. The hitherto insufficiently appreciated construction which permitted Bartolus to prove the legislative sovereignty of the people, was the *equiparatio* of the tacit and explicit consent of the people: once the efficacy of the former was recognized in the shape of customary law, there was indeed no obstacle to ascribe the same efficacy to the explicit consent of the people. And Bartolus took this small, but highly significant step and thereby arrived at the legal (as distinct from the political) conception of the State. This State therefore derives its structure and mechanism, its aim and policy, in other words, its whole substance and essence from its own sovereign, the people, which is, legally, tautological with the State itself.

This Bartolist doctrine of popular sovereignty involves a transference of the seat of authority from one source to another, with the vital consequence that whilst the *princeps* stood outside the *populus*, he is now inside the *populus* itself and is part and parcel of the people: the *populus* is its own *princeps*, its own *superior* (56): « Ipsamet civitas sibi princeps est » (57) or which is the same: « Populus liber nemini subditus ... est princeps » (58). But since the people itself is the sovereign, that is the *princeps*, all the maxims relating to the *princeps* can now be transferred to this sovereign (59), which means that the laws passed by the Council in the name of the people, demand the same obedience

---

(55) Cf. Ercole, op. cit., pp. 140-1.

(56) *Comm.* ad Dig. 48.1.7, no. 15: « Quaelibet civitas Italiae hodie, praecipue in Tuscia, dominum non recognoscit, in seipsa habet liberum populum et habet merum imperium in seipsa, et *tantam potestatem habet in populo quantam imperator in universo* ».

(57) *Comm.* ad Dig. 4.4.3, no. 2, fol. 133rb.

(58) *Comm.* ad Dig. 43.6.2, no. 1, fol. 147va, and *Comm.* ad C. XI.XXXI.3, no. 2, fol. 35vb: « Dico, quod in civitatibus, quae in temporalibus non recognoscunt superiorem, ut est civitas Perusina, et sic populus liber est, ut notatur in l. Hostes, ff. de cap., quod venditio rerum immobilium possit fieri auctoritate eius concilii, apud quod est omnis potestas. *Illud enim vicem imperatoris gerit in civitate illa* ». Cf. also *Comm.* ad Dig. 49.1.1 § Si quis, no. 10, fol. 207va.

(59) Cf. also ERCOLE, op. cit., pp. 117-8, referring to the *plenitudo imperialis potestatis* which is now applicable to the *civitas sibi princeps*: to this « infatti, si applicano ... direttamente i testi di quel diritto pubblico romano imperiale... ».

as those passed by the prince. More than that, the sanctions for non-obedience to the laws of the people are exactly the same as those for non-obedience to the prince's laws. Bartolus, in order to prove this equality refers to canon law and applies the *princeps* in an alleged statement of Gregory I to the people — « Qui non obedierit principi, morte moriatur » — as well as to the statement of St. Paul which he slightly modifies to suit the situation, and consequently concludes that disregard of the law of the superior, be he people or prince, is a mortal sin leading to damnation (60):

> Si quis facit contra praeceptum legis, peccat mortaliter, ut extra, de maj. et ob., c. II (Extra: I.XXXIII.2), qui non obedierit principi, morte moriatur. Et alibi Paulus ad Rom. XIII, 'Omnis anima subdita sit principi' (*sic*) et infra, Et qui voluntati eius resistit, Dei voluntati resistit et damnationem sibi acquirit. Cum ergo *superior populus* vel princeps *hoc praecipiat,* si quis facit contra legem, peccat mortaliter.

Perhaps nothing shows Bartolus' full grasp of the implications of his doctrine better than his substitution of the *princeps* for the Pauline *potestas sublimior* (61). By this modification Bartolus indicates beyond any reasonable doubt that he is perfectly aware of the Achilles heel of the theory of popular sovereignty (62).

I would not like to leave this topic without drawing particular attention to the fructification of the Bartolist doctrine with regard to the development of the notion of citizenship. Once the *populus liber* is recognized as a *universitas,* that is as a corporation to which the ordinary corporation laws are found applicable, it was only a small step to extend their operation and to apply them to the making of individuals, of the *extranei,* full citizens, that is, members of the corporation. Bartolus himself came very near to it (63), but the full consequences of his standpoint were drawn out by the following generation of jurists, notably by Baldus. The highly significant notion of *civilitas* — citizenship, *Staatsbürgerschaft, cittadinanza* — assumes its im-

---

(60) *Comm.* ad C. II.XXVIII: *Authentica*: *Sacramenta,* no. 15, fol. 85vb.

(61) *Rom.* XIII.1: « Omnis anima *potestatibus sublimioribus* subdita sit ».

(62) Which some five centuries later Austin will exploit to the full.

(63) Cf. supra at note 21.

portant meaning (64). Thus *civilitas* means that the citizen is « de eodem civili corpore et universitate active et passive » as Baldus had it (65), and it will not be long before the distinction will be made, on the basis of Bartolist thought, between the natural citizenship — *civilitas originalis* — and the acquired citizenship (66). In this development towards the notions of the citizen and the foreigner, the *Staatsbürger* and *Ausländer,* lies more than a whiff of modern times.

III

Any comparison of Bartolus' theory of popular sovereignty and of Marsilius' doctrine must duly emphasize the entirely different starting points of the two writers. Bartolus is nothing but a jurist: nowhere does he operate with anything but the law, either in the shape of the Roman or in that of the canon law; hence his terminology and phraseology are exclusively legal, and so is his theory (67); in the true legal tradition everyone of his statements and everyone of his objections must be buttressed by the law. Marsilius on the other hand is nothing but a political writer: it is Aristotle, whether correnctly understood by him

---

(64) Although the terms are the same, I do not think that this *civilitas* has much in common with DANTE'S *humana civilitas* in his *Monarchia*, I. 3; cf. also ibid. 2 (ed. C.A. Volpe, Modena, 1946), p. 32. DANTE'S was more a sociological notion, whilst the late fourteenth-century term belonged entirely to the juristic sphere.

(65) *Consilia* (Frankfurt, 1589), I.349, no. 4, fol. 84ra.

(66) See the *Consilium* of FRANCISCUS ALBERGOTUS, printed in the *Consilia* edition of BALDUS, V. 64, no. 2, fol. 15ra: « Considero quod civilitas quaedam est quae non potest induci nisi *per naturam*, ut *civilitas originalis* ... quaedam est civilitas quae potest induci *per constitutionem humanam* et ista vere inducitur per statutum ». Cf. also BALDUS himself, ibid., V. 29, fol. 7ra.

An equally important application of this is the acquisition of citizenship of the husband by the wife who was before her marriage an *extranea*. Cf. BARTOLUS, *Comm.* ad Dig. 50.21.4 and quite especially BALDUS, *Cons.* V. 100, no. 1, fol. 19va: the wife obtains the husband's citizenship, because « pars corpis viri effecta esset et est de Castellione durante matrimonio. Nam matrimonium est istius virtutis ac naturae, quod transfundit originem uxoris in originem viri ... sed est major unio quam unio conjugalis per quam vir et uxor efficiuntur una caro etiam et est una substantia in duabus personis ».

(67) In one place he even seems to pour scorn on ARISTOTLE by declaring that this sort of language does not appeal to legists: *De regimine civitatis*, no. 7.

or not (68), who supplies the intellectual equipment; Roman law is in a few places alluded to, but not quoted; nor is any Romanist cited; the terminology and phraseology are non-juristic, and hence also open to more than one interpretation. And yet, in their substance the two doctrines show an extraordinary kinship, in so far as both insist on the popular will as the basis of the validity and applicability of this popular legislation. One real difference between the two systems lies in that Marsilius envisages his on a universal scale: his is to be applicable to any community, and the result is therefore the purely « political » complexion of his thesis. Bartolus' system is applicable only to small communities in which a practical « democracy » he considers feasible. To him there is still — how could it be otherwise with a Post-Glossator? — the *de jure* lordship of the emperor: true when put to the test, very little of even this theoretical imperial power remains; this *de jure* position of the emperor is to Bartolus a juristic construction rather than a workable constitutional reality. Or differently expressed, the *leges* assume very much the same function as the *jus gentium* or the *jus naturale*: they are higher laws in so far as they provide a kind of norm the infringement of which deprives any other legal enactment of its validity and force (69). However, even of this remnant there is no trace in Marsilius, and if he does deal with the emperor's position, it is not on the traditional theocratic lines at all, but on his own premisses and within the framework he himself has provided.

Another difference but of a more fundamental nature, lies in the composition of the *populus* and therefore also in the kind of laws which it can create. To Marsilius the *legislator humanus* comprises all those who answer the description of a *civis;* hence it does not include children, slaves, foreigners and women (70), but does include the clergy. Marsilius' *legislator* is all-inclusive and comprehensive. Bartolus, on the other hand, although he too excludes by reason of their incapability of having a *habilis*

---

(68) Cf. on this MARIO GRIGNASCHI, « Le rôle de l'aristotelisme dans le Defensor Pacis de Marsile de Padoue » in *Revue d'histoire et de philosophie réligieuses*, XXXV (1955), pp. 301-40.

(69) Cf. in this context the analysis of WOOLF, op. cit., pp. 160-1.

(70) *Defensor Pacis*, I.XII.4. I have used the edition by R. SCHOLZ in *Fontes juris germanici antiqui* (Hannover, 1932).

consensus, minors under 25 years of age, mentally sick and women (71) and for obvious reasons foreigners, he nevertheless does not include in his *populus* the clergy. This exclusion of the *clerus* reflects the legalistic bonds of Bartolus which, so to speak, impeded the pursuit of his own theory to its logical conclusion — or perhaps it was again the vicinity of Rome that prevented him from including the clergy in the *populus*. Clerks and laymen form two separate « populi » (not estates) which is proved by each of them having separate tribunals (72); the former have therefore nothing in common with the *populus* (73). On the general principle of the operation of the *consensus*, the clergy are not bound by the customs of the lay people, and consequently also not by their statutes, unless clerical consent has been obtained (74). Hence according to Bartolus a cleric is not a *civis*. And the consequence is clear: legislation of the people has no effect upon the clerics, whilst for Marsilius the *universitas civium* which comprises the clerics and is therefore all-comprehensive, can legislate equally all-comprehensively.

In other fundamental topics there is, however, a very great agreement between the two doctrines. We may select the one or the other to bring their resemblances into clear relief. Both authors, as we have said, are emphatic on the operation of the people's will; both base themselves on the element of representation. But it seems that Marsilius's statement lacks precision and definition: he declares that the authority to establish laws belongs « ad solam universitatem aut eius valenciorem partem »; and he

---

(71) Cf. *Comm.* ad C. VIII.LII.2, no. 13, fol. 114rb, where he states that it is necessary « habilem consensum ad legem vel consuetudinem inducendam ».

(72) Ibid., no. 38, fol. 117ra: « Quia clerici et laici sunt diversi populi, quod patet, quia habent diversos judices, arg. ff. de off. ass., 1. Si eadem (Dig. 1.22.3) ». Here one might have expected a reference to the *Decretum* (XII.I.7: St Jerome) instead of relying on an argumentum. Perhaps it was the term « genera » in this passage which prevented BARTOLUS from citing the passage. If this assumption is correct, it would once again prove the subtle perspicacity of BARTOLUS: he was concerned with the *populus*, and this populist attitude of his militates against adducing the colourless and indifferent term *genera*.

(73) Ibid., referring to C. I.III.17 and VI.XXIII.23, neither of which is, strictly speaking, pertinent.

(74) Ibid.: « Non ligantur eorum (scil. plebeiorum) consuetudine et statutis, nisi consenserint ». All he concedes is that a clerk suing in a secular court is subjected to the procedural laws of this court, but nothing else: « servetur consuetudo et statutum populi, quod est ad litem ordinandam, alias non ».

goes on to state: « Hoc autem est civium universitas aut eius pars valencior *quae totam universitatem repraesentat* » (75). Superficially looked at, this statement seems to be almost identical with that of Bartolus, and in a way it is, in so far as a part of the people represents the whole. But whilst Bartolus as clearly as one might wish, shows how his representative organ comes about (the Council), namely through election, there still remains open a very wide scope for differing interpretations of the Marsilian *pars valencior*. Is it an organ of the *universitas civium* as with Bartolus; or is it « a definite portion of the *populus* which by consent of all may act for (*repraesentare*) it » (76); or is it « almost the whole body of citizens » (77); or is it « la majorité de l'assemblé générale des citoyens » ? (78). What is certain that the *pars valencior* of Marsilius does not come about through election (79). It may tentatively be suggested that Marsilius' *pars valencior* is identical with Bartolus' *Concilium majus* or *Parliamentum* or *Adunantia generalis*. In their structural elements the two bodies seem to be very much the same: the only difference I can see is that for Bartolus the *Parliamentum is* the people, whilst for Marsilius the *pars valencior represents* the people. With Bartolus the idea of representation begins to operate as the result of the election of the Council, whereas for Marsilius the *pars valencior*, solely by virtue of its being the *pars valencior*, « represents », that is, is taken for, the whole (80). Seen from a different angle, Bartolus' Council being representative of the people, is always answerable to the people, whereas the Marsilian *pars valencior* itself is autonomous and in nobody's control, just as the *Adunantia generalis* or the *Concilium majus* of Bartolus is under nobody's control. However, when we come to the Bartolist « administratores » and to their Marsilian counterparts, there is again

---

(75) *Def. Pacis*, I.IX.5, ed. cit., p. 65.

(76) C.H. McILWAIN, *Growth of Political Thought in the West* (London, 1932), p. 304.

(77) A. GEWIRTH, *Marsilius of Padua: The Defender of the Peace* (New York, 1951), I.189.

(78) G. DE LAGARDE, *La naissance de l'ésprit laique au moyen age: Marsile de Padoue*, 2nd ed. (Paris, 1949), II.196.

(79) Cf. also A. GEWIRTH, op. cit., I.188.

(80) *Def. Pacis*, I.XII.5 (ed. cit., p. 66): « Hoc autem fieri optime per civium universitatem tantummodo aut eius valenciorem partem, *quod pro eodem de cetero supponatur*, sic ostendo... ».

a very close resemblance between the two authors: both are insistent upon the function of these officials who merely act in the name of the people (81). Both therefore employ an almost identical terminology. Bartolus speaks of « aliquibus committi (possit) quod faciant statuta » and Marsilius on this very same point refers to « aliquibus commiserit (universitas civium) faciendum (scil.leges) » (82): the conclusion is obvious, namely that the identical view leads to an identity of expression, no matter how much the views differ in their premises.

The functions which Marsilius attributes to the *pars principans* are virtually the same as those ascribed to the *Concilium* by Bartolus, namely government by law. And for both the primary cause of the efficacy of the laws is the will of the people, although, again, the construction chosen by the two authors differs: for Bartolus it is the juristically valid and *expressus consensus*, for Marsilius it is the (Aristotelian inspired) philosophically conceived will of the *universitas* civium which imparts enforceability to the laws. The one chooses a juristic construction, the other a philosophic-political device, but the effect is the same, namely, the exclusion of an external legislator: in both authors legislation forms an essential facet of the *populus* itself which alone is *superior* and therefore does not recognize any *superior* outside itself. Bartolus presents the Marsilian political thesis in the guise of the law — Bartolus' legal sovereignty of the people is Marsilius' political sovereignty of the people. But as law and politics at all times in the Middle Ages were tautological expressions for one and the same thing, namely coercive government by means of the law, Marsilius' and Bartolus' systems are substantially the same. Marsilius' preoccupation with law and with the nature and roots of the *praeceptum coactivum* (83) no less than his description of the *lex* as an « oculus ex multis oculis » (84) reflects his realization of the « political » character of the law as the crux of government; this is for Bartolus the self-evident *point d'appui*, and his analysis way well be considered complementary to the Paduan's

---

(81) Ibid., I.XIII.8, p. 77: « Eligi debent viri ... *vicem et auctoritatem* universitatis civium *repraesentantes* ». For BARTOLUS see supra at note 48.

(82) Ibid., I.XII.3, p. 64.

(83) *Def. Pacis*, I.X.4, pp. 49-50; II.XII.3-5, pp. 264-7; etc.

(84) Ibid., I.XI.3, p. 57.

influential theme. What needs pointing out is that despite the divergent starting points both authors fetch the law down from heaven and let it grow up from the native soil of the people, the one arriving at this conclusion through a superb mastery of the law in conjunction with the recognition of incontrovertible facts, the other through the employment of naturalistic Aristotelian themes. The one is a legalistic analysis, the other a philosophic one. By a circuitous route both authors, probably without realizing it, return to the primaeval conception of law and government (85).

There seems hardly any need to indicate the effects of this ascending conception of law as propounded by Bartolus. When once the ascending character of law — emanating as it did from the *populus* — was understood in all its implications, the result could be none other than the end of all the traditional forms of theocratic government, be it papal or royalist. Then indeed nothing could remain, even in theory, of the *de jure* lordship of the emperor — for the Ruler as standing outside the community enthroned in the clouds and supremely issuing forth his commands, there was no more room: his rulership *divina favente gratia* or *Dei gratia* evaporates, is divested of its commanding halo and provides no longer a title deed to rule (86). That title deed can be had, in order to be effective, no longer from divinity, but from the people itself represented in the appropriate organ (87). But thereby the whole function and position of the Ruler has radically changed from a separate estate outside and above the people into an essential part within and of the people. The Ruler

---

(85) See supra section I.

(86) It is perhaps worth pointing out that at this very same time and also as an effluence of Aristotelian themes the nature of the Church as a merely mystical body came more and more to the foreground of discussion, with the consequence that being a purely mystical-sacramental body its claim to coercive jurisdiction was denied: only « human » organisations can make this claim and are in need of this kind of jurisdiction. On this basis too the later conciliarism was the answer, as it conceived the Church in its visible shape alone as being endowed with full jurisdictional power which, for purposes of administration and government, it hands over to the pope as its representative. Cf. further text.

(87) The English formula (coined considerably later) of the « King in Parliament » which is the supreme constitutional authority, expresses the combination of the ascending and descending conceptions of law and government. It is at the junction of the « King in Parliament » that popular sovereignty and theocratic rulership meet.

— like the law itself — is fetched down from the heavens to the humdrum workaday world: he becomes one of the people. The full realization of the Bartolist doctrine and its consistent application on a universal scale heralds the dawn of the modern era.

But this is a merely indirect political effect of this exclusively legal doctrine. What is of more direct concern is its infiltration into and permeation of the traditional canonistic doctrine of government. The papal-canonistic theory of government in its classical form corresponds entirely to the secular theory of the Ruler as a separate estate, but with perhaps more justification than the royalist theory, the papal conception of governing the Church operated with the thesis of an avowedly divine institution of government, the papacy itself, and with the consequential descending conception of law and government. And quite in consonance with this fundamental theme of papal government the point of view is understandable that within the Church — itself a divine institution — the only law that mattered was that of its monarch. Nevertheless, the events in the second half of the fourteenth century furnished a fertile soil upon which Bartolus' ascending theory of the law could bear fruit. For what else is the conciliarist theme but an application of the populist theory of government on a universal scale? Is it a mere coincidence that the most eminent canonists came out in favour of conciliarism? Is it a mere chance that the General Council was considered as a *concilium quod repraesentat congregationem fidelium* and that out of the pope, the Master, became the pope, the servant, of the *congregatio fidelium?* The pope ceased to be a separate estate and became incorporated in the corpus of Christians. Does not the whole conciliarist scheme show an extraordinary kinship with Bartolus' structure of his *civitas?* Just as it is the *populus* of the *civitas* that is the bearer of legal sovereignty, so it is here with the Church that the *populus christianus* is the bearer of this legal sovereignty, with the consequence that the pope derives his power from below and is answerable to, and controllable by, the Christian people. And just as the Bartolist *concilium repraesentat totum populum,* so also, as the assembled wisdom of Europe at Constance decreed — *concilium generale repraesentat totam catholicam ecclesiam.* This representative nature of the General Council is a faithful replica of the Bartolist doctrine. The preponderantly legal character of conciliarism is now satisfactorily explicable: next to its purely canonistic roots (88) there is the acknowledged and unacknowledged influence of Bartolus himself: it is the victory of the idea of representative government, the victory of the idea of the human State. To draw attention to these unnoticed features and influences is a duty incumbent upon those who are assembled to pay homage to the man and jurist Bartolus.

---

(88) About which see W. ULLMANN, *The Origins of the Great Schism* (London, 1948), pp. 193 ff.; B. TIERNEY, *Foundations of Conciliar Theory* (Cambridge, 1955).

XI

THE UNIVERSITY OF CAMBRIDGE AND THE GREAT SCHISM

AMONGST the hitherto unnoticed documents preserved in the Archives of the University of Cambridge are two which warrant some attention here. Until very recently, these Archives had a rather insecure existence which partly accounts for the disappearance of many of the medieval records and partly for the bad preservation of surviving documents. Moreover, as is well known, during the riots between the town and the University in 1381[1] the bulk of the documents perished in a huge bonfire. Chance, however, has preserved a number of original documents which have not apparently been the object of an earlier investigation, and it may well be that further systematic searches will necessitate a revision of the unfortunately rather generally accepted low estimate of the standing of the University in the Middle Ages.[2] The documents with which this paper deals, would prove that Cambridge, certainly in the later Middle Ages, enjoyed a reputation in no wise below that of other *studia*.

I

The first document that invites our attention is the considered opinion of the University on the proposal of a withdrawal of English obedience from Boniface IX, in 1398.[3] The circumstances leading to the consultation of the University by the king, Richard II, were, briefly, these.

Of the three possibilities of ending the Great Schism—the *via cessionis* (resignation of both popes), the *subtractio obedientiae* (withdrawal of obedience), and the convocation of a General Council—the University of Paris and the French court in 1395 strongly favoured the first. Whilst France upheld the cause of the Avignonese pope, England unwaveringly supported the claims of the Roman pope.[4] In the autumn

---

[1] See H. Rashdall, *The Universities of Europe in the Middle Ages*, ed. F. M. Powicke and A. B. Emden (Oxford, 1936), iii. 285.

[2] Cp., e.g., Brian Twyne, *Antiquitatis Academiae Oxoniensis Apologia* (Oxford, 1608), 269–70; H. Denifle, *Die Entstehung der Universitäten des Mittelalters* (Berlin, 1885), 367 ff.; Rashdall, op. cit. iii. 284, 292, &c. ('third-rate University'; 'medieval insignificance', &c.), although the editor of the third volume has considerably mitigated the harsh judgement of Dean Rashdall, cp. iii. 284 n. 2.

[3] For Boniface IX, the Roman pope, cp. E. Vansteenberghe in *Dict. d'histoire et de géographie ecclésiastiques*, ix. 909–22.

[4] Cp. E. Perroy, *L'Angleterre et le Grand Schisme* (Paris, 1933), 51 ff.; W. Ullmann, *The Origins of the Great Schism* (London, 1948), 102 ff.; E. F. Jacob in his edition of *The Register of Henry Chichele* (Oxford, 1943), i. xxvi.

54

of 1395 Charles VI dispatched an embassy to Richard II, and the University of Paris sent a letter to Oxford in which the arguments in favour of a *cessio* were set forth.[1] Although it is strange that the Parisian Masters' long document[2] should have been sent to Oxford only, no evidence has so far come to light which would justify the assumption that the University of Cambridge was also approached, but negative evidence of this kind should, of course, never be accepted as foolproof.[3] The reply of Oxford (17 March 1396) was an unequivocal, well-argued, and calm rejection of the Parisian arguments: the Oxonians wholly denied the Parisian suggestion that *cessio* was a safer method of ending the Schism; they adduced scriptural, patristic, and canonistic arguments to prove that only a General Council convoked by Boniface IX, the Roman pope, could end the Schism.[4] On this basis no *rapprochement* between the two popes nor between France and England could result.

By 1398 Paris came out in favour of a *subtractio obedientiae*. King Charles VI convoked a synod for 22 May 1398; the French episcopate and the representatives of the University took part in it and thoroughly examined the question of how best to achieve the resignation of the adamant Benedict XIII (Peter de Luna);[5] that is, whether a partial or a total withdrawal of obedience should be advocated and a corresponding proposal submitted to the king. The synod decided in favour of a total withdrawal as the most appropriate way of forcing Benedict's abdication.[6] The University of Paris in its own memorandum of 11 June 1398 strongly supported the *via subtractionis* and advised Charles VI accord-

[1] For details see N. Valois, *La France et le Grand Schisme d'Occident* (Paris, 1901), iii. 75 ff.; E. F. Jacob, 'Some English Documents of the Conciliar Movement', in *Bulletin of the John Rylands Library*, xv (1931), 362 ff., re-edited in *Essays in the Conciliar Epoch*, 2nd ed. (Manchester, 1953), 57 ff.; E. Perroy, op. cit. 365 ff.

[2] Analysed by E. F. Jacob, art. cit. 361–3 (= op. cit. 60 f.).

[3] This so-called 'General Epistle' of the University of Paris, not yet edited, is known in only one copy to which E. F. Jacob was the first to draw attention (B.M. Royal 6 E. iii, fols. 77–80). It is addressed: 'Universis Christi fidelibus tempore scismatis universitas studii Parisiensis perlacitissima [*sic*] pacis, salutem et in edificium sacrosancte militantis Ierusalem caritatis vinculo conveniri.' The *Incipit* and *Explicit* are transcribed by E. Perroy, op. cit. 367 note O. This MS. is of Oxonian origin.

[4] The reply is printed *in toto* by C. Bulaeus, *Historia Universitatis Parisiensis* (Paris, 1688), iv. 776–85; analysed by E. F. Jacob, art. cit. 364 ff. (= op. cit. 61 ff.) and by E. Perroy, op. cit. 368 ff. MSS. of the reply are signalled by N. Valois, op. cit. iii. 77 n. 2.

[5] About him cp. L. Jadin in *Dict. d'hist. et de géogr. ecclés.* viii. 135–63 (with copious literature).

[6] The proceedings and speeches are reported in Bulaeus, op. cit. iv. 829–44 under the heading: 'Acta concilii tertii Gallicani pro unione ecclesiae.' Cp. also Valois, op. cit. iii. 148–63.

ingly, namely that it was in the interest of union 'a Benedicti ipsius obedientia ex nunc cessare totaliter atque recedere'.[1] On 27 July 1398 Charles VI gave the royal order for the total withdrawal of obedience.[2]

As he had been three years earlier, Richard II was again approached by the French court and in particular by his father-in-law, Charles VI, and by the University of Paris, with a view to persuading him to adopt the same course, that is, to withdraw English obedience from the Roman pope, Boniface IX. Although the French embassy arrived in September 1398,[3] Richard II took no steps until 20 November 1398 when he issued writs to the Universities of Oxford and Cambridge, ordering the two Universities to give him their opinion on the French proposal. If Thomas Rymer had not, one might almost be tempted to say, by accident, mentioned that an *a-pari* copy of this writ to Oxford was also dispatched to Cambridge, it is not unlikely that not even this fact would have been known.[4] Oxford's reply has been common knowledge for a long time, having been published by Raynaldus in his *Annales Ecclesiastici*.[5] Of the Cambridge reply nothing has been known.

It is fortunate that the original writ of Richard II has been preserved in the Archives of the University.[6] It is addressed to the Chancellor, commissary, and proctors of the University as well as 'universis et singulis magistris et doctoribus, regentibus et non regentibus ac aliis graduatis studii universitatis predicte'. The writ is dated, like the Oxford counterpart, on 20 November 1398: 'Teste meipso apud Westmonasterium xx die Novembris, anno Ricardi secundi vicesimo secundo', and bears in its right-hand corner the name of Stanley, the keeper of the rolls.[7] Richard, after lamenting the Schism within the Church, orders the University, under pain of forfeiture of its liberties and privileges, to forward to him the considered opinion of the Masters on the proposal of the *subtractio obedientiae* from Boniface IX; he encloses the letters

---

[1] Bulaeus, iv. 845–7, at 846.

[2] Bulaeus, iv. 853–63; cp. also Valois, iii. 183 n. 2 for the correct date and for the originals of the royal decree. For details cp. also J. Hefele–H. Leclercq, *Histoire des Conciles* (Paris, 1915), vi–2, 1210–42.

[3] About this embassy see N. Valois, iii. 289 ff., and E. Perroy, 384 f. For the instructions given to the two legates Nicholas Paynel and Jean Courtecuisse, see Appendix XV in Perroy, 416–18.

[4] T. Rymer, *Foedera*, Hague ed., 1740, iii–4, 153; *Calendar Close Rolls*, vi. 354.

[5] Raynaldus, *Ann. Eccles.*, ed. A. Theiner (Bar-le-Duc, 1874), xxvii. 34–36.

[6] This writ is not preserved in the Archives of the University of Oxford, as the Archivist, Mr. Pantin, has kindly informed me.

[7] There are some slight, but inessential, variants between the writ directed to Oxford (printed in Rymer, loc. cit.) and that directed to Cambridge, so that a full transcription does not seem called for. C. H. Cooper, *Annals of Cambridge* (Cambridge, 1842), i. 144, refers to this writ, but was clearly unaware of its existence in the Archives, since he based himself on Rymer and the Close Rolls.

56

sent to him by the French king and the University of Paris.[1] The answer was required 'citra festum Carniprivii proximi futurum sub communi sigillo studii universitatis', that is, by Ash Wednesday of the following year, 12 February 1399.

There is a second writ in the Archives which does not seem enrolled or calendared or otherwise known or referred to. It is dated 6 January 1399 and was obviously a reminder to the University, being couched in entirely identical terms with the exception of one word: in the place of the original 'quas (*scil.* litteras) vobis mittimus' the second writ has: 'quas vobis misimus'. The assumption is not unjustified that this second writ of 6 January was related to the order of Richard II, issued on 2 January, which convoked the regular and secular clergy to Oxford for Monday after the feast of the conversion of St. Paul, that is, 27 January 1399.[2] It seems that Richard wished to have the opinion of Cambridge at the earliest date, and possibly in time for the meeting on 27 January.

If this is so, the Cambridge Masters did not disappoint the king, for they replied on Friday, 24 January 1399, in a Congregation of regent and non-regent Masters[3] specially summoned for this purpose. It is not without some interest to note that the Oxford reply came nearly a fortnight later, on Wednesday, 5 February. Moreover, there would appear some indications that the Oxonians were acquainted with the arguments of Cambridge of which an echo might be detected in the Oxford document.

The text of the Cambridge reply[4] is written on rather thin paper, and was mounted on a strip of modern paper probably in the nineteenth century.[5] The document measures $20 \times 9\frac{1}{2}$ inches and is very carefully written by an extremely neat and regular small book hand of the late

[1] 'Vobis, sub fide et ligeantia, quibus nobis tenemini, districtius quo possumus, injungimus et mandamus, quod, attenta arduitate ac summa utilitate felicis successus et expeditionis negotii antedicti visisque insuper et diligenter circumspectis tenoribus duarum literarum harum [*harum* om. in Rymer], unius videlicet carissimi patris nostri Francie et alterius studii Parisius, materiam predictam concernentium, nobis etiam exhibitarum et ostensarum, quas vobis mittimus sub pede sigilli nostri, vos, super materia predicta diligenter deliberetis. . . .'

[2] This writ of 2 January 1399 is calendared in *Cal. Close Rolls* vi. 367–8; a copy of this writ is in B.M. Cotton Cleopatra E. ii, fol. 224, see N. Valois, iii. 293 n. 1, and E. Perroy, 386 n. 2.

[3] In medieval times the term 'non-regent' does not entirely correspond to its modern connotation: the Master who has become a Doctor in a higher Faculty was also a non-regent. But the term also included, as in modern times, the Master who had retired.

[4] The reply (as well as the writs of Richard II) are listed by H. R. Luard, 'List of the Documents in the University of Cambridge from 1266 to 1544', in *Communications of the Cambridge Antiquarian Society*, iii (1876), no. 82; the writs are numbered 80 and 81.   [5] Cp. Luard, loc. cit. 386.

fourteenth century. It may well be presumed that the document now in the Archives was actually the one read out in Congregation. In only one place a correction of the text has apparently been attempted, although it cannot be said that this attempt improved the style.

The document can easily be divided into three distinctive parts. The first, the introductory part, consists of the Arenga which is characterized by the usual somewhat bombastic and pompous style. In it the Cambridge Masters—'ad terram prostrati' before the king, Richard—adopted a solemn, not to say, unctuous tone, most formally protesting their allegiance and obedience to the 'metuendissimus rex', Richard. They managed to weave biblical passages and allusions into the texture of their affirmations quite skilfully, and to introduce some interesting observations on the office of the king. The second part, the argumentative section of the document, deals with the substantive arguments set forth by the Parisians and Charles VI in favour of a withdrawal of obedience, whilst in the third, the constructive part, they make counter-proposals. Both these sections are well reasoned and, in contrast to the irate Oxford reply, calm and concise in tone, matter-of-fact, and devoid of all flourish. The reply clearly indicates that a good deal of thought had gone into its making and that the Masters were fully conscious of the 'arduitas negotii' and of the weight and responsibility attached to their counsel. Above all, and again in contrast to other University replies, Cambridge considered it undignified to display argumentative fireworks for the mere sake of display, and its constructive proposals, considering the nature of the conflict in general and the personality of Benedict XIII in particular, must be reckoned as feasible and sound. A short analysis of the main contents may be advisable.

As in modern days, the *brevitas temporis* seems to have also weighed upon the Cambridge Masters in the late fourteenth century, for they offer their apologies to the king on this score as also on that of the *paucitas consulentium*; whether this latter term was to be taken in the quantitative or qualitative sense, may be left undecided. After summarizing the French proposals, the University declared that they set out from misconceived premises. For Boniface IX and Benedict XIII cannot be put on the same level: the former was at all times a free agent, never having made any promises regarding the termination of the Schism. The anti-pope, Benedict, however, had promised on oath, on the occasion of his election, that he would take any conceivable steps, including the *via cessionis*, to bring the Schism to an end,[1] but he not

---

[1] For this promise see the *Cedula conclavis*, printed by Bulaeus, iv. 730–1, with the signatures of the cardinals, including Peter de Luna; cp. also ibid. 750–1, and, furthermore, S. Baluzius, *Vitae Paparum Avenionensium* (Paris 1693), i. 567

58

only resisted all demands by his own cardinals to take any effective measures, but even forbade them to initiate any action on their part. Hence, however excellent the reasons of Charles VI were for withdrawing French obedience from Benedict, they were quite inapplicable to 'our' pope, who never bound himself in any way and who on no account can be said to have provoked the Schism:[1] on the contrary, the continuation of this lamentable Schism is due entirely to the *ambitio dominandi* by which Benedict is obsessed—and the truth of this assertion was amply confirmed by subsequent events. Boniface, on the other hand, merely pursued his own right: 'quia juris ordine papatum admisit nec scisma facit, qui suo jure utitur, nec fructus consumit, quos ob juris sui defensionem legaliter exponit.'

In his statements Charles VI had referred to the affairs of Pope Anastasius II and of Guido, Archbishop of Vienne.[2] Both these cases were to show that there were historical precedents for lawful withdrawals from a legitimate pope. Anastasius II, it may be recalled, served as the medieval paradigm of the erring pope—and for this reason a very resourceful argument in the literature before and during the Schism[3]— but it was not an argument that greatly impressed the Cambridge Masters: he was *heresi respersus* and, consequently, they implied that

and ii. 1107 (= ed. G. Mollat, Paris, 1914, i. 540–1). See also N. Valois, iii. 15 n. 1, and M. Souchon, *Die Papstwahlen in der Zeit des Grossen Schismas* (Braunschweig, 1898), i. 212–30, edition of these so-called *Wahlkapitulationen*, ibid. i. 298–300; see also Hefele–Leclercq, vi–2, 1155 ff.

[1] This was clearly intended as a hint at the part played by Peter de Luna after the election of Urban VI in 1378. For a judicious account of Peter de Luna's conduct in the summer months of 1378 see M. Seidlmayer, 'Peter de Luna und die Entstehung des Grossen abendländischen Schismas', in *Gesammelte Aufsätze zur Kulturgeschichte Spaniens*, ed. H. Finke (Münster, 1933), iv. 206–31, edition of new documents, ibid. 232–47. See also the reference to Peter de Luna's statement in the testimony of Cardinal Adam Easton, ed. by L. Macfarlane, 'An English Account of the Election of Urban VI', in *Bulletin of the Institute of Historical Research*, xxvi (1953), p. 84, lines 117 ff.

[2] See Charles VI's decree, in Bulaeus, iv. 861: 'Si multi clerici a communione Anastasii pro longe minori causa, etiam sine sententia et declaratione se canonice abegerunt, si etiam Guido archiepiscopus Viennensis postmodum factus Calixtus secundus una cum prelatis tunc in concilio Viennensi assistentibus a Paschalis II obedientia recedere tunc decrevit, multo maiori pro vitanda videlicet notorietate scandali fautoria scismatis, subversionis ecclesiae et animarum periculo, ambitioneque et cupidine contendentium eorundem jubemur a Domino per Moysem ab huiusmodi pravissimorum hominum consortio separari.'

[3] For the case itself see *Liber Pontificalis*, ed. L. Duchesne (Paris, 1886), i. 258, editorial note 3, ibid., and the Introduction, pp. xlii–xliii. The relevant passage was incorporated by Gratian in his *Decretum, Dist.* xix, c. 9, which became the *locus classicus*. For a cautious estimate of the affair see E. Caspar, *Geschichte des Papsttums* (Tübingen, 1933), ii. 85–87, 758, and for the canonistic utilization of the passage cp. Brian Tierney, *Foundations of Conciliar Theory* (Cambridge, 1955), 38, 42, 50, 70–71.

withdrawal from him was in order. The second example adduced by the French was very weak indeed and was an historical tergiversation, since their statement that Guido of Vienne had withdrawn from Paschal II was not true. In actual fact, Guido was the leader of the French opposition to Paschal II who was asked by the synod of Vienne (1112) to rescind the 'compact' he had made with Henry V in the matter of investitures: the decrees of this synod were submitted to the pope with the request for confirmation and the synodists declared that if the pope were to refuse confirmation, they would withdraw from him.[1] The Cambridge Masters, who, for understandable reasons, were ignorant of the actual facts, and had therefore to rely on the French presentation of the case, had no other means of meeting the argument than by stigmatizing Guido's conduct as 'male' and by declaring that 'facti penitens ad obedientiam predictam (scil. Paschalis) rediit et postea Calixtus secundus effectus est'. Just as the French assertion of Guido's withdrawal was untenable, so was the Cambridge statement that he had returned to obedience: Guido never receded, since Paschal II confirmed the decrees of the synod.[2] Nevertheless, the Cambridge argument was quite apposite to the issue: the French argument was actually made to recoil upon the French themselves who should now take the example of Guido of Vienne to heart.

Consequently, the University correctly perceived that the whole issue of the Schism was legal and in matters of law the question is,

---

[1] Under the chairmanship of Guido, the synod resolved that (1) lay investiture was heresy; (2) the document signed by Paschal in 1111 was extorted from the pope and therefore null and void; (3) Henry V was to be excommunicated. The synodists, in their letter to Paschal, say this (after reciting the decrees): 'Illud etiam cum debita reverentia vestrae suggerimus pietati, quod si nobiscum in his steteritis, si hoc, sicut rogamus, confirmaveritis, si deinceps ab ipsius crudelissimi tyranni et nuntiorum eius, litteris, locutione, muneribus abstinueritis, unanimiter nos, sicut decet, habebitis filios et fideles. Si vero, quod minime credimus, aliam viam aggredi coeperitis et nostrae paternitatis assertiones predictas roborare nolueritis, propitius sit nobis Deus, quia nos a vestra subjectione et obedientia repelletis. Valete', Mansi, *Conciliorum Collectio* (Venice, 1776), xxi. 75–76. Only Ekkehard of Aura, from a German standpoint, had to say this: 'Ex hac occasione Viennensis archiepiscopus cum suis complicibus novum scisma nostras in partes seminare et gladium anathematis in imperatorem molitur extendere', *Chronicon*, in *M.G.H. SS.* vi. 246. For Guido (Calixtus II) see, furthermore, *Liber Pontificalis*, ed. cit. ii. 322, and *Liber Pontificalis prout extat in Codice manuscripto Dertusensi*, ed. J. M. March (Barcelona, 1925), 192; Baronius, *Ann. eccles.*, ed. cit. xviii. 228; M. Maurer, *Pabst Calixt II* (Münster, 1886), 54 ff.; U. Robert, *Histoire du pape Calixte II* (Paris, 1891), 30–34 (the best account); G. Meyer von Knonau, *Jahrbücher des Deutschen Reichs unter Heinrich V* (Leipzig, 1907), vi. 240–4; and A. Fliche, *La Réforme Grégorienne et la reconquête chrétienne* (Paris, 1946), 367, 378.

[2] For Paschal's answer see Mansi, xxi. 76.

60

not what is, but what should be.[1] Basing itself on this axiom the University proffered—perhaps gratuitously—the advice that Benedict should return to Boniface IX and that Charles VI and France should do likewise. That 'Urbanus sextus fuit verus papa' was, after all, known from the public statements of the cardinals themselves after the election of Urban, and one could not easily presume that such eminent men would have suggested *toti christianismo* a false vicar of Christ and deceived the whole world. When the cardinals later asserted the opposite and proceeded to another election, thereby causing the Schism, they could no longer claim to deserve credibility. In a somewhat lofty manner the Masters expressed an encouraging approbation for Charles's step of withdrawal: he was on the right way and should take another step and recognize Boniface IX.

The considered opinion of the University was that Richard should on no account recede from Boniface. For how could a faithful son of the Roman Church lawfully withdraw from the pope? A withdrawal of obedience, moreover, would indicate vacillation: 'si fieret obedientie subtractio, quod absit, inconstantia universaliter per totum mundum vobis et regnicolis cito imponeretur, et pagani, azephali, scismatici non immerito nuncuparemur.' A step like this would also be an encouragement to rebellion everywhere, would entail insecurity, undermine stability, and lead to the destruction of the State: 'Nam politia omnis destrueretur et cito universum vacillaret.' The *medium subtractionis*, as suggested by Paris, 'credimus injustissimum, pessimum Deo et toti ecclesie catholice dampnatissimum, cum non sit medium inducens, sed potius excludens per quod ecclesia poterit reformari'. Only worse things could follow from a withdrawal of obedience.

In the third and last part in which the University puts forward constructive proposals, two concrete suggestions are made. The first seems somewhat unrealistic and was not apparently taken seriously by the authors themselves, for they propose that after the resignation of Benedict XIII—a step to which he had pledged himself—Boniface would be at liberty to resign himself 'absque coactione, minis et precum importunitate', provided that adequate arrangements could be made about the creation of a future pope. The Masters realized that, quite apart from the intrinsic difficulties inherent in this plan, a proposal of this kind would not be well received by the other side, and they therefore propounded an alternative solution: if the resignation of both claimants should not prove feasible, Boniface, always ready for a peaceful solution,[2]

---

[1] 'Inspicitur enim a jure, non quod fit, sed quod fieri debet.'

[2] Cp. Boniface IX's letter in L. d'Achéry, *Spicilegium* (Paris, 1664), vi. 49–53, and also ibid. 57–60.

should summon a General Council which should have as its agenda, firstly, the termination of the Western Schism; secondly, the termination of the Schism between East and West; and thirdly, reformatory measures within the Church. To the General Council there should be specially invited all adherents of Boniface as well as Benedict himself and his accomplices, and in general everyone who asserted that he had a *jus et interesse* in the papacy of Boniface IX. In order to expedite the actual summoning the princes should prevail upon Boniface *honesta prece*. Benedict's party should be given a full hearing in the General Council, so that justice be done.

The mere acceptance of Boniface's invitation by Benedict's party might well imply their acknowledging him as pope and in this case an effective step towards the actual ending of the Schism would already have been taken. But, considering the obstinacy of Benedict, the possibility had to be faced that he (and his followers) would disregard the invitation, in which case the University proposed that *in penam contumacie ipsorum* the mere fact of Urban's election (in 1378) should be put to the discussion, examined, and a decision reached as to whether it be accepted as valid, or cancelled or annulled; in the latter case the Council should declare itself as to the necessity of a resignation of one or both claimants.

This advice, again, was quite adroit, for through their failure to appear at the General Council convoked by Boniface, the anti-papal party would have lost the opportunity of publicly impugning the validity of Urban's election, the exordium of the whole conflict. On the other hand, if Benedict's party were to follow the summons, they would implicitly recognize Boniface as true pope, in which case there was no need to discuss the legality of Urban's election and position. In a skilful manner the University provided an inescapable dilemma for the antipapal party. Amongst the numerous proposals put forward by other universities, by corporations, by learned men, and so forth, the Cambridge proposal stands out as having the merit of saneness and directness.

It may not be unprofitable to look at the reply which the University of Oxford sent to Richard II, almost a fortnight after Cambridge had advised the king. Indications are not wanting that the Cambridge reply was not unknown to the Oxford Masters.[1] Although shorter than the

---

[1] The reply is preserved in the Vatican collection of documents relating to the Schism (Vatican Archives: *Armarium LIV: Libri de scismate*, tom. xxvi, fol. 268) and printed in Raynaldus, *Ann. eccles.*, ed. cit. xxvii. 34–36, dated 5 February 1399. The Bodleian MS. Digby 188, fol. 47ʳ et seqq. purports to contain 'Epistola universitatis Oxoniensis ad Ricardum II regem Anglie: responsoria ad epistolam Parisiensis studii' (see W. D. Macray, *Catalogue of Digby Manuscripts* (Oxford, 1883), pp. 200–1), which is certainly not a copy of an actual reply: it is undated and appears to be the copy of an early draft of a reply to be sent to Richard, who is

62

Cambridge answer, Oxford's answer would appear to have followed the Cambridge document in general layout and structure. It is, however, on the whole characterized by an ill-tempered and irascible tone[1] and, in contrast to the earlier reply (1396), does not excel in analytical or constructive argumentation.

Cambridge, as we have seen, had dealt with the substance of the cases of Anastasius and Guido of Vienne, and stated in conclusion that in matters of law the question is, not what is, but what should be. Oxford, in its turn, repeated the substance of the Cambridge conclusion, also adjoining it to the two cases which were bracketed together (although they had nothing in common) and which were dealt with rather superficially.[2] Cambridge had emphasized that as a loyal son of the Roman Church Richard could not withdraw from the legitimate (Roman) pope.

addressed sometimes in the second person singular, sometimes plural; it lacks all finish and the argumentation is still rather incoherent; the biblical quotations (fol. 48^r–48^v) would appear to be more appropriate to a tract on the relations between *regnum* and *sacerdotium* and quite irrelevant to this issue ('Ozias rex a Domino lepra percussus est [cp. Thomas Becket's identical formulation in *Materials for the History of Thomas Becket*, Rolls Series (London, 1881), v. 273] qui sacerdotii officium usurpare non timuit . . .' (cp. 2 Paral. xxvi. 21); 'Salvator de sacerdotibus suis dicit "Qui vos spernit . . ."' (Lk. x. 16, and see again Becket, p. 273); 'et alibi per prophetam "Nolite tangere christos meos . . ."' (Ps. civ. (cv) 15)); even Gelasius's well-known statement is adduced ('religiosi principis est Dei sacerdotes honorare atque tueri, ad quos, que ecclesie disponenda sunt, pertinere voluit Deus, non ad seculi potestates, que cum filii ecclesie sint et non presules, suas excusationes [*sic*; *recte*: exsecutiones] ecclesiasticis presulibus subdere debent . . .' (cp. again Becket, p. 274)); whoever the author may have been, he calls this 'letter' an 'opusculum' (fol. 54^r: 'multa, que ob prolixitatem huic opusculo non inserimus') and 'presens epistolarum compendium' (fol. 61^r); there are many scribal errors, and so forth. On this piece cp. A. Wood, *History and Antiquities of the University of Oxford* (Oxford, 1792), i. 533–4 (sub anno 1398); E. F. Jacob, art. cit. 366 (= op. cit. 64); E. Perroy, op. cit. 386 n. 3.

[1] Cp. also its characterization by E. F. Jacob: '(it) betrays more than a touch of irritation' (loc. cit.).

[2] Raynaldus, loc. cit., 35A: 'Quod vero ad chronicas de Anastasio et Guidone, quas pro fundationis corroboratione sumpserunt; cum forsan auctoritate universalis ecclesiae vel alia justa causa, utpote haeresis damnata, sicut est de facto, in casu proposito, quem non exprimit chronica, haec facta fuerunt, vel si facta fuissent aliter, non ad exemplum trahenda, cum non quae fuit [*sic*], sed quae fieri debent admittimus, pro solutione talium motivorum non multum duximus insistendum.' It should be noted that the phrase 'non ad exemplum trahenda' is legal: cp. *Cod. Just.* VII. xlv. 13; W. Engelmann, *Die Wiedergeburt der Rechtskultur in Italien* (Leipzig, 1938), 74–75; W. Ullmann, *The Medieval Idea of Law* (London, 1946), 117 ff. In the draft of a reply the case of Anastasius is dealt with in this manner (fol. 57^r): 'Arguunt, quod multi clerici a communione pape Anastasii recedere decreverunt etc. Sed revera non hoc ut assumitur ex minori (fol. 57^v) causa fecerunt, sed quia iste Anastasius nedum hereticus, sed herichiarcha [*sic*] fuerat eo quod fautor et defensor extitit ipsius Achatii propter heresim ab ecclesia condempnati.' I have found no reference to the case of Guido of Vienne.

Oxford held that a withdrawal from any constituted authority was wrong and that even from wicked kings and pr:·sts no obedience should be withdrawn; consequently, Oxford denied that the French had a right to withdraw from Benedict. Let us juxtapose the two passages.

Cambridge	Oxford
Quo enim jure seu *qua fronte* posset ecclesie Romane filius dominum nostrum Bonefacium pro *papa indubitanter* habitum nominatum et publice pro tali per vos et regnum vestrum admissum et reputatum absque heresi spernere seu *obedientiam* eidem *subtrahere*, nullo videmus jure.	*Qua* ergo *fronte* a *pape indubitati obedientia*, qualem utraque pars suum asserit, erit *recedendum*?

Whilst, furthermore, Cambridge had justified its statement by quoting some well-known biblical passages, Oxford, in its justification of its own thesis, clearly had in mind the same passages, though they were referred to in general terms only.[1]

The appeal of Cambridge to Richard to hold fast to Boniface, because of the evil effects of a withdrawal on the State, might possibly be seen to have found an echo in Oxford's statement 'cum turbato sacerdotio turbatur et patitur respublica, nec solidum censetur imperium, cuius subditorum fides aut religio discrepat'. Oxford, like Cambridge, proposed, in its third part, the convocation of a General Council.[2] The subtlety of the Cambridge reasoning in case of non-appearance of Benedict and his party does not, however, seem to have been properly appreciated by the Oxford Masters, who merely say that both contestants should take an oath to the effect that they would abide by the decisions of the General Council *quoad papatus titulum*. As a last resort Oxford suggested the use of force by the Catholic powers.

II

Since the Universities during the Schism played a very active role in creating and influencing public opinion and since, moreover, they took

---

[1] 'Nam obediendum est prelatis et prepositis etiam discolis, et reprobatis a Deo principibus et sacerdotibus subtractam obedientiam non legimus; imo iis, quorum in dubium probabiliter versum est jus et titulus, quousque fiat super titulo dubio declaratio, secundum canones est parendum', loc. cit. 34B.

[2] 'Dominus noster Bonifacius apostolici culminis verus pastor, quem secundum predecessores electionis unitas, temporis et possessionis prioritas, jure possessorio dilucidant et declarant, pro sedatione tam seditiosi scismatis generale concilium convocet per decretum non solum sibi subditos adhaerentes, quinetiam suum adversarium apostaticum Petrum de Luna, jam se Benedictum temere nominantem, cum suis anticardinalibus et antiprelatis adhaerentibus universalis ecclesiae nomine pariter atque suo ad interessendum in ipso concilio citet', loc. cit. 35B.

64

from the very beginning a lively interest in the theological and legal questions raised, it was understandable that both kings and popes should treat the Universities with great respect. Hence, during the Schism the practice grew up of notifying the Universities of a new papal election, the most likely reason being to curry favour with the University addressed.

Again, it is not yet fully appreciated that in influential European circles Cambridge enjoyed a reputation equal to that of other *studia*. There are two documents which would illustrate this point. One of them has been noted, but seems otherwise to have escaped attention, whilst the other has only recently come to light. So far there is no evidence that Oxford was the recipient of corresponding communications.

It is common knowledge that on the occasion of the election of a successor to Innocent VII[1] the cardinals subscribed to a number of stringent conditions in case one of them should be elected pope.[2] In the end, the Venetian Cardinal Angelo Correr emerged as the unanimously elected pope—Gregory XII—who immediately after the immantation was made to repeat the solemn pledges upon oath in the presence of the papal notaries and other official witnesses.[3] Outstanding amongst these promises was his pledge to notify his opponent, Benedict XIII, of his intention to abdicate if Benedict were to do the same and to announce to the Christian world this undertaking within one month after his coronation.

Punctiliously, Gregory XII dispatched on 11 December 1406, hence before his coronation (19 December), a number of letters to archbishops and bishops, kings, and also to some Universities. Of the letters to Universities so far only two are known, namely, those to the Universities of Paris and Vienna,[4] although it is likely that other Universities were also informed.[5] That the University of Cambridge was also the recipient

[1] Innocent VII was the immediate successor of Boniface IX and died on 6 November 1406.

[2] For these *Wahlkapitulationen* see Raynaldus, *Ann. eccles.*, ed. cit. xxvii. 156–7; D. Wilkins, *Concilia* (London, 1737), iii. 286–8; M. Souchon, op. cit. i. 95–114, edition of the articles subscribed, ibid. i. 285–95; N. Valois, op. cit. iii. 485 f.; Hefele–Leclercq, op. cit. vi–2, 1030 ff.

[3] See Souchon, op. cit. 113–14.

[4] For Paris, see Martène–Durand, *Thesaurus novus anecdotorum* (Paris, 1717), ii. 1286–7; for Vienna, see A. Aschbach, *Geschichte der Universität Wien* (Vienna, 1865), i. 244; the letter is preserved in the Archives, cp. ibid., note 2.

[5] For instance, the cardinals wrote to the University of Cologne, see Martène–Durand, ii. 1280–1. It should be remembered that this University was founded by Urban VI and hence special connexions between the Roman curia and the University may have existed. Apart from this, it is certainly noteworthy that it was always the same Universities which appear as recipients of a letter by the pope or by the cardinals: Paris, Cologne, Vienna, and Heidelberg (see below), in

of a letter by Gregory XII has been observed by Valois, though apparently no use of this information has been made.[1] Unfortunately, however, the original of this letter is no longer extant, but only a copy of it made by William Cole[2] from the transcripts of Robert Hare.[3] In his 'Extracts from volume 3 of Mr. Hare's collections relating to the Town and University of Cambridge temp. Hen. 4ti' William Cole heads this letter as 'Bulla Gregorii 12mi universitati transmissa, de pace et unione facienda in papatu', but transcribed not the whole of the communication, but only its substantial parts. The address reads:

Gregorius episcopus, servus servorum Dei, dilectis filiis Rectori (sic) et Universitati studii Cantebrigiae, salutem et apostolicam benedictionem.

An edition of this letter can be dispensed with, since it is entirely identical with the one sent by Gregory XII to Arundel on the same day and printed in full by Wilkins.[4] Assuming that Martène published the whole document, it would seem that Gregory, in contrast to his procedure adopted in his letters to Canterbury and Cambridge, did not insert in his communication to Paris a copy of the letter he had sent to his opponent, Benedict XIII.[5]

Of greater interest is the notification which the University received from the cardinals and which appears to have escaped the attention of historians. Martin V was elected at Constance on 11 November 1417, an election that brought this dismal story of the Schism to an end. The new pope and the cardinals announced the election to the Christian world: this time the University was the recipient of a letter written, not by the pope, but by the cardinals who had elected Martin and who, in their letter, gave a brief account of the actual procedure and the subsequent events.[6]

other words, those Universities which in one way or another had given their opinion on the ending of the Schism; cp. Henry of Langenstein, Conrad of Gelnhausen, Gerald of Calcar, &c., and my *Origins of the Great Schism*, p. 92 n. 3. It may not be unreasonable to suppose that Cambridge, for the same reason, was accorded a similar position.

[1] See Valois, iii. 487 n. 2.
[2] About whom see *D.N.B.*, s.v.
[3] B.M. Add. MS. 5843, fols. 361–2 (new foliation, fol. 176r–176v).
[4] Wilkins, *Concilia*, pp. 284–6.
[5] See Martène–Durand, ii. 1287.
[6] The letter is listed by Luard, loc. cit., no. 96. For details of Martin's election cp., *inter alia*, the critical examination of most of the sources by B. Fromme, 'Die Wahl des Papstes Martin V', in *Römische Quartalschrift*, x (1896), 133–61, and J. Hollnsteiner, 'Studien zur Geschäftsordnung am Konstanzer Konzil', in *Festschrift f. Heinrich Finke* (Münster, 1925), 240–56; the diary of Cardinal Fillastre is partly edited by H. Finke in his *Quellen und Forschungen zur Geschichte des Konstanzer Konzils* (Paderborn, 1889), 163 ff., esp. 232 ff., and for the edition of the whole diary see *Acta Concilii Constanciensis*, ed. H. Finke

66

The importance of this find is heightened by the fact that this seems to be the only extant original of the cardinals' communication.[1] It is true that they had also written to the University of Cologne,[2] but it is difficult to say whether the original has survived. Moreover, the letter to Cambridge is not a mere copy of the one they had written to Cologne: it is slightly rephrased in parts, especially in those dealing with the new pope's coronation; nor is the date the same: the letter to Cologne bears the date of Martin's coronation day (21 November 1417), whilst their letter to Cambridge is dated on 22 December 1417, and no other copy of a letter written by the cardinals on that day has ever come to light. As far as the available evidence goes to show, the archbishop of Canterbury does not seem to have been informed of the election directly, for in the Convocation of 26 Nov. 1417 he read out a letter of the 'Council of Constance' addressed to the Duke of Bedford which contained the announcement of the new election.[3] Again, to judge by the entry in the records of the English nation at Paris, it seems that the University of Paris was in receipt of a letter from the cardinals, but whether it is extant I have been unable to establish.[4] These circumstances would make it advisable to edit the cardinals' letter to the University. Although they

(Münster, 1923), ii. 13–170, esp. 157 ff.; see, furthermore, ibid. iv. 201. For another detailed eyewitness account see Ulrich von Richental, *Chronik des Constanzer Concils*, ed. M. R. Buck (Tübingen, 1882), 116 ff. Cp. also Peter of Pulkau's letters, ed. by F. Firnhaber, 'Peter de Pulkau, Abgesandter der Wiener Universität am Concilium zu Constanz', in *Archiv f. Kunde oesterr. Geschichtsquellen*, xv (1856), numbers 25–28, pp. 56 ff.

[1] If I understand the late H. Finke aright, the letter of Martin and the cardinals to the University of Heidelberg is preserved in a copy only, Vat. MS., Cod. Pal. 701, fol. 224^v; cp. *Acta Conc. Const.*, iv. 201 n. 5.

[2] Cp. Martène–Durand, *Thesaurus*, ii. 1690–2 (= Mansi, xxviii. 898–901).

[3] See *Register of Henry Chichele*, ed. cit. iii. 33: 'Archiepiscopus intimavit eisdem prelatis et clero nova iocundissima, videlicet de assumpcione et eleccione sanctissimi in Christo patris et domini nostri Domini Martini divina providentia pape quinti in concilio generali Constan' in die sancti Martini episcopi ultimo tunc preterito ut asseritur graciosissime celebrata, prout, ut asseruit idem reverendissimus pater [*scil.* archiepiscopus], per quasdam litteras de concilio generali predicto inclitissimo principi Domino Johanni duci Bedford' custodi Anglie transmissas, quas ibidem publice idem reverendissimus pater perlegi fecit, sibi certitudinaliter tunc constabat, pro quibus novis idem reverendissimus pater ac confratres sui predicti ceterique prelati et clerus inibi congregati cum decantacione ympni *Te Deum laudamus* . . . atque laudes devotissime persolverunt.'

[4] See *Chartularium Universitatis Parisiensis: Auctarium* (Paris, 1937), ii. 238: from the *Liber procuratorum nationis Anglicanae* for 23 December 1417: 'Fuit congregatio universitatis facta in eodem loco super quatuor articulos. Primus erat super una littera missa de curia Romana, in qua continebatur qua die summus pontifex in concordia fuerat electus . . . Quantum ad primum (articulum) natio regratiabatur Deo omnipotenti de coronatione facta summi pontificis.' But cp. Bulaeus, v. 307 and also 331.

say that the pope himself is going to write to the University, I have found no trace of this papal notification.[1]

The text is written in pale brown ink on fairly thick paper, having been mounted, probably in the nineteenth century, on modern paper. There are few abbreviations, the letters are quite large and spacious, and the whole is well laid out. There are of course no ornamentations or any other features typical of papal documents. Only the initial M of the first word is enlarged, but otherwise the text does not call for any comment,[2] except that there are one or two indications of some scribal hastiness and carelessness. The document measures $16\frac{1}{2} \times 8\frac{1}{2}$ inches; the seal is lost.

The contents of the letter can be summarily dealt with. After briefly recalling the effects of the long Schism, the cardinals refer to the laborious negotiations between them and the commissaries (deputies) of the various nations represented at the Council. These negotiations led to the decree in which the electoral procedure was embodied.[3] This decree (30 October 1417) laid down that each of the five nations should send six delegates into the conclave and, according to the old papal election decree,[4] which was extended to this unusual case, a two-thirds majority was necessary for election. There were therefore thirty national 'co-electores' in addition to the twenty-four cardinals.[5] On Monday,

---

[1] The only addressees of Martin V's letter, in which he announced his election (*Inc.*: 'Misericors et miserator Dominus unigenitus Dei Filius . . .') I could trace are the following (date of letter in brackets): University of Cologne (21 Nov.), ed. Martène–Durand, ii. 1688–9 (not in Mansi); his brother Renzio di Colonna (22 Nov.), ed. Mansi, xxviii. 896–7; the city of Velletri (22 Nov.), ed. Alexander Borgia, *Istoria della chiesa e città di Velletri* (Nocera, 1723), 349–50; the city of Viterbo (11 Nov.), ed. F. Bussi, *Istoria della città di Viterbo* (Rome, 1742), 429–30 (= Mansi, loc. cit. 898–9); the city of Corneto (27 Nov.), ed. A. Theiner, *I due concilii generali di Lione e di Costanza* (Rome, 1861), 49–50. It will be noticed that these three cities were situated in the papal state. The only original of this papal letter that seems to survive is in the Colonna Archives (III B. xvi. 5), cited by L. Pastor, *Geschichte der Päpste* (Freiburg, 1886), i. 159 n. 2; a MS. copy of the mid-fifteenth century is in Codex Lucensis 540, fol. 551, see *Acta Conc. Const.*, iv. 201 n. 4. For the University of Heidelberg, see ibid., n. 5 and above, p. 64, n. 5.

[2] The observations of P. M. Baumgarten as regards the documents emanating from the *Camera* of the College of Cardinals would appear to be applicable to this letter too, cp. his *Untersuchungen und Urkunden über die Camera Collegii Cardinalium* (Leipzig, 1898), pp. clxxxvi ff.

[3] For this decree, its sources, &c., see Valois, iv. 396–402.

[4] See Alexander III's decree in *Liber Extra*, i. vi. 6 (*Licet de vitanda*).

[5] The names of the 6 English 'co-electores' were these (reconstructed from C. Eubel, *Hierarchia catholica medii aevi* (Münster, 1913), i. 33 n. 7): the bishop of London, Richard Clifford; the bishop of Bath and Wells, Nicholas Bubwith; the bishop of Lichfield, John Catterick; the bishop of Norwich, John Wakering; the abbot of St. Mary's, York, Thomas Spofford; the dean of York, Thomas

68

8 November, at 4 o'clock in the afternoon this fairly large assembly retired into the conclave which was held in the Town Hall at Constance, where on Thursday, 11 November, at 10 o'clock in the morning Cardinal Oddo of Colonna was unanimously elected.[1] The cardinals immediately enthroned him[2] and paid the customary homage to him. Ten days after the election the new pope's coronation took place in the presence of Sigismund, the emperor, and enormous crowds *cum inexplicabili letitia.* The letter concludes with the usual assurances and wishes to the University.

These three documents would create a strong presumption in favour of the view that, in the age of the Great Schism at any rate, the University of Cambridge, so far from being a 'third-rate university' and of no importance, stood in the estimation of both king and papal curia on a level with any other European seat of learning. It may well be true that its Masters had not been infected with the malaise of vociferous self-advertisement, but what cannot be denied is not only that they were approached in such delicate and highly politic matters to which the documents bear witness, but also that, as their reply to the king shows, they knew how to handle complex material in a manner which stands in contrast to the acrimonious statements issued by many another contemporary university.

APPENDIX

A

*The University of Cambridge advises King Richard II against accepting the French proposal of a withdrawal of obedience, declares Urban VI and Boniface IX to be the legitimate popes, and submits proposals for ending the Schism.**

Cambridge, 24 Jan. 1399

Serenissimo christianissimo et victoriosissimo in Christo principi et

Polton (later bishop of Hereford). About the intervention of Thomas Polton at a crucial moment at the Council, see H. Finke, 'Die Nationen in den spätmittel-alterlichen Konzilien', in *Hist. Jahrb.* lvii (1937), 329. The English participants, according to Finke, art. cit., 337 n. 21, were: 10 bishops, 2 bishops-elect, 2 proto-notaries, 7 abbots, 16 doctors of theology, 11 doctors of both laws, 25 M.A.'s, more than 60 proctors of chapters, &c., and over 100 'literati'. Cp. also Ulrich von Richental, ed. cit. 168–9, 176, 186; *Reg. Chichele*, iii. 13.

[1] He was a cardinal deacon and in actual fact only a sub-deacon: he was ordained deacon on 12 November, priest on the following day, and on Sunday, 14 November, consecrated bishop when he said his first mass. Cp. H. von der Hardt, *Magnum oecumenicum Constantiense Concilium* (Frankfurt and Leipzig, 1699), iii. 1486–7.

[2] But cp. the statement in von der Hardt, op. cit., ed. cit., 1482, according to which it was Sigismund who enthroned Martin.

* Original draft (O) in the Archives of the University of Cambridge: plan press, second drawer. I should like to thank Mr. R. M. Ogilvie, of Clare College, for his valuable suggestions on some points of the text.

domino nostro metuendissimo domino Ricardo, Dei gratia regi Anglie et
Francie, domino Hibernie et duci Aquitanie illustrissimo, vestre celsitudinis regalis devotissimi oratores fideles et ligei cancellarius et universitas
vestra studii generalis Cantebriggie ad terram prostrati fidelitatem,
devotionem et subjectionem ligeam in eo,[1] per quem reges regnant et 5
principes dominantur.

Regalis vestra sublimitas, nobis et regno ac sacrosancte Romane
ecclesie iugiter pro(s)tensa, floribus ubertatis copiosa et irrigua et mentis
nostre speculo radios sue latitudinis assidue infundens, gratiarum et
laudum preconia tanto culmini indesinenter referre nos urget atque im- 10
pellit, retinentes in archivis nostris, quod velut princeps catholicus summo
creatori et ipsius vero vicario in cathedra piscatoris residenti devotus,
firmus et stabilis ac ut basis aurea[2] defensor extitistis et existitis propitius,
prout magnifica vestre celsitudinis opera in publicum manifestant. Ipsa
namque veluti virtuosus pugil ecclesie Romane ac integritatis eiusdem 15
zelator eximius ad hoc sua vota direxit suaque tempora sub felici pro-
secutione deducit, ut ab unitate segregatos ad rectam emulationem revocet
et tam fidei quam fidelium terminos valeat dilatare, attendens nichil esse
quod clarius credatur prefulgere quam recta fides in principe. Ex alto
quippe prospicitur vestra amplitudo regalis quam potentie univit im- 20
mensitas, dirigit altitudo consilii redditque plenitudo virtutum conspicuam
quod non solum a populis vobis subiectis, sed etiam ceteris nationibus
canticum laudis, honoris et glorie vestro nomini decantatur.

Digne igitur humana preconia vestrum affatum collaudant, ipsum
honorant atque glorificant, quem ipse[3] rex regum hiis ita dignum in orbe 25
statuit sub regio titulo singularem; licet enim sensualitatem assequentes
ecclesiam sanctam, que una est, scindere non valeant, eo quod unitas
divisionem non patitur, sese tamen scindant ab eadem magnificentia;
nichilominus vestra regalis sinderisi[4] fulcita exemplo David tendit ad
yma dum sic canit[5]: Accedit homo ad cor altum et exaltabitur Deus. . . . 30
Archa enim, per quam ecclesia sancta designatur, tunc vincit cum
leditur, tunc intelligit cum arguitur, tunc secura fit cum superata videtur,[6]
inundationibus concutitur, sed elevatur[7] in sublime. Quare confidendum
est, quod ille, qui post nubilum dat serenam inclitam sponsam succedenti-
bus turbationum fluctibus agitatam, oculo clementiori ex alto respiciet et 35
non feret eam in sui numinis iniuriam diutius conculcari. In nomine enim

---

[1] Cp. Prov. viii. 15–16.   [2] Cant. Cant. v. 15.   [3] Cp. 1 Tim. vi. 15.
[4] sinderisi(s): a most unusual and unique form of addressing a king in an
official document. The term expresses (as Dom David Knowles, Regius
Professor of Modern History, kindly informs me) the habitual knowledge of
the principles prompting moral actions. Cp. St. Thomas Aquinas, S. Theol.,
Ia IIae, qu. 94, art. 1, ad 2 (ed. Venice, 1593, 203): 'Synderesis . . . est habitus
continens praecepta legis naturalis, quae sunt prima principia operum huma-
norum'; see also D.T.C. xiv. 2992–5, with examples from SS. Jerome, Bona-
venture, &c. What the Masters had probably in mind was the king's 'public
conscience' which directs the actions of his subjects.
[5] Ps. lxiii. 7–8.   [6] Cp. Lk. vi. 48.   [7] Cp. Gen. vii. 17.

70

Christi semper superat, semper vincit, et quantum alii insidiantur, tantum
ista dilatatur, et fluctus quidem illi dicuntur, sed fundamentum,[1] quod
supra petrum est, non quassatur. Unde in figura ecclesie[2] dixit Christus
Petro:[3] Ego rogavi pro te, ut non deficiat fides tua, quoniam[4] tu es petrus
5 et super hanc petram edificabo ecclesiam meam, et porte inferi, id est,
scisma et hereses, que sunt aditus ad infernum, numquam prevalebunt
adversus eam. Ex hiis igitur spiritus letitie et firmioris spei in nos assu-
mentes, degeneres filios in agro dominico zizaniam[5] serentes surculo vestre
ditionis regalis relicta palea ad verum granum temporibus vestris credimus
10 revocandos.

Ideoque multa sub compendio concludentes nedum videamur intricare
scripturas et auditoris aures gravare sermone, maiestatem vestram
regalem attenta mente deposcimus, quatenus iura ecclesie sancte, ut
hactenus, in sua soliditate conservare dignemini in futurum, ne videantur
15 presidentie vestre tempora aliquorum sophisticatione quomodolibet
sustinere ruinam, quod nullatenus evenire posse pensamus. Et nos vestre
celsitudinis oratores iuxta modicitatis nostre arbitria iniunctionibus vestris
pariter et mandatis parentes contra tunicam[6] Domini lacerantes non
subterfugimus,[7] quominus decreto ipsorum sentire nostrum absque
20 arrogantie titulo explicabimus, et omne consilium Dei,[7] ne sanguine
eorum contaminemur, si eis salutare consilium pronuntiare nollemus,
serenitati vestre studuimus adaperire in omni reverentia et honore.

Aggredientes demum iniuncta vestre celsitudinis regalis pariter et
mandata eadem ad mulieris paupercule instar[8] in gazophilacium post
25 multos divites scientie profunditate et discretionis titulo insignatos,
iactantes optimis viribus nostris iuxta complacentie vestre regalis modum
utinam per nos scitum, licet temporis brevitas et negotii arduitas ac
consulentium paucitas se offerant in medium, nostri avisamenti modulum
aliorum respectu exile seu nullum humiliter promovere, protestationis
30 tamen nodum adicientes, quod in correctionis culminis vestri almifici seu
consilii vestri aut alterius cuiuscumque regula residere afficimur voto
communi, per presentes scripturas igitur labores pariter et decreta sata-
gentium, ut asserunt, scisma presens pestiferum et dampnabile per ipsos
tamen, ut cum eorum pace loquamur, suscitatum et exortum radicitus
35 extirpare et ecclesiam sanctam in suis membris laceratam sanctius red-
integrare, diligenti studio inspeximus, ex quibus intentio ipsorum finalis
et unanimis existit, quod a Benedicto pretenso, adversario domini nostri,
quem suum reputant papam, de papatu cum domino Bonefacio, quem
verum papam tenetis et indubie, contendente, obedientia quecumque tam

4 *pro* inserted above the line.　　26 O: *optannis*.　　30 fortasse: *modum.*

[1] Cp. Lk. vi. 48.
[2] Cp. St. Augustine, *In Johannis Evang.*, tract. 124, cap. 5 (*P.L.* xxxv. 1973);
Sermo CCXCV, cap. 2 (*P.L.* xxxviii. 1349); *Sermo* LXXVI, cap. 1 (*P.L.* xxxviii. 479).
[3] Lk. xxii. 32.　　　　[4] Mt. xvi. 18.　　　　[5] Mt. xiii. 24 ff.
[6] John xix. 23.　　　　[7] Acts xx. 27.　　　　[8] Cp. Lk. xxi. 1 ff.

in temporalibus quam in spiritualibus subtrahi debet, prout cum cause
cognitione et per ipsorum decretum in scriptis redactum[1] proinde pro
parte sua subtraxerunt, requirentes itaque magnificentiam vestram
regalem, ut credimus, minus iuste quatenus contra dominum nostrum
Bonefacium papam nonum, de quo vestre serenitati scribentes nullam 5
faciunt mentionem, cum sibi, ut dicunt, numquam obediverunt nec
obedire debent, ut carnaliter et pompose asserunt, in futurum acies[2]
vestras consimiles dirigeretis et obedientiam quamcumque, quam ut
medium putant melius, brevius et sanctius ad scisma presens sedandum,
subtraheretis ab eodem.   10
    Christianissime et metuendissime princeps, licet enim Karolus pater
vester illustris universis Christi fidelibus per litteras suas insinuat, quod
a Benedicto pretenso, quem suum reputat papam, obedientiam sub-
traxerit omnem, illud tamen in litteris eisdem inserit[3] fecisse propter
periurium, quod idem pretensus extra casum iuris voluntarie asseritur 15
incurrisse; nam, ut testantur littere predicte, prefatus adversarius domini
nostri contra frequentem requisitionem cardinalium suorum devotamque
pariter et lacrimosam eorundem, uno dumtaxat excepto,[4] in cupidine
dominandi demersus viam pacis pro scismate presenti sedando contra
suum iuramentum elegit intricatam et quasi impossibilem sicque idem 20
ambitione peccatisque aliis involutus viam pacis recusavit cardinalibus
suis inhibens expresse, ne quid facerent in premissis vel fieri consentirent,
sed dominus noster Bonefacius in sua semper remansit et remanet libertate
promissionibus, iuramentis seu asseveramentis huiusmodi minime
obligatus, occasionem talem vobis minime subministrans. Sicque ad 25
paria cum suo adversario judicari non debet.
    Cessant ob illud Karoli patris vestri illustris rationes in suis litteris
contra dominum nostrum et suum adversarium pro cessione utriusque
facte, dum per ipsum adversarium et eius predecessorem suam sumpsit
originem et scandalum subintravit. Ambitioque ipsius dominandi, cum 30
non per ostium, sed aliunde pontificii se immiscet dignitati, manifeste
patet. Sicque rationes hee et alie prefatum adversarium dumtaxat urgent
ad cedendum vel expelli deberet a sede et dum nostrum Bonefacium

---

9 O: *cedandum.*   17 A corrector tried to insert between *requisitionem*
and *cardinalium* an *aut*, but misjudged the space available and managed to write
only an *aū*, which is not really a recognized abbreviation for *aut*. As the grammar
and sense are perfectly clear without the *aut*, I have omitted this word. Cp. also
line 21.   In the margin of this line there is a *Nota* sign.   19 O: *cedando.*
21 *recusavit*] Here the same corrector inserted an *aut*, but this time above the line.

---

[1] Cp. Bulaeus, op. cit. iv. 853 ff.   [2] Cp. Gen. xiv. 8.
[3] See Bulaeus, op. cit. iv. 858 and 859.
[4] This was Cardinal Martin de Salvis (Zalva), called 'Pampilonensis', created
by Clement VII on 21 July 1390, died 27 October 1403; cp. M. Souchon, op. cit.
i. 236, and C. Eubel, *Hierarchia*, i. 28, note 30; and especially F. Ehrle, 'Neue
Materialien zur Geschichte Peter's de Luna', in *Archiv f. Literatur und Kirchengeschichte*, vi (1892), at 247–53.

72

minime tangunt, quia iuris ordine papatum admisit, nec scisma facit, qui
suo iure utitur, nec fructus consumit, quos ob iuris sui defensionem legaliter exponit. Nec exemplo multorum recedentium a papa Anastasio[1]
incitamur, quoniam heresi respersus fuit, nec urget factum Guydonis
5 Viennensis, qui una cum aliis ab obedientia Paschalis male recessit et se
inobedientem constituit, sed facti penitens ad obedientiam predictam
rediit, et postea Calixtus secundus effectus est. Inspicitur enim a iure,
non quod fit, sed quod fieri debet. Retorquentur igitur predicte rationes
in capud adversarii dumtaxat, ut et ipse utinam sublato cecitatis velamine
10 ad obedientiam domini nostri valeat resilire.

Nec titubat homo noster interior seu dubitaret homo catholicus quiscumque,[2] deposito private affectionis sedere de titulo felicis recordationis
domini Urbani sexti et nunc nostri Bonefacii pape noni, cum de habitis
factis et gestis cardinalium intra conclave tempore electionis eiusdem
15 Urbani constare non poterat cuiquam nisi per ipsorum assertionem et
relationem clero et populo Romano publice patefactam ac deinde per
scripturas eorundem cunctis pene mundi principibus divulgatas, quod
Urbanus sextus fuit verus papa; quibus fides adhiberi debuit, cum non sit
verisimile ipsos cardinales in suis scripturis inserere nisi quod mente
20 agitarunt nec presumitur tante auctoritatis viros toti christianismo falsum
proposuisse Christi vicarium et populum ad obedientiam et venerationem
eiusdem dolose invitasse, si titulus defuisset. Nec relatio ipsorum
cardinalium a diu posterior sue prime contraria, qua patrem vestrum
Karolum predictum illustrem et prelatos Francie seduxerunt, ipsos ab
25 ecclesie unitate dividendo, Clementem olim et nunc Benedictum pretensum in suum papatum nominando, amplectenda foret a diligenter
intuente, cum prefatis cardinalibus contrarium sui primi dicti et facti
astruere intendentibus, tamquam inconstantie et variationis filiis, fides de
iure adhiberi non debet. Indignum enim iudicatur, quod quis sua voce
30 dilucide est protestatus, illud in casum infirmare seu proprio resistere
testimonio permittatur; ipsorum igitur Karoli illustris et scribentium
progressus contra Benedictum pretensum, dum tamen sancta procedat
intentione, incipit esse meritorius et fortior cresceret, si domino nostro
Bonefacio adhererent.

35 Requisitio tamen eorundem iniusta, dampnabilis et scandalosa patet
cuicumque fideli Christiano. Quo enim iure seu qua fronte posset ecclesie
Romane filius dominum nostrum Bonefacium pro papa indubitanter
habitum, nominatum et publice pro tali per vos et regnum vestrum ad-
missum et reputatum absque heresi spernere seu obedientiam eidem
40 subtrahere, nullo videmus iure. Hortatur enim nos Christus in evangelio,[3]

---

4 *factum* inserted above the line by corrector.   24 *et* conjectured: the word
is written over the crease and has become illegible.   28 O: *intentibus*.

---

[1] For the following cp. above, pp. 58–59.
[2] Cp. the speech of the abbot of St. Michael before Richard II in 1395,
reported in Bulaeus, op. cit. iv. 756–7.   [3] Mt. xxii. 21.

Reddite que sunt Cesaris Cesari et que sunt Dei Deo, et Paulus com-
memorat,[1] Reddite, inquit, omnibus debitum, cui tributum, tributum, cui
vectigal, vectigal, cui timorem, timorem, cui honorem, honorem, et alibi,[2]
Obedite prepositis vestris et subiacete eis, ipsi enim pervigilant quasi
rationem pro animabus vestris reddituri. In veteri etiam testamento 5
inobedientia sacerdoti ministranti morte puniebatur, quanto magis in
novo a Christi vicario recedere et cervicem contra ipsum erigere dampnabile iudicatur et Deo offensurum teste apostolo,[3] Qui potestati resistit, Dei
ordinationi resistit, qui autem resistunt, ipsi sibi dampnationem adquirunt.

Execrabilis igitur erit omnibus, qui diligunt Deum, qui subtrahit, quod 10
Dominus iubet prestari, et si fieret obedientie subtractio, quod absit,
inconstantia universaliter per totum mundum vobis et regnicolis cito
imponeretur, et pagani, azephali, scismatici non immerito nuncuparemur
et, quod timendum verisimiliter foret, subditi contra suos dominos tam
in temporalibus quam in spiritualibus hoc intuito rebellirent sententieque 15
et censure ordinariorum vilipenderentur. Nam politia omnis destrueretur
et cito universum vacillaret. Multa quoque ex subtractione huiusmodi
sequerentur inconvenientia Deo detestabilia, que in longum protrahere, ne
vestram fatigemus celsitudinem stilo prolixo, hic subticemus. Quare sub
serenitatis vestre correctione prostrati dicimus et cum humilitate, reve- 20
rentia et devotione, qua possumus aut valemus, vestre solertie regali
respondemus, quod a domino nostro Bonefacio papa nono propter scisma
huiusmodi ab ipso vel vobis eidem adherentibus minime exortum, subtrahi obedientia non debet. Sicque medium illud, quod adversarii eiusdem
putant sanctissimum et saluberrimum pro scismate presenti cessando, 25
credimus iniustissimum, pessimum Deo et toti ecclesie catholice dampnatissimum, cum non sit medium inducens, sed potius excludens per quod
ecclesia poterit reformari, non scismatis corruptivum, sed potius genera-
tivum, non pacem procurans, sed gladium, cum ex subtractione huiusmodi maiora orirentur scismata tam in ecclesia quam in conscientiis 30
perfectorum.

Sed inferri possunt alia media ad presens scisma extirpandum, prout
nostris ingeniorum modulis perspicimus in presenti. Si enim via cessionis,
per quam ecclesia possit plenarie et sine mora quietari, tamquam sancta
et Deo grata admitteretur, et dominus noster Bonefacius post cessionem 35
sui adversarii pure, sponte et libere absque coactione, minis et precum
importunitate cedere decerneret adhibita primitus cautela bona collegi-
orum eorundem de futuro substituendo Romano pontifice, ne novissimus
error fieret peior priore,[4] unitas ecclesie reformaretur et cuncta sopirentur,
amboque contendentes sacrificium Deo gratius et curie celesti accepta- 40
bilius offerre putarentur. Si autem cessiones huiusmodi per contendentes
minime sint accepte nec adversarius domini nostri ex se cedere seu ipsum

---

[1] Rom. xiii. 6 ff.   [2] Heb. xiii. 17.   [3] Rom. xiii. 2.
[4] With this formulation should be compared the diction in the Oxford draft:
if *subtractio obedientiae* were adopted 'sic fiat novissimus error scismatis peior
priore' (MS. cit. fol. 52[r]).

74

dominum nostrum Bonefacium ad possessionem suam, quatenus in ipso
consistit, restituere decreverit, prout affectant restitutionem omnia iura
et clamant omnino ex ordinata iustitia, expediens tunc fore credimus
honestum atque utile quod dominus noster Bonefacius, dominandi
5 cupidine iniuste diffamatus, pronus semper ad pacem, prout littere eiusdem Karoli illustris affirmant, quod ipse eundem Karolum illustrem con-
stanter requisivit, quod viam rectam inveniret et ipse consentiret, ad ora
obstruenda detractorum cunctis publice offerat pacem et iustitiam
poscenti omni sine suspitione se indulgere. At ex hoc ipse solus et insoli-
10 dum non tantum propter flebile scisma presens, sed propter futurum, si
eveniat, quod absit, celerius extirpandum necnon et inobedientiam
Grecorum et alia in ecclesia Christi salubriter reformanda, ad concilium
suum generale sibi adherentes ac Benedictum pretensum et alios suos
complices in specie, necnon et omnes alios et singulos ius et interesse in
15 papatu contra ipsum Bonefacium se habere pretendentes seu non pretendentes in genere, valeat et velit ad locum tutum convocare, ad quod celerius
exequendum poterunt principes catholici eundem invitare honesta prece.
In quo quidem concilio, si pars Benedicti pretensi pro iure suo decreverit
interesse, audiatur et fiat iustitia inspecto altissimo absque favore aliquali.
20 Si autem pars ipsius pretensi seu alius quiscumque contra eundem dominum nostrum oppositor in concilio generali predicto adesse minime cura-
verit, tunc in penam contumacie ipsorum huiusmodi factum verum et
nudum electionis felicis recordationis domini nostri Urbani pape sexti
publice proponatur et diligenti studio examinetur, et prout iustum et
25 visum fuerit concilio memorato, approbetur seu cassetur et annulletur
affectione carnali quacumque semota seu alias in concilio memorato
declaretur, an cessio utriusque seu alterius eorundem contendentium
fieri debeat pro ecclesie pace. Sicque scisma presens repetitis malleis
crebrisque tunsionibus ecclesiam Christi infestans iustitie et iuris titulis
30 potest honeste terminari.
    In hac igitur procella tempestuosa manus dignemini apponere adiutrices,
quoniam[1] navicula iactatur fluctibus, quia ventus est contrarius, nam
speramus et pro certo tenemus, quod si presens negotium ditionis vestre
presidio meruerit decorari, grata perfectione letabitur nec suspendetur in
35 mora. Que omnia et singula non arroganti stilo sub correctione vestra
consiliique vestri ac cuiuslibet alterius melius in hac parte sentientis
vestre transmittimus celsitudini regali intuenda, quam ad regni regimen
ecclesie catholiceque tutamen dirigat in prosperis per tempora diuturna
ipsius ecclesie capud Christus Ihesus, qui facit utraque unum vivens in
40 secula seculorum.
    Scriptum Cantebriggie in congregatione nostra regentium et non re-
gentium ad hoc specialiter congregata sub sigillo nostro communi

---

12 O: *consilium.*   18 O: *consilio.*   O: *pretensus.*   21 O: *consilio.*

---

[1] Cp. Mt. viii. 24 and xiv. 24; Lk. v. 3.

vicesimo quarto die Ianuarii, anno Domini millesimo trecentesimo nona-
gesimo octavo.

B

The College of Cardinals announce to the University of Cambridge the
election and coronation of Martin V*

Constance, 22 Dec. 1417

Miseratione divina episcopi, presbyteri ac diaconi sacrosancte Romane
ecclesie cardinales dilectis nobis in Christo Rectori et Universitati studii
Cantabrigiensis salutem in Domino sempiternam.   5

Pater futuri seculi, princeps pacis de throno eius ineffabilis pietatis
atque clementie ad statum Petri navicule,[1] variis et calamitosis undarum
turbinibus fere per quadraginta annorum lugenda curricula ob scisma
pestiferum lacrimabiliter lacessite, prospiciens ac misertus iam tandem
super illam, nec passus diutius sacrosanctam Romanam catholicam 10
ecclesiam post cessionem iuris papatus dudum per olim Johannem XXIII
et subsequenter Gregorium XII in eorum obedientiis nuncupatos factas
et depositionem a papatu de dicto olim Johanne per sacrosanctam et
generalem synodum Constantiensem ac deinde de Benedicto XIII in eius
etiam obedientia nuncupato et per ipsam synodum legitime celebratas, 15
suo presule viduatam in maximum et enorme preiudicium animarum et
corporum ac interitum deplorandum fidelium Christianorum, ipsius
viduitatis ulterius deploranda incommoda, per infusionem spiritus sancti
paracliti[2] diebus preteritis in corda hominum inspirare in maximo rerum
turbine, nam ubi vult spirat,[3] inestimabiliter est dignatus, ut post multos, 20
diutinos, varios laboriososque tractatus inter nos et deputatos per com-
missarios nationum in presenti synodo degentium, quas divina maiestas
ad pacem et reformationem et unionem dicte ecclesie de universis Christianitatis et nonnullis aliis partibus in unum mirabiliter adunavit, super
electione summi Romanique futuri proximi pontificis habitos, in ipsa 25
generali synodo concorditer provisum extitit et conclusum[4] super modo et
forma electionis ipsius Romani ac futuri proximi pontificis, quod Collegio
nostro prefate ecclesie cardinalium sex coelectores pro qualibet quinque
nationum in ipso concilio seu synodo existentium ad peragendam una

---

3 ac] *et.*   4 dilectis nobis] *egregiis viris.*   8 om. *fere.*   15 om. *etiam.*
17 ac] *et.*   18 O: *deplorare*; M: *deplorande non ferens.*   19 diebus preteritis]
diebus his proximis.   21 om. *per.*   22 degentium] *existentium.*   23 pacem et]
om. *et.*   25 Romanique] *et.*   futuri] *tunc.*   27 ac] *et.*

---

* Original letter (O) in the Archives of the University of Cambridge: plan
press, second drawer. Collated with Martène–Durand, *Thesaurus novus anecdo-*
torum, ed. cit. ii. 1690–2 (M). Unless otherwise stated, the variant readings refer
to M.
[1] Lk. v. 3. Cp. H. Rahner, 'Navicula Petri', in *Zeitschrift f. katholische Theo-*
logie, lxix (1947), 3–35.
[2] John xiv. 26.
[3] John iii. 8.
[4] H. v. der Hardt, *Magnum oecumenicum Const. Conc.*, ed. cit. iii. 1452–6.

76

nobiscum electionem huiusmodi adiungerentur: ita tamen, quod electus
in papam per duas nostri Collegii et duas alias partes coelectorum cuiuscumque nationum predictarum, concorditer a cunctis Christifidelibus pro
unico, vero ac indubitato pontifice prefate ecclesie catholice haberetur,
5 prout in decretis ipsius synodi latius denotatur. Postque nationes ipse
supremis aspirantes affectibus, ut pro universali bono Christianitatis
electio ipsa in Altissimi gratia concluderetur celeriter, ad electionem
coelectorum huiusmodi procedentes, sex prelatos et alios viros gradibus,
scientia et virtute conspicuos ad electionem huiusmodi pro earum quin-
10 que nationum qualibet, nobis et nostro Collegio adiunxerunt; et deinde
dictorum sex pro natione numero triginta coelectorum ad electionem
ipsam celebrandam, electio per nationes, ut premittitur, celebrata, in
eadem synodo fuit confirmata solenniter cum potestate in decreto dicti
concilii alias declarata.
15 Quibus opportune peractis, die lune octava mensis Novembris proximi
preteriti circiter horam quartam post meridiem nos et dicti coelectores,
servatis de more servandis decretum, conclave in domo communitatis
Constantiensis notabili et accommoda libertate atque securitate amplissimis
communitum,[1] ad omnipotentis Dei laudem et gloriam, pacem, statum et
20 unionem predicte ecclesie ac totalem extirpationem scismatis predicti in
spiritus sancti nomine exultantes intravimus. Illoque qui de supero ubi
vult spirat[2] ac fidelium corda vivificat[3] et illustrat, corda nostra et coelectorum nostrorum inestimabiliter ac divinitus inspirante, die XI dicti
mensis circa horam decimam, et ad tam sacratissimum negotium eodem
25 spiritu humillime, prout tam sublimis materia exposcebat, ab intimis
precordiis invocato, unacum coelectoribus prefatis consultatione et deliberatione mature prehabitis super statu ipsius ecclesie, tranquillitate fidelium, ac electione huiusmodi prefatique scismatis confusione universali,
vota nostra cum eisdem coelectoribus unanimi consensu ac libera volun-
30 tate, nemine discrepante, in reverendissimum in Christo patrem dominum
Oddonem de Columpna, tunc sancti Georgii ad Velum aureum diaconum
cardinalem confratremque nostrum, eiusdem ecclesie verum et indubita-
tum pontificem suprema cordium nostrorum affectione direximus, ac
ipsum elegimus et prefecimus eidem Romane ecclesie in huiusmodi
35 pontificem et pastorem.
Moxque cum hymnis de more et canticis ipsum, mutato Oddonis
nomine in Martinum papam quintum solenniter inthronizavimus[4] et

3 *predictorum.*　4 ac] *et.*　8 sex] *inter.*　9 O: *eorum.*　12 O and M:
electione.　15 opportune] *et solenniter.*　15 octava] *instantis mensis.*
18 om. *et.*　20 predicte] *prefate.*　21 supero] *cardine.*　22 ac] *et.*　corda
nostra] *mentes nostras.*　23 die] *Iovis.*　dicti] *presentis.*　26 O: *unacum
cum.*　27 *maturis.*　om. *prehabitis.*　28 ac] *et.*　*prefati.*　31 *Odonem
de Columna.*　32 *confratrem.*　36 *Odonis.*

[1] v. der Hardt, iii. 1471–2; 1479.
[2] John iii. 8.　　　[3] Ibid. vi. 64.　　　[4] Cp. above, p. 68.

adoravimus iuxta morem, confectis super hiis omnibus ad futuram rei
memoriam publicis documentis ac deinde celeberrimis sacrisque celebratis circa consecrationem ipsius in Constantiensi ecclesia serenissimo
principe ac domino, domino Sigismundo Romanorum et Hungarie etc.
rege in regalibus infulis ac maiestate cum prelatorum, ducum, procerum 5
ac nobilium suorum illustrium comitiva, cleri populique multitudine
copiosa ibi adstantibus, in iubilo prefati domini nostri XI Kal. Decembris
proximi preteriti, sue coronationis in thalamo fuere de more ad Altissimi
gloriam, pacem et salutem ipsius ecclesie solennia,[1] cum omni copiosissime
multitudinis atque perceleberrime tam regis quam nostra, prelatorum, 10
principum, cleri ac reliquorum inexplicabili letitia[2] celebrata. Que licet
idem dominus noster devotionis vestre affectibus latius per suas litteras
intimet, nos etiam significare decrevimus ad letitiam singularem, offerentes
nos prona semper affectione dispositos apud ipsum dominum nostrum
tranquillitatem vestram pariter et honorem paternaliter amplexantem 15
pro omni statu et honore vestris interponere, totius vigilantie nostre curas,
casu quolibet ingruente. Vos autem, prout de eiusdem vestre devotionis
integritate erga statum, honorem et gloriam prefatorum et ecclesie abunde
confidimus, sic vos exhibeatis diligentissimos et solertes, ut eadem vestra
devotio merito valeat in Altissimis collaudari ac condigne remunerationis 20
impendia promereri.

Datum Constantie, provincie Maguntie, sub trium priorum nostrorum
sigillis, die XXII Decembris, ab assumptione pontificalis culminis ipsius
domini nostri, anno primo, MCCCCXVII.

2–11 *Et deinde solenniis iuxta ritum prefate Romane ecclesie hac presenti die in*
ecclesia Constantiensi canonice et solenniter celebratis, adstante multitudine per-
celebri, in presentia serenissimi principis domini Sigismundi regis Romanorum et
Ungarie illustris, prelatorum, procerum, nobilium ceterorumque ipsius domini nostri
coronationis insignia celebravimus cum exultatione premaxima.   10 *O: om.*
quam. There is a corrector's dot in the text between *regis* and *nostra.*   12
dominus circumspectioni vestre latius affectibus.   15 *fraternaliter am-*
plectentem.   16 *totiusque.*   17–18 *de vestra circumspectione et integritate.*
18 *prefatorum] domini nostri.*   19 *diligentissimum et solertem.*   19–20
ut merito valeatis in Altissimo.   23 *XXI Novembris.*   24 MCCCCXVII]
indictione decima.

[1] Cp. v. der Hardt, iii. 1489–91.
[2] Cp. 1 Pet. i. 8.

XII

THE RECOGNITION
OF ST BRIDGET'S RULE BY MARTIN V

It is not generally known that in the history of the Bridgettine Order the intervention by one of the great canonists of the time, a Benedictine Abbot and Archbishop of Palermo, played a crucial role. As is well known, Martin V gave on 7 April 1419 recognition to the Order which was the technical and canonical act according full monastic status to the whole Order. What assumes however a particular significance in this context is that only the year before, in 1418, the same pope had revoked all the privileges granted to the Order by other popes. It may be profitable to review briefly this somewhat unusual procedure, so as to throw into clear relief, on the one hand, the debt which the new Order owed to the eminent Nicholas de Tudeschis (variously also styled Panormitanus or Abbas Modernus), and, on the other hand, the influence which he exercised upon the papacy.

The peculiarity of this new Order established by St Bridget[1], the widow of a Swedish nobleman, accounts for a certain amount of reticence on the part of the popes in granting full canonical status ; it is perhaps significant that Urban V on 5 August 1370 gave only recognition to the monastery at Vadstena, founded by St Bridget, and not to the Rule as such[2]. Moreover, a comparison between the constitution approved by Urban V and the Rule confirmed later, would go to show that the former contained the proviso of the government of two monasteries, a facet which puts an altogether different complexion upon the Order[3]. However, Pope Urban VI on 3 December 1379 gave general recognition to the Rule composed by St Bridget, the *Regula sancti Salvatoris*[4].

---

1. About the deep spirituality and fervent mysticism of St Bridget see the excellent article/by F. VERNET in *Dict. de Spiritualité*, I (1937), cols. 1943-58.

2. See *Acta Sanctorum* (Boll.), October, IV. 446-7.

3. Cf. also the pertinent observations by J. BIRGER in his account in the *AA.SS.*, *cit.*, at p. 421 B and C ; see also Dom Stephan HILPISCH, *Die Doppelklöster: Entstehung und Organisation* (in *Beiträge zur Geschichte des alten Mönchtums*, vol. xv) (Munich, 1928), p. 84: "Urbans Bestätigung legt allerdings Wert darauf zu betonen, dass es sich um zwei Klöster handelt, die beide die päpstliche Gutheissung finden".

4. For the text of the bull — *Ad perpetuam rei memoriam* — see *AA.SS.*, *cit.*, 466-7 ; about the date cf. *ibid.*, p. 467 A-B.

The obvious difficulty arising out of this recognition of the Rule lay in that is was granted during the Great Schism by a pope who was certainly not acknowledged as pope in all parts of Christendom. Hence continuous efforts were made by the youthful Order to gain universal recognition throughout the period of the Great Schism from other popes as well as from the Council assembled at Constance. It was actually during this period that the English kings Henry IV and Henry V sought to introduce the Bridgettines into England, and the latter king, after overcoming some considerable obstacles, obtained a decree from Martin V on 18 August 1418 granting the establishment of the Order at Syon[1]. The decree of Martin can be likened to that of Urban V : in each case papal approbation concerned only an individual foundation, and did not refer to the Rule itself.

It is worth while to keep this point in mind, for although it is usually assumed that the final canonical establishment of the whole Order, following barely a year afterwards, came, so to speak, as a matter of course, it becomes clear from the abundant source material that in the intervening period the pope had in fact revoked all privileges granted to the Order by his predecessors. This revocation decree was based upon the view that the Rule of St Bridget established double monasteries, an institution that was canonically forbidden and consequently the pope forbade the Bridgettines to receive any more novices[2]. It is nevertheless

---

1. For this see Margaret DEANESLY, *The Incendium Amoris of Richard Rolle of Hampole* (Manchester, 1915), pp. 93, 127 ; for the letter of Henry V to Martin V, see *ibid.*, pp. 130-7, and the pope's reply *ibid.*, pp. 139-42 ; for a fresh and succinct survey see Dom David KNOWLES, *The Religious Orders in England* (Cambridge, 1955), II. 175-9. In fact, the pope sent two letters, one addressed to Henry V and edited in W. DUGDALE, *Monasticon Anglicanum* (London, 1830), VI. 543-4 (*Incipit*: "Eximie devotionis et sinceritatis affectus...") and the other addressed to the Archbishop of Canterbury, the Bishop of London and the Abbot of St Albans, preserved in a Transsumptum and for the first time edited by DEANESLY, *op. cit.*, pp. 137 ff. Cf., furthermore, T. TANNER, *Notitia Monastica* (Cambridge, 1787) : Middlesex no. XI.

2. For the decree and a summary see Dom HILPISCH, *op. cit.*, pp. 84-5. The so-called "double monasteries" were proscribed by both civil and canon law ; for the former see *Cod. Just.*, I. III. 19 and 44 ; *Novella* CXXIII, cap. 36 : in this latter passage the term "duplicia monasteria" occurs for the first time : διπλᾶ μοναστήρια· For the canon law see Gratian's *Decretum*, XVIII. II. 20 ff., and for earlier pronouncements see Dom U. BERLIÈRE, *Les monastères doubles aux XIIᵉ et XIIIᵉ siècles* in *Mémoires publiés par l'académie royale de Belgique : Classe des lettres*, vol. XVIII (1924), fasc. 3, pp. 21-2. For the history of these "double monasteries" see Mary BATESON, *Origin and early history of the double monasteries* in *Transactions of the Royal Historical Society*, new series, vol. XIII (1899), pp. 137-98 ; St. HILPISCH, *op. cit.*, and A. HAMILTON THOMPSON, *Double Monasteries and the male element*

192

worth pointing out that whilst the Swedish Bridgettines never actually saw this decree, Nicholas de Tudeschis, to judge by the way he refers to it, had been given an opportunity of seeing the decree itself. Little imagination is needed to perceive what sudden blow this papal measure must have meant for the Bridgettines, having been virtually condemned as an outcast and illicit organization.

At least seven letters were despatched by Swedish personalities on 10 December 1418, that is, two from Vadstena monastery, three by King Eric XIII to three cardinals and one to the pope himself, and one letter by Queen Philippa to another cardinal. In all these letters the revocation of the privileges by Martin V is made the sole grievance and the pope is entreated to withdraw his step. On the same day, 10 December 1418, special ambassadors as bearers of these communications were despatched to the Roman curia, that is, Johannes Haquini and Johannes Hillebrandi[1].

The whole unedifying story is perhaps best revealed in the moving and sorrowful letters written by the nuns of Vadstena to the nuns of Syon[2], from which communication we actually learn that the Bridgettines only heard of the revocation by way of rumour :

Ut fama referente didicimus, dominus apostolicus omnes indulgencias datas ab obitu Gregorii XI ad instar alterius indulgenciae in estate

---

in nunneries in Ministry of Women : A Report by a Committee appointed by the Archbishop of Canterbury (London, 1919), pp. 145-64 (for Syon abbey, see pp. 163-4). Only in an untechnical sense can the Orders of Fontevrauld (see Kirchenlexicon, IV. 1598-9 ; M. HEIMBUCHER, Die Orden und Kongregationen der katholischen Kirche (Paderborn, 1934), I. 327-9) and of Gilbert of Sempringham (see Dom KNOWLES, Monastic Order in England (repr. Cambridge, 1950), pp. 205-7, and HILPISCH, op. cit., pp. 71-75) be called double monasteries. About the Bridgettine Order which, as Panormitanus convincingly proves, was not a double Order in any sense, cf. HEIMBUCHER, op. cit., I. 620-25 ; P. DEBONGUIC in Dict. d'archéologie chrétienne et de liturgie, X (1938), cols. 728-31 ; and BIEHLMEYER-TÜCHLE Kirchengeschichte, 12th ed., (Paderborn, 1948), II. 453 f; here also further literature.

1. See Diarium Vadstense, ed. E. BENZELIUS (Upsala, 1721), p. 60 (ad annum 1418) : "Sabbatho ante III dominicam adventus emittebantur duo fratres nostri, videlicet Johannes Haquini et Johannes Hillebrandi, ad Romanam curiam pro reformandis privilegiis et indulgentiis nostri ordinis." The former ambassador returned early in January 1420, see ibid., p. 61 (ad annum 1420), and the latter returned in June of the same year, ibid., pp. 61-2.

2. Diplomatarium Suecarum, ed. C. SILFVERSTOLPE (Stockholm, 1902), no. 2552, pp. 390-1. For this letter see also T. HÖJER, Studier i Vadstena Klosters och Birgittenordens Historia (Upsala, 1905), p. 176 ; this author also refers to other unedited material dealing with the supplications to the pope in this matter, p. 178 n. 4 and p. 179 n. 2.

praeterita revocavit, sed hanc revocacionem, ut nos intelleximus, non fecit publice nec de communi consensu omnium nacionum, sed tantum de consilio et consensu nacionis germanicae posuit huiusmodi revocacionem inter regulas cancellarie[1], aliis quatuor nacionibus[2] super hoc minime consencientibus, et forsitan propterea non fit aliqua mencio in regno Angliae de indulgenciis talibus revocatis[3].

Hence the nuns of Vadstena request the nuns at Syon to enlist the support of Henry V: he should at once send an embassy to the Roman curia to support their own, so that the pope may be persuaded to change his mind[4]. In a most dignified letter to the pope the king himself submits the request for a papal confirmation of the Rule[5], whilst in the letters to the cardinals he hopes to solicit their support[6]. One quotation will suffice to show how profoundly the king was affected by the papal revocation :

Quia indulgencias monasteriorum sanctarum Marie Virginis et Birgitte de Watzstena dolenter audivimus per dominum apostolicum revocatas et quia eadem monasteria et ordinem totis diligimus visceribus ac illorum felicem conservacionem et profectum devotissimis faucibus esurimus, idcirco dileccionem vestram, de qua magnam gerimus confidenciam, instantissime deprecamur quatenus latores presencium, dictorum monasteriorum et ordinis procuratores, velitis totis conatibus erga dominum apostolicum promovere et omnibus viribus cooperari[7].

No less touching was the letter which the queen herself sent by the same post to a cardinal[8]. There can be no doubt that the cancellation by the pope created consternation and dismay in the

---

1. For this cf. E. OTTENTHAL, *Regulae Cancellariae Apostolicae : Die päpstlichen Kanzleiregeln von Johann XXII bis Nikolaus V* (Innsbruck 1888), pp. 195-6, nos. 38-41, especially no. 39 ; cf. also B. HÜBLER, *Die Constanzer Reformation und die Concordate von 1418* (Leipzig, 1867), p. 155 and notes *ibid.*, 99-102 ; and J. HEFELE-H. LECLERCQ, *Histoire des Conciles* (Paris, 1916), VII-1, pp. 548, 562.
2. That is the natio *Gallicana, Italica, Anglicana* and *Hispana.*
3. *Dipl. Suec., cit.*, p. 390.
4. *Ibid.* To the agitation of the Lübeck clergy attention should be drawn, *ibid.*, pp. 390-1 : "Quia dilectissimi nostri confratres de monasterio Mariewold, quod est situm in Saxonie partibus iuxta civitatem Lybicensem, nobis nuper per suas epistolas lamentabiliter intimarunt, quod cum ipsi cepissent circa ad vincula sancti Petri ordinis nostri indulgencias publicare, mox totus clerus in dicta civitate Lybicensi, que est imperialis et magna, et similiter in aliis circumiacentibus civitatibus tam religiosi quam clerici saeculares insurrexerunt contra eos, publice dicentes omnes indulgencias ad instar tempore scismatis concessas, totaliter fuisse revocatas et fundant se in regulis cancellarie..."
5. *Dipl. Suec.*, no. 2555, p. 393.
6. *Ibid.*, no. 2554, p. 392 ; no. 2556, p. 394 ; no. 2558, p. 395.
7. *Ibid.*, p. 394.
8. *Ibid.*, no. 2557, p. 394-5.

194

highest ecclesiastical and civil circles. With one stroke of the papal pen the destiny of the whole Order seemed doomed ; it was a wholly undeserved fate caused, in part at least, by an odious rivalry.

It must have been in the autumn or winter months of 1418 that the services of the outstanding canonist of the day were enlisted. The *Consilium* of Panormitanus is not dated, but his reference to the revocatory letter by Martin V in the body of the *Consilium* proves that it was given before the final approbation of the *Regula sancti Salvatoris* on 7 April 1419[1]. Indeed, the great canonist at the very end of his *Consilium* can, with justifiable gratification, say this :

> Vidi post hoc consilium litteras bullatas domini Martini confirmantes praedictam religionem secundum decisionem huius consilii. Laus Deo et sanctae Brigidae[2].

The *Consilium* itself gives no indication by whom it was requested. The question submitted (the *casus consilii*) to Panormitanus was:

> Quaeritur an religio instituta per beatam Brigidam, quae fuit per papam confirmata et demum per successores in papatu in dubium revocata, dicatur esse contra sanctorum patrum decreta seu canonicas sanctiones, praesertim quod in tali religione instituendi sunt etiam sacerdotes seu fratres, qui debent deservire eisdem monialibus in divinis.

Indeed, the possibility that it was Swedish circles who asked the canonist's expert opinion, cannot be excluded.

Nicholas de Tudeschis was one of the most eminent canonists in the early fifteenth century. At an early age he entered the Benedictine Order and, at Padua, became a pupil of Cardinal Franciscus Zabarella[3]. In 1411 he was already professor at Bologna, later migrating to Parma and Siena. In the meantime (1425) he had been elected Abbot of Mineo in the diocese of Messina (hence his name *Abbas Siculus*) and in 1435 he became Archbishop of Palermo (hence also called Panormitanus)[4]. In contradistinc-

---

1. Printed in *AA. SS., cit.*, p. 477 C-E ; and in *Dipl. Suec.*, no. 2615, pp. 438-9 ; another bull of 1 July 1419, *ibid.*, no. 2657, pp. 468-9.

2. *Consilium* VIII in the edition Venice, 1571, fol. 6ᵛ et seqq.

3. About whom cf. W ULLMANN, *The Origins of the Great Schism* (London, 1948), Appendix, pp. 191-231 ; B. TIERNEY, *The Foundations of Conciliar Theory* (Cambridge, 1955), pp. 220 ff.

4. For these details see J. F. SCHULTE, *Geschichte der Quellen und Literatur des Canonischen Rechts* (Stuttgart, 1877), II. 312-13 ; A. VAN HOVE, *Prolegomena ad Codicem Juris Canonici*, 2nd ed. (Mechlin., 1945), pp. 497-8; here also further literature.

tion to the *Abbas antiquus* [1] he was named *Abbas Modernus*. With every justification it has been said that "entre tous les bénédictins qui se firent un nom dans l'étude du droit, Nicolas de Tudeschis est certes le plus célèbre. Peut-être fut-il, après Jean André, le plus grand canoniste du moyen âge [2]". Whilst Johannes Andreae was called by his contemporaries the *Tuba juris*, Panormitanus was distinguished by being referred to as the *Lucerna juris*. Even the critical Schulte declared that Panormitanus belonged "unstreitig zu den bedeutendsten Kanonisten des Mittelalters"; what characterized him was "ein scharfes Urteil, einen auf die Bedeutung der Rechtsfragen für das Leben gerichteten Sinn [3]". That a canonist of this standing was frequently consulted in difficult legal questions is not indeed surprising : his *Consilia* show a sound and practical common sense and avoid all embellishments, frills and the display of an undigestible array of citations—the great malaise of contemporary legal scholarship.

It was in fact these very same qualities which are manifested in his *Consilium* on the canonical legitimacy of the Bridgettine Order. After invoking the help of Christ, of the Virgin and of St Bridget herself [4], he proceeds in the usual scholastic manner by first stating the negative proposition, namely that this Order is against the canon law. In particular, the Rule of St Bridget seems to contradict chapter 23, C. XVIII, *quaestio* ii [5], because, at least "sub clausula generali", priests and brothers "constituuntur in monasteriis puellarum"; moreover, chapter 22 of the same *quaestio* would seem to be violated by this Rule, since double monasteries, even if monks and nuns form a separate juristic entity, that is, a separate *collegium*, are prohibited [6]. The underlying reason for the prohibition of double monasteries is the

---

1. That is Bernardus de Montemirato. His identity was established by St. Kuttner, *Wer war der Dekretalist Abbas Antiquus?* in *Zeitschrift der Savigny Stiftung f. Rechtsgeschichte, Kanon. Abtlg.*, xxxvi (1937) pp. 471 ff. ; cf. also E. Meijers, *Responsa Doctorum Tolosanorum* (Haarlem, 1938), pp. 43, 56.

2. Dom Philibert Schmitz, *Histoire de l'ordre de Saint-Benoît* (Maredsous, 1949), v, p. 194.

3. Schulte, *op. cit., loc. cit.*

4. This is the *Incipit* of the *Consilium* : "Christi, eiusdem Matris ac ipsius Brigidæ, cuius factum agitur, praesidio invocato."

5. This canon reads : "Monasteria puellarum longius a monasteriis monachorum aut propter insidias diaboli aut propter oblocutiones hominum collocentur."

6. Fol. 6ᵛ ed. *cit.* : "Monachi et moniales non debent in uno monasterio cohabitare ; quinimo etiam duplicia monasteria prohibentur a jure, vel ubi sunt duo collegia monachorum et monialium... si ergo dicamus esse unicum monasterium, in quo fratres et sorores sunt, sive sint diversa collegia et diversa monasteria a jure videntur prohibita, saltem propter propinquitatem et familiaritatem."

proximity of monks and nuns which may on the one hand occasion the "crimen incestus" and on the other hand may give rise to "mala opinio" as well as to the inevitable "oblocutiones hominum". It may be said that it is precisely these reasons which "urgent et militant adversus dictam religionem sanctae Brigidae". But quite apart from these considerations, it is the provision in the Rule of St Bridget that the Abbess "debet esse caput et domina monasterii" and hence that she may appear to be the "caput omnium, tam virorum quam mulierum" which is apt to arouse opposition and hostility. For a provision such as this "sonat in absurdum", because "vir debet esse caput mulieris, et non econtra ¹". Lastly, Panormitanus says that there is no need to labour the point at all, since Pope Martin V had most recently maintained that the Rule of St Bridget violated canon law in so far as double monasteries were to be established.

> Ultimo videtur amplius non insistendum, cum ipse dominus papa Martinus quintus hodiernus expresse in suis litteris revocatoriis asserat per illam regulam duplicia monasteria constitui contra jus prohibitionis, et verbis papae standum est omnino.

Panormitanus was too good a jurist not to realize that all these objections did not carry much legal weight. "Sed his non obstantibus oppositum puto de jure verum"—with these words he introduces the constructive part of the *Consilium*. The only proper way of finding out whether or not this Rule is legitimate is the juristic examination of those of its chapters which have a bearing upon the disputed point. What he does in the second part of the *Consilium*, is to subject some of these chapters to a juristic test. This test yields one certain result, namely that the Bridgettine Order does not contradict the law or the constitution of the Church.

In the first place, an unbiased reading of the important chapter 10 of the Rule proves that St Bridget had no intention of founding two monasteries nor of making men and women live within the precincts of one and the same monastery : what she intended to found was one monastery or *collegium monalium* to which clerics should administer the divine sacraments, so however that these clerics were there, not as a corporate body or *collegium*, but merely as individuals ². In fact, this same chapter of the Rule says that

---

1. With a reference to Gratian, XXXIII. v. 12, 13, 17.
2. After quoting the text of this chapter of the Rule, Panormitanus says : "Ex quibus verbis primo pondero, quod intentio beatae Brigidae non fuerit

the clerics have their own *curia*, that is, their own house or quarters, entirely separated from the monastery of the nuns. The juristic import of this stipulation is that the clerics can on no account be said to constitute a *collegium* or a separate monastery or establishment ; these clerics, being there merely as individuals, can in all respects be compared with any other priests who serve a female monastic establishment [1]. Plainly, therefore, in law and in fact this is the only satisfactory arrangement available to the nuns :

> Cum enim non possunt sorores sine sacerdotibus esse eis divina ministrantibus, melius est, quod habeant istos homines aptiores seu sanctiores electos institutos per tam devotissimam sanctam quam quod habeant alios, ex quibus forte ad mala facilius perveniant.

That the clerics attached to the nunnery do not form a corporate entity, that is, a legal *collegium* in the technical sense, is manifest, since the Confessor General receives his authority from the Bishop—both in respect of the power of the keys and the disciplinary power of correcting the subordinate clerics. For if the clerics constituted a *collegium*, it would be they as the members of this corporate body who elected their superior, that is, the Confessor General, who afterwards only would receive his confirmation from the Bishop. As it is, according to the Rule it is the Bishop who appoints the Confessor General [2].

---

conlocare seu instituere duo monasteria, scilicet virorum et mulierum, neque in uno monasterio instituere masculos et foeminas, sed dumtaxat instituere moniales seu collegium monialium, et quod isti clerici seu fratres non essent ibi tamquam facientes collegium, sed tamquam singulares et servitores in divinis. Quod patet clare ex illis verbis, cum dicit "clericos habebunt". The numeration of the chapters of the Rule by Panormitanus does not agree with the numeration of chapters adopted in the printed editions; I have used the edition of Rome, 1628, II. 351 ff. The chapter referred to is 12 (not 10), see p. 359.

1. "Item ex aliis verbis dum dicit in eodem capitulo, quod isti clerici habebunt unam curiam per se ita, quod sint omnino separati a monasterio sororum. Quae verba sonant, quod isti clerici seu fratres non faciunt per se monasterium, nec est nisi unum monasterium sororum, cum dicatur, quod a monasterio sororum sint omnino separati. Sed curia significat etiam locum habitationis, sicut fieri videmus hodie in omnibus monasteriis monialium, quae non valent per se propter defectum sexus celebrare missas et praedicare, ut capitulum Nova, De poenitentiis et remissionibus (*Extra* : V. xxxviii. 10) ; habent sacerdotes et saeculares prope monasterium eis celebrantes et praedicantes, pro qua observantia facit capitulum Dilecta, De excessibus praelatorum (*Extra* : V. xxxi. 14) et capitulum finale, De statu monachorum (*Extra* : III. xxxvi. 8), et fratres seu clerici substituuntur loco illorum ; et cum praesumantur sancti omnes propter multas austeritates, quas promittunt observare, praesumendi sunt honestiores, XVI qu. prima, capitulum Doctos et Nulli" (*Decretum* : XVI. 1. 21 and 62).

2. "In dicto capitulo dicitur, quod confessor generalis monasterii debet ab

198

An arrangement such as this should not and could not give rise to charges of familiarity or of "living together", not only because the residence of the clerics is situated quite apart from the monastery proper, but also because the Rule itself expressly stipulates that the Confessor General or any other clerics, be they priests or brethren, are allowed to enter the monastery on only two occasions, that is, in order to administer the sacraments to sick nuns or in order to bury a deceased nun, but these are occasions on which also mere secular clerics are allowed to enter the monastic precincts, and is therefore nothing extraordinary. Even the confession of the nuns is, according to the Rule, so arranged that they can only be heard, but not seen, by the officiating priest. Hence the Rule itself, according to Panormitanus, certainly gives no more rise to scandalous gossip than the Rule of any other female monastic institution[1]. Considering all the probable grievances which may have been raised against this new and devout Order, it must have been a very welcome relief for the Bridgettines to have their Rule interpreted and understood in this sound manner.

A further attentive reading of the Rule convinces Panormitanus that in the preamble to the Rule, in which the late Saint had propounded her intention of founding a monastery for nuns in honour of the Virgin, speaks only of women and does not even mention clerics or brethren. How then can one say that this Rule establishes a double Order ? Moreover, chapter 13[2] lays down that the priests have to attend only to the divine office and have to abstain from all other business of the nuns, and this again is a clear indication that the Rule does not envisage a "commune monas-

---

episcopo loci recipere potestatem ligandi et solvendi, corrigendi atque reformandi omnes sacerdotes, fratres et ceteros, per quae verba etiam arguitur fratres non esse ibi ut collegium persistens. Nam si essent ut collegium, eligerent sibi praelatum, qui ex sola electione et confirmatione episcopi subsecuta, consequeretur dictam potestatem ligandi, solvendi et corrigendi alios fratres." The statement, therefore, made by Dom HILPISCH, *op. cit.*, p. 79 that the Abbess "ernennt den Beichtvater" is inaccurate. The relevant chapter (14) says this : "Abbatissa etiam unum de XIII sacerdotibus in quem una cum omni congregatione sororum et fratrum consentit, in confessorem omnium eligat ipsumque episcopus constituat et confirmet." The interpretation by Panormitanus is therefore perfectly correct.

1. "Item in capitulo 22 Regulae dicitur, quod numquam confessor generalis vel aliquis presbyterorum vel fratrum monasterium monialium ingrediatur, nisi quando infirmis ponenda sunt sacramenta vel soror mortua sepelienda ; quibus casibus etiam saecularibus clericis liceret... quando sorores confitentur, audiri quidem possunt, minime videri." The chapter referred to is chapter 25 of the printed editions, cf. ed. cit., p. 366.

2. This is chapter 15 ; cf. ed. cit., p. 361.

terium" at all. The priests function there merely as "servitores in divinis". No other juristic meaning can reasonably be attributed to the provision that the "abbatissa in negotiis et bonis monasterii semper est consulenda". This provision also shows that the authority of the Abbess is exercised solely and exclusively over the monastery itself[1]. Even if—which is certainly not the case with the Bridgettine Order—the Abbess had authority over men, this would be comparable to a queen ruling her subjects by virtue of hereditary succession: "Immo mulier ratione successionis in regno posset habere jurisdictionem plenissimam in omnes subjectos[2]".

One may even go so far as to claim that the Rule of St Bridget is in entire accord with canon law. For the relevant canon[3] declares that "monasteria virginum (in provinica Baetica) monachorum administratione et praesidio gubernentur[4]". Panormitanus holds that just as in this canon "deputati fuerint monachi ad regendum et gubernandum monasteria monialium", so in the present instance the clerics may be "deputari administrare divina dictis sororibus". There is only one monastery, that of the nuns who assign and attach to themselves clerics for the divine offices[5]. This arrangement is in fact dictated by both usefulness and necessity, since the clerics assigned must not reside too far away from

---

1. "In casu nostro abbatissa ratione dignitatis suae habet jurisdictionem supra dictum monasterium, et posset habere jurisdictionem in clericos saeculares, licet in casu nostro nullam jurisdictionem habeat in fratres." Again, Dom HILPISCH's statement (op. cit., p. 78) that "Die Nonnenklöster hatten einen dienenden Mönchskonvent zur Seite, der unter der Leitung der Aebtissin stand" is open to criticism.

2. With a reference to *Extra* : I. XLII. 4, in which decretal Innocent III fully acknowledged the jurisdictional authority of a reigning queen. Cf. also *Decretum*, XII. II. 8.

3. See *Decretum*, XVIII. II. 24.

4. The canon continues : "Tunc enim salubria Christo dicatis virginibus praebemus, quando eis patres spirituales eligimus, quorum non solum gubernaculis tueri, sed etiam doctrinis aedificari possint." This canon originated in the Council of Seville (619) under the chairmanship of Isidore of Seville ; cf. J. D. MANSI, *Concil. Coll.*, (Florence, 1764), x. 560-61 (cap. XI). See furthermore, HEFELE-LECLERCQ, *op. cit.*, III-I, p. 257, and also Mary BATESON, *art. cit.*, pp. 190-91 and HILPISCH, *op. cit.*, p. 52.

5. Fol. 7ra : "Non obstat cap. Monasteria (*Decretum* : XVIII. II. 23) quia loquitur, quando duo monasteria aeque principalia sunt fundanda, tunc enim cum nulla necessitas cogat seu utilitas suadeat, debent ut evitetur malum reipsa et opinione, distantia inter se collocari. Sed si bene consideretur regula, casus videtur esse prorsus diversus, cum unicum sit monialium monasterium tantum, sed sacerdotes seu fratres tamquam deputati ad serviendum tantum in divinis habeant quandam habitationem dumtaxat omnino separatam a monialium monasterio, ut supra in dicta regula continetur."

the nuns, if they are to do their duties adequately[1]. Wisely enough, Panormitanus reminds those who are easily perturbed by loquacious and malicious tongues that what matters is the truth, and nothing else. "Nec curandum quod os loquentium inique loquatur, dummodo non recedatur a tramite veritatis".

In short, there is nothing in the *Regula sancti Salvatoris* that violates the existing canon law : the monastic way of living as set forth in the Rule has at no time been proscribed by the law. There is neither a double monastery, because the clerics do not constitute a separate legal entity or *collegium*, nor a single monastery housing both men and women, because the former live in separate quarters and have no access to the nuns except on the two occasions mentioned[2].

The papal revocation decree remained nevertheless a serious stumbling block for Panormitanus. This was certainly a rather delicate point requiring not only tact, but also a good deal of juristic dexterity. For Panormitanus had so far given his decision in open contradiction to the papal decree, and however well-reasoned his *Consilium* was, it stood in direct opposition to a most recent papal ruling. How can this obstacle be removed ? Panormitanus would not have been the great jurist he was acclaimed, had he not also at his disposal the juristic skill to render this papal decree innocuous. Perhaps nowhere emerges the acumen of the Benedictine canonist better than in the way in which he dealt with this obstacle. No doubt, he made it considerably easier for the pope to retract his step. From the purely juristic point of view Panormitanus's argumentation on this score is perhaps the most valuable part of this *Consilium*.

A papal letter can command authority only in so far as the juristic deductions and arguments of the pope are based upon true facts ; if therefore the pope was wrongly informed or based himself upon dubious facts, the papal injunctions and prohibitions deriving from this insecure basis are devoid of legal validity[3]. In other

---

1. *Ibid.* : "In casu nostro subest ratio utilitatis et necessitatis, cum habeant eis deservire in dictis officiis, quod de facili non possent quotidie, si longius starent, venire in dictum monasterium, maxime cum non decet dictos fratres et tamquam Deo deditos devotissimos fratres quotidie exire cunctis horis per vicos et plateas civitatis".

2. "Si ergo ponderentur verba Regulae et omnia praedicta, non potest dici eas habere monasteria duplicia. Nec quod habitent in uno monasterio, cum debeant stare fratres separati omnino a monasterio sororum, nec ad eas est familiaris accessus. Unde saltem negare non possumus istum modum vivendi non fuisse hactenus jure prohibitum".

3. This is, incidentally, the reason why in papal letters and decretals there

words, if the basis is wrong, the conclusions too must be wrong and therefore cannot be binding.   A papal ruling is valid, Panormitanus declares, "quando papa fundat intentionem suam super facto proprio, secus si super facto alieno".   In the latter case it is open to doubt "cum papa in facto alieno de facili posset errare". But in the present instance the pope was obviously wrongly informed when he said that the Rule of St Bridget envisaged the establishment of double monasteries—"quod reipsa falsum est", since, as shown before, there is only one monastery.   The juristic versatility of Panormitanus lies in that he rightly considered the Rule as constituting a question of fact, and not as forming a question of law.   And in questions of fact the pope can very well be the victim of deception.   "Dominus papa sic ex falsa ratione potuit verisimiliter esse deceptus, cum dicta Regula consistat in facto, et non jure."   This is certainly a first-class juristic argumentation which effectively removed this obstacle of the papal revocation decree ; at the same time it must have paved the way for the final approbation : without this juristic argument—unanimously acknowledged by contemporary legal scholarship—it would have been very difficult indeed for the pope to set aside his own decree within so short a time.

> Concludo ergo meliori judicio et maxime Domini nostri semper salvo, dictam religionem sanctae Brigidae non esse aliquatenus violandam ex eo, quod monasteria dicantur duplicia vel quod in eodem monasterio habitent masculi et foeminae.

Whoever consulted this distinguished canonist could not have chosen a jurist of greater calibre nor one who had a deeper understanding of monasticism and its contemporary needs.   It was the fortunate combination of the monk and the canonist in the *Abbas Modernus* which may well be said to have saved the Bridgettine Order at a crucial moment of its existence.

Cambridge.

---

occurs so often the phrase : "si res ita se habeant" or "si res ita est" or phrases to the same effect.

XIII

EUGENIUS IV, CARDINAL KEMP, AND ARCHBISHOP CHICHELE

WHILST earlier conflicts between Canterbury and York, though not devoid of picturesque embellishments, were of purely local-provincial interest and therefore never left any imprint on the law of the universal Church, the dispute between Henry Chichele, archbishop of Canterbury, and John Kemp, archbishop of York, though hardly known, affected the common law of the Church so much that the pope's decision is cited as a *pièce justificative* in the most recent legal enactments of the Roman Church. The significance of the verdict given by the pope, Eugenius IV, is that it fixes authoritatively and officially the status of the cardinals and, what is equally important, for the first time reveals the views of the papacy on the nature of the cardinalate. It may not be out of place to review this conflict in a volume that is dedicated to one of our great medievalists, himself *quondam alumnus Oxoniensis*, and to offer him a contribution that attempts to portray the historical and canonical importance of a contest in which two such distinguished *Oxonienses* of the fifteenth century figured prominently. May he accept this essay as a humble token of personal friendship and respect.

I

ENGLISH historiography does not seem to have taken much notice of this *cause célèbre*, for apart from Arthur Duck's *Life of Henry Chichele*[1] which gives a brief summary of this conflict, I have not found any other account of it.[2] Now, according to Duck, this very sharp dispute between Canterbury and York arose in 1432 in the parliament of Westminster.[3] This, as will be presently seen, is not accurate, for John Kemp was not created a cardinal until 18 December 1439. Duck based his account on Cardinal Dominicus Jacobazzi's *De Conciliis*. Jacobazzi wrote this inordinately long work

---

1. Engl. translation from the Latin, London, 1699, at p. 147.
2. The *D.N.B.* entry, *s.v.* Kemp, John, relies on Duck, and so do W. F. Hook, *Lives of the Archbishops of Canterbury* (London, 1867), v. 106-7, and Folkestone Williams, *Lives of the English Cardinals* (London, 1868), p. 115. On the other hand, Johannes Palatius, *Fasti cardinalium omnium* (Venice, 1703), ii. 226, though calling John Kemp a ' magnus theologus,' knows nothing of this dispute. Nor do Alph. Ciaconius and Aug. Oldoinus, *Vitae et res gestae PP.RR. et S.R.E. cardinalium* (Rome, 1677), ii. 902.
3. He links this up with the convocation of September 1432 : *Register of Henry Chichele*, ed. E. F. Jacob (Oxford, 1946), iii. 230 ff.

between 1512 and 1522,[4] and it seems that he was the first authority who mentioned the case and also rendered the letter of Eugenius IV *in toto*. He says that he has found[5]

> in quibusdam meis reportatis litteras papae Eugenii IIII directas super ista materia ad archiepiscopum Cantuariensem (de qua facta est mentio supra), pro qua consuluit Dominum Antonium de Capharellis. Erat enim controversia inter archiepiscopum praedictum, qui est legatus natus . . . et est metropolitanus Cantuariensis provinciae et primas regni Angliae, et inter cardinalem s. Balbinae in sedendo, in loco et in voto at aliis in parliamentis regni Angliae.

But it is not only English historiography which has taken so little notice of this case : there is no mention of the affair in any of the official records of the time.[6]

Unfortunately, Jacobazzi does not give the date of this letter, but merely has : ' Datum Florentiae etc.' This decree of Eugenius IV—*Non mediocri dolore*[7]—was given in abbreviated form by Raynaldus in his *Annales ecclesiastici* under the year 1439, but he amplified the dating by ' Datum Florentiae . . . pontificatus nostri anno VIII.'[8] Mansi corrected this date so as to read : ' pontificatus nostri anno IX.'[9] But even this emendation is in need of improvement. Furthermore, this letter also makes its appearance in all the editions of the *Bullarium Romanum*[10] as well as in the *Bullarium*

---

4. For details see J. Klotzner, *Kardinal Dominikus Jacobazzi und sein Konzilswerk* (in *Analecta Gregoriana*, xlv (1948)). He was as a young man professor of law at the University of Rome, and later for 40 years in the service of the curia and on two occasions a papal candidate : auditor of the Rota, then dean of the Rota, bishop of Nocera and *vicarius urbis* until created a cardinal in 1517. His tract has been printed several times : first edition, Rome, 1538, and last in Mansi, *Sacr. Conc. Coll.*, (ed. Paris, 1903), pp. 1-560. I quote from the edition in *Tractatus illustrium jurisconsultorum* (Venice, 1584), xiii-1, fo. 190 ff.

5. I. i, no. 251, fo. 203 va.

6. Neither the rolls of parliament nor the records of the Privy Council nor Beckington, contain the slightest hint of any altercation. To judge by these sources, there was never anything amiss between Chichele and Kemp.

7. The letter begins : ' Non mediocri dolore afficimur, cum inter fratres nostros episcopos seu alios ecclesiasticos dissidii aliquid exortum esse percipimus, tum propter malum quod inde in populis exemplum provenit, tum quia contemptus et detractionis praebet occasio.'

8. Raynaldus, *Ann. eccles.*, ed. A. Theiner (Bar-le-Duc, 1874), xxviii. 323.

9. Mansi in his editorial note *ad locum*.

10. That is, the *Magnum Bullarium Romanum*. I have consulted the following editions : Lyons (1592), i. 351-2, no. 15 ; Rome (1617), i. 282-4, no. 15 ; Lyons (1655), i. 351-3, no. 15 ; Luxembourg (1727), i. 332-4, no. 15. Cherubini's son, Flavius, treats of it in his *Compendium Bullarii*, (Rome, 1623), i. 58-9 and (Lyons, 1624), i. 105. Charles Cocquelines also has this letter : *Bullarium privilegiorum et diplomatum RR.PP.*, (Rome, 1743), iii. 21-4. Laertius Cherubini's first edition, *Bullarium sive collectio diversarum constitutionum*, (Rome, 1586), does not contain the letter, the probable reason being that this work has only bulls in the proper sense.

Taurinense.[11] But no entry has any dating which is fuller than that given by Raynaldus. It is therefore all the more regrettable that amongst the surviving Registers of Eugenius IV this letter is not traceable.[12] Although nobody has ever doubted the genuineness of this letter, it would have been highly convenient, if the original Register entry could have been produced, for it is justifiable to assume that because of its intrinsic importance this letter would have been enregistered. That by virtue of his status as dean of the Rota Cardinal Jacobazzi had access to the then still extant Registers is plausible ; it is equally plausible that Raynaldus as well as the editors of the *Bullaria* had actually copied from the Register. The fact that Eugenius IV resided at Florence from January 1439 until 7 March 1443 [13] is of little help to us in our attempt to fix the date of this papal decision.

Let us therefore turn to the *casus* itself. Jacobazzi says that the trouble between the two dignitaries arose in a parliament. Now the only parliament that comes into question is that which began its session on 12 November 1439 at Westminster and which was prorogued on 21 December 1439 to Reading for Hilary of the following year, 1440, because there was no time left before Christmas to transact the outstanding business.[14] Both Chichele and Kemp appeared in this parliament as triers of petitions, the former for England, Ireland, Wales and Scotland, the latter for Gascony and other parts of the kingdom. It is nevertheless worthy of note that in the parliament roll Cardinal Henry Beaufort, bishop of Winchester, preceded Chichele, designated as he was ' cardinal of England.'[15] Henry VI in his letter to Eugenius IV, written on 22 January 1440 from Shene, thanks the pope in warm terms for elevating Kemp.[16] Two days later, on 24 January, the king writing again to the pope, but this time from Reading, once more expresses his thanks for the promotion of Kemp (as well as for that of the archbishop of Rouen), and asks that both may be allowed to keep their preferments.[17] Finally, and still from Reading, Henry VI

11. *Bull. Taurinense*, (ed. Turin, 1860), v. 34-8.

12. I wish to record here my sincere thanks to the Prefect of the Vatican Archives, Msgr. Martino Giusti, who has taken infinite trouble to trace this letter, but unfortunately without success ; my thanks are also due to Msgr. M. Maccarrone and to Fr. L. Boyle, O.P., for their help in the Archives. About the still missing Register volumes of this pope, cf. *Cal. Papal Registers : Letters* (London, 1955), xiii-1, p. xiv.

13. C. Eubel, *Hierarchia Catholica* (Munster, 1914), ii. 7 n.4.

14. *Rot. Parl.* (18 Henry VI), v. 4, no. 11.

15. *Rot. Parl., ibid.*

16. *Official Correspondence of Thomas Bekynton*, ed. G. Williams (Rolls Ser., London, 1872), i. 38-9 : no. xxx.

17. Beckington, pp. 50-2 : no. xxxvi. The dating of this letter should be emended from 1439 to 1440, since the consistory in which Kemp was elevated, did not take place until 18 December 1439. The editor has noted the wrong dating of no. xxxi, pp. 39-41.

issued letters patent on 4 February 1440 in which he commends the new cardinal in most laudatory terms.[18] It is not unjustifiable to assume that this conflict between Chichele and Kemp started at the Reading session of parliament in the second half of January 1440.

It was not resolved in the summer of 1440. For we have independent evidence which also at the same time corroborates the statement of Jacobazzi. This evidence comes from the papal collector in England, Piero da Monte. He wrote from London two letters on the subject, one to the pope personally, and the other to the College of Cardinals, dated 1 August 1440. In both he gives vent to his indignation about the ' inaudita extollentia ' of Chichele, the latter's ' nova superbia ' who

> nimis profecto proterve atque impudenter contendere cepit, asserens sibi et ecclesie sue Cantuariensi priorem ac superiorem locum deberi, in prestandis quoque suffragiis tam in concilio regis quam alibi, cum de statu publico agitur, anteriorem sibi nititur vendicare.[19]

From this letter we also gather that Chichele had issued an official declaration publicly in which he presumably set forth the ' privileges ' of the see of Canterbury ; Piero da Monte enclosed a copy of this declaration.[20] It would be fascinating to know which privileges Chichele quoted here, but our curiosity must, for the time being, remain unsatisfied. In somewhat rhetorical language the collector refers to the ' non mediocris iniuria dignitatis quoque et auctoritatis lesio ac diminutio ' which Chichele had inflicted upon the College of Cardinals—no less than to the ' insolita perturbatio ' of the whole ecclesiastical hierarchy.[21] He suggests therefore ' ne parvus ignus ingens incendium esuscitet ' that stern measures be adopted

18. Beckington, pp. 41 ff., no. xxxii—Rymer, *Foedera* (ed. Hague, 1741), v-1, pp. 74-5.

19. The correspondence of the collector has been edited by the late Johannes Haller, *Piero da Monte : ein Gelehrter und päpstlicher Beamter des* 15. *Jahrhunderts* (Rome, 1941) ; the letter referred to is no. 150, pp. 168-9, written to the pope. He begins by saying that a new and unheard of affair touching the ' dignitas et majestas ' of the Roman Church had emerged which he is forced to report to the pope. Despite his respect for Chichele ' non desistam tamen ea sanctitati vestre nota facere, que in gravem apostolici throni offensam ipse (Chichele) nuperrime fecit. Is namque, nescio quo spiritu ductus, quo consilio fretus, de prioritate loci cum reverendissimo domino Eboracensi . . . contendere cepit. . . .'

20. ' Eam prioritatem ecclesie sue privilegiis sibi deberi pertinaciter affirmat, quod protestatio per ipsum publice facta, cuius exemplum cum his litteris sanctitati vestre mitto . . .'

21. ' Qualis autem et quantus sit in ecclesiastica ierarchia cardinalium ordo quamque supremo ecclesie capiti immediate coniunctus, atque ob eam rem quantus honor illi quantaque reverentia debeatur, supervacuum censeo sanctitati vestre scribere . . . facile enim fieri potest ut quod a tanto tamque honorabili membro ecclesie agitur, si impunitum relinquatur, trahatur a reliquis in exemplum. Scribendum itaque est quam acerbe eidem domino Cantuariensi mandandumque sub penarum comminatione, ut suis terminis contentus superiorum iura invadere nullo modo presumat . . .'

against Chichele, so that in future he may know that he cannot with impunity set aside the proper hierarchical ordering. In the same vein Piero da Monte addresses himself to the College of Cardinals to whom he reports that Chichele ' ausu temerario ' had damaged the dignity, status and authority ' sacri ordinis vestri ' ; and he encloses therefore a copy of his letter to the pope ' ut status vestri gloriam, excellentiam ac splendorem defendatis illumque a nemine maculari aut conculcari patiamini.' Piero certainly sensed the temper in the College of Cardinals correctly.[22]

These pieces of evidence would strongly warrant the assumption that the contest started in the Reading session of parliament in late January 1440 and was not yet over by 1 August 1440. The testimomy of Piero da Monte deserves all the more credibility as he was continually moving amongst the highest government circles[23] and it would of course have been senseless to write in the tone in which he did, if the case had already been decided. On the other hand, there is no warrant to assume that he was ignorant of the decision : he was not the man whose attention this kind of papal letter could have escaped for more than four months ; on the contrary, he was the man whose perspicacity little that concerned the curia had eluded. In other words, the dating of Eugenius's letter by Mansi, namely the ninth pontifical year, cannot easily be accepted. Eugenius became pope on 3 March 1431 and was enthroned on 11 March 1431. Hence the ninth pontifical year ended on 11 March 1440. Assuming that the journey from London to Florence took at least three weeks—a very conservative

22. This letter has not been edited by Haller and I think it would be worth while to print it, in view of the importance which the matter clearly has. MS. Vat. Lat. 2694, fo. 234 vb-235 ra : ' Sacro Collegio Reverendissimorum dominorum Cardinalium. De his que adversus statum, dignitatem et auctoritatem sacri ordinis vestri ausu temerario fieri sentio, reverendissimi patres et domini, mearum partium esse arbitratus sum, sacrum cetum vestrum facere certiorem ut eam erga sanctam Romanam ecclesiam vestrasque, reverendissimi domini, fidem, studium atque observantiam copiosius cognoscatis. Cum itaque pontifici maximo cuius principaliora membra estis cuique vestra quotidie consilia auxiliaque impenditis inauditam quandam superbiam et insolitam elationem temerariamque pre-eminentiam domini Cantuariensis contra honorem et dignitatem sacri ordinis vestri meis scribam, earum exemplum duxi pro mea erga vos, reverendissimi patres, reverentia eisdem transmittere, ut status vestri gloriam, excellentiam ac splendorem defendatis illumque a nemine maculari aut conculcari patiamini idque cum pontifice agatis, ut hi qui se minime cognoscentes in tantam labuntur dementiam tantamque elationem ut superiorum iura violare aut eorum lora violare contendant : debita coertione corrigentur atque composcantur, ita ut eorum exemplo eligant ceteri solide potius subsistere in se quam superbe et inaniter ferri supra se. Vestras, reverendissimi domini, feliciter custodiat altissimus quibus me humillime commendo. Ex Londoniis, Kal. sextilis, 1440.'

For a description of the MS., see Haller, op. cit., p. *109 f. It is an autograph of Piero da Monte, a very steady, appealing and neat Renaissance hand.

23. Cf. the excellent characterization of the man by Haller, pp. * 73 ff., although Haller may have underestimated the intellectual capabilities of Piero da Monte.

estimate in view of the winter months—and considering further that the pope had at this very time his hands full with many other and more pressing matters, it seems highly unlikely that the decision would have been reached within the remaining three weeks of the ninth pontifical year. Moreover, at no time was curial business distinguished by speed. But to these considerations comes also the following.

Apparently incensed not only by Kemp's elevation, but also by the latter's quick apprehension of the situation resulting in his claim for precedence, Chichele appointed a proctor in the curia in the person of Antonius de Capharellis. Clearly, Chichele was adamant and in a pugnacious frame of mind which is also demonstrated by the public declaration he had issued in England.[24] What great importance he in fact attached to the case, can be seen from his appointing Antonius de Capharellis, one of the most brilliant and successful advocates at the time—the Marshall Hall of the fifteenth century—known to be most vehement in the presentation of a case ; he is said to have had a very large and highly lucrative practice.[25] Now this proctor had to be briefed ; he had to prepare his case—and it is not to be assumed that de Capharellis was particularly familiar with the English situation—and the case had to be argued before the pope.[26] All these circumstances make it highly unlikely that the letter *Non mediocri dolore* could still have been issued in the ninth pontifical year : the report of Piero da Monte of 1 August 1440 is consequently additional reason for rejecting Mansi's emendation of the date, and for suggesting that the letter was written in Eugenius's tenth pontifical year, that is, between September 1440 and 11 March 1441. Lastly, when referring to the cardinalate of Henry Beaufort, the pope says in his decision that he had been a cardinal for 'fourteen years and more '[27] and hence if the decision in Chichele's case had been taken in the ninth pontifical year, the statement would obviously be wrong. Some arithmetical error cannot be excluded, but together with the other evidence this statement would indeed seem to be correct and support our suggestion of the decree being issued in the latter part of the tenth pontifical year.[28]

24. See Piero da Monte's statement supra at note 20.

25. In fact he spent so much time in making money that he left no legal writings. For all these details see Vespasiano da Bisticci, *The Vespasian Memoirs*, transl. W. George and E. Waters (London, 1926), p. 430. A search through the *Chartularium studii Bononiensis*, vol. xiii, yielded no results ; he may very well have graduated in some other University.

26. There is not the faintest record in Chichele's register about all this. Nor is the decision of the pope enregistered. Equally, there is nothing in the—as yet—unedited register of John Kemp as archbishop of York.

27. See the passage cited infra note 34. He was created a cardinal on 24 May 1426, see C. Eubel, ii. 6.

28. Cf. also infra note 71. In all this we shall of course bear in mind that the term *parliamentum* was not restricted to parliament in the technical sense, but comprised also any meeting or council of an official character.

II

WHAT precisely the pleadings of Chichele-de Capharellis were, is no longer possible to ascertain. One thing, however, is clear and that is that the ' ancient privileges' of Canterbury were not adduced as points of legal relevance, since the pope nowhere in his decision refers to any such privileges. Chichele's proctor was too good a jurist to make use of the ' privileges' in this case, because Kemp's rested on his being a cardinal : his claim to precedence had nothing to do with his function as archbishop of York, but solely with his being a member of the College of Cardinals. In this feature lies the fundamental difference in complexion between this conflict and earlier conflicts between Canterbury and York.

The only direct information about the arguments employed by de Capharellis comes from Jacobazzi. Dealing with the position of non-curial cardinals, he cites the arguments of Chichele's proctor who had claimed that this class of cardinals, by virtue of their non-residence in the curia, could not be put on the same level as curial cardinals. A cardinal bodily separated from the pope, was an anomaly and something like a fish out of water. His contention therefore was that the usual privileges enjoyed by cardinals were inapplicable to a non-curial cardinal.[29]

Indirectly, the letter of Eugenius IV permits us to gather some more arguments brought forward by de Capharellis. Although it never refers specifically to him, it is clear that some of the arguments dealt with could have had relevance only in this case. One of these was that an ecclesiastical dignitary partook in royally convoked assemblies as an incumbent of his own church, that is, not as a cardinal—a dignity unknown within a kingdom —but ' ut suae ecclesiae praelatus.' He coupled this with the assertion of a priority in time, and Chichele being prior in time as ' primas Angliae ' should therefore keep his precedence.[30] Another point made by the proctor

---

29. Jacobazzi, fo. 203, no. 246 : ' Hoc plurimis rationibus tenuit etiam solennis Doctor Dominus Antonius de Capharellis in quibusdam suis allegationibus a fortiori in primate Cantuariensi et in presbytero cardinali, tum ratione loci juris-dictionis, tum ratione separationis a praesentia papae eum illustrante, et ideo dicitur, quod cardinalis absens a curia est sicut piscis extra aquam.' Baldus in his *Commentaria ad Dig. Vet.* (*Dig.* 1. 16, Rubrica, ed. Venice, 1616, fo. 60), had this : ' Cardinales in curia sunt digniores quam extra.' It may be that the proctor relied on Baldus and applied the latter's statement that the non-curial cardinals were like the Gascons who recognized the English king only when he was in Gascony : Baldus, *Commentaria ad Decretales* (ed. Lyons, 1551), ad 1. 33. 1, no. 2, fo. 157 : ' Vascones dicunt, quod non subsunt regi Angliae, nisi ipso praesente.' Cf. also *idem, ibid.* ad 1. 5. 4, no. 4, fo. 73 : ' Cardinales residentes in curia aequiparantur stellis fixis, quae non moventur nisi motu orbis, sic cardinales non moventur nisi motu papae.'

30. ' Si quis forte objecerit prioris dignitatis potius esse rationem habendam quam cardinalatus de novo collati, cum in regiis tractatibus ac parliamentis quilibet ut suae ecclesiae praelatus, non ut cardinalis intersit . . .'

was that the claim was raised within the territory of Chichele's jurisdiction and that therefore the archiepiscopal position could not be overridden by a cardinal who had no rights in another's province ; hence setting out from his contention that no specific cardinalitian rights could be attributed to a non-curial cardinal, Kemp could only act as archbishop of York, and as such he was, within the province of Canterbury, no more than a private person.[31]   An argument that suggested itself was that Kemp had only been made a cardinal-priest and consequently, even if specific cardinalitian rights could flow from his being a non-curial cardinal (which he denied), Kemp was, as regards his clerical *ordo* definitely placed below the archbishop : it was clear that the episcopal *ordo* surpassed the priestly *ordo*,[32] and as a cardinal, Kemp was, so to speak, divested of his episcopal *ordo* and was given a mere priestly *ordo* in his capacity as a cardinal.

It will be seen that in so far as they can be reconstructed, de Capharellis's pleadings did not constitute a formidable array of arguments : in fact, they almost lent themselves to an easy refutation ; they offered many targets no longer defensible, and the pope had little difficulty in rendering them harmless and ineffective.   On the other hand, Chichele certainly was unfortunate in choosing his ground of complaint on the basis which he actually did.   Firstly, he never had any quarrel with Cardinal Beaufort, the bishop of Winchester, on this score and always yielded precedence to him. And Eugenius could probably not understand what made Chichele adopt this intransigeant attitude towards Kemp : it was, as he said in the letter, a *nova et insolita res*.[33]   In no uncertain terms Chichele is told that it would have been ' decentius ' to have consulted the pope in this matter before any

31. This was of course ancient doctrine and could be maintained only on the presupposition of the distinction between the two classes of cardinals.   Baldus had even declared (ad *Extra*. 1.6.42, *ed. cit.*, fo. 97 va) that a cardinal if he voluntarily left the papal residence was a deserter, though he had primarily in mind the schismatic cardinals in 1378 : ' Cardinales sunt de clero et in clero Romano . . . et qui sponte recedunt ab ea (scil. urbe) sunt quodammodo transfugae.' This was precisely the point raised by the decree of Innocent X in 1646 in which he called those cardinals leaving Rome, deserters, see *Bull. Rom.*, (ed. Luxembourg, 1727), v. 432, no. 15.

32. This, according to later writers, was indeed held long before the 15th century.   Cf., e.g., Augustinus Barbosa (1589-1649), *Juris ecclesiastici universi libri tres* (Lyons, 1718), i. 71, no. 24 who says that down to Alexander III, ' cardinalitia dignitas inferior haberetur episcopatu quocumque, exinde factum fuit, ut et honor cardinalitius admirabiliter fuerit auctus, et ad eum coeperint aspirare non episcopi tantum, sed etiam archiepiscopi.'   Cf. also Al. Guerra, *Pontificiarum constitutionum epitome* (Venice, 1772), i. 386, though referring this to Boniface VIII.

33. It is possible that the proctor had referred to Chichele yielding precedence to Beaufort, but he may have justified this by the latter's being the uncle of the king.   See the pope's statement in the following note.

trouble started.[34]   Secondly, for at least two generations the problem of
the cardinalate had been one of the most prominent topics discussed in
the literature, and the general tenor of this literature was to boost the
position of the cardinals enormously.   The decisive role played by the
cardinals in the events since 1378 had moreover brought their standing
into clear relief.[35]

It is nevertheless true that both literature and actions were exclusively
concerned with the relations between cardinals and pope ; in attempting
to clarify these relations the cardinals had constructed a veritable edifice of
specific cardinalitian rights and privileges.   The important point is, however,
that although these latter were set forth with a view to establishing a kind
of oligarchic form of government, they could nevertheless be made service-
able for the present dispute.   The case no doubt presented for this reason
considerable difficulties for the pope : on the one hand, on understandable
historical and canonical grounds, he could not very well tolerate Chichele's
high-handed manner, but on the other hand the papacy had so far not had
an opportunity to pronounce officially and authoritatively on the reasons
which raised the cardinalate above all other ecclesiastical functions.   There
was, to be sure, a formidable literature dealing with precisely these reasons ;
there were also explicit decrees by previous popes providing special penal
protection for the cardinals.   But there never had been an explicit and official
papal statement setting out the reasons why the cardinals were to be on a
level different from all other ecclesiastical dignitaries.   The case of Chichele
thus forced the papacy to declare itself.

34. ' Non parum audisse displicuit dissensionem illam quam cum dilecto filio
nostro Johanne, tit. s. Balbinae presbytero cardinali, nuper tua fraternitas habuit,
cum nova et insolita res ipsa sit, quae nunc attentatur.   In primis autem admiramur
satis cum per quatuordecim annos et amplius cum dilecto filio nostro Henrico,
s. Eusebii presbytero cardinali, in sedendo et in ferendis votis sine altercatione
vixeris, et nullam secum super hoc prorsus habueris disceptationem, quid causae
sit quod nunc primum in contentionem venias cum ipso Johanne cardinali, eadem
dignitate.   Nec quidem generis regii erga ipsum Henricum ratio praetendi potest,
quoniam et antequam cardinalatus ipsam foret dignitatem adeptus dumtaxat
existens Vintoniensis episcopus, et voce et loco tibi cedebat, postea autem quam
in cardinalatum per f.r. Martinum praedecessorem nostrum assumptus est, jure
tibi et aliis antepositus fuit, et nunc anteponitur.   Quod si sola cardinalatus dignitas
hanc in alio praelationem operata est, cur in isto id idem non efficietur, cum tamen
ipse archiepiscopus, ille episcopalem obtineat dignitatem, et illius ecclesia tuae sit
suffraganea, istius vero nullo jure subjecta . . . nolis in lite mota persistere, immo
apostolicae sedis stare judicio, cuius inter alia privilegia, quae manutenere et
defendere protestaris, hoc etiam est, ut de quibuscumque ambiguis quaestionibus,
quae in ecclesia Dei accidunt, valeat judicare et sua auctoritate finem imponere,
quamquam longe decentius fuisset ante motam controversiam sedem apostolicam
consulere.'

35. I think it is impossible to assume that Chichele could have hoped, as a
result of the recent steps taken by Eugenius IV, that the pope would make this a
test case against cardinalitian aspirations.

Now it would have been the easiest course for Eugenius to accept the arguments so vociferously broadcast during the tumultuous times of the Schism and afterwards, arguments that is which so severely limited the pope's government by aiming at an oligarchic form of government. But this was a course which Eugenius could never adopt. For, quite apart from every other consideration, it was Eugenius himself who had, so to speak, suffered from the concrete application of the cardinalitian arguments, namely the papal electoral pacts : in the conclave which elected him, he himself had entered into the pact [36] which as pope he promptly discarded and for which he cared nothing.[37] One of the arguments forming the doctrinal justification for concluding these electoral pacts (*Wahlkapitulationen*) was, however, that the cardinals were constituent parts of the Roman Church and the cardinalate was an institution decreed by divine law, and hence the pope could not set aside the divinely appointed members of the curia. He had to act in consonance and in agreement with them.[38]

Consequently, to adopt these views would have amounted to Eugenius not only denying himself, but also to his officially denying the monarchic role of the pope and endorsing an oligarchy. Considering the situation of the papacy in the year 1440, it was a serious dilemma in which Chichele had placed the pope. He extricated himself from the dilemma by most skilfully skirting the danger points, that is, by using the cardinalitian arguments not as proof for the divine origin of the cardinalate, but as mere illustrations. In brief, the biblical passages hitherto adduced were no reasons for asserting the divine ordination of the cardinalate, but were merely examples which showed that the institution of the cardinalate was somehow modelled on biblical instances. Nowhere does Eugenius speak of a *jus divinum cardinalatus* or says anything which would justify the conclusion that the cardinals had a pedigree in the Bible. Although he sometimes moves frightfully near the danger zone, the decree as it stands does not

---

36. See Raynaldus, *Ann. eccl.*, ad. 1431.

37. It is in our context not without significance that in his first pontifical year Eugenius issued the important bull *In eminenti sedis apostolicae specula* which dealt with the function of the College of Cardinals (26 October 1431).

38. I have dealt with these points in my paper, 'The legality of the papal electoral pacts' in *Ephemerides Juris Canonici*, xii (1956), 246 ff. In general, cf. P. Hinschius, *Kirchenrecht der Katholiken und Protestanten* (Berlin, 1869), i. 309 ff. ; J. B. Sägmüller, *Die Tätigkeit und Stellung der Cardinäle bis auf Bonifaz VIII* (Freiburg, 1896), pp. 165, 210 ff. ; V. Martin, *Les cardinaux et la curie* (Paris, 1930) ; B. Tierney, *Foundations of Conciliar Theory* (Cambridge, 1955). For the earlier history cf. S. Kuttner, 'Cardinalis : the history of a canonical concept,' in *Traditio*, iii (1945), 129 ff. ; for the emergence of the College of Cardinals in the 11th century cf. H. W. Klewitz, 'Die Entstehung des Kardinalskollegiums,' in *Sav. Z., Kan. Abt.*, xxv (1936), 115 ff. ; for the 14th and early 15th centuries see G. Mollat, 'Le sacré collège de Clément V à Eugène IV,' *Rev. d'hist. ecclés.*, xlvi (1951), 88 ff., although this letter to Chichele seems to have escaped Mollat's attention.

lend support to the cardinalitian thesis of a *jus divinum*. The well-known decretal of Innocent III had so often been quoted to show that the cardinalate had an Old Testament ancestry. Now Eugenius merely cites it, without drawing any conclusion from it ; and the manner of his citation leaves it completely open whether or no he adopted the cardinalitian interpretation of this decretal.[39] The other stock device of the cardinals to show the divine origin of the institution was to speak of themselves as the successors of the 70 elders. Here again, Eugenius refers to it as an example to be followed by the pope—'nam cum summus pontifex vices gerit Dei in terris, decuit quemadmodum Moysi praeceptum fuit, ut omnia ad exemplum faceret, sicut ei ostensum erat in monte'[40]—and it is certainly not without some interest to note that this same Old Testament passage was adduced by contemporaries to prove nothing more than the necessity of a division of labour in all strata of ecclesiastical officers.[41]

There is also the evidence of a negative character. Eugenius very much stresses the monarchical status of the pope, calls St. Peter's chair the *apostolicus thronus*, drives home the function of the Roman Church as *caput omnium ecclesiarum* (and hence also of Canterbury), but nowhere does he adopt the cardinalitian argument that the cardinals share the pope's plenitude of power—one of their most favourite themes ; nor does he refer to the cardinals as constituting the Roman Church ; [42] nor is there anything in the document which would allude to any corporational thesis ; nor to the other cherished cardinalitian argument with a 'democratic'

39. He says this : ' Immo, ut *inquit* Innocentius tertius, ex veteri testamento jussu Dei traxit originem (scil. cardinalatus). *Asserit* enim id, quod Deut. XVII dicitur, ut pro difficultate et ambiguitate judicii accedatur ad sacerdotes levitici generis . . . de summo pontifice intelligendum esse et fratribus eius, i.e. S.R.E. cardinalibus, qui ei jure levitico in executione sacerdotalis officii coadjutores existunt (*Extra* : 4.17.13). Itaque (!) et *ab exordio ecclesiae* sicut et hodie summis pontificibus in regenda gubernandaque universali ecclesia *assistebant*.'

40. Continuing : ' Quod ad instar illius coelestis hierarchiae in hac nostra ecclesia tres constituerentur ordines assistentium papae . . .' The first mentioning of Num. xi. 16 in this context seems to be in the spurious constitution of John VIII, *Constitutio de jure cardinalium* (Mansi, xvii. 247 B), about which see *Ephem. juris can.*, cit., at note 30 (with further literature and the reference to St. Bernard). But there are some substantial differences between this constitution and Eugenius's wording.

41. See the fifteenth-century chancellor of Oxford, Thomas Gascoigne, who applied Num. xi. 16 to the episcopal curia in order to establish the principle of a division of labour, *Loci e libro veritatum*, ed. J. E. Thorold Rogers (Oxford, 1881), p. 23.

42. A good contemporary illustration is the statement of Ludovicus Romanus Pontanus (cf. infra note 60) in his *Consilium* no. 498, no. 10, fo. 263 : 'Romanam ecclesiam constituunt papa et cardinales, ut ex se notum est (!), unde cardinalium collegium dicitur ipsius Romanae ecclesiae gremium . . .' For earlier statements to the same effect, cf. B. Tierney, *op. cit.*, pp. 42, 43, 80, 233-4, and *Ephem. iuris can.*, p. 273 n. 69 and p. 275 n. (Petrus Olivi).

flavour, namely that the College of Cardinals represented the whole Church, representing the *congregatio fidelium*. All the themes supporting an oligarchy are carefully omitted. In fact, far from partaking in the pope's government, the cardinals are merely assistants of the pope and it is this point which prompted Eugenius to illustrate it by referring to the Old Testament examples.

At the same time it is worth while pointing out that Eugenius with equally great skill avoids the anti-cardinalitian argument that the cardinalate was merely an institution of the positive human law.[43] Whilst thus not supporting the cardinalitian thesis of a divine origin nor the anti-cardinalitian theme of the cardinalate as an issue of positive canon law, Eugenius steers a middle course by emphasizing that the cardinalate originated in St. Peter himself. He does indeed adopt the argument that the cardinals were the successors of the Apostles, but he does this merely to show their function as assistants of Christ, whilst Christ was still on earth, whereas the bishops succeeded the Apostles after the Resurrection. In other words, he draws a parallel between himself as vicar of Christ and Christ Himself.[44] It is therefore of the greatest moment when Eugenius states that the office of the cardinals was *instituted* by St. Peter himself.

> Quippe etsi huius dignitatis nomen, quod modo in usu est, ab initio primitivae ecclesiae non ita expressum fuit, *officium* tamen ipsum *a*

43. This was the point made by Bishop Teodoro de Lelli and the eminent canonist Andreas de Barbatıa. About the former cf. J. B. Sägmüller, *Ein Traktat des Bischofs von Feltre und Treviso*, ed. in Suppl. vol. of *Römische Quartalschrift* (Rome, 1893); about the latter cf. the article cited supra note 38.

44. 'Decuit etiam, cum summus pontifex, qui Christi repraesentat personam, ut quemadmodum Christo conversanti in terris *assistebant apostoli*, ita etiam cardinalium coetus apostolicum (scil. coetum) repraesentans, coram papa assisteret, reliqui vero episcopi ubique diffusi apostolos repraesentant ad praedicandum per orbem missos.' This point of view is derived from Egidius Romanus who equally insisted on the cardinals as assistants in which function they were successors of the apostles during the life of Christ. See his *De Renuntiatione papae*, cap. xi, in I. T. Roccaberti, *Bibliotheca maxima pontificia* (Rome, 1698), ii. 33 B : ' Si quaeras, qui sunt illi in ecclesia, qui gerunt vices apostolorum ? Dicemus, quod cardinales et episcopi alii etiam, qui non sunt cardinales gerunt vices apostolorum, aliter tamen et aliter, quia apostoli et Christo astiterunt, et per diversas partes mundi fuerunt dispersi, quia unus apostolus accepit in sortem praedicationis suae hanc partem orbis et alii aliam partem orbis. Cardinales itaque qui assistunt papae gerunt vices apostolorum prout apostoli assistebant Christo, episcopi vero habentes curam secundum diversas partes orbis gerunt vices apostolorum, prout apostoli per diversas partes orbis fuerunt sparsi.' A similar point was made, apparently independently of Egidius, by Augustinus Triumphus in his *Summa de ecclesiastica potestate* (Rome, 1584) Qu. VIII, art. 4, pp. 70-1: 'Ipsi (cardinales) repraesentant personas apostolorum ut fuerunt assistentes . . . facti sunt enim episcopi ab eo post resurrectionem quando (Jo. xx. 22-3) dixit : " Accipite spiritum sanctum, quorum remiseritis peccata, remittuntur eis." '

beato Petro eiusque successoribus *institutum* evidenter invenies.[45]

This construction chosen by Eugenius is ingenious : it not only avoids the crucial problem of the divine origin of the cardinalate,[46] but also serves him as an instrument that enables him to clarify the nature of the cardinalate itself.

Anyone acquainted with the problem of the cardinalate will appreciate how much this problem was aggravated by the lack of any precise designation—did the cardinalate constitute an office or was it a mere dignity ? If it was the former, the immediately emerging question was, of what character was this office ? Furthermore, being an office, it must have been conferred and could consequently be taken away. If it was a mere dignity, the whole cluster of questions surrounding the problem itself, would in any case have made little sense ; apart from this, no special or tangible rights or privileges could follow from a mere dignity.[47] Or was the cardinalate a specific function connected with the *ordo* of the individual cardinal ?

To few papal documents dealing with constitutional questions can be attributed so fundamental an importance as to this letter of Eugenius IV. It authoritatively and officially pronounces the cardinalate to be an office, as distinct from a mere dignity, an office, moreover, which is entirely unrelated to the actual clerical *ordo* which the cardinal may or may not have. Furthermore, this office is of a jurisdictional nature. In itself this

45. There may well be an echo in this passage of the decree of 769 under Stephen III to which Eugenius himself refers, but there is again a great difference between the point which is to be established by this decree and that of Eugenius. He quotes it quite correctly : ' Ex concilio Stephani papae colligitur dicentis : Oportebat ut haec s. domina Romana ecclesia *juxta quod a b. Petro et eius successoribus institutum est*, rite ordinaretur . . .' For the decree itself see Mansi, xii. 719 B=Gratian, D. 79 c. 3 ; cf. also *Liber Pontificalis*, ed. L. Duchesne (Paris, 1886), i. 476 in the *Vita Stephani* : ' Nullus unquam praesumi laicorum . . . nisi per distinctos gradus ascendens diaconus aut presbyter cardinalis factus fuerit ad sacrum pontificatus honorem promoveri.' This view might possibly go back to the *Vita Cleti*, in *Lib. Pont.*, i. 122, cf. also editorial note 3, *ibid*. On this Roman Council of 769 cf. also S. Kuttner *art. cit.*, p. 149, and W. Ullmann, *The Growth of Papal Government* (London, 1955) pp. 87 f.

46. With this diction of Eugenius should be compared, for instance, the statement of Petrus d'Alliaco (Pierre d'Ailly) in his *Tractatus de ecclesiae . . . auctoritate*, i. 3 (ed. in Joh. Gerson, *Opera Omnia* (Antwerp, 1706), ii. col. 934) : ' Ex praemissis infertur, quod sicut status papae, sicut post eum, status cardinalium ad ordinem hierarchicum ecclesiae, *ex Christi institutione*, pertinet.' On him relies heavily Johannes de Turrecremata in his *Summa de ecclesia* (Venice, 1560), i. 80, fo. 82 : ' Est enim cardinalium status a Christo solo originaliter et primordialiter institutus.' Turrecremata was created a cardinal on the same day as John Kemp.

47. In parenthesis it may be remarked that Chichele's proctor had probably this in mind when he distinguished between curial and non-curial cardinals, the latter having merely a dignity.

372

papal *pronunciamento* is not so startling, because implicitly at any rate, though never explicitly, the papacy had held this view.[48] A correct reading of Alexander III's election decree—*Licet de vitanda*—can leave no doubt on the view of the papacy about the nature of the cardinalate. For alone of all medieval election procedures this decree enacts the numerical majority principle (two thirds majority) for papal elections, instead of the usual qualitative principle, that is, decision by the *pars sanior*. This quantitative majority in the election decree can satisfactorily be explained only by the electors being equals, that is, having the same function and offices. On this basis the qualitative principle could not of course have been invoked, as there was no difference between their offices. The decree of Alexander III was therefore a rather clear pointer.[49]

Eugenius considers this office as pertaining exclusively to the public-jurisdictional sphere. The cardinals' special jurisdictional power comes into play by their sitting in judgment—together with the pope—over all ecclesiastical officers, including patriarchs and archbishops, of the whole Christian world, whilst by virtue of their office they are subjected only

48. Thus *en passant* Innocent III speaks of himself before becoming pope as constituted *in minori officio*, *Extra*. 1.6.24; cf. also *Clem*. 3.16.1. Cf. furthermore Bartolus, *Commentaria ad Dig. Nov*. (Turin, 1577), ad *Dig*. 49, 1, § Si quis (fo. 207, no. 4): 'Similiter videmus in cardinalibus, qui non habent majorem dignitatem quam habent episcopi, sed *majus officium*.' Baldus ad *Extra* : 1.5.4, *ed. cit*., fo. 73, no. 1: 'Cardinalatus est officium, non ordo episcopalis.' But neither refers to any law or other writer. Later writers attributed this *theoretical* view exclusively to Bartolus (e.g., Barbosa, *loc. cit*. (supra note 32), p. 71 no. 25) or to Baldus (e.g., Prosper Fagnani (1588-1678), *Jus canonicum* (Rome, 1661), ii. 210, no. 65).

49. No other construction, I think, can explain the otherwise unintelligible papal election decree. As far as I can see, this rather essential point is overlooked in modern literature; cf., apart from Gierke and Esmein, some recent works : E. Ruffini-Avondo, 'Il principio maggioritario nella storia di diritto canonico,' in *Archivio giuridico*, xciii (1925), 15 ff.; N. Hilling, *Der Grundsatz der pars sanior bei kirchl. Wahlen* (Veröff. d. Görresges., fasc. 40, 1923), esp. 228 ff.; A. Petrani, 'Génèse de la majorité qualifiée,' in *Apollinaris*, xxx (1957), 430 ff.; L. Moulin, 'Sanior et major pars—Note sur l'évolution des techniques éléctorales . . .', in *Rev. hist. de droit francais et étranger*, xxxvi (1958), 368 ff. The same conclusion as regards the papal view of the cardinalate as an office, may be reached by a different route, that is, by considering the deposition of a cardinal. Deposition, by its very nature, can refer to an office or to a function only, and not to the *ordo*. I know of only two such depositions since 1059 and before the fifteenth century. Cardinal Hugh the White was deposed by Gregory VII who with his usual inimitable succinctness of language declared : 'Ugonem cardinalem tit. s. Clementis . . . ab omni sacerdotali *officio* privamus.' (*Reg*. v. 14a, no. 4, ed. E. Caspar, p. 369), whilst Boniface VIII's diction in his decree deposing the Colonna cardinals is not so succinct : 'Deposuimus Jacobum et Petrum a cardinalatibus eiusdem (Romanae) ecclesiae, et ab omni cardinalatus commodo et honore' (*Sext*. 5. 3. 1.). There is some resemblance in diction between this and the decree of Innocent IV, *ibid*., 2. 14. 1.

to the pope's jurisdiction.⁵⁰ Moreover, the jurisdiction of an archbishop over his province takes into account merely local interests—the *privata utilitas unius patriae*—whilst the jurisdiction of the cardinals is concerned with translating the dictates of the *publica utilitas* for the whole Christian people ; hence archiepiscopal jurisdiction relates to one church only ; the cardinals' jurisdiction to the whole Church.⁵¹

What however gives this document its special flavour and importance is the argumentation adopted by Eugenius in his consideration of the *potestas jurisdictionis* and the *potestas ordinis*. He brings into clear relief the relation between the two *potestates* and in so doing this document marks a very definite advance. We have just seen how he dealt with the apostolic succession of the cardinals and the bishops : the argument is quite clearly aimed at establishing the higher rank of the cardinals, even if they are not ordained, in comparison with the bishops. The important point is that from the governmental point of view—and it is this which always stood in the forefront of papal reasoning—it is not the clerical *ordo* that determines the standing of an ecclesiastical person, but his jurisdiction or his office. Nobody should say, Eugenius declares,

> quod ordo episcopalis presbytero major sit, quoniam in eiusmodi praelationibus *officium* ac dignitas sive *jurisdicto praeponderat ordini*.

The whole ecclesiastical organism, as far as public power is concerned, is fixed by the kind of jurisdiction conferred, and not by the *ordo*. Hence, the archdeacon, though not ordained, ranks higher than the archpriest—an old canonical principle⁵² which Eugenius applies to the cardinalate. It is a highly welcome application because it permits us to fathom the mind of the papacy on a crucial point. But most welcome perhaps is Eugenius's declaration that for the exercise of true governmental-jurisdictional power the consecration of the elected bishop is no presupposition.

> Sic et electus ad ecclesiam cathedralem et *confirmatus, quamquam nondum consecratus, ratione jurisdictionis* cunctis in sua diocesi praeeminet.

Here we have a very neat separation of the *potestas jurisdictionis* from the *postestas ordinis*. When we now in this context give due weight to the statements of Eugenius that it was from the Roman Church that all

---

50. ' Et cum a nemine nisi a solo papa judicentur, ipsi et patriarchas, archiepiscopos et reliquos ecclesiae gradus cum summo pontifice judicant.' This goes back to the late eleventh-century *Descriptio sanctuarii Lateranensis*, cf. the passage cited in *Papal Government, cit.*, p. 325 n. 2.

51. Who would not see, Eugenius asks, that the archbishop's jurisdiction ranks lower than that of a cardinal, ' quia illa privatae unius patriae praesit utilitati, ista publicae totius populi christiani, illa dumtaxat regit unam ecclesiam, ista cum sede apostolica universas.'

52. See *Extra.* 1.24.1. to which Eugenius makes no specific reference. The *gl. ord.* drily remarks, s.v. ' subesse' : ' in potestate et in ordine differt alter ab altero.' The pope says this after the passage in the preceding note : ' Quemadmodum jure cautum est, ut archidiaconus non presbyter suae jurisdictionis obtentu, archipresbytero praeferatur.'

ecclesiastical orders took their origin, that all patriarchates, archbishoprics, etc., had been instituted by the Roman Church, that it was the Roman Church which enlarged and restricted the scope of authority of individual office holders,[53] when in other words we properly appreciate this what for want of a better name may be called derivational thesis of organised Christian life,[54] we shall gain a better insight into the argumentation that underlies this letter. For the theme upon which this decision is based— and let us be clear once again that the views expressed in these statements were aired over 1000 years before—is the fundamental theme of the *potestas jurisdictionis* being transmitted downwards by the pope. It is the theme which not only makes accessible to proper understanding the concept of the vicariate of Christ—which is outside the scope of this essay[55]—but

53. Cf., e.g., this passage : ' Omnes patriarchales, archiepiscopales, episcopales cathedrales aliasque dignitates *Romana ecclesia fundavit*, sicutque licuit uni ecclesiae amplam, alii ampliorem et alii amplissimam prout expedire judicavit, *tradidit potestatem* . . . quis ergo jam dubitarit eum qui talia jura et canones condidit, et talem aliis *tribuit potestatem*, posse eandem, cum vult, et *majorem* suis membris *tribuere*? '

54. He continues : ' Omnes enim tamquam unius arboris rami ab una eademque radice et ut diversi aquarum rivuli ab eodem fonte prodierant, licet unus alio copiosior atque uberior.' This metaphor of a source and the rivers flowing from it (hence *de-rivare*) is one of the oldest themes in papal ecclesiology : cf., e.g., Innocent I, *Ep.* 29 (Migne, P.L., xx. 583 B) : ' velut de natali suo fonte ' all the other churches derived their power from the Roman Church. Almost the same words occur throughout the following centuries, cf. 900 years later the passage of Clement V cited in *Texte und Untersuchungen zur Gesch. d. altchristl. Literatur*, lxiv (1957), 161 n.1. It is on this derivational view that the concept of the Roman Church as *caput et mater* or as the *fundamentum totius christianitatis* is based. From the point of view of government, however, this thesis represents what I call for want of a better term the *descending* form of government : all power comes, metaphorically, from above and is distributed downwards, hence not only the intrinsic importance of the vicariate of Christ, but also of the axiom of the pope's being the transmitter of *gratia* (in the widest sense), manifesting itself, for instance, in the appellation of the bishop as 'Dei et *apostolicae sedis gratia* episcopus.' This is the theme underlying Eugenius's letter. Opposed to this view is the *ascending* form of government, according to which power resides with the people and rises upwards. The conciliarist (and partly also the cardinalitian) standpoint is only one practical application of this ascending theory. For some preliminary remarks cf. *Rev. d'hist. du droit*, xxvi (1958), 361 ff., and my forthcoming paper, ' De Bartoli sententia : concilium repraesentat mentem populi.'

55. Though the discerning reader will no doubt bear in mind that the conception of the pope as *vicarius Christi* had received particular attention and precision the year before this letter was written, namely at Florence, on 6 July 1439, in *Laetentur coeli*, where we read : ' Item diffinimus sanctam apostolicam sedem et Romanum pontificem in universum orbem tenere primatum, et ipsum pontificem Romanum successorem esse b. Petri, principis apostolorum, et verum Christi vicarium . . . et ipsi in b. Petro *pascendi, regendi ac gubernandi* universalem ecclesiam a Domino nostro Jesu Christo *plenam potestatem* traditam esse ' (Mansi, xxxi. 1031 E). With this may be compared Eugenius's phrasing supra note 53. H. Jedin, *Geschichte d. Konzils von Trient* (Freiburg, 1949), i. 14, rightly remarks that this definition became ' die Magna Charta der päpstlichen Restauration.'

which also explains why Eugenius is so emphatic, on the one hand, on the nature of the cardinalate as a jurisdictional office, and on the other hand on its having been instituted by St. Peter and his successors. For the papal view was that the *potestas jurisdictionis* resided solely in the pope[56] who according to his discretion and according to the exigencies of time, place and persons, hands part of it on to others. The *ordo*, on the other hand, was directly derived from Christ and could neither be modified nor enlarged nor restricted ; hence it was also of an indelible character.[57] Jurisdictional power, however, residing only in the pope, is flexible and capable of expansion and modification and, above all, is quite independent of the *ordo*. This view of the *potestas jurisdictionis*—which, seen from a different angle, is the same as the *plenitudo potestatis* of Leonine coinage[58]—had been simmering under the surface for a very long time with particular reference to the relations between the pope and the bishops. What Eugenius did was to apply this view of the *potestas jurisdictionis* to the cardinalate which enabled him not only to circumvent the vexatious *jus divinum cardinalium*,[59]

56. For an ingenious combination of the *potestas jurisdictionis* (=*plenitudo potestatis*, see further text) with the Joannine dictum (Jo. i. 16) cf. Innocent III : ' cuius (scil. Romanae ecclesiae) pastor ita suas aliis vices distribuit, ut caeteris vocatis in partem sollicitudinis (Leo I : *Ep.* 14, c. 1), *solus* retineat plenitudinem potestatis, ut *de ipso post Deum* alii dicere possint : " Et nos de plenitudine ipsius accepimus," ' (*Reg.* i. 320 : P.L. ccxiv. 286 C).

57. Hence Baldus ad *Extra*. 1.5.4, no. 2, *ed. cit.*, fo. 73, states quite clearly : ' Ex his patet, quod si cardinalis deponitur, quod non retinet dignitatem (i.e. the office), tamen retinet sacrum ordinem, qui erat impressus.'

58. And which represents the papal exegesis of Matt. xvi. 18 f., namely that the Petrine commission was wholly of a jurisdictional character constituting the only and exclusive link between heaven and earth ; hence the promise of the *claves regni coelorum* to St. Peter alone (cf. also the passage cited infra note 66) and the fulfilment of this promise in Jo. xxi. 15 f., which was bracketed with Ezek. xxxiv. 16 and 17 ; hence the continual emphasis on the nature of the papacy as primarily an institution concerned with jurisdiction, that is, government ; hence also, as Leo I had it as clearly as one might wish, the view that the other apostles had derived their jurisdictional power from St. Peter. For some details cf. the paper cited infra note 65.

59. Nevertheless, this unambiguous thesis of Eugenius was not always correctly understood by later writers ; on the contrary, he was invoked for the view that the cardinalate was an issue of divine law. Cf., e.g., Jacobus Cohellius, *Notitia cardinalatus* (Rome, 1563), cap. 1, p. 1 : he opens his discussion with Eugenius's letter and says that accordingly ' ab ipso Christo salvatore nostro institutum fuisse cardinalatus officium . . . (p. 2) satis probatum videtur cardinalatus officium originem ex jure divino, tam ex veteri, tam novo testamento . . .' ; cf. also cap. 8, p. 16. On the other hand, Lud. Thomassin, *Vetus et nova ecclesiae disciplina* (Venice, 1766), I. ii, cap. 114, p. 398, no. 1, strongly emphasized Eugenius's view on the Petrine origin of the cardinalate and says in this context ' de jurisdictione hic agi, non de ordine.' Rob. Bellarmin, *De controversiis* (ed. Naples, 1857), ii. 175, whilst pointing out the jurisdictional nature of the cardinalate (on the basis of Eugenius's letter), is silent on the divine or human origin of the cardinalate, and so is Muratori, *Antiquitates italicae medii aevi* (Milan, 1741), v. 155 f., Diss. 61.

376

but also to utilize in a most innocuous manner a number of cardinalitian arguments[60] which, so far, had been designed to buttress the oligarchic form of papal government.

He can therefore state, without fear of his statement being turned against him, that the cardinals are part of the pope's body : ' Partem sui corporis summi pontifices eos (scil. cardinales) appellant.' It may be recalled that the cardinalitian argument deduced therefrom the cardinals' share in the pope's plenitude of power, but when it is kept in mind that the cardinals' (jurisdictional) office is derived from the pope, the statement is perfectly harmless.[61] Equally, Eugenius can speak of the cardinals as the pope's *contigua membra*, who because they derived their very special status, function and office from the pope, are in a particular way protected by severe penal sanctions : an offence against a cardinal is an offence against the *apostolicus thronus* and hence constitutes the *crimen laesae majestatis*.[62] Moreover, this conception of the cardinalate as a jurisdictional office explains why the patriarchs are to be placed below the cardinals in rank. The significance of this is that Eugenius by tacitly setting aside the consequences drawn from the ancient papal view of the patriarchs being those bishops who occupied an episcopal chair founded by an apostle,[63] brings into relief the

60. The address given by Ludovicus Romanus Pontanus in commemoration of St. Thomas Aquinas before the Council of Basle, is a particularly good example for marshalling all the cardinalitian rights and arguments. The speech is printed in his *Consilia* (ed. Frankfurt, 1577), Appendix, fo. 286-8. He was a most determined opponent of Eugenius IV and the role he played at Basle is well known ; cf. *Concilium Basiliense*, v (1904) and vi (1926). He died in the summer of 1439 at Basle, having been at night suffocated in his room by smoke fumes ; see Diplovataccius's notice in J. F. Schulte, ii. 395 n.1.

61. It is so often overlooked that this, one of the stock arguments in favour of an oligarchic government, is derived from the Roman law. In a law of the Emperors Arcadius and Honorius dealing with the penal protection of the members of the Roman senate, they refer to the senate as *nostrum consistorium* and to the senators as forming part of our body : ' nam et ipsi pars corporis nostri sunt ' (*Cod. Just.*, 9.8.5). It was probably with this Roman law passage in mind that St. Peter Damian made his well-known statement about the cardinals forming the senate of the Roman Church, cf. *Papal Government*, p. 320 n.6 ; S. Kuttner, too, seems to have overlooked this probable genesis of Damian's passage (*art. cit.*, p. 174). His designation is still in use to-day. cf. *C.I.C.* c. 230 and Pius XII in *Acta Apost. Sedis*, xlvi (1954), 528.

62. Cf. already Honorius III : *Regesta Honorii III*, ed. P. Pressuti (Rome, 1895), no. 5726, printed in Raynaldus, *Ann. eccl., ed. cit.*, xx. 507-8 ; furthermore, *Sext.* 5.9.5.

63. See Nicholas I, *Ep.* 99, cap. 92, in *MGH. Epp.* vi. 596, lines 31 ff. : ' Veraciter illi habendi sunt patriarchae, qui sedes apostolicas per successiones pontificum optinent, id est, qui illis praesunt ecclesiis, quas apostoli instituisse probantur, Romanam videlicet et Alexandrinam et Antiochenam.'

jurisdictional position of the pope as vicar of Christ and consequently of him as dispenser of the *potestas jurisdictionis*.[64]

This decree of Eugenius IV reveals itself therefore as a document of first-class importance. He manages to avoid a most perilous position by applying on the one hand the principle that had been at work in the papacy itself, namely that the pope from the moment of his election assumed full jurisdictional power, quite irrespective of whether or not he was ordained or consecrated, that in other words what counted for the exercise of papal power was the jurisdictional office which the pope received from the moment of election,[65] and on the other hand the principle relating to the bishops that although their *potestas ordinis* was divinely derived, they none-theless had their *potestas jurisdictionis* conferred upon them by the pope.[66]

64. It is not therefore without reason that the *Annuario pontificio* (ed. 1958 at p. 35) sees in Eugenius's letter (here designated as a bull) the constitutional source for the precedence of the cardinals before the patriarchs.

65. Cf. the election decree of 1059, in *MGH. Const.*, i. 539, no. 382 ; and for the application of this view by Gregory VII see W. Ullmann, ' Romanus Pontifex indubitanter efficitur sanctus : D.P. 23 in retrospect and prospect,' in *Studi Gregoriani*, vi (1959), 229 ff. at 249 ff. About the early 14th century see M. J. Wilks, ' Papa est nomen jurisdictionis,' in *J. of Theol. Studies*, viii (1957), 71 ff., 256 ff., at 265 ff. For the current law see Pius X in *Vacante Sede*, of 26 Dec. 1904, no. 88: from the moment of election the candidate is ' verus papa ' and ' plenam absolutamque *jurisdictionem* supra totum orbem acquirit et exercere potest ' and if he is not ordained or consecrated, this shall be done, no. 90 ; the same in Pius XII's constitution, in *Acta Apost. Sedis*, xxxviii (1946), no. 100 and 107, pp. 97, 98. Cf. also *C.I.C.* c. 219.

66. This was, and still is, one of the trickiest ecclesiological problems. Although the weight of opinion, both amongst canonists and theologians (esp. Thomas Aquinas) was in favour of the episcopal derivation of the *potestas jurisdictionis* from the pope—because only in this way could the cancer of episcopalism be held in check—both the *Tridentinum* and the *Vaticanum* shirked an explicit statement. If I am not mistaken, this centuries-old problem has been somewhat unobtrusively settled by Pius XII in *Mystici Corporis* (in *Acta. Ap Sedis*, xxxv (1943), 211-2). Doctrinally perhaps the best statements come from Augustinus Triumphus who utilizes the metaphor of source and rivers as well as that of the tree and its branches (cf. Eugenius supra note 54) for the purpose of demonstrating that whilst the episcopal *ordo* is directly transmitted, the episcopal jurisdiction comes from the pope : ' auctoritas jurisdictionis non conceditur nisi per claves ecclesiae, sed claves ecclesiae Christus non concessit nisi Petro singulariter . . . derivata est in eis (episcopis) a Christo, *mediante papa*, quod patet tali ratione sicut se habent rivuli ad fontem, et radii ad solem, rami ad arborem, sic se habet potestas episcoporum ad potestatem papae . . . ergo potestas jurisdictionis episco-porum non est immediate a Christo, sed derivata in eis, mediante papa,' *ed. cit.*, I.i., pp. 2-3. For an excellent discussion cf. Wilks, *art. cit.*, 84 f. Hence juris-dictional power was quite independent of the *ordo* and a layman could be given ecclesiastical jurisdiction, cf. *ibid.* 259 (a good illustration of this in an earlier period is the conferment of legatine powers on King Roger I of Sicily by Urban II in 1098. This at one time hotly debated privilege (P.L. cli. 596) can only be explained by the possibility of conferring the *potestas jurisdictionis* on a layman,

It is superfluous to remark that it would have been neither advisable nor prudent nor expedient for Eugenius, under the conditions prevailing in the year 1440, to have gone further in his letter and to have specifically invited attention to this delicate and sore episcopal-papal relationship. The exquisite compositorial craftsmanship that characterizes this document shows itself perhaps best in the following statement which explicitly avoids any reference to a divine or human origin of the College of Cardinals, and yet drives home the crucial role of the Roman Church.[67]

> Itaque si justis ex causis et spiritus sancti instinctu quo hanc sedem regi credendum est, *Romana ecclesia* venerabilem *cardinalium coetum* ad coelestis hierarchiae similitudinem *conditum*, et tamquam sui corporis partem his privilegiis et honoribus illustrare *decrevit*, nec tua ecclesia cui *per* apostolicam sedem *praefectus* es, nec quisquam alius ecclesiae gradus ab eodem similiter apostolico throno *originaliter institutus*, quae omnia de ipsorum nostrorum fratrum consilio acta sunt, ullam succensendi aut conquerendi causam habeat.

The conclusion therefore is that the cardinals by virtue of their office have precedence over all other ecclesiastical officers, including patriarchs and metropolitans.[68] The pleas of Chichele's proctor could consequently be demolished with great facility. According to Eugenius there was no distinction—as there still is none—between curial and non-curial cardinals, because there is no distinction as regards their offices. The proctor's argument

so that he acts as a legate of the Roman Church in his kingdom. Of course, any action falling within the *potestas ordinis*, was excluded. It is strange that this explanation of Urban's step has not been offered before). Johannes de Turrecremata constructed the same theme largely on Leonine passages : *De pontificali . . . auctoritate* (Venice, 1563), fo. 16v. no. 22 : ' Ceteri apostoli non immediate a Christo jurisdictionem acceperunt, sed *mediante Petro*.' This view presented some practical difficulties, however, in regard to the doctrinal justification of the translation or deposition of a bishop by the pope : the bishop's *matrimonium* with his diocese was held (by the conciliarists) to be indissoluble, cf. the interesting case in Pontanus's *Consilium* no. 467, *ed. cit.*, fo. 250. Innocent III had anticipated the difficulty, cf. *Reg.* i. 336, P.L. *cit.*, 292 A-B.

67. Cf. also this : ' Et sicut tu vis, ut privilegiis ecclesiae tuae ab hac sede concessis, aliae deferant inferiores ecclesiae, ita eadem ratione par est, ut *ab eadem ecclesia huic coetu instituto* tu similiter deferas et reverentiam praestes.'

68. This, he asserts, is also shown in the seating arrangements in the present Council of Florence, and it could also be observed in the two Lyons councils, and all this ' nullo umquam contradicente.' But the one argument which I miss in this letter is the one current since Hostiensis (and also Johannes Andreae) that the cardinal priests and deacons do not need to take an oath of obedience to the pope (by virtue of their very special connexion with the Roman Church), whilst every ordinary bishop had to swear obedience and fidelity. The reason for this silence may be the consequence which the cardinals were wont to draw from their not taking this oath : because they considered themselves as constituent members of the Roman Church, this oath would have meant, so they argued, that they had taken it to themselves, which was a legal impossibility.

that Cardinal Kemp took part in parliament in his function as the archbishop of York, and not as a cardinal, could hold no water according to
Eugenius, because it is his duty and not only his right, to uphold the
privileges of the Roman Church.[69] With this falls also to the ground the
further point that Kemp is in the province of Canterbury a private person.
Lastly, the argument that Kemp was a mere cardinal-priest, whilst Chichele
was archbishop (and primate) made little impression upon Eugenius : if
this were correct, one could hardly say that a cardinal had been promoted,
but rather demoted when he assumed the status of a cardinal.[70] Chichele is
curtly told that he desist from pursuing this ' irrationalis causa ' which
could well lead to disturbances ' in quolibet rei publicae statu.' For the
universal Church would soon be thrown into chaos, Eugenius concludes
using the memorable declaration of Gregory I, though without acknowledging his source, ' nisi eam huiusmodi magnus differentiae ordo servaret
ecclesiasticus, quia confunderetur ordo, si cuique sua dignitas non
servaretur.'[71]

Symbolism is an excellent historical source for heuristic and inter-
pretative purposes. The conflict between Chichele and Kemp, though
outwardly concerned with ' mere' precedence, nevertheless in reality
went deeper than this merely external apparel. Admittedly, the ancient
rivalry between Canterbury and York may have supplied a special stimulus
and for this reason may blur an otherwise pretty clear issue. These questions
of precedence had considerable practical value in the great ecclesiastical
assemblies, such as General Councils, particularly in the order of seating,
and it is from this angle that Jacobazzi actually approached the problem
as to whether cardinals took precedence over patriarchs. This matter was
unequivocally decided by Eugenius IV. We are now in the fortunate
position to be able to call upon an exceptionally well informed witness,

---

69. ' Huic objectioni evidens respondet ratio, nam cum personae sint ecclesiasticae, sicut statuta et privilegia suarum ecclesiarum in his actibus servant, multo
magis Romanae ecclesiae, cui vinculo obedientiae astricti sunt, privilegia et statuta
servare tenentur. Quibus nec ipsae personae ecclesiasticae nec alii quicumque
tamquam inferiores derogare quomodolibet possunt.' And yet Dean Hook,
op. cit., v. 106, wrote that the claim of Kemp ' so far as the House of Lords was
concerned, was so preposterous that it was soon settled. A cardinal was a foreign
prince, but no foreigner could of right possess a seat in the English parliament.'

70. The pope, Eugenius says, ' non amplius sub nomine ecclesiarum, sed titulo
cardinalatus scribit (scil. cardinali) quasi (ad) majorem dignitatem et jurisdictionem
assumpserit, alioquin non ascendisse, sed descendisse, non honorari, sed dehonorari
viderentur.'

71. Gregory I in Reg. v. 59 (MGH. Epp., i. 371, lines 15f), repeated by
Gregory VII, cf. Papal Government, pp. 41, 289. In his letter to the pope Piero
da Monte had also borrowed from Gregory I (though not this passage), and there
are some other notable verbal similarities between his and Eugenius's letter, but I
think it would be somewhat hasty to conclude therefrom that the pope actually
borrowed from Piero, because so much of this terminology was common property.

380

namely the papal Master of Ceremonies at this very time, Augustinus Patricius Piccolomini. He informs us in his book on papal ceremonies composed by order of Innocent VIII (which had a somewhat adventurous history)[72] that whilst earlier the patriarchs were ranked with the kings amongst the cardinal-bishops—in alternating order—'nowadays and in the time of Eugenius IV they no longer sit amongst the cardinals nor is their train carried.'[73] The theoretical arguments employed by the pope in his letter to Chichele were immediately put into practice—and one of the surest means of so doing was to translate theory into symbolic reality.

There was another case which, though apparently quite independent of Chichele v. Kemp, nevertheless showed extraordinary kinship with it. This case concerns the Polish bishopric of Cracow and the archbishop of Gnesen.[74] The bishop of Cracow, Sbigneus Olesnicki, was created a

72. The dedicatory epistle to Innocent VIII of 1 March 1488 is in P.L., lxxviii. 1399-1402. The work was not destined for publication, but the archbishop of Corfu, Christopher Marcellus, through the services of a cardinal, obtained a copy of the work and published it under his own name and the title : *Rituum ecclesiasticorum sive sacrarum caeremoniarum s. Romanae ecclesiae libri tres*, at Venice, 1516. The papal Master of Ceremonies (Paris de Grassis) raged with fury at this gratuitous revelation of the secret and sacred ritual used in the Roman Church and considered the publication a ' contemptus apostolicae sedis ac pontificiae dignitatis ' ; he proposed burning of the book and of its plagiarist author. See his diary and letter to Leo X in P.L., *cit.*, cols. 1401-6. The work carried a flowery dedication to Leo X ; nevertheless it was the first book on papal ceremonies on which Piccolomini had worked for three years ' incredibili studio et exacta diligentia ' having filled ' plures annos magistratum caeremoniarum egregie et scite ' (col. 1404). For some remarks cf. also *Dict. d'archaéol. et de liturgie chrétienne*, *s.v.* Cérémonial, ii-2, 3296-7. I have used both the *editio princeps* and the edition, Venice, 1582, to which the folio references apply.

73. Fo. 195v under the title, *De ordine sedendi in capella papae* : ' Quatuor vero patriarchae principales, videlicet Constantinopolitanus, Alexandrinus, Antiochenus et Iersolomytanus, sedere consueverunt inter episcopos cardinales, ut supra diximus de regibus, et in curia Romana ferebant continuo cappam et faciebant sibi deferre caudas ut cardinales : nostris autem diebus et tempore Eugenii quarti papae, neque sedent inter cardinales neque portatur eis cauda.' Cf. also fo. 31v under the title, *De convivio solenni pontificis* : ' consueverunt antiqui ponere patriarchas quatuor ecclesiarum principalium inter episcopos cardinales mixtim, nostro tempore . . . ponuntur immediate post cardinales.' About the distinguished seating arrangement for the emperor (the pope's *filius specialis*) cf. fo. 195r ; it is interesting to note that the Eastern emperor—the ' imperator Graecorum '— was ranked amongst the kings. There was no change in the seating of kings who therefore kept their seats in the ranks of the cardinals—a highly instructive and illuminating symbolic arrangement in view of the cardinalate being a jurisdictional office. The importance of Eugenius's pontificate for these ceremonial matters seems recognized by Onuphrius Panvinius (1492-1568), *De episcopatibus . . . cardinalium liber* (Paris, 1609), pp. 36, 43 (his *De origine cardinalium* was not accessible to me). From the view that kings and cardinals were of equal standing, followed some practical consequences, cf. *South African Law Rev.*, iii (1956), 92 ff.

74. Both were founded by Otto III on the occasion of his Gnesen campaign, see Robert Holtzmann, *Geschichte d. sächsischen Kaiserzeit* (Munich, 1943), p.361.

cardinal in the same consistory as John Kemp,[75] but there was a slight complication, unconnected with the dispute he had with the archbishop of Gnesen, because he had the unique distinction of being also made a cardinal by the anti-pope, Felix V, four months later.[76] He appears somehow to have managed to accept both creations.[77] The archbishop of Gnesen, however, acted in exactly the same manner in which Chichele had acted, namely he refused to accord precedence to the newly created cardinal of Cracow. The case seems to have dragged on, for it was not until 1449 that the hat was sent to him by Nicholas V, the successor of Eugenius IV, who at the same time dispatched a letter, not to the archbishop of Gnesen, but to the barons of Poland.[78] Although he insists that in public royal assemblies the cardinal of Cracow must have precedence in rank,[79] Nicholas makes a small concession in so far as in the actual voting the archbishop could cast his vote before the cardinal, the reason being—in fact the very point which Chichele's proctor had unsuccessfully pleaded— that in these assemblies it was the church whose head he was that counted, and not the cardinalate which was a personal distinction.[80] It is likely that at least the contents of Eugenius's letter were known in Poland,[81] for

75. C. Eubel, *cit.*, ii. 8.

76. *Ibid.*, p. 9 : 12 April 1440; cf. also p. 383.

77. *Ibid.*, n. 4 History does not relate whether he actually made use of his amphibious cardinalate. Johannes Palatius (*supra* note 2) ii. 242, no. 30, says that for a time he became a neutral.

78. Raynaldus, *Ann. eccl.*, ad 1449, who renders the letter *in toto* : Licet dudum f.r. Eugenius papa, dated 28 July 1449. This letter is not in the *Bull. Rom.* For the case itself cf. also Johannes Palatius, *loc. cit.*, and L. D. d'Attichy, *Flores historiae sacri collegii cardinalium* (Paris, 1660), i. 146 ff., at 156. Thomassin (supra note 59), p. 399 no. III is incorrect when he says that it was Eugenius who had sent to the bishop of Cracow 'cardinalitium galerum.' For possible reasons of the delay cf. H. Zeissberg, *Die polnische Geschichtsschreibung des Mittelalters*, (Leipzig, 1873) pp. 201 ff., although he knows nothing about the dispute itself or of the letter sent by Nicholas through Jan Dlugosz (Johannes Olugosth as designated in the letter itself) ; nor does M. Schlauch, 'A Polish vernacular eulogy of Wycliff,' in *J. of Eccles. Hist.*, viii (1957), 53 ff., who though dealing with Sbigneus as a central figure in these very years, makes him not only the archbishop of Cracow (although her own extracts have him as a bishop), but also asserts that 'in order to obtain confirmation (*sic*) of his status as cardinal which had been delayed in Rome,' he may have ingratiated himself in the curia by exaggerating the danger of Polish heresies (p. 59) : a characteristic case of historical 'reconstruction.'

79. 'Volumus tamen, ut cardinalis propter sedis apostolicae auctoritatem et dignitatis suae excellentiam, primum locum honoris et sedendi teneat.'

80. 'Certificamus . . . ut in omnibus parliamentis et conventionibus privatis et publicis archiepiscopus Gnesensis prior votum suum et sententiam dicat, cardinalis vero eo loco votum suum pronuntiet, qui ex ordine ad ecclesiam suam spectat . . . infertur neque honor eius (archiepiscopi) in aliquo diminuitur, cum dignitas ipsa non ecclesiae Cracoviensi, sed personae cardinalis attribuatur.'

81. For the sometimes quite unexpected 'migration' of Western sources to Poland, cf. Jacub Sawicki, 'Die Entwicklung d. Kirchenrechtswissenschaft in Polen,' *Oesterr. Archiv. f. Kirchenrecht*, ix (1958), 243 ff. at 259.

382

although Nicholas did not mention it or make the point of a cardinal's precedence over a patriarch, the historian dealing with this dispute, the bishop of Ermland,[82] somewhat apprehensively states that 'they'—he does not reveal whom in point of fact he has in mind—want a cardinal priest and cardinal deacon to be superior even to a patriarch.[83] But the archbishop of Gnesen did not yield: on the very next occasion, in December 1449, upon seeing that the cardinal of Cracow entered the council chamber, the archbishop immediately rose and walked out 'ne principem locum amitteret.'[84] Although this meeting had to take place in his absence, the king, Casimir III, afterwards insisted on the instructions of the pope being carried out.[85]

In view of the fundamental importance of the letter of Eugenius IV it is not surprising that it became the *locus classicus* in all later discussions on the status of the cardinals ; it would only be tedious and unnecessary in the present context to enumerate the long list of popes and authors who quote the letter,[86] down to Phillips and Hinschius,[87] although it cannot be said

82. Martin Cromer was secretary of King Sigismund and prefect of the royal archives, later bishop of Ermland, took a prominent part in the Council of Trent and was virtually an official historian. He died in 1587. For details see A. Eichhorn, *Der ermländische Bischof Martin Cromer* (Mainz, 1868) ; also *Dict. théol. cath.*, iii. 2363-4.

83. *Id.*, *De origine et rebus gestis Polonorum* (Basle, 1558), lib. xxii, p. 510 : ' Volunt enim cardinalem etiam presbyterum et diaconum majorem esse dignatione quam episcopum, archiepiscopum atque etiam patriarcham.' He does not give his source of information. This statement follows immediately the one cited in the next note.

84. *Ibid.* : ' Decembri demum mense rex in Poloniam ad comitia Petricovensia (i.e., Petrikau) revertit, ubi magna exorta est inter proceres propter Sbigneum episcopum, cui a duobus pontificibus prius cardinali presbytero creato Nicolaus paulo ante insignia honoris miserat. Nam illo in senatum veniente, Wladislaus archiepiscopus, ne principem locum amitteret, cum omnibus majorum Polonorum proceribus . . . discessit.'

85. *Ibid.* It is not possible to say whether Chichele's absence from the parliament following Eugenius's decision, is to be explained on similar grounds. Cf. *Rot. Parl.*, v. 36, where only the ' cardinal of England ' and the ' cardinal and archbishop of York ' are named as triers of petitions. This parliament of Westminster lasted from 25 Jan. until 27 March 1442. On 10 April, for reasons of age and debility, Chichele asked the pope for leave to resign ; cf. also Henry VI's letter of 24 April supporting the application (Beckington, pp. 148-50, no. cvii).

86. For instance, Vincentius Petra (1662-1747) in his *Commentaria ad constitutiones apostolicas* (Venice, 1739), deals with it twice, once on John XV's *Cum conventus* (Mansi, xix. 169-72, of 3 February 993, which is the first papal canonization decree (St. Udalric)), i. 91 no. 25, where he couples it with the Gnesen case, and once *ad locum*, iv. 293-5 : ' Eugenius fortissimis argumentis perstringit Cantuariensem . . .' Or cf. Ant. Diana, *Coordinatus seu omnes resolutiones morales* (Lyons, 1667), ix. 373-5, who quoted the letter in full introducing it : ' Quia supradicta quoad amplitudinem cardinalitiae dignitatis mirifice confirmantur ex epistola Eugenii papae IV, visum est mihi per extensum apponere.' But he does not give his source. The dating is the same as in the *Bull. Rom.* and in Raynaldus.

87. And the *Dict. dr. can.*, ii. 1318 (by A. Molien).

that its interpretation has always been what its author intended it to be. That the jurisdictional complexion of the cardinalate was of vital constitutional significance, is in no need of further elaboration. Above all, this letter forms the *Grundgesetz* for the respective enactments in the modern canon law.[88] And in the recently promulgated code for the Oriental Church this letter is again treated as a fountain head of wisdom for the chapter on the Roman cardinals.[89] Though buried in historical obscurity, the conflict between Chichele and Kemp provided the occasion for a basic papal pronouncement which substantially contributed to the law valid to-day. The pontificate of Eugenius IV which, after disastrous decades, saw the reassertion of papal authority bear fruit, assumes in this much neglected topic also its true significance. His decision made explicit what had been only implicit : the cardinalate being an office of a jurisdictional nature, was therefore the effluence of the comprehensive papal *potestas jurisdictionis*, and in so far the decision, in its genetical assumptions and in its future influence, manifests once again the extraordinary continuity of ideas animating the substance of the papal government.

88. See the *Apparatus fontium* in the edition of the *C.I.C.* by Cardinal Gasparri (Rome, 1918), ad cc. 230, 231, 239.

89. See *Acta Apost. Sedis*, xlix (1957), 483 f. : cc. 175 ff. : *De S.R.E. cardinalibus*.

XIV

THOMAS BECKET'S MIRACULOUS OIL

THE legend of the Sainte Ampoulle, according to which an angel brought oil from heaven during the baptism of Chlovis, was at all times of immeasurable value to the French kings, because nobody else could boast of so eloquent a distinction as the *Rex christianissimus*.[1] It was not until the reign of Edward II that English kings realized the potentialities inherent in a heaven-sent oil and attempted to attain a similar distinction: in 1318 documentary 'evidence' was produced which was to prove that, whilst in exile, Thomas Becket was given by the Virgin Mary a golden eagle which contained a phial of heaven-sent oil for the consecration of English kings. The pope, when approached on the matter, considered it prudent not to pronounce upon the merits of the story submitted to him by Edward II.[2]

It does not seem that this miraculous oil played any role in the coronations that occurred in the fourteenth century. In 1399, however, Richard II seized upon the eagle and the phial which until then had had a rather checkered and insecure existence[3] and which he discovered in the Tower of London. He requested the archbishop of Canterbury, Thomas Arundel, to reanoint him with this miraculous oil, but the request met with a curt refusal by the archbishop: 'dicens sibi sufficere quod semel per manus suas sacram suscepit in coronatione pristina unctionem, quae habere non debuit iterationem'.[4] Nevertheless, it was in the same year 1399 that the miraculous oil first came to be used at the coronation of Henry IV, obviously to buttress the rather shaky claim of the new

[1] The French coronation *Ordo*, the so-called *Ordo* of Rheims of *c.* 1270, points this out: 'Qui solito [*amended to*: solus] inter universos reges terre hoc glorioso prefulget privilegio, ut oleo celitus misso singulariter inungatur', U. Chevalier, *Sacramentaire et Martyrologe de l'Abbaye de Saint-Remy* (Paris, 1900), p. 224; the edition of this *Ordo* occupies pp. 222–6.

[2] For the legend cp., *inter alia*, H. A. Wilson, 'The English Coronation Orders' in *J.T.S.* ii (1901), pp. 490, 501; A. Taylor, *Glory of Regality* (London, 1820), pp. 59–60, 348; Rupert Taylor, *The Political Prophecy in England* (New York, 1911), pp. 99–100; L. Wickham Legg, *Coronation Records* (London, 1901), p. xxxvii; P. E. Schramm, *History of the English Coronation* (Oxford, 1937), p. 131. The papal reply to Edward II is printed in Wickham Legg, op. cit., pp. 69–76, and the description by Thomas Becket of the delivery of the oil, ibid., pp. 169–71.

[3] See Thomas Walsingham, *Historia Anglicana*, ed. H. T. Riley (Rolls Series, London, 1864), ii. 239.

[4] Walsingham, op. cit., pp. 239–40.

king to the throne.[1] After this event, the miraculous oil as well as the eagle with the ampulla containing it, fade into obscurity, and nothing seems to have been heard of them any more. In fact, the foremost modern authority on medieval coronation symbolism, Percy Schramm, writes: 'The discovery [by Henry IV] does not seem to have made a great impression, for the *Ordines* make no mention of any special oil and no trace remained of this fresh attempt to secure recognition for this heaven-sent oil for England as well as for France.'[2] Wickham Legg, on the other hand, surmised that the use of the eagle as the proper container of the chrism was probably due to the efficacy of the Becket legend.[3] Evidence, however, has come to light recently which shows that the use of the eagle as well as of the miraculous oil was in fact authenticated in a copy of the *Liber Regalis* of the mid-fifteenth century.

It may be recalled that the *Liber Regalis* of the fourteenth century contains the medieval coronation service in its final form.[4] Since the king was anointed first on the head with the oil of the catechumens and afterwards with chrism in the same place, these two kinds of oil had to be supplied. Consequently, the *Liber Regalis* directs that the sacrist of Westminster should provide two phials, the one which is of silver, for the oil, the other which is to be of gilt, for the chrism.[5] The first docu-

---

[1] Walsingham, loc. cit.; H. A. Wilson, art. cit., locc. citt.; Schramm, op. cit., p. 137.

[2] Schramm, op. cit., p. 138. A. Taylor had said this: 'What was the practice afterwards [after Henry IV] with the vessels of the legend, we are not informed', op. cit., p. 349.

[3] Op. cit., p. xxxvii.

[4] Ed. Wickham Legg, op. cit., pp. 81–130. A useful historical introduction is in E. C. Ratcliff, *The Coronation Service of Her Majesty Queen Elizabeth II* (London & Cambridge, 1953), pp. 11 ff., and for the ceremonial directions of the *Liber Regalis*, ibid., pp. 67 ff. The historical account in R. M. Woolley, *Coronation Rites* (Cambridge, 1915), pp. 56–90, is not free from inaccuracies. The genealogy and filiation of the English coronation *Ordines* (on the basis of the available MS. material) are exhaustively treated by P. E. Schramm in *Archiv für Urkundenforschung*, xv (1938), pp. 305–91.

[5] Ed. cit., p. 93: 'Et prevideatur a sacrista quod ampulle tam de oleo quam de crismate, quarum una deaurata est et in se continens sanctum crisma, altera vero solum argentea et in se continens oleum sanctum, sint preparate.' For the three kinds of oil, cp. H. A. Wilson, *The Gelasian Sacramentary* (Oxford, 1894), no. xl, pp. 69 ff.; no. lxxii, pp. 114 f.; no. lxx, p. 113; L. Eisenhofer, *Grundriss der Liturgik* (Freiburg, 1950), 5th ed., pp. 130–1; J. A. Jungmann, *Der Gottesdienst der Kirche* (Innsbruck, 1955), p. 218. For the historical development of the three kinds of oil see Ph. Hofmeister, *Die heiligen Oele* (Würzburg, 1948), pp. 18 ff. This is not the place to go into the question whether chrism was introduced only for the coronation of Edward II in 1308 or whether chrism had always been used, in England at least, but so much seems certain that the *Anselm Ordo* of the twelfth century prescribes anointing on the head with chrism; see the rubric in MS. Trinity College, Cambridge, B. 11. 10, fol. 106[r],

mentary evidence of the use of the eagle—of which no mention is made in the *Liber Regalis*—appears in a writ of Henry VI issued on the day of his coronation, 6 November 1429: it directs that the 'golden eagle' together with the phial should be delivered to John Merston, the keeper of the royal jewellery, for safe custody.[1] It is certainly possible that the golden eagle here mentioned contained the phial with the miraculous oil.[2] This possibility becomes a virtual certainty through the evidence provided by the hitherto unknown copy of the *Liber Regalis* of the fifteenth century.

The public library of Evora, Portugal, possesses a manuscript of unique value and importance.[3] It contains a description of the royal chapel in Henry VI's time which is, as far as can be ascertained, the only account of the English royal chapel in medieval times.[4] Composed by William Say, the dean of the royal chapel and later dean of St. Paul's,[5] at the special and repeated request of Count Alvaro Vaz

on which a marginal gloss of the thirteenth century comments: 'Dicit tamen Innocentius III in titulo De sacra unctione, quod rex non debet inungi in capite, sed in brachio, humero vel armis.' Innocent III's ruling seems to have had little effect, cp. E. Eichmann in *Hist. Jahrbuch* (1925), p. 543. The great canonist of the thirteenth century, Hostiensis, in his *Summa* ad h. t., says that since this was a 'prisca consuetudo', it may continue.

[1] T. Rymer, *Foedera* (ed. Hague, 1740), iv. 4, p. 151: '*De ampulla benedicta.* Sexto die Novembris anno VIII apud Westmonasterium concordatum et concessum fuit, quod fuit warantum directum thesaurario et camerariis de scaccario, de liberando Johanni Merston, custodi jocalium domini regis, aquilam auream cum ampulla, qua reges consecrari solebant, ad eas salvo et secure ad opus regis custodiendas.' Although A. Taylor, op. cit., p. 382, had printed this, it does not seem to have been taken notice of by subsequent scholars.

[2] Cp. also Walsingham, loc. cit., p. 239: 'Hoc unguentum in aquila aurea et ampulla lapidea conservatum, latuit per multa tempora. . . .'

[3] Biblioteca pública e Arquivo distrital, Evora, MS. CV. The text in the volume takes up 37 folios; at the end of the volume there are 8 folios with miscellaneous notes scribbled in Portuguese. Fuller details will be given in the forthcoming edition.

[4] The first traceable papal confirmation of the immunities and liberties of the royal chapel is by Gregory IX, on 27 April 1236; see his *Register*, ii. 380, no. 3133. But this is only a confirmation; when the original grant was made, I have been unable to find, since the twelfth-century Registers have been lost.

[5] See R. Newcourt, *Repertorium ecclesiasticum parochiale Londinense* (London, 1708), i. 44, 167, 187, 221, 285. William Say died on 23 Nov. 1468. He came from Winchester and entered New College in 1427; he was proctor of his University in 1441 and in this capacity delivered 'an eloquent oration in Henry VI's presence at Oxford in praise of the two Universities', see *Thomas Bekynton's Correspondence*, ed. G. Williams (Rolls Series, London, 1872), i. 207, ii. 412. He was a pluralist of the usual kind; the last papal dispensation (for three otherwise incompatible benefices) seems to be that of Paul II of 8 April 1465, *Calendar Papal Letters*, xii. 426. He was also archdeacon of Northampton, privy councillor, master of St. Anthony's Hospital in London and rector of the Confraternity of Jesus, London.

d'Almada, a Portuguese nobleman who was created a knight of the Garter on 11 July 1445,[1] the volume is richly ornamented, obviously written by a court scribe and carefully corrected throughout. The count was apparently so impressed by the ceremonial he had observed at the court of Henry VI that he wished to have a concise account of it for his own king.[2] Indeed, the manuscript has all the appearances of having been written for royal perusal. The count himself was killed in the battle of Alfarobeia on 20 May 1449,[3] and it is of course possible that the king of Portugal never got to see the account which cannot have been written later than the year of Alvaro's death.[4] It contains, amongst other hitherto unknown details of the royal chapel, the coronation *Ordo* of the *Liber Regalis*, but with some significant additions concerning the participation of the members of the royal chapel, the actual music sung, and also the point relative to the miraculous oil. After the statement in the *Liber Regalis* about the two phials, the manuscript has a reference mark in the text to the bottom of the folio where the following entry will be found:[5]

Sic solebat antiquitus fieri. Modernis autem temporibus sacra aquila in qua continetur oleum miraculose inventum per sanctum Thomam Cantuariensem, quo presentes reges inunguntur, more processionali cum lumine a palatio regio ab aliquo episcopo pontificaliter induto per medium ecclesie ad summum altare honorifice defertur, cui venienti humiliter rex coronandus assurgit, et deinde cetera peraguntur ut supra.

The importance of this piece of evidence can be considered under three heads. Firstly, there is a striking resemblance between the procedure described here and the procedure adopted in the coronation of the French kings. The *Ordo* of Rheims, too, had laid down that the 'sacrosancta ampulla' was to be 'processionaliter cum crucibus et cereis'

---

[1] F. Menestrier, *Le Blason de la noblesse ou les preuves de noblesse de toutes les nations de l'Europe* (Paris, 1683), pp. 493, 503; *The Register of the Most Noble Order of the Garter*, ed. J. Anstis (London, 1734), i. 38–39; Rymer, *Foedera*, ed. cit. v. 1, pp. 146–7, where the royal decree will be found.

[2] The MS. begins: 'Forma sive ordinatio capelle illustrissimi et christianissimi principis Henrici sexti regis Anglie et Francie ac domini Hibernie, descripta serenissimo principi, Alfonso regi Portugalie illustri, per humilem servitorem suum, Willelmum Say, decanum capelle supradicte. Quoniam, illustrissime ac serenissime princeps, vir clarissimus Alvarus Alfonsi, vestre majestatis servitor humillimus, totam formam atque ordinationem capelle excellentissimi principis et christianissimi regis Anglie et Francie sibi per me etiam humilem servitorem vestrum describi jam sepius postulavit. . . .'

[3] See Visconde de Santarem, *Quadro elementar das relações políticas e diplomáticas de Portugal*, xiv (Paris, 1853), p. clv.

[4] That Say was dean of the royal chapel in this year is confirmed by the grant made to him in this capacity by the king, see *Calendar Patent Rolls* (27 Henry VI), p. 259.

[5] Fol. 18ʳ.

brought to the cathedral by the monks of St. Remigius; they handed it over outside the cathedral to the archbishop of Rheims who 'venit processionaliter more solito ad altare, cui venienti debet ibi astans rex assurgere reverenter'.[1] Secondly, in constrast to the *Liber Regalis*, there are no longer two anointings, one with oil and one with chrism, but only one with the miraculous oil, supposedly still more potent than chrism. The French kings, too, were anointed only once, with the heaven-sent oil. Thirdly, the eagle-shaped vessel is the only recognized container of the miraculous oil; in this one might possibly detect an advance upon the French pattern. Whilst the shape of the vessel, even if not the vessel itself,[2] has remained in use down to our own days, the miraculous oil of Thomas Becket was not destined to have so great a future. When it actually vanished one cannot say, although the possibility exists that it played some role as late as the coronations of Elizabeth I and James I.[3] The change effected in Henry VI's time was evidently a forerunner of the later ceremony of one unction instead of two as well as of the eagle-shaped container. It is a link, however tenuous, with the miraculous oil of Thomas Becket.

[1] See the directions in the *Ordo* of Rheims, ed. cit., p. 223, and compare their wording with our text which adopts the same terms; the last sentence could almost have come straight from the French *Ordo*. The only difference concerns the place of custody of the oil. At Rheims it was the monks of St. Remigius who kept it, hence it was they who took it to the cathedral; in England it was kept by the royal custodian of the jewellery, see Henry VI's writ, already quoted.

[2] In the Inventory of the Regalia made in 1606 there is recorded an 'Eagle of golde called the Ampull', see Wickham Legg, op. cit., p. 243.

[3] See especially H. A. Wilson, *J.T.S.* ii (1901), p. 501, note 4, and the evidence cited there.

XV

THE LEGAL VALIDITY OF THE PAPAL ELECTORAL PACTS

The utilization in 1059 of the existing organization of the Roman clergy, primarily for the purpose of creating an electoral machinery and secondarily for providing the pope with a permanent body of counsellors [1], was at the time a step that was, if not dictated, at least imperatively suggested by the governmental exigencies of the papacy itself. The creation of this electoral and senatorial body in which Cardinal Humbert was particularly instrumental [2], entailed no doubt disadvantages the full implications of which may not have been apparent to everyone at once. From the strictly constitutional point of view, the sole right and duty of the cardinals was the election of the future pontiff, but by virtue of the demands of a highly complicated governmental machinery they steadily assumed also the role, not indeed on a constitutional basis, but on that of a *de facto* practice, of papal advisers in the manifold questions affecting the pope as monarch of the body of the faithful [3]. This role the cardinals exercised in their more or less regular meetings with the pope : the consistory came to oust the local Roman synod and grew, so to speak, into the papal cabinet [4].

But the lack of a constitutional and legal arrangement concerning the mutual relationship between pope and cardinals should not conceal the fact that the cardinals took an ever increasing share in the pope's government, with the consequence that out of the papal need for an advisory body there grew on the other hand a custom that

---

[1] *Mon. Germ. Hist., Constitutiones*, i. no. 382, pp. 539-40.

[2] See A. Michel, « Humbert und Hildebrand bei Nikolaus II » in *Festschrift für* G. *Schreiber* (= *Hist. Jahrbuch*, lxii, 1953), pp. 143 ff.

[3] For further details cfr. W. Ullmann, *The Growth of Papal Government in the Middle Ages* (London, 1955), pp. 319-25, with further literature.

[4] For the Byzantine model of Constantine's *Sacrum Consistorium* see G. Ostrogorski, *Geschichte des byzantinischen Staates* (Leipzig, 1940), p. 20. The allegorical expression that the cardinals formed « pars corporis papae » originated with the imperial decree of Arcadius and Honorius (*Cod. Just.* IX. viii. 5) in which the Roman senators were said to be « pars corporis nostri (*scil.* imperatoris) ». Cfr. also ibid., XII. i. 8.

the cardinals be at least consulted on the major issues of papal policy. This virtually unchallenged participation of the cardinals in papal government was indeed the consequence of the multifarious demands made upon the nerve centre of the Christian body politic, but at the same time also accounted for the latent tension between pope and cardinals. Precisely because there was only a clear definition of cardinalitian rights and duties when there was no pope — that is, in the case of a papal vacancy — and because paradoxically enough there was no definition of their rights and duties vis-à-vis a reigning pope, a conflict between pope and cardinals was at all times a contingency. That the cardinals were anxious to turn the practice of participating in the pope's government into a constitutional right, fixed by a constitutional law, is, from their own point of view, understandable ; on the other hand, that the popes resisted the cardinalitian ambition, is equally understandable. The latent tension within the curia resolved itself into monarchy *versus* oligarchy. Had the cardinals' participation become one of right, it would severely have impinged upon, not only the concept of papal monarchy, but also upon the actuality of this monarchy. The problem was not consequently one of a mere constitutional character, but, more importantly, also one of a dogmatic nature. The most promising way to secure the cardinals' constitutional participation in Church government was on the occasion of the election of a new pope : the electing cardinals in their function as electors, could bind each other to agree on certain points in case one of them were elected pope and in this way they could impose quite formidable restrictions on the monarchic exercise of the papal government by the future pope.

Considering therefore — and leaving aside the details of the intervening period — the relations between popes and cardinals in the mid-thirteenth century [5], it is highly significant that Gregory X at the

---

[5] Cfr., *inter alia*, J. B. Sägmüller, *Die Stellung und Tätigkeit der Cardinäle bis Bonifaz VIII* (Freiburg, 1896) ; idem in *Theologische Quartalschrift*, lxxx (1898), pp. 596 ff. ; lxxxiii (1901), pp. 45 ff. ; lxxxviii (1906), pp. 595 ff. ; C. Wenck in *Göttinger Gelehrte Anzeigen.*, 1900, pp. 139-75 ; art. « Cardinal » in *Dict. Droit Canonique*, ii. 1310 ff. ; B. Sütterlin, *Die Politik Kaiser Friedrichs II. und die römischen Kardinäle* (Heidelberg, 1929) ; J. Lulvès, « Die Machtbestrebungen des Kardinalskollegiums gegenüber dem Papsttum » in *Mitteilungen des oesterr. Instituts für Geschichtsforschung*, xxxv (1914), pp. 455 ff. ; V. Martin, *Les cardinaux et la curie* (Paris, 1930) ; and so forth.

second Lyons Council promulgated *Ubi periculum* which exhaustively dealt with the procedure to be adopted in papal elections. What appears most symptomatic is that this decree was issued in a Council — « hoc sacro concilio approbante » — which might well indicate that the pope wished to exclude himself as the sole legislative agency and throw the burden upon the Council itself ; on the other hand, it may also not seem unreasonable to suggest that in view of the stipulations concerning the cardinals, any resistance on their part could be expected to be suppressed by the other members of the Council. The prohibition that the cardinals must not, on the occasion of an election, enter into any pacts, conventions, treaties, and so forth, and the declaration that such compacts are to be null and void, even if solemnly confirmed by oath, are no less significant, and bearing in mind the later development, this section of the decree reads like a prophetic anticipation of things to come. Although no evidence has emerged which would prove that already in the second half of the thirteenth century the cardinals had entered into such pacts during an election procedure, this possibility indeed cannot be entirely dismissed, if due regard is had to the concise and pregnant wording of the decree itself.

Nevertheless, there was still left a loophole. If the cardinals were forbidden to enter into binding obligations during an election, it might still be possible to say that, apart from this specific occasion, the college of cardinals could during a vacancy exercise that kind of legislative authority which was properly the pope's. Consequently, and in circumvention of *Ubi periculum*, the cardinals could have issued a decree in which their constitutional participation in the pope's government was laid down. At the turn of the thirteenth and fourteenth centuries and quite especially after the stormy pontificate of Boniface VIII there was noticeable particularly amongst cardinals who were professional canonists [6], the view that during a vacancy it was the college of cardinals that exercised papal jurisdiction. It was a view which could never become the law, however much it was propagated with an ingenious array of arguments, because Clement V in *Ne Romani* [7] unam-

---

[6] See especially B. Tierney, *The Foundations of Conciliar Theory* (Cambridge, 1955), pp. 150 ff. ; 184 f. The tract of Augustinus Triumphus *De potestate collegii mortuo papa* directly bears upon this question : ed. in R. Scholz, *Die Publizistik sur Zeit Philipps d. Schönen* (Stuttgart, 1903), pp. 501-8.

[7] About the origin of this decree see E. Müller, *Das Konzil von Vienne* : 1311-1312, *Seine Quellen und seine Geschichte* (in *Vorreformationsgeschichtliche Forschungen*, ed. H. Finke, vol. xii) (Münster, 1934), pp. 642 ff. ; about the views of Durantis, ibid., p. 596.

biguously and unequivocally declared that the college of cardinals did not exercise papal jurisdiction during a vacancy. Hence both avenues were barred to the cardinals if they wished to secure a constitutional foothold for participating in the pope's government — to turn, in other words, the papal monarchy into an aristocratic oligarchy.

When at Avignon the consistory acted constitutionally as the supreme court of appeal with the consequence that the important and high-level judicial business was transacted within this assembly of pope and cardinals, the latter's aspiration to have a share in the pope's government was considerably nearer to realization. There can, in fact, be little doubt that at Avignon the oligarchic tendencies of the college of cardinals were given a strong stimulus [8], in so far as the actual exercise of governmental functions, by virtue of the enormously increased scope and extent of government business, necessitated some form of « consultative » government, for which the consistory provided of course the readiest instrument [9].

It was in order to safeguard the oligarchic state of affairs and to perpetuate the oligarchic practice of government constitutionally, that on the occasion of the election of Innocent VI the cardinals drew up what became known as the first electoral pact (*Wahlkapitulation*), at any rate the first pact of this kind preserved. What is certainly noteworthy is that this pact is both in its letter and in its spirit a clear violation of *Ubi periculum* — the only explanation for its conclusion one may find is that the practice of government had, in

---

[8] A proper appraisal of the rise of the cardinals must take into account Clement IV's ruling that a cardinal-legate had ordinary jurisdiction : hence the death of the pope did not affect the legate's jurisdictional powers. See *Sextus* : I. xv. 2. According to canonistic doctrine only cardinals could be *legati de latere*, because they formed « part of the pope's body », therefore overrode the jurisdiction of the *legati nati* and were, of course, superior to the *nuntii*. Cfr. the Speculator, Guilelmus Durantis, *Speculum juris* (ed. Frankfurt, 1592), I. i. De Legato, § 3, n. 1, p. 30 concluding that « nec est credendum quod ipsi (scil. cardinales laterales) aliter judicent quam ipse dominus papa judicaturus esset ».

[9] For details cfr. G. Mollat, « Le sacré Collège de Clément V à Eugène IV » in *Revue d' Histoire Ecclésiastique*, xlvi (1951), pp. 80 ff. ; and cfr. p. 593 : « L'afflux des affaires soumises à la cour pontificale à la suite de la centralisation réalisée par les papes d' Avignon explique tout naturellement les innovations introduites. Les cardinaux eussent été submergés par la besogne qui leur aurait incombé ». The governmental ambitions of the cardinals at Avignon are only parallelled by their greed for material wealth, cfr. Mollat's exposition of their incomes, art. it., pp. 61 ff.

the opinion of the cardinals, already gone so long a way that it only needed a small step to turn this practice into law, in other words, to legalize it. It is significant that the very first stipulation concerns the creation of new cardinals : the future pope was not allowed under any circumstances to create cardinals unless their number had shrunk to 16 and that he was bound by the « counsel and consent » of at least a two-thirds majority of the cardinals [10]. Equally, the deposition and excommunication of a cardinal by the pope depended upon the consent of the whole college for its validity [11]. Other provisions of this electoral pact were that the pope could not alienate any territory or city situated in the papal state without the cardinals' consent ; that their right to half of all the papal revenues was established ; that the pope could not remit the tenths and the like without their consent and that the future pope promises not to impede the free deliberations of the college [12].

These stipulations are not so revolutionary as they may at first appear, for what they embody was the actual state of affairs as practised. For instance, their right to receive half of the papal income was given to them more than a generation before, by Nicholas IV and appears here merely as a confirmation ; the restrictive provision about

---

[10] See Raynaldus, *Annales ecclesiastici*, ed. A. Theiner (Bar-le-Duc, 1874), xxv. 540, ad annum 1352, n. 26 : « Deliberatione plena habita pro bono publico, concordant omnes domini cardinales, nemine discrepante. In primis quod summus pontifex, Domino providente, creandus, nullo unquam tempore ex quavis causa procedat ad creationem cardinalium nisi secundum modum et formam inferius denotatas, videlicet quod non creet seu faciat aliquos cardinales donec numerus cardinalium venerit ad numerum sexdecim cardinalium, aliis qui essent supra numerum sexdecim de medio jam sublatis ; et tunc assumat, si ei videbitur, tot quot ascendant ad plus usque ad numerum viginti et non ultra, praedictis sexdecim aut paucioribus, si forte tunc superessent, in viceno numero computatis. Quos quidem cardinales per papam creandos, ipse creare et ordinare habeat de omnium cardinalium tunc superexistentium seu duarum eorundem corsilio et consensu ». For a discussion of this pact cfr. Mollat, cit., pp. 99 ff.

[11] Raynaldus, ibid. : « Item quod papa non procedat ad depositionem seu personae captionem alicuius cardinalis sine corsilio et consensu omnium fratrum, nemine discrepante, nec ad excommunicationem vel aliam censuram ecclesiasticam, ad suspensionem vocis vel consistorii seu portationis capelli, nec ad privationem, nec ad suspensionem beneficiorum ipsorum cardinalium sine consensu omnium fratrum aut duarum partium eorundem. Item quod papa nullo modo ponat manum in bonis quorumcumque cardinalium, eis viventibus vel defunctis ».

[12] Raynaldus, *loc. cit.*

alienation and so forth was surely only the formal declaration of the existing practice. What may appear new was the pope's restriction of freedom to create new cardinals — how the Avignonese papacy proceeded before this conclave is not yet quite established, but it is certain that some informal consultation had taken place between pope and cardinals prior to the actual creation [13]. Nevertheless, as I have said, both in the letter and in the spirit of *Ubi periculum*, this pact presents itself as a violation of a clear legal enactment.

Although himself a party to this pact, Innocent VI declared it null and void in a bull — *Ad perpetuam rei memoriam* — issued on 30 June 1353. His reasons were of a formal and of a substantial nature. Formally, the promise was inoperative because it contradicted the decree of Gregory X (*Ubi periculum*). As to its substance Innocent VI had no difficulty in showing that adherence to this compact would entail a drastic reduction of the pope's monarchic powers — the pact « in diminutionem et praejudicium plenitudinis potestatis ex ore Dei collatae soli dumtaxat Romani pontifici dignoscitur procul dubio redundare » — since a divinely conferred plenitude of power was here limited « ab homine ». At the same time it was plainly insane to maintain that the Roman pope, the successor of St Peter and vicar of Christ, had not been called by Christ to exercise his full monarchic powers.

---

[13] The *Ordo Romanus XIV* (in Mabillon's numeration) composed by Cardinal Gaietano Stefaneschi at Avignon would bear out this assumption. See cap. cxvi (PL. lxxxviii. 1259): « Die Mercurii quatuor temporum dominus papa in consistorio consuevit quaerere a cardinalibus an expediat fieri creationem novorum cardinalium, faciendo ibi primitus aliqualem brevissimam collationem, quod expediat creare novos cardinales. Cardinales vero postea omres quilibet secundum ordirem suum consueverurt respondere et corsulere an expediat fieri vel non. Quo facto, dominus papa consuevit dicere: ' Nos sequimur consilium dicentium quod fiat ' vel ' non fiat ' .... et ubi eligit viam quod fiant immediate, interrogat cardinales de quanto numero videtur eis faciendum. Quo responso per eos ut supra, dominus papa dicit ' Nos sequimur consilium dicentium, quod fiant usque ad talem numerum '. Deinde ibidem dicit: ' Cogitabimus et cogitetis de personis nominandis, et die Veneris proxima agemus super iis Deo dante ». On the occasion of the actual creation and after having heard the proposals of the cardinals the pope says: « Deo gratias, nos habemus de personis concordiam omnium fratrum ». Cfr., furthermore, Mollat, art. cit., pp. 39 ff., and on the *Ordo* itself see M. Andrieu, *Le Pontifical Romain au Moyen Age* (Città del Vaticano, 1941), iii, 35 ff., and also W. Ullmann in *Journal of Ecclesiastical History*, vi (1955), pp. 26 ff. (here also further literature).

Accordingly, and after having had consulted with « some » cardinals
and jurists, the pope rescinded the whole compact [14].

It was indubitably due to the energetic and unambiguous language
of Innocent VI that no further electoral pacts were made in the following decades, that is, pacts which aimed at securing a « constitutional » basis for an oligarchic form of government. The electoral pacts
concluded during the Great Schism do not belong to this category [15],
as they were exclusively concerned with finding ways and means of
ending the Schism. Nevertheless, the pact concluded on the occasion
of Innocent VII's election (1404) caused some misgivings on his part,
if the report of Dietrich of Niem is correct [16], but the fundamental
question as to whether a pact of this kind was at all legally permissible, does not seem to have been ventilated [17]. Apart from this
it would be true to say, however, that the Great Schism itself was
perhaps the most important causative agent for bringing the problem
of the cardinalate so much to the fore, that it could almost be said
that they (and not the popes) dominated the scene. Through the adamant attitude of the rival popes and their quite obvious unwillingness to take any effective steps towards ending the Schism, the always
latent aspirations of the cardinals were given far more outlet than in
more normal circumstances. There is little doubt, equally, that at least
some cardinals were genuinely anxious in bringing to a close this tragedy — and the most readily accessible means of so doing was to bind

---

[14] The whole bull is printed in Raynaldus, *Ann eccles.*, cit., ad annum 1353,
n. 29 (ed. cit., pp. 561-2): *Sollicitudo pastoralis officii.*

[15] See also J. Lulvès, « Päpstliche Wahlkapitulationen » in *Quellen und Forschungen aus italienischen Archiven und Bibliotheken*, xii (1909), pp. 212 ff., at, p. 214.

[16] « At Innocentius per certos ambasiatores nonnullorum principum et per
quosdam suos curiales fecit fieri scrutinium ibidem in Viterbio, an dictam unionem
facere teneretur, ponens tunc in dubio quod, dum de electione ageretur in conclavi,
omnino expediri decebat ; ex quo contra Innocentium curialium non modica orie-
batur suspicio murmurantium invicem et dicentium, quod unionem revera facere
nollet .... » quoted from M. Souchon, *Die Papstwahlen in der Zeit des Grossen Schismas* (Braunschweig, 1898), i. 81 note 1.

[17] For some doubts on the part or the cardinals of Benedict XIII's adherence,
cfr. Souchon, *op. cit.*, i. 220 note 2. Petrus de Ancharano, the eminent canonist, gave
several *Consilia* on the obligation of the cardinals arising from these electoral pacts,
cfr. his *Consilia* (ed. Lyons, 1532), n. LXVI, fol. 115 vb-117rb ; n. CCLXXXI, fol.
24vb-25rb ; and see Souchon, *op. cit.*, ii. 241-56. Cfr. also Petrus de Ancharano's
gloss ad *Sextum* : *De regulis juris*, cap. 42 (ed. Bologna, 1583), pp. 605-7, n. 20.

the future pope by delineating his course of action, once elected. It should be pointed out that none of the electoral pacts concluded during the Schism referred to the model of 1352 which feature only goes to show how much these pacts were prompted by the unusual and quite unprecedented situation. What is remarkable is the acknowledgment by the Council of Constance that the pope was bound by his oath to implement the pact : in its 37th Session the Council condemned Benedict XIII as a *perjurus*, because he had failed to act in accordance with the oath he had taken [18].

This view expressed as it was by the most distinguished theologians and canonists assembled at Constance, throws a very significant light upon the prevailing mentality : it was, in oblivion of the explicit enactment in canon law, obviously taken for granted that the cardinals were legally entitled to limit the pope's monarchic powers by imposing upon him restrictions. In a word, Constance was loyal to itself, for this view was a manifestation of their own conciliarist theory. However much influence the wider conciliarist doctrines lost after the election of Martin V, the tension between pope and cardinals was not relieved. On the contrary, one might be tempted to say that by virtue of their close relationship with the popes during the recent schismatic times the appetite of the cardinals was whetted, and their aspirations received an invigorating lease of life.

Whilst at the election of Martin V, for understandable reasons, no opportunity had offered itself to draw up a compact, on the next occasion, in 1431, the college of cardinals, for the first time since the termination of the Schism, proceeded to lay down restrictions upon the pope to be elected, restrictions which went further than those of 1352, clearly the pattern for 1431. This pact demanded — in the fashion of the time — the « reformatio tam in capite quam in membris » through a General Council to be convoked by the pope and further prohibited that the pope moved the Roman curia without the consent of the cardinals ; the stipulations of 1352 were repeated in somewhat accentuated form [19]. That Eugenius IV cared nothing for this pact is well known : his attitude — as that of his successors Nicholas V and

---

[18] See von der Hardt, *Concilium Constantiense* (Frankfurt, 1699), iv. 1375 (the final condemnation of Benedict XIII) ; cfr. also ibid., pp. 970-1, 988.

[19] Printed in Raynaldus, *Ann. eccl.*, cit., ad 1431, nos. 5-7 ; cfr. L. Pastor, *Geschichte der Päpste*, 2nd ed. (Freiburg, 1891), i. 232 ; Lulvès, art. cit., p. 214.

Calixtus III — was that of the true papal monarch, and it was probably
due to this deliberate disregard of cardinalitian « rights » that the election of Pius II in 1458 was again preceded by a compact which reiterated
in sharper measure that of 1431, adding the duty of the pope to continue the war againts the Turks in accordance with the binding advice of the cardinals ; the financial stipulations of the earlier compacts
were tightened up — the pope had to pay any cardinal whose income fell
short of the 4000 ducates, a monthly stipend of 100 ducates until
the figure of 4000 was reached — and more so than before the papal
monarchy was purely nominal. In order to prevent an escape from the
obligations entered into, the elected candidate was to confirm the pact
immediately after his election and in his function as pope, before the
election was made public. Moreover, at least once year the assembled
college of cardinals was to examine how far the pope had adhered to
the pact, and if he was found wanting he was to be admonished three
times. What this really meant is not clear at all and was probably no
more than empty threat palpably revealing their constitutional weakness and in fact enabling the pope to disregard the compact safely [20].

In the immediately following conclave the cardinals agreed upon
still more stringent restrictions. But the pope who emerged, Paul II,
apparently troubled in his conscience about the obligatory character of the oath he had taken, took the way which seemed the only sensible one, that is, he consulted some eminent jurists. The reason why his
immediate predecessors had not taken this step may well be that canonistic scholarship did not on the whole favour the pure monarchic
position of the pope, and the fact that a pope did consult canonists,
would indicate that the tide was running in favour of the papal monarchy again [21].

The two authorities approached were Bishop Teodoro de' Lelli and
the canonist Andreas de Barbatia. The Bishop's tract, written in
1464, the year of Paul's election, has been edited by J. B. Sägmiiller [22] :
his conclusion was that these electoral pacts were devoid of all legal

---

[20] For details see Raynaldus, ad 1447, 1455.

[21]. For details see Raynaldus, ad 1464 ; furthermore, L. Pastor, *op. cit.*, ii. 8 f. ;
Lulvès art. cit., p. 215 f. ; H. Jedin, *Geschichte des Konzils von Trient* (Freiburg,
1949), i. 66. About the papal « restoration » see the excellent pages in Jedin, pp. 16 ff.

[22] J. B. Sägmüller, *Ein Traktat des Bischofs von Feltre und Treviso, Teodoro
de' Lelli*, ed. in Supplement Helft of *Römische Quartalschrift* (Rome, 1893).

validity. The opinion of the canonist, though sometimes referred to[23], has never been adequately examined : from the purely juristic point of view, Andreas de Barbatia's *Consilium* stands on a higher plane than that of Lelli ; it deserves all the greater attention as it clearly shows the change of opinion that was taking place at that time, for some 16 years earlier he had written a long tract *De praestantia cardinalium*, in which he warmly defended the rights of the cardinals against the popes ; in particular he maintained in this tract that all the *causae majores* or *arduae* (in accordance with the electoral pacts) have to be treated jointly by the pope and the cardinals, in other words, that in fundamental questions affecting the whole Christian body politic, the oligarchic form of government replaced the monarchic [24].

Andreas de Barbatia's argumentation appears firm and well knit together. His conclusion that these pacts display no validity is based upon a thorough knowledge of the law — not without reasons have his contemporaries styled him the *utriusque juris monarcha* — no less than on his mastery of juristic literature, and above all on a proper conception of the papal office itself. At the same time it should be said that his *Consilium* is indicative of that malaise from which all contemporary scholarship was suffering, namely the almost endless citation of authorities. Nevertheless, in agreeable contrast to other writings of the time, his *Consilium* shows the infiltraton of the « humanistic » trend manifesting itself in reference to, and quotations from, Cicero, Virgil, Lucan, and so forth [25].

One of the main contentions current at the time and lending a superficial force to the argument was that the cardinalate was an item of divine law [26], a theory that was particularly in vogue in the mid-

---

[23] L. Pastor, *op. cit.*, ii. 293 note 4 ; Lulvès, art. cit., p. 219 ; Jedin, *op. cit.*, i. 68.

[24] The tract is edited in *Tractatus universi juris* (Lyons, 1549), xiii. 349 ff. Some of his points have been treated by me in *South African Law Review*, iii (1956), ₚₚ. 92 ff. For biographical details of Andreas de Barbatia, a layman, see J. F. Schulte, *Geschichte der Quellen und Literatur des canonischen Rechts* (Stuttgart, 1877), ii. 306-7 ; A. van Hove, *Prolegomena ad Codicem Juris Canonici*, 2nd ed. (Mechlin-Roma, 1945), p. 500 (with further literature).

[25] I have used the edition of his *Consilia*, Venice, 1509, where the *Consilium* is the first printed occupying fol. 2ra-12vb.

[26] This point of view was very much propagated by Cardinal Johannes Monachus, see Sägmüller, *Cardinäle*, cit., pp. 211-15 ; Tierney, *op. cit.*, pp. 183 f.

dle of the fifteenth century through the influential writings of Cardinal Johannes de Torquemada [27]. Andreas de Barbatia would have none of this : according to him the cardinalate was wholly an item of positive-human law — « cardinalatus fuit inventus a jure positivo, ergo dicitur esse juris positivi » — for it was introduced by the papacy for some specific and well-defined purposes, although « now » the cardinals no longer fulfilled the role originally allotted to them. It is a historic fact that at the time of Constantine's Donation there were no cardinals at all, and it was only afterwards in a special synod that Pope Silvester himself created them [28], a point of view derived from one of the spurious Symmachan decrees [29]. This fact alone makes it evident that the cardinalate is an issue of human-positive law : « Ergo sequitur quod cardinalatus esse dicitur de jure positivo, ex quo fuit introductum de jure positivo ».

It might conceivably be objected that although the name of cardinal was introduced by positive law, the thing and the institution itself, the cardinals' power and office, were of divine origin ; and for this view some support might be derived from Innocent III's *Per Venerabilem*, in which the pope said that

> sunt autem sacerdotes Levitici generis fratres nostri, qui nobis jure Levitico in executione sacerdotalis officii coadjutores existunt [30],

---

[27] See his *Summa de Ecclesia* (ed. Venice, 1561), Lib. I, cap. 80-83, fols. 92-95v, where all the « reasons » for considering the cardinalate as an issue of divine law, are marshalled with his customary lucidity. It needs no longer to be stressed that most of the cardinalitian « rights » claimed, go back to canonists who were cardinals (Hostiensis, Johannes Monachus, Zabarella, etc.). Andreas de Barbatia is rather caustic about them : « quia erat cardinalis » ; or « non est credendum in eo, quia caro et sanguis sibi revelavit et non spiritus loquitur, et in causa sua non creditur », and many similar expressions.

[28] With a reference to Oldradus de Ponte's *Consilium* 62 Andreas says : « Tempore quo Constantinus fecit donationem beato Silvestro, non erant cardinales, sed postmodum congregavit sinodum universalem, ubi introducti fuerunt cardinales, II qu. IV, c. praesul (II. iv. 2) ».

[29] About the transmission see St. Kuttner, « Cardinalis : the history of a canonical concept » in *Traditio*, iii (1945), pp. 189 ff.

[30] *Extra* : IV. xvii. 13. For an allegedly similar view of John VIII cfr. G. Phillips, *Kirchenrecht* (Regensburg, 1864), vi. 68, 126, 256 ; Sägmüller, *Cardinäle*, pp. 5, 8, 212. The genuineness of this so-called *Constitutio de jure cardinalium* by John VIII has been impugned for the first time by Kuttner, art. cit., pp. 193-6, and with good

and it has been suggested that Innocent III had here in mind the cardinals. If this were correct, then indeed they would derive their « potestas et officium » from divine law, that is, from the Old Testament [31], no matter whether or not the name of cardinal actually occurred. Andreas de Barbatia, however, rightly objected to this interpretation, since Innocent III only spoke in this place of the bishops, and not of the cardinals [32]. The opposite view can only be maintained as a result of a wrong interpretation of this decretal. It has always been held that the term *fratres nostri* referred to bishops only, and not to cardinals, because the former, and not the latter, were the successors of the apostles, equals of St Peter and therefore of the pope, certainly with regard to the *potestas ordinis* [33]. The appellation *fratres nostri* can therefore only apply to the cardinal-bishops, themselves a minority compared with the cardinal-priests and cardinal-deacons who « non potuerunt succedere in locum sacerdotum Leviticorum », but whom the pope may well address as « fratres ex quadam benignitate apostolica » [34]. In any case, neither cardinal-bishop nor cardinalpriest or deacon would have the temerity of addressing the pope as brother [35]. Neither the

---

reasons. Whether Innocent III relied on this or on the similar expressions of Bernard cannot be decided. Cfr. St Bernard, *De consideratione*, IV. iv (PL. clxxxii. 778) :« Tuum est undecumque evocare et adsciscere tibi exemplo Moysi senes, non juvenes, quos tu nosti, quia senes populi sunt ».

[31] For Peter Damian's point of view, see Sägmüller, *op. cit.*, p. 211 and Tierney, *op. cit.*, p, 183 note 4, although it is not quite accurate to say, as virtually all medieval canonists (cfr., e. g., the Speculator in his *Speculum*, ed. cit., De Legato : « cardinales enim sunt sacerdotes Levitici generis ») and the two modern authorities do that Innocent III spoke of the cardinals as the successors of the Levitic priests ; cfr., furthermore, text ; G. Phillips, *op. cit.*, vi. 256 already doubted this interpretation.

[32] This whole argumentation might well have been directed against the letter of Eugenius IV to Archbishop Henry Chichele of Canterbury, see infra n. 70, ... but Andreas does not mention this papal communication and he refers in a rather guarded manner to this view : « Et si quispiam non levis auctoritatis doctor dixit, Amice, licet quoad nudum nomen cardinalatus fuerit introductus a jure positivo, tamen eorum potestas et officium sunt de jure divino, hoc decidit textus d. c. Per Ven., § rationibus .... » Cfr. with this diction that of Eugenius IV, infra n. 70.

[33] « Quinimo dico, quod loquitur (Innocentius) de episcopis, quod sic ostendo, nam illa verba ' fratres nostri ' potius congruunt episcopis quam cardinalibus ... secundo, fratres papae proprie sunt episcopi .... tertio, episcopi sunt equales papae quoad ordinem successorium, quia equales Petro quoad ordines ... pari consortio honorem et potestatem acceperunt ».

[34] Fol. 5rb.

[35] Fol. 7ra.

primitive church nor any decretal would lend support to the view that the cardinalate was of divine origin. Quite the contrary is true : just as the Roman senate was an issue of positive law, so was the senate of the cardinals, and since the cardinalate is a human institution, it is wrong to say « quod de jure papa teneatur adhibere in arduis consilium cardinalium » ; it would, on the other hand, be accurate to say « quod Romani pontifices possunt extinguere cardinalatum, quia eius est tollere, cuius est condere » [36]. There is consequently no need at all for the pope to consult the cardinals in any business : although they are styled « pars corporis papae », this too is merely the effluence of human law : « non ex dispositione juris divini aut veteris aut novi testamenti, sed ex dispositione juris positivi Romanorum pontificum » [37].

The same conclusion may be reached by a different route, that is, by the adequate appraisal of the pope's monarchic function. Andreas begins this section by the statement that « potestas papae est amplissima .... facit enim tribunal unum cum Jesu Christo » — how should one then assume that he should be bound by the advice of the cardinals ? There is no council whose decrees are not subject to the pope's veto — it is he who infuses binding power to conciliar decrees — a significant statement in the mid-fifteenth century — and how much more can this be applied to the college of cardinals :

> Ex quo infertur vera et indubitata conclusio quod cardinalatus receperit esse et subsistentiam a papa, non poterunt cardinales praefigere legem papae.

The Petrine commission, the true foundation of the papal monarchy, is all-embracing : « quia universaliter locutus est, nichil excepit (scil. Dominus) a jurisdictione Petri ». In his exposition Andreas relies to a large extent on Innocent IV' s commentary [38] when he declares that

---

[36] Fol. 5va.
[37] Fol. 6vb.
[38] Cfr. Innocent IV, *Commentaria super libros quinque decretalium* (ed. Frankfurt, 1570), ad *Extra* : III. xxxiv. 8, fol. 430, n. 4 : « Item ipse Petro et successoribus eius dedit claves regni coelorum et ei dixit, ' Quodcumque ligaveris .... ' Omnes autem fideles quam infideles oves sunt Christi per creationem, licet non sint de ovili ecclesiae, et sic per praedicta apparet, quod papa habet super omnes jurisdictionem et potestatem de jure, licet non de facto ».

Per illa verba « Quodcumque ligaveris .... » et « Pasce oves meas » Petrus et eius successores receperunt potestatem non solum super fidelibus, set etiam super infidelibus, juxta illud evangelicum Fiat unum ovile .... et sic papa omnia potest ut Deus excepto peccato.

This correctly understood monarchic position of the pope manifesting itself in his vicariate of Christ [39] and epitomized in the statement « unde omnia judicat et disponit prout sibi placet » excludes indeed any duty on the part of the pope to consult the cardinals. Both in the gospels [40] and in the Acts [41] St Peter appears as the chief of the apostles and the only one to whom jurisdictional power was given [42].

In his further argumentation Andreas de Barbatia falls back on the old allegorical description of the pope as the source (the *fons et origo*) of all Christian life : there are many branches of the tree, « set robur unum radice tenaci fundatur » ; there are many rays, « set unum lumen » ; there are many rivers, but only one source. « Unum tamen caput et una origo, una mater ecclesia copiosa fecunditatis » [43]. Hence,

---

[39] With a reference to Innocent III's « vicem non puri hominis, sed veri Dei gerens in terris », in *Extra* : I. vii. 3.

[40] Matt. xvi. 19 ; xvii. 26-7.

[41] Acts, xi. 71 ; xv. 7-11, etc.

[42] According to Andreas the « great sheet » (« linteum ») in Acts xi. 5 symbolizes the « mundus cum hominibus diversorum situum, et manducare et occidere non erat aliud in Petro quam perversos mores rescindere », whilst in Matt. xvii. 27 the « hook » (« hamus ») signifies the « jurisdictio qua Petrus praefuit aliis, quia hamo, i. e. ferro secantur carnes putridae ». Cfr. also St Ambrose in Gratian, XXIV. i. 8. That St Peter was the leading figure after the Ascension becomes quite clear from Acts xv : « Petrus habuit principatum inter ardua ». Just as St Peter did not consult with anyone on this occasion so the pope has no obligation to consult the cardinals (fol. 5vb). Although St Peter did not personally intervene in every church, he nevertheless exercised a supervisory function over all churches : « Petrus non poterat exercere personam suam personaliter in omni ecclesia, sicut hodie etiam papa non ministrat in omni ecclesia, tamen quoad universalem administrationem Petrus impedivit se de universis, ut apparet in conciliis factis tempore apostolorum » (foll. 12rb).

[43] This is also the theme of his contemporary Piero da Monte in his as yet inedited tract *Contra impugnantes sedis apostolicae auctoritatem*, which also clearly portrays the re-orientation towards, and restoration of, the traditional outlook. See MS Vat. Lat. 4145, fol. 22r : « Quis est autem, qui non videt radium a sole, ramum a radice a fonte rivum, a capite membra, influxum, motum ac vitam recipere ? ....

the Church as the one and indivisible body of Christians demands proper monarchic government for the sake of achieving the end of all its members and therefore unity.

> Cum ergo ecclesia unum corpus existat, oportet si ista unitas debeat servari, quod sit aliqua potestas regitiva respectu totius ecclesiae.

This is as true of the whole body of believers as it is of the exigencies of the Roman Church itself. It is the pope alone who creates the cardinals and it is the pope alone who is entitled to deprive them of their office [44]. Hence the restriction imposed upon the pope in the electoral pact concerning these points, is obviously devoid of any basis in law.

The monarchic position of the pope is in entire accordance with the position which Christ conferred upon Peter — « confirma fratres tuos et pasce oves meas, id est, loco mei » — so that the pope acts in the same way in which Christ wished Peter to act. The monarchy of the pope alone will ensure that unity of the *populus christianus* will come about, but the electoral pacts are the best means of preventing the exercise of the divinely conferred monarchy for the good of the whole Christian body politic.

> Sicut ergo in uno speciali populo Christiano requiritur unus episcopus, qui sit totius populi caput, ita in toto populo christiano requiritur, quod sit unum totius ecclesiae caput, ergo papa solus erit caput et solus reget ecclesiam, et non cum cardinalibus [45].

Non aliter inferiores praelati potestatis suae influxum a summo pontifice recipiunt .... ». Although he accepts that the cardinals are the « sacerdotes Levitici generis » (fol. 45r), he denies that they have jurisdictional powers, fol. 43r. On Piero da Monte, at one time papal collector in England and later Bishop of Brixen, see J. Haller, *Piero da Monte* (Rome, 1941) who would seem, however, to have greatly underestimated the capabilities of da Monte.

[44] Referring to Panormitanus, Andreas says: « Solus papa potest deponere cardinalem suis demeritis exigentibus .... ergo sequitur, quod papa potest creare cardinalem, cum solus potest illos deponere ».

[45] It should be noted that, contrary to some modern « interpreters » of medieval ecclesiological views, Andreas de Barbatia, like all medieval writers, equated the *populus christianus* with *ecclesia*. Their identity makes it impossible that a distinction could be drawn between the *ecclesia* on the one hand and the *populus christianus* or *christianitas* on the other hand. In this context the parallel between the *ecclesia*

XV

This monarchic government instituted by Christ may well be likened
to the kind of government which a king exercises : amongst a number
of ministers the king puts his particular trust in one through whom
he carries out his government, and in the same manner Christ wished
Peter to be His chief minister [46]. The pre-eminence of Peter must necessarily be conceived in jurisdictional terms, the evidence for which
lies not only in Matt. xvi. 19 and John xxi. 15, but also in Matt. xvii.
27 by which Christ in a singular way bestowed on St Peter jurisdictional powers — an interpretation of the passage which is at once unique and as far as can be seen new in canonistic literature [47]. The
only permissible conclusion to be drawn from the biblical evidence is that

> cum piissimus salvator noster Jesus Christus fecit opus per-
> fectissimum Petrum suum vicegerentem faciendo ita quod
> ad ipsum solum spectaret gerere vices Dei in terris, et non
> ad apostolos.

But according to the electoral pact it would be be possible, « uno
contradicente », to render nugatory any papal decision and in fact
vitiate the whole government of the *populus christianus*. If this view
were correct, it would amount to a denial of the continuously effective « merita beati Petri », for it is these which make the papal office
holder « sanctus » [48], and « reddunt Romanum pontificem perfectum

---

riumphans and the *ecclesia militans* suggested itself. Once more heavily leaning on
Innocent IV, our canonist declares that the former is to be the model for the latter,
and therefore the monarchic government of the former is reflected in the latter by
a single vicar of God, the pope : « Sicut in ecclesia triumphante est unus solus, cui
cuncta obediunt, ita in hac ecclesia militante debet esse unus solus vicarius Dei,
qui omnibus praesit » (fol. 9ra).

[46] « Sicut rex praeter particulares thesaurarios vult habere unum, cui magis
confidit super omnes thesaurarios et per cuius manum omnia transeunt .... sic et
Christus super ones thesaurarios suos regni coelorum voluit esse unum principem
et universalem thesaurarium, qui haberet plenam dispensationem totius thesauri, »
fol. 6rb.

[47] See supra n. 42.

[48] Cfr. Gregory VII in his *Dictatus Papae*, cap. 23 : « Romanus pontifex ....
meritis beati Petri indubitanter efficitur sanctus » (ed. E. Caspar, p. 270). Piero da
Monte wrote in a similar vein : « Summi itaque pontificis sententia et diffinitio in his,
quae fidem concernunt, errare nullatenus potest Deo propter continuam assistentiam
eum in errorem labi nequaquam permittente » (MS cit., fo. 25v).

et capacem ad regendum ecclesiam et gregem dominicum ». It would indeed be a « signum magnae imperfectionis » if the pope were bound by the advice of the cardinals. The recourse to such constitutional devices as the electoral pacts entails not only setting aside the efficacy of the « merita beati Petri » but also the very obvious distinction between the pope as a private and a public person. In his former capacity the pope is a mere « homo », perfectly capable of sinful conduct, but from this alone does not follow that he cannot, in his public function, « bene administrare papatum, quia possibile est, quod aliquis sit malus in se et peccabilis, et tamen in communi sit bonus et bene administrat ; concedo, quod papa potest peccare in quantum homo ». The reason advanced sometimes for the necessity of concluding these electoral pacts, namely that they were the only means of preventing misgovernment by the popes, must therefore be rejected, on general grounds. But this reason must also be rejected on the special ground that it would presuppose the application of the civilian principle which makes the heir responsible for the misdeeds of the deceased. This is quite inapplicable to the papacy, because no pope succeeds, in law, to another pope but succeeds St Peter directly : the pope « non habet jus ab illo predecessore mortuo ».

Nobody has ever included in the term « Roman pontiff » the cardinals, however much they may be spoken of as parts of the pope's body, because the Petrine commission was purely personal. Accordingly, as Johannes de Lignano put it, the pope has « quandam potestatem generalissimam » and is therefore rightly conceived as the « dominus orbis in spiritualibus et temporalibus » [49]. Within a correctly understood papal monarchy there is simply no room for a statutory and binding consultation of the cardinals by the pope. But apart from this dogmatic reflexion there is also one of positive law, that is, an *argumentum a minori ad majus*. For it is plain and admitted on all sides that the cardinals have no right whatsoever of disposing of papal revenvues : since even the financial administration of the papal *camera* is outside their competence, it follows with cogent reasons that the imposition of conditions upon the future pope's government is all the more outside their rights. Assuredly, « dignior est ipsa potestas et ipse magistratus Petri in universo orbis terrae quam sint redditus temporales (scil. camerae apostolicae) » [50].

---

[49] Referring also to Gratian, IX, iii. 17 and 21 ; *Dist.* xxi. 2.

[50] Fol. 8vb. He continues : « Si ergo non possunt disponere de minimis, ergo multo fortius de ipsa potestate et imperio beati Petri .... ».

It may be recalled that an influential body of canonists maintained the view according to which during a papal vacancy the college of cardinals exercised the jurisdictional power of the pope himself and therefore could issue a constitution restricting the future pope, as in fact the electoral pacts tried to do [51]. But this view cannot be reconciled with *Ne Romani* which excludes this very claim, and consequently a constitutional decree of this kind presupposes exactly this jurisdictional power which the cardinals do not possess [52].

> Coetus cardinalium vacante sede non potest facere constitutionem, quia concedere constitutionem est jurisdictionis.

Hence the electoral pact assuredly coming within the category of constitutional laws, is null and void — « cui ergo non competit jurisdictio non potest statuere .... coetus cardinalium non potuit facere illa capitula per modum constitutionis et per consequens sunt nullius efficaciae » [53]. As Baldus had declared, the imperial electors were not entitled to change the constitution of the empire during a vacancy, nor could they even together with the emperor alter the form of an imperial election for the future [54], so the same must hold good for

---

[51] See B. Tierney, *op. cit.*, p. 234 (Zabarella), and cfr. Baldus, *Infortiatum* (ed. Venice, 1615), fol. 29v, n. 3 (ad. Dig. 25. 5. 19 (Ubi absunt) : « Electio papae debet spectare ad patriarchas, si omnes cardinales sint mortui, Jacobus de Arena. Item est argumentum mortuo papa papalis jurisdictio est penes cardinales secundum Ubertum ». On Ubertus de Bobbio, a civilian, see J. F. Savigny, *Geschichte des römischen Rechts im Mittelalter* (Heidelberg, 1850), v. 143 ff. In the estimation of Johannes Andreae Ubertus « fecit opus ita confusum, quod particulariter difficile allegatur », see Johannes Andreae's *Additio* to the *Speculum juris*, ed. cit., Proemium, p. 4. For Augustinus Triumphus see *supra*, n. 6.

[52] This is actually the opinion of Johannes Andreae in his gloss ad *Clem.* I. iii. 2, s. v. « non consonam », attacking Hostiensis who gave clearest expression to the idea that the college of cardinals during a vacancy had « papal » powers : he operated with the analogy between a cathedral chapter in the case of an episcopal vacancy and the college of cardinals. Johannes Andreae, not unjustifiably, dubbed Hostiensis's view as an « absurditas », because taken to its logical conclusion, there was no need at all to elect a pope.

[53] Fol. 6va, Even if a practice such as this had grown up, it could never create any prescriptive rights, « quia esset prescribere contra supremam potestatem papae, contra quam non valet aliqua prescriptio ».

[54] With a reference to Baldus's commentary on *Licet de vitanda*, Andreas says : « Sicut electores imperii simul cum ipso imperatore non possunt mutare formam electionis futuri imperatoris, ita non possunt cardinales facere talem ordinationem », fol. 8vb.

the pope, and therefore « remanebimus sub regula prohibitiva, ut cardinales non possint onerare futurum papam ». The cardinals' sole right and duty is to elect a pope, and whatever is outside this task of theirs, has no foundation in law : « Quicquid agunt extra vel praeter electionis actum, est ipso jure nullum .... non potuerunt facere illam ordinationem, quia habent legem resistentem ».

History also proves that popes had transacted the most difficult governmental business without even having had a body of cardinals at their side ; the case which came readily to Andreas's mind was that of Childeric's deposition by Pope Zacharias. In actual fact, the Church was well governed before there ware any cardinals [55]. Of course, this does not exclude that the pope voluntarily consults the cardinals : the canon law itself (*Extra* : I. vi. 17) says as much, but to deduce therefrom or from the employment of the phrase in decretals *De consilio fratrum nostrorum* a papal duty, is quite a different matter : what this phrase simply designated was that a consultation had taken place, not that it was bound to take place. « Ponitur in potestate papae et voluntate, si velit petere eorum consilia ». According to Albericus de Rosciate this phrase « magis emanavit de honestate quam de necessitate » [56].

---

[55] « Antequam essent cardinales introducti in ecclesia Dei, papa erat, et ecclesia Dei bene et beate regebatur et gubernabatur » (fol. 11ra). The phrasing of this idea is strangely reminiscent of the famous French pamphlet of the early 14th century : « Antequam essent clerici, rex erat .... ».

[56] See Albericus de Rosciate, *Super Codice* (ed. Lyons, 1545), *Rubrica* : *De legibus et constitutionibus*, fol. 46v, n. 3 : « Utrum papa sine cardinalibus possit leges sive decretales facere ? Laurentius tenuit quod non generales, pro hoc infra eod., Humanum (*Cod.* I. v. 9). Communis opinio est in contrarium, et etiam de facto videtur. De hoc notatur per Archidiaconum, XXV Qu. I, Quae ad perpetuam (XXV. i. 3) et cap. Sunt quaedam (ibid., c. 6), et De officio ordinarii, c. Quamvis, libro VIo (*Sextus* : I. xvi. 8). Unde illa clausula ' De fratrum nostrorum consilio ' magis videtur decentiae quam necessitatis ». Cfr. the Archdeacon (Guido de Baysio), *Super Sexto* (ed. Venice, 1534), ad I. xvi. 8, fol. 51v, n. 1 « Saepius vidi in curia quaeri, quid operentur ista verba D. f. n. c. Dici potest, quod sunt ad bonam ordinationem papae, qui habet uti consilio potissime fratrum, unde in multis juribus antiquis et novis dicitur ' Habito fratrum nostrorum consilio', sed non quantum ad necessitatem .... sed potissime in magnis negotiis tali debet uti consilio, cum alios inferiores velit ita facere ». The accent seems to lie on the last clause. Baldus, *Super Codice* (ed. cit.), ad VI. lxi. 7, had maintained that not only *consilium*, but *consensus* of the cardinals seems to be necessary, if the pope wished to carry out an infeudation, for which opinion he was stigmatized by Andreas de Barbatia as a

The latest electoral pact goes even so far as to say that the advice of the cardinals must be unanimous — « istud est durissimum auditu et dictu » — a proposition which puts the pope on an infinitely lower level than any bishop or abbot, because the latter's chapters at least work on the majority principle. This stipulation is therefore « contra omnem juris censuram » and in itself deprives the pact of its validity. The implementation of the pact would simply mean that the pope was not pope at all, at least as far as its stipulations go [57]. Moreover, compared with the imperial government, the papal government would be hamstrung to an extent to which no emperor had ever consented, for according to the imperial constitution the emperor is in no need to consult his barons and dukes — but the pope is supposed to be bound by the veto of one cardinal : this proposition once again shows the dogmatically and legally ill-conceived nature of the electoral pacts. Due weight should also be given to the bad example which this sort of pseudo-constitutional law may set for others : once accepted in the nerve-centre of Christendom as a regular procedure, there is nothing to prevent other churches and secular governments from adopting the same device, with the consequence that all orderly government would soon come to an end [58] — a reflexion which certainly had a realistic ring — but the public interest demands proper monarchic government : « sed publica utilitas est, ut ecclesia regatur per unicum monarcham, et non per plures ».

One can go further and say that even if the pope wished a curtailment of his powers, this wish could not be respected. For a design of this kind tends to be to the detriment of the Church as whole and of the apostolic see in particular — « papa non potest consentire in id,

---

« peregrinus », because « istud esse videtur singulare mendacium, quia in nullo jure censura reperietur illud verbum De fratrum nostrorum consensu, sed bene dicitur ' de consilio ' ». (fol. 10va).

[57] « Quinimo plus videtur quod non videtur esse papa quoad omnia, nam quoad illa XL capitula videtur quod non habeat potestatem liberam, quom consuetum est Romanum pontificem habere » (fol. 9va, referring to a similar point of view of Johannes ab Imola).

[58] « Praeterea ponderetur accurate, quia dicta ordinatio videtur cedere potius ad deterius quam ad bonum, quia ex juris dispositione domini cardinales teneantur facere provisionem utilem et valde necessariam toti mundo providendo de sponso ecclesiae idoneo .... quia ecclesia Romana est speculum omnium .... videtur, quod sit causa pessimi exempli ut aliae ecclesiae sic faciant, ut regna et regnicoli suis futuris regibus conveniant et gravent et onerent suos futuros dominos » (fol. 8va).

quod tendit ad opprobrium sedis apostolicae, quia videtur irrogare injuriam piissimo nostro salvatori, cuius est vicarius » — because it would be tantamount to a breach of trust, just as no cleric can consent to be tried by a secular court, and for the same reason : « Unde papa non potest renuntiare illi privilegio .... cum principaliter non concernat utilitatem suam, sed Dei et ecclesiae » [59]. Whenever therefore any act of a pope appears harmful to God and His Church, it is unlawful : but each and everyone of the stipulations contained in the electoral pact is clearly detrimental to the Church [60].

This argumentation clears the ground for answering the rather intricate question concerning the oath taken by the cardinal who became afterwards pope. How far is this oath valid ? Indeed, this is a crucial question which may well have troubled the conscience of more than one pope. The reply which Andreas gives, is unequivocal : if the pope were to act in consonance with the oath, he would in fact inflict so much harm to the whole Christian body politic that it would amount to a desertion of his office and his duties [61].

> Ubicumque peius est servare juramentum quam non servare, tale juramentum non valet, quia tendit in peiorem exitum [62].

---

[59] Referring to Panormitanus Andreas says : « Quod papa non posset subjicere clericos judicio saeculari, quia hoc privilegium fori habent clerici a Deo ». Cfr. also Innocent IV, ad *Extra* : I. xxxiii. 2 (ed. cit., fol. 156v, n. 1) : « Sed quaeris, quis exemit clericos de jure imperatoris, cum prius subessent ei ? Respondeo .... quod exempti sunt a Deo .... vel dic, quod papa .... quia clerici res spirituales sunt et ex toto corpus et animam dederunt in servitium et sortem Christi .... per consequens papae in judiciis et constitutionibus subsunt ». For some observations on this point cfr. also W. Ullmann in *L' Europa e il Diritto Romano* (Milan 1954), i. 127 ff.

[60] « Et sic potest formari ratio inconvincibilis : factum papae non tenet quotiescumque tendit ad opprobrium Dei et suae ecclesiae, set quod non possit facere cardinales, et quod non possit infeudare terras temporaliter subjectas ecclesiae, et quod non possit conferre beneficia, et quod non possit facere ardua ex officio suae potestatis papalis, set quod oporteat quod habeat consensum omnium cardinalium adeo, quod uno contradicente non possit disponere circa contenta in dictis XL capitulis, diminuitur honor ecclesiae, cuius est sponsus ille piissimus salvator noster Jesus Christus » (fol. 9rb).

[61] « Per huiusmodi juramentum, votum et promissionem decoloratur status et honor sedis papalis, et per consequens non ligabitur tali voto seu juramento » (fol. 9rb).

[62] Ibid., referring to Baldus, *Super Codice* (ed. cit., ad IV. i. 4 (Si ad excludendam), fol. 4v, n. 7 : « Omnia juramenta sunt inducta ad finem veritatis probandae vel servandae, tamen in juramento promissorio quod vocatur cautionale, requiritur

An oath of this kind is « naturaliter malum » ; it is moreover « contra bonum publicum » and it would be the height of temerity to suggest
that the pope should divest himself of the means through which the
public interest can be promoted. If the pope were to act as « promised », the result would be that « per indirectum et obliquum aperiretur
via ad illud, quod recta fieri non posset ». Hence juristically no release
from this oath is necessary, and neither layman nor cleric can be
held to it. The disregard of this oath does not stamp one a « perjurus »
nor does one become a « fractor voti » ; its observance « est potius perju-
rium » [63]. At the same time the view might be — as in fact it was —
advanced that, apart from the oath, the cardinals had made a contract with the pope and therefore he was bound by virtue of the contractual obligation. But this view overlooks the simple fact that the
contract was made between equals, that is, between the cardinals when
there was no pope — « ideo falsum est dicere, quod contractus fuit
celebratus cum papa ».

In short, the introduction of an oligarchic form of papal government cannot be squared with the dogma, law, Bible or history. For
this oligarchy would mean that there is not one head, but several heads
of the Church — « quod esset error suppinus ». The view that these electoral pacts have constitutional validity must be rejected — « primo
hoc non probatur jure ; secundo nos videmus Romanos pontifices
servare contrarium ; tertio illud dicitur a doctoribus, qui fuerunt cardinales ». However eminent the latter may have been, their views can
never invalidate the clear letter of the law : « Ubi habemus casum legis,
tunc enim cessant dicta doctorum ». The *Consilium* concludes with
the advice to the pope — an advice, no doubt prompted by the personalities of contemporary cardinals — only to create those cardinals
who are fit to fill so high an office, and in considering candidates not
to be influenced by nepotism :

---

veritas intentionis, judicium discretionis et justitiae impletio .... unde si ex imple-
tione juramenti sequeretur injustitia, puta propriae salutis dispendium vel alterius
detrimentum, non obligat sacramentum .... et ubicumque peius est juramentum
servare quam non servare, non valet, quia vergit in deteriorem exitum. Hoc autem
contingit sex modis. Primo quando juramentum est malum in se naturaliter .... »
(citing *Dig.* 2. 14. 7).

[63] The opinion of Lulvès, art. cit., pp. 233-4, that the oath was « vom juristischen Standpunkt an sich gültig » is therefore very much open to doubt. Teodoro
de' Lelli too denies the binding character of this oath, see *op. cit.*, ed. cit., II. xiii,
pp. 163-8.

Sit tamen memor sanctitas sua, ut provideat ecclesiae, et non personis, ut sanctos viros litteratos et valde disciplinatos et illustres promoveat ad tantam dignitatem.

A brief comparison between Andreas de Barbatia's *Consilium* and Teodoro de' Lelli's work may not be out of place. Both products were prompted by the electoral pact concluded on the occasion of Paul II's election ; both arrived at the same negative conclusion ; both were written as a result of this pope's request ; both expressed the views of a contemporary section rapidly rising to ascendency. Above all, both quite independently covered very much the same ground and yet, there are some noticeable differences. Lelli's tract is considerably longer than Andreas's *Consilium* : it is a veritable *opusculum* to which its author had clearly devoted a considerable amount of preparation, but there is little doubt that he was not particularly versed in this *genre* of writing. This is all the more remarkable as Lelli was a jurist — it was at Padua that he graduated as a *Juris Utriusque Doctor* [64] — but the abstract juristic argumentation does not seem to have been his strength ; possibly, his employment in the Rota and on papal legations made him a practician rather than a theoretician. Although on the whole far better composed than the *Consilium* and also more interestingly written, the points are by no means as trenchantly and pungently made as in the Bolognese professor's work. It is no disparagement to say that the tract was written primarily from the biblical-theological standpoint ; therefore, we find quite often a lengthy biblical exegesis and considerably more reliance on patristic literature than is the case with Andreas de Barbatia. On the other hand, his exposition and interpretation of the canon law — and after all the whole problem was one of constitutional law — must be classed as decidedly inferior to that of the Bolognese. It was as if Lelli himself felt his weakness, and the reader of the tract senses the tentative and groping manner in which Lelli proceeds. He cites not a single civilian and the few canonists he refers to are not quoted in anything approaching exactness, but in a way that indicates how unsure he felt himself in this line [65]. Andreas de Barbatia's strength lies precisely in his

---

[64] See J. B. Sägmüller, ed. cit., p. 15.

[65] Cfr., for example, his reference to the Archdeacon, ed. cit., p. 107 : « .... ut quidam juris canonici commentator refert, videlicet archidiaconus Bononiensis » without any indication where the Archdeacon is supposed to have made the point

mastery of both corpora of laws and of the juristic literature — a mastery freely acknowledged by all his contemporaries — whilst his knowledge of extra-canonistic literature and doctrine nowhere approaches that of the Bishop of Treviso.

In fact, both works complement each other very well : the one was a literary product, easily readable and attractive and on its own ground very well argued ; the other wholly a juristic product, by no means attractive as a piece of literature, but at the same time manifesting all the logical acumen and the legal punch characteristic of a first class Bolognese Master. The perusal of these two works creates the definite impression that, amongst certain strata of contemporary intellectual society, there was a wholesome re-orientation in favour of the traditional papal monarchy. And what is more, both try with the limited amount of material at their disposal, to go back to the *ecclesia primitiva*, in order to illustrate how much the proposed limitation of papal power is at variance with the ancient set up. The interesting point is that their opponents too, and quite especially the conciliarists, had taken the route to the primitive Church and were also looking backward in the hope to justify their own reformatory measures. This infiltration of the historic element into the dogmatic discussion appears to me a not insignificant feature of the fifteenth-century literature, and became more pronounced as time went on, though it can not be maintained that this historic orientation always produced salutary effects.

Considering therefore the dogmatically, theologically and legally untenable character of the electoral pacts — so plainly demonstrated in these two works —- the historian is nevertheless confronted with the crucial question. What explanation can be found for the continued conclusion of these electoral pacts, well into the second half of the sixteenth century [66]. Until an exhaustive examination is made of the relationship between cardinalate and papacy in this period [67] only a very tentative answer can be given. Whatever final explanation

referred to ; cfr. also, p. 162 and the loose reference to Innocent IV, Hostiensis and Durantis ; on p. 141 he declares that Huguccio did not follow the doctrine of Johannes Monachus ; etc. All this may be read in a badly prepared doctoral dissertation.

[66] See the enumeration of these *Wahlkapitulationen* by Lulvès, art. cit., pp. 216 ff.

[67] Cfr. also the observation of Mollat, art. cit., pp. 593-4. For the earlier part of the fourteenth century see H. Hofmann, *Kardinalat und kuriale Politik in der ersten Hälfte des vierzehnten Jahrhunderts* (Leipzig, 1935) which is, however, in need of a good deal of supplementation.

may be forthcoming, however, no answer can leave out of account the indirect effects of the Avignonese papacy, the direct effects of the Great Schism, and the over-all effects of canonistic teachings. It is assuredly no coincidence that the first electoral pact was concluded at Avignon where by virtue of the enormously increased and complicated curial business the cardinals, one might well be tempted to say, automatically enhanced their authority and weight vis-à-vis the pope. The centralization of governmental business at Avignon, paradoxically enough, was instrumental in releasing the hitherto more or less latent oligarchic designs of the cardinals. That the Schism itself was overwhelmingly occasioned by the clash between (papal) monarchic and (cardinalitian) oligarchic designs, seems no longer disputable and that, the longer the conflict lasted, the more decisive the role of the cardinals became, also seems beyond dispute : without them none of the rival popes could have hoped to assert himself ; moreover, it was largely through the cardinals that the secular powers tried to influence the course of the conflict. To this must be added the loss of prestige and reputation of the office of the papacy in the eyes of contemporaries — few (then as now) could distinguish between the office and the person of the office holder — and the undignified exhibition which some popes gave of themselves, that is, even without the additional propagandistic embellishments gratuitously contributed by cardinals and other adherents of the rival obedience, cannot but have left deep marks which, for understandable reasons, could not easily be effaced.

In practical terms the most obvious effect was concentrated upon the tenet of the divinely conferred monarchic primacy of the pope. It was an article of faith, and nothing can shake faith more than the corroding influence of doubt. And the events — again, without the contributory nature of polemical propaganda — had fostered this doubt to a hitherto unknown extent, a doubt, moreover, the seed of which had been planted by agencies entirely independent of the schismatic situation. It is not unreasonable to maintain that doubt in the primatial position of the pope had in the early fifteenth century deepened into implicit denial, as is manifested in *Sacrosancta*, according to which the bearer of all power was the Church, from which all other ecclesiastical officers, including the pope, derived their status and function [68].

---

[68] The return to the traditional standpoint is also demonstrated in Piero da Monte's view : « Superiorum autem haec sit conclusio omnem ecclesiasticam potestatem a summo pontifice causalitatem et dependentiam habere, ipsius autem supre-

Can there be better proof of the disrespect in which the pope was held by the cardinals than the terrifying spectacle of several of them attempting his assassination — on the very eve of the great European revolt ? What, in short, the electoral pacts make abundantly clear was the implicit denial of the monarchic function of the pope by the cardinals who, so to speak, were historically conditioned for their oligarchic-aristocratic role in Church government. But the cardinals resisted not only the proper papal monarchic government — they also resisted the designs of the conciliarists. For, although in justifying their electoral pacts they occasionally invoked *Frequens*, this decree served them merely as a figleaf for their eventual aim and its invocation should not deceive anyone about their hostility to the underlying ideology of the conciliarists.

So much would seem to be certain, since we here still move within the precincts of the ascertainable and indisputable. When one approaches the question from the purely doctrinal point of view, however, there would appear to be a considerable margin of uncertainty. Doctrinally, the oligarchic designs of the cardinals would seem to be explicable only by the very flexible and vague notion of « Roman Church ». Assuredly, it was their main contention that the college of cardinals constituted a structurally integral part of the Roman Church and by virtue of their forming an essential element of the Roman Church, they claimed their due share in the governmental business of this self-same Roman Church [69]. That is why the Innocentian passage was giv-

---

mam atque plenissimam a solo Deo esse institutam, quam cum ipse secundum quandam immensitatem recepisse videatur, aliis tamen distribuit secundum aliquam mensuram » (MS. cit., fol. 26r).

[69] All cardinals who were professional canonists held that the Roman Church consisted of the cardinals and the pope. Following Johannes Monachus, Cardinal Zabarella declared : « Ecclesia Romana non censetur esse solus papa, sed ipse papa cum cardinalibus, qui sunt pars corporum papae seu ecclesiae, quae constituitur ex papa tamquam ex capite et ex cardinalibus tamquam ex membris » (Commentary ad *Extra* : I. vi. 6) ; cfr. also ibid. : « Romana ecclesia (quae) *representatur* (!) in papa tamquam in capite et in cardinalibus tamquam in membris ». For a discussion of this and other similar passages cfr. my *Origins of the Great Schism* (London, 1948), pp. 203-4, and B. Tierney, *op. cit.*, pp. 233-4. In this latter work will also be found the ancestral sources for this view on the constitution and structure of the Roman Church ; see especially, p. 42 (Huguccio) : « Romana ecclesia dicitur papa et cardinales » ; p. 43 (early thirteenth-century anonymous gloss) : « Ecclesia Romana dicitur .... papa cum suis cardinalibus ; » p. 80 (*Summa Et est sciendum*) : « Accipitur pro capite et membris, id est, papa et cardinalium collegio ». Andreas de Barba-

en an interpretation according to which the cardinals were the Christian Levitic priests, consequently had an Old Testament pedigree and for this very reason could claim an origin in divine law — a contention which if correct would give strong support to a possibly more distinguished ancestry than the pope's own ; above all, this assertion would lend some colour to their claim of being integrated in the Roman Church : without their participation no pope could legitimately govern ; theirs was a right based on divine law which the pope must at all times respect. That the Innocentian decretal could not bear this interpretation is obvious and Andreas de Barbatia had no qualms in saying so, and he deserves all the more credit for it, as he was the first to interpret the passage in its proper juristic context and, as I have hinted before, possibly with an eye to the letter of Eugenius IV to the Archbishop of Canterbury [70].

It would be appropriate at the same time to point out that it was in fact the papacy itself which from the time of instituting the cardinals had always associated them closely with the Roman Church. One has only to look at the very suggestive announcements made during the early years of the corporate existence of the college of cardinals as the senators of the pope to realize the potency of such pronouncements as those made, for instance, by Cardinal Humbert, pronouncements which were never revoked, on the contrary endorsed by both popes and

---

tia commenting on Zabarella's view says : « Pro certo dominus cardinalis sine lege loquitur » (fol. 12ra). In this context the assertion was often made that it was only the flatterers of the popes and the hunters for benefices who expounded the « extreme » views of the papal plenitude of power, whereupon Andreas de Barbatia comments : « Miror vehementer quod potuerit suaderi alicui Romano pontifici quod possit facere illicita ex libito voluntatis .... et quod plus posset quam Deus .... ».

[70] This letter has not attracted the attention which is its due ; it also seems to be unknown to M. Mollat. In it Eugenius IV rather severely takes Henry Chichele to task for denying precedence of rank to John Kemp, the Archbishop of York, recently made a cardinal. The pope wholly adopts and even amplifies the wrong interpretation of the Innocentian decretal by saying : « Et si huius dignitatis nomen, quod modo in usu fuit, ab initio primitivae ecclesiae non ita expressum fuit, officium tamen ipsum a beato Petro eiusque successoribus institutum evidenter invenies, imo ut inquit Innocentius tertius, ex veteri testamento jussu Dei traxit originem ; asserit enim id, quod Deut. XVII dicitur, ut pro difficultate et ambiguitate judicii accedatur ' ad sacerdotes Levitici generis .... ' (Deut. xvii. 8), de summo pontifice intelligendum esse et de fratribus eius, id est, S. R. E. cardinalibus, qui ex jure Levitico in executione sacerdotalis officii coadjutores existunt .... datur manifeste intelligi hos fratres nostros, qui inter cardinales loquantur, tempore beati Petri extitisse .... ». I hope to deal with this letter of Eugenius IV separately.

cardinals [71]. But a concise definition or an exegetical clarification and exposition of what was the Roman Church, was at all times missing : Who constituted the Roman Church ? It was a question which, it may be recalled, had already engaged the cute mind of the author of the York Tracts, and which spasmodically flashed across canonistic writings, without however being made the focus of a systematic analysis [72]. But on the answer to this fundamental problem depended the constitutional standing of the *Cardinales sanctae Romanae ecclesiae.* Do they or do they not belong to the Roman Church constitutionally and structurally ? Once again, this was a concept which in earlier times had proved a signal source of strenght to the papacy, but in the later Middle Ages proved to be more a papal liability than an asset. The statement, oftentimes made in the fourteenth century, that « Ubi est papa, ibi est Romana ecclesia » indicates that the problem was seen particularly in connexion with the physical removal of the papacy from Rome to Avignon — but as it is with all epigrammatic statements, it helps little to clarify this difficult constitutional issue and the structural concept of the Roman Church. What appears a justifiable deduction from the doctrinal pronouncements and actions of the cardinals in the fourteenth and fifteenth centuries is that they merely expanded, amplified and applied the earlier very largely allegorical statements. An allegory — such as, for example, that the cardinals were the hinges or that they were « pars corporis papae » and the like — however alluring and useful it may originally have been in driving home a point, turns out to be not only a source of confusion, but, worse still, a source of doctrinal danger when once the allegory is pressed into a juristic framework. As long as the structural hierarchy of the Roman Church was not sharply delineated — and the *Consilium* of Andreas de Barbatia does little to clarify the notion [73] —

---

[71] In this context due consideration should also be given to the nature of the charge preferred in the case of an injury inflicted upon a cardinal, namely, that of high treason (*Sextus* : V. ix. 5) because of the cardinal's close association with the pope ; to the legates having ordinary jurisdiction, see supra n. 8 ; to the exclusive papal jurisdiction over a cardinal (see *gl. ord.* ad *Extra* : III. iv. 2) ; etc. All these features are explicable only as a result of the cardinals ' intimate connexion with the Roman Church, cfr., especially the reasoning of Boniface VIII in *Sexto*, cap. cit.

[72] See the statements supra n. 69.

[73] Although he has seen the problem, he does not solve it, but sidetracks the discussion, ensnared as he was by the appeal of the allegory. Setting out from the premisse that the Bishop requires the collaboration of the cathedral chapter (*Dist·*

both the claims of the cardinals as integral parts of the Roman Church and consequently their aspirations to share in the pope's government as well as the pope's denial of these aspirations, are understandable : because of the papal denial the cardinals insisted upon drawing up the electoral pacts. For if they are constitutionally members of the Roman Church, they have every right to shape its constitution in a suitable manner -- and the only suitable manner was through the instrumentality of the electoral pacts. The « problem of the cardinalate » [74], born as it was with the institution itself, was in reality the problem of what was constitutionally the Roman Church. None perceived this problem with greater clarity than the man who himself played so great a role in establishing the functions of the cardinals, namely Cardinal Humbert. Who is to judge the pope if he becomes a heretic ? The answer implied by Humbert and expressed by canonists later [75], was that the Roman Church, that is, the cardinals, judge the pope : the reason advanced was that they as co-bearers of the primacy formed a corporative entity with the pope, and therefore all the norms governing a corporation were held to be applicable [76].

---

xxiv. 6 ; X. ii. 1 ; XVI. iii. 1 ; *Extra* : III. x. 3, etc.), but that on the other hand (IX. iii. 4) this requirement is inapplicable to the Roman Church, it follows that the Roman Church « est privilegiata in hoc » and that therefore « sequitur necessario quod intelligitur sine consilio cardinalium, ex eo quia collegium cardinalium dicitur esse capitulum ecclesiae Romanae ». And he concludes :

> Ex hoc tollitur quod posset opponi, videlicet quod appellatione Romanae ecclesiae venit papa et cardinales, quia sunt membra papae et faciunt unum corpus cum ipso papa, quia ego fateor quod sunt membra hoc modo, quia ex quo assistunt lateri papae dicuntur esse membra papae, set non sunt proprie ita membrum ut in homine, quia caput esset nichil si non habet et membra .... Dicuntur membra quoad favorem ipsorum cardinalium, ut si aliquis offendat cardinalem dicatur offendisse membrum papae ad hoc ut puniatur offendens acrius tamquam offenderet membrum Christi .... » (fol. 7vb-8ra).

It cannot be said that this discussion is particularly helpful.

[74] Which I have mentioned elsewhere, cfr. *Growth of Papal Government*, cit., p. 321.

[75] Cfr. W. Ullmann, « Cardinal Humbert and the Ecclesia Romana » in *Studi Gregoriani*, iv (1952), pp. 111 ff. ; cfr. also P. E. Schramm in *Göttinger Gelehrte Anzeigen*, 1953, pp. 128-30.

[76] See especially Hostiensis, *Lectura* (ed. Paris, 1512), ad IV. xvii. 13 (fol. 38va) : « Multo magis et multo excellentius et major est unio inter papam et col-

It can hardly be disputed that the electoral pacts introduced a not negligible amount of tension into the Roman curia. Tension always saps energies and, in order to be relieved, diverts attention to other than immediately pressing tasks. Instead of directing the concentration on meeting vigorously and radically the challenge issued by the « Reformers » in the early sixteenth century, the curia dealt with it in a way which suggests turbidity and sluggishness. The great powers which stood behind the cardinals and which, in any case, had so enormously increased their authority and influence at the expense of the papacy in the fifteenth century, enchained the popes at this vital moment in European history. The mere fact of concluding electoral pacts with the future pope and, still more, their underlying idea could not but help to demonstrate to the world the low esteem with which the cardinals themselves (including the pope who emerged from their midst) viewed the papacy, and above all to lower still more an already much debased papacy in the eyes of influential strata of society — even if the precise contents of the electoral pacts were not publicly known, their general tenor assuredly was — and a not negligible contributory reason for the rapidity with which the « Reformers' » ideas spread, can be found in the constitutional devices of the cardinals. It may be safe to say that for the general upheaval in the early sixteenth century the college of cardinals cannot escape its due share of responsibility : it was very largely they as the highest ecclesiastical officers and dignitaries who mainly through the instrument of electoral pacts had eroded the papal office and exposed an already weakened papacy to the virulent attacks of the « reforming » party.

---

legium Romanae ecclesiae quam inter aliquem alium patriarcham et capitulum suum .... multo fortius ergo decet papam consilia fratrum suorum requirere, nam et firmius est judicium quod a pluribus queritur .... unde et dicti sunt cardinales a cardine quasi cum papa mundum regentes .... non solum papa sed et cardinales etiam includerentur in expressione plenitudinis potestatis». Petrus Olivi in his tract *De renuntiatione papae* ed. in *Archiv. Franciscanum Hist.*, xi (1918), by L. Oliger, went so far as to say that St Francis had understood by the term «Roman Church» «solum collegium cardinalium, qui proprie et anthonomastice sunt ipsa sedes ecclesiae Romanae» (p. 353-4). It may be that the modern canon law (*C. I. C.*, can, 100, § 1 with § 2) solves this problem by the theory of the corporation sole; cf. most recently also the code for the oriental Church in *Acta Apostolicae Sedis*, xlix (1957), p. 444, can. 28.

Appendix

It is well known that very few papal decretals issued in the fourteenth century were fortunate enough to be commented upon or glossed. This is all the more strange as there were quite a number of decretals which supplemented, modified or applied earlier papal pronouncements and which might well have formed the basis of a gloss or a commentary. It is therefore all the more remarkable that the bull of Innocent VI, *Sollicitudo pastoralis*, came to be glossed : the very fact of this bull being glossed would indicate the fundamental importance which canonists attributed to it. The gloss together with the text of the bull itself is in MS. Bibl. Nat. Lat. 1478 [1] which is a paper codex of miscellaneous contents and which forms one of the volumes entitled *Tractatus de schismate*, of which the remaining volumes are in other B. N. codices [2]. As far as could be established, this is not only the one extant copy of this gloss by a canonist whose identity escaped detection, but also certainly one of the very few specimen of a gloss on a fourteenth-century pronouncement issuing forth from the Avignonese papacy.

These somewhat unusual features would warrant a few remarks on the gloss itself. It cannot, however, be said that the gloss is very profound : the main intention of the unknown glossator was quite clearly to prove that Innocent VI propounded nothing startingly new and that therefore the substance of the bull was in entire agreement with previous papal legislation and canonistic doctrine. The glossator concentrates upon the problem of the binding character of the oath taken by the cardinals during the conclave. This problem is stated quite succinctly in the proemium :

---

[1] Noted by G. Mollat, art. cit., p. 102, n. 1.

[2] For details and description see Ph. Lauer, *Catalogue général des manuscrits latins* (Paris, 1940), ii. 28-9, sub n. 1478. The paleographical evidence would indeed indicate that text and gloss were written simultaneously, probably in the first half of the fifteenth century. Both are on fol. 15r-17v. There is some difference in the dating of the bull itself : here it is dated « II non. Julii », whereas in Raynaldus the date is « II kal. Julii ». This may be only a scribal error. The volume opens with a memorandum on the cardinals who were present at the death of Clement VII on 16 September 1394 ; cfr. S. Baluzius, *Vitae Paparum Avenionensium*, ed. G. Mollat (Paris, 1914), i. 537.

Illa concordata in scriptura, de quibus hic agitur, et super quibus prestita juramenta videbantur servanda, cum illa observanda non vergant in dispendium salutis eterne, immo sunt licita.

But this proposition cannot withstand criticism, for although the stipulations in the pact are valid and permissible in themselves, it is their consequences and effects which deprive them of their legal and binding character.

Scilicet illa in se licita sint, tamen quia a jure prohibita effecta sunt illicita, non quia in se mala sint, sed propter malum, quod inde sequi potest.

Amongst these consequences the glossator mentions the delay in the electoral proceedings themselves, the inevitable prolongation of the vacancy, the distraction of the electors from the proper election, their concern with the stipulations of the pact to be concluded, and so forth. Moreover, it cannot be argued that the good intention of those who take the oath, could validate an otherwise illicit oath :

Nota ergo quod rectus zelus jurantis non validat illicitum juramentum [3].

This electoral pact is also invalid from another point of view, namely from that of the papal plenitude of power. « Nota quod verbum quod potestas pape inquantum limitatur vel coartatur, tollitur » [4]. And such opposition or assertion is not only temerarious, but also, as the pope said here, insane : temerarious, because against human law ; insane, because against divine law [5]. The term « insane » may also denote the state of mind of a heretic, as the glossator believes was the doctrine of the Archdeacon, because only a heretic can be so devoid of sense as to limit the pope's plenitude of power [6]. All the

---

[3] Gloss s. v. *rectum zelum* : with a reference to *Extra* : II. xxiv. 18, and *Decretum*, XIX. iv, p. t.

[4] Gloss s. v. *divinitus*.

[5] Gloss s. v. *temerarium* : « Est ergo talis oppositio vel assertio temeraria, id est, illicita et juri contraria, sic exponitur XVII, qu. IV, c. diffinitio (35) et XI, qu. III, cap. temerarium (49), et De jure jur., c. Sicut ex litteris *(Extra* : II. xxiv. 13). Et temerarium est quia contra jus humanum, insanum vero quia contra jus divinum ».

[6] Gloss s. v. *insanum* : with a reference to the *Rosarium*, XIX. i. 2.

cases ennumerated in the pact, in which the pope was obliged to consult the cardinals, the glossator thinks are well covered by the existing canon law. Nevertheless, he declares a consultation by the pope of the cardinals would be « satis honestum », though « non tamen potest effici necessarium, cum apud solum papam plenitudo potestatis resideat » [7]. Therefore, although the stipulations in themselves contain nothing dishonest, « papa non potest obligari nec astringi ad contenta in hoc articulo ». Still less can the pope be restricted as regards the tenths [8]. What, however, appears less certain to the glossator is the illegality of the pope's restriction concerning the appointment of the marshall of the Roman curia and of the rectors of towns situated in the papal state [9] : the conferment of these offices is not an issue of the power ot the keys at all, and therefore this prohibition is aimed at restricting nepotism (carnalitatis affectus) :

> Nota quod provisio talium officiorum non videtur directe pertinere ad generalem et illimitatam potestatem clavium et tamen non potest restringi, licet hic videbatur reprimi carnalitatis affectus et per consequens videretur rem licitam continere, De preb., Grave (III, v. 29).

Probably written in the first half of the fifteenth century, this gloss would in fact be a further witness of the re-assertion of the traditional point of view : surely the only purpose of this gloss was to prove that the rescission of the electoral pact by Innocent VI was in entire accord with the canon law no less than with the constitution of the Church ; conversely that the electoral pacts were an innovation devoid of all legal and constitutional justification. In view, however, of the subsequent practice of concluding electoral pacts it cannot be maintained that this gloss exercised any influence, but its historical value lies in its symptomatic nature, as it is apt to demonstrate that even amongst French canonists this practice was considered illegal.

---

[7] Gloss s. v. *consilio.*

[8] Gloss s. v. *decimarum* : «Nota ex hox et sequenti articulo quod potestas pape non potest restringi vel limitari etiam ad illa, que fienda sunt secundum conscientiam et rectum zelum rationis quamvis alias teneatur ad illa».

[9] This stipulation in the pact ran : «Item quod ad officium marescalli Romanae curiae et rectorum terrarum seu provinciarum Romanae ecclesiae nullus de consanguinitate vel affinitate Romani pontificis assumatur». (Raynaldus, *Ann. eccles.,* cit., p. 540).

XVI

JULIUS II AND THE SCHISMATIC CARDINALS

IT would seem that in the assessment of the forces prevalent on the eve of the Reformation too little attention has been paid to the determined steps which a number of cardinals initiated in 1511 when they took it upon themselves to convoke a general council at Pisa. The cardinals and the ensuing council have never had a good press. In fact there seems a unanimous condemnation of their initiative: they were labelled schismatics paradoxically because they tried to prevent a schism; they had proved themselves, so it was alleged, as mere instruments of French expansionist policy and had acted against the interests of papacy and Church prompted as they were by personal considerations and animosity against Julius II. It seems almost 'heretical' to question this general verdict.

Yet as far as I can see no detailed investigation has been undertaken to arrive at a more equitable and balanced verdict which, moreover, takes into account the actual and juristic background of the cardinals' initiative. The purpose of this communication is to invite attention to some features which do not seem to be adequately appraised or even analysed. And these features belong almost wholly to juristic categories of thought in conjunction with the reality of the situation. The cardinals moved entirely within the juristic thought pattern. Three points must be made straight away. First that before his election Pope Julius II had entered into the by then quite common electoral capitulations in the conclave and promised under oath that among other things he would convoke a general council within two years of his election.[1] What distinguished this capitulation from most previous ones was that the College of Cardinals insisted on Julius II repeating his promise *after* his election which he did; he also solemnly declared in his function as pope that neither he himself not anyone else could absolve him from

---

[1] For these capitulations see [O. Raynaldus,] *Ann[ales] Eccl[esiastici]* (ed Bar-le-Duc 1877) xxx, p 537: anno 1511 no 3, where the relevant parts of the capitulations are given verbatim. For the general juristic problems caused by these capitulations see W. Ullmann, 'The legality of the papal electoral pacts' in *Ephemerides iuris canonici*, XII (Rome 1956) pp 212ff.

the obligation sworn to.[1] For just under eight years following his election there is no evidence whatsoever that Julius took any steps towards implementing the promises given under oath. The second point is that the whole pontificate of Julius was overshadowed by a tension between him as pope and the College of Cardinals, amongst whom – and they were the articulate, learned and also independently-minded – there were outspoken opponents of the monarchic idea of the papacy as represented by Julius's manner of government and his aims. He made not only no concessions to the prevailing mood amongst the more educated and critically inclined clerical and lay sections, but also adopted a veritably retrograde policy which showed him a mixture of a crafty and at times violent renaissance prince and a wily medieval pope. The third point is that amongst the cardinals there were men who as far as one can judge by their deeds, were perfectly aware of the needs of the time and who sensed the perilous nature of the policies pursued by this renaissance pope.[2] What a small section of the cardinals realised was that if nothing concrete was done to quell the spiritual unrest, decomposition, demoralisation and protest of contemporary Christendom, if in other words some effective measures were not taken at least to initiate a 'reform in head and members', a complete cataclysm could hardly be avoided. Moreover, amongst these far-sighted cardinals were some who were quite outstanding as canonists, such as Johannes Antonius de s. Georgio who in his lengthy and somewhat diffuse commentary (written before he had become a cardinal) faced the question crucial at the time – what to do with a pope whose government proved deleterious to the cause of Christendom, who refused to summon a general council and who could be shown to be suspected of heresy by his actions, teachings and the scandal he inflicted upon Christendom.[3]

[1] See especially *Ann Eccl* p 397a, 1503, no 6: 'Ego Julius secundus electus...praemissa omnia et singula promitto, iuro et vovo...et sub poena periurii et anathematis, a quibus nec me ipsum absolvam nec alicui absolutionem committam.'

[2] This present communication deals with Julius as pope, and not with the man who in so magnificent a manner had largely made Rome what it has become. It will be recalled that it was Julius II who granted Henry VIII the dispensation from the marriage impediment, see *Ann Eccl* p 402a–b, 1503, no 22 where the papal decree is dated 26 December 1503.

[3] See Johannes Antonius de sancto Georgio, *Commentaria super decretorum volumina* (ed Lyons 1522) hereafter Songiorgio, ad D.a.c.1, *Dist* 17, no 3, fol 66ra, and *Dist. ead.c.*1 (Synodum) no 5, fol 66va. The extremely detailed presentation by Sangiorgio would warrant a study of its own. He devotes no fewer than six folios to the question of pope and general council. On him see [F. J.] Schulte, [*Geschichte der Quellen und Literatur des canonischen Rechts*](Stuttgart 1877) II, pp 338–41; A. van Hove, *Prolegomena ad Codicem Iuris*

Julius II and the schismatic cardinals

That the government of Julius II caused serious apprehension in the
College of Cardinals was therefore comprehensible, especially when his
total inability as well as unwillingness to enact any of the necessary
reformatory measures was considered. In view of the papacy's immediate past record there was considerable justification for the cardinals
insisting upon the implementation of the electoral capitulations. To
them therefore the general council appeared as the only appropriate
forum to enact on a universal and comprehensive scale the *reformatio in
capite et membris*. But Julius would have none of this. A man of iron
will, pertinacity, and stubbornness Julius preferred petty Italian power
politics to any attempt at an improvement of the spiritual, disciplinary
and moral standards of which contemporary Christianity was ostensibly
in need. This is not to say that his restoration of some order in the papal
state was not a considerable achievement but is simply to point out the
singularly one-sided interest which he displayed as pope. The other
side of his interest – regeneration and rebirth on not only artistic and
architectural levels – was conspicuously absent, and if he ever realised
the need for this regeneration or rebirth, he never showed it in his
public or official acts. Assuredly, there was more of a military commander and a king in him than of a pontiff.[1] Perhaps not so manifest
as in recent pontificates nepotism of cardinalitian appointments still
reached quite respectable dimensions: no fewer than four members of
his family (the della Rovere) received the cardinal's hat in successive
creations. Julius's over-all governmental concept culminated in the
restoration of the papacy as a universal power: once more it was to be
the nerve-centre of the christian world.[2] The means to achieve this
end were the full deployment of papal-monarchic powers based on
the traditional petrinological argument. That neither the plan nor its

Canonici (2 ed Mechlin-Rome 1945) p 498. He was created a cardinal by Alexander VI
in 1493, having been appointed an auditor of the Rota by Innocent VIII in 1481 (see
A. Cerchiari, *Capellani papae et apostolicae sedis auditores* (Rome 1926) II, p 69). He was
professor of Roman and canon law at Pavia and was one of the most outstanding jurists
of the late fifteenth and early sixteenth centuries. He died in March 1509 (see Schulte,
p 339).

[1] One can hardly disagree with [L.] Pastor's judgment, see his [*Geschichte der Päpste im
Zeitalter der Renaissance*] (Freiburg 1895) III, p 526. See further the unnecessarily reticent
view of G. Schwaiger on Julius II in L[*exikon für*] T[*heologie und*] K[*irche*] v (Freiburg
1963) p 1205: 'hinter der gewaltigen politisch-militärischen Tätigkeit trat das geistliche
Wirken sehr stark zurück.' Here are good bibliographical details.

[2] Once more we can cite Pastor's view, III, p 527: 'Der Hauptgedanke: die Weltmacht
des Papsttums neu zu beleben, dem heiligen Stuhl durch einen festgefügten Staat
Unabhängigkeit und Ansehen zu verschaffen, stand von Anfang seiner Regierung an
unverrückt vor der Seele des neuen Papstes.'

execution met with the support of the College of Cardinals, would not seem surprising. Indeed, some of the alert and reflective cardinals felt not only justifiable apprehension, but also alarm on account of the policy consistently pursued by Julius. The view which Luther – in common with many other contemporaries – formed of this pope when on a visit to Rome during Julius's pontificate, may well have reflected the sentiment of a great many non–Italians: 'a blood-sucker', 'a cruelly violent animal'.[1]

The dichotomy between promise and achievement can hardly have been more obvious than in this pontificate. It is not difficult to visualise how agonising the situation must have been for these members of the curia who realised the need for drastic measures. That both the French king Louis XII and the German emperor-elect Maximilian – for reasons which may well have been different from those which prompted a number of cardinals to leave the curia – displayed animosity against the pope by 1510 and early 1511, no doubt weighed heavily with the faction of cardinals who now began to take matters into their own hands. Even by contemporary standards the situation had indeed reached intolerable dimensions on account of the military policy of Julius who by 1510 was not merely the nominal, but the real supreme commander of the army in the field. Nevertheless, with his permission five cardinals left the curia: they had clearly sensed the futility of acting as advisers of the pope who had threatened some of the independently-minded cardinals with ecclesiastical censures and had actually incarcerated some of them. There can be no doubt that contact was established between the French king and those cardinals who had left the curia, yet it would be erroneous to see in this contact anything more than a diplomatic *rapprochement* strongly reminiscent of the situation exactly a century earlier. Indeed, the situation in 1407 culminating in the secession of a number of cardinals from both popes and resulting in the Council of Pisa in 1409, provided the men of the early sixteenth century with a pattern, even in regard to the locality. It is not generally known that the cardinals who seceded in 1407 obtained the opinion of some very eminent jurists, such as Antonius de Butrio (canonist) and Paulus Castrensis (civilian):[2] exactly the same procedure was followed by the cardinals in 1511.

[1] Quoted from *Reallexikon für Theologie & Kirche*, ed A. Hauck, IX (Tübingen 1907) p 624.

[2] See the latter's *Consilia* (ed Frankfurt 1582), *cons* 419 by him himself (fol 216va); no 420 by Antonius de Butrio (fol 218ra); and no 421 by two other Bolognese doctors. Nor is it generally known that Baldus de Ubaldis dealt at some length with the with-

Julius II and the schismatic cardinals

On 16 May 1511 nine cardinals of whom the outstanding Carvajal[1] was clearly the leader issued their summons for a general council to be opened on 1 September at Pisa. These cardinals were by no means all French – only two of them were ostensibly so – and it would be a somewhat *simpliste* assumption and facile explanation to say that they were the tools of Louis XII or of Maximilian. That there had been negotiations between the two rulers and the cardinals their convocation edict explicitly mentions; it goes even so far as to say that both Louis and Maximilian had agreed through their proctors to their step. But before initiating this fateful measure the cardinals had – like their predecessors of a century earlier – consulted some of the most eminent jurists: Phillipus Decius,[2] Jason de Mayno,[3] Franciscus Curtius and Paulus Picus[4] were some of those who initially advised the cardinals on the legality of convoking a general council. Only the *consilium* of the first-mentioned is known, though to the best of my knowledge it has never been properly analysed.[5] An analysis of their convocation edict shows that the cardinals relied entirely on the juristic advice proffered by these outstanding canonists and civilians. Neither the iurists nor the cardinals considered that this convocation of a general council constituted a schismatic action or turned them into schismatics.

The main points in the cardinals' summons were first that because the pope had neglected to implement the promise to convoke a general council, the duty to do so developed upon them in order to deal with the sorry state of the Church and to effect a reform in head and mem-

---

drawal of the French king from the anti-pope Benedict XII in 1397; see Baldus, *Lectura in decretales* (ed Venice 1615) ad *Extra*: 1.iii.25 (Olim), fols 53rb–53va. See further [Petrus de] Ancharano, [*Consilia*] (ed Lyons 1539) cons 281, fols 116ra ff which is a very subtle and lengthy treatment of the juristic points raised by the cardinals who had receded from both obediences; see further Domenicus Geminianus, *Consilia* (ed Lyons 1533), cons 88, fols 51ra–vb.

[1] On him see [C.] Eubel, [*Hierarchia catholica medii aevi*] (Münster 1914) II p 22 and III p 4; further J. Wodka in *LTK*, II (1957) pp 959–60: cardinal since 1493 and curial legate in Germany in 1496 and 1507–8.

[2] For him see [F. C.] Savigny, [*Geschichte des römischen Rechts im Mittelalter*] (Heidelberg 1850) VI, pp 374ff; Schulte, II, pp 361ff and [M. P.] Gilmore, [*Humanists and Jurists*] (Cambridge, Mass. 1963) pp 73ff. See also M. Ascheri, *Un Maestro del 'Mos italicus': Gianfrancesco Sannazari della Ripa* (Milan 1970) pp 27–9.

[3] See Savigny, VI, pp 397–418, Gilmore, pp 68–72 with further literature.

[4] See Savigny, VI, p 381.

[5] See Pastor, III, p 649 (a mere mentioning); [H.] Jedin [*Geschichte des Konzils von Trient*] (Freiburg 1949) p 86 (only a few lines) (Engl transl 1957, at p 106). Jedin also refers to an anonymous *consilium* which he himself had discovered in Rome, Vatican MS Bibl Barb Lat 843; see furthermore J. Hefele–H. Leclercq, *Histoire des conciles* (Paris 1917) VIII, p 316, and for a very brief summary, Gilmore, pp 75–7.

bers.[1] Moreover, the Council of Constance in the decree *Frequens* had stipulated that a general council should be held every ten years, and though the present pope had sworn to convoke one within two years he had done nothing in this direction. The cardinals considered him 'nedum negligens in praecepto ecclesiae et concilii set et voti et iuramenti huiusmodi transgressor'. In so far they merely re-echoed Julius II's own words.[2] By his unwillingness to convoke the council the pope had adversely affected the well-being of the Church: the duty to convoke it developed upon them.[3]

It is difficult to see in these statements of the cardinals anything that formally or constitutionally could be called schismatic, since there was no suggestion whatsoever that the cardinals (or for that matter Louis or Maximilian) considered a separation from the Roman Church or from the pope.[4] On the contrary, as the second point in their documents makes amply clear the cardinals had so little intention of being the agents of a schism that they humbly and most respectfully invited the pope to give his assent to the council envisaged and convoked, and to honour it either by his own personal presence or by his legates.[5] By no stretch of imagination could this be seen as a schismatic step nor as one that showed any disrespect to the pope. Throughout their lengthy document there is no indication that the cardinals viewed Julius as anything else but the lawful pope whose wrath in case of independent action they nevertheless had cause to fear, as they also made abundantly clear when they explained the reason why their convocation was not issued from the curia but was nailed on the church doors at Modena, Reggio, Parma, and so on: the pope, they said, had thrown some cardinals into the dungeons and had imprisoned others

---

[1] See *Ann Eccl* xxx, p 538: 'pro vera pace christianorum fundanda et sufficienti bello contra infideles et pro extirpatione haeresum et errorum in diversis mundi partibus superiorum negligentia pullulantium et similiter schismatum ac divisionum necnon potissime pro reformatione morum universalis ecclesiae in capite et membris plurimum collapsorum ac emendatione criminum gravissimorum notoriorum, continuorum aut incorrigibilium universalem ecclesiam scandalizantium'.

[2] See above, p 178 n 1.

[3] See *Ann Eccl* xxx, p 538b.

[4] The statement by [J. J.] Scarisbrick, [*Henry VIII*] (London 1968) 26, that Louis XII summoned a schismatic general council to meet at Pisa in May 1511 'which would have on its agenda nothing less than the deposition of Julius himself' does not seem accurate.

[5] *Ann Eccl* xxx, p 538b: 'Quapropter cum omni reverentia et humilitate ac instantia sanctissimum dominum nostrum Julium papam nomine quo supra supplicamus et per viscera misericordiae Dei nostri requirimus, ut huic vocationi concilii pro dictis causis assentire dignetur et illud personaliter vel per legatos suos honorare et confirmare.'

Julius II and the schismatic cardinals

contra ius gentium – these were notorious facts, they maintained, which caused them to be apprehensive of their safety, hence the unusual method of publication.[1]

What must be stressed is that there is no shred of evidence that the cardinals intended to charge the pope with any particular crime or offence. All they did was what the pope should have done. In so far the nine cardinals did not go beyond what the moderate section of canonists had held to be legitimate. In any event the juristic problem raised by their convocation of a general council was certainly not that of pope versus council. Because of the gravity of their step they wished to be assured of its legality, and that was why they sought the expert opinions of famous jurists. As a matter of fact, one of their own colleagues who had died only two years previously, the already mentioned Johannes Antonius de s. Georgio, had advocated a scheme of things which was fully embraced by the great Jason de Mayno in his *consilium*. The late cardinal had maintained[2] that if the pope's conduct had caused scandal, the cardinals *quasi ex necessitate* were entitled to convoke a general council. And once they had convoked the council and assembled together, they should request the pope to be present and authorise the council as a general council. Only if the pope were to refuse he could then be treated as someone suspected of heresy and be deposed. The essential point of cardinal Sangiorgio was that a pope could be charged and condemned and deposed only for heresy: for no other crime could he be brought to trial.[3] Jason de Mayno literally followed the cardinal's

---

[1] *Ibid* p 539a: 'Quia tutum non esset nobis procuratoribus dictam convocationem concilii et protestationem in praesentia sanctissimi domini nostri facere, qui sanctae universalis ecclesiae cardinales fratres suos et ecclesiam universalis principes carceribus aliquando mancipandos minari fecit oratoresque principum contra ius gentium detineri, prout notorium est et pro notorio allegatur, ideo decrevimus per affixionem huiusmodi schedulae.'

[2] I am unable to understand the statement by Jedin, p 87 (Eng trans p 108) that 'Sangiorgio blieb bei Julius II.', because he had been dead for two years by the time the cardinals convoked the general council; he died on 14 March 1509, see Schulte, above p 178 n 3 and Eubel, II, p 22, n 3.

[3] See Sangiorgio, fol 66ra: 'Satis videtur cum papa ex hoc videtur scandalizareuniversalem ecclesiam, poterunt cardinales quasi ex necessitate convocare concilium ...ubi congregati fuerint (possint) rogare papam ut adsit et auctorizet congregationem, quod si fecerit monendus erit ut se corriget...quod si neque venire neque auctorizare voluerit vel se corrigere recusaverit tamquam suspectus de haeresi poterit deponi, c.si papa (=Dist. xl.c.6).' About the provenance of this chapter in Gratian see W. Ullmann, 'Cardinal Humbert and the ecclesia Romana' in *Studi Gregoriani*, IV (Rome 1952) pp 111ff; here also further literature. In another place Sangiorgio declared that in case of scandal caused by the pope, the council could well proceed against him 'non intelligo ad iudicandum eum, sed ad monendum et inducendum eum ad correctionem, quia a nemine excepta causa haeresis iudicari potest' (fol 66va, no 5).

exposition by copying his words in his own *consilium* and adding that such a solemn and charitable exhortation issued formally by a general council could not fail to produce the desired result.[1] Since the nine cardinals adopted a point of view which was wholly consonant with the most moderate section of canon lawyers, it is hard to understand why they should have attracted the opprobrious charge of being schismatics. What needs stressing is that both Sangiorgio and Jason rejected the standpoint put forward by the *glossa ordinaria*[2] which was generally accepted. These two jurists restricted the accountability of the pope before a general council to matters of heresy, while Phillipus Decius adopted the view of the *glossa* and held that for *any* notorious crime the pope could be charged and condemned by a general council. The *glossa ordinaria* (based as it was on Huguccio)[3] as well as the common opinion maintained that incorrigibility and negligence (*contumacia*) of the pope amounted to heresy and therefore was a chargeable crime.[4]

That Pisa was chosen as the locality of the forthcoming general council had again its explanation in the model situation of exactly a century earlier. Indeed, Antonius de Butrio and Panormitanus had already pointed out that nobody had ever charged the cardinals who had left Gregory XII, with the crime of schism. And Gregory XII's case was not at all unlike that of Julius II: he too had sworn in conclave and repeated the promise under oath as pope that he would renounce the papacy and would not create new cardinals in order to bring the schism to an end – and yet did neither. That the pope could not absolve himself from the oath he had taken, was common opinion which Julius himself had endorsed.[5] By not adhering to his own promises the

---

[1] See Jason de Mayno, *Consilia* (ed Frankfurt 1609) IV, *cons.* 95, pp 349ff at no 41, p 356b: 'Item per concilium generale poterit fieri charitativa admonitio et exhortatio papae circa eius correctionem denuntiando ei qualiter pernicioso vitae suae exemplo universam ecclesiam scandalizaret et conturbaret. Quae exhortatio sic a tota ecclesia facta cum tanta sollenitate et auctoritate non est dubium quin magna virtutis et efficaciae esset ad animum papae in bonum convertendum.'   [2] On *Dist.* xl, c. 6.

[3] See further Baldus, *Lectura ad tres priores libros decretalium* (ed Venice 1615) ad *Extra*: I.iii.25, no 22, fol 53vb: after referring to Huguccio 'quod papa potest removeri propter notorium crimen enorme. Tene menti.' The outstanding Ludovicus Romanus Pontanus held in his *Consilia* (ed Frankfurt 1577) *cons.* 523, no 15, fol 285rb that 'papa stans in crimine notorio scandalizante totam ecclesiam desistere nolens incidit in suspicionem haeresis...potest ut haereticus condemnari atque consequenter deponi a papatu.'

[4] See *gl. ord.* ad *Dist.* xl, c. 6. [Phillipus] Decius in his [*Consilium*], ed in Melchior Goldast, *Monarchia Romani imperii* (Frankfurt 1668) II pp 1767ff at p 1771, no XIII, lines 25ff: 'Illa enim incorrigibilitas seu contumacia dicitur haeresis secundum glossam, et tali casu non requiritur quod sit haereticus proprie.' See also Ancharano above, p 180 n 2.

[5] See above, p 178 n 1. See further Antonius de Butrio, *Commentaria ad decretales* (ed Lyons 1556) ad *Extra*: I.ii.1, no 10, fol 9vb: 'Et papa astringitur voto et iuramento ac promis-

Julius II and the schismatic cardinals

pope had given an example which all too easily could influence lower placed officers and hence all Christians: 'scandalum generatur mentibus laicorum dicentium, Ubi est deus clericorum?'[1]

A difficult juristic point was this: could the cardinals who convoked the general council be said to constitute the majority of the College of Cardinals and represent its opinion? That numerically they did not form the majority of the College, could hardly be disputed. But did they render themselves culpable of the charge of causing a schism by wilfully setting aside the majority view? There was general agreement that in case of need the College itself was entitled to summon a general council. Certainly, the present contingency of only nine cardinals issuing an invitation to a council was not provided for in law.

Decius devoted a great deal of space and argument to this intricate problem. The argument by which he chose to solve it, was not unlike the one which canonists of an earlier generation had advocated in settling a similar question. In their manner he operated with the analogy of a cathedral chapter. If, so it was pointed out, the bishop was negligent or remiss in his duties, the cathedral chapter stepped into his place, and if the chapter itself was negligent, the right to act devolved upon the individual canons.[2] As a matter of fact, the great civilian Paulus Castrensis had dealt with exactly the same problem in his *consilium* on the situation in 1407–9.[3] His conclusion appeared to be directly applicable to the contingency in Julius II's pontificate. Decius

sione nec ab illis stante vinculo seipsum absolvere potest...ex quibus patet Gregorium XII qui in conclavi ante papatum tamquam cardinalis et post papatum promisit, iuravit et vovit renuntiare pro sedando schismate quod duraverat XXX annis...quod et publicavit per universum orbem, suo astringitur iuramento et voto et promissione... cardinales pene omnes ab eo de Luca recesserunt Pisas.' Cf. further Panormitanus, *Super quinto libro decretalium* (ed Lyons 1512) ad *Extra*: v.xxxix.44, no 5, fol 248ra, as well as Decius in *Cons.*, p 1772, no XVII, lines 30ff. The latter pointed out that the oath came within the precincts of divine law, from which, by general consent, the pope could not dispense.

[1] Decius, p 1770, lines 3–5.

[2] *Ibid*, p 1774, no XXVI, lines 58ff. For earlier similar views see [B.] Tierney, [*Foundations of conciliar theory*] (repr Cambridge 1969) pp 127ff.

[3] See Paulus Castrensis, *Consilia* (ed Frankfurt 1582) I, *cons.* 419, who went even so far as to say that 'si cardinales persistant in eius obedientia [Gregory XII] videntur eius esse fautores et participare in crimine praestando ei auxilium et favorem'. See also Antonius de Butrio, *cons.* 420, fol 217rb who held a similar opinion. Cardinal Zabarella had indeed envisaged the possibility of a divided College of Cardinals in which case he counselled recourse to the emperor, obviously an advice that could not be adopted in the present instance, see his *Consilia* (ed Lyons 1552), *cons.* 150, fols 90vb–92rb, at no 5, fol 91ra: 'ipse [imperator] repraesentat totum populum christianum' with a reference to the *lex regia*. About Zabarella see W. Ullmann, *The Origins of the Great Schism* (repr London 1967) pp 191ff.

therefore held that in the interests of the universal Church even individual cardinals were entitled to convoke a general council 'propter negligentiam papae et collegii cardinalium'.[1] And the negligence of the pope was amply proved by his failure to convoke a council as he had promised to do within two years after becoming pope. Nor was any further admonition necessary, because where a promise remained unfulfilled after the appointed time no special admonition was called for.[2]

There was another argument according to which individual cardinals were entitled to proceed to a convocation of a general council. Negligence on the part of the pope redounded to the detriment of the universal Church, and hence the summoning of a council could be viewed as a defensive measure. This indeed was a standpoint that was closely linked with the whole question of negligence of a superior, even if he were pope. For if he proved himself to be a *malus praelatus* even an excommunicated individual was entitled to take the necessary steps to remove him – 'ubi agitur de repellendo de malo praelato, dicitur defensio necessaria, ideo etiam excommunicatus admittitur'. The conclusion which Decius reached – and indeed he was able to muster the common opinion in his favour[3] – was that individual cardinals were fully entitled to act where the defence of the Church was concerned. Hence they could from the strictly legal standpoint speak on behalf of the whole College of Cardinals which as a legal corporation was impeded in its actions and consequently incapable of expressing its own point of view.[4] 'Totum ius collegii in ipsis [cardinalibus] residere videtur.'[5] And lastly, according to the commonly accepted

[1] Decius, p 1775, lines 12ff and lines 23ff: 'Quia collegium deprehenditur in negligentia, haec provincia ad cardinales deferri videtur, ut omnes doctores tenent.'

[2] Decius refers to Baldus, *Lectura in Codicem* (ed Venice 1615), v.i.2, fol 149vb, but this appears hardly relevant, as Baldus dealt here with the unfulfilled promise to marry within two years, in which case no special warning was necessary.

[3] See for instance, Panormitanus, [*Super primo libro decretalium*] (ed Lyons 1512) ad *Extra*: I.v.2, no 9, fol 77ra: '...quaeritur numquid ius universitatis possit remanere in uno solo omnibus aliis mortuis vel privatis...tota potentia collegii residet in isto solo ...iste tamen solus non poterit seipsum eligere'. See also Petrus de Monte, *De potestate pontificis*, ed in *Tractatus universi iuris* (ed Venice 1579) XIII, I, fol 147va: 'ius universitatis potest esse in uno residente.' This standpoint had already been clearly expressed by the *gl. ord.* on *Extra*: I.v.2, s.v. 'Pauciores'. For Petrus de Monte compare also A. Black, *Monarchy & Community* (Cambridge 1970) pp 58, 62ff.

[4] See further the *gl. ord.* on *Extra*: I.v.2; and Panormitanus, no 5, fol 76vb.

[5] Furthermore, the right of the College of Cardinals could devolve on one cardinal only, as the corresponding *universitas* in Roman law also could consist of one member only, according to Decius, p 1775, no XVIII, lines 51, 55ff referring to *Dig.* 3.4.7 §2: 'ius omnium in unum reciderit et stet nomen universitatis.'

Julius II and the schismatic cardinals

doctrine, one sole remaining member of a chapter can elect the prelate, and hence 'in uno solo cardinali ius collegii residere potest et ipse poterit papam eligere'.

These were some of the main points made by contemporary *lumina iuris* whom the cardinals had consulted. It will be readily seen that from the formal and juristic standpoint the charge of having caused a schism could not be made against the cardinals. They had powerful doctrinal support and had not even adopted the commonly accepted viewpoint of the *glossa ordinaria*: they limited the case of an accusation of the pope to that of an alleged heresy, a charge which they had not raised. In their edict there was therefore no suggestion that they would proceed to an election of another pope or that they would take measures which could conceivably be construed as schismatic.

Paradoxically enough, the most convincing vindication of the cardinals' step came from the pope himself. There can be no doubt that he was galvanised into the very action and procedure which formed the case of the cardinals. The edict now issued by Julius II completely changed the situation and gravely affected the standing of the cardinals who had taken the initiative. Two months after the cardinals had despatched their edict, Julius II issued on 25 July 1511 the decree (dated 18 July 1511) by which he summoned a general council (the Fifth Lateran Council) for 19 April 1512 at the Lateran. In order to defuse the – admittedly dangerous – situation Julius attempted to wrest the initiative from the cardinals and did what he should have done some time within the preceding eight years.

What strikes the reader of this papal communication[1] is that Julius was far more concerned with attacking the cardinals than with the question of how to effect some concrete 'reform in head and members of the Church', a terminology which is conspicuously absent in this document. Instead, the cardinals were called 'sons of darkness' who had 'mendaciously acted as true schismatics'. Their envisaged council was no more than 'a schismatic conventicle'[2] or a synagogue of Satan provoking a malignant schism – *pessimum noviter pullulans schisma*.[3] The cardinals had neither the power to convoke a general council nor a legitimate cause. In any event, Pisa was a notoriously unsafe place. Again and again, Julius (and those cardinals who had remained with him) returned to the charge and accused their opponents of treasonable and schismatic conduct: the papal edict declared that they took the step 'ad scindendam et scandalizandam universalis ecclesiae unitatem',[4]

[1] *Ann Eccl*, pp 540b–545b.   [2] *Ibid* p 543b.   [3] *Ibid* pp 543b, 544a.   [4] *Ibid* p 543b.

hence their proposed measure was pronounced totally invalid 'ne cancerosus morbus invalescat'. Severe sanctions were threatened against individuals, groups and localities willing to render any help to the schismatic cardinals. In contrast to the lengthy and diffuse vituperations and condemnations of the cardinals the papal document becomes rather economical, if not tantalisingly vague, when it approaches the reason for convoking the general council: all the edict said was that the council would do everything to exalt and preserve the unity of the Church and activate its reform so that heresies and schisms were to be extirpated.[1]

In the annals of the medieval papacy it is indeed rare to find a document which in so one-sided a manner and without giving the cardinals accused and convicted of the crime of schism a chance to defend themselves, so completely disregarded fundamental principles of law applicable to the lowliest villein, a feature that was pointed out by cardinal Jacobazzi at the time.[2] Yet from the purely formal and constitutional standpoint the summoning of a general council was the master stroke of the experienced, shrewd and ruthless diplomat that Julius II had proved himself throughout his pontificate. Clearly, there was a very real dichotomy between the constitutional position of the pope and his undoubted right (and duty) to convoke a general council on the one hand, and the reasons which prompted him to act, that is, the action of the cardinals on the other. Their alleged schismatic action was the reason for the pope's summons – nevertheless, according to the solid body of established juristic theory and the opinion of the most outstanding jurists as well as according to the cardinals' own intentions the charge raised against them stood on extremely shaky foundations.

There is need for a more balanced assessment of the cardinals' step than it has so far received. For, as pointed out, on any strict analysis they could not be stigmatised as schismatics, because one of the pre-suppositions of schism in the juristic sense was absent: the essence of the crime of schism was rupture of the unity of the Church by separating parts of the Church from the pope, that is, withdrawal of obedience from him.[3] But this was precisely not the case here: on the contrary the cardinals had invited the pope to confirm and attend the council.

[1] *Ibid* p 544b.
[2] In his lengthy work *De concilio*, lib. vii, art. 1, ed in *Tractatus universi iuris* (Venice 1584), XIII-1, fol 302.
[3] Gratian, XXIV.i.34; also Panormitanus in the heading on the *gl. ord.* on *Extra*: v, 8.

Julius II and the schismatic cardinals

Nor had they, as already mentioned, created or intended to create an anti-pope. But Julius II was all out to smash the initiators of the Pisan Council as well as the conciliar idea itself with the help which conciliarism provided. Indubitably, the cardinals had forced his hand. The question was not simply council versus pope, but whether the council summoned by the pope or that initiated by the cardinals was to be the instrument by which reform was to be carried out. The pope spoke vaguely of a 'reformatio morum tam ecclesiasticorum quam saecularium personarum'[1] – an unobjectionable and laudable aim, but hardly one that touched the core of the matter – and as the first sessions of the Fifth Lateran Council proved, nothing of any consequence in the direction of reform was in fact enacted. The pope merely used the device of a general council to render harmless the intentions of the cardinals. The design of the cardinals to effect the 'reformatio in capite et membris' – and this is one of the crucial points – was brought to naught by the papal summons. But from the formal juristic standpoint the papal action cornered the cardinals: for by continuing to pursue their plan *after* the papal summons had gone out, they now formally and constitutionally began to become schismatics.

This indeed was also the opinion of contemporaries who had displayed great sympathy with the cardinals' cause. For instance, cardinal Jacobazzi[2] in common with many others held that while before the papal summons the cardinals could not possibly be called schismatics,[3] their standing afterwards assumed an entirely different complexion: they now had become schismatics *vere et proprie*.[4] Julius II knew how to derive the greatest profit from his constitutional position and relentlessly drove home his undoubted right which he used to the fullest possible extent and advantage: in the early autumn of 1511 he set the cardinals a term within which they had an opportunity of recanting. When the ultimatum expired, in public consistory on 24 October 1511

---

[1] *Ann Eccl*, p 544.

[2] For Jacobazzi see W. Ullmann in *Medieval Studies presented to Aubrey Gwynn*, ed J. A. Watt, J. B. Morrall, F. X. Martin (Dublin 1961) p 360, n 4, with further literature.

[3] See *De concilio*, no 80, fol 302vb: 'Non videntur dicendi schismatici [cardinales] quia nullam scissuram in ecclesia fecerunt...cum ergo per discessum ipsorum cardinalium adhuc nulla reperiatur illicita divisio per inobedientiam ab unitate ecclesiae, sequitur quod adhuc praedicti cardinales non possunt dici schismatici.'

[4] *Ibid* no 82, fol 303ra: 'Vereor si post intimatum concilium per sanctissimum dominum nostrum ad quem hoc spectat, se non subiecerunt voluntati eius, et a suis coeptis non destiterint volendo a seipsis concilium tenere et antipapam erigere, quod tunc erunt vere et proprie schismatici, quia tunc quicquid fecerunt, ambitiose factum esse ostenderent.' See also *ibid* no 87, fol 303rb. Jedin has rightly stressed the importance of Jacobazzi's standpoint, p 89 (Eng trans p 107).

the chief actors amongst them were excommunicated and deprived of their cardinalate.[1] Herewith the cardinals were publicly exposed as seditious schismatics. The first session of their council did not take place until 5 November 1511 – the delay was caused by a number of factors of which the papal summons, the lukewarm support by Louis XII and the detached attitude of Maximilian were in the foreground – and it was a council without a constitutional head and entirely in the hands of formally condemned schismatics who had been excommunicated in a juristically unimpeachable manner.

In a word, the situation had changed quite drastically by the autumn of 1511. Considering the profound issues at stake, was the display of legal formalism really sufficient and adequate to stem the rapidly advancing tide of a far more serious schism, the contours of which could clearly be discerned on the not too distant horizon? Assuredly, the College of Cardinals had, as also in previous pontificates, shown considerably greater awareness of the very pressing needs of the time than the papacy – one has but to recall the high-powered commissions of cardinals appointed by Pius II and Alexander VI and their terms of reference – but what does strike the distant observer is the conspicuous and fundamental divergence in the juristic and theological approach to the issues at stake. Frequently enough do we obtain just more than a mere glance in the protagonists of either side of some deep-seated aversion from the other's point of view.[2]

What must be emphasised is that the jurists were quite ostensibly aware of the necessity for some quick, drastic and effective measures if the collapse of a united and uniform Christendom was not to come about. They certainly had their ears more to the ground than their theological colleagues. What is particularly interesting and what also needs to be stressed is that the jurists did not employ any new arguments, still less propound radical solutions, but entirely relied on established doctrine and the more recent exposition of the constitutional law of the Church. Here we find a feature which is not at all unfamiliar to those who have some acquaintance with the development of juristic themes in the Middle Ages. What fifteenth and early six-

---

[1] *Ann Eccl*, pp 553-7, with testimonies of eye witnesses and actual texts of sanctions promulgated.

[2] See, for instance, Decius, no XI, p 1770, lines 50ff: 'Non curandum est quod theologi aliter dicant, quia in ista materia magis standum est doctoribus canonum quam theologiae magistris, quia hoc non exigitur de articulis fidei, sed de moribus et integritate vitae, quo casu magis credendum est professoribus canonum.' See also no XII, p 1771, lines 20ff expressing a similar point of view.

Julius II and the schismatic cardinals

teenth-century jurists advocated was merely a practical application of already accepted doctrine – this indeed is a parallel case of the conciliar theme itself which, as has been shown by one of my pupils, was virtually as old as canonistic doctrine itself was.[1] Here we have exactly the same situation: in themselves perfectly harmless juristic theses gained the greatest topical significance when applied to a concrete situation. Apparently when set forth in lectures, glosses, commentaries and books, these themes were considered innocuous and abstract enough, but once applied to a real contingency, they assumed an unexpectedly dangerous complexion. Yet looking at the scene as the fateful second decade of the sixteenth century opens, one can hardly resist the temptation to think that they might well have offered some solution of the crucial problems besetting contemporary Christendom. One can go further and say that juristic doctrine in the fifteenth and early sixteenth centuries attempted to accommodate the law to the exigencies of the time by simply adapting well-worn abstract themes to reality. And in this canonistic jurisprudence showed itself fully alive to its vocation and mission as a social science.

On the other hand, the theologians showed themselves, as their numerous statements amply prove, wholly impervious to the exigencies of the time. There is no doubt that the papal convocation edict was inspired by one of the greatest theologians of the time – and one who was unsuccessfully to confront Luther only six years hence: Thomas de Vio, commonly known as Cajetan. His mastery of theology was never in doubt;[2] what might legitimately be doubted was whether the theological arguments as set forth by him, were suitable and relevant at this particular juncture of time. His theology showed an inflexibility and rigidity that admitted of no adjustment or accommodation to newly emerging problems. It was a regurgitation of stale hierocratic themes and axioms which bore little relation to the changing conditions of the time. The very able and eloquent Dominican General proved himself a highly gifted pupil of Bernard of Clairvaux and of Innocent III but nevertheless had not their sense of realism.[3] His bitterness about the canonists was proportionate to the contempt in which the latter held the former. It was the unyielding dogmatic position concerning the pope which acted as an additional solvent of the one and universal Church. The theological stance not inconsider-

---

[1] See Tierney, especially pp 96ff.
[2] See Scarisbrick, p 166: 'probably the most considerable Catholic theologian of the century.'   [3] See also the assessment by Jedin, p 91 (Eng trans p 114).

ably contributed to the cataclysm which paradoxically enough it was designed to avoid. Neither legal formalism nor old-fashioned hierocratic arguments were adequate means to effect a cure of the endemic disease from which contemporary Christianity suffered. These ills could not be cured by stigmatising cardinals as heretics, merely because they proposed to do what the pope had failed to do. Nor were the craftiness of Julius II, his political sagacity, astuteness and alertness, his reliance on the conservatism of the curia and the theologians apt to ward off the clearly discernible break-up of Christendom. What would seem to me a very necessary research task is the detailed analysis of the part which the professional theologians and the professional jurists played on the eve of the Reformation.

The year 1511 with its dramatic and swiftly following events would seem to assume profound significance in the involved and complex contingencies on the eve of what technically and from the medieval standpoint was a schism. We should not forget that it was also in the same summer months of 1511 that the emperor-elect Maximilian made determined attempts to become pope himself.[1] That the convocation of the Fifth Lateran Council was nothing but a manoeuvre on the part of the pope, can hardly be disputed. Its early sessions, still in his pontificate, demonstrated this, and they also demonstrated that contemporaries had looked through this manoeuvre – the pamphlet *Julius exclusus e coelis* was a persuasive pointer.

Above all, could the hierocratic theme of papal monarchy still make much impact in the early sixteenth century? Was not this the very age in which constitutionalism, that is, the restriction of monarchic prerogatives, had already made great strides? Once again, it would seem that the jurists – and they were civilians as well as canonists – were on the whole more alive to the constitutional needs of the period than their theological colleagues. And the jurists among the cardinals incurred the charge of being schismatics because *inter alia* they advocated a governmental scheme that appeared better attuned to the social and legal needs than the theologians cared to admit. The problem besetting christian society as seen by the jurists was in other words not so much a matter of faith as one of law and order.[2] Great issues seem to be telescoped within the few summer months of 1511. Was not the papal endeavour to re-establish papal monarchy, not with the help of

[1] See Pastor, III, p 564; more recently H. Wiesflecker, 'Kaiser-Papst Plan Maximilians i.J.1511' in *Mitteilungen des Instituts für österreichische Geschichtsforschung*, LXXI (Vienna 1963) pp 311–32.
[2] See Decius above, p 190 n 2.

Juilus II and the schismatic cardinals

jurists, but with the help of theologians, anachronistic in the situation of the early sixteenth century? Did not this papal intention contribute to a still greater alienation of currently critical opinion from the papacy and all it stood for? Did not papal intransigence prove itself to be a factor which unwittingly but all the more potently promoted schismatic aspirations? Insistence on outworn principles of government can hardly be called a sign of prudence, wisdom or statesmanship.[1]

Yet contemporaries who across the Alps watched the situation from the distance, could not but see a confirmation of their deep apprehension concerning the state of the Church, the papacy and officially endorsed theology. It was perhaps not so much the fact of the pope excommunicating and deposing eminent cardinals – the most intimate counsellors of the pope, always designated as *partes corporis nostri* [*papae*] – as the manner in which the punitive measures were taken against them and still more the reason for invoking the heaviest sanctions which must have been grist to the mills of the critics of the papacy. The policy of Julius II and the pitiable performance of both the Pisan and the Lateran councils could not but fail to impress the in any case critical contemporaries: Luther – soon to join the ranks of heretics and schismatics – can be cited as a witness for the general feeling of frustration and disillusionment at the efforts – unsuccessful as they were – to lift the universal Church out of the quagmire into which it had fallen.[2]

[1] There was of course consistency in Julius II's basic aims. Two years earlier, on 2 July 1509, he had issued his decree *Suscepti regiminis*, ed in *Bullarium* [*Magnum Romanum*] (Lyons 1692) I, pp 511–12, in which any appeal to a general council against a decree or law by whomsoever initiated, made the appellant at least suspected of heresy. This, incidentally, is still the law in the modern *Codex iuris canonici* (c.2332). But this decree of Julius II was an extension of Pius II's decree *Execrabilis* of 18 January 1459: it was the first time that an appeal from a decree or verdict of the pope to a general council incurred the penalties of the crime of *lèse-majesté* (ed in *Bullarium*, I, p 386).

[2] See his *Resolutiones* (ad annum 1518) in conclusio 89, *WA* (1883) I, p 627, lines 27ff. 'Ecclesia indiget reformatione, quod non est unius hominis, pontificis nec multorum cardinalium officium sicut probavit utrumque novissimum concilium, sed tocius orbis, immo solius Dei.' On this see esp C. Stange, 'Luther und das Konzil von Pisa von 1511' in *Zeitschrift für systematische Theologie*, x (Tübingen 1933) pp 681ff at pp 685–8, 709–10.

XVII

The Medieval Papal Court as an International Tribunal

For a medievalist pure and simple to be invited to contribute to a *Festschrift* that honours Hardy Cross Dillard's elevation to the highest judicial tribunal and office in the world is at once an undeserved privilege and a challenge. Has a medievalist anything useful at his disposal that can be of any interest to so illustrious an honorand? Is there anything within the orbit of the modern International Court of Justice that could conceivably have any affinity with a medieval court? The very question indicates the deep chasm that exists between the medieval and the modern ideas and systems of law and its administration. In choosing the papal court in the Middle Ages as a specific topic I can only hope that the great *lumen iuris* may find the one or the other point which possibly evokes his interest. The purpose of this short contribution is to invite attention to some basic features in the structure of the medieval law and in so doing to find a possible avenue to the answer as to why the International Court of Justice today has (what is technically called) no compulsory jurisdiction, is unable to act as a tribunal which authoritatively *dicit ius* (unless explicitly requested by both parties in a dispute) and has no means nor machinery to enforce its decisions. The papal court in the Middle Ages disposed of precisely these three appurtenances—it had compulsory jurisdiction, authoritatively laid down, explained, interpreted and developed the law, and could reasonably anticipate the enforcement of its decision. How can one explain this difference? It is a difference which in the Occident highlights far more clearly than any lengthy disquisition could hope to do both the development in the sphere of public law, especially public international law, and the development of the concept of law.

I

Two points in modern international law [1] require a brief restatement. First, disputes which the International Court of Justice is competent to try and to decide are only those which occur between sovereign states—the concept of state sovereignty is therefore an integral element of modern international law and is at the same time an essential structural feature of the international tribunal itself. Secondly, the judicial machinery can be set in motion only if all the parties involved expressly consent to its operation. In some ways therefore the International Court of Justice strongly partakes of the

---

1. Throughout this paper only public law is considered.

procedure characteristic of arbitration machinery. Although at first sight it may seem that the two presuppositions are quite unrelated to each other, they nevertheless have a close relationship, a point that will emerge with all the greater clarity once it is thrown against the medieval background.

That the papacy and its courts acted throughout the central period of the high Middle Ages in the manner of a tribunal possessing compulsory jurisdiction is so well known that this fact needs only to be stated to be adequately appreciated. And the jurisdiction was comprehensive and all-embracing; the papal court could act both as a tribunal of first instance and as an appellate court. It could become active on its own motion or upon the complaints of a party, be that an individual or a group or a corporate body or a Ruler. Its jurisdiction was unrestricted as to subject-matter, persons, or territories. No prescriptive time impeded its working. Thus treaties between governments were submitted to the papacy for approval, confirmation and ratification, but treaties and compacts could also be annulled by the papal court without any foregoing papal ratification or confirmation.

The papacy could, as indeed it did, give orders to belligerent parties to refrain from further belligerent action, to enter into peace negotiations or to establish a truce. The papal court issued decrees by which the continuance of commercial relations between certain territories or with certain groups of persons were to be severed. Similarly, reprisals against towns and the confiscation of public property were ordered by the papal court. Unjust tolls or fees exacted on public highways and rivers were forbidden by the papacy in its judicial function. By the verdict of the papal tribunal governments could be changed and governmental power transferred to organs other than those who in actual fact possessed public power. In support of warring and hard pressed goverments the papacy judicially ordered the dispatch of armed troops, just as it decreed that belligerent governments were to be assisted by other governments, provided always that the cause of the war was papally approved. By the same token the papal court could prohibit assistance to troops which had invaded or were about to invade territory. Rulers, including kings and emperors, were by the decision of the papal court deprived of their governing powers, either by formal deposition or by excommunication. Any municipal law could be declared invalid and the people of a particular region or country forbidden to adhere to this or that law or accept the laws of this or that government.[2]

It should be kept in mind that these papal judicial decisions affected the public law and public relations in Europe from the Iberian peninsula to Western Russia, from Scandinavia and Scotland to Sicily, and

---

2. For all instances, see W. ULLMANN, PRINCIPLES OF GOVERNMENT AND POLITICS IN THE MIDDLE AGES 82-86 (2d ed. 1966) [hereinafter cited as PRINCIPLES OF GOVERNMENT]. For numerous extracts from medieval papal documents see G. BALLADORE-PALLIERI & G. VISMARA, ACTA PONTIFICIA IURIS GENTIUM USQUE AD ANNUM MCCCIV (1947).

to some extent also territories outside Europe, especially when the full effects of the crusades came to be felt, such as was the case in Georgia in Asia Minor. I think it is no exaggeration to say that this kind of universal (that is, by contemporary medieval standards, universal) jurisdiction had not been witnessed in antiquity nor is it in the modern period. The idea that within the framework of a judicial process and through the instrumentality of a centrally situated court boundaries of countries could be changed or fixed, Rulers and governments be replaced, and punitive measures against organizations and corporations be decreed, was assuredly alien to the world of antiquity. Yet to say, as it is said frequently enough, that the absence of the idea of sovereignty made possible this compulsory and comprehensive jurisdiction or accounted for the non-existence of the very idea of an international law,[3] would not seem to furnish an entirely adequate explanation of this phenomenon. For we should bear in mind that the idea of sovereignty in the sense in which most modern writers use the term is itself the outcome of a rather complex historical and ideological process; what is commonly understood by it today is territorial sovereignty or state sovereignty which indeed did not in conceptual form emerge until the later Middle Ages, and in so far the *communis opinio* is correct.

But it does not go far enough, because the notion that preceded territorial or state sovereignty was personal sovereignty. It was this sovereignty which was operational in medieval Europe from the ninth century onwards and which emanated from the office which the Ruler occupied. As the incumbent of the office, the Ruler formed an estate of his own, standing over and above the people committed to his government and his care.[4] This kind of personal sovereignty was observable with all medieval Rulers. However, although this personal sovereignty displayed all the effects which came to be associated later with territorial or state sovereignty, it nevertheless was no obstacle to the exercise of a veritably universal jurisdiction on the part of the papal court. The disregard of the effects of personal sovereignty can bring us nearer to an understanding of why the papal jurisdiction was compulsory, effective and authoritative.

In order to appreciate this medieval phenomenon two sides of the same coin should be recognized: the so-called ecclesiological theme on the one hand, and the governmental theme as propounded by the papacy on the other hand. Both are different facets of one and the same thing, which is technically called the primatial position of the papacy, or what was also termed its *principatus*. And both facets went back—or rather were traced back by the medieval papacy—to the biblical passage in which a particular body as well as its government were established *uno ictu*. That is to say, according to the bibli-

---

3. *Cf.*, *e.g.*, J. L. BRIERLY, THE LAW OF NATIONS 4-7 (6th ed. H. Waldock 1963) [hereinafter cited as BRIERLY].

4. *See* PRINCIPLES OF GOVERNMENT, *supra* note 2, at 115-19.

cal passage [5] Christ was held to have created the Church and at the very same time also provided for its government.[6] Now the creation of the Church as the body of all the faithful—clergy and laity alike— supplied the so-called ecclesiological element and furnished the pre-supposition for the interpretation of this passage in an exclusively monarchical sense. According to this interpretation—adopted in actual fact by the papacy from the mid-fifth century onwards—the binding and loosening powers of which the passage spoke, were Christ's own, but were vicariously handed over to St. Peter, so that the latter was said to act on behalf of the former. Recent exegesis has made it clear that the tenor, substance and significance of this basic passage was partly of Old Testament origin, and partly of Roman law provenance. The effect of combining biblical and Roman elements was a thorough-going juristic construction. The "binding and loosening powers" were the allegorical expression for the Old Testament legalism, and their vicarious possession by Peter was the basis of the further juristic theme, according to which the pope was a successor to these petrine powers. The Roman law of inheritance served as a prototype, and from the mid-fifth century down to the end of the medieval period, if not beyond, the pope called himself "the unworthy heir of St. Peter" (*indignus haeres beati Petri*). The crucial point here is that according to Roman law the heir continues (in a purely legal sense) the legal personality of the deceased person whom he inherits. All the assets and liabilities of the dead person were transferred to the heir. This Roman law principle was applied by the papacy to the powers and office which Christ was alleged to have conferred on St. Peter and which, by way of inheritance, were said to have been possessed by the pope as the heir of petrine functions and status.

With regard to the present topic, the essential point is that genetically and historically the pope as successor to the petrine office and powers was, and was intended to be, a monarch in the literal sense of the term, hence the adoption of the Roman notion of *princeps* for the pope and *principatus* for the institution of the papacy. Monarchy was not however merely a name or a convenient governmental nomenclature, but was conceived as the sum-total of all governmental power in the public field. And this governmental power could not—once more on the basis of the Roman law model—be understood in any sense other than the legal one, so that its exercise was nothing but either the creation of new law or the application of already existing

---

5. *Matt.* 16:18-19.
    And I say unto Thee, that thou art Peter, and upon this rock I will build my church . . . and whatsoever thou shalt bind on earth shall be bound in heaven: and whatsoever thou shalt loose on earth shall be loosed in heaven.
6. For details see Ullmann, *Leo I and the Theme of Papal Primacy*, 11 J. THEOLOGICAL STUDIES 25 (1960); *see also* W. ULLMANN, THE GROWTH OF PAPAL GOVERNMENT IN THE MIDDLE AGES 18-28, with references to additional literature at 462-63 (3rd ed. 1970).

law. *Iurisdictio* was the hallmark of *gubernatio*: he who *dicit ius* also *gubernat*. The *gubernator* was he who authoritatively laid down what the law in a special case was to be.

It readily can be seen how closely linked were the ecclesiological and the monarchic themes, and this close link is of special importance in the present context, for by virtue of all Christians having been members of the Church, the pope as monarch presided over them, without regard to the status which an individual member may have possessed in the public field by virtue of his functions. The Church as conceived in this context consisted of those Christians who accepted the papal interpretation of the fundamental biblical passage. In other words, the ecclesiological point of view—as disseminated throughout the Latin West—rested not so much on a rational and critical acceptance of the one biblical statement as upon the conviction that its interpretation by the papacy was correct. This is the same as saying that the integrating, structural and essential element of the ecclesiological standpoint was the element of faith—faith in the institution of the papacy, faith in its function as the governing organ of the Church (in the sense defined), faith in it as the divinely established special agency by which the ecclesiological unit was to be led to its eventual destination. This is not the place to expand on the inherent teleological substance of this governmental idea. What is of immediate concern is the means by which the papacy was to fulfill its function, for as far as the public sphere came into question, the one effective instrument at the papacy's disposal was the law.

What therefore needs particular emphasis is the essence of the law as handled and issued and applied and modified by the medieval papacy. That law embodied all the features which characterized the ecclesiological and governmental themes. Above all, it reflected the element of faith to exactly the same degree to which it formed part of the Church and the papacy itself. Because (Latin Western) Christians believed in the papacy as the divinely decreed governmental organ, its claims that its law and individual verdicts constituted in actual fact the concrete manifestation of the divine will itself, were in the ecclesiogical basis accepted. One might go further and say that the medieval papal idea of law was a necessary consequence of the ecclesiological and primatial presuppositions. Faith in the divinely appointed government of the divinely established Church was the indispensable requisite and material ingredient of the papally issued law and judicial sentence. The descending theme of government and law found its classic expression in the medieval papal government. Negatively expressed, what was not in evidence and what was a necessary ideological absentee, was the notion of consent as a material ingredient as far as the papal law and government were concerned. Faith alone was the prime and sole basis of the government as exercised by the papacy and therefore of its law and judicial decisions.

This recognition of the faith as the structural repository of the medieval papal law [7] has direct relevance to the present enquiry. Not only does it explain the commanding position of the papacy itself, but also, and above all, the efficacy of the papal law and of papal jurisdiction in general. By virtue of the efficacy of the element of faith, the problem of sanctions hardly arose. Precisely because the Latin Christians had faith in the institution of the papacy as the divine instrument of government, they accepted without scrutiny and detailed enquiry the rulings the papal court gave, however little an individual decision was appreciated by those who were adversely affected by it. This faith was not imposed upon contemporaries; it was, as so much else in the Middle Ages, taken for granted and was a self-evident condition and basis of private and public life. And within the precincts of the law it is especially important to point out that this faith itself was subject to the rulings of the papacy. Faith in the divinity of the papacy as a governmental institution brought forth the law of this institution, and this in turn regulated the faith itself. Three points deserve special emphasis in this context.

First, the exercise of practical judicial functions by the papacy as the supreme court of Western Christendom was contingent upon the availability of a body of law that was capable of being administered and applied by the papacy. This contingency occurred in the mid-twelfth century, and it was only from then onwards that the papacy rapidly emerged as a central, universal and supreme organ which acted as a *gubernator* exclusively through the vehicle of the law. The age subsequent to the publication of Gratian's *Decretum* was the age in which the monarchic role of the papacy came to full fruition by means of the law, and not least in those situations which would nowadays be classed as "cases in international law," such as in fact have been instanced.

The second point to be made is that because the papacy operated with the law, that law was contained, not in statutes or general ordinances, but in individual decretal letters: they dealt with one specific case only, it is true, but by virtue of the ruling having been given by the papal court as a universal judicial tribunal, it had necessarily universal applicability and was regarded as such. The incorporation of a decretal in one of the official collections of canon law (for instance, in the *Liber Extra*, or the *Liber Sextus*, and so on) did not create the binding and enforceable and universal character of the ruling, but merely assisted its availability. It stands to reason that a law is easier to apply if without great difficulty it can be traced in a codex within two stiff covers, instead of having to be searched for in a number of repositories. But what needs special underscoring in this context is that in issuing a decretal the papacy functioned at

---

7. See generally PRINCIPLES OF GOVERNMENT, *supra* note 2, at 95-97; *cf.* C. FRIEDRICH, THE PHILOSOPHY OF LAW IN HISTORICAL PERSPECTIVE 8-12 (1958).

once as a legislative organ and as a judicial tribunal. Legislative and judicial functions were not only not separated, but were functions which were intrinsically, ideologically and programmatically fused, for the papal court pronounced the law of the pope himself, because in the overwhelming number of cases he presided over the court, and he presided both as a monarchic Ruler and as a judicial officer.

The third point concerns not the subject matter of law, but the persons to whom it applied. By virtue of the universality of the papal law and of its scope on a universal plane, the rulings of the papal court applied to all Christians—the very test of the ecclesiological theme—which meant that neither king nor emperor nor any other dignitary was excluded from the effects of papal decisions. And one of the most conspicuous features of the papal judicial decisions was that they denied the personal sovereignty of those Rulers they affected[8]; the papal judicial decisions exempted neither persons nor things.[9] Again, this can be explained without great intellectual efforts by the character of the government and the body over which the government was exercised: the universality of both supplied the explanation.

It is in connexion with this third point that the element of faith enters once again into the discussion. Precisely by virtue of their being members of the Church, precisely by virtue, moreover, of Rulers having been "Kings by the grace of God," they, as the most directly affected individuals, automatically accepted (or were supposed to accept) the rulings of the papal court. By resisting them the Rulers would have been said to have resisted divinity itself and would have exposed themselves to the charge of unfaithfulness which was tantamount to apostasy and heresy.[10] Faith was an integral part of the law, and without the acceptance by the people of the ultimately divinely decreed function of the papacy as a judicial organ, papal verdicts would not have been considered binding on the Ruler. The papacy as a judicial institution depended for the "enforcement" of its decrees and verdicts on the belief held by the people at large in its being the mouth-piece of divinity: the papacy had no militia, no

---

8. This was precisely what evoked the wrath of affected Rulers who nevertheless found themselves caught on the horns of a dilemma. On the one hand they claimed special personal sovereignty by virtue of divinity having entrusted to them Rulership (through the grace of God), and on the other hand they questioned the papal right to interfere with their position as God's vicegerents. One cannot have it both ways.

9. *Cf., e.g.,* Gelasius I, *Epistola* 30, cap. 12 in EPISTOLAE ROMANORUM PONTIFICUM GENUINAE 445 (A. Thielm ed. 1862) Gregory VII, *Register*, II.51 in MONUMENTA GERMANIAE HISTORICA: EPISTOLAE SELECTAE 193 (E. Caspar ed. 1955) *Reg.,* VII.21 in *id.* 557; and especially *Reg.,* IV.2 in *id.* 294; *see also* Innocent III, LIBER EXTRA I.XXXIII.6. It was only another way of expressing the same theme when Gregory VII declared that the papal government was a *universale regimen*, as he did in his *Reg.,* II.44 in MONUMENTA GERMANIAE HISTORICA *supra*, at 180.

10. For the legal consequences see LIBER EXTRA V.VII.13.

police force or other paraphernalia with which its laws and decisions could have been enforced.

However severe papal judicial measures were in regard to Rulers or even groups, the backing—even if only silently, and as often as not unenthusiastically—by the populace, was a presupposition of their efficacy. Whether it was a deposition or a decision in a contested royal election or a boundary dispute or an order to dispatch troops or to arrange a truce—the papal verdict could always rely on the support or at least the acquiescence of the (inarticulate) people at large. This was really the crux of the whole juristic situation: what in ancient Roman times was the consent of Roman citizens was supplanted by the faith of the members of the Church who were the subjects of the monarchically ruling pope. And because they were subjects, they could also be made to suffer the penalty of collective measures, that is, the papally decreed interdict in the case of their reluctance, and all the more so in the case of resistance or disobedience to papal judicial verdicts which were nothing but decisions made on a supra-regal, supra-tribal and supra-national plane.

Since the papal law and papal decisions incorporated as their material ingredient faith and thus moved within purely spiritual, that is, incorporeal precincts, the sanctions partook of the same spirituality. This indeed is perhaps the best means to test the character of the papal canon law and its efficacy on a "global" scale. It was effective because it was accompanied by sanctions which themselves came from the same arsenal as that from which the law stemmed and accorded with the sentiments of society at large. That society manifested an ideology which itself emanated from the same spiritual quarter as the law and its sanctions did. The descending theme of government and law was possibly the most conspicuous expression of this ideology. The sanctions—excommunication, interdict, and so forth—were as incorporeal measures commensurate to the law itself; yet they displayed their effects on the social plane, effects which were felt as drastically as if they had primarily and exclusively been of a purely temporal character.

The efficacy of papal rulings in matters which would today be classed as international disputes, can effortlessly be explained by the unquestioned assumptions upon which medieval society rested. It was these assumptions, overwhelmingly religious in substance, which created the ideology of that self-same society, a society to all intents and purposes identical with the Church. Within this Church every Christian (of the Roman persuasion in contrast to the Byzantine adherents) was a member with definite roles allocated. The efficacy of a papal decision was, so to speak, built-in. *Per se,* it did not need the armed assistance by police or militia, because it presupposed faith; without it papal law and papal judicial decisions were unthinkable, and the sanctions reflected in a singularly persuasive manner the essence of the law no less than the ideology of which the law was a prominent offspring.

That the idea of law was in actual fact embodied in the dominant ideology which was the social and governmental manifestation of the religious sentiment, can be shown by evidence from another sector. The metaphorical antithesis of *anima* and *corpus* brought into clearest possible relief that particular facet of the medieval concept of law according to which the law as a social norm expressed in the public realm what in the private realm was "the soul." The role which was assigned to the soul in the individual body, was assigned to the law in the collective body, be that the Church, a kingdom or other body public. Just as the soul—one of the undisputed axioms of medieval Christianity—ruled the body, in the same way the law fulfilled the function of a norm which ruled the (public) collective body.[11] This meaning of the allegory presented the fullest confirmation of the legalism prevalent in the Middle Ages, that is, that a public body could live, develop and reach its end only through the instrumentality of the law which thereby became the soul of the body public. The *anima* was the vivifying organ of the individual as well as of the public body.[12] Hence the ready recourse to the law and the courts of law, and also the ready recourse to the supreme and generally acknowledged court of the papacy to settle "international" disputes.

All this tallied of course with the ecclesiological premise. The papal law and tribunal were seen as the mouth-piece which was alleged to have made known the will of divinity in regard to contemporary society viewed as the Church. The latter's well-being, so it was held, would have been seriously affected if the organ charged with its government had not decreed "peace" in the most authoritative manner

---

11. W. ULLMANN, THE INDIVIDUAL AND SOCIETY IN THE MIDDLE AGES 47 (1966); W. ULLMANN, PAPST UND KÖNIG 38-40 (in Salzburger Universitätsschriften, fasc. 3, 1967).

12. This allegory is of the greatest significance in understanding the idea of medieval law, pervaded as it was by religious tenets and maxims. This antithesis of soul and body was not a medieval invention, but was bequeathed to the Middle Ages by early Christian doctrine. In a statement of the fourth century one reads that the king had power to dispose over the body only, while the bishop had power over the soul as well as the body. PRINCIPLES OF GOVERNMENT, *supra* note 2, at 93. But once the soul was equated with the law as the vivifying element of the body public, this purely religious opinion of early Christianity was to assume an entirely different complexion in the high Middle Ages. On its basis proper governing and legal power of the papacy was claimed to extend through the medium of the law (*i.e.* soul) to the purely temporal (*i.e.* bodily) concerns of the body public. This was clearly the case from Innocent III onwards. The feature which has sometimes caused misgivings, that is, the indirect jurisdiction of the papacy over the so-called temporal (*i.e.* bodily) matters, can find a ready explanation in the meaning attached to the *animacorpus* metaphor. The seventh-century Visigothic laws contained a statement which leaves nothing to be desired as regards clarity: 'Lex est . . . anima totius corporis popularis' (MONUMENTA GERMANIAE HISTORICA, LEGES VISIGOTHORUM, I.II.2 at 41).

it could do, that is, by deciding a dispute in a final papal verdict that was issued *auctoritate omnipotentis Dei*. Negatively expressed, the vivifying element of the collective body, the Church, would have been believed to be found wanting. The supply of this life blood to the ecclesiological unit might have appeared deficient. Seen from yet another angle, the sempiternity of the body public that could be achieved only by the law [13] would have been jeopardized if no papal decision in law had been made in regard to the matters which seemed to the contemporary papacy to call for a final and authoritative ruling in order to preserve the integrity and sempiternity of the collective *corpus fidelium*. The papal law as promulgated in the individual decisions was viewed as an instrument of order and peace, not necessarily as an instrument of morals or virtuous living.

In brief, the descending theme of government and law makes understandable why the decisions of the papal court were not only of direct interest to the internal structure of the Church, but were also, and to exactly the same extent, relevant to matters which impinged upon the order and peace of this self-same Church that was viewed as medieval society. The very existence of the one and only body which knew no boundaries of an ethnic, linguistic or biological character explains without undue effort why the rulings of the papal tribunal were, if not explicitly, at any rate implicitly, effective judicial decisions of a kind that nowadays applies only to judicial verdicts within the precincts of municipal law. Indeed, what the observer witnesses is that both the papal law and the papal decisions were by virtue of their finality nothing else but "municipal law writ large."

II

There is no text-book on international law which does not in one way or another convey the generally accepted viewpoint according to which international law presupposes the nation state whereby the accent appears to lie on the concept of the State. One has only to read what one of the great teachers of this century has taught, that is that a fundamental postulate of international law is the existence of a number of states, secular, national and territorial.[14] It would seem, however, that within this framework the concepts of "State" and "nation" are interchangeable—hence also the nomenclature of the "law of nations"—which implicitly presupposes that within one and the same State there could exist only one nation. Be that as it may, the current opinion has nevertheless a great deal in its favour, although one may question whether from the genetic point of view there is not an essential element missing, and that element concerns jurisprudence. Or seen from a different angle, current opinion needs to be qualified by considerations which are the proper métier of legal

---

13. *Cf.* Ullmann, *Historical Jurisprudence*, in LA STORIA DEL DIRITTO NEL QUADRO DELLE SCIENZE STORICHE 194-211 & n.10 (B Paradisi ed. 1966).

14. BRIERLY, *supra* note 3, at 5-7.

history. It is particularly advisable in the present context to point out the jurisprudential substratum, for if the element of faith as a structural, indispensable and material ingredient of the idea of law makes understandable the efficacy of papal judicial decisions concerning "international" disputes, we must also enquire what it was that eventually relegated the papal court to so minor a role within the international orbit that it has to all intents and purposes long ceased to exist as an effective judicial organ. On this occasion only a few tentative remarks can be made.

That the papal judiciary declined in authority and prestige steadily from the late thirteenth century onwards is a factor which is indubitably true, relevant and also important in itself; however, this decline needs to be seen against a larger canvas and against the background of an intellectual revolution that gained momentum in the succeeding period. It is furthermore true that there was a corresponding decrease of appeals and of cases dealt with by the papal court—not so much a quantitative as a qualitative decrease as the fourteenth century wore on, for although appeals concerning internal feuds of individual churches, monasteries, and so on, in fact increased, fewer and fewer of the "great questions" came to be decided by the papal court. And for obvious reasons during the schismatic age the latter kind of jurisdiction to all intents and purposes ceased. The so-called conciliar movement of the early fifteenth century culminating in the decrees of the Council of Constance adopted some of the essential dogmas which characterized the intellectual revolution and raised them to the platform of universally binding laws. The bearers of this intellectual revolution were jurists, philosophers, theologians, practical lawyers and polemicists. Their concern was the adaptation of Aristotle and of his doctrines to the science of law.

The result of this process of adaptation and accommodation was a jurisprudential theme which was substantially and essentially the very opposite of what the high Middle Ages had witnessed. While there the descending theme of government and law predominated, the absorption of Aristotelian theorems yielded the ascending theme of government and law, according to which all power was located in the people, hence one can also speak of a populist theme. The conceptual substance of this ascending theme was the change of the status of the individual from a subject to that of a citizen. Evidently, the law-creative process was greatly affected by this change, for within the terms of the ascending theme the law embodied the consent of the citizens, and not, as within the orbit of the descending theme, the faith of the subjects in the law-creating organ. The citizens themselves participated in the creation of the law, either directly or through their elected representatives. The element of consent became thereby within the ascending theme a structural element of the law and replaced the function of faith. Of course, there are crucial differences between faith and consent. The former was focused on the authority of the papacy and its divine establishment as the organ directing and governing the Christian body public by means of the law that was *given* to the faithful subjects; the latter was focused on the exercise of rational assessment and critical evaluation of concrete situations and circumstances by the autonomous citizens who thus became (either directly or indirectly) the creators of the law. The law was therefore *made* by citizens, not given to subjects.[15]

No great intellectual imagination is required to realize the profound effects which this Aristotelian-inspired jurisprudence exercised in the sphere of public government and law. If, metaphorically speaking, power was located "down below" and "rises," the whole function and complexion of the governmental apparatus, its *raison d'être* and philosophy underwent a drastic change. And what is of immediate interest is that the judicial powers of the papacy could deploy efficacy only as long as the parties concerned expressed their consent. In practice this consent by the parties was given by the governments in question which themselves rested upon the consent of their citizens. The government acted on behalf of the people, since the government was its representative organ. It was this ideological development in the late Middle Ages which accounted for the radical transformation of the situation in the public sphere. In parenthesis it may be remarked that a similar development took place in the purely religious field leading to the Reformation of which one feature was the appeal to a critical apraisal of the Bible by the individual Christian.

The juristic development led to a close definition of those who as citizens could effectively participate in the law-creative process. In other words, the unit or entity which could reasonably cope with the exigencies of public government was either the city-state or the territorial state, a more or less closely confined region. And this was exactly the picture which the late Middle Ages show. The result was that the State as a territorial unit began to exhibit all the characteristics of sovereignty—the territorial sovereignty was either substituted for the personal sovereignty or placed next to the latter. What mattered was that this territorially confined region became the operational unit: it operated through the active participation of its citizens. An immediate consequence, and one that directly bears on the problem investigated, was that the territorial unit had to enter into relations with similar other units. What is termed international law was therefore in the last analysis the outcome of a jurisprudential evolution which itself was the direct offspring of the intellectual revolution engendered by the absorption of Aristotelian theses.

---

15. The stimulating chapter, *Sovereign and Subject*, in H. HART, THE CONCEPT OF LAW 49-76 (1961) would have gained greatly in depth if the law-creative process and the change in the individual from a subject to a citizen had been thrown against some historical canvas. *Cf.* J. FAWCETT, THE LAW OF NATIONS 31-40 (1968).

The decline of papal judicial authority in the late Middle Ages was the direct result of this ideological and jurisprudential re-orientation. In fact, the further one removes oneself from the properly medieval period, the more conspicuous becomes the paucity of the cases in which the papal tribunal was involved and which could be termed international disputes. The place of the judicial verdict was taken by pastoral exhortation which lies outside a juristic framework. It may well be true as a great authority on international law has stated that the problem of the limitations of the function of law in the settlement of disputes is largely the creation of the doctrine of sovereignty,[16] but, as already indicated, it would seem profitable to realize that the concept of sovereignty itself was very largely the result of a purely legal and jurisprudential reasoning. The undisputed modern doctrine that the jurisdiction of an international tribunal does not come into operation unless and until the individual State has accepted it, is effortlessly explicable by the postulate that municipal law is to be based upon the consent of the citizens of the particular State. Hence the consent of the citizens is bound to come into operation—through their government—in the case of submitting a dispute to an international tribunal. Seen from the strictly legal-historical angle, "international" law becomes, through the consent of the State to the jurisdiction of an international court, national; that is, municipal law in the particular instance. Once more one can say, international law, looked at from this standpoint, is nothing more than municipal law writ large. Furthermore, considered from this viewpoint, the papal court could, if the parties so wished, become the judicial tribunal for an international dispute at least theoretically, with the important proviso that the judicial function of this papal tribunal would not be based on the "faith" of the parties, but solely on their consent.

These considerations open up further vistas. By virtue of the absence of the concept of territorial sovereignty in the high Middle Ages, papal judicial decisions dealt with persons or clearly defined groups of persons only. The abstract entity of the "State" was as yet unborn in the central medieval period. The papal decision affected the standing of persons who were the objects of the dispute, whether this was a duke, prince, king, or emperor or guild; in short the principle prevailed that only disputes between persons were justiciable. What mattered, to express the same idea in different words, was the concept of personal sovereignty,[17] or the idea that only human persons could embody power, not "countries," "nations," "estates," that is, abstractions. In short, only individual persons could be bear-

---

16. H. Lauterpacht, The Function of Law in the International Community 3 (1933).
17. Cf. Ullmann, Juristic Obstacles to the Emergence of the State in the Middle Ages, Annali di storia del diritto 41-64 (Calasso Memorial Vol., xii-xiii, 1968-69).

ers of rights, and especially of the rights which appertained to sovereignty.

It was not until the ascending theme of government and law came to be worked out in theory (and partly also adopted in practice) that the concept of the State emerged, the State, that is, as a legal abstraction which was considered an independent, autonomous, self-sufficient and above all sovereign unit, precisely because it was sustained by its own inner force and, as it was expressed in late-medieval terminology, was a product of nature. What matters in this context is that the idea and concept of the State in this sense could not come about without the individuals becoming citizens who were capable of giving informed consent to proposed legislative measures. The sum-total of the citizens capable of expressing valid consent was epitomized in the abstract entity of the State, or, in the current late-medieval coinage, of the *universitas civium*.[18]

On the model of the Roman-law *universitas* the State was seen as a corporation. This corporation came to be "personified" in so far as it was viewed as a fictive person (*persona ficta*) with its own rights and right-subjectivity, and could thus be accommodated within the then usual thought-patterns. The State was conceived to be a body corporate to which belonged rights and duties, and these were viewed to exist aside and apart from the rights and duties which belonged to the individual citizens who constituted this body corporate. In other words, a new personality, albeit an artificial and purely notional personality, had come into being, and this new personality acquired a sovereign status on the analogy of the sovereign status with which the persons of the Ruler had hitherto been invested. And it was this fictive person, the State, that became the subject of international law. The State alone assumed this role because it was a sovereign entity. The ascending theme of government and law could not lead to any other conclusion, with the consequence that, as has been noted, as a sovereign body it had to give its consent to the jurisdiction of an international tribunal. The fictive personality of the State was the bearer of the sum-total of rights and duties—in no wise different from the individual Ruler's very real human personality to which, in the high Middle Ages, personal sovereignty was ascribed.

This status of a personal sovereign was expressed by the highly characteristic term of *maiestas*, that is, *maioritas* (or *superioritas*) of the Ruler in his relations to his subjects. This attribute of sovereignty signified the higher status of the personal Ruler, hence also the very expressive linguistic addresses of *La sua altezza, Your Highness, Hoheit*, and the like.[19] Now as a result of the State having acquired sovereign status, these attributes, formerly belonging to the

18. This was the definition given by Marsilius of Padua, Defensor Pacis, I.IV.5; also I.III.4 and 5.
19. In international language this reappears in the still current diplomatic expression of "The *High* Contracting Powers . . ."

370

personal sovereign, could be, as indeed they were, transferred to the fictive conceptual personality of the State, with the consequence that *Hoheit, maioritas,* and so on, were ascribed to the State itself which, according to late medieval doctrine, was nothing more than a *nomen iuris.* And because it was a mere incorporal, a-human thing, this entity had no will of its own and could become active only through its human representatives which was the government.[20] In the present context this meant that it was the government of the State which alone could give the required consent; the power of the government was based on the consent of the citizens, and since only humans could and can consent, the human persons who acted on behalf of the fictive person which was the State, who in other words "represented" the citizens, was the government. Hence it was the government which appeared as the *Hoheitsträger.*

III

An assessment of some recent developments in international law would seem to show that, within limits, there is some awareness of the very crux of the inefficacy of international law and specifically of an international court of justice. It is with considerable hesitation that I venture into this particular thicket of international law, but on the present occasion at least a short reference might perhaps seem justified. There has been quite vociferous opposition to the point of view expressed and acted upon in this century that because international law was concerned with the actions of sovereign States, it did not refer to individuals. The most noteworthy instance has been the trial before the International Military Tribunal of the German war criminals. Despite a very fierce opposition to making individuals responsible within the framework of international law, it would appear that individual responsibility was simply a recognition that the civilian and military leaders of a State were the real *Hoheitsträger* as organs representing the purely fictive, legal concept of the State. For just as it is the government of the State in the shape of human persons who as actualized *Hoheitsträger* consent to international agreements and the jurisdiction of international tribunals, in the same way it is human persons, and not purely abstract legal entities, who commit crimes against the international community, and this once more in their function as apparent *Hoheitsträger.*[21] The significance of this development lies in not only making concrete, at least

---

20. *See* Innocent IV in his commentary on LIBER EXTRA V.XXXIX. 64. There is a competent exposition of the theory of the *persona ficta* (which was actually Innocent IV's theory) in the work of a former pupil of mine, B. TIERNEY, FOUNDATIONS OF CONCILIAR THEORY 98-107 (repr. Cambridge 1969).

21. CHARTER OF THE INTERNATIONAL MILITARY TRIBUNAL art. 7 states: "The official position of Defendants, whether as Heads of State or responsible officials in Government Departments, shall not be considered as freeing them from responsibility or mitigating punishment."

within criminal law, the accountability for crimes committed, but also, and perhaps more importantly, in rendering international law and its application more effective than it had hitherto been.

With this consideration a further reflexion is linked. It concerns the first tangible steps towards a greater efficacy of international law, though here too it was the last war which accelerated this development. According to the Charter establishing the International Military Tribunal (London, 8 August 1945), crimes against humanity were established as a specific category of criminal conduct perpetrated during the war. Here too there was a vociferous opposition, because, so it was asserted, a new offense was created and thereby the age-old principle of *nullum crimen sine lege* was violated: at the time when these alleged crimes were said to have been committed, they were not punishable.[22] Both the International Military Tribunal and the Military Tribunal III (U.S.A.) rejected this point of view, and rightly so; apart from its pure formalism, this standpoint also overlooks the vital principle that all the actions which constituted the crime against humanity, were punishable as crimes of the most serious order in all civilized countries and states. In other words, each individual State belonging to the community of civilized nations recognized in its own municipal laws the criminal character of conduct falling into the category of this crime. There was therefore a common consent to make this conduct punishable, though the individual municipal laws may have varied in detail, scope and nomenclature, but certainly not in principle.

From the strictly legal point of view, therefore, the London Charter of 1945 was declaratory, and not constitutive. It merely declared in international law a crime against humanity what had already been a crime (of possibly different connotation) in national law. But considered from the genetic angle, this latest development makes new use of the principle of consent and applies it to the sphere of criminal law. At least constructively one may say that by proscribing crimes against humanity and declaring them part of international law, this specific instance would go to prove that international law is municipal law writ large. As the history of civilization demonstrates, criminal law and jurisdiction was always one of the most effective means to establish and maintain peace and order, and criminal law was frequently enough the begetter of other and perhaps more refined systems of law. Perhaps, then, there are hopeful signs of an approximation towards that efficacy of "supra-national" jurisdiction which was a feature of the high Middle Ages. There is indeed some prospect of turning into law on the largest possible scale what has so aptly been called *la conscience juridique de l'humanité.*

---

22. See *also* BRIERLY, *supra* note 3, at 410-411.

XVIII

The Papacy as an Institution of Government in the Middle Ages

A FTER reading the title of my paper, you may well have wondered
whether anything worth while or useful can still be said
about the mediaeval papacy. Your apprehension would certainly be justified, if I were concerned merely with its history, but
of recent years the institution has not been so much the subject of
purely narrative treatment as of the underlying principles and aims.
And here so great a variety of views has been set forth that an outsider might well feel somewhat perplexed by the contradictory views
propounded. Why does the mediaeval papacy evoke such divergent
interpretations?

This question, I think, is all the more justified as there is no other
institution which presents the inquirer with so rich and abundant
material as the mediaeval papacy. Divergencies of views are usually
the result of insufficient and incomplete evidence which leaves a
large margin to the enquiring historian's imagination and conjectures. But this is precisely not the case with the mediaeval papacy,
and we are faced with the paradoxical situation that despite the
abundance of evidence, despite the uncommonly precise nature of
the contents of evidence, there is a remarkable variety of interpretation. Why is this so?

There are, as can readily be understood, several ways in which
the papacy, as an institution of government, can be dealt with. The
richness of the surviving material makes the mediaeval papacy easily
a playground for the antiquarians: they do not ask questions which
go beyond the vision of a mole, they are not interested in anything
outside the sphere of their self-imposed limits, they are in fact a

The Papacy as an Institution of Government in the Middle Ages

classic example of self-abnegation: they treat of the minutiae in the papal state, in papal administration, in papal liturgy and symbolism, in papal prayer texts, in papal law, and have developed a remarkable skill in suppressing very effectively any problem of a historical nature. The antiquarians are on the whole tolerant, conscious of their limitations and satisfied with digging up the one or the other fact irrespective and oblivious of its historical relevance. This is quite a harmless group, and I can leave it at that.

There is another group of researchers into the institutional machinery of the papacy. They, too, can quickly be dismissed, because to them the papacy was still merely one more governmental institution on a level with the institution of mediaeval kingship or a mediaeval town government, and the like. As historians of the institution of the papacy, they cannot raise high stakes, because they have not yet penetrated deeply enough to see that in treating of the mediaeval papacy something more is required than merely a narrative account of purely external and superficial features, however much this treatment is enlivened with moral judgements: naturally, remaining as they do on the surface, untouched as they are by contact with the sources, and relying as they do on secondary literature, they have little else but their own purely subjective-moral evaluations with which their presentation is interleaved. When one knows no sources, except perhaps those conveniently selected in well-known compendia, one virtually must take refuge in moralising judgements; how else is one to paint a picture?

There is, thirdly, a group of historians which does attempt to penetrate into the texture of the mediaeval papacy, which does try to see the principles upon which the papal government worked in the Middle Ages, but having made this valiant attempt, they at once realise the implications and the logical conclusions to which the full recognition of principles must necessarily lead: the result is that instead of spreading out a comprehensive system of the vital principles of government animating the mediaeval papacy, they shirk this task and withdraw either into commonplace and meaningless generalisations or—much more frequently—present a picture which is, historically seen, a travesty of the truth. This group is far less numerous than their vociferously publicised views would in fact suggest, but I am bound to say a few words about them, because they propound views which cannot be squared with the sources, views, that is, which can be put forward only when either the sources are deliberately neglected or, if not neglected, their historical relevance and efficacy is suppressed. Their historical matter is set forth in a manner which is attuned to modern views and which readily appeals to the uninitiated, whom indeed they have primarily in mind. The expectation that the uninitiated will accept their views has here and there met with some success: their victims, precisely because they are so blissfully uninitiated, little realise how far their credulity has been taxed and misused.

What explanation can be offered for the tergiversations on the part of this vociferous group, for their readiness to disregard, if not to bend, the sources? In attempting to answer this crucial question, we ought to try to find out what motives and reasons there may be for this pseudo-historic attitude. When one looks at their writings, one detects at once a defensive note: they try to present the mediaeval papacy in a manner which—to the connoisseur anyway—appears so distorted, so twisted, that one has difficulties in recognising the mediaeval papacy. The answer to the question I have asked, is, I think, intimately connected with one of the most pronounced features of the papacy itself.

The papacy is the only historic institution which has come down to us from late antiquity; it can legitimately boast of a continuity which, considered purely historically, is indeed baffling. For this continuity it is very difficult to find a parallel, at least within the Western orbit. The claim to unbroken continuity back to the post-apostolic period is the hallmark of the papacy. When we give due attention to this vital feature, we shall perhaps also understand why certain historians are anxious to present the mediaeval past of the papacy in a way which is more in line with present-day requirements than with the requirements of historic truth. Differently expressed, mediaeval papal history easily becomes contemporary history. By virtue of the claim to uninterrupted continuity, in fact by virtue of the claim to the sameness, to the identity of the papacy at all times, certain features of the mediaeval papacy may well appear disconcerting or disturbing: hence the attempt to tailor mediaeval papal history to modern requirements, to adjust and to attune it to the somewhat different climate in the present age. Admittedly, the principles on which the mediaeval papacy worked tally rather badly with those which this or the last generation has come to adopt: but if the claim to historic continuity and historic identity is taken seriously enough, one can readily understand that there is an almost irresistible temptation to project present-day axioms back to any period in history in which the papacy operated. But no historian worth his calling should succumb to this temptation. It is not really the fault of a historian if mediaeval papal history has become contemporary history. The historian has not created the papacy in any age: when there are discrepancies in papal principles, when there are deviations between, say, the Gregorian or Innocentian papacy on the one hand, and some modern pontifical pronouncement, there is no justification for a historian to tailor history to suit contemporary needs. The spectre which haunts those so-called historians who are so anxious to fit mediaeval papal history into modern categories is the consideration that, precisely because of the thesis of historic continuity and identity, undesirable conclusions may be drawn. Whether the modern emphasis on continuity is an asset or a liability, I do not know, but there can be no legitimate doubt that this assertion of continuity was in the Middle Ages of most profound and decisive significance.

In this mediaeval assertion of continuity lies to my mind one of the main reasons for the success of the papacy in the Middle Ages. One might be almost tempted to say that the historian is here presented with a conservatism for which it would be difficult to find appropriate parallels. This conservatism appears in a twofold form: partly genuine, that is, a conservatism nurtured by the ready availability of previous documents and official statements in the well-kept archives; partly a conservatism artificially created by inventing statements which had allegedly been made in the far distant past.[1] The older the authority was, the more patina it had accumulated, the greater weight it had. This very marked inclination to rely on the

[1] This spurious kind of conservatism should not, however, be evaluated by our modern somewhat refined standards: the spurious document, the forged or falsified statement, and the like, had, as often as not, a non-papal provenance, though in course of time the papacy itself adopted and incorporated it in its own statements. There are very few instances in which an entirely new point of view or principle was propounded: what was done was to project a statement back into the distant past, whilst perfectly genuine models of a more recent date might have been available. For instance, in the Symmachan forgeries of the early sixth century we find a statement made at a spurious council that the pope cannot be judged by anyone. In actual fact, there would have been perfectly genuine statements about the same matter in the pontificates of Felix III and Gelasius I, and there would have been the statement of Zosimus in the early fifth century, cf. PL 20, col. 677=*Avellana* (in *CSEL*, xxxv, 116).

older instead of on a more recent (and genuine) statement, this
inclination to a genuine or artificial conservatism and, above all, the
stress on the continuity of thought, ideas, and resulting principles,
was not only peculiar to the papacy, but seemed also to have
originated with the institution. Certainly in the Roman administration and constitution we find few traces of anything approaching
this kind of continuity.

How did this feature come about? The conservatism did not
affect so much the actual doings of the papacy, as the principles
underlying intended or performed actions: it was, in short, a conservatism relating to principles and far less one relating to facts. How
is one to explain this? In the vast output on papal historiography one
will look in vain for a recognition of this problem which has not yet
been seen to exist. I cannot offer you a cut and dried answer, but
merely a tentative approach to a solution of what would seem to me
a fundamental problem.

There seems now to be general agreement that the period
between the pontificate of Damasus I in the eighties of the fourth
century and of Leo I in the mid-fifth century was the period of
gestation, as far as the establishment of papal principles of government was concerned. Within these two generations the papacy
entered public life and began to work out some of its fundamental
axioms relating to the government of the Christian body. There are
both doctrinal and historical reasons which apply with particular
force to that period. It was within that period that, to begin with, the
Bible became generally available in an idiom which was readily
understandable by the cultured and educated Roman classes. The
requirement for an intelligible, readable, and universally acceptable
Latin text became especially pressing after the basic decree of
Gratian, Valentinian, and Theodosius I of 27 February 380—
Cunctos populos,[1] according to which all the peoples of the empire
should live in consonance with apostolic discipline and biblical
doctrine: *secundum apostolicam disciplinam et evangelicam doctrinam*.
But, surely, the presupposition, in Rome anyway, was that the Bible
was accessible in an idiom readily and generally understandable by
those classes which mattered. It is certainly no coincidence that it
was the contemporary pope, Damasus I, who emphasised the need
for a good translation of the Bible and who persuaded St Jerome to

---

[1] *Cod. Theod.* XVI, i, 2=*Cod. Just.* I, i, 1.

The Papacy as an Institution of Government in the Middle Ages

undertake this herculean task,[1] after the same pope had initiated in liturgy the transition from the Greek to the Latin language.[2] The availability of the Bible in the shape of the Vulgate would appear to be of crucial importance: it came to form the only available basis of organised Christianity, and it was now also available in the very language to which the educated governing classes of Rome were attuned. Over and above these two features there was the fact of the Roman Church having been credited with a certain pre-eminence in the Roman-Christian world. But there was as yet no attempt to prove by explicit reference to the Bible the institutional pre-eminence of the Roman Church concerning its function as a supreme governmental authority. This somewhat serious gap was in fact highlighted by the decree *Cunctos populos* which declared also that the faith should be that which the divine apostle Peter had handed over to the Romans.[3]

As far as we are concerned at the moment, the doctrinal establishment of the papacy's exclusive governmental authority began in the period immediately following the pontificate of Damasus. I am persuaded that this again can be no coincidence. The invocation of the crucial Matthean verses now begins its triumphant career, first with the help of the *Epistola Clementis*, considerably inflated in its Latin translation,[4] and then with the display of juristic arguments drawn from the arsenal of the Roman law and Roman constitution. What should never be lost sight of is that the translated Bible employed Latin terms and notions which fell on very fertile soil and in actual fact suggested borrowings from Roman jurisprudence. One has but to think of the terms *ligare* and *solvere* and their juristic overtones to

[1] I am of course well aware that Latin translations of some parts of the Bible began to appear from the late second century onwards, but the historically decisive translation was that of St Jerome. According to Christine Mohrmann, *Études sur le Latin des Chrétiens* (in *Storia e Letteratura*, LXV, I (1958), 357) Jerome was 'a clever and thoughtful artist in language . . . we can have nothing but the greatest admiration for Jerome's feeling for language and style.'

[2] Cf. Th. Klauser, 'Der Uebergang der römischen Kirche von der griechischen zur lateinischen Sprache,' *Miscellanea G. Mercati* (in *Studi e Testi*, LXXXI, I (1946), 467-9) (possibly suggested by St Ambrose); Christine Mohrmann, 'Les origines de la latinité chrétienne à Rome,' *Vigiliae Christianae*, III (1949), 47-50, 163-80; ead., *Études sur le Latin des Chrétiens*, loc. cit. II (1961), 40-58; cf. also L. Eisenhofer, *Grundriss der Liturgik des römischen Ritus*, 5th ed. by J. Lechner, Freiburg 1950, 214.

[3] '. . . quam divum Petrum apostolum tradidisse Romanis religio usque adhuc ab ipso insinuata declarat.'

[4] For this cf. W. Ullmann, 'The significance of the Epistola Clementis in the Pseudo-Clementines,' *JTS*, XI (1960), 295-320.

realise the impact which they were bound to make on receptive ears. The employment of such terms as *potestas*, *imperium*, *gubernacula*, *iurisdictio*, *sententia*, *iustitia*, and so forth, evoked unmistakable echoes amongst the attentive personnel in the Roman Church.[1] The point I wish to make is that the pronounced reliance, purposeful as it was, of the Roman Church on the Bible for establishing papal governmental authority, suggested the construction of an indestructible linkage between the papacy and the alleged source of its authority, the Bible. Let us keep in mind that it was not the Bible in its original Hebrew or Greek text, but in the Latin text, which rather faithfully reflected the cultural and above all legal milieu of Rome. Once this link between the papacy and the Bible, and in particular with the Matthean passage, was established, the path for the papacy was pre-portrayed and pre-designed. For the Bible, anyway, in the shape of the Vulgate, was held to be immutable, unchangeable, unmodifiable; and when the pope's function was—with the help of Roman law—derived from the Bible, the further development appears not only understandable, but also determined. If, as the papacy, and especially the Leonine papacy, insisted, the pope was successor of St Peter, that the *plenitudo potestatis* given to St Peter by Christ, was inherited by the pope, and that the pope as heir continued to be Peter himself, then we can indeed understand the future development as well as also the theme of continuity. One might well say that historically considered the standpoint taken by the papacy in the fifth century was both retrospective and prospective. Retrospective, because of the insistence of the papacy that its function was derived from the Bible; prospective, because of the comprehensiveness of the principles thus derived, to which feature I will turn in a moment. Since the biblical Peter had only one successor in the Roman pope, the pope's monarchic function was held to be identical with that of Peter of the Bible; and since the pope was not the vicar, but the successor of the biblical Peter, and thus governed with the same authority with which papal biblical exegesis had credited him, the papacy assumed thereby the function of an

---

[1] The infiltration of Roman jurisprudential ideas and terms into the Latin Bible and the echoes they were bound to evoke, would indeed be worthy of a special study. For some remarks cf. W. Ullmann, 'The Bible and Principles of Government in the Middle Ages,' *Settimana Spoleto 1962*, Spoleto 1963, 184-6. Christine Mohrmann touches on the juristic Latin vocabulary in connection with liturgical questions, cf. *Études sur le Latin*, loc. cit. II (1961), 105.

institution which claimed to be not merely the instrument of the
Bible, but the actualised Bible itself, the divine word made manifest
within space and time. The immutability of the Bible and the thesis
of the papacy that it alone was its divinely appointed mouthpiece
necessarily induced a continuity of thought and development.

We can from here perhaps also understand why the statements of
the fifth-century papacy were repeated a thousandfold in the
centuries to come, why we read of statements made in the fourteenth century which were made in almost the same terms in the
fifth century,[1] although we can be fairly certain that the fourteenth-
century pope did not know of the fifth-century passage, why views
flowed into the pen of a thirteenth-century pope which were to all
intents and purposes identical with those expressed by an allegedly
post-apostolic literary product,[2] why above all the function of St
Peter as the builder of the Church was seen to be continued—and I
mean continued—in the pope, and why therefore the pope did not
succeed his predecessor, but succeeded St Peter himself directly and
without intermediary. Having claimed the role of the sole and exclusive interpreter of the divine will, having solely in its possession the
keys of salvation and damnation, the papacy put forward the juristic
theme of the identification of Peter and pope as well as the juristic
thesis that the institution of the papacy was specifically biblical.

Let me give you an example of a papal principle with a biblical
basis. The historian of canon law knows that all *causae maiores* had
to come before the pope's court. Now this was laid down by Innocent I
in 404, and when one analyses the language of the passage, one will
find that it is quite clearly modelled on Exodus xviii, 22, though the
place of Moses was taken by the *apostolica sedes*; even the Latin term
referre and its subjunctive reappears in the papal rescript.[3] This
incidentally is also quite a good example of how the papacy substituted a biblical basis for an imperial basis: a few years earlier, in 378,
there was an imperial rescript according to which metropolitans
could be tried by the Roman pope only: Innocent I substituted the
Bible for this jurisdictional measure and went far beyond the

---

[1] Cf. W. Ullmann, *The Growth of Papal Government in the Middle Ages* (P.G.),
2nd ed. 1962, additional *n.*4, p. 8 (p. 462), and idem, 'Leo I and the theme of papal
primacy,' *JTS*, XI (1960), 44, *n.*4.
[2] Cf. the *Didaskalia* and Innocent III, cited in W. Ullmann, *Principles of Government
and Politics in the Middle Ages* (P.G.P.), 1961, 92-4.
[3] *Ep.* 2, c. 6; see W. Ullmann in *Settimana Spoleto*, loc. cit. 221, at *n.*170.

imperial decree. But this is merely an instance of how the papacy attempted to master reality by substituting a biblically founded theme for a historically conditioned fact.[1] Further, the absorption of the characteristic Roman legal and constitutional vocabulary into the system of the papacy was considerably facilitated by the latinised Bible, for it was here that such terms as *principatus* could be read. Can one really be surprised that Roman constitutional notions and biblical notions flowed into one resulting in the *principatus Romanae ecclesiae*?[2] If the concept of 'Roman' is extended to include also the latinised Bible, one can well subscribe to Gabriel Le Bras when he said: 'L'église romaine demeure la plus véritable héritière de l'empire et du droit de Rome.'[3]

One should beware, however, of thinking in purely doctrinal terms. Doctrine as such can never be more than an influencing agent in society; what it cannot do is to serve as a substitute for the law. And this is the second limb, so to speak, of the problem of continuity. However much a doctrine is alleged to be divine in origin, it needs for the transaction of public and social matters the force of the law behind it. The physiognomy of the papacy as the actualised Bible, or if you like as the actualised divine word, needed to be complemented by the legal halo surrounding the pronouncements of mere doctrine—which is a necessary prerequisite to turn the papacy into a fully fledged institution of government. Here it is merely necessary to mention the notion of Rome to realise the fecundity and receptivity of the soil in which the Church of Rome lived and prospered. Moreover, it is not without some interest to note that from the very beginning of the fifth century there was observable an acceleration of jurisprudential activity throughout the empire—down to the *lex citationis*[4] and the *Codex Theodosianus*, to mention but two outstanding landmarks. Roman government—even at the approaching nadir in the fifth century—was nothing but the application and adminis-

---

[1] On the subject itself cf. E. Caspar, *Geschichte des Papsttums*, Tübingen 1930, I, 307.

[2] For some remarks cf. W. Ullmann, *P.G.* ed. cit., 8-12, and for some of the semantic problems raised in the Latin Bible, id., *Settimana*, loc. cit. 188-9 and 225-7, and especially Chr. Mohrmann, loc. cit. II (1961), 18-25. Cf. also A. Stein, 'Das Fortleben des römischen Prinzipatsgedankens,' *Bulletin of the International Committee of Historical Sciences*, x (1938), 191.

[3] In *Rev. historique de droit français et étranger*, XXVII (1949), 398-90.

[4] Cf. H. F. Jolowicz, *Historical Introduction to the Study of Roman Law*, 2nd ed. 1952, 482, and for purposes of orientation cf. F. Pringsheim in *Studia et Documenta Historiae et Iuris*, XXVII (1961-2), 235.

The Papacy as an Institution of Government in the Middle Ages

tration of the law. Given the presuppositions, it would have been miraculous if the Church of Rome had not also worked with the law in its attempt to secure its governmental authority. I have already mentioned how much Roman legal atmosphere radiated from the Latin Bible; one should also realise how strongly permeated the Bible, and especially the Old Testament, is with legal concepts and matters. The more one penetrated into the Bible, the more one began to understand the importance of the law in matters of government. It was also in this same fifth century that the interpretation of the Bible began to differ widely between East and West. In the West, in Rome, the Bible was treated as in no wise different from the text of a statute or a decree or a law; in the East it was theological speculation, if not theological metaphysics, which characterised the treatment of the Bible, but in the West, Roman jurisprudential thought engulfed the very matter of the Bible, the Latin language of which no doubt greatly facilitated this juristic method.[1]

The harnessing of the law by the papacy to its doctrine in the Roman milieu strongly marks off the Roman Church from any other contemporary Church: it is a feature which will distinguish it from all other Churches throughout the Middle Ages and beyond. But the essential and conclusive point is that once doctrine was endorsed and reinforced with the law, it itself became an enforceable rule, and one the substance of which was allegedly biblical. Thereby the link between the papacy and the Bible became fundamentally strengthened. On the other hand, this enveloping of doctrine with the law put also, as we shall presently see, considerable fetters on the papacy. In short, what the papacy laid down was not merely doctrine originating in divinity, but also, and for public matters more important, the law —obedience to which secured salvation, disobedience damnation. The elaboration of papal principles of government induced of necessity a continuity of development and of thought. When in the thirteenth century Innocent IV designated the papal canon law as *ius divinum*,[2] he merely expressed the equivalent character of biblical and papal law.

I am well aware of the following objection: how can you, I might be asked, square the theme of continuity and the consequential rigid

---

[1] For the legalism in the Western Church, beginning in fact with the jurist Tertullian (and also Cyprian), see A. Harnack, *Lehrbuch der Dogmengeschichte*, 4th ed., Tübingen 1909, II, 179-80, III, 350-69.

[2] *Sextus* V, vii, 21; cf. also Innocent III in *Reg.* I, 320.

adherence to earlier views with the thesis that the pope was autonomous and sovereign, which in practice meant that by a stroke of the
papal pen an entirely new situation may be created, so new that it
may even contradict antecedent rulings? Fundamentally, the objection would seem justified. The pope as supreme law-giver is not
accountable to anyone and cannot be made responsible to anyone—
papa a nemine iudicatur—who can set aside any previous law and
consequently any previous doctrine: this thesis may be difficult to
reconcile with the avowal of biblical continuity and the inflexibility
of papal views. Although this again is a problem that has not yet
been recognised in all its profundity, there is at least a remote possibility of solving the antinomy. I am sure you are acquainted with
the mediaeval views on the pope's dispensing powers, that is, how
far the pope by virtue of his *plenitudo potestatis* can do away, legally
and legitimately, with antecedent laws? This much discussed topic is
in actual fact an issue of the far more extensive problem of reconciling
the legislative omnipotence of the pope with the dictates of continuity of government.

The solution of this problem may perhaps be less difficult than it
looks. I think it is best if I were to give an example. When Leo I by
an unsurpassable command of Roman law established that the pope
was an *indignus haeres beati Petri*, he thereby made perhaps the most
notable contribution to papal governmental principles which any
pope has made. And anyone only vaguely acquainted with papal
government and documentation will readily admit the significance
of this contribution. Now, theoretically, that is, if we take the papal
thesis of legislative omnipotence seriously, it would be quite feasible
that a later pope either implicitly or explicitly denied this function of
the pope:[1] theoretically, any pope could have decreed that it was not
St Peter, but St Paul whose successor he was (and as a matter of fact,
this would at least have had some resemblance to the actual influence
of the *doctor gentium* upon the papacy). But there was no pope who
had asserted anything like this, although the fully developed doctrine maintained often enough that the pope could lay down any
law he liked, not, however, without at the same time asserting (in
what may appear as a contradiction) that the pope could not change
the *status ecclesiae* or issue any law against the Bible. If we lift these

[1] See now on this specifically M. J. Wilks, *The Problem of Sovereignty in the later
Middle Ages*, Cambridge 1963, 470, *n.*2.

The Papacy as an Institution of Government in the Middle Ages

restrictions on to a more general level, we might well be justified in saying that, in regard to *essentialia* of the pope's government, his legislative omnipotence, his *plenitudo potestatis*, was not operative, but only *in inessentialibus*. Essential elements were those which had in fact been declared by antecedent popes as based on the Bible. I think that the distinction between essential and inessential elements opens up a road to a reconciliation of the two apparently contradictory propositions. No principle of continuity is violated, if, say, chancery practices were changed in order to accommodate administrative needs to contemporary exigencies, that is, no link between the production of the papal chancery and the Bible was ever envisaged. The objection to this point of view, namely who decides whether or not a particular item belongs to the category of essentials, can easily be met by the simple reflection that a disregard of essential elements by a pope would have redounded to his own detriment, would have inflicted irreparable damage to his own function and position. He himself would have undermined his own position, he himself would have committed suicide in his function as pope. The intimate connection with the Bible rather effectively prevented discontinuity. Because the papacy considered itself as the actualised Bible and divine word, because the papacy was believed to have an indestructible link with the Bible, because the papacy had asserted that its own principles of government were nothing but concrete applications of biblical themes,[1] any deviation from principles allegedly based on the Bible would have taken the ground away from under the feet of the popes themselves. The asserted continuation and actualisation of the Bible in the papacy gave birth to continuity of thought and government. The one bred the other, restricting the pope's space of movement and hedging him in as far as matters were essential and basic to his function.

We can with great facility test this conclusion by giving no more than a perfunctory attention to the lack of official papal statements which would have asserted that any of their predecessors had wrongly pronounced on a matter of doctrine or on a matter of governmental principle. In the vast papal output of the Middle Ages I myself have not come across a statement in which a pope had accused any of his predecessors of erroneous interpretation of the Bible or of erroneous principles. This is not the same as saying that

---

[1] For the pope as 'living evangelical oracle' see Wilks, op. cit. 372.

later papal doctrine or principles did not, in some cases, at least put the emphasis, if not also state the substance, differently from an antecedent pope, but there was never, to my knowledge, any overt rebuke of a predecessor for erroneous views. Why not? Mediaeval popes were not known for their tender-heartedness or gentility, and considering the numerous rebukes they so easily, and often light-mindedly, administered whenever it appeared advisable to them, one is indeed struck by the silence towards their own predecessors. Whether living or dead, neither king nor emperor, neither cardinal nor patriarch or metropolitan was exempted from often very drastic strictures for erroneous views, steps, or actions, but never do we read of anything like this towards papal predecessors.

The explanation of this phenomenon may once again be sought in the direct link with the Bible: if a predecessor had been charged with pronouncing wrong doctrines or principles, this would in reality have meant that St Peter himself had pronounced erroneously, because the pope considered himself to be St Peter. It is this consideration which I feel is at the centre of the whole cluster surrounding the infallibility problem, but this is really a modern issue, and so I had better refrain from saying any more. We may go a step further: often enough in the course of my academic duties have I been confronted by the question: when did the papacy disavow Pseudo-Isidore? When was it that the papacy admitted—or withdrew, as I am sometimes also asked—the forgery of the Donation of Constantine? I am sure I am not the only one to whom these and similar questions are addressed. The answer is a very simple 'Never.' Never has the papacy officially declared that Pseudo-Isidore was an enormous fabrication, nor that the Donation of Constantine was pure invention—dozens of other examples could be cited. The explanation here is the same as in the case of the silence of a rebuke against a predecessor: the matters which were covered by these forgeries no doubt fall into the category of the *essentialia* of papal government, and therefore could not be disowned: they affected in a vital way the very basis of a number of substantial papal principles of government.

One can perhaps now understand how precisely as a result of the theme of continuity there accumulated in the course of time such a welter, such a mass of precedents, such a weight of conservatism, such an incubus of tradition that what was once an asset came to be turned into a liability. There can be no doubt that the theme of

The Papacy as an Institution of Government in the Middle Ages

continuity was, as I have already indicated, of the greatest possible advantage to the mediaeval papacy: it really needs no great historical imagination to visualise the impression created by a reference to a statement of, say, a second-century pope (even if it was of pseudo-isidorian provenance) or, to take an example from another field, by St Peter himself writing a letter to Pippin, and so on: all that was needed was to take a volume from the shelves of the archives. Further, this constant emphasis on simply continuing the ancient ways, because they were alleged to be founded on the Bible, could not but help to produce in the popes themselves a state of mind which itself manifested the theme of continuity. Both the recipient of a papal decree and the pope himself were engulfed in this process—a circle from which there was no escape. But in course of time it would seem that this accumulation could well be a hindrance to a free development and above all to an adjustment to emerging exigencies. Whilst earlier the popes referred to themselves as the governors of the Church, carrying a *gravissimum pondus*, it might well towards the end of the Middle Ages have looked as if the principles, maxims, axioms, and doctrines of the papacy themselves became a *gravissimum pondus* on their shoulders, so heavy in fact that the theme of continuity and conservatism appeared to exercise a suffocating effect. One has but to think of the conciliar epoch in the early fifteenth century to realise the stultifying effects of the weight of tradition in precisely those matters of government which would have profited from an infusion of new principles, particularly in regard to the laity: the price of continuity in matters of government was rigid formalism and externalism deprived of the invigorating effects which can result from new and 'unauthorised' interpretations, but which, when propounded, were at once branded as heretical, because contradicting tradition and threatening continuity.

One more reflection comes here into operation, and this concerns the very concept of history within the papal framework. Anyone who has worked on the mediaeval papacy will have been struck by the unhistorical methods it employed. How is one to explain the readiness to invoke a view or a law made centuries before and attuned to a quite different situation? How is one, to put the question differently, to explain this absence of a historical sense? The lack of historicity in the Middle Ages has often enough been observed, but I think that the close connection with the Bible may here again serve at least as part of an explanation.[1] Although discernible in all mediaeval sections, the lack of historical sense is quite especially marked with the papacy. The constant preoccupation of the papacy with translating the Bible into the workaday world could not but help to stunt the historical sense rather effectively. The Bible was held to be valid for all times; its themes to have immediate relevancy and applicability; within its framework there was no today and no yesterday; it was ever present, ever valid, because it was the embodiment of the divine word, for all time and all contingencies. And this divine word must be the same for today and yesterday. What one witnesses here is something of a short-cut or even of a short-circuit which rather effectively prevented the emergence of a historical sense. Today biblical exegesis asks in what context, in what situation, in what relation this or that biblical statement was made; today one compares the present with the biblical period; today the thinking is time- and space-conditioned; today biblical allegory, symbolism, and mythology are separated from historical facts. But this is not how a mediaeval writer proceeded, and to a most pronounced degree we see the papacy actively short-circuiting the Bible of yesterday and the situation of today. This kind of reliance on the Bible promoted the atrophy of a historical sense, and in the final resort the explanation is that the Bible was the unchangeable *auctoritas*, and the papacy as its mouthpiece represented the same *auctoritas*. The Bible was viewed as one block hewn by divinity itself and given to mankind as one piece. If we attach due importance to the kind of Bible upon which the papacy worked, that is, the Vulgate, we may be able to see further. It was a translation, a Latin translation, made within the Roman surroundings of the fourth and fifth centuries, and one has to give merely a cursory attention to the restrictive character of language as a medium of conveying sets of ideas and institutions to a public for which they were really quite incomprehensible, to realise how much the Vulgate itself accounts for the stunting of the historical sense. The divine word was understood to have been expressed in Latin. One has here to bear in mind the associative power of the word, its overtones and its undertones, evoking mental associations which were wholly in consonance with the Latin usage

---

[1] Cf. e.g. P. Koschaker, *Europa und das römische Recht*, Munich 1947, 48-50; P. Kirn, *Das Bild des Menschen in der Geschichtsschreibung von Polybios bis Ranke*, Göttingen 1955; etc.

The Papacy as an Institution of Government in the Middle Ages

of a term, but not necessarily with the Hebrew or Greek meaning. That there resulted a confluence of biblical with Roman-Latin doctrine, and that the Latin language itself was largely responsible for the arrested historical sense will be readily understandable,[1] and when the papal edifice came to rest on these foundations, one can also understand why not only the Vulgate has been declared authentic, but also why there had always been a strong opposition to vernacular translations. To quote a mid-sixteenth-century writer, a translation into the vernacular is *periculosa, damnosa*, and *scandalosa*.[2] Thought-processes and mental associations of the papacy were Roman-conditioned, conditioned by geography and language; metaphorically, it seems as if the Jordan had become the Tiber.

When one considers the papacy as an institution of government—and that indeed was what the papacy itself so insistently claimed to be from the time it entered the historic scene—the intimate connection, nay, the intimate fusion of faith and law will now not only be more readily understandable, but will also be seen as a vital factor in the theme of continuity itself. Faith demands that its basis is constant, permanent, stands, in other words, before us like a rock. Within the terms of the papacy it was not so much a somewhat vague Christian faith or a faith in Christ, but the specific faith in the function of the pope as the biblically constituted organ charged with 'the building of the Church' and transmitting the divine will to the members of the Church. Because the Bible itself was the basis of the faith and because the papacy had presented itself as the actualised Bible, notably as a result of the exegesis of the Matthean and Johannine verses, faith in the Bible—I merely try to follow papal ways of thought—automatically entailed faith in the function of the pope. Without faith in the efficacy of the Petrine powers the papacy falls to the ground: it was the papacy which authoritatively expounded the Bible—and, conversely, faith in the Bible presupposed faith in the papacy. We are here led back to the already mentioned indestructible linkage between Bible and papacy, only seen from a different angle. What needs to be stressed is that faith in the divinely instituted and biblically founded institution brought forth the law of this institution. The pope was not only the *armarium iuris*,

---

[1] For some observations on this cf. *Settimana*, cit. 180-3 with further literature.
[2] Arnoldus Albertinus, in *Tractatus Universi Iuris*, Venice 1584, XI, 98vb-99rb, qu. 28, nos. 34-5.

but also the *armarium scripturae*.[1] The law of the papacy was so much based on the faith in the function of the papacy, that, from the point of view of government, the one could not exist without the other. In a memorable passage Gregory VII had once said that his predecessors and he himself had always striven to lead the Christians to their salvation by *legalibus disciplinis*.[2] It is, I think, largely due to this feature of the faith in the largest possible sense that the papacy was able to exercise so overwhelming an influence in the Middle Ages. Nowadays it is an axiom that no government can exercise influence without physical strength: one has but to think of defence policies and all the attendant consequences and paraphernalia. Yet, the mediaeval papacy is a classic example of a government which had no armed forces, no militia, no police force in the accepted sense, whose *precipua membra* were in fact barred from bearing arms; but on the other hand it is no exaggeration to say that in mediaeval Europe the papacy was the fulcrum, so much so that both Western and Eastern Europe hinged on the papacy, which with consummate skill fostered and strengthened the faith in its function, even if only by prohibiting disputations amongst—significantly enough—lay people concerning the faith[3] and, if necessary, by employing the appropriate inquisitorial machinery. When Luther made a bonfire of the papal canon law, this was not so much a symbolic protest against the law, as a sign of remonstration that he had no faith in the institution of the papacy. And because he had no faith, the papal law had no more binding force on him.

If due attention is paid to the interlacing of faith and law, we shall perhaps be able to explain the papacy's rigid adherence to its earlier pronouncements. Nothing undermines faith as much as change; nothing is more detrimental to faith than inconsistency and inconstancy. If the close and intimate link between Bible and papacy had been allowed to be cracked in one small—and possibly even unimportant—part, the consequences might well have been—as in course of time they were to be—disastrous for the papacy. Hence it

---

[1] See on this M. J. Wilks, op. cit. 156 with *n*.4, where further literature will be found.
[2] Gregory VII, *Reg.* II, 76.
[3] Cf. Alexander IV in *Sextus*: V, ii, 2, where the *gl. ord.* cannot refrain from asking: 'Quid enim est dicere, quod ruralis clericus disputando de fide non incidat in hanc poenam (i.e. excommunication) et doctor decretorum laicus incidat?' The glossator is obviously afraid of arguing his own case, as he continues: 'Tamen sufficit ita esse scriptum, et solum duo sunt christianorum genera, clerici et laici.'

The Papacy as an Institution of Government in the Middle Ages

was a dictate of prudence and self-preservation not to castigate doctrine or laws of a predecessor as erroneous, although a later pope might well have, by implication, given an entirely different ruling. The result was again expected: the accumulation of laws, decrees, statements which, because they were stored up in the memory of the papacy—that is, the archives—assumed the function of precedents which in themselves induced a sense of continuity. Over and above this, there was in any case the papal decision issued *auctoritate* or *iudicio omnipotentis Dei*. A moment's reflection will show how much faith in Christ or in the Bible would have been detrimentally affected, if the *iudicium omnipotentis Dei* was seen to be subjected to change: the papacy would then have itself suggested the mutability of divine judgements and would itself have become an instrument in the corrosion of faith. These premisses make in fact clear why continuity was in reality forced upon the papacy.

One may well object to the view here propounded by saying that the theme of continuity of governmental principles precluded any kind of development. In one sense the objection is justified. Once more we are thrown back to the distinction between *essentialia* and *inessentialia*: within the former there was no change. What the discerning historian witnesses is that in course of time there was deepening, greater elucidation, and penetration into a once established principle of government: its structural elements came to be seen in all their implications and applications, in all the possible ramifications. One has but to think of the distinction between office and the person of the office holder which began as a small point and reached in course of time dimensions of a major importance; or the thesis of the pope being the vicar of Christ which took a very long time to crystallise, in fact not before the twelfth century;[1] the Leonine *plenitudo potestatis* could be pressed home to its fullest advantage when the Petrine powers were seen to be vicarious powers, with the result that the statements of Christ himself and about himself were applied to the pope;[2] thus when St Paul had said that God had put all things under Christ's feet (Eph. i, 22), the concept of *plenitudo potestatis* served to justify a thirteenth-century pope to

[1] About the juristic meaning of the notion cf. W. Ullmann, 'Romanus pontifex indubitanter efficitur sanctus: D.P. 23 in retrospect and prospect', *Studi Gregoriani*, VI (1959), 229-64.

[2] Cf. Innocent III in his *Reg.* I, 320; hence also the application of 'All power is given unto me . . .' to the pope; cf. W. Ullmann, *Mediaeval Papalism*, 1949, 152-8.

apply this Pauline statement to himself,[1] and because the pope was vicar of Christ, Christ was corporally present in the pope;[2] or to take the derivational theme, first enunciated by Innocent I: the Roman Church was the source of all the churches,[3] from which developed the thesis that all ecclesiastical power—that is, the *potestas iurisdictionis*—was derived from the pope, and the third Innocent could say that the Roman Church was the *fundamentum totius christianitatis*. What we see at work is a merciless and ruthless logic which uncovered ever greater depths and layers, and which penetrated ever deeper into the structural elements, of a principle. Is it really surprising that what would seem to be a fundamental Christian-Pauline principle—that is, What I am, I am by the grace of God—became by the same process of relentless logic a supreme principle of government with the papacy? That, in other words, the *gratia Dei* became the *gratia apostolica* or the *favor apostolicus*[4] without which neither any legitimate Christian power could exist nor, more specifically, any governing power, including imperial and royal power? Rulership was the effluence of the divine good will, was a *beneficium divinum*, to use a fifth-century pope's expression with a great future,[5] to which no king or emperor had any right or claim: the pope standing in the place of Christ on earth claimed to be the organ which in actual fact conferred this divine good deed. It is the concatenation of faith and law[6] which facilitates the understanding of the mechanism worked by the papacy. And it is on the basis of the pope's actualising the Bible that the axiom arose that an appeal from the pope to the Bible or to God was a sign of heresy, that the *consistorium papae et Dei unum et idem censendum est* and that *papa est Deus.*[7] Of course, the juristic identification of the pope with Peter or Christ would stimulate these themes.

[1] Cf. also *P.G.P.*, 53, with the full quotation from Urban IV; see also Ps. viii, 8.

[2] Cf. *P.G.*, 444 *n.*1 (Innocent IV).

[3] Cf. *P.G.P.*, 48–52; also W. Ullmann, 'Eugenius IV, Cardinal Kemp and Archbishop Chichele', *Studies in Mediaeval History presented to A. Gwynn*, Dublin 1961, 374, *n.*54. Cf. also Jer. ii, 13.

[4] In proximity to this stands the appellation of the pope as *apostolicus* himself, cf. W. Ullmann in *JTS*, loc. cit. 43, *n.*2; also M. J. Wilks, 'The apostolicus and the bishop of Rome,' ibid. XIII (1962), 290–317; XIV (1963), 311–43; see also L. M. Dewailly in *Mélanges de science religieuse*, V (1948), 141–52.

[5] For this cf. also W. Ullmann in *Miscellanea Historiae Pontificiae*, XVIII (1954), 107–27; idem in *Cambridge Historical Journal*, XI (1955), 233–52.

[6] On this cf. *P.G.P.*, 95–8.

[7] About the juristic construction of these themes cf. art. cit. above, p. 95, *n.*1.

The Papacy as an Institution of Government in the Middle Ages

In realising the potentialities of a general principle the juris-prudential equipment of the Roman papacy, its familiarity with Roman law, played a decisive role. The secret lay in the abstract, general, comprehensive formula, at which only a trained jurist could arrive. The formula or statement or view must be expressed in such a manner that it could embrace all sorts of contingencies. Therein lies the secret skill of the good lawyer. If the notion or principle is conceived wide enough and comprehensive enough, it is not too difficult to fit into it a number of subordinate notions and principles. This juristic method was in fact considerably buttressed by the Bible itself, the importance of which was only heightened by the Latin of its text. The *'Quodcumque ligaveris . . .'* in the Matthean passage presents the comprehensiveness of a formula *kat' exochen*: it received in course of time its stamp of all-embracing practical applicability. The statement of a fifth-century pope in regard to this is no different from that of a ninth-century or a thirteenth-century pope,[1] leading in fact to the claim that only the pope could open the gates to paradise.[2] What differed were the circumstances to which the formula was applied: the principle underwent no change, what changed were the circumstances to which the principle was found applicable. A similar observation can be made about the Pauline *'Princeps non sine causa portat gladium,'* or the pregnant view expressed in 1 Corinthians vi, 3, and of course numerous other instances spring to mind. What they all show is that the formula was a shell which had to be filled with contents, supplied by the emerging circumstances.

We may go further and say that it was precisely the width of the programme, the comprehensiveness of the papal blue-print, which enabled it to incorporate also elements into its scheme of government which originally had not grown on its own soil. Precisely because the programme was so comprehensive, it could absorb an enormous variety of circumstances and elements—and yet, when challenged, the papacy could still maintain that this was in line with the principle which was therefore continuously applied. In this feature one may well see the source of the papacy's flexibility, adjust-ability, resilience, and easy accommodation to new circumstances.[3]

---

[1] See *P.G.* 20, *n.*1.   [2] See *P.G.P.* 51.

[3] It may be apposite to quote what P. E. Schramm once said: 'The papal court had always been the unsurpassable master in the art of justifying each of its steps by reference to the divine order, morals, law and tradition,' cit. in *P.G.*, 225, *n.*1.

So far from hemming in the papacy and restricting it, its rigid adherence to the comprehensively expressed principles gave it a freedom of action for which an adequate parallel cannot easily be found.

The consequential constancy of aims, enshrined in the programme of the papacy, led to the pursuit of policies which, however much the methods adopted varied to suit changing circumstances, remained remarkably stable. We can follow this up in virtually every major point of the mediaeval papacy. Take, for instance, the relations between the papacy and Byzantium. Constantinople did not recognise the jurisdictional primacy of the Roman Church, and pushed it into a position of one of several patriarchates. The Roman Church, on the other hand, could not, for understandable reasons, acquiesce in this state of things—hence the first serious schism between East and West, the Acacian Schism in the late fifth century, incidentally arising in the first flush after the fixation of vital papal principles. Although patched up, the papacy was unable to push its primatial claim towards Constantinople. The popes would have been oblivious of their function, had they simply allowed this state of affairs to continue, but on the other hand, they were subjects of the emperor, and therefore remonstrations on their part against imperial rulings entailed serious constitutional consequences for them. The presupposition for an active policy culminating in the establishment of Roman jurisdictional primacy in Constantinople was that the popes were freed from the constitutional fetters which their membership of the Roman Empire had imposed upon them. Hence the first step: the extrication of the city of Rome and surrounding districts from the imperial framework, and the establishment of a papal state, recognised as an independent entity by the West. The alleged retransfer of the imperial crown from Byzantium and the coronation of Charlemagne constituted a further link in the pursuit of this policy: the Roman-imperial crown could be on the head of a Latin Christian only, and not on that of a Greek, more than merely tainted with heresy. But there were now two entities, each calling itself 'Roman empire,' one in the East and one in the West—if the two could be made into one, the result would be to make Christendom into one, that is, to make Roman jurisdictional primacy also operative in the East. The plan of Pope Leo III of marrying the widowed Irene to Charles would be just about the answer to the problem:

The Papacy as an Institution of Government in the Middle Ages

then indeed both 'Roman empires' would be one, in which, one might well be tempted to say, Roman primacy would automatically be established. The plan came to naught, but the union of East and West was an ever-present *desideratum* of the papacy.

There is no need to depict the involved story, unedifying as it is in the ninth and tenth centuries, and it must suffice to state that with the final break of 1054 the methods of establishing the primacy in Constantinople assumed a somewhat different complexion. On the one hand, by the mid-eleventh century there was a firmly established Roman-imperial government in the West, whose aim was the *dominium mundi* which in practical terms meant the reduction, if not the absorption, of Constantinople; we witness the pursuit of the Western imperial policy unmistakably from the ninth century onwards, through the various stages of Eastern mission, colonisation, and expansion far into the East European space. We bear of course in mind that the idea of a Latin-Roman empire was the intellectual offspring of the papacy itself who thereby created on a universal scale its prolonged arm, the *brachium saeculare*. On the other hand, there was on the papal side the emergence of the crusading idea, precisely twenty years after the final break with Constantinople. Gregory VII in his appeal for the crusade made the establishment of Roman primacy in Constantinople his principal aim.[1] The policy of the West Roman emperors towards Byzantium in the twelfth century considerably prepared the ground for the ensuing steps in the early thirteenth century. Not only had Frederick I claimed, by virtue of the Roman emperorship and under the cover of a crusade, the government over Byzantium and had directed his army against Constantinople itself, but his son Henry VI managed to marry Irene, the daughter of Isaac, to his brother Philip of Swabia, and Irene was the indubitable heir to Byzantium. Nothing else was now demanded by Henry VI than the cession of the whole Byzantine empire. When Henry died in 1197, the fearful encirclement of Byzantium had become a fact. His successor Philip of Swabia, as plainly as one might wish, had promised to Innocent III in 1203 that if the Almighty would enable him to subdue the kingdom of the Greeks, 'I will subject the Church of Constantinople to the Roman Church.'[2]

---

[1] *Reg.* II, 31. C. Erdmann, *Die Entstehung des Kreuzzugsgedankens*, Stuttgart 1936, 252, commented: 'Wir dürfen es ihm aufs Wort glauben, dass dieser Plan, eine Union ... und den römischen Primat dort zur Geltung zu bringen, sein Hauptmotiv gewesen ist.'

[2] MGH, *Constitutiones*, II, 9, no. 8, § 7: 'Si omnipotens Deus regnum Graecorum

Both empire and papacy therefore pursued the same end—the sub-jection of Byzantium to Western rule, and when as a result of the combined preparations by the Latin empire and the papacy Constantinople was captured in 1204, Innocent III triumphantly exclaimed: 'now by the grace of God the Church of Constantinople has returned to her mother, the Roman Church, and now there is *unum ovile, unus pastor.*' [1] The end was achieved—Roman primacy was implanted in Constantinople. It was a very long route, but the principle and the aim had always been the same, though the means to achieve the aim differed: negotiations, discussions, formulae, marriage proposals, actual marriages, use of force or threat of force by the *brachium saeculare*, and finally the crusading idea, which covered a multitude of ambitions and aims. One might well say that here, as in so many other instances, papal principles of government supplied their own impetus, supplied their own dynamic force.

You have allowed me to delve a little below the surface of well-established papal principles of government in the Middle Ages: in so doing the inquiring searcher and researcher inevitably comes upon the feature which itself had been the central axiom of the mediaeval papacy, that is, the principle of continuity. Its efficacy in the mediaeval period shows that the papacy was, as I have termed it on other occasions, a government *sui generis*. No government in the Middle Ages had been able to forge that intimate direct link with Scripture as the papacy had done. Other governments indeed invoked the Bible often enough for support, illustration, and exemplification: what they did not do was to assert that they were the Bible made directly manifest and they simply the organ to translate the Bible within space and time. Once this is grasped, one will also understand not only the absolutist character of papal doctrine, but also the severe restrictions placed on the papacy: it could not go beyond what it had once declared biblical and say at a later date that it was unbiblical; it could not revoke what had once been firmly fixed; it became, so to speak, its own prisoner. On the other hand, precisely because of the comprehensiveness of papal principles, because of the generality of its fundamental axioms, they could be applied, with the

mihi vel leviro meo subdiderit, ecclesiam Constantinopolitanam Romanae ecclesiae bona fide et sine fraude faciam fore subiectam.' For the whole question see A. Frolow, *Recherches sur la déviation de la IVᵉ Croisade vers Constantinople*, Paris 1955.

[1] *Regestum de negotio Romani Imperii*, no. 113, of 29 October 1204; see further *Reg.*, VII, 203; VIII, 19, 24, 26, 153; etc.

The Papacy as an Institution of Government in the Middle Ages

indispensable assistance from Roman jurisprudence, to virtually illimitable sets of circumstances, situations, and contingencies. It is no paradox to say that the bounds set were those of divinity and logic, and not those set by the actual reality. That a good many features of the mediaeval papacy may become more easily accessible to under-standing, if these presuppositions are taken into account, is not an unreasonable hope—for one must try to see the papacy as it saw itself in its numerous amply documented self-portraits. That is the only task—but a very difficult one—for the historian who is not, by virtue of his profession, called upon to answer the question whether the biblical theme of the papacy was correct. That is the task of the theologian or philosopher, but not of the historian who has merely to recognise the facts as history presents them. And one of them is continuity.

INDEX